WX 159 AAN

THE HANDBOOK OF LEADERSHIP DEVELOPMENT EVALUATION

Bottom row from left to right: Kelly Hannum, Claire Reinelt, Jennifer Martineau

Second row from left to right: Manuel Gutiérrez, Heather Lewis-Charp, Karl Umble, Alison Ellis, Darlene Russ-Eft, Prisca Collins, Maenette Benham

Top row from left to right: Barry Kibel, Deborah Meehan, Sally Leiderman, Hazel Symonette, Nilofer Ahsan, Teri Behrens, Bart Craig, Michelle Gambone, Tania Tasse, John Baum

Not photographed: Nancy LeMay, John Grove, Patti Phillips, Jack Phillips, Larry Peters, Todd Kern, Rodney Hopson, Kim Jinnett, Jane Davidson, Taylor Haas, Kim Howard, Hanh Cao Yu

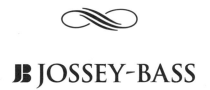

**Center for
Creative
Leadership**

NORTH AMERICA   EUROPE   ASIA

www.ccl.org

THE HANDBOOK OF LEADERSHIP DEVELOPMENT EVALUATION

Kelly M. Hannum
Jennifer W. Martineau
Claire Reinelt
Editors

Foreword by Laura C. Leviton

John Wiley & Sons, Inc.

Published by Jossey-Bass
A Wiley Imprint
989 Market Street, San Francisco, CA 94103-1741   www.josseybass.com

Jossey-Bass books and products are available through most bookstores. To contact Jossey-Bass directly
call our Customer Care Department within the U.S. at 800-956-7739, outside the U.S. at 317-572-3986,
or fax 317-572-4002.

Jossey-Bass also publishes its books in a variety of electronic formats. Some content that appears in print
may not be available in electronic books.

Library of Congress Cataloging-in-Publication Data

The handbook of leadership development evaluation/by Kelly M. Hannum, Jennifer W.
Martineau, Claire Reinelt, editors; foreword by Laura C. Leviton.
        p. cm.—(A joint publication of the Jossey-Bass business & management series and
the Center for Creative Leadership)
   Includes bibliographical references and index.
   ISBN-13: 978-0-7879-8217-1 (cloth)
   ISBN-10: 0-7879-8217-2 (cloth)
   1. Leadership-Evaluation. I. Hannum, Kelly. II. Martineau, Jennifer. III. Reinelt,
Claire.
   HD57.7.H3563 2007
   658.4'092—dc22

                                                                    2006027163

Printed in the United States of America
FIRST EDITION
HB Printing   10 9 8 7 6 5 4 3 2 1

A JOINT PUBLICATION OF

THE JOSSEY-BASS

BUSINESS & MANAGEMENT SERIES

AND

THE CENTER FOR CREATIVE LEADERSHIP

CONTENTS

FOREWORD

The term *leadership* means many things to many people. It is one of the big societal concepts, and it is of the same size and importance as "access to medical care" or "quality of education." Leadership encompasses many talents and skills. There are different styles of leadership, and there are different factors affecting how leaders are regarded. There is authoritarian leadership, democratic leadership, and most recently, collaborative leadership. After hundreds of studies and many years of research, we still find ourselves playing with a few pebbles on the shore of this vast sea of subject matter.

It is in that context that this handbook on evaluation of leadership development is presented. Although the topic is vast, there are certain evaluation approaches and subjects that have proven their value. Several vital and generic evaluation topics are presented in these chapters: how to study implementation; how to present evaluation findings; designs for evaluating leadership development; and using theories of change to inform the choice of measures for evaluation. They are a valuable foundation.

At the same time we can ask, Leadership of what and for what? Leadership always takes place in context. So does evaluation. In this book we find some remarkably different programs that see leadership in different ways. An argument can be made for each of them, and they all merit evaluation. We have personal transformation leadership efforts, leadership development to achieve organizational change, and leadership development for neighborhood transformation. It is heartening that the field of evaluation is flexible enough to apply its frameworks and methods to such a range of development initiatives.

Evaluation helps us to understand leadership in other ways. For example, the term *leadership* is highly vulnerable to rhetorical use and abuse. Are we entirely sure that a program that includes "leadership" in the title is truly about this big concept? Or, is the concept being used for some other agenda unrelated to leadership by even the broadest definition? One advantage of evaluation is that it seeks to operationalize the big concepts. Evaluation *has* to do this, because it is systematic inquiry about programs' logic, resources, activities, outputs, and outcomes. Systematic inquiry requires a highly specific understanding of the principles and concepts being employed. Evaluation separates real outcomes from wishful thinking, slogans, or overly vague program aspirations.

Even when we do know what we are trying to achieve in a leadership program, we may still not know quite how. Evaluation can assist by providing neutral, constructive observations to guide a program's inevitable changes and evolution. Once a program is established, evaluation continues to contribute by assisting the program managers to optimize their use of resources on behalf of the participants.

Finally, even when we are not entirely sure what leadership is supposed to be, what it consists of in a given context, or how to develop it, evaluation helps us. Many leadership programs have never been tried before. By definition, they are ventures into the unknown, aspiring beyond the tried and true. From that point of view, evaluation is about discovery, understanding what is possible to achieve, and even helping to define and characterize new kinds of leadership.

What we do know is that leadership is an essential ingredient for personal and social change. So is evaluation, as seen in decades of learning from fields as disparate as education, health, community and social welfare. These two essential tools of change come together in this volume.

September 2006   Laura C. Leviton
                                                                                           Princeton, New Jersey

Laura C. Leviton is a senior program officer for the Robert Wood Johnson Foundation and former president of the American Evaluation Association. She has conducted evaluations in the health area ranging from fellowships and scholarships to quality of medical care and prevention of disease.

PREFACE

Why did the Center for Creative Leadership (CCL), the Leadership Learning Community (LLC), the Robert Wood Johnson Foundation (RWJF), and more than thirty authors collaborate to write a book about the evaluation of leadership development? Quite simply, because there is considerable demand for guidance in evaluating leadership development by those who practice and fund development and evaluation in commercial and nonprofit organizations. There is no single source that provides practical content, examples, and tools from many different settings and perspectives. As practitioners of leadership development evaluation, we are aware of the substantial need for this type of resource. In this volume, we bring together distinguished authors with knowledge and expertise about leadership development evaluation, whose contributions can benefit leadership development evaluators, practitioners, and ultimately those participating in leadership development.

The pace of change in contemporary organizations and communities creates new challenges for individuals, organizations, and communities. Many fields of practice are feeling the impact of these phenomena. Leadership development is no different. When CCL was founded in 1970 for the purpose of understanding and developing leadership, few institutions were offering leadership development. Since then, leadership development has grown into a strategy that is utilized globally by organizations of all types. Individuals, groups, teams, organizations, and communities seek to become more effective and strategic in their leadership. Organizations and foundations invest in leadership development for individuals and groups of individuals in order to achieve the broader strategic and social change objectives they seek and to realize their missions.

Leadership development is frequently used as a strategy to help prepare individuals and groups of individuals to address the complex challenges they face. Numerous tools, processes, and programs to develop leadership are being implemented, and although many are being evaluated, there is even more need for evaluation to answer important questions, improve practice, and inform decisions. Funding agencies, designers, sponsors, and participants (among others) frequently have a variety of questions about leadership development, including:

- Is the time and money spent on leadership development worthwhile?
- What difference does leadership development make?
- What development and support strategies work best to enhance leadership?
- What outcomes can be expected from leadership development?
- How can leadership development efforts be sustained?

The complexity of leadership development requires innovative models and approaches to evaluation in order to answer those questions. Traditional evaluation approaches (such as use of control groups, and pretests and posttests, for example) can be impractical, incomplete, and sometimes inappropriate models for evaluating leadership development initiatives in some contexts. An increasing number of innovative models and approaches to evaluate leadership development that are more appropriate and useful in other contexts have evolved over time, and presenting them to a professional audience is the purpose of this book.

Many organizations and foundations have created innovative models and approaches of leadership development evaluation. The LLC Evaluation Learning Circle has posted many of these models and approaches in its Knowledge Pool located at www.leadershiplearning.org (many of the resources cited in this handbook are also posted there). However, few people have had the opportunity to learn about these innovations and apply them in their own work. It is through this process of application, adaptation, and subsequent learning that the field of leadership development produces knowledge about how to support and develop individuals and organizations so that greater impact can be achieved.

We want to underscore the intent of this book. We believe that leadership development and its evaluation will meet the needs of those who rely on it to address the complex challenges of today's world only if evaluators and other interested practitioners and stakeholders share their experiences and expertise. This book aims to lay a foundation for this exchange of ideas and practices.

How We Created This Book

The process of conceptualizing, organizing, writing, and evolving this book was highly collaborative. We share this story with readers so that they might consider adapting similar strategies and apply them to their own learning projects.

The concept of a book addressing leadership development evaluation emanated from two different places simultaneously. Kelly Hannum and Jennifer Martineau of CCL had for more than a decade been leading their organization's efforts to evaluate leadership development and had amassed specific expertise that, because of CCL's mission as an educational institution, they wanted to share with other evaluators and leadership development practitioners. They also knew that there were others out in the field who also had valuable knowledge to contribute. At the same time, the Leadership Learning Community (see Chapter Eighteen for more information) had formed an evaluation learning circle (convened by Claire Reinelt) whose members were motivated to move the practice of leadership development evaluation forward by sharing their expertise, tools, and resources with each other and with a broader, virtual community of practice. The leadership development evaluation goal of both of these organizations is to advance the practice of leadership development and support so that leadership (both individual and collective) can more effectively lead change that will have a positive impact on society and the world. This book shares knowledge and expertise that will help leadership development and evaluation practitioners and users achieve this goal.

As we conceptualized the book and its contents, we focused on the three general areas that are detailed in the book's three parts: Design, Implementation, and Use. We scanned the field of leadership development evaluation to identify ideal chapter topics and authors for those chapters. In addition, we also agreed that the group of authors participating in this project should form a community of practice in order to create a more coherent, integrated volume and not simply produce the separate and distinct chapters typically found in an edited book. With the financial support of the Robert Wood Johnson Foundation and the provision of facilities by CCL and RWJF, the community of authors met twice during the writing process: first, after the chapter outlines were complete; and second, between the first and second drafts of the chapters. During these conferences and through e-mail exchanges, the authors shared chapter outlines and drafts. All of the authors received feedback that they incorporated into their chapters. We also conducted a series of dialogues that resulted in better understanding of the many facets of leadership development evaluation. The content of the Introduction and Afterword include the output from those dialogues.

Evaluation as a Way of Life

Of the many things we have to say about the evaluation of leadership development, perhaps the most important is this: approaching issues from an evaluative perspective enables one to consider multiple perspectives and draw lessons as a natural part of the way work is done. People can improve their effectiveness by challenging assumptions and drawing lessons from the many challenges they face by adopting an evaluative perspective. This kind of thinking is in fact a quality of good leadership. Leaders who learn from the successes and trials of their work are typically more successful than those who do not. What our readers—whether they are evaluators, stakeholders, or leaders—may not always recognize is that evaluation is learning, and learning is evaluation. Evaluation should not be something that is forced upon the unwilling, nor should it be misused to harm others. Evaluation can be and should be a vibrant and engaging activity that leads to powerful learning and well-informed action. We encourage you to find the relevant value of this book's contents for your leadership development and evaluation work, and to discover the value it brings to you in your role as a leader.

September 2006   Kelly M. Hannum
Greensboro, North Carolina   Jennifer W. Martineau
                                                                             Claire Reinelt

ACKNOWLEDGMENTS

We editors would like to thank the Robert Wood Johnson Foundation, the Leadership Learning Community, the Center for Creative Leadership (CCL), and Jossey-Bass for their support of this project.

CCL colleagues Tracy Patterson, Meena Wilson, and Laura Santana supported us during the authors' conferences by contributing their time, facilitating, and taking notes, and we thank them for that. Other very important people are the authors of the chapters. This dedicated group devoted untold time and contribution of self to the project. We also thank the many other contributors, reviewers, and thought partners who worked with the authors and editors to make this book better. They include Rebecca Aced-Molina, Deborah Brown, Jill Casey, Sarah Clark, George Consolver, Mike Copland, Linda Darling-Hammond, Jacqui Darroch, James Dean, Ron Martinez Looking Elk, Rick Foster, Susan Fowler, Joan Galer, Danis Gehl, William Graustein, Miguel Guajardo, Joe Hafey, Patricia Moore Harbour, Laura Harris, Linda Helstowski, Paul Hill, Hartley Hobson, Sarah Johnson, Seema Kapani, Kerri Kerr, Mike Knapp, Amy Carter Knight, Shamali Kuru, Johanna Lacoe, Karen Lassner, Don Lauro, Matthew Leiderman, Ken Leithwood, Elizabeth Long, Hannah McKnight, Deborah Meehan, Deb Meyerson, Inca Mohamed, Joe Murphy, Sister Gerrie Naughton, Dale Nienow, Phil Novick, Beth Peterman, Lourdes de la Peza, Andy Porter, Janet Porter, Pam Putney, Chris Riordan, Carla Roach, Jim Roach, Cecilia Roddy, Kwesi Rollins,

Karma Ruder, Craig Russon, Sharon Rudy, Rire Scotney, Eric Schaps, Karen Seashore, Karen Sherk, Cynthia L. Sipe, Barry Smith, John Sommers, Sengsouvanh Soukamneuth, Erica Spielman, Rochelle Thompson, Zita Unger, Kyle Voorhees, Sylvia Vriesendorp, Kyla Wahlstrom, Bill Weber, Suzi Weber, Wendy Wheeler, and Susan Wright.

We are also very thankful to each other for being thoughtful collaborators, for being dedicated to learning and sharing knowledge, and for forgiving each other's mistakes—both big and small. Two people provided the behind-the-scenes work that made this collection of chapters become a book. A big thank-you goes to Laurie Merritt for keeping us grounded and moving forward and to Pete Scisco for his savvy editing and insight.

From Jennifer W. Martineau

I thank my husband, Jim, and our children, Sarah, Christopher, and Grace, for their love and unending support of me during the many long hours spent writing and editing this book. You are my inspiration and the loves of my life. I would also like to thank my parents, Herb and Ellen Wells, and my mother-in-law and father-in-law, Judy and Bob Martineau (whom we recently lost to cancer), for their strong examples of the value of education, curiosity, and hard work.

From Kelly M. Hannum

I thank my family and friends for their support, encouragement, and understanding. I especially want to thank Bart Craig for being a great coauthor, and even more important, a wonderful friend. I also thank Keith Erickson for providing the unconditional love necessary in any challenging endeavor.

From Claire Reinelt

I thank Suzi Weber, Bill Weber, Cecilia Roddy, and the rest of the Development Guild/DDI staff for their support and encouragement of my participation in this book project. I would also like to thank Rick and Emma for their understanding and patience as I worked on this book many evenings and weekends. I dedicate my work on this book to my husband, Rick, and my daughters, Julia and Emma, for all the wonderful years that we have had together and for our support of each other's passions and pursuits.

THE AUTHORS

Nilofer Ahsan is an associate at the Center for the Study of Social Policy. She is the author of *Protecting Children by Strengthening Families: A Guidebook for Early Childhood Programs, Domestic Violence and Family Support Programs: Creating Opportunities to Help Young Children and Their Families,* and *How Are We Doing?—A Program Self-Assessment Toolkit for the Family Support Field.* She has a master's degree in public policy from the University of Chicago.

John Baum is professor of professional practice in leadership in the Neeley School of Business at Texas Christian University. He received his Ph.D. in organizational behavior and industrial relations from the University of Wisconsin-Madison. He is principal and president of Corporate Education Resources, Inc., which provides development resources to firms that are committed to developing their managerial talent into business leaders.

Teresa R. Behrens is the director of evaluation at the W. K. Kellogg Foundation in Battle Creek, Michigan. Her efforts focus on developing effective systems to monitor and measure the results of funded projects and activities. She also is responsible for developing tools for programming staff to work with grantees on evaluation. She received her Ph.D. in psychology from North Carolina State University.

Maenette K. P. Benham is a professor in the educational administration department of the College of Education at Michigan State University. She earned her doctoral degree in education from the University of Hawai'i-Mānoa. Her books include *Culture and Educational Policy in Hawai'i: The Silencing of Native Voices, Let My Spirit Soar! The Narratives of Diverse Women in School Leadership,* and *Indigenous Educational Models for Contemporary Practice: In Our Mother's Voice.*

Prisca M. Collins is the coordinator of the American Evaluation Association/Duquesne University Graduate Education Diversity Internship Program. She holds a Ph.D. in health and rehabilitation science from the University of Pittsburgh. Her writings include *Clinical Outcome from Mechanical Intermittent Cervical Traction for the Treatment of Cervical Radiculopathy: A Cases Series* and *The Role of Faith Practices and Religiosity in the Utilization of Available Health Services by Inner City African Americans.*

S. Bartholomew Craig is an assistant professor of psychology at North Carolina State University, an adjunct research scientist at the leadership development consultancy of Kaplan DeVries Inc., and an adjunct program evaluator at the Center for Creative Leadership. He is coauthor, along with Sigrid Gustafson, of the Perceived Leader Integrity Scale, a multirater tool for assessing leaders' ethical integrity. He holds a Ph.D. in industrial-organizational psychology from Virginia Tech.

E. Jane Davidson is director of Davidson Consulting Ltd., a New Zealand–based evaluation and organizational consulting firm. She received her Ph.D. in organizational psychology (with substantial emphasis on evaluation) from Claremont Graduate University. She is the author of *Evaluation Methodology Basics: The Nuts and Bolts of Sound Evaluation,* a step-by-step guide to the use of evaluation-specific logic and methodology.

Alison Ellis has twenty-five years' experience working in international family planning and reproductive health. She is currently team leader of the Monitoring, Evaluation, and Communication unit of the Leadership, Management, and Sustainability Program of Management Sciences for Health. She coauthored the Management chapter of the *Compendium of Indicators for Evaluating Reproductive Health Programs* and "User's Guide on Planning and Managing a Quality Survey in Reproductive Health Programs."

Michelle Alberti Gambone is a sociologist who has been conducting research on youth development, community mobilization, and youth policy and program effectiveness for the past fifteen years. She is currently the president of Youth Development Strategies, Inc. She also continues the work of Gambone & Associates, a consulting firm that assists organizations in developing planning, management, and evaluation tools for youth development initiatives. Her Ph.D. in sociology is from Princeton University.

John T. Grove is a founder and past director of the Sustainable Leadership Initiative, where the EvaluLEAD approach and tools began. Currently, he is the team leader for monitoring and evaluation with the Centers for Disease Control and Prevention Global AIDS Program in Zambia. He coauthored *EvaluLEAD: A Guide for Shaping and Evaluating Leadership Development Programs*. He holds an M.A. in education from the University of San Francisco.

Manuel Gutiérrez is presently the director of the Division of Applied Research and Evaluation at Metis Associates, a national research and consulting firm. He holds a Ph.D. in clinical psychology from Temple University. He is the principal author of *Next Generation Leadership Program: Final Assessment Report* and *Strengthening Families to Promote Youth Development*.

Taylor Haas is a consultant providing technical assistance with planning, research, writing, and evaluation for programs in nonprofit and private sectors. She received her M.S. in population studies from the London School of Economics. She coauthored the guidebook *EvaluLEAD: A Guide for Shaping and Evaluating Leadership Development Programs* and the Institute of International Education's *Population Experts in Developing Countries: A Summary Report and Directory*.

Kelly M. Hannum is an enterprise associate in the Global Leadership and Diversity and Design and Evaluation groups at the Center for Creative Leadership. She holds a Ph.D. in educational research, measurement, and evaluation from the University of North Carolina at Greensboro. She coauthored *Evaluating the Impact of Leadership Development: A Professional Guide* and *Evaluation in North America* in *Cross-Cultural Evaluation: An International Annotated Bibliography*.

Rodney K. Hopson is Hillman Distinguished Professor, associate professor, and chair of the Department of Educational Foundations and Leadership and faculty member in the Center for Interpretive and Qualitative Research at Duquesne University. He has undergraduate and graduate degrees from the University of Virginia, and has postdoctoral and visiting research and teaching experiences from the Johns Hopkins Bloomberg School of Hygiene and Public Health, the University of Namibia, and Cambridge University.

Kim Ammann Howard is the director of evaluation and organizational learning for BTW Consultants. Her publications include *Leadership Matters: An Evaluation of Six Family Planning and Reproductive Health Leadership Programs Funded by the Packard and*

Gates Foundations and *One Story, Many Voices: The Impact of the California Wellness Foundation's VPI Leadership Program.* She holds a Ph.D. in health policy and management from the Johns Hopkins School of Public Health.

Kimberly Jinnett is research director of the Integrated Benefits Institute, a nonprofit membership organization providing research, analysis, and information on health and productivity management. She received her Ph.D. degree in sociology and health services organization and policy from the University of Michigan, Ann Arbor. Her publications have appeared in *Medical Care, Health Services Research, Social Science and Medicine, Journal of Mental Health Policy and Economics, Advances in Medical Sociology,* and other forums.

Todd Kern currently serves as chief knowledge officer of New Leaders for New Schools, a national not-for-profit organization that promotes high academic achievement for every child by attracting, preparing, and supporting the next generation of outstanding leaders for our nation's urban public schools. He completed his graduate work in public policy at the University of Chicago, focusing on education reform, urban poverty, and community-based economic development strategies.

Barry M. Kibel is a senior research scientist at the Pacific Institute for Research and Evaluation (PIRE), having joined the institute in 1991 and having created and been director of PIRE'S Results Mapping Laboratory since 1997. He holds a Ph.D. in city and regional planning from the University of California-Berkeley. He is author of *Success Stories as Hard Data,* an exploration of the use of stories in evaluation, and of numerous professional publications.

Sally Leiderman is president of the Center for Assessment and Policy Development, a nonprofit policy, research, and evaluation organization founded in 1988. She coauthored *Flipping the Script: White Privilege and Community Building,* partnered in the development of *Training for Racial Equity and Inclusion: A Guide to Selected Programs,* and coauthored *A Community Builder's Toolkit: 15 Tools for Creating Healthy, Productive Interracial/Multicultural Communities.* She graduated from Temple University with a B.A. in urban studies.

Nancy Vollmer LeMay is senior program officer for the Monitoring, Evaluation, and Communication unit of the Leadership, Management, and Sustainability Program of Management Sciences for Health, where she participates in all aspects of program evaluation for field and virtual projects. She holds an M.P.H. in international health from Yale University with a focus on epidemiology.

Heather K. Lewis-Charp is a social scientist at Social Policy Research Associates. She received a master's in education research from the University of California-Santa Cruz. She is lead author of "Youth Opportunity Grant Initiative: Ethnographic Final Report," *Extending the Reach of Youth Development Through Civic Activism: Outcomes of the Youth Leadership Development Initiative,* "The Influence of Intergroup Relations on School Engagement: Two Cases," and *School Connections: U.S. Mexican Youth, Peers, Schools Achievement.*

Jennifer W. Martineau serves as director of the Center for Creative Leadership's Design and Evaluation Center. At CCL since 1993 and with more than fifteen years' experience in the field of evaluation, she has focused her attention on the evaluation of leadership development programs and initiatives. Her work can be found in book chapters, peer-reviewed journals, and practitioner-oriented publications. She holds a Ph.D. in industrial and organizational psychology from the Pennsylvania State University.

Deborah Meehan is the founder and executive director of the Leadership Learning Community (LLC). The LLC strengthens the practice of leadership development by linking the inquiry, practice, and resources of those who fund, run, study, and provide services to leadership programs. Many of her publications are available on the LLC Web site at www.leadershiplearning.org. She is a graduate of the University of California-Berkeley.

Larry Peters is professor of management in the Neeley School of Business at Texas Christian University. He received his Ph.D. in industrial/organizational psychology from Purdue University. He has coauthored two case books and was the senior editor of *The Blackwell Encyclopedic Dictionary of Human Resource Management.* He is founder and president of LH Peters and Associates, LLC. He has provided consulting, training design, training, meeting design, facilitation, and applied research services to business, nonprofit, and government organizations.

Jack J. Phillips is chairman of the ROI Institute, Inc. Through the institute, he provides consulting services for Fortune 500 companies and major organizations in forty-one countries. He has a Ph.D. in human resource management from the University of Alabama. His most recent books include *Proving the Value of HR: When and How to Measure ROI, The Leadership Scorecard, The Human Resources Scorecard: Measuring the Return on Investment,* and *The Consultant's Scorecard.*

Patti Phillips is president and CEO of the ROI Institute, Inc., and chairman and CEO of the Chelsea Group, Inc. Her Ph.D. is in international development. Her most recent publications include *The Bottomline on ROI,* the ASTD *In Action* case-books, *Measuring Return on Investment Volume 3, Measuring ROI in the Public Sector,* and *Retaining Your Best Employees.*

Claire Reinelt is research and evaluation director for the Leadership Learning Community. She holds a Ph.D. in sociology from Brandeis University. She is an author or coauthor of the following publications: *Evaluating Outcomes and Impacts: A Scan of 55 Leadership Programs, Developing Leadership in an International Context,* and *One Story, Many Voices: The Impact of VPI Leadership Programs.*

Darlene F. Russ-Eft is currently an associate professor in the Department of Adult Education and Higher Education Leadership in the College of Education at Oregon State University. She received the ASTD Research Article award for "Customer Service Competencies: A Global Look," appearing in *Human Resource Development International* in 2004, and has coauthored several texts. She holds a Ph.D. in psychology from the University of Michigan.

Hazel Symonette is senior policy and program development specialist with the University of Wisconsin-Madison and the University of Wisconsin System Administration. She advocates assessment/evaluation as a participant-centered self-diagnostic resource for continuous improvement and strategic image management. She holds two master's degrees and a Ph.D. from the University of Wisconsin-Madison in social work/community organization, sociology/social demography, and educational policy studies/sociology of education respectively.

Tania Tasse, formerly a senior project manager at the OMG Center for Collaborative Learning, is currently working for Metis Associates in New York. She holds an M.A. in public policy from the Johns Hopkins University. An important aspect of her education has been her involvement in community service and service learning programs, including the Peace Corps (Romania, 1997–99) and AmeriCorps.

Rosalie T. Torres is president of Torres Consulting Group, an evaluation and management consulting firm specializing in the feedback-based development of programs and organizations. She earned her Ph.D. in research and evaluation from the University of Illinois. She has authored or coauthored numerous books and articles, including *Evaluation Strategies for Communicating and Reporting: Enhancing Learning in Organizations,* 2nd edition, and *Evaluative Inquiry for Learning in Organizations.*

Karl E. Umble received a Ph.D. in adult education from the University of Georgia. At the North Carolina Institute for Public Health at the University of North Carolina-

Chapel Hill School of Public Health, he plans and evaluates continuing education and distance learning programs for public health professionals and teaches program evaluation. His publications have appeared in the *American Journal of Public Health, Public Health Reports, Evaluation and the Health Professions,* and other forums.

Hanh Cao Yu is a vice president and senior social scientist at Social Policy Research Associates. She received her Ph.D. in education at Stanford University. Her writing has appeared in *Anthropology and Education Quarterly, Phi Delta Kappan,* and the *American Educational Research Journal.* She coauthored *Adolescent Worlds: Negotiating Family, Peer, and School Worlds* and *Extending the Reach of Youth Development through Civic Activism: Outcomes of the Youth Leadership Development Initiative.*

INTRODUCTION

Jennifer W. Martineau, Kelly M. Hannum, and Claire Reinelt

This book provides broad and practical information about how to conduct leadership development evaluations using a variety of approaches, many of which have been recently developed. We have intentionally sought authors from a variety of sectors (nonprofit, academic, for-profit, and governmental agencies) to increase the diversity of perspectives, expertise, and experiences represented in these pages. The target populations and program designs covered in this handbook are also diverse; we believe this book represents a powerful opportunity for cross-program and cross-sector learning.

This handbook is divided into three parts, each of which begins with an overview chapter. Part One is devoted to designing leadership development evaluations. The chapters in this section address a variety of approaches and considerations that come into play when designing a method for evaluating leadership development initiatives. Part Two, Leadership Development Evaluation in Context, presents chapters addressing specific environments for designing and implementing leadership development, ranging from a stand-alone leadership program for developing evaluators of color to a change initiative intended to transform school leadership and performance. Finally, in Part Three, Increasing Impact through Evaluation Use, the book addresses ways in which evaluation can and should be used to maximize impact, rather than serving only to measure and document.

Who This Book Is For

This book supports the daily work of people responsible for developing, implementing, and evaluating leadership development programs and initiatives. These can be human resource managers, instructional and learning designers, trainers, consultants, funders, evaluators, and others from a wide range of organizations: for-profit, nonprofit, governmental, educational, religious and faith-based, community, and more. People who study and research evaluation, leadership development, or both (such as students, scholars, and staff at foundations, think tanks, or research organizations) form a secondary audience for this book. While we focus on our intended audiences, we sincerely hope that others will benefit from the knowledge, practices, and resources presented in this handbook.

We invite those of you interested in the field of leadership development evaluation to learn from each other and broaden the scope of questions you are asking and the evaluation approaches you are using and testing. Our intent is that this handbook will move the field of leadership development evaluation forward by creating more interaction between practitioners in the for-profit and nonprofit, governmental, and educational fields, pushing their collective thinking ahead by exposing them to areas of practice they might not otherwise have access to in their daily work.

How to Use This Book

This book is first and foremost a resource for its readers, to be used in whatever manner they see fit. We encourage readers to find and read those chapters that are most immediately valuable to them, given the context of their work and the questions they are asking. For example, if you have a question such as, How do other evaluators design an evaluation when control groups are not possible?, you can find answers in Chapter One. If you ask, How do I evaluate leadership that is focused on systems transformation?, you will find guidance in Chapter Eleven. And if your stakeholders want to know how you plan on sharing the results of the evaluation, consult Chapter Seventeen's discussion of communication. While each chapter has a specific focus, you are likely to find relevant information and advice on a variety of topics in many different chapters, especially those chapters that describe how leadership development is implemented in a specific context. For that reason, we encourage readers to make liberal use of the book's index and to read the introductions for each of the book's three parts, which provide an overview of the ideas expressed by the chapters in that part.

What This Book Is Not

This book is not about the programs or initiatives that are being evaluated; rather it is about the evaluations of those programs or initiatives. Similarly, this book is not about leadership development evaluation findings other than those that are relevant to evaluation design, implementation, and use. Program or initiative information is given to provide the reader with the contextual information about the evaluation.

Second, this is not a basic evaluation text. There are many very good resources available for readers wishing to learn more about how to evaluate in general (for example, Davidson, 2005; Fitzpatrick, Sanders, and Worthen, 2004). We assume that you have a basic understanding of evaluation (see Exhibit I.1) that will let you delve into the specifics of leadership development evaluation.

EXHIBIT I.1. BASIC STEPS IN EVALUATION.

Evaluations rarely follow a linear process, but the steps outlined here represent typical activities an evaluator facilitates during an evaluation.

- Identify stakeholders for the initiative and the evaluation.
- Articulate the initiative and evaluation purposes.
- Specify at what level impact is expected to occur (for example, individual or organizational).
- Specify the type and timing of impact (for example, a change in a specific behavior within six months after the program).
- Determine and prioritize critical evaluation questions.
- Identify or create measures or processes for gathering information about the initiative and its impact.
- Gather and communicate information.
- Share and interpret information from the evaluation.
- Use the information from the evaluation.

Third, this book does not promote one evaluation approach over another. We believe that different leadership development programs, different organizational or community contexts, and different evaluation questions demand a broad variety of approaches. The multitude of effective and appropriate evaluation approaches is one of the reasons we felt it was so important to draw this collection of information together.

Fourth, there are contexts for leadership development evaluation that are not adequately covered by this book, including leadership development outside the United States and in many more diverse communities and cultures than we can cover in one book. For example, we concentrate on leadership efforts that target adults. While we have sought diverse perspectives in a variety of contexts, we hope future work will illuminate lessons about leadership and leadership development in diverse cultures and communities worldwide.

Finally, though we hope and believe that the information provided in this book will lead to more effectively and appropriately designed leadership development efforts, the focus of the book is not about designing leadership development initiatives.

Key Concepts

Because this book explores the intersection of leadership development and evaluation, we think it is useful to orient the reader to concepts about what leadership development and evaluation together offer each other.

Leadership Development

In *The Center for Creative Leadership Handbook of Leadership Development* (McCauley and Van Velsor, 2004), a key distinction is made between *leader development* and *leadership development*. Leader development is directed toward individuals to expand their "capacity to be effective in leadership roles and processes" (p. 2). In this definition, leadership roles and processes are those that "facilitate setting direction, creating alignment, and maintaining commitment in groups of people who share common work" (p. 2). Leadership development is the "expansion of the organization's capacity to enact the basic leadership tasks needed for collective work: setting direction, creating alignment, and maintaining commitment" (p. 18). Granted, the term *tasks* can evoke a cold and mechanistic view of leadership; however, in this context the tasks needed for collective work are authentic and relational. The Center for Creative Leadership (CCL) pioneered the study and practice of leader development, particularly through feedback-intensive programs such as 360-degree assessments and developmental coaching. In recent years, its focus has expanded to include team and organizational development and what is being called "connection development"—the interdependency among individuals, groups, teams, and whole organizations. The purpose of connection development is to strengthen relationships so that the collective work of organizations can be carried out more effectively.

In a recent GrantCraft guide for funders of leadership development, two broad categories of approaches to leadership development are identified. One seeks to support greater organizational effectiveness among nonprofit organizations and uses leadership development "as a way to support specific individuals and provide them with skills, experiences, and resources that will make them and their organizations more effective" (GrantCraft, 2003, p. 6). The second approach seeks to strengthen communities and fields by developing leadership "as a way to change what is happening in a particular community or in a field by increasing skills, role models, credentials, resources, and opportunities for people who work in the community or field and by bringing them into contact with new perspectives or approaches to social change" (GrantCraft, 2003, p. 7). These two categories are very similar to those set out by CCL. Because GrantCraft and CCL serve many organizations, their ways of categorizing the work of leadership development indicate broad acceptance of this understanding and practice in the field.

Within the categorizations of leader and leadership development, there are many different types of leadership that are being developed and supported. One of the earliest distinctions was between transactional and transformational leadership (Burns, 1978). *Transactional leadership* is an exchange of something that has value for both leaders and followers. *Transformational leadership* is a process that leaders and followers engage in that raises one another's level of morality and motivation by appealing to ideals and values. Another way in which transactional and transformational leadership are distinguished is between what leaders do and who leaders are (see Chapters Six and Thirteen).

Early understandings of leadership focused almost exclusively on the traits, characteristics, and capacities of individual leaders. Currently, there is growing interest in collective leadership—sometimes called *shared leadership, connected leadership, collaborative leadership,* or *community leadership.* Collective leadership focuses on leadership as a process, on the relationships between people, their interdependency, and their ability to act upon a shared vision (see Chapter Nine).

Leadership development can be used to achieve many different goals. Some of the purposes of leadership development may include

- Expanding the capacity of individuals to be effective in leadership roles and processes
- Developing the pipeline of leaders within an organization or field
- Identifying and giving voice to emerging and/or invisible leadership
- Strengthening the capacity of teams to improve organizational outcomes
- Supporting the creation of new organizations or fresh approaches to leading
- Encouraging collaboration across functions, sectors, and industries
- Creating a critical mass of leaders that can accelerate change in communities and countries to address key issues and problems

Evaluation

Evaluation is a process of inquiry for collecting and synthesizing information or evidence. There is considerable variation in how information or evidence is gathered, analyzed, synthesized, and disseminated; and there are different purposes for which these things are done.

In the *Encyclopedia of Evaluation,* Fournier (2005) describes evaluation as a process that "culminates in conclusions about the state of affairs, value, merit, worth, significance, or quality of a program, product, person, policy, proposal, or plan" (p. 139). In this definition, evaluation is primarily about determining value and worth. In other definitions there is more emphasis on use. The Innovation Network has articulated a use-focused definition of evaluation as "the systematic collection of information about a program that enables stakeholders to better understand the program, improve its effectiveness, and/or make decisions about future programming" (Innovation Network, 2005, p. 3). For a more in-depth discussion of evaluation use, consult Part Three of this book.

In recent discussions about multicultural evaluation, emphasis is placed on the inquiry process itself and those engaged in it. Because people have different worldviews and value systems, proper data gathering, synthesis, and interpretation requires more than applying a set of tools. To be relevant and valid, data collection, analysis, and dissemination strategies need to "take into account potential cultural and linguistic barriers; include a reexamination of established evaluation measures for cultural appropriateness; and/or incorporate creative strategies for ensuring culturally competent analysis and creative dissemination of findings to diverse audiences" (Inouye, Cao Yu, and Adefuin, 2005, p. 6). Practicing culturally competent evaluation involves understanding how history, culture, and place shape ways of knowing and the ways in which knowledge gets used (see Chapters Four and Nine).

You may wonder how evaluation is different from research. The two activities are multifaceted and at times are quite similar. Both research and evaluation depend on empirical inquiry methods and techniques, but often differ in their purpose. For instance, evaluation traditionally focuses on determining the quality, effectiveness, or value of something, but research seeks to understand relationships among variables or describe phenomena on its way to developing knowledge that can be generalized and applied. The distinction between evaluation and research blurs when complex initiatives are evaluated. Oftentimes, research methods are used to gather data to assess whether an initiative's strategies are convincingly linked to change, such as when school performance rises (see Chapter Eleven). This information is used to improve those strategies and determine how resources will be allocated.

Sometimes calling an inquiry process an *evaluation* can suggest a methodology to prove or disprove success. The emphasis on proof instead of learning has negatively impacted some programs, initiatives, and communities. As a result, there are contexts in which evaluators may use alternative terms, such as *documentation* (see Chapter Fourteen) or *appreciative inquiry* (Preskill and Coghlan, 2004) to describe a process of systematic inquiry. By focusing evaluation on improvement instead of proof, evaluation becomes an asset in these communities rather than a liability.

Leadership Development Evaluation

Leadership development evaluation brings together leadership development and evaluation in a way that expands and deepens the dialogue regarding what constitutes effectiveness in both. Leadership development, when it uses evaluation effectively, accelerates desired changes by being intentional about what is being achieved and why. Evaluation can also be used to better understand and document the unintentional outcomes of leadership development. This knowledge can then be used to improve development programs. Evaluation that embraces leadership development pays more attention to how evaluation gets used, who defines success and for what purpose, and what methods are developed to measure and document changes that result from leadership actions. In this book, we hope to facilitate the transfer of learning about leadership development and evaluation across contexts and to improve practice in both areas.

Purposes of Evaluating Leadership Development. Leadership development is a particularly complex process; it is not something that is fully knowable in a short period of time. Leadership development programs seed changes in and connections among individuals, groups or teams, organizations, and communities that continue to emerge over time. There are many reasons to evaluate leadership development:

- To demonstrate more fully how participants, their organization, and communities do or might benefit from their leadership development program experiences
- To fine-tune a proposed or existing leadership development intervention so that it has farther reach and might better meet its goals
- To show how participation in leadership development experiences connects to such visions as improving organizational performance or changing society for the better
- To promote use of learning-centered reflection as a central evaluation activity
- To pinpoint what leadership competencies are most appropriate in particular settings
- To encourage more comprehensive discussion about what works and why

Leadership Development Evaluation Roles

Leadership development evaluators have many different and often overlapping roles, depending on the context in which they are evaluating and the purposes for which the evaluation is being done. Some of the roles include

- *Assessor.* Evaluators assess the value and quality of a leadership development program or intervention in order to determine if it has achieved its desired outcomes without doing harm or provided a valuable return on investment.
- *Planner and designer.* Evaluators assist stakeholders in using evaluation findings and processes to improve and sometimes to design a new program or

intervention. They also engage designers to identify what outcomes are desired, what will demonstrate success, and what program elements will contribute to or cause these outcomes.

- *Trainer and capacity builder.* Evaluators educate stakeholders so that they might design, implement, and use evaluation effectively. Often this is done by facilitating gatherings where stakeholders participate in the evaluation process and learn how to use evaluation tools.

- *Translator and boundary spanner.* Evaluators cross boundaries to listen to and search for multiple perspectives and interpretations. As they move back and forth across boundaries, evaluators carry perspectives and findings with them and share those with the other groups in ways that those groups can hear and understand.

- *Advocate.* Evaluators present evaluation findings in public forums that are intended to influence decisions about a program, policy direction, or allocation of resources. Evaluators can give voice to ideas, perspectives, and knowledge that normally go unheard or unknown because the groups that espouse them are ignored by groups with more resources and power. Evaluators advocate for taking the time and investing the resources to reflect, inquire, study, and assess programs and interventions because this process increases the likelihood of success and impact. In their role as advocates, evaluators may find that they are asked to modify or couch their findings in ways that will have positive results for a particular audience. Evaluators have an ethical obligation to do their best to maintain the integrity of the evaluation.

- *Reflective practitioner.* Evaluators learn from their own thoughts, reactions, and experiences through a systematic process of interaction, inquiry, and reflection (see Chapters Four and Seven).

Leadership Development Evaluation and Assumptions About Change

It is a common assumption that change is a linear process that happens over time. The program logic model or pathway model is a linear diagram that specifies inputs and expected short-, intermediate, and long-term impacts. These models assist stakeholders to better delineate and agree on the changes they seek over time, how these changes are linked to each other, and how they are linked to the inputs. Evaluations typically test the logic between the parts in these kinds of models.

However, leadership development and its outcomes rarely fall into a neat, linear progression, and sometimes profound change can happen very quickly (see Chapter Three). Recent leadership development evaluations have designed evaluation approaches that are based on systems theories (see Chapters Three and Eleven). These approaches seek to capture the complexity of changes that are occurring and how leadership development contributes to or is linked with those changes.

Where to Look for Change

There are many different domains of impact where results from leadership development interventions can be measured or captured.

- *Individuals.* Leadership development evaluators look for results among the individuals who participate in a program (by far the most common domain). They look for changes in knowledge, skills, values, beliefs, identities, attitudes, behaviors, and capacities.
- *Groups and teams.* In an organizational context, when specific groups or teams are the target of leadership development efforts, evaluators may look for changes in workgroup climate, collaboration, productivity, and so on.
- *Organizations.* Leadership development programs may seek to influence strategy, sustainability, and quantity and quality of products or services delivered. Evaluators look for changes in decision making, leadership pipelines, shared vision, alignment of activities and strategy, and key business indicators.
- *Communities.* Leadership development programs may seek changes in geographic communities or communities of practice. Evaluators look for changes in the composition of leaders who are in decision-making positions, in social networks, in partnerships and alliances among organizations, in ways in which emerging leaders are identified and supported, and in the numbers and quality of opportunities for collective learning and reflection.
- *Fields.* Leadership development programs may seek changes in language, paradigms, and how knowledge gets organized and disseminated. Evaluators look for changes in language, shifts in paradigm, the demographics of participants in a field, and the visibility of ideas within a field.

- *Networks.* In a community or field context, when network building is a core focus of the leadership development effort, evaluators may look for changes in the diversity and composition of networks, levels of trust and connectedness, and their capacity for collective action.
- *Societies/social systems.* Leadership development evaluators sometimes seek to measure or capture social or systems change. Because it typically takes longer to occur, it may be difficult to see in the timeframe of most evaluations. Evaluators look for changes in social norms, social networks, policies, the allocation of resources, and quality of life indicators.

Conclusion

Throughout this book, its authors delve into the concepts we introduce here and into other ideas. We hope that you will find this book useful and thought provoking, and that you will be interested in learning more and contributing your knowledge and experiences to advancing the field of leadership development evaluation. For more information and resources related to topics in this handbook, visit the book's companion Web site at www.leadershiplearning. org/evalhandbook.

References

Burns, J. M. *Leadership.* New York: Harper & Row, 1978.

Davidson, E. J. *Evaluation Methodology Basics: The Nuts and Bolts of Sound Evaluation.* Thousand Oaks, Calif.: Sage, 2005.

Fitzpatrick, J. L., Sanders, J. R., and Worthen, B. R. *Program Evaluation: Alternative Approaches & Practical Guidelines* (3rd ed.). Boston: Addison-Wesley, 2004.

Fournier, D. M. "Evaluation." In S. Mathison (ed.), *Encyclopedia of Evaluation.* Thousand Oaks, Calif.: Sage, 2005, pp. 139–140.

GrantCraft. "Leadership Development Programs: Investing in Individuals." [www. leadershiplearning.org/community/files/download?version_id=1247]. 2003.

Innovation Network. *Evaluation Plan Workbook,* 2005. [www.innonet.org].

Inouye, T., Cao Yu, H., and Adefuin, J. *Commissioning Multicultural Evaluation: A Foundation Resource Guide.* In partnership with Social Policy Research Associates. Oakland, Calif.: The California Endowment's Diversity in Health Education Project, January 2005.

McCauley, C. D., and Van Velsor, E. (eds.). *The Center for Creative Leadership Handbook of Leadership Development* (2nd ed.). San Francisco: Jossey-Bass, 2004.

Preskill, H., and Coghlan, A. (eds.). *Using Appreciative Inquiry in Evaluation.* New Directions for Evaluation, no. 100. San Francisco: Jossey-Bass, 2004.

PART ONE

DESIGNING LEADERSHIP DEVELOPMENT EVALUATION

Each chapter in this part of the book addresses a different approach to or perspective on designing leadership development evaluation. Part One provides ideas and techniques to stimulate your thinking and enhance your evaluation practice. The chapters in this part do not represent the full spectrum of design possibilities. Chapter authors provide references and resources so you can learn more about a wider variety of ideas and approaches.

Every evaluation design has strengths and limitations associated with it. Understanding the benefits and liabilities of various approaches in the context of your initiative will not only help you make a better selection but also help you explain and defend the choices you make. Combining multiple approaches may allow you to meet the needs of multiple stakeholder groups and gain a multifaceted and deep understanding of the leadership development initiative and its impact.

The Purpose of an Evaluation

When designing an evaluation, one of the most important steps is determining the ultimate purpose of the evaluation. The questions following are aimed at surfacing and summarizing the information needed to craft and prioritize evaluation needs and purposes.

- What are the critical questions the evaluation should answer? From whose perspective are the questions likely to be posed? When would a person (or group of people) need to have information related to their question?
- What are the objectives of the leadership development initiative? What aspects of the initiative address those objectives?
- What logical connections can be made (or should be investigated) between initiative outcomes and the intended impact?
- What levels or domains of impact are of interest?
- What outcomes are possible to measure, given the timing of the evaluation in relation to the implementation of the leadership development initiative?
- How will the information from the evaluation be used?

Evaluation Resources

Evaluators also need to know what resources are available to them in terms of money, time, and staff. The cost of the evaluation depends on how complex the initiative and the evaluation are. Complex initiatives with complex evaluations are likely to require a more highly skilled evaluator and more evaluation resources. Evaluators need to consider several factors when determining the complexity of an initiative or evaluation.

- *How the initiative is implemented.* Implementation methods might include face-to-face, electronic, or multiple modalities.
- *Duration of the initiative.* Time frames can range from a single one-hour event, for example, to a multiphase, multisite, multicohort initiative.
- *The embeddedness of the initiative.* Is the leadership development part of a larger effort? Is the evaluation part of the leadership development initiative?
- *Continuum of learning or mastery.* Where does the intended learning outcome fall along a line from increasing awareness (learning new terms, models, and so on) to skilled performance (being able to fluidly apply the learning in different contexts)?
- *Domain of outcomes.* What type of knowledge, skill, and other attributes is expected to change (for example, giving feedback, being culturally aware, and so forth)?
- *Levels of training.* At what level is the initiative being delivered? Levels can include individual, group, team, organizational, community, field, institutional, system, societal, and others.

- *Levels of outcomes and measurement.* At what level can the outcomes or impact of the development be observed (for example, individual, group, team, organizational, community, field, institutional, system, societal, and so on)?
- *Timing of outcomes and impact.* Is change expected over the short term, over an intermediate time frame, or long term? These time periods can mean different things in different contexts, so having a conversation about when would be an appropriate time to measure is important.

Methodological Concepts

There are a few general methodological concepts that are important to understand when designing evaluations. The concepts are not terribly complicated; however, there can be subtle shifts in meaning when the concepts are discussed in the framework of a particular approach.

Causal Attribution. Causal attribution is the logical connection between the initiative and changes occurring after the initiative. Several primary elements help establish a causal relationship between an initiative and the outcomes of an initiative. The elements described below are adapted from information available at: www.socialresearchmethods.net/kb/causeeff.htm.

Temporal Precedence. This means establishing that the cause came before the effect. In terms of leadership development initiatives, it means proving the change occurred after the initiative.

Logical Relationship Between Cause and Effect. There must be some sort of logical link between the initiative and the outcomes of the initiative. For instance, if skills related to providing developmental feedback are discussed and practiced during an initiative, then one would expect to see changes in participants' skills and behaviors related to providing developmental feedback.

Empirical Relationship Between Cause and Effect. This is a measured relationship between the cause and effect (for example, a high correlation between initiative attendance and the observed change).

No Plausible Alternative Explanations. This aspect of the causal chain involves ruling out other factors that may have led to the observed changes. For instance, if a leadership development initiative occurred at the same time as a conflict resolution workshop, it would be difficult to tie a drop in employee conflicts to either initiative specifically. This element of the causal argument rests firmly on the internal validity of an evaluation design (see Chapter One for more information).

In gathering information about causal attribution, evaluators seek to answer the question, Was the change caused by the program? This question is primarily answered through the design of the evaluation. Given the complexity of leadership development initiatives and the contexts in which they occur, not all evaluations of leadership development seek to establish a strong causal link. It is pertinent in all cases to understand the link between information gathered about changes occurring and the initiative. This can be in the form of statistical relationships or stories about how a program has resulted in change. More information about this aspect of evaluation can be found in Chapters One and Three.

Validity. Validity is the degree to which evidence and theory support the interpretations included in and resulting from an evaluation. *Validity* is a term applied to studies as well as one applied to assessments. When it comes to assessments, validity is the combination of two ideas: (1) the degree to which an assessment measures what it claims to measure; and (2) the usefulness of an assessment for a given purpose. Chapter One discusses validity in some detail.

Validity can also be thought of as the truth of an evaluation. Since there are many perspectives and experiences related to leadership development, it is important to consider the truth from multiple perspectives. Chapter Four addresses the complexity of trying to find the truth and challenges us to think more deeply about the unacknowledged and unexplored assumptions and values we bring to leadership development and evaluation.

Reliability. Reliability is the degree to which an assessment produces consistent results. If an assessment does not produce consistent scores, you may be getting more error than information. In the evaluation of a leadership development initiative, it is important to have a sense of how reliable the information is. More information about reliability can be found in Chapter One.

Generalizability. This is the extent to which results for one group apply to another group, and is usually related to external validity evidence. If a leadership development initiative worked for a group of Fortune 500 chief executive officers, how do you know it will work for community leaders in rural areas? Most evaluation studies are interested in the results of a specific initiative for a specific group and are not concerned with generalizing findings to other groups. However, if the initiative being investigated is a pilot run of an initiative that will eventually be offered to other groups or in other contexts, then the generalizability of the findings is an important consideration.

Chapter Summaries

Chapter One. This chapter focuses on experimental and quasi-experimental evaluation approaches. The authors provide an overview of key features and descriptions of specific designs that fall into these two types of designs. Contextual considerations and other issues that are likely to have an impact on these designs are discussed and solutions to common challenges are explored. Circumstances that challenge the validity of experimental and quasi-experimental designs are examined in depth.

Chapter Two. The theory of change approach, which emphasizes making the underlying theory of programs clear in order to evaluate them, forms the basis of the process called *pathway mapping,* which is at the heart of this chapter. Pathway mapping helps evaluators determine what types of evidence they should look for in order to measure program success, and helps stakeholders gain clarity about how and why a leadership development initiative should lead to identified objectives.

Chapter Three. The authors of this chapter propose that evaluations be framed within a holistic design. They suggest that evaluations extend beyond looking for results solely amongst program participants to exploring results in the arenas in which they interact. The authors describe EvaluLEAD, a framework for marrying program activities with more far-reaching results, as a model that places primary focus on what the program is doing to seed change simultaneously at individual, organizational, and community or societal levels.

Chapter Four. This chapter proposes that evaluation is part of the development process. By engaging and including multiple voices and views in the evaluation process and by integrating evaluation into the natural rhythms of life and work, the evaluation itself becomes an ongoing and embedded component of effective program development, implementation, and improvement.

Chapter Five. The final chapter in Part One focuses on measuring the impact of leadership development using a return on investment (ROI) methodology. The chapter provides specific information about measures and ROI calculations.

CHAPTER ONE

EXPERIMENTAL AND QUASI-EXPERIMENTAL EVALUATIONS

S. Bartholomew Craig and Kelly M. Hannum

Experimental and quasi-experimental approaches to evaluation are the focus of this chapter, and they provide a structured means to think about designing evaluations. Though leadership development initiatives and quasi-experimental designs have both been around for decades, few published resources address the challenges of applying experimental or quasi-experimental designs to leadership development.

Two challenges faced by many, if not all, evaluators of leadership development initiatives are (1) the need to measure changes in leadership or leadership outcomes—two complex and sometimes nebulous areas; and (2) determining the relationship between the leadership development initiative in question and the changes measured. Experimental and quasi-experimental approaches provide a means to address both challenges.

Research and evaluation can be thought of as distinct but related activities. This chapter represents the overlap between research and evaluation and uses a research framework for thinking about evaluation. Research designs are typically categorized in one of three ways: nonexperimental, experimental, or quasi-experimental. Exhibit 1.1 illustrates the key elements of each design. Nonexperimental designs are observations about something without any intervention in what is being studied. Because there is no intervention in

EXHIBIT 1.1. USEFUL TERMS AND DEFINITIONS.

Control Groups. A control group contains people who did not participate in the initiative being studied. This is the group against which data from those who did participate in the initiative are compared.

Random Placement. Individuals are assigned to participate in a program or not through a random method and not on the basis of any characteristic they possess or any other non-random process.

Nonexperimental Design. Observations are made in the absence of any intervention in the phenomena being studied. Relative to the other designs, nonexperimental designs are comparatively inexpensive and simple to execute, but provide only hints about possible cause-and-effect relationships. *Example:* Examining the relationship or correlation between leaders' uses of rewards and team performance, without making any attempt to influence either, would be an example of a nonexperimental design.

Quasi-Experimental Design. Observations are made about an intervention. Control groups are typically used, but groups are not created using random assignment. These designs are more complicated to implement than nonexperimental designs, but provide more information about possible cause-and-effect relationships. *Example:* Leaders choose whether to participate in a leadership development program or not. Those participating in the program are compared to themselves before the program or to other groups who did not participate in the program.

Experimental Design. Observations are made about an intervention. One or more control groups are used, but groups are created using random assignment. Because random placement reduces the need to prove that groups are roughly equivalent, results from these designs can be less complicated to interpret than those from quasi-experimental designs and can provide the most information about possible cause-and-effect relationships. *Example:* A group of leaders is identified as appropriate for a leadership development program. The group is randomly divided into two cohorts with one group participating in the leadership development program first. Those participating in the program are compared to the group that has not yet participated in the program.

The table following provides an overview of the key distinctions among the three approaches to research addressed in this chapter.

	Nonexperimental	Quasi-Experimental	Experimental
Control Groups	No	Usually	Yes
Random Placement	No	No	Yes

nonexperimental studies, no evaluation would be considered nonexperimental. Experimental and quasi-experimental designs involve interventions of some kind. Almost all program evaluations could be considered to be at least quasi-experimental in nature, because the program being evaluated represents an intervention that would not have occurred otherwise. In the context of evaluation, however, the terms *experimental* and *quasi-experimental* usually imply that data from different groups are to be compared in some way. This comparison may be made across time, as when the same participants are assessed before a leadership development program and then again afterward; or, the comparison may be made across people, such as when managers who participated in a development program are compared to managers who did not.

When comparisons are made among groups of people, the distinction between experimental designs and quasi-experimental designs comes into play. In experimental designs, individuals are randomly assigned to participate in programs. The group not participating in the program is usually called a *control group*. The control group is the group against which those participating in the program are compared. In quasi-experimental designs, individuals are put into groups on the basis of some nonrandom factor. For example, if leaders are allowed to choose whether or not to participate in a given program, then any evaluation of that program would be, at best, quasi-experimental, because participants were not randomly assigned to participate.

Random assignment is the reason why experimental designs can be more effective at establishing whether the program actually caused the changes that were found. Randomly assigning participants into a program (or not) allows evaluators to assume that any preexisting differences among individuals are evenly distributed between the group participating in the program and those in the control group. For example, some individuals are more ambitious than others. If individuals are allowed to decide for themselves whether to participate in a leadership development program, a greater number of ambitious individuals may become participants versus individuals who are not ambitious. If the evaluation later finds that program participants tended to rise to higher levels in the organization than did nonparticipants, there would be no way to know whether that difference existed because of the program or because the participant group was more ambitious and therefore engaged in other processes that furthered their careers. By randomly assigning people to participate in leadership development, the evaluator can assume that program participants are no more ambitious, on average, than control group members. A similar issue arises when supervisors are asked to recommend individuals for program participation; they may be more likely to recommend high performers in order to maximize return on the organization's investment in the program. The list of factors that can influence group membership in quasi-experimental designs is nearly endless.

If the evaluator could anticipate all the factors that might influence whether individuals end up participating in the program, it would be a simple matter to compare the group participating in the program to those who did not participate in the program, because the evaluator could statistically account or control for any differences that existed prior to the program. Unfortunately, there is no way for an evaluator to be certain that all possible variables have been considered. The main strength of random assignment is that the evaluator is relieved of that burden. When people are assigned to groups at random, individual differences can be assumed to be evenly distributed across the groups (for example, intelligence, personality, work experience, sex, and race). The goal of an experimental design is to engineer a situation in which the only difference between the groups being compared is participation or nonparticipation in the program. Even with randomization it is possible, though unlikely, to get nonequivalent groups; you have experienced this if you have ever tossed a coin and had it come up heads far more often than tails. Therefore, it is recommended that randomly assigned groups be spot-checked on a few key variables of interest in order to confirm that randomization succeeded. If the groups are found to be nonequivalent, randomization can be repeated or the variables on which they differ can be controlled for with statistical techniques. When experimental designs are impractical, as is often the case in the leadership development context, quasi-experimental designs may be used to increase confidence regarding causality.

We began this chapter with two challenges faced by evaluators of leadership development initiatives. The two challenges are related to two broad questions, the answers to which are often sought as part of evaluations. The first question is, What changes have occurred? Answers to this question might include the specific domains where change was found (for example, self-awareness), the direction of the change (for example, increase or decrease), the magnitude of the change (for example, by 21 percent), and the level at which the change occurred (for example, individual, team, or organizational). In most cases quasi-experimental and experimental evaluations of leadership development programs are concerned with change reported at the individual or team level. (It would be a difficult but illuminating study to look at organizations conducting leadership development and compare them to organizations not conducting leadership development.)

The second broad question is, Were the changes caused by the program being evaluated? Change can occur for a variety of reasons. It is usually not sufficient for an evaluation to describe how people changed around the time of a leadership development program; we want to know whether that change occurred *because* of the program. Summative evaluations focus primarily on those two main questions. Formative evaluations also consider questions specifically related to the process or functioning of an initiative with an eye toward how it might be improved.

This chapter is organized around the two questions just mentioned. First, we address some issues associated with measuring change. We then proceed to the problem of linking the changes found to the leadership development initiative. Evaluations are often conducted to help make decisions about resources. If the desired changes are not happening or are not the result of a program, then changes to the program or an entirely different program might be needed. Those using information from evaluations must balance the risk of altering or dropping a program that is performing well, even though the evaluation is not able to pick up on the benefits of the program, with the risk of continuing to put resources into a program that may not be delivering results despite the positive spin around the program. Before delving into these two evaluation questions, we first consider the context in which the evaluation is to occur. The context is critical because it offers clues into what type of evaluation is most appropriate.

Evaluation Context

Leadership development programs, and evaluations of them, are conducted in a wide variety of settings for a wide variety of purposes. The specific context in which the evaluation is to take place has implications for whether or not an experimental or quasi-experimental design is appropriate and, if so, what specific design may be most suitable. Several aspects of the context that should be considered are discussed next.

Clarity of Objectives and Outcomes

All too often, leadership development initiatives are implemented without a clearly stated set of objectives or outcomes. Goals for the program might be stated in vague terms, such as "improve leadership capacity" or "develop our leadership pipeline" with no specific objectives or outcomes associated with the goals. In such cases, different stakeholders may have different ideas about what the program is supposed to accomplish because the goals are open to interpretation. Part of an evaluator's role is to help ensure that stakeholders have a shared understanding of the program's objectives and outcomes. Chapter Two provides helpful advice about how to facilitate and document conversations about stakeholders' expectations for an initiative. This clarification provides necessary information about what changes are expected to occur. Most leadership development initiatives are expected to cause change in several areas, such as participant self-awareness, interpersonal skills, or approaches to problem solving. The direction in which the change should occur should also be clarified with stakeholders. For example, self-awareness might increase, decrease, or stay the same. In almost all cases, measurement strategies should be selected that are capable of detecting change in any direction.

In addition to creating confusion among stakeholders, vaguely stated goals are difficult to measure. Before specific measures can be selected or developed, desired objectives and outcomes must be stated in unambiguous language. Ideally, this clarity should be attained early in the design of the leadership development initiative. Several experimental and quasi-experimental evaluation designs involve collecting data before the initiative begins (pretests). If the desired objectives and their outcomes are not articulated until after the initiative has begun, then pretests are less likely to be useful or may not be possible at all. An initial evaluation may be needed to gather qualitative evidence about what changes occur that can later be used to develop or select more targeted measures.

In situations where stakeholders are not clear about the changes they expect to see after a leadership development initiative, an experimental or quasi-experimental design may not be the best approach. It may be wise to begin first with a more flexible approach that can help deepen understanding about what changes are occurring after an initiative, the results of which could be used to help design an experimental or quasi-experimental evaluation. Chapter Three in this book describes an open-systems approach that may be helpful in contexts that may not be appropriate for experimental or quasi-experimental designs.

Availability of Sound Measures

Even when stakeholders have clearly stated their objectives and outcomes for a leadership development initiative, some of the desired objectives and outcomes may not be easily measurable. For instance, a program goal may be to improve participants' ability to adapt to a changing competitive landscape. But exactly how you measure "ability to adapt to a changing competitive landscape" may be far less clear. How would we quantify this dimension so that participants could be compared, either to themselves before the program or to a control group?

In addition to measuring specific changes, it is important to consider the amount of detail needed about "how much" change has occurred. For instance, you may want to administer a measure of self-awareness that could detect improvement by 5 percent or by 75 percent, or it may be enough to know that, in general, there were signs of improvement. There is little point in using an 18-point response scale when all that is needed to address stakeholder questions is a simple Yes or No.

In some cases, an objective or outcome may be so specific to a particular organizational context that established measures of it do not exist. When outcome criteria are difficult to quantify, evaluation designs that require comparisons among groups will be difficult to implement. Certainly, objective performance data such as revenue or employee turnover rate lend themselves to quantitative comparisons, but there may not be a strong enough logical link between changes in these measures and the leadership development initiative being evaluated. Sometimes individuals will want to make comparisons among data that are readily available without using sound logic to link the measure and the initiative. When thinking about what kind of measure to use, it is important to be sure that what you want to know about can in fact be measured relatively accurately and that there is a reason to think that the initiative will have a fairly direct impact on what is being measured.

Availability of Adequate Sample Size

Experimental and quasi-experimental designs involve comparisons, typically conducted using statistics that explain whether the differences between the groups are likely to be chance fluctuations or real impact. For comparisons to be defensible, fairly large sample sizes may be needed. If a leadership development initiative is only implemented with a small number of individuals (twenty, for example), such comparisons may not be statistically viable (Tourangeau, 2004). If there is not an adequate number of people participating in the program to conduct statistically meaningful comparisons, it does not make sense to invest the time and money into an experimental or a quasi-experimental design. Some resources for determining sample size requirements are listed at the end of this chapter.

Initiative Time Span

One of the key ways in which evaluation designs differ from each other is in terms of the timing of data collection. For example, pretests typically are thought of as occurring before an initiative starts and posttests as occurring after the initiative ends. But some leadership development initiatives may not have definite beginning or end dates. This is often true in the case of systemic leadership development initiatives. Systemic approaches to leadership development may involve a sequence of developmental job assignments or mentoring relationships that are ongoing, with no specific end date. Leaders participating in this kind of development usually do not move through the system as an intact group or cohort; different individuals are at different stages at any given point in time. Evaluations of such initiatives cannot wait for the program to be completed; evaluators must employ designs that collect data at meaningful time points that may be different for different participants, which increases the complexity and complicates the interpretability of experimental and quasi-experimental designs.

Environmental Stability

One of the most important and challenging aspects of leadership development evaluation is establishing the program as the cause of the observed changes. People may change for a variety of reasons that have nothing to do with participation in the program being evaluated. Changes in the organizational context can lead to changes in individuals. For example, if the goal of an initiative were to increase participants' willingness to take risks, and the organization underwent a merger during the course of the program that caused some managers to fear losing their jobs, measures of "risk taking" taken after the program might not accurately reflect the program's efficacy in that domain. In fact, the environmental event (the merger) might decrease the apparent effectiveness of the program by causing it to appear that participants were actually more risk averse after attending the program. Other environmental events that could produce similar results include organizational restructuring, changes in organizational leadership, changes in funding or budget allocations, the entry of new competitors into a market, the introduction of new policies and procedures, new rewards and recognition systems, changes in the regulatory or legal landscape, and changes in the political regime of the country in which the organization operates. The list of possibilities is extremely long and highly dependent on the context in which the evaluation is being conducted. Ideally, evaluations should be timed so as to be as insulated as possible from potentially disruptive environmental events. When evaluations must take place in unstable environments, evaluators should make careful note of the relative timing of the events. When possible, evaluators should also take separate measurements of the events' effects to have the best possible chance of being able to separate their effects from those of the program. In unstable environments, using control groups who experienced the same environment as participants but who did not participate in the program is especially useful.

Measuring Change

A critical part of the design process is deciding what kinds of change will be measured and how. Measuring leadership outcomes and linking them to a specific initiative in dynamic and fluid contexts is by no means simple. Ideally an evaluator would work with stakeholders to determine the areas in which change can be expected and linked to the leadership development initiative and to determine how the change can best be measured. Once the domains are identified, appropriate and accurate measures for assessing that domain can be identified or developed. For example, an evaluator may decide to measure participants' self-awareness by comparing self and others' ratings on a 360-degree assessment instrument, or the evaluator might interview participants' colleagues to ask how effectively participants communicate their visions for the future to others. As part of this process it is also important to identify the level(s) at which change is expected (for example, individual, group, organizational, community), when the change is expected, and from whose perspectives the change can be seen and measured.

It may seem obvious, but it is critical to be certain that the measures you are using are as accurate and as appropriate as possible. In many cases, positive behavioral change is an expected outcome of leadership development. Accurately measuring behavioral change is difficult and much has been written about this topic (for example, Collins and Sayer, 2001; Gottman, 1995; Harris, 1963). Relying on instruments with established, well-researched psychometric characteristics is one way to help ensure accurate and appropriate measures. The two indicators of most interest are reliability and validity. They are related concepts, but they have distinct meanings and are assessed differently.

The reliability of a measure can be thought of as the consistency of results (see Exhibit 1.2). For example, if a scale indicates you weigh 120 pounds on one day and then on the next day it indicates you weigh 220 pounds, those results are inconsistent, which means the scale is not a reliable measure of your weight. Reliability can be estimated a number of ways and is usually indicated on a scale from zero to one. Typically, reliability estimates above 0.80 are considered reasonably good (Nunnally, 1978). However, it is important to keep in mind that some things can be measured more objectively (for example, the frequency with which a manager provides feedback) while other areas can only be measured subjectively (for example, the quality of the feedback provided). Objective measures are more likely to have higher reliability estimates. Reliability is important because if a measure is providing inconsistent results, you may not want to put too much stock in the data you collect with it.

When using a preexisting measure, it is also important to make certain that the measure is a good fit for the situation, which leads us to the appropriateness of the measure or the measure's *validity*. A measure of coaching behaviors developed for use with sports team coaches is not likely to be a good measure for the coaching learned in a leadership development program for a manufacturing setting. Similarly, an assessment developed for use with university students in Sweden may not be appropriate for university students in Venezuela. There are various approaches to determining a measure's validity. Exhibit 1.2 provides an overview of some of the more common approaches to validity.

Cause and Effect

Whether or not, or how confidently, the second basic question of evaluation—Was the change caused by the program?—can be answered depends on the design of the evaluation. Typically an evaluation design provides a logical plan

EXHIBIT 1.2. RELIABILITY AND VALIDITY OF A MEASURE.

Reliability is the degree to which an assessment produces consistent results. If an assessment does not produce consistent scores, you may be getting more error than information. Reliability is never truly measured, but it can be estimated. The same test will likely have different reliability estimates depending on how reliability is calculated and on the sample used. The appropriate reliability level depends on the situation. Reliability is usually reported on a scale ranging from 0 to 1, with estimates closer to one being preferred. Three ways to assess reliability are

1. *Internal consistency,* which provides information about whether items on a scale are measuring the same or closely related concepts. Usually Cronbach's alpha is used to measure internal consistency. The Instrument Review Team at the Center for Creative Leadership, for example, recommends alphas of 0.70 or higher.

2. *Interrater agreement,* which provides information about the degree to which ratings agree. *Feedback to Managers* suggests interrater reliabilities should be between 0.40 and 0.70 for 360-degree assessments (Leslie and Fleenor, 1998).

3. *Test-retest,* which provides information about the stability of items and scales over time. In this case, the test is administered and then administered again after a short period of time. Reliabilities of 0.70 or higher are generally considered acceptable.

The validity of a test is a combination of two ideas: (1) the degree to which an assessment measures what it claims to measure; and (2) the usefulness of an assessment for a given purpose. Validity is a multifaceted concept and an extremely important consideration when developing or using assessments. Multiple types of evidence are needed to establish test validity. Validity evidence should be gathered in the varying situations and with the varying populations for which the assessment is intended. Validity has to do with the test, the people taking the test, the purpose of the test, and the consequences of the test. Types of validity evidence for assessments include:

- *Content validity.* The extent to which the assessment adequately and comprehensively measures what it claims to measure.

- *Construct validity.* The relationship between test content and the construct it is intended to measure. Typically, this type of evidence involves logical and/or empirical analysis including statistical comparisons to other assessments and expert judgments of the relationship between the assessment and the construct.

- *Criterion validity.* The relationship between the assessment and a criterion such as effective performance (for example, looking at the relationship between an assessment of job performance and job performance ratings). Concurrent evidence refers to criterion data collected at the same time the test is administered and predictive evidence involves criteria collected at a later point in time.

EXHIBIT 1.2. RELIABILITY AND VALIDITY OF A MEASURE, Cont'd.

- *Consequential validity.* Evidence supporting the benefits and consequences of testing are examined in this type of study. Consequences of tests are considered aspects of validity when they are related to construct underrepresentation or construct-irrelevant components of a test. This is particularly important in high-stakes testing. The consequences associated with test use are not universally accepted as an aspect of validity.

We sometimes take for granted that an assessment is providing accurate, useful, and appropriate information. Assessments do not always do that. Validity studies are one way that item or test bias or unfairness can be revealed. Bias is the presence of an item or test characteristic that results in differential performance for individuals of the same ability but from different groups (for example, ethnic, sex, cultural, social status, or religious groups). Bias often stems from limitations of our perspective and understanding. No test is free from bias, but item and test bias and unfairness can be detected and reduced. How might bias enter into an assessment? Items that use vocabulary, content, structure, or an administration mode that improve the performance of one group over another are potentially biased or unfair items. For example, a test written in English might be biased against individuals for whom English is a second language. Other potential sources for bias or unfairness include offensive, demeaning, or emotionally charged items. While there are strategies and tools for assessing bias in tests and items, it can be difficult to figure out how much difference is too much, the root of the difference, and the appropriate course of action. The process can get complicated and expensive. The consequences of not addressing bias in assessments can also be complicated and expensive. Assessments are only as good as we make them. How accurate an assessment needs to be depends on many things including the intended use and consequences of use associated with the assessment.

---

for what will be assessed, how it will be assessed, when it will be assessed, and from what sources data will be collected. Linking changes in leadership outcomes to a leadership development program cannot be accomplished without a good evaluation plan. Drawing conclusions about cause and effect is almost never straightforward. A general discussion about causal inferences is included in the overview for this part of the book. How confident we can be that the changes we measured can be attributed to the leadership development program in question depends heavily on how the evaluation was designed.

Factors that reduce our confidence about causality are called *threats to validity.* Threats to validity are possible alternative explanations, not related to the program, about why changes may have been observed. For instance, if participants received a large monetary bonus during the time period when the leadership development program occurred, that—rather than the program—might be the reason for any increase in organizational commitment. As we discuss in detail later, different types of evaluation designs are vulnerable to different types of threats to validity. Understanding validity and threats to validity is essential for making methodological choices.

Validity

Validity is the truth of inferences based on the results of your evaluation. Validity, as we discuss it in this section, is about the evaluation rather than a specific measure (see Exhibit 1.2). Strong validity requires accurate, appropriate, and sufficient evidence. An evaluation is said to have adequate internal validity if we can be confident in its conclusions about cause-and-effect relationships. For example, if an evaluation provides compelling evidence that managers' participation in a leadership development program caused their sales teams to increase their orders in the month following the program, then the evaluation study would demonstrate strong internal validity. What is considered compelling evidence is a matter of judgment. In order for us to have confidence in such a cause-effect relationship, the study's design must enable us to rule out other plausible explanations for the increased sales, such as seasonal fluctuations or a broad change in market demand. In many ways the situation is similar to a legal argument; is there convincing evidence that the program caused or contributed to the changes indicated? It is important to consider that different stakeholder groups may have very different ideas about what they consider convincing evidence and may be able to offer differing perspectives on the logic of arguments.

External validity is the degree to which conclusions from an evaluation are true for people, places, or times other than the ones actually evaluated. For instance, if another evaluation conducted a year later on a different group of participants found the same effect on sales orders, we would say that the first study demonstrated external validity. An evaluation study must have internal validity in order to have external validity, but having internal validity does not guarantee external validity.

Threats to Internal Validity

Factors that weaken confidence in conclusions that changes were caused by the program being evaluated are called *threats to internal validity.* As mentioned earlier, different evaluation designs are vulnerable to different threats, so an understanding of common threats to internal validity is important to anyone charged with designing or interpreting an evaluation study.

Systematic Differences Between Program Participants and Nonparticipants.

As mentioned earlier, a key goal of an experimental or quasi-experimental design is to create a situation where the only difference between program participants and nonparticipants is their participation in the program. This is an almost impossible goal in today's dynamic environments, but the closer you can get to it, the more confidence you can have that the changes observed are because of the program evaluated. This is generally achieved by randomly assigning individuals to the program (experimental) or measuring and controlling for factors that may be different between participants and nonparticipants (quasi-experimental). Several potential threats to achieving such a state of affairs are explained below.

Selection. Any factor that causes people with certain characteristics to be more likely to participate in the program than people without those characteristics is a threat to internal validity. For leadership development initiatives, two common practices are self-selection and boss-selection. If participants are permitted to choose whether to participate (self-selection) or their superiors select or nominate them for participation (boss-selection), then people with certain characteristics may be more likely to be excluded from the program group (for example, managers with more hectic schedules, lower ambition, lower or higher job performance). In cases where self-selection or boss-selection is used to identify who will participate in leadership development, randomly creating two cohorts allows for a control group that is likely to have similar characteristics. For example, if fifty individuals were selected by themselves or their bosses to participate in leadership development then twenty-five could be randomly selected to participate in the first cohort, while the remaining twenty-five could be used as a control group until their participation in the program.

Other potential problems include conducting the program at a time when certain types of people are not available or in locations that are more accessible to some types of leaders than others (for example, conducting a program during a time when individuals from a specific region are involved in opening a new office). Such factors can result in *preprogram* differences between groups that may later be confused with program effects. Selection can also be an issue when not all program participants are included in the evaluation and the individuals participating in the evaluation are different from those who do not participate.

Attrition. This problem is similar to the selection issue except that attrition occurs when participants with certain characteristics are more likely to drop out of the program (or the evaluation) before its completion. The end result is the same as with selection: the groups being compared are different for reasons other than the program. For example, leaders who have difficulty delegating or who work in small organizations may be more likely to have to drop out of a program in order to deal with a crisis within their organizations. Attrition can occur in the context of the evaluation as well, with certain types of individuals dropping out of the evaluation (that is, failing to complete evaluation measures). For instance, individuals who did not experience benefits from the leadership development initiative may not want to spend more of their time by participating in the evaluation. If those who feel similarly also drop out, then the results of the evaluation are compromised. At a minimum, it is a good idea to follow up with individuals who drop out of the initiative or the evaluation to find out more about why they dropped out. In cases where a large number of people have dropped out, you may want to randomly follow up with a smaller subset of the individuals who dropped out.

Regression to the Mean. This issue concerns the tendency for those scoring extremely high or low on a measure to be less extreme during the next test. For example, if only those who scored poorly on a leadership capacities test are included in the program, they might do better on the next test regardless of the program just because the odds of doing as poorly the next time are low. Similarly, if only those scoring high on the leadership capacities test are selected, they may not do as well on the next test simply because achieving a higher score when one is already near the top of a range is difficult (there is less room for improvement). Selecting or developing a measure that more fully represents the knowledge, skills, abilities, or behaviors of those in the group targeted for development is one way to help guard against this threat.

Changes Not Caused by the Program. Whereas the threats discussed previously concern differences between groups that might mask change or be mistaken for change, the next two threats to validity exist when changes do occur in program participants, but those changes are caused by some factor other than the program being evaluated.

Maturation. People are always changing and developing even when they are not explicitly involved in development programs. We tend to become better at our jobs with experience and our personalities can change with age. Distinguishing between changes resulting from natural biological or psychological development and changes caused by the program can sometimes be difficult, especially in evaluation designs that do not use control groups and continue over an extended period of time. Although maturation can be a threat in the evaluation of long-term systemic leadership development initiatives, this type of threat is less likely to occur in traditional leadership development situations of shorter duration (unless the program is specifically for new hires or new placements who might develop a variety of skills in a short time based on learning from their new job experiences). However, it can be a problem when the program is brief, but the time intervals between evaluation measurements are long, such as when pretests are conducted long before the program starts or posttests are administered long after it ends.

History. As discussed earlier, evaluations can be compromised when changes in participants' environment occur around the same time as the program and cause participants to change their behavior in ways that might be confused with effects of the program. Such events can occur in the internal environment of the organization or in its external environment. For example, a corporate merger could cause employees to fear for their jobs, or an economic recession might cause a downturn in organizational performance that could mask the otherwise positive effects of a leadership development program. Changes due to such historical events are more likely to be temporary than changes from maturation and can often be detected by collecting data at multiple points in time. Using a control group allows an evaluator to better tease out programmatic effects, since both those participating in the program and those in the control group should experience the same events and shifts.

Problems with Measures. Sometimes the evaluation process creates threats to its own validity. Although it can be useful to think of evaluation as a kind of intervention with its own set of outcomes, those outcomes can be problematic when they inhibit the evaluator's ability to accurately assess the effects of the program. Two evaluator-generated threats to internal validity are discussed here.

Testing. You have probably heard the adage that "practice makes perfect." If identical measures are administered before and after a program, the preprogram test can act like a practice session that serves to improve performance on the postprogram test. This effect can occur for at least two reasons. One is familiarity; when participants take the test following the program, they have already seen it at least once before and that familiarity may serve to increase their scores the second time around. The other reason is that the pretest may provide participants with clues as to which parts of the program's content they should pay close attention to. By sensitizing participants to the specific areas on which they will be tested again after the program, the pretest serves as a study guide. In some ways this increased focus can be seen as a benefit, if knowing which areas are the focus of the program helps participants meet a learning objective. However, the result can be that the posttest scores become biased indicators of program effectiveness, usually overestimating how much participants learned in the program. If, however, the pretest is part of the initiative and there is no identical posttest that is part of the evaluation, testing is not likely to pose a threat to validity.

The testing threat is an issue primarily with knowledge or skill assessments that are completed by participants and contain items scored as right or wrong. This type of assessment is not very common in leadership development contexts, but it is used often enough that evaluators should be wary of the testing threat.

Instrumentation. Instrumentation bias occurs when measurements taken at different times are not meaningfully comparable. This can occur even when the measures have been taken with identical instruments. When instrumentation bias is operating, calculating the difference between scores from any two occasions can produce a misleading estimate of change. This can occur when instruments are completed by participants' coworkers, such as in the case of 360-degree leadership assessments. If the exact same group of coworkers is not surveyed at each time point, then differences in ratings may be due to the changes in the composition of the rater group rather than actual changes in participants.

Instrumentation bias can also occur in self-report instruments completed by participants. One reason for this phenomenon is often referred to as *response shift bias.* Response shift can occur because the leadership development program changes the way participants think about the behaviors assessed by the instrument (Howard and Dailey, 1979; Rohs, 1999, 2002). For example, prior to the program a manager might rate herself as a "3" on a 5-point scale measuring her empowerment of her subordinates. During the program she learns about many new ways to empower subordinates that she had not considered before. When she rates herself again after the program, she realizes that she really should only have rated herself a "2" earlier, but because she has improved following the program she now rates herself a "3." Because both the pretest and posttest were 3s, a simple comparison of the two scores would suggest that no improvement occurred. But the change in the participant's frame of reference regarding what constituted a "2" versus a "3" prevents us from meaningfully comparing the scores. This change in frame of reference can be a positive outcome of the program, indicating that participants' knowledge in a particular domain has increased. But whether or not such a shift is considered to be a desirable outcome, it creates measurement problems and it is important to keep in mind that pre- and postprogram scores cannot be meaningfully compared when such an effect is present. Unfortunately, methods for detecting response shift bias involve sophisticated statistical procedures that are not accessible to all evaluators (for details, see Craig, Palus, and Rogolsky, 2000; Millsap and Hartog, 1988; Schmitt, 1982). As an alternative, some researchers have recommended the use of retrospective pretests that are administered at the same time as posttests in order to ensure that both measures are completed with the same frame of reference (Howard, 1980; Howard and Dailey, 1979). Retrospective measures require that individuals accurately remember behaviors exhibited in the past— frequently, a few months in the past. Thus retrospective measures depend on potentially faulty human memories, so there is at present no easy solution to the problem of response shift bias. In cases where different measures are used to assess the same construct or domain, then the two measures should be comparable in terms of content and response scale. This comparability is referred to as measurement equivalence and also requires sophisticated statistical techniques (Cronbach and Furby, 1970; Facteau and Craig, 2001).

Threats to External Validity

While an evaluation study's internal validity is a necessary requirement for external validity, it is not sufficient alone. *External validity* is the extent to which the evaluation's findings apply to people, places, or times other than the ones actually studied. In some cases, evidence about the external validity of an evaluation study may not be critical. This is especially true when an organization wants the results only for use regarding a program in a specific context and for a specific group of individuals. However, in situations when program evaluation findings are intended to be reflective of results one might expect of a program across different types of individuals in different contexts, then guarding against the threats to external validity becomes important. In the paragraphs that follow we discuss some common threats to external validity that can occur even in a study with high internal validity.

Selection-Treatment Interaction. The pool from which participants are selected, even when they are randomly assigned to a program, can limit the generalizability of evaluation findings. For instance, assume a health care organization decided to evaluate its leadership development efforts intended for the high-potential leaders in the organization. A successful leadership development initiative for those participants, in that context, may not be effective for at-risk participants coming from the financial sector. Therefore it is important to consider the program within the context where it was implemented; for instance, in terms of the individuals participating, and the sector and region in which they are working.

Multiple Treatment Interference. In the context of leadership development, this type of threat can occur when participants have attended a previous development program (for example, a program on personal responsibility) and the effect of the prior program affects or interacts with the leadership development program. Future participants in the leadership development program who have not also experienced the personal responsibility program might exhibit different types of change than would have been expected based on the earlier evaluation. This situation limits the generalizability of evaluation findings because it is difficult to determine the effects due exclusively to the leadership development program. In cases where other initiatives are known to have been offered, the evaluator could list different development opportunities and request individuals to indicate in which ones they participated. Alternatively, an open-ended question could be asked about other types of development the individual has experienced recently. These data could be used to track which participants had participated in other development programs and analyzed to determine the contribution of participation in other development initiatives.

Specificity of Variables. Deciding exactly how to measure the specific elements of the domain identified as the area of change after a leadership development program is difficult. If a domain is measured in very specific terms that only apply to a certain group or a certain context, it will be difficult to argue that similar findings are likely in other settings. For example, many leadership development programs require participants to set goals for specific projects taking place in their organizations (for example, "hire three new members for the health care IT team by August"). Progress toward such situation-specific goals may be hard to generalize to other settings. Conversely, if the measures are couched in very general terms, they may be more applicable to different settings or groups but lack the specificity necessary to provide clear evidence for the particular group being evaluated. Generally, it is better to be certain to measure what is most important in the context of the evaluation rather than to become overly concerned about generalizing results to other situations.

Treatment Diffusion. Individuals attending a leadership development program may communicate what they are learning in the program with people outside the program. In some cases, that is an intended and valuable outcome of leadership development initiatives. For example, many leadership development programs encourage participants to share what they have learned and their development plans with their bosses in order to gain their support for the participants' change efforts. However, the situation creates a problem for evaluators because individuals who did not attend the program are experiencing elements of the program. If an individual in a unit is a member of the control group while another individual in the same unit is participating in the program, it is possible that the individual in the control group could make some improvement in his or her leadership simply because of conversations with the individual in the program. Such treatment diffusion could make the differences between the program participants and the control group appear smaller than they really are, leading to an underestimation of the program's impact.

Experimenter Effects. Conscious or unconscious actions of researchers that affect participants' performance and responses are called *experimenter effects.* An example in the context of leadership development would be an evaluator providing feedback to participants, based on observations, that improves participants' performance. While improving participants' performance is the goal of the initiative, it may be that a primary reason for the improvement was the feedback from the evaluator rather than the initiative itself. Experimenter effects can even occur simply because the evaluator discloses details of the evaluation design to participants. If participants know exactly what the evaluator is trying to measure, they may behave differently with regard to the domains being assessed.

Reactive Effects. Merely knowing that an evaluation is taking place may affect participants' behavior. These effects are sometimes called *Hawthorne effects* or *John Henry effects.* In the context of leadership development, individuals selected to participate in the program may be more confident in themselves because their organization has made an investment in them. Alternatively, if a leadership development program is perceived to be the last effort an organization makes before firing someone, participants may begin looking for other employment when they learn they have been selected to participate in a program. Increased turnover subsequent to the program may therefore not be related to the program itself, but rather the reputation of the program.

Factors to Consider in Choosing a Design

The collection of concepts and terms presented in this chapter may seem daunting, but it is not necessary for you to memorize them. Our intent is to acquaint you with a way of thinking about evaluation design that considers what kinds of questions you want your evaluation to answer and what factors might influence the evaluation's ability to answer those questions. No evaluation is perfect. This chapter can serve as a useful reference that you can refer to on an as-needed basis. You cannot successfully defend against all the threats to validity, but understanding more about the various threats enables you to better account for these elements in the design of the evaluation and in the interpretation and use of results. After all, evaluations are used to make decisions about funding and other resources, so it is important to think about the quality, accuracy, and appropriateness of the data on which decisions are based.

Following are some suggestions for incorporating the ideas presented here into the decisions you make in the design of your evaluation.

Evaluation Purpose

For an evaluation to be effective, one needs to understand the overall purpose of the evaluation from the perspective of key stakeholders. Understanding the purpose of an evaluation helps determine what kind of an evaluation is most likely to meet that purpose. If stakeholders are looking for answers to questions related to the general questions, What changes have occurred? and Were the changes caused by the program being evaluated? then an experimental or quasi-experimental design with one or more control groups is worth considering. Keep in mind, however, that there are other methodologies that can provide information that may augment information gathered as part of an experimental or quasi-experimental design or may even be more appropriate.

Understanding what contributed to or diminished change after a leadership development initiative may be best achieved using a mixed methodology approach. Collecting stories or examples of specific changes and the barriers to and facilitators of those changes can be accomplished through interviews or focus groups. This type of information is often very helpful in providing examples that "speak" to stakeholders and can provide meaningful clues about why an initiative achieved its goals or why not. It can be even more compelling when stories collected from participants are compared to stories collected from nonparticipants for evidence of change due to the program. These data combined with quantitative data about the program can provide a more comprehensive view of the program.

Typically, quantitative data, such as 360-degree leadership ratings, are shared with stakeholders in aggregate form, indicating trends across or within groups of individuals, rather than highlighting specific individual examples or creating a deep understanding of why an initiative worked or not. Qualitative data can provide rich insight into participants' subjective experiences with the program. The evaluator's understanding of how the results of an evaluation will be used and the specific questions the evaluation seeks to answer are essential to creating or selecting the appropriate design. Both quantitative and qualitative data can be used in quasi-experimental and experimental designs.

On the following pages we present and comment on the most common experimental and quasi-experimental designs. Russ-Eft and Hoover's (2005) discussion of experimental and quasi-experimental designs provides additional information about various designs in the context of organizations.

Single-Group Designs

In a single-group design, only individuals who participated in the leadership development initiative are studied. There are essentially three ways to organize this type of design:

1. Posttest only
2. Pretest-posttest
3. Repeated measures

In the posttest-only approach, participants are measured after they have engaged in leadership development. The problem with this approach is that it is impossible to establish whether high scores are the result of the initiative or if they were preexisting. No objective measures of change can be taken, though participants can be asked to reflect and report how they think they have changed. Individuals with whom the leadership development participant interacts can also be asked to report how they think the participant changed. Keep in mind that if you are asking others about the changes in the participant, the questions need to address things someone other than the participant would be able to notice.

In contrast, a pretest-posttest approach provides information about the amount of change that occurred, although the lack of a control group still limits confidence in the program as the cause. Retrospective pretest-posttests are a variation of the general pretest-posttest approach, with the distinction being that retrospective pretests are administered after the program. In either case, it is difficult to prove the program caused the change. Any observed change might be due to another event experienced by the group, such as layoffs or annual salary increases (see the previous section on Threats to Validity for more information). If all participants show change and they are from different contexts (different sectors or organizations, for example), there may not be another plausible explanation for the change and it would therefore be easier to argue that the program caused the change.

Repeated measures designs involve collecting multiple measurements typically before the program, during the program, and after the program. Exhibit 1.3 provides an example of a longitudinal approach. Longitudinal data collected on three or more occasions allow us to track the group's scores over an extended period of time, providing evidence of trends. If there is a trend of improvement it can be more convincing than improvement measured at a single point in time. Looking at data over time is especially appropriate when there is reason to expect a dip in performance before improvement. For instance, you may expect individuals to be a bit awkward using newly acquired skills at first (they may be used to a very different style), but over time their performance might climb to a new high as they gain proficiency and comfort.

EXHIBIT 1.3. A LONGITUDINAL APPROACH TO DATA COLLECTION.

Preprogram	During the program	3 months after the program	6 months after the program	9 months after the program
Baseline measure taken	Measure progress	Measure progress	Measure progress	Measure progress

Thus, data collected at multiple points in time will reflect all parts of the performance curve.

Designs with Two or More Groups

Even when a strong repeated measures design shows change, there is still the possibility that the improvement is due to something other than the leadership development program. For this reason, evaluators should prefer designs using at least two groups.

These types of designs have the same basic variations as single-group designs (that is posttest only, pretest-posttest, or longitudinal), but at least two groups are studied in order to provide a comparison. If participants show positive change in the identified areas and those who did not participate in the initiative do not show positive change (or show less change), that provides more convincing evidence for the effectiveness of the initiative than assessing only a single group.

Ideally the groups to be compared are formed using random placement. Although it might be impractical to completely withhold a development program from some individuals at random, a random process can be used to determine the order in which individuals participate and thus achieve nearly the same result. Consider, for example, a repeating series of initiatives intended for large numbers of individuals preselected by the human resources department to participate. If the pool of selected candidates were 250, then 125 could be randomly assigned to participate as the first cohort and the remaining 125 would be assigned to participate at a later time as the second cohort. In the interim, the second group could function as the control group for the first cohort, since the groups should be similar; however, this process may not guarantee that the two groups will remain equivalent throughout the study. Members of the participant group may drop out before completing the program, or members of either group may not be able to be located for follow-up purposes for reasons that are systematically related to the impacts of the program. Members of the control group could also be affected by treatment diffusion.

Identifying a Control Group

When random placement is not an option, there are two alternative approaches to identifying a control group: (1) matching participants and nonparticipants on important characteristics; and (2) statistically controlling for differences between groups during data analysis. Note that both of these methods require that the evaluator be able to anticipate which variables might affect the outcomes being measured. Matching participants and nonparticipants on key traits can be difficult when multiple characteristics must be considered, which is often the case with leadership development. Some characteristics to consider often include geographic location, department or function, age, gender, organizational level, and job performance indicators. If additional personal information is available, such as scores on ability, performance, or personality tests, those may also provide useful matching variables.

Often the matching can lead to other issues. For instance, if you match a participant with a nonparticipant who is in the same group and shares the same boss, you may be introducing treatment diffusion or expectation effects. The participant may talk about or model knowledge or skills gained in the initiative, thereby exposing the nonparticipant to aspects of the initiative. It is also possible that the boss may treat differently, or have different expectations of, the participant, which can lead to a change in performance (or another area measured).

Statistically controlling for differences assumes you are aware of the variables on which the groups differ and have measures to quantify them. Statistical control requires considerable statistical savvy to execute properly and likely will require additional data collection; therefore it may not be the best option in some cases. In addition, the amount of testing required to gather the data needed in the analysis may be too burdensome.

Planning for Data Analysis

Once measures have been selected or developed, and you have decided on the groups, you can begin to determine what kinds of analyses you intend to conduct. At this point, it is important to check the available sample size, especially if generalizability is a goal. It may not be possible to obtain groups large enough to make meaningful statistical comparisons (Tourangeau, 2004). Even if the sample size was determined to be adequate prior to beginning the initiative and the evaluation, it is often the case that not all the identified individuals will complete the initiative and participate in the evaluation. In small organizations, complex statistical analyses are often not viable because it may be impossible to gather data from enough individuals to permit meaningful comparisons.

Conclusion

Used appropriately, experimental and quasi-experimental designs can be an effective tool for determining the effects of leadership development initiatives. This chapter introduces some of the core elements and issues related to using this approach as an evaluation tool for leadership development. In Exhibit 1.4, we summarize the main points of this chapter into a succinct list of recommendations for evaluators of leadership development initiatives and include a worksheet as Exhibit 1.5 to help you identify threats to internal validity that might affect your evaluation. The Resources provided at the end of the chapter are intended to help you locate additional information.

EXHIBIT 1.4. RECOMMENDATIONS FOR EVALUATORS OF LEADERSHIP DEVELOPMENT INITIATIVES.

- Use complementary methods to illustrate, qualify, and strengthen the understanding of the measured change and its causal link to the program.
- Use equivalent control groups when possible to help guard against arguments that the changes were due to something other than the leadership development initiative.
- Use multiple measures (triangulate methods and sources). If an evaluation is able to demonstrate positive impact the next question is usually "Why?" Collecting diverse information from diverse sources leads to results that are able to meet a variety of stakeholder needs.
- Make sure an appropriate sample size is available for the types of comparisons planned.

EXHIBIT 1.5. THREATS TO INTERNAL VALIDITY WORKSHEET.

Threats to internal validity are listed following, along with questions that can help you reveal and think about these threats in leadership development contexts.

Selection

- How are participants selected to participate in the leadership development initiative?

- What records are kept about the selection process?

- Is a specific type of person more likely to participate in the leadership development initiative?

- How might the selection process have an impact on evaluation efforts?

Mortality or Attrition

- What processes are in place to monitor initiative participation and track demographic (and perhaps other) information about those who complete or do not complete the initiative?

- Are resources available (for example, budget) to follow up with individuals who drop out of the initiative or the evaluation?

Statistical Regression

- If participants are selected on the basis of their performance on a measure or if there is baseline information about performance on a measure, how does the observed range of scores compare to the possible range of scores?

Maturation

- How likely is it that participants would perform better on the measures selected for the evaluation because of natural development trends (such as more time on the job)?

History

- What about the context in which individuals and groups are performing has changed or might change?

- What processes are in place to track the changes likely to have an impact on the initiative or the evaluation?

- What impact might these changes have on results?

EXHIBIT 1.5. THREATS TO INTERNAL VALIDITY WORKSHEET, Cont'd.

Testing

• Is a pretest being administered as part of the evaluation?

Instrumentation

• Is there evidence that the measures being used (for example, pretest and posttest) are reliable?

• Are the pretest and posttest the same measure? If different measures are being used, are the two measures directly comparable? If the same measure is being used, what impact might response shift have on results?

Resources

For more detailed technical information about experimental and quasi-experimental research designs, see Campbell and Stanley, 1963; Cook and Campbell, 1979; Russ-Eft and Hoover, 2005; Shadish, Cook, and Campbell, 2002.

Existing measures can be identified and evaluated using information provided by the Buros Institute of Mental Measurements, which has a searchable Test Directory online at www.unl.edu/buros/bimm. The site also provides guidance about selecting and using appropriate measures.

There are many Web sites that offer online calculators for estimating sample size requirements as well as guidance that can be helpful, for example:

www.surveysystem.com/sscalc.htm

www.stat.uiowa.edu/~rlenth/Power

www.isixsigma.com/library/content/c000709.asp

References

Campbell, D. T., and Stanley, J. C. *Experimental and Quasi-experimental Designs for Research.* Boston: Houghton Mifflin, 1963.

Collins, L. M., and Sayer, A. G. *New Methods for the Analysis of Change.* Washington, D.C.: American Psychological Association, 2001.

Cook, T. D., and Campbell, D. T. *Quasi-Experimentation: Design and Analysis for Field Settings.* Chicago: Rand McNally, 1979.

Craig, S. B., Palus, C. J., and Rogolsky, S. "Measuring Change Retrospectively: An Examination Based on Item Response Theory." In Jennifer Martineau (chair), *Measuring Behavioral Change: Methodological Considerations.* Symposium presented at the annual conference of the Society for Industrial and Organizational Psychology. New Orleans, April 2000.

Cronbach, L. J., and Furby, L. "How We Should Measure Change—or Should We?" *Psychological Bulletin,* 1970, *74,* 68–80.

Facteau, J. D., and Craig, S. B. "Are Performance Appraisal Ratings from Different Rating Sources Comparable?" *Journal of Applied Psychology,* 2001, *86,* 215–227.

Gottman, J. M. *The Analysis of Change.* Mahwah, N.J.: Lawrence Erlbaum Associates, 1995.

Harris, C. W. (ed.). *Problems in Measuring Change.* Madison: The University of Wisconsin Press, 1963.

Howard, G. S. "Response Shift Bias—A Problem in Evaluating Interventions with Pre/Post Self-Reports." *Evaluation Review,* 1980, *4*(1), 93–106.

Howard, G. S., and Dailey, P. R. "Response-Shift Bias: A Source of Contamination in Self-Report Measures." *Journal of Applied Psychology,* 1979, *64*(2), 144–150.

Leslie, J. B., and Fleenor, J. W. *Feedback to Managers: A Review and Comparison of Multi-rater Instruments for Management Development.* Greensboro, N.C.: Center for Creative Leadership, 1998.

Millsap, R. E., and Hartog, S. B. "Alpha, Beta, and Gamma Change in Evaluation Research: A Structural Equation Approach." *Journal of Applied Psychology,* 1988, *73,* 574–584.

Nunnally, J. C. *Psychometric Theory* (2nd ed.). New York: McGraw-Hill, 1978.

Rohs, F. R. "Response Shift Bias: A Problem in Evaluating Leadership Development with Self-Report Pretest-Posttest Measures." *Journal of Agricultural Education,* 1999, *40*(4), 28–37.

Rohs, F. R. "Improving the Evaluation of Leadership Programs: Control Response Shift." *Journal of Leadership Education,* 2002, *1,* 50–61.

Russ-Eft, D., and Hoover, A. L. "Experimental and Quasi-Experimental Designs." In R. A. Swanson and E. F. Holton (eds.), *Research in Organizations: Foundations and Methods of Inquiry.* San Francisco: Berrett-Koehler, 2005.

Schmitt, N. "The Use of Analysis of Covariance Structures to Assess Beta and Gamma Change." *Multivariate Behavioral Research,* 1982, *17,* 343–358.

Shadish, W. R., Cook, T. D., and Campbell, D. T. *Experimental and Quasi-Experimental Designs for Generalized Causal Inference.* Boston: Houghton-Mifflin, 2002.

Tourangeau, A. E. *Evaluation Study of a Leadership Development Intervention for Nurses.* Final Report to the Change Foundation, Ontario, Canada, January 2004.

CHAPTER TWO

LEADING WITH THEORY

Using a Theory of Change Approach for Leadership Development Evaluations

Manuel Gutiérrez and Tania Tasse

When faced with the task of designing evaluations of leadership development programs, evaluators are likely to wonder what types of evidence they should look for in order to measure program success. Leadership development initiatives often have very broad and highly ambitious objectives that are not easily measurable. In addition, staff and stakeholders of leadership programs may not be totally clear—or in agreement about—how and why their program's activities should lead to these objectives or what are the signs of progress along the road to success.

To help overcome these challenges, we rely on a process called *pathway mapping* as the first step in evaluating leadership programs. Pathway mapping has its roots in an evaluation approach called *the theory of change approach*, which emphasizes making the underlying theory of programs clear in order to evaluate them. In pathway mapping, the staff and other stakeholders of a program examine and make explicit their theories and assumptions about how the program works from start to finish. The final product of this process, a pathway map, is a flowchart documenting how program activities are believed to lead to results over time. Pathway maps are a critical tool in planning evaluations of leadership development programs and can be extremely valuable to program staff and stakeholders as a means of describing program theory, making decisions about the future of programs, and as a tool for those managing programs.

Figure 2.1 provides an example of a pathway map for a community-based employment program. In this example, developed by the OMG Center for Collaborative Learning, where both authors conducted much of the work described in this chapter, we present the basic elements of a pathway map: a contextual analysis for the program, the program's strategic focus, its actions and activities, and its intended outcomes (short-term and long-term improvements). Very important, we also include the program's core assumptions that underlie the connections between the basic elements of the pathway map. Later in this chapter, we provide additional details about and examples of pathway maps. We also describe a step-by-step process for creating pathway maps.

Theory of Change Approach to Evaluation

The theory of change approach to evaluation gained popularity and wide acceptance in the 1990s through its innovative use in the evaluation of comprehensive community initiatives (CCIs). By definition, CCIs are community-based initiatives that seek multiple-level outcomes (that is, for individuals, families, and neighborhoods) across several programmatic areas, such as education, health, housing, and employment. Given the inherent complexity of CCIs, evaluators found serious limitations in traditional evaluation approaches and were forced to come up with other approaches that would be suitable for these initiatives. The work of the Aspen Institute Roundtable on Comprehensive Community Initiatives for Children and Families was extremely important in legitimizing and expanding the understanding of the applicability and limitations of the theory of change evaluation approach (Connell, Kubisch, Schorr, and Weiss, 1995; Fulbright-Anderson, Kubisch, and Connell, 1998). Notably, the Aspen Institute Roundtable provided a forum for funders, evaluators, and practitioners to refine the approach by sharing tools and lessons learned from conducting theory of change evaluations.

The basic description of a theory of change approach to evaluation was defined by Carol Weiss (1995). Essentially, Weiss proposes that a theory of change approach requires that the designers of an initiative articulate the premises, assumptions, and hypotheses that might explain the how, when, and why of the processes of change. As part of this approach, program designers

FIGURE 2.1. EXAMPLE PATHWAY MAP.

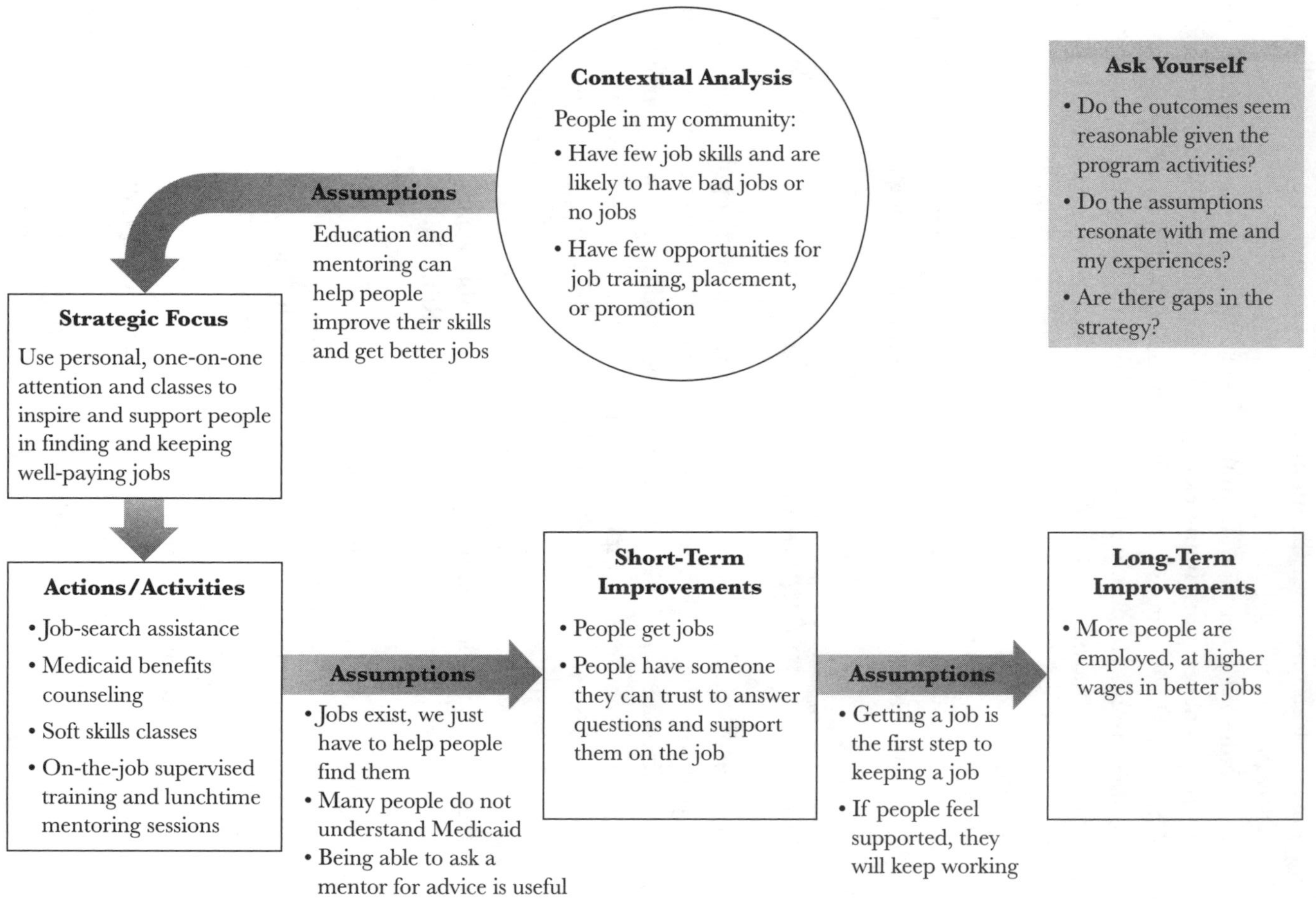

Ask Yourself

- Do the outcomes seem reasonable given the program activities?
- Do the assumptions resonate with me and my experiences?
- Are there gaps in the strategy?

Contextual Analysis

People in my community:

- Have few job skills and are likely to have bad jobs or no jobs
- Have few opportunities for job training, placement, or promotion

Assumptions

Education and mentoring can help people improve their skills and get better jobs

Strategic Focus

Use personal, one-on-one attention and classes to inspire and support people in finding and keeping well-paying jobs

Actions/Activities

- Job-search assistance
- Medicaid benefits counseling
- Soft skills classes
- On-the-job supervised training and lunchtime mentoring sessions

Assumptions

- Jobs exist, we just have to help people find them
- Many people do not understand Medicaid
- Being able to ask a mentor for advice is useful

Short-Term Improvements

- People get jobs
- People have someone they can trust to answer questions and support them on the job

Assumptions

- Getting a job is the first step to keeping a job
- If people feel supported, they will keep working

Long-Term Improvements

- More people are employed, at higher wages in better jobs

© 2002 OMG Center for Collaborative Learning.

with other key stakeholders are asked to identify key programmatic elements and to indicate how these interventions might lead to the anticipated short-term, intermediate, and long-term outcomes. This process is commonly referred to as "articulating an initiative's or a program's theory of change." Once the theory of change is made explicit, then it becomes possible for the evaluator to test the assumptions that underlie the initiative or program and to assess its outcomes.

Theory of Change and Logic Model: Are They the Same Thing?

The terms *theory of change* and *logic model* are often used interchangeably, which may leave one wondering whether they are in fact the same thing. Logic models have been used in program planning and evaluation since the 1980s (Bickman, 1987), preceding the popularization of theory of change evaluation. A logic model is a flowchart that depicts the inputs, processes, outputs, and outcomes associated with a program.

While the terms are often used interchangeably, some evaluators have attempted to differentiate between theories of change and logic models. Clark and Anderson (2004) describe logic models as placing greater emphasis on the representation of actual program components: the basic inputs, outputs, and outcomes of programs. In contrast, they describe theories of change as involving higher order critical thinking, articulating hypotheses about why something will cause something else, and having greater explanatory power. Although this differentiation may be accurate when comparing theories of change to simple logic models, we find that many evaluators consider logic models to have comparable characteristics to those ascribed to theories of change.

The Kellogg Foundation's *Logic Model Development Guide* (W. K. Kellogg Foundation, 2003), an invaluable resource for planners and evaluators, provides a different perspective on the relationship between logic models and theory of change. In this guide, the authors describe three types of logic models: theory approach models, outcomes approach models, and activities approach models. According to this classification, theory approach models "emphasize the theory of change that has influenced the design and plan for the program" (p. 9) and are used to illustrate how and why the program will work (in other words they describe the big picture of the program). Outcomes approach models describe the program's anticipated outcomes or impacts over time, going from short-term to intermediate to long-term outcomes. Activities approach models describe program implementation, providing the specific phases and steps for program operations. From this perspective, theories of change are one type of logic model.

In our experience, the theory of change approach to evaluation requires the integration of the theory approach and outcomes approach models but may or may not place much emphasis on the activities approach model. The important elements are the assumptions underlying program strategies, the articulation of anticipated outcomes, and the linkages between them. We have more to say about this later in this chapter.

So, are a theory of change and a logic model the same thing? We would answer that it depends. Logic models that reflect a program's theory of change must include the following three characteristics: (1) the underlying assumptions about how and why the program will achieve its anticipated results; (2) the identification of anticipated outcomes over time; and (3) the connections between strategies and outcomes. In cases where all three characteristics are present, we would say that a logic model reflects a theory of change approach.

Theory of Change Evaluation and Leadership Development: A Good Fit

There are many valid approaches for conducting an evaluation of a leadership development program. Some of those approaches are presented by other authors in this book. Often, factors such as the characteristics of the specific program, the nature of the evaluation questions, and the resources designated for the evaluation are likely to influence the type of evaluation that will be selected. We believe that in most cases a theory of change approach is a good fit for evaluating leadership development programs for the following reasons:

Leadership and leadership development are terms with multiple meanings and definitions. Given the various definitions of leadership and the wide array of existing leadership development programs, the theory of change approach focus on articulating premises and assumptions is an effective process for clarifying a program's view of leadership and how this view shapes program activities.

Leadership development is a complex psychological and social process. Describing the change process for individuals participating in leadership development programs may be as complex and challenging as describing the neighborhood change process in comprehensive community initiatives. For that reason, a theory of change evaluation represents a promising approach for systematically tracking and understanding the personal change process in individuals.

Leadership development programs typically hold the expectation that individual-level changes will lead to organizational-level, system-level, and societal-level outcomes. Moving from individual-level outcomes to organizational-level or community-level outcomes adds further complexity to a leadership development program evaluation. In this context, the theory of change approach provides a framework that articulates the anticipated pathways of change and allows evaluators to gather data in order to test out whether, to what extent, and in what contexts individual-level change leads to broader outcomes. Chapter Three in this handbook also describes a process for linking these levels of outcomes.

Leadership development programs typically involve multiple components. In this case, the observed complexity derives from the nature and layering of the components or interventions. This layering takes place over time as well as across various didactic and experiential activities, reflecting the program design. In addition, it sometimes occurs across groups, for those programs that incorporate network activities bringing together participants from different program classes or cohorts. Given this programmatic complexity, the theory of change evaluation approach can help ascertain how and to what extent different program components contribute to the attainment of anticipated outcomes.

Pathway Mapping and Pathway Maps

Over time, through multiple engagements involving the evaluation of comprehensive community initiatives and single-focus programs, we have used a process called *pathway mapping* to engage stakeholders in order to articulate an initiative's or program's theory of change.

More specifically, pathway mapping is the process of specifying a program's desired outcomes and linking those outcomes to program actions and strategies. The pathway-mapping process also requires making program assumptions explicit, challenging them when they appear inconsistent or unclear, and reaching consensus on those program assumptions and sequences of events that describe why and how a program works—the pathways to change. The pathway-mapping approach is a specific planning process that articulates a program's theory of change using a logic model framework.

The pathway-mapping process produces pathway maps. Pathway maps place emphasis on the assumptions linking a program's strategies, activities, and outcomes. We prefer using the term *pathway map* rather than *logic model* because it connects the process (mapping) to the product (map) and emphasizes the concept of pathways of change that links to the program's theory of change. For us, then, a pathway map is a particular type of logic model that surfaces a theory of change. A pathway map is a blend of the theory approach model and outcomes approach model discussed earlier in this chapter.

Pathway Maps and Leadership Programs

Over the past few years, we have used pathway mapping to evaluate three established leadership development and recognition programs: the Rockefeller Foundation's Next Generation Leaders (NGL), the Eisenhower Fellowships' (EF) international exchange programs, and the Ford Foundation's Leadership for a Changing World (LCW). The LCW and NGL evaluations also included implementation studies. (For more information on these programs, readers can turn to this chapter's Resource section.) We draw on our experiences evaluating these programs to illustrate the value of theory of change approaches to evaluation and pathway mapping in particular.

These three programs are quite diverse in their views on leadership, their goals and intended outcomes, the characteristics of program participants, and the strategies used to achieve their goals. Nevertheless, in spite of their diversity, we find that the theory of change approach provides a flexible framework for evaluating each program (see, for example, Gutiérrez and Stowell, 2004; Gutiérrez and Tasse, 2005).

Details of a Pathway Map

The EF pathway map shown in Figure 2.2 includes program activities or inputs such as: the nomination and selection processes that precede the fellowship, joint program planning, the actual fellowship experience, and resources provided to alumni. The pathway map also includes critical assumptions about how change will happen through this program; for example, through experiential learning. It details the outcomes that are expected to occur for the individual fellows (for example, enhanced professional knowledge), for their organizations (improvements and/or growth in the organization), and for their communities or societies (new programs, institutions, policies being put in place). Ideal outcomes were included in this pathway map to convey the vision that the program is ultimately striving to contribute to; however, they are formatted differently in the pathway map to indicate that these are ideals and that the program does not necessarily expect to be able to measure progress toward them. The arrows from left to right reflect the order in which the Eisenhower Fellowships believe outcomes develop.

The content, format, and layout of pathway maps may vary extensively from client to client. For example, while EF chose to depict outcomes according to the level at which they occur (individual, organizational, and societal), many programs prefer to state their outcomes according to the time period over which they are expected to occur, and thus they use such category headings as *short-term, intermediate,* and *long-term outcomes.* Another common variation is that in addition to program inputs and outcomes, some pathway maps include a problem statement or contextual statement describing why the program was first started, under what conditions, and what problems it addresses. For example, one program's pathway map begins with a contextual statement that includes the following language: "There is a lack of conviction in the public that leadership exists and that local/community leaders can impact social issues" (Gutiérrez, Tasse, and Bergson-Shilcock, 2006). The program activities and desired outcomes in the program's pathway map are driven by this statement.

The length and degree of detail shown by a pathway map are other variables to be decided upon. We have worked with programs to produce in-depth pathway maps and also to produce simpler ones. It requires a significant amount of time to fully describe the conditions that led to a program, the activities and resources comprising the program, and the assumptions delineating how and why outcomes are thought to occur. The resulting document is generally several pages long and requires the full attention of a reader to grasp. This type of pathway map is valuable for some purposes, including building consensus around program theory when establishing a new program and rethinking program design. Regardless of the length of the document, evaluators working with program staff need to balance the level of detail provided on a pathway map with the level of information required to understand the program. Typically, the inclination is to add as much detail as possible to the pathway map. However, very detailed pathway maps will look cluttered and will be hard to interpret.

Shorter pathway maps (like that illustrated in Figure 2.2) are generally one or two pages long and highlight only the key activities and expected outcomes

FIGURE 2.2. EISENHOWER FELLOWSHIPS PROGRAM ACTIVITIES AND ASSUMPTIONS.

Activities

Nominating and Selecting Fellows

- Selection criteria conveying clear standards
- Diverse in-country nominating committees, including EF alumni, rigorously applying selection criteria
- Final selection by EF staff (Philadelphia) with input of trustees

Program Planning

- Fellows identify their interests
- Fellows and program officers plan individual itineraries with participation from trustees, alumni, professional contacts, and so on

Fellowship Experience

- EF seminars
- Travel and individualized itineraries
- Spousal participation
- Discussions and networking with trustees and sponsors

Alumni Resources and Network

- Online resources: directory of fellows, discussion forums
- Hosting and meeting with current fellows or alumni fellows visiting country
- Countrywide associations of alumni
- Conferences
- Ongoing communications and stewardship via EF newsletters, Webnews, reports, messages from the president, and so on
- Hosting and meeting with trustees and stakeholders visiting country

Assumptions

EF selects "the right people" to become fellows, and the program's success is closely tied to the selection process.

Leadership is understood differently across various cultures, and the program does not support one definition of leadership over others. However, it does seek to heighten fellows' awareness of themselves as leaders and their comfort in assuming leadership roles.

Access to new and high-level contacts will propel fellows to a new professional level. By arranging appointments between fellows and high-level professionals in another country and providing a cohort of qualified fellows, EF provides access to a new and high-caliber network of professional contacts.

The learning that occurs during EF is experiential learning and happens mainly through exposure to different people and viewpoints.

Individual Level

- Broadened perspective

- Enhanced professional knowledge

- Improved leadership awareness and capacity, including:
  - Self-confidence
  - Assertion of leadership
  - Recognition of leadership by others
  - Motivation

- New relationships, networks, and alliances with:
  - Professional contacts, often high level, from United States (or country visited)
  - Fellows in cohort
  - EF alumni
  - EF staff, trustees, PAC, and sponsors

- Heightened cross-cultural and international perspective

- More comprehensive understanding of the United States and its key institutions (or of the country visited, for U.S. program)

Organizational Level

- Application of broader perspective and/or knowledge gained during EF to work in current or new fields

- Assuming positions of greater influence and scope; exerting more effective leadership

- Strong personal and professional networks

- Strong EF network

- Ongoing relationships, communication, and partnerships with contacts from United States, fellows in cohort, EF alumni, country associations, and so on

- Sharing knowledge and perspective gained during fellowship with others

- Improvements or growth in fellows' organizations and institutions

Societal Level

- Fellows make more and deeper impacts in current or new professional fields

- Fellows develop strategic collaborations that result in new and/or improved activities, programs, or institutions, with benefits extending to a broader constituency

Ideal

- Progress and advancements that benefit society

- Greater mutual understanding and peace

Source: Gutiérrez, M., and Tasse, T. *Eisenhower Fellowships: Final Evaluation Report.* Philadelphia: OMG Center for Collaborative Learning, 2005.

of a program. These pathway maps may be less helpful in presenting why the program exists or the details and logic behind the program and activities. On the other hand, they are simpler to understand, and thus they can be used to illustrate a program's logic to audiences that are unfamiliar with the program, or to those who do not require *all* of the details behind it. In general, the content, format, and layout of a pathway map should be presented in whatever style that best reflects the program at hand, and the degree of detail should be decided based on why the program is doing the pathway map and how it is likely to be used in the future. Even when pathway maps are presented in a simpler layout, key elements of the theory of change, such as program context and assumptions, are presented as accompanying text.

No matter what the finished document looks like, if a pathway map effectively captures the logic behind a program, it can be used as a roadmap to guide the evaluation. It specifies what results evaluators should look for, and it often specifies at what time periods those results should occur. Pathway maps also provide a list of key program activities, which is critical if the evaluation includes an assessment of the program's implementation. Once the pathway map is completed, the evaluator's next step is to select methods and design data collection activities.

It is important to note that in the absence of an experimental or quasi-experimental design such as described in Chapter One (which is often not a realistic design for the evaluation of leadership programs), the theory of change evaluation approach provides a good alternative to the limitation of the lack of a control group. If an evaluation can show that program activities were fully implemented and that outcomes developed in the way envisioned by staff and stakeholders and documented on the pathway map, then credibility is built for the program theory through documentation of the process. In other words, even if causal links have not been firmly established using a control group, the theory of change approach makes it easier to believe that the program contributed to outcomes in the way depicted by the pathway map because the pathways are well articulated and evaluation data document the movement along the pathways, providing support for the theory.

Usefulness of Pathway Maps

In addition to providing a framework for assessment activities, pathway maps also provide a useful structure for evaluation reports. The first section of a report would describe the logic and assumptions behind the program, as well as the inputs and expected outcomes. The next sections would describe whether or not the program was implemented according to its design, and whether outcomes occurred in the way envisioned by the staff and stakeholders in the pathway map.

Beyond their usefulness to evaluators, pathway maps can be valuable tools for program staff and administrators because they provide a level of clarity and explicitness about program theory that many programs do not capture in writing. Pathway maps can be used for program planning, management, and development purposes, as well as to present and explain programs to those who are not familiar with them. For example, pathway maps are useful when orienting new staff to the mission and purpose of a program, or to inform critical programming decisions like whether or not new activities that are being considered make sense in light of the other inputs and goals. The inputs section of a pathway map can be used as a programming checklist, against which a program manager may ask the questions, Are these activities in place? and if so, Are they in place at the right intensity to lead to these outcomes? Or, if certain activities are not in place, then which outcomes are not likely to occur?

Additionally, when a program uses a pathway-mapping process as part of the program design phase, it increases the likelihood that everyone involved has a shared understanding about how the program will look and work, and what is expected to happen as a result of it. For example, we conducted pathway mapping with one program during the design phase, and the staff of the program continue to use the document to reexamine and refine program activities and logic. In this respect, it is important to note that a pathway map should be considered a dynamic tool for incorporating evaluation findings, reflecting midcourse corrections, and capturing other program evolutions. A pathway map should not be considered etched in stone, but rather as a roadmap that is likely to show some changes over time, given new knowledge about the program. Those changes, of course, would be an important part of the story that a theory of change evaluation should be able to tell (for a different approach to pathway mapping, see Exhibit 2.1).

The Pathway-Mapping Process

In this section we discuss how to prepare for the mapping sessions, offer suggestions for conducting the mapping sessions, and point out the various roles that evaluators play in the mapping process.

EXHIBIT 2.1. CREATIVE PATHWAY MAPS.

Some organizations have developed creative ways to present their programs to others. ARISE, a grassroots organization in Alamo, Texas, that combines personal development, leadership, and community organizing training for women living in southern Texas *colonias,* created a visual and kinesthetic representation of their work consisting of multiple footprints and hearts spread across the floor (each footprint or heart is drawn on a piece of paper so that they can be used repeatedly). Inside the footprints and hearts are ARISE's guiding principles and values statements. The footprints "walk" across the floor, scattered among the hearts. They lead to the organization's vision statement, which is displayed on the wall.

Although ARISE doesn't use the term *logic model* or *theory of change* to describe this depiction of its program, it serves a similar purpose as a pathway map: to communicate the program's logic and to connect the everyday activities of ARISE to the organization's vision. Sister Gerrie Naughton, founder and executive director of ARISE, came up with the idea for this tool, and the program staff created the footprints, hearts, and vision statement. Sister Gerrie says that the guiding principles, values, and vision statement already existed on paper, but that the tool was developed because there was a need to see, to visually connect, how the everyday work of ARISE (the inputs) lead to the vision (outcomes). ARISE uses it for training purposes when they hire new staff and for sessions of renewal and rededication to the vision of ARISE for all staff persons, experienced as well as new.

Preparing for the Mapping Sessions

It is ideal to develop a pathway map and evaluation plan at the same time that a program is being designed. It is important to document the context, assumptions, and objectives of a program from the beginning. Also, both pathway mapping and evaluation planning are processes that tend to raise questions about inputs, desired outcomes, and resources that may help to inform program design. While this is the ideal situation, it is more often the case that an evaluator is asked to develop a pathway map and evaluate a program that is already underway.

Assuming that you are asked to evaluate a program already under implementation, the pathway-mapping process begins with a review of written program documents, including the program's Web site, application or nomination forms, participant handbooks or other materials describing the program's activities, annual reports, newsletters and publications, and any prior evaluations that have been conducted. When reviewing these documents, try to identify the key activities of the program; the short-term, intermediate, and long-term goals; and the assumptions about how and why the program should cause the desired goals to occur.

The next step is to interview (in person or via telephone) key stakeholders of the program. Interviews may be conducted with different types of stakeholders for different purposes. For example, it is often useful to interview the individuals who originally designed a program in order to gather in-depth contextual information about how and why the program was started. Also, interviews should be conducted with individuals who are influential to the program; for example, those involved in program planning, implementation, or decision making (staff, executive directors, board of trustee members, and so on) but who may not be available to participate in the next step of the process, the working sessions. Lines of questioning for these interviews include why the program was originally designed, why or how the set of program activities was decided upon, what are the program impacts that the interviewee has witnessed or heard about from those who have participated in the program, and what are the perceived strengths and weaknesses of the program.

After the interviews, the evaluator schedules a series of working sessions with key staff and any other individuals whom the program decides to include in the development of the pathway map. This may include individuals who have participated in the program (alumni), board members, or former staff. Since the working sessions are highly interactive and their success depends on participation from all group members, we recommend that no more than ten people be included. Also, since the sessions are intense, we recommend at least two separate sessions. In our experience, two three- to four-hour sessions are generally sufficient to produce a basic, one- or two-page pathway map. More detailed maps may require additional sessions or longer sessions.

Conducting the Mapping Sessions

Based on the initial document review and stakeholder interviews, the evaluator drafts a preliminary pathway map and presents it at the first working group meeting. The draft serves two purposes: first, since most people are unfamiliar with pathway maps, it provides an example of what the document looks like; second, concerning content, the draft gives the working group something to react to instead of having to start from a blank slate. It is important when presenting the draft to frame it as a preliminary document whose contents are entirely open to change, since the working group sessions are the most in-depth and critical component of the pathway map development process.

Over the course of the working group sessions, the group should review the program inputs (or activities) and come to agreement on a list of critical activities. Next, they should discuss outcomes. Since most programs already have mission statements outlining their long-term goals, it generally makes sense to start with these and work backward to the short-term and intermediate outcomes. Short-term and intermediate outcomes are changes or results that one would expect to occur in the interim between the program's implementation and its ultimate goal. They are markers of progress along the longer road to success. The pathway-mapping process should include a discussion about when short-term and intermediate outcomes are expected to occur. There is no standard time frame that can be used by all programs; this element of the pathway map varies depending on the types of outcomes being sought and the assumptions behind the design. Keep in mind that the time frames depicted on the pathway map will have implications for evaluation activities. For example, if a new program specifies that their short-term outcomes will be discernible after two years, then evaluation activities should not be commenced until participants have been out of the program for at least two years (unless the evaluation includes an implementation study).

During discussions about short-term and intermediate outcomes, it is critical that evaluators not only identify the outcomes but also that they surface and examine the group's assumptions concerning why certain activities will lead to certain outcomes. These assumptions can be considered the pathways in the pathway map: they are the logic behind the arrows leading from program inputs to program outcomes.

For example, it is not uncommon during pathway mapping for staff of a program to list a set of short-term and intermediate outcomes that make sense given the long-term goals of the program but do not follow logically from the program's activities. For example, if a program's activities focus on strengthening the capacity of individual leaders to do their work, but the program lists greater public knowledge and awareness of leadership as an outcome, then it would be important for an evaluator to examine the assumptions of the group. Why do they believe activities being conducted with individuals will affect public opinion? Did they forget to list key activities in their pathway map, or are the program's activities misaligned with its vision?

Another question for consideration during pathway mapping is whether the pathways between activities and outcomes are based on research results (tested theory, proven logic) or represent a new approach being tried by the program (untested theory, new logic). In some pathway maps, it may be important to distinguish between these types of links and possibly to focus evaluation resources on examining the experimental pathways, since such examinations can contribute to further learning in the field.

During the course of the working sessions, evaluators should expect to encounter disagreement among participants. There are at least two different types of disagreement that can occur: those concerning the wording and organization of the pathway map and those concerning the contents and assumptions within it. Disagreements reflecting the first category are fairly easy to resolve. For example, staff of a program may argue about whether the fifteen key activities should be grouped into three, four, or five categories or headings. Some staff may see three natural categories, while others see four, and still other see five. However, all participants agree that the fifteen activities are the key activities for the program. A sharp evaluator can recognize and diagnose this type of disagreement, and once participants see that their differences are not fundamental to their understanding of the program, it is usually resolved by compromise. Sometimes, these differences point to a more fundamental disagreement about the nature or goals of the program.

Disagreements about program content, goals, and assumptions are a more serious challenge to the pathway-mapping process. These disagreements are more likely to arise when a program is producing a detailed pathway map, because the more details being depicted in the document, the greater the number of things that staff must discuss and agree upon. When disagreements occur around core goals or assumptions underlying a program, it is important to hear all viewpoints and allow participants to engage in discussion. Sometimes, what seems like a disagreement is actually the result of individuals expressing the same thing differently. A helpful facilitation technique in the development of a pathway map is to provide a glossary of terms to participants. This ensures that every participant is familiar with the pathway-mapping language (the use of terms like *strategies, activities, outcomes,* for example). We have also found that it is very helpful to use the same technical terms that a program has been using (*indicator* versus *measure, results* versus *outcomes*). When developing the pathway map it is also helpful to avoid wordsmithing during the work session. We typically insist on trying to get the main idea and then working on the language with one or two members of the group after the work session. Otherwise, the process becomes too slow and frustrating for the group.

In some cases, participants are able to work through disagreements themselves. (The fact that pathway mapping is a time-intensive process usually means that participants are open to compromises that will move the process forward.) However, in cases when true disagreement exists around the key activities or goals of a program, it is necessary to seek out the input of individuals who designed the program or those who are most knowledgeable and ultimately responsible for the program's direction. Participants can look to these individuals for clarity about the purpose and vision of the program.

Following the working sessions, the evaluator revises the draft and provides the participants with a second draft. Ideally, all the members of the working group will come together for another session to review, discuss, and comment on the document. However, if not all workgroup members are able to meet, the evaluator will make sure to get everyone's comments before or after the meeting. The evaluator receives all comments and makes revisions to the pathway map. Assuming that there are no further issues to clarify or resolve, the pathway map is then finalized. If any unresolved issues emerge during the revision process, one should continue to work with the stakeholders until they are able to reach a consensus. While there may never be consensus around every detail of a pathway map, all stakeholders should feel that the pathway map accurately represents the program.

Evaluator Roles

Evaluators play different roles when engaging stakeholders in the pathway-mapping process. These roles include being a facilitator, an expert researcher, a challenger of assumptions and conventional wisdom, a mediator, a consensus builder, and a synthesizer. While it may be possible for an individual to effectively fulfill all of these roles, we have found that it works much better to have a team of two evaluators involved in the pathway-mapping process. That way, roles can be shared or balanced, as needed, by the evaluation team members. Since we recommend that no more than ten stakeholders be included in the pathway-mapping sessions, it makes sense to limit the number of evaluators participating in the session to no more than two or three. Having more than two or three evaluators participating in the process may be overwhelming or confusing for the participants.

As it should be evident by now, conducting effective pathway-mapping sessions with stakeholders requires sound knowledge of program design, program implementation, and evaluation issues, as well as strong skills in group dynamics. Since the pathway map is a critical product for evaluators and program staff, it is extremely important that program staff see the mapping process as an opportunity to engage in reflective practice and not just as a mechanical exercise to satisfy evaluator demands.

Lessons Learned with Pathway Mapping

Our experience provides some lessons for others who may use pathway mapping in the future. The first lesson concerns the usefulness of benchmarking, or indicating to what degree an outcome is expected to occur. This is important because it allows evaluators to interpret findings related to program outcomes. For example, EF's pathway map lists new and/or improved activities, programs, or institutions benefiting a broad constituency as a program outcome (see Figure 2.2). For this evaluation, data collection focused on assessing the extent to which fellows (participants in the EF program) had contributed to such improvements. We found that approximately 50 percent of fellows had contributed to this outcome; however, we didn't know whether 50 percent was low, acceptable, or high. We did not know how to interpret the finding. As a result, we recommend that the pathway-mapping process include some discussion of how much or to what extent a particular outcome is expected.

Another word of caution concerns the level of outcomes that programs include in a pathway map. As mentioned previously, leadership programs tend to have very broad and idealistic goal statements (for example, achieving mutual understanding and peace or changing the way leadership is understood). While these may be effective visioning statements for galvanizing an organization, they should not automatically be incorporated into a pathway map. The outcomes listed in a pathway map should be ones that can serve as accountability measures. They should be specific enough and realistic enough that a program can be held accountable to them. For evaluation purposes, the outcomes need to be measurable.

Finally, there is a lesson about having clients understand the value of pathway mapping. Since accountability is the primary concern of most clients who seek evaluation services, they are most interested in assessment activities that generate findings related to program impacts and sometimes view pathway mapping as an unnecessary part of the evaluation. They do not realize that pathway mapping is a planning and evaluation tool or process that allows for outcomes to be collected in a more focused and productive way later on in the evaluation. In the past, when we have described proposed evaluation activities based on a theory of change approach (pathway mapping followed by a combination of surveys and focus groups or interviews) to prospective clients, some clients have responded that they would like to skip the pathway mapping and go straight to the data collection activities.

When and if this happens, it is important to let clients know that the pathway mapping produces a framework which is critical to a systematic evaluation of program outcomes. In addition, we have found that it is very useful to offer clients good descriptions of the various uses of pathway maps and the valuable reflections that are generated by the pathway-mapping process.

Another argument for including pathway mapping in the evaluation design is that, unless the evaluator is already familiar with the program, time must be devoted up front to informing the assessment team about the program. Since this level of effort is required, it makes sense to fully invest in the pathway-mapping process and have the evaluator document what she is learning about the program in a way that will serve both the evaluation and the program. In other words, the process of pathway mapping needs to happen to a greater or lesser extent for an evaluator to become familiar enough with a program to conduct an evaluation. If the process is already happening, it makes sense to have it formalized and documented so that the program reaps the benefits as well.

If a client chooses not to engage in pathway mapping, there is the risk that the evaluation that is devised will not provide evidence about critical strategies and assumptions underlying the program's theory of change. Further, since program stakeholders generally have slightly different unspoken understandings and assumptions about a program, the evaluation may meet the needs of some stakeholders more than it meets the needs of others.

Conclusion

Throughout this chapter we discuss the usefulness of a theory of change evaluation approach called pathway mapping and argue that this type of approach is a good fit for evaluating leadership programs. But when would the use of a theory of change approach not represent a good fit for a leadership program? We think that there are two program contexts where the theory of change evaluation may not be a good fit, although both cases are arguable. The first one is a stable program that undergoes periodic evaluation and that has already identified, with good clarity, its objectives, interventions, and intended outcomes. This type of program shows internal cohesion, its anticipated outcomes appear reasonable, and measures have already been identified and used to assess its anticipated outcomes. A theory of change evaluation, then, might not add much value, and a more traditional approach would be completely suitable. The argument to this context is that even those programs that have a logic model may not update and revise the model regularly, and would benefit from doing so. This is a situation where clients and evaluators need to figure out the relative benefits of investing resources into the review and possible rearticulation of the program's theory of change.

The second context that may not be amenable to a comprehensive theory of change evaluation approach would involve an exploratory, pilot program in which program designers are not ready to specify clear pathways of change and need to better understand the effects of specific program components or their interactions with different types of participants. In this case, it might be useful to generate a preliminary theory of change for the program at a very high level. This document would serve as a sketch that evaluators could change and refine as time goes on. This way, the theory is flexible and can be revisited as the program evolves. In this case, evaluation activities should be more exploratory and use different methodologies to attempt to understand how the program works and the types of results it produces.

A common challenge to theory of change evaluation is how to reconcile multiple theories of change representing the views of distinct stakeholders. Although differences among stakeholders (staff, participants, alumni, board) of leadership programs focusing on individuals come up, it is generally possible to reach consensus as the program represents a narrow slice of experience. When evaluating that type of leadership program, we push for consensus on the theory of change whenever possible. If not possible, we will work with multiple theories of change, although this has been rare. This situation becomes more complicated when the leadership program is set up as a place-based program or initiative (for instance, a neighborhood-based program or a citywide initiative) and the program directly targets individual and community change. This type of program or initiative represents a much broader slice of experience. In this situation, program participants who are community members may hold quite different views than the program's funder about the nature and sequence of change in their communities. While consensus should also be sought in this situation, it would be realistic to expect to have multiple theories of change representing the perspectives of distinct groups of stakeholders. The evaluation should allow for these differences and attempt to test the different theories if possible.

The theory of change evaluation approach has often been criticized for representing a linear progression of change in a world where change is not linear. This is a complex epistemological issue that is beyond the scope of this chapter. However, we argue that a good theory of change evaluation needs to be open to change in whatever form or sequence it occurs, whether anticipated or not, and we urge evaluators using this approach to remain flexible during the evaluation and not to grow overly confident on the accuracy of a program's articulated theory of change or the details of a pathway map or logic model. We need to remind ourselves that a theory is just a set of beliefs that helps explain events and guide actions and that we are continually evolving in our understanding of complex phenomena such as leadership development. Thus, we need to be open to new knowledge and possible reinterpretation of previous beliefs and assumptions. After all, a theory is just a theory.

Resources

Aspen Institute Roundtable on Community Change. [www.aspeninstitute.org/site/c.huLWJeMRKpH/b.612045/k.4BA8/Roundtable_on_Community_Change.htm]. This resource describes the work of the roundtable and includes links to resources concerning theory of change and community-building topics.

Eisenhower Fellowships. [http://eisenhowerfellowships.org]. This source describes the mission and goals of the Eisenhower Fellowships as well as program activities. It lists news pertaining to alumni achievements and announces upcoming events. Also includes a link to the OMG Center's evaluation study (in the "About Us" section).

Leadership for a Changing World (LCW). [http://leadershipforchange.org]. This resource describes the LCW program and includes announcements about new and current award winners and their social justice work and accomplishments. Includes links to research being conducted by the Research Center for Leadership in Action at NYU concerning social justice leadership.

Pathways Mapping Initiative. [www.pathwaystooutcomes.org/]. This resource provides information about strategies that have been effective, appear to be working, or are promising, in community initiatives taking place in particular locations. It also discusses how pathways are designed to guide choices about investments, programs, and policies made by multiple stakeholders.

Next Generation Leaders. [www.nglnet.org]. This resource includes information about the background of the Next Generation Leadership program, and the program's alumni network.

W. K. Kellogg Foundation Logic Model Development Guide. [www.wkkf. org/Pubs/Tools/Evaluation/Pub3669.pdf]. This electronic publication gives an introduction to logic models for program planning and evaluation, and includes exercises and examples focused on developing basic logic models. It also discusses program theory and theories of change.

References

Bickman, L. "The Functions of Program Theory." In L. Bickman, *New Directions in Program Evaluation: Using Program Theory in Evaluation*, no. 33. San Francisco: Jossey-Bass, 1987.

Clark, H., and Anderson, A. "Theories of Change and Logic Models: Telling Them Apart." Presentation at American Evaluation Association conference. Atlanta, November 2004.

Connell, J. P., Kubisch, A. C., Schorr, L. B., and Weiss, C. H. *New Approaches to Evaluating Community Initiatives: Concepts, Methods, and Contexts*. Vol. 1. Washington, D.C.: Aspen Institute, 1995.

Fulbright-Anderson, K., Kubisch, A. C., and Connell, J. P. *New Approaches to Evaluating Community Initiatives: Theory, Measurement, and Analysis*. Vol. 2. Washington, D.C.: Aspen Institute, 1998.

Gutiérrez, M., and Stowell, B. *Next Generation Leadership Program: Final Assessment Report*. Philadelphia: OMG Center for Collaborative Learning, 2004.

Gutiérrez, M., and Tasse, T. *Eisenhower Fellowships: Final Evaluation Report*. Philadelphia: OMG Center for Collaborative Learning, 2005.

Gutiérrez, M., Tasse, T., and Bergson-Shilcock, A. *Leadership for a Changing World: Final Evaluation Report* (unpublished). Philadelphia: OMG Center for Collaborative Learning, 2006.

W. K. Kellogg Foundation. *Logic Model Development Guide.* Battle Creek, Mich.: Author, 2003.

Weiss, C. H. "Nothing as Practical as Good Theory: Exploring Theory-Based Evaluation for Comprehensive Community Initiatives for Children and Families." In J. P. Connell, A. C. Kubisch, L. B. Schorr, and C. H. Weiss, *New Approaches to Evaluating Community Initiatives: Concepts, Methods, and Contexts.* Vol. 1. Washington, D.C.: Aspen Institute, 1995.

CHAPTER THREE

EVALULEAD

An Open-Systems Perspective on Evaluating Leadership Development

John T. Grove, Barry M. Kibel, and Taylor Haas

Leadership assumes widely different forms and is expressed through varied personal and cultural styles. Furthermore, a leader's understanding of her mandate and license for personal, organizational, and social change varies. Successful development programs and evaluations accommodate these variations. It is hoped and anticipated that the recipients of leadership development programs will translate their learning to fruitful action through various exchanges with others within the diverse organizational and community settings in which they practice their leadership. But programs themselves typically remain at least one step removed from organizational and community-level results.

In this chapter, we introduce an approach for sound and holistic evaluation strategies within this challenging context. As you can see from Chapter Two, it is difficult to assess the value added by a leadership development program to those directly served, as each participant or team comes with different skill sets, perspectives, and readiness to be influenced by the program. It is even more difficult to assess the value added by the program to the individuals, organizations, and communities with which it does not have direct contact but reaches indirectly through the follow-through actions of program participants. And yet frequently this is the justification for a leadership development program: to create broader change (such as on collaborative work of organizations in target communities, on state policies, or on the content and quality of social dialogue) through its influences on those it reaches directly.

Attempts to evaluate links between program actions and organizational or systems-level results are doomed to prove less than satisfactory to those seeking strong and irrefutable evidence of a contributory or causal relationship. However, we do not suggest that evaluations focus only on those more proximal results that can be linked to the program with more confidence (for example, hours trained or shifts in skill mastery levels from pre- to postintervention). Instead, or rather in addition, we propose that evaluations be framed within a holistic design that includes proximal and distal results. We suggest that evaluations extend beyond looking for results solely among program participants to exploring results in the arenas in which they interact, and that places primary focus on what the program is doing while working with participants to seed (not directly cause) change in these more distal arenas.

Evaluating programs in this way generates data, feedback, and insights with a breadth and richness that evaluations focused only on proximal changes lack. Program staff can draw on this type of evaluation to learn what, if anything, is leading to distal change and why. They can then make critical changes in program design and delivery to better equip and motivate participants to aim for the changes that sponsors and funders likely had in mind when they established the programs.

In short, to more clearly relate leadership development programs to systems change, the inquiry must be extended beyond direct participant changes. Programs whose purpose and mode of operation attend to subsequent participant relationships and interactions occurring within and across organizations and communities demand open-systems evaluations, which attune to both proximal and distal changes and dynamics. This perspective recognizes the importance of (1) capturing and seeing the whole picture, perhaps vague and misinformed at the outset but increasingly clearer and with more insight as evaluation inquiries proceed; and (2) drawing on this understanding to revise the practices upstream in anticipation of more attractive and compelling results downstream. *Upstream activities* refer to the direct influences of the program on its participants, while *downstream results* allude to what these participants do with the skills and insights they glean from the program as they engage as leaders.

In this chapter, we feature EvaluLEAD, a framework for marrying leadership development activities with systemic results beyond those immediately obtained with program participants. EvaluLEAD was developed over a three-year period by the authors of this chapter with contributions from more than 100 colleagues. Work on EvaluLEAD began in 2001 with the launch of the Leadership Evaluation Advisory Group sponsored by the Population Leadership Program of the Public Health Institute. During the next two years, the emerging framework was refined and expanded, building on feedback from experts in the field. EvaluLEAD and its foundational concepts were explored by a variety of leadership development programs in a field test sponsored by the W. K. Kellogg Foundation and with design support of the U.S. Agency for International Development (USAID).

A preliminary version of the EvaluLEAD schema (see Figure 3.1) was re-examined and refined throughout this three-year period. The schema underwent a number of changes as we deepened our collective understanding of what an open-systems approach to leadership development program evaluation entails. For example, initially evidential approaches were labeled as "more tangible" and evocative approaches as "less tangible." We recognized that this was representing evidential as "more" and evocative as "less" and subsequently

FIGURE 3.1. THE EVALULEAD FRAMEWORK.

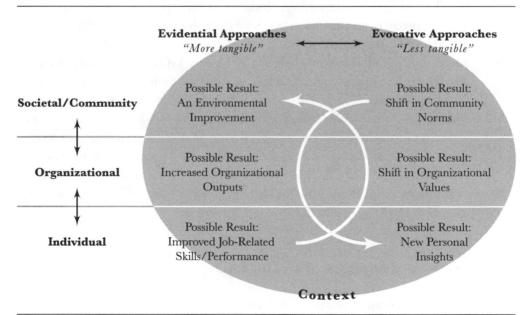

USAID/WKKF/PHI/PLP/SLI©

adjusted the language to designate evocative approaches as being "more holis-tic" as a counterpoint to evidential approaches being "more tangible." This better defines both as being important, but for different reasons. As a second example, the distinction among episodic, developmental, and transformative modes of change was introduced and became a critical part of our thinking, leading to a nine-cell matrix format (featured elsewhere in this chapter) rather than the six-cell format represented in Figure 3.1.

During the formative stages of development of EvaluLEAD, the W. K. Kellogg Foundation (2002) had independently funded a scan of fifty leader-ship programs to determine what each program deemed important and ex-amined in terms of outputs, outcomes, and impacts. We had the opportunity to examine and map these varied results within the emerging EvaluLEAD nine-cell matrix. More than 900 outcomes were mapped to gauge the results emphasized by programs. This analysis demonstrated that the programs par-ticipating in the scan were mindful of the importance of organizational- and society/community-level results, including those that did not lend themselves to quantification. This reinforced our contention that a framework and a tool were needed to marry upstream and downstream results, as well as to en-courage both evidential and evocative forms of inquiry.

This chapter presents the foundational concepts for using an open-sys-tems approach and then describes how these concepts are embedded within EvaluLEAD. We provide two case examples of applications of the approach. One case is the International Health Programs' GOJoven initiative, a Public Health Institute program working in its pilot year with youth health leaders in Latin America. The second case is Public Allies, an established national or-ganization in the United States with a multisite leadership development pro-gram that aims to facilitate community development. We conclude with a short discussion of the challenges associated with promoting use of an open-systems approach of this type within a field that is still dominated by the use of more closed-systems frameworks (largely cause-and-effect assessments fo-cused on proximal results) for evaluating success.

Foundational Concepts of EvaluLEAD

In practice, current efforts to understand and assess the worth of leadership development programs often focus solely on aspects of program delivery, ask-ing questions such as the following:

- How large a program staff is there and what roles do individual staff members perform?
- How many leaders have been or are being trained?
- How frequently do participants meet and for what purposes?
- In what ways are participants different at the end of the program than they were at the beginning?
- How did participants enjoy the program? What was the best part for them?
- What are participants' immediate and longer-term intentions?

While these questions may be useful, tracing and gauging a program's multiple and broader influences requires a broader set of questions to illuminate distinctly different yet interconnected aspects of a leadership development program's results.

As an increasing number of participants exit from any given leadership development program and begin to exercise their new learning and insights, there is a corresponding increase in the quantity, quality, variety, and duration of outputs, outcomes, and impacts whose emergence they may have helped influence. This complexity of results builds from cohort to cohort, soon challenging the abilities of program team members and others to keep up with, record, measure, and assess these results. Consequently, the full value of the program becomes difficult to assess.

Human reality is also capricious. Certain events and behaviors can be predicted with a fair amount of certainty; others cannot. The more chaotic the environment in which we find ourselves engaged, the farther we reach into the future, and the deeper we delve into human nature, the less we know and can control or predict. It would be nice, and is in some cases possible, to link cause to effect and assume that logic. However, that assumption may not be warranted.

Why an Open-Systems Perspective?

A useful distinction is made in general systems theory between simple, closed systems and complex, open systems. Examples of simple, closed systems are the electrical and plumbing systems in a home. Such physical systems are viewed as closed to suggest that a conceptual boundary can be placed around all critical components essential for full understanding of that system. In some sense, all systems are open to influences beyond their respective boundaries. A power outage, for example, would affect the working of the electrical system in the home.

However, except in rare situations, these outside factors can be ignored, and the system can be considered as closed.

Most human systems are open in both the sense that the actors within them are able to exercise free will and are subject to continual influence from outside sources at both the individual and systems levels. To illustrate, consider first a human system that is relatively closed: an elementary school. The activities of the children in the school are scheduled and regimented and the teachers follow curricula. Still, the learning of children will be impacted among other things by how much sleep they had, their relationships outside of school, and their physical and mental health—as well as by how personally motivated they are to learn. Similarly, the quality of the learning experiences offered by specific teachers will be influenced by outside factors such as family pressures and physical and mental health. Further, shifts in the national and state economy might create budget shortfalls that translate to dropped extracurricular programs, tutors not hired, and overcrowded classrooms, all contributing to teacher frustration, burnout, and less-than-ideal classroom performance.

Returning to our discussion of leadership development programs, adopting an open-systems view of interactions and connectivity between activities, programs, people, organizations, and communities implies recognizing that participants benefiting from leadership development programs also experience a multitude of nonprogram stimuli. Participants will be influenced by innumerable interactions and requirements on their time and attention that are not linked to program demands and expectations.

An open-systems perspective means that we assume that both predictability and unpredictability cooperate. As such, attributing causal relationships between program activities and upstream program outputs may be reasonable; attributing causal relationships between these same activities and downstream results is less reasonable due to the multitude of other factors at play. Accordingly, an open-systems perspective implies that evaluative investigations of the results of leadership development programs should be journeys of discovery rather than proofs of success. These journeys may uncover findings that are pivotal to changing the program for the better (such as to get more downstream results) but which would not have been included within a tightly designed, causal model for that program. The intent of evaluative exploration is to build a holistic picture of both the near and far-reaching promise of the program. In doing so, stakeholders benefiting from evaluation feedback will be better informed and more intuitively sensitive to the productivity and potentials of the program, and what is needed to produce more, and perhaps more dramatic, results.

We propose that evaluative discovery in this context is primarily formative and has three purposes:

1. To better understand the direct linkages and more casual (not causal) associations among the varied results observed in the individual, organizational, and societal domains
2. To gain an overall sense from observed patterns and examples of how a program works to accomplish its objectives and broader mission
3. To share these understandings with key program stakeholders and use them as a basis for modest to major program enhancements

An excursion into open-systems inquiry begins with mapping all the possible types of results to which a program might expect to contribute. After that, approaches for capturing, documenting, and illuminating these results for others are considered. This mapping and exploration of possible results (and associated protocols for capturing these data) provide a basis for subsequent prioritization and orchestration of data collection, and initiates the process of building a body of information (numbers plus narratives) for capturing the program's multiple contributions. This mapping further serves to help program staff, evaluation facilitators, and other stakeholders to truly grasp the potential consequences of their work and begin to think about what it will take to realize this potential.

Parameters for Analysis

Mapping program results requires identification and examination of four parameters.

1. *Result types,* or forms of change, characterized as Episodic, Developmental, and Transformative
2. *Domains of impact,* or social areas in which a leadership development program's results occur, identified as Individual, Organizational, and Societal/ Community
3. *Forms of inquiry* that can be employed in a complementary manner to gauge and illuminate results, described respectively as Evidential and Evocative

4. *Context,* which refers to the purposes, assumptions, and expectations surrounding both leadership as defined by the project and the evaluation
   process

The first three parameters define the potential results space of the program. Considerations of context inform decisions regarding which types of
results in which domains ought to be given priority and which forms of inquiry ought to be featured in the evaluation.

Result Types

There are three fundamentally different yet interrelated forms of change that
leadership development programs seek. Figure 3.2 provides an illustration of
these three forms of change.

Episodic changes are of the cause-and-effect variety. An intervention is made
and predictable results ideally follow. Episodic changes are typically well-
defined, time-bound results stimulated by actions of the program or its participants and graduates. Examples might include knowledge gained, a proposal
written, a conference held, and an ordinance enacted.

Developmental changes occur across time; include forward progress, stalls, and
setbacks; and proceed at different paces and with varied rhythms for participating individuals, groups, and communities. Results are open-ended, and less
controllable and predictable than for episodic changes, due to, among other
factors, external influences and internal willingness and ability to change. Developmental results are represented as sequences of steps taken by an individual, team, organization, or community that reach toward and may actually

FIGURE 3.2. VISUAL REPRESENTATION OF TYPES OF CHANGE.

Episodic	Developmental	Transformative
Learn 25 basic French phrases	Complete 6-month course in conversational French	Become a Francophile

achieve some challenging outcomes. Their pace may be altered by unantici-pated or uncontrollable conditions and events. Examples include a sustained change in individual behavior, a new organizational strategy that is used to guide operations, and the implementation of a phased economic development program.

Transformative changes represent fundamental shifts in individual, organiza-tional, or community values and perspectives that seed the emergence of fun-damental shifts in behavior or performance. These transformations represent regenerative moments or radical redirections of effort, and they are often the prize to which programs aspire. Transformative results represent a crossroads or an unanticipated new road taken for the individual, organization, or com-munity, whereas episodic and developmental results are not nearly so un-expected or so potentially profound in their consequences. Examples of transformative results include substantial shifts in viewpoint, vision, or par-adigms, career shifts, new organizational directions, and fundamental socio-political reforms. These results are emergent over time but may appear episodic when noticed.

Within an open-systems perspective, episodic, developmental, and trans-formative changes are seen as concurrent. This contrasts with closed-systems frameworks and logic models, where changes are frequently arrayed in chrono-logical sequence—with outputs leading to outcomes leading to impacts—as is the case with the experimental or quasi-experimental designs discussed in the first chapter of this handbook.

To illustrate the concurrent nature of these changes, we ask you to con-sider a program graduate attending an annual gathering of graduates and coming away with some new insights or a renewed contact. This would be an episodic result. That same individual might be campaigning for a seat on the local school board as a step toward her ultimate aim of gaining a seat in the U.S. Congress. Should she succeed, this would be a developmental result along her career pathway. Her election could be considered as an isolated episodic result, but contextual considerations argue for it being considered develop-mental. As part of the campaign, she visits some classrooms in the inner city and, during one visit, gains an insight that profoundly impacts the way she views public education and its possibilities, giving rise to a radically different leadership agenda and purpose. This is a transformative result. It appears episodic, but the readiness to be so influenced might likely have been building for some time, reaching a critical threshold during the classroom visit. A single program objective, such as enhancing organizational performance, might embody all three types of results.

Domains of Impact

There are three multi-tiered levels—or domains of impact—within which leadership development programs typically seek results and are addressed within the EvaluLEAD framework: individual, organizational, and societal or community.

The *individual domain* typically centers on individuals currently participating in the program. Program graduates from previous cohorts constitute another important set of beneficiaries. Both current participants and graduates are positioned to influence the personal learning or growth of other individuals (for example, peers from work or comembers of a community task force). Within the individual domain, program-associated results might be expected from current participants, graduates, and secondary contacts.

The *organizational domain* includes agencies, departments, programs, teams, alliances, or other structured groups of persons organized for a particular purpose where program participants and graduates are affiliated and might be expected to apply their newly acquired leadership skills and perspectives. Within the organizational domain, program-associated results may occur within the home organizations of program participants and graduates and/or within outside organizations with which these individuals or their organizations interact.

The *societal/community domain* refers to the broader neighborhoods, communities, social or professional networks, sectors of society, or ecosystems to which the influences of program participants and graduates may extend, either directly or through their organizational work. The mission and raison d'être of many programs may, in fact, be to influence such results. In such cases, it is critical to include this domain within the evaluation schema.

Since learning is occurring all the time, and there are feedback loops among individuals, their organizations, and their communities, change can also be concurrent in multiple domains. For instance, a change in the organizational domain might trigger new behaviors for individuals. Further, since the relationship between a program and the individual participants may be extended (such as through ongoing technical support or periodic seminars for program graduates), the flow of results from the individual to the organization and/or community may be activated on multiple occasions and lead to multiple rounds of results that reinforce, complement, or undermine others.

Forms of Inquiry

Evaluations of programs that aim to affect the lives of participants they serve have frequently been criticized for focusing on numbers and not on people themselves—for counting bodies while missing souls, failing to capture the human drama and associated opportunities for affecting individuals or communities in profound ways. Figure 3.3 provides an illustration moving from examining cause-and-effect change to synchronistic change and the associated shift in the methods and tools we use to understand the different types of change. By employing different types of inquiry within a comprehensive framework, proximal and easily measured participant experiences, as well as more distal developmental and transformative factors, can be brought together to broaden and deepen understanding.

To do this, we encourage the strategic use of two distinctly different, yet complementary, forms of inquiry to gauge and illuminate results: evidential and evocative.

Evidential inquiry attempts to capture and represent the facts regarding what is happening to people (and by extension, to their organizations and communities). It seeks descriptive, numeric, and physical evidence of program impact,

FIGURE 3.3. BALANCE OF TOOLS OF INQUIRY BETWEEN CLOSED AND OPEN SYSTEMS.

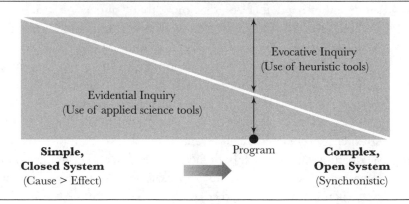

and supports analytic and deductive assessment of a program's influence and worth. In evidential inquiries, we identify facts, track markers, and compile other conventional forms of hard evidence to determine what is taking place that can be associated back to the program or its participants and graduates. Quantitative and qualitative methods may be used, with results presented as representational data. Evidential inquiries should contribute to an improvement in analytical reasoning regarding the program and its effects.

Evocative inquiry seeks the perspectives and sentiments of those influenced by the program—either directly as program participants or as subsequent beneficiaries of participants' actions. This feedback is obtained and conveyed as stories, viewpoints, or discourse through methods such as open-ended surveys, case studies, anecdotes, journals, and video diaries, and plays to the intuitive sensitivities of those interested in assessing the program. Evocative inquiries attempt to capture and re-create some of the richness and human dimension of what is happening or has happened. Evocative inquiry is employed to assess a reaction to the change process as a whole rather than its parts. These reactions may range from "This makes no sense!" to "I didn't realize how much impact this was having!" Evocative inquiries should contribute to heightened intuition and holistic comprehension regarding a program and its effects.

The evidential-evocative distinction is different than the quantitative-qualitative distinction that permeates the fields of evaluation and social science. The evidential-evocative distinction reflects the recognition that a balance needs to be struck between valuing both what can be measured and analyzed and what cannot. In the truism that "the whole is more than the sum of its parts," evidential inquiries focus on the parts and their measurement, generally using fragmented or reductionist approaches. Evocative inquiries, on the other hand, focus on the "more than" dimension, using integrating approaches that strengthen awareness, appreciation, and affinity for that which is being studied. Put another way, evidential inquiry supports deductive reasoning, while evocative inquiry supports inductive judgment. (See Grove, Kibel, and Haas, 2005, *EvaluLEAD: A Guide for Shaping and Evaluating Leadership Development Programs*, Section II, Step 8 for further discussion.)

Both modes of inquiry are applicable to all three types of change: episodic, developmental, and transformative. For example, episodic results can be documented through both facts (evidential) and opinions about the overall experience (evocative). Because episodic results are of a cause-and-effect variety, facts offer specific and concrete evidence that the results of interest have occurred. They include, for instance, counts of individuals reached and types of services provided, dates and descriptions of events of note, comparisons of pre- and posttests, and reports of new changes; and will comprise the bulk of episodic evaluative inquiry. To extend our understanding or appreciation for these black-and-white facts, however, opinions are solicited from program participants or other critical observers. These may include participant ratings of services received; structured, open-ended feedback from key informants on the implications of processes introduced; or public opinion surveys.

Developmental results can be documented equally through achievement of markers (evidential) and associated stories or case studies (evocative). Markers are used both as evidence of progress toward some long-term goal and to acknowledge milestones reached along the way. For added dimensionality, case histories or stories are captured to reveal challenges and struggles behind the gains observed. Stories fill in the spaces between the markers and put human faces on the data, thereby evoking better understanding of what has been achieved and for whom.

Transformative results are most immediately captured through personal reflections (evocative) of those with firsthand knowledge of what has occurred and, for harder results, through documentation of shifts in macro-level indicators (evidential) of health or life status of individuals, organizations, or communities affected. Because these results are unique to the individual, organization, or community realizing them, those most profoundly affected are best positioned to reflect on and share the implications of what has occurred. Such reflections may be captured through journals, interviews, focus groups, or other forms of self- or group expression. Concrete evidence of change, such as improvements in personal health (physical, mental, and/or spiritual), organizational climate, or community health statistics and quality-of-life indicators, should follow the declarations in relatively short order if the results truly are transformative.

Results Space

An evaluation that explores the three types of results (episodic, developmental, and transformative) across all three levels (individual, organizational, and societal/community) yields nine distinct lenses for focusing on the results of a leadership development program. This is a program's unique *results space*, which represents the full scope of potential results sought. Each of these nine lenses is bifocal, to suggest options for both evidential and evocative inquiry (see Exhibit 3.1). For example, one such activity might use evidential inquiry to measure an

EXHIBIT 3.1. PROTOTYPICAL NUMBER OF EVALUATION ACTIVITIES FOR FULL SCOPE OF RESULTS.

Result Types (3)		Domains (3)		Forms of Inquiry (2)		Prototypical Evaluation Activities (18)
Episodic Developmental Transformative	×	Individual Organizational Societal/Community	×	Evidential Evocative	=	

episodic result occurring in the organizational domain. A second activity might use evocative inquiry to illuminate that same result. A third activity might use evocative inquiry to illuminate a transformative result in the individual domain.

Applying nine unique bifocal lenses to the study of a leadership development program may appear a formidable or totally unworkable proposition. In *EvaluLEAD: A Guide for Shaping and Evaluating Leadership Development Programs* (Grove, Kibel, and Haas, 2005), we offer a practical step-by-step process for (1) taking a quick look at the program through each of these lenses; (2) setting priorities regarding where to concentrate resources and attention based on time, budget, stakeholder interest, ease of data collection, and other criteria; and (3) striking the right mix between evidential and evocative approaches.

For relatively simple systems (of varying degrees of complication but with well-defined human behaviors), applied science tools are suggested with minimum attention to evocative approaches. However, to investigate relatively complex systems with high levels of interaction, relation building, and improvisation, an evaluation design that makes extensive use of evocative approaches, but with supporting evidential approaches, is suggested.

Thinking Holistically

To make best use of an open-systems perspective in evaluation, one needs to assume a perspective that relates each new lesson back to a whole program picture. Each lesson, when viewed as a piece of a larger puzzle (rather than a piece in isolation) both informs all previous learning and sets conditions for future learning. What is learned about some episodic result at the organizational level, for example, should be interpreted in terms of both earlier results observed or documented at the individual episodic and developmental levels and potential results at the societal level.

Consistent with this perspective, each result listed in any of the nine cells is stated in the present tense. For example, instead of "Program X will train thirty team leaders," we suggest that the result be framed as "Thirty leaders are being trained." One of the EvaluLEAD field-test participants shared an insight that truly captures the power inherent in use of the present tense for results: "What I like best about the EvaluLEAD framework is that it encourages a program to think about transformation as if it is already happening here-and-now and being lived and experienced by participants, rather than as a vision to be realized perhaps some time out in the distant future."

EvaluLEAD in Practice: Case Examples from International Health Programs' GOJoven Program and Public Allies' Core Apprenticeship Program

In this section of the chapter, we demonstrate the EvaluLEAD approach and supporting tools through two case examples. One example is provided by the Public Health Institute's International Health Programs' GOJoven program for leadership development among youth in reproductive and sexual health, a small program with limited resources working in Central and South America. The second case focuses on Public Allies, a national program facilitating community development as a sustainable addition to the AmeriCorps experience. We chose these two programs as case examples because they represent different ends of the organizational spectrum between start-up and established programs and international versus domestic target groups; and both had experienced program evaluators participating in the field test who could contrast this approach with others they had employed. The GOJoven case demonstrates use of EvaluLEAD in the process of establishing foundational evaluation approaches with a view toward long-term assessment at the societal level. The Public Allies case highlights solutions and challenges in introducing fresh approaches set within broader organizational shifts and existing traditional methods.

In each of these cases, we provide information about the program: its purpose, vision, goals, and desired results, as well as whom it involves, where it focuses geographically, and who are its target participants. In addition to presenting their use of EvaluLEAD tools, we also share their successes, challenges, and lessons learned in implementing them. For each case we present

- A completed program results map
- The process and results of the program's prioritization exercise
- An investigation worksheet example for one prioritized area for evaluation

A program results map can be used ideally with all stakeholders, including funders, to create shared agreement of the shape and evaluation of a leadership program. When viewed in its entirety, the nine-cell program results map offers a compelling and comprehensive picture of a program. The map also makes clear that an evaluation of all aspects might be both costly and time consuming, perhaps dwarfing the program itself. Still, all cells in which stakeholders hope to see results (potentially as many as nine) deserve at least some attention to sustain a holistic view.

The program results map is used as a menu from which each stakeholder can suggest where the evaluation ought to focus to learn the most about what interests them. A prioritization exercise is designed to answer the question, Where and how should the bulk of evaluation resources be expended? and to bring the evaluation design within manageable limits by setting priorities regarding the level of effort that will be devoted to each of the nine results areas identified on the map.

Exhibit 3.2 represents the intersection of assessment of the data collection challenge against stakeholder priority, which helps programs establish a priority ranking for each result area (cell) of potential evaluation inquiry. Working alone or with other key stakeholders, programs estimate how challenging it will be to gather the needed data and solicit the desired feedback for each result. This is weighed against the priority that stakeholders place on a particular result—for example, how important are demonstrations of individual change versus organizational gains to individual stakeholders?

This process can be adapted and expanded to be as methodical, democratic, or directive as needed based on the group's needs and decision-making style. For example, a program could generate a set of priority scores based on program staff input and then establish separate scores with board members or donors. The two sets can then be averaged or juxtaposed and used in a joint discussion of the program.

Once the results map has been completed and specific results prioritized, developing specific evaluation strategies begins. Starting with the highest pri-

**EXHIBIT 3.2. PRIORITIZATION EXERCISE MATRIX OF
STAKEHOLDER PRIORITIES AND DATA COLLECTION CHALLENGE.**

		Data Collection Challenge		
		Easy	Feasible	Difficult
Stakeholder Priority	H I G H	3 Definitely collect	2 Worth collecting	2 Consider an alternative
	M E D	2 Worth collecting	1 Collect if have time	1 Collect if have time
	L O W	1 Collect if have time	1 Collect if have time	0 Ignore

ority cell, one investigation worksheet is completed for each cell in the results map with priority scores greater than zero (refer to Exhibit 3.5 as an example). The worksheet provides prompts for

- Revisiting the results statement, domain, and type of results
- Suggesting specific evidential and evocative strategies
- Noting the suggested evaluation approach depending on the type of change identified (track markers, capture stories, and so on)
- Considering opportunities and challenges that might be faced in using the proposed strategies

The process is iterative. Most programs will work and rework the sheets several times before commencing data collection.

Case I. GOJoven. Laying the Foundation for Long-Term Assessment

The Youth Leadership in Sexual and Reproductive Health Program (GOJoven) is a three-year leadership development initiative to improve adolescent sexual and reproductive health in four countries in Latin America. GOJoven is implemented by the Public Health

Institute's (PHI) International Health Programs (IHP) and is funded by the Summit Foundation. The project is operated in coordination with in-country partners in each focus country.

GOJoven's overall program approach is to develop an influential cadre and network of young leaders (Summit Fellows) who have the knowledge, skills, and commitment to increase young people's access to youth-friendly sexual and reproductive health policies, programs, and services at local and national levels. At the end of its initial three-year program, IHP expects to have strengthened the enabling environment of each focus country by introducing and supporting efforts to improve adolescent sexual and reproductive health policies, practices, and institutions. Specifically, the primary objectives of GOJoven are to

- Build the capacity of 56 emerging leaders ages 18–30 by strengthening their vision, capacity, and commitment to improving adolescent sexual and reproductive health services and programs and influence the development and improvement of sexual and reproductive health policies for adolescents in Belize, Guatemala, Honduras, and Mexico
- Increase the institutional commitment and capacity of five organizations or agencies per country to focus on adolescent sexual and reproductive health issues and support emerging leaders with an adolescent sexual and reproductive health focus within their home institutions
- Influence adolescent sexual and reproductive health programs, services, and policies by creating a regional network of emerging and established leaders participating in GOJoven and in the International Family Planning Leadership Program who are working together to create lasting positive changes in the field of adolescent sexual and reproductive health within their countries and throughout the region.

GOJoven's Evaluation Coordinator has overall responsibility for coordinating and planning the evaluation for GOJoven. Under IHP's program and organizational structure, GOJoven's program director and program manager work with the evaluator to review and approve GOJoven's evaluation plan, assess evaluation instruments, collect data, monitor information for the program, and write reports on the progress of the program for the funding agency. Country representatives in each focus country collect and compile data and information for the program. The evaluator led EvaluLEAD related activities with key support from other IHP staff members.

Program Results Map

Using the Program Results Map tool, IHP examined and solidified their intended results for GOJoven. In the process, they relied on the original funding proposal and the project's preliminary evaluation plan. This plan detailed traditional evaluation elements of goals and objectives, as well as input, process, output, outcome, and impact indicators. Qualitative and quantitative methods of assessment were specified.

The GOJoven evaluator used an iterative process to develop the Results Map. First, she mapped and prioritized the high-level intended results (goals and objectives) of the program, based on her analysis of the outcomes most closely associated with the projected program activities and her perceptions of stakeholder interest. This map, shared as Exhibit 3.3, provides a broad overview of the GOJoven program and the interconnections between the program's proposed interventions and the spheres in which it intended to have influence. Then, the evaluator transferred and adapted the detailed results and specific indicators that key stakeholders agreed upon to each domain of impact and its result type (see Exhibit 3.4). This task helped her to think about new evaluation strategies and to consider capturing alternative information.

One challenge faced in using EvaluLEAD was determining the appropriate way to best express what the program expects to achieve. Outcome statements were typically expressed as "will increase," "will improve," "will be strengthened." Switching from future tense to present tense was a break from the evaluator's prior evaluation experience as well as a philosophical shift, and ultimately something the evaluator opted not to do.

Prioritization Process

The evaluator noted that prioritization was particularly difficult because everything felt to her like a priority. With each result area, she had to reflect on what IHP was really trying to accomplish through GOJoven.

A number of considerations informed evaluation priorities: GOJoven's start-up status and its immediate three-year time horizon, the emphasis within IHP on evaluation for program improvement, the flexibility of the Summit Foundation, and financial and human capacity within the program and organization to support evaluation.

Consistent with IHP's mission and stakeholder preferences, GOJoven wanted to see results in the organizational and societal domains as depicted in the prioritizations in their first results map (see Exhibit 3.3). However, as depicted in the second, more detailed, iteration of GOJoven's results map (see Exhibit 3.4), the program staff decided to focus on evaluation at the level of the individual. They consciously noted this as a priority since it was their first year of operations. They decided to focus on individual participants' perceptions of their own change, if any, and verify these changes with nonparticipant sources. They anticipated that in the program's second year they would focus more effort on understanding results at the organizational level. They built in flexibility to allow for change as they established new relationships with partners.

EXHIBIT 3.3. GOJOVEN'S COMPLETED INITIAL PROGRAM RESULTS MAP WITH PRIORITIZATIONS.

Project: GOJoven: Youth Leadership in Sexual and Reproductive Health—International Health Programs/Public Health Institute

	Societal/Community Episodic (S1)	2	Societal/Community Developmental (S2)	0	Societal/Community Transformative (S3)
			*Youth leaders and partner organizations will expand youth-friendly reproductive health policies, programs, and services in the communities they serve.		*Decreased rates of adolescent pregnancy, youth maternal mortality, infant mortality, sexually transmitted infections, and HIV-AIDS in communities served.
Gather facts	*Collect opinions*	*Track markers*	*Compile stories*	*Measure indicators*	*Encourage reflection*

3	Organizational Episodic (O1)	2	Organizational Developmental (O2)	3	Organizational Transformative (O3)
*Partner organizations in each country will receive technical assistance in institutional capacity building and facilitated mentoring processes.		*In three years, five partner organizations per country will demonstrate increased commitment and capacity to address adolescent sexual and reproductive health issues, develop and support youth leadership, and implement facilitated mentoring processes.		*A network of reproductive health youth leaders and partner organizations will be formed to advocate for expanded reproductive health policies and programs for youth.	
Gather facts	*Collect opinions*	*Track markers*	*Compile stories*	*Measure indicators*	*Encourage reflection*

EXHIBIT 3.3. GOJOVEN'S COMPLETED INITIAL
PROGRAM RESULTS MAP WITH PRIORITIZATIONS, Cont'd.

3	Individual Episodic (I1)		3	Individual Developmental (I2)		2	Individual Transformative (I3)	
*48 Summit Fellows (50% women) will complete the GOJoven leadership development program in reproductive health (four Fellows per four countries per three years).			*Summit Fellows will demonstrate increased knowledge, skills, and heightened commitment in leadership development and adolescent reproductive and sexual health.			*Summit Fellows will exercise increased decision-making power and influence in their organizations and communities. *An increased number of youth leaders will choose a career in adolescent sexual and reproductive health.		
Gather facts	*Collect opinions*		*Track markers*	*Compile stories*		*Measure indicators*	*Encourage reflection*	

Source: Youth Leadership in Sexual and Reproductive Health Program (GOJoven). International Health Programs/Public Health Institute.

Investigation Worksheet

GOJoven's individual domain result states, "Summit Fellows will increase their knowledge, skills, and heightened commitment in leadership development and adolescent reproductive and sexual health." This outcome, an individual developmental result, called for markers to be tracked (evidential) and stories to be compiled (evocative). The evaluator created a plan for conducting self-assessments and identifying Summit Fellows from whom to gather stories. She also presented evaluation strategies for addressing challenges and opportunities she anticipated. Exhibit 3.5 provides a sample of a completed investigation worksheet.

Two constraints influenced the ability of the program to implement the evaluation strategies that were proposed. GOJoven was unable to establish a control group of youth to compare with youth who were accepted to the program, primarily because the recruitment and acceptance process turned out to be different than imagined. In addition, human resource constraints within the program prevented GOJoven's implementation of 360-degree assessments. Instead, interviews were conducted with Fellows' supervisors and partner organizations.

EXHIBIT 3.4. GOJOVEN'S REVISED DETAILED PROGRAM RESULTS MAP WITH YEAR 1 EVALUATION PRIORITIZATIONS.

Project: GOJoven: Youth Leaders in Sexual and Reproductive Health— International Health Programs/Public Health Institute

Societal/Community Episodic (S1)		0	Societal/Community Developmental (S2)	0	Societal/Community Transformative (S3)	
			*Improved quantity and quality of media coverage of adolescent sexual and reproductive health issues. *Increase in number of adolescent sexual and reproductive health programs and service sites.		*Improved implementation of existing adolescent sexual and reproductive health laws and policies. *Increase in number of new national policies and laws promoting adolescent sexual and reproductive health and improvements in Ministry of Health policies or guidelines.	
Gather facts	*Collect opinions*	*Track markers*	*Compile stories*	*Measure indicators*	*Encourage reflection*	

Organizational Episodic (O1)	0	Organizational Developmental (O2)	0	Organizational Transformative (O3)
*A minimum of eight partner organizations will receive training in facilitated mentoring processes, development and fundraising, evaluation, leadership, and so on.		*Facilitated mentoring processes will be operating in all four focus countries. *Organizations will demonstrate improved implementation of youth-friendly programs and policies focusing on the provision of sexual and reproductive		*Organizations will increase their vision, commitment, and capacity to design, manage, and evaluate adolescent sexual and reproductive health programs and policies. *Strengthened collaboration and networking among

EXHIBIT 3.4. GOJOVEN'S REVISED DETAILED PROGRAM RESULTS MAP WITH YEAR 1 EVALUATION PRIORITIZATIONS, Cont'd.

Organizational Episodic (O1)	0	Organizational Developmental (O2)	0	Organizational Transformative (O3)	
		health services and information. *Partner organizations in each country develop a program plan to institutionalize an adaptation of GOJoven. *Increase in number of NGOs with staff involved with adolescent sexual and reproductive health activities.		key organizations and heightened capacity to conduct local- and national-level advocacy.	
Gather facts	*Collect opinions*	*Track markers*	*Compile stories*	*Measure indicators*	*Encourage reflection*

3	Individual Episodic (I1)	3	Individual Developmental (I2)	1	Individual Transformative (I3)
*48 Summit Fellows will complete the GOJoven sexual and reproductive health leadership program over three years (four Summit Fellows per four countries per three years). *Four Summit Fellows from each country will form a country team each year.		*Summit Fellows will increase their knowledge, skills, and heightened commitment in leadership development and adolescent sexual and reproductive health. *Summit Fellows will expand their vision of sexual and reproductive health.		*Summit Fellows will exercise increased decision-making power and influence in their organizations and communities. *An increased number of youth leaders will choose a career in sexual and reproductive health.	

EXHIBIT 3.4. GOJOVEN'S REVISED DETAILED PROGRAM RESULTS MAP WITH YEAR 1 EVALUATION PRIORITIZATIONS, Cont'd.

3	Individual Episodic (I1)	3	Individual Developmental (I2)	1	Individual Transformative (I3)
	*Each Fellow will create a Personal Leadership Development Plan (PLDP). *Each year 100% of Fellows will be mentored by an IFPLP Fellow or sexual and reproductive health leader. *100% of Fellows assigned/ working in an organization that supports their work in improving adolescent sexual and reproductive health practices and policies. *Summit Fellows will participate in the IFPLP Network by attending regional network meetings, participating in mentoring relationships, and communicating via the IFPLP LA Web site. *Summit Fellows will participate in other sexual and reproductive health leadership networks conducted by Packard, Gates, and MacArthur grantees in focus countries.		*Each country team will design and implement a collaborative leadership activity to improve adolescent sexual and reproductive health through a Leadership Action Plan (LAP). *At least two mentoring pairs per year in each country report increased capacity to address adolescent sexual and reproductive health issues. *Fellows will activate a regional network of Summit Fellows, communicating via the GOJoven Web site. *By the end of three years, 75% of Fellows will be active participants in the GOJoven network, functioning in all four focus countries. *Increased participation of Summit Fellows in existing national, regional, and international leadership networks to incorporate a youth perspective. *Regional network of Summit Fellows will support one joint effort to improve		*A critical mass of multi-generational sexual and reproductive health leaders (Summit Fellows, IFPLP Fellows, and Gates, Packard, and MacArthur Fellows) collaboratively implement joint projects that influence policies to improve adolescent sexual and reproductive health and increase popular understanding of adolescent sexual and reproductive health issues.

EXHIBIT 3.4. GOJOVEN'S REVISED DETAILED PROGRAM RESULTS MAP WITH YEAR 1 EVALUATION PRIORITIZATIONS, Cont'd.

3	Individual Episodic (I1)		3	Individual Developmental (I2)		1	Individual Transformative (I3)	
			sexual and reproductive health for adolescents in the region. *Summit Fellows in each focus country will present GOJoven to government and NGO officials and representatives to seek support for adolescent sexual and reproductive health initiatives.					
Gather facts		*Collect opinions*	*Track markers*		*Compile stories*	*Measure indicators*		*Encourage reflection*

Source: Youth Leadership in Sexual and Reproductive Health Program (GOJoven). International Health Programs/Public Health Institute.

Successes, Challenges, and Lessons Learned

IHP has experience with using monitoring and evaluation for program improvement and program evaluation. However, it has seldom attempted to systematically measure long-term results, mostly because of funding limitations. With EvaluLEAD it was provided with a way to systematize program learning and evaluation, including measuring long-term impacts and outcomes of leadership development programs. IHP restructured and improved GOJoven's evaluation plan and framework using the EvaluLEAD approach.

Using the results map helped IHP staff to identify gaps in GOJoven's original program evaluation plan, highlighting where the evaluation was strongly designed to collect some types of data and weak in taking the opportunity to capture other important data. In turn, the results map influenced the design of instruments for collecting program information, the analysis of data and information, and the preparation of reports for the funding agency. The results map was more useful than a logic model in helping program stakeholders think about the relationships between their interventions and the results areas they hoped the program would influence. The EvaluLEAD results map

EXHIBIT 3.5. GOJoven'S INVESTIGATION WORKSHEET EXAMPLE FOR ONE PRIORITIZED AREA.

Project: GOJoven: Youth Leadership in Sexual and Reproductive Health—
International Health Programs/Public Health Institute SHEET #5

Outcome/Objective: Summit Fellows will increase their knowledge, skills, and heightened commitment in leadership development and adolescent reproductive and sexual health.	INDIV	ORG	SOC	EPISOD	DEVEL	TRANS
	x				x	

EVIDENTIAL INQUIRY:
☐ **Gather Facts**　　　☑ **Track Markers**　　　☐ **Measure Indicators**

Evaluation Strategy: Measure change in confidence, skills, and knowledge of Summit Fellows. Collect information from program application submissions and by conducting a now-before self-assessment with Summit Fellows during the training. Track information on Summit Fellows' professional development activities and pursuits. Measure Summit Fellows' commitment to adolescent sexual and reproductive health by collecting information on participation rates and activeness levels of Summit Fellows in GOJoven.

Context Opportunities and Challenges: We are exploring the feasibility of piloting the use of a control group in one of the countries to measure/compare changes between Summit Fellows accepted into the program in years 1 and 2.

Evaluation Constraints:

EVOCATIVE INQUIRY:
☐ **Collect Opinions**　　　☑ **Capture Stories**　　　☐ **Encourage Reflection**

Evaluation Strategy: Through open-ended questions in posttraining on-the-job questionnaires, collect case examples from Summit Fellows on how the acquisition of knowledge and skills has made a difference in their professional and personal lives. Gather case stories on commitment of Summit Fellows by conducting detailed interviews with a sample of Fellows from each country: Where do they see themselves in five years? What is their level of sexual and reproductive health knowledge (knowledge = interest = link to commitment)?

Context Opportunities and Challenges: We are exploring the feasibility of conducting 360-evaluations on a sample of Summit Fellows with their peers, colleagues, and supervisors in partner organizations.

Evaluation Constraints:

Source: Youth Leadership in Sexual and Reproductive Health Program (GOJoven). International Health Programs/Public Health Institute.

accentuated the multiple dimensions of the work. The framework assisted GOJoven staff to map the interconnectedness of activities and contexts within the program and document its more complex results.

Though they did not prioritize organizational or societal/community-level results in their first year, they recorded these data as they came in, especially as stories. Because they had a results map that specified multiple result areas, they had a way to represent the information as transformative, developmental, and episodic, and consider it in relation to other result areas and overall program accomplishments.

The Summit Foundation was aware that there was no easy and direct route between a leadership development intervention and their ultimate goals of improving population-level health indicators in the focus regions. Thus, this funder remained open to changing and improving processes and pathways toward end results.

In-the-field evaluation efforts were specifically designed to capture not only evidential data but also evocative data. In addition, program staff made a shift in their use of evaluative language, from distinguishing between quantitative and qualitative to distinguishing between evidential and evocative. Strategically, IHP thought the GOJoven team's new focus on collecting and capturing evocative information and results was important because this information captivated the attention and commitment of the funding agency, as well as the staff and beneficiaries of the program. For example, IHP provided a summary of GOJoven evaluation results to the Summit Foundation's board of directors that included both evidential and evocative expressions of results, as well as lessons learned and issues being addressed to improve the program.

In addition, staff found that personal stories of development and changes in perspective and attitude forged bonds among everyone directly connected to the program, including GOJoven's funders, staff, and beneficiaries. IHP's deputy director observed, "I listened raptly to an hour of transformational stories from a small cohort of young leaders. In the middle of these incredible descriptions of individual and team transformations—acts of true bravery, adaptations of new, and sometimes dangerous, conceptual frameworks, one story after another of the light bulb being lit, and the understanding that it could not ever be turned off—my 'Aha!' experience came to me—it occurred to me that evaluation can be inspiring as well as informing."

IHP and GOJoven continue to use the concept of transformation within the context of their program and its evaluation. They continually ask, What does transformation mean in this context? What does it look like? Is this truly transformative? While specific examples of community transformation come to mind, the evaluator finds it is something she can more readily observe than absorb in written accounts or questionnaires.

Unlike a traditional model of evaluation where there is linear movement from one element to the next (inputs lead to outputs lead to impacts), EvaluLEAD reflects the multidimensionality of the interplay between relationships and activities. This open-systems perspective can be used more effectively to build a model for long-term program

improvement because the tools employed take into account a broader view of a program's many areas of influence and allows for ongoing review and change in focus.

Case II. Public Allies.
Seeking Inward and Outward Meaning

Through the AmeriCorps program, Public Allies provides a ten-month leadership program targeting talented young adults from diverse backgrounds. The Public Allies
leadership model is based on values of collaboration, diversity, community assets, integrity, and continuous learning. Through full-time apprenticeships, team service
projects, and intensive training programs, young adults gain skills intended to help
them build healthier and more empowered communities, make nonprofits more effective and responsive, and increase civic engagement among themselves and the
communities they serve.

Public Allies uses a mixed-method approach for evaluating program process and
outcomes at individual, organizational, and community levels. Their Comprehensive
Continuous Learning and Improvement process includes (1) an online personal impact and service documentation tool to track participants' service outputs and outcomes; (2) 360-degree reviews; (3) annual year-end surveys of participants and partner
organizations; and (4) Presentations of Learning, during which participants demonstrate how they have met their service and learning outcomes. At the end of each year,
the Center for Urban Initiatives and Policy Research at the University of Wisconsin-
Milwaukee compiles Public Allies' data across tools and compiles reports to Public Allies that they use to improve programming.

Public Allies was interested in investigating current and potential evaluation strategies and methods related to three main areas. The first was assessment of the impact
Public Allies has on the partner organizations with which its Allies work. Though they
assessed this impact through an end-of-year survey of partner organization supervisors,
they wanted to more fully understand how deeply Public Allies' culture and values per-
meated partner organizations in the long term. They felt they needed to improve their
community-level measures to do this.

A second area was assessment of Public Allies' impact on the communities in
which they work. Public Allies has been established in some communities for ten years
or more. Although they developed and centralized many data collection and evaluation procedures, previous data collection was the responsibility of individual sites and
could be sporadic and inconsistent.

A third area they wanted to better understand was program participants' (known
as *Allies*) attitude, knowledge, and behavior change throughout the course of the pro-

gram year. For example, all Allies participated in a 360-degree process that provided a baseline assessment in month 4 of the program year. After individual Allies were coached through personal development plans, the 360-degree assessment was again administered in month 8 of the program year. Public Allies suspected that social desirability bias and/or response shift bias were negatively affecting the results. To alleviate these biases, they considered adopting retrospective pretest methods to supplement the 360-degree assessments.

Finally, Public Allies had some specific organizational challenges. The organization had not always been well coordinated nationally, leading to inconsistencies in programming. As they revised program curricula components, the organization was interested in adding rigor. Public Allies was also interested in learning from other programs about how they measured civic engagement in leadership programs.

Program Results Map

Public Allies underwent a process of developing their organizational theory of change. They identified immediate changes resulting from Public Allies' core apprenticeship program, changes as a result of specific alumni programming, and long-term community-level changes that they hoped to see happen, most likely over the next 10–20 years.

These were then translated into more tangible intended results and put within the EvaluLEAD framework, which helped them articulate a level of specificity that they needed to establish a concrete evaluation plan.

The organization's vice president of programs (VP) and the continuous learning officer (CLO) were primarily responsible for this process, coordinating with different people at different points to get reactions to their thinking as the evaluation team. Public Allies' national Continuous Learning Team, which included site-level program staff and national program support staff, developed and revised outcomes in the framework and provided advice to develop the evaluation plan for their core apprenticeship program. The Alumni Relations Team developed and revised outcomes in the EvaluLEAD framework that pertained to alumni programming.

During the process of formulating their EvaluLEAD program results map (see Exhibit 3.6), the VP and CLO had to reconcile two diverse contexts: the national service field (as an AmeriCorps program) and the leadership development field. This entailed a continuous questioning of what each intended result meant in terms of AmeriCorps on the public service side and in terms of diverse young leaders strengthening communities on the leadership development side. If Public Allies had been dealing with only one audience, it would have had an easier time designing the evaluation plan. With multiple audiences, the plan needed to respond to multiple evaluation needs.

EXHIBIT 3.6. PUBLIC ALLIES'
PROGRAM RESULTS MAP WITH PRIORITIZATION.

Project: Public Allies' Core Apprenticeship Program

0	Societal/Community Episodic (S1)	0	Societal/Community Developmental (S2)	0	Societal/Community Transformative (S3)		
*(More) People engage in activities that improve their community.		*Nonprofit and community leaders see young people as assets in creating community and social change. *Communities experience an increase in civic engagement from diverse populations.		*Communities experience more just and equitable solutions to social problems.			
Gather facts	*Collect opinions*	*Track markers*	*Compile stories*	*Measure indicators*	*Encourage reflection*		

3	Organizational Episodic (O1)	3	Organizational Developmental (O2)	0	Organizational Transformative (O3)		
*Partner organizations receive capacity-building benefits from the Allies' service in the ten-month program.		*Partner organizations have a sustained or ongoing increase in capacity beyond the ten-month program. *Nonprofits create systems to develop diverse young leadership.		*Nonprofit organizations are inclusive, collaborative, asset based, continuously learn and improve their work, and have integrity.			
Gather facts	*Collect opinions*	*Track markers*	*Compile stories*	*Measure indicators*	*Encourage reflection*		

EXHIBIT 3.6. PUBLIC ALLIES'
PROGRAM RESULTS MAP WITH PRIORITIZATION, Cont'd.

3	Individual Episodic (I1)		3	Individual Developmental (I2)		3	Individual Transformative (I3)	
*Allies engage with their communities in ways they haven't before.			*Allies exhibit attitudes and behaviors that define Public Allies' leadership. *Alumni become leaders in influential roles with control of resources.			*Alumni become effective change makers in public life and are committed to creating community and social change. *Allies embrace values-based leadership and believe it can work toward creating a more just and equitable society.		
Gather facts	*Collect opinions*	*Track markers*	*Compile stories*			*Measure indicators*	*Encourage reflection*	

Source: Public Allies, Milwaukee, Wisc.

National Public Allies staff engaged in a conversation about implications for potential changes in departmental work as a result of a new focus on results and aimed to provide all internal staff with another way to think about mission achievement. Public Allies' Continuous Learning Team prepared the working group on national staff for a two-day retreat to incorporate Public Allies' current logic model into the EvaluLEAD framework.

Prioritization Process

Priorities for evaluative effort are represented by the numbers in the top left corners of each cell in Public Allies' program results map, with 3 indicating very high priority and 0 indicating extremely low priority. The priorities reflect a compromise between maintaining continuity with existing evaluation practices and incorporating new areas of inquiry. However, a number of considerations played into the final decisions about where to evaluate.

Not all of the performance measures that Public Allies is required to report under their AmeriCorps funding are reflected in the map. Rather than look at new approaches as extra work, the Public Allies team asked, How can we modify what we're already doing to provide information that is closer to the essence of who we are? Upon reflection, it chose to add some new measures.

At the societal level, there was not unanimous understanding as to what the results statements meant in concrete, operational terms. Some results were expected only in the very long term; for these, Public Allies decided not to prioritize measurement right away. It did decide to keep its options open to collect additional data, if and when methods became more readily available and the information easier to collect. (Capacity to implement evaluation strategies is always an issue, in terms of what is feasible to ask local sites to do without it being viewed as a burden.)

In the end, Public Allies decided to place the highest priority on individual-level results. The majority of its assessment instruments were participant centered, and local sites were already trained and experienced in their use. Thus, Public Allies had existing capacity on which it felt it could easily build.

Public Allies also had hundreds of nonprofit partner organizations being exposed to asset-based development and learning from young people. Where some tracking was already being done, it prioritized organizational-level episodic and developmental results. The organization made some adaptations in the instruments to track these results. These changes were easily incorporated because the ability to evaluate at this level was already quite high.

There were results and goals that were very important but not prioritized because they were seen as extremely long term, based on Public Allies' current program design, or were extremely difficult to track. Exhibit 3.7 provides an example of one of their completed investigation worksheets.

EXHIBIT 3.7. PUBLIC ALLIES' INVESTIGATION WORKSHEET EXAMPLE FOR ONE PRIORITIZED AREA.

Project: Public Allies' Core Apprenticeship Program SHEET #2						
Outcome/Objective: Partner organizations have a sustained or ongoing increase in capacity beyond the ten-month program.	**INDIV**	**ORG**	**SOC**	**EPISOD**	**DEVEL**	**TRANS**
		x			x	

**EXHIBIT 3.7. PUBLIC ALLIES' INVESTIGATION
WORKSHEET EXAMPLE FOR ONE PRIORITIZED AREA, Cont'd.**

EVIDENTIAL INQUIRY:
☐ **Gather Facts**   ☑ **Track Markers**   ☐ **Measure Indicators**

Evaluation Strategy: There are a variety of benefits that organizations receive from partnering with Public Allies—from developing new collaborative relationships to gaining new and diverse perspectives on the work they're doing. In addition, partnership with Public Allies should increase the partner organizations' abilities to carry out their missions or program goals. Annual surveying of partners will ask those who worked closest with Allies to quantify the increase their organization experienced as a result of their involvement with Public Allies.

Context Opportunities and Challenges: Again, with such a wide range of the types of organizations with which we partner it will be difficult to understand the true picture of increased capacity when looking solely at this data set. It is likely that a smaller, younger organization will experience increased capacity than a larger, more established one.

Evaluation Constraints: As this is a developmental outcome, we would like to be able to track markers at various stages—as they develop, and specifically. It would be good to identify what types of capacity have been increased—both on an annual partnership basis and for the organizations that we work with ongoing, for multiple years.

EVOCATIVE INQUIRY:
☐ **Collect Opinions**   ☑ **Capture Stories**   ☐ **Encourage Reflection**

Evaluation Strategy: Partner organization focus groups will give us insight as to how perspectives of staff may be enhanced or shifted as a result of working with their Allies, and will give us data on how their organizations are able to support young adults and their leadership development. Focus groups will be convened midyear and hosted by external facilitators.

Context Opportunities and Challenges: For organizations with which we partner episodically, through a one-year partnership, we should not expect organizational systems to develop diverse young leadership to be achieved. However, for those organizations that rely on Public Allies to carry out their missions, and for those with which we partner for multiple years, outcome achievement should take place in this context.

Evaluation Constraints: Supporting young adults and developing systems to do so involves many factors, including professional development, management practices, relationship building, organizational culture, and so on. We would like to be able to develop a way to track markers of these organizational development factors. Evocatively, we would like to be able to capture stories of how nonprofit professionals change the way they see young adults in the workplace and in mission fulfillment.

Source: Public Allies, Milwaukee, Wisc.

Successes, Challenges, and Lessons Learned

By using EvaluLEAD, Public Allies gained a new perspective on evaluating leadership development. It was able to clarify the domains of change in which it was already seeing achievement and identify those in which it would like to see future achievement. An open-systems perspective helped it craft the big picture of its program. It was a flexible approach more congruent with Public Allies' program and the program's essence than more prescriptive and structured approaches, such as those required by its federal government funder.

Its EvaluLEAD evaluation plan enabled Public Allies to improve its evidential approaches to data collection, and to an even greater extent it pushed Public Allies to think more creatively about the role of evocative inquiry in evaluation. Public Allies explored data collection systems for looking at both text analysis and narratives or stories in its evaluation plan. Although these data were collected, they were only used anecdotally and the quality of data varied. The evaluation team restructured how individual leadership portfolios and Presentations of Learning were organized and used. In addition, the team considered using comparison between multiple case studies to show transformational change in Allies and alumni over the course of time.

Over the past five years, Public Allies has become more intentional about using individual reflective practice focused on values as part of its program activities. EvaluLEAD affirmed that reflection is a powerful tool to use in eliciting the voice of people in the program and that it is a legitimate way of affirming and knowing about the experiences of participants.

Public Allies expended considerable effort improving instruments that focused on collection of evidential information to include both more robust evidential questions, especially the 360-degree process and baseline assessment. In the process, Public Allies' follow-up assessment became a retrospective 360-degree assessment that acted as both an intervention and evidential evaluation instrument.

Its ongoing hope is to implement more evocative approaches, especially in a long-term evaluation strategy. It plans to collect anecdotal cases that can be used for this purpose in the near term. The greatest challenge to collecting and analyzing these cases over time is a lack of staff time devoted to evaluation at both the national office and at the local level. Though some local sites might choose to employ evocative approaches on their own, the national office is not in a position to mandate their use. In this evaluative context, Public Allies decided to incorporate more evocative components to methods currently in use. In facilitated feedback sessions following the 360-degree assessment process, participants were invited to share face-to-face feedback with each other to provide evocative insights and facilitate individual and team learning.

Public Allies also used the EvaluLEAD framework to help plan activities and efforts for new program options for both Allies and program alumni. They used EvaluLEAD as an intermediary tool between the theory of change and program planning processes and as a starting point for designing new initiatives. Having EvaluLEAD at the forefront of its thinking at the beginning of new program development was exciting because it had the opportunity to look at how context shapes the development process and to think about the interconnectedness of individual, organizational, and societal domains as they articulated the types of changes Public Allies hoped to see as a result of new initiatives.

Communication within Public Allies about the framework and its implications for future evaluation was a part of the organization's iterative learning process. The CLO observed, "The open-systems approach helped us acknowledge the wide range of factors contributing to program participant leadership development. Allies are all placed at different nonprofits, come from diverse backgrounds, and work in a broad range of fields. Acknowledging and accepting all of these influences as factors contributing to the achievement (or not) of outcomes opened up our ability to see context, and to see the expectations we have for our program in a different light. This awareness was primarily held within our program department, but was shared amongst some members of senior management as well."

The development of Public Allies' theory of change in concert with EvaluLEAD concepts was an opportunity and an accomplishment for Public Allies. It believes that a key challenge in further developing its theory and consequent evaluation plan is the diversity of contexts that shape leadership development. While Public Allies believes that its way of developing young community leadership can carry over nationally, results of leadership development may differ depending on the context (for example, results in the state of Delaware may differ from results in the city of Los Angeles). These differences do not necessarily mean that the overarching social change model is not sound, but they do require an exploration of other factors that may be contributing to these different outcomes.

Implications: Cases Compared

These two cases illustrate how EvaluLEAD can be used to shape and assess individual programs as well as organization-wide systems. The cases have several similarities in how internal program evaluators used EvaluLEAD to catalyze organization-wide reflection on their program's purpose and desired outcomes. In the process, they found they needed to reconfigure existing statements of goals, objectives, and indicators without abandoning prenegotiated items upon which funding and performance were based. They also had to incorporate existing reporting templates with which they were expected to be compliant. Application of EvaluLEAD meant striking a balance between meeting preexisting requirements and making room for new, open-systems understandings of program design, purpose, and methodological approaches.

Public Allies and GOJoven each struggled with how to include the full scope of their intended outcomes in their program results maps. These cases illustrate notable differences in how they pursued defining their program and evaluation scopes and what decisions they made about allocating resources to their application. For example, in GOJoven's case, it found it useful to explore each program component in light of a series of key objectives they had determined in program planning phases. In the Public Allies case, it found itself concurrently involved in a process that included board and senior management-level representatives exploring the question, How can we modify what we're already doing to provide information that is closer to the essence of who we are? It identified changes it sought from its core apprenticeship program and from specific alumni programming, including long-term (10–20 years) community-level changes.

As with any evaluation, each program makes decisions about where to apply the bulk of its evaluative effort based on available resources and time. Each makes determinations about which domains and types of inquiry are priorities to pursue. GOJoven was initially overwhelmed by the prospect of examining all nine cells on its initial map. Since GoJoven was in its first year of programming, it limited its inquiry to the individual domains and opted to collect organizational- and societal-level outcomes some time in the future. At the same time, GOJoven staff, participants, and funders embraced evocative inquiry as a method that more holistically captured key results among its program's participants. Evocative inquiry approaches became a standard component of program assessment and ongoing learning as a result.

Public Allies chose to explore individual and organizational domains. Because it perceived capacity limits and time constraints to gathering evocative information, at least in the short term, Public Allies' national office decided not to develop or require other new evocative approaches to be used by local sites. However, Public Allies highly valued this type of inquiry and found ways to incorporate evocative approaches within existing instruments and established assessment processes such as additional questions on a 360-degree assessment.

Two observations arise from these cases. One is a concern that programs may not continue to keep a holistic picture of what transformation looks like if they do not indeed develop their evaluation approaches to organizational-level and societal-level results in the short term, if not from the outset. The true strength of operating from an open-systems orientation is visualizing and assessing transformation of societies and communities as both a starting point and an endpoint of leadership development. Program staff and funders should make every effort to utilize every cell of the results map, even if to simply imagine desired outcomes without placing heavy resources on assessment at that level. However, exploring a mix of evidential and evocative approaches may prove feasible, especially if innovations in using these approaches can be developed that are less costly. For example, gathering a sampling of stories from community members might prove quite viable for exploration of a societal-level outcome as opposed to population-based opinion polling. Second, we propose that solely integrating evocative inquiry into existing instruments may not permit for the spontaneous element so critical to the essence of evocative information. This challenges those espousing evocative approaches to continue to explore efficient and practical methodologies to support this type of inquiry on its own merits rather than as an add-on to evidential-based tools.

Based on these programs' positive experiences with organization-wide dialogue and reflection, we encourage stakeholders using EvaluLEAD to use processes that involve a broad set of implementers, recipients, and decision makers in shaping and assessing their leadership programs. As EvaluLEAD and other open-systems approaches are used and studied critically, we anticipate that more programs will feel comfortable developing program maps that include the full scope of domains with a confident appreciation of myriad interrelationships between them. Clearly, EvaluLEAD needs to be implemented with sensitivity to the context of the organization using it. In some cases, it may be advisable to employ only the concepts and components on which consensus can be reached, omitting those that represent too much of a stretch for the organization to embrace. Folding in new ways of thinking as organizational readiness develops is always preferable to forcing the use of a model that the organization is not ready for.

Challenges to the Use of an Open-Systems Perspective

Let us return briefly to the challenge we presented at the opening of this chapter. It is not possible or reasonable to hold leadership development programs entirely responsible for downstream results and yet it is these results that

funders and supporters want to see to justify their investments of time and resources. So what should the legitimate focus of program evaluations be? Stay
focused on what can be measured accurately and attributed to the program
reasonably? Or, consider all reasonable and compelling possibilities that become visible when considering the broader changes that programs seek? Explicitly, we opt for this latter option with EvaluLEAD. It is up to each program
to choose the approach that works best in its context.

Implied in EvaluLEAD is a readiness on the part of evaluators, program
staff, funders, and other stakeholders to move beyond causal logic to embrace
synchronicity, serendipity, and synergy. *Synchronicity* implies that things happen
only when—and precisely when—there is appropriate alignment of factors
and forces, some of which we still do not understand. *Serendipity* points to the
fortuitous results that occur when life trajectories intersect by chance or acci-
dent. *Synergy* is defined as the emergence of higher-order characteristics or
properties when two or more parties interact so as to give birth to them. The
legitimacy of the open-systems perspective for evaluation ultimately is linked
to the premise that synchronicity, serendipity, and synergy can be induced by
intention and skillfulness—they need not be chance occurrences. To do this
effectively, evaluators must pay attention to and learn from the dynamics of
synchronicity, serendipity, and synergy. As a parallel and complementary
process, new ways of engaging in deeper learning and uncovering meaning
about complex interconnected issues require practice and mastery. We must
be careful to marry theory to method as we move forward.

Open-systems applications are currently relatively rare. We suggest that
there are three primary reasons for this. First, those responsible for providing
the funds for leadership development programs or who are paying directly for
these services want insured results for their significant or modest investments.
The programs need to demonstrate that they can deliver on these results, and
evaluation resources, which typically are limited, are directed at proving those
results.

Second, the practice of generating systemic results (synchronicity,
serendipity, and synergy) is relatively young. And frankly, it is harder to wrap
one's mind around than the practice of generating causal results. While there
are a growing number of publications on this realm, there are still very few
best practices to draw upon. In fact, the very notion of best practices may run
counter to the systems paradigm in the sense that intuition and spontaneity
appear more critical to success than deduction and replication.

Third, for success, the practice demands shifts in behavior toward more concentrated and intimate modes of interaction and inquiry than are typically encouraged by conventional society. These shifts must occur not only in the leaders being trained, but they in turn must cultivate such nontraditional behaviors in key players within the organizations, communities, and sectors they aim to transform.

In light of these three formidable barriers, how good are the chances that an open-systems perspective will penetrate into evaluations of leadership development programs? Actually quite good, for two reasons. First, the body of science and practice that supports this perspective is growing rapidly and is very compelling for those who take the time to consider what is being put forth. Second, the causal perspective is not antithetical to the systems perspective. Rather it is a limited and constrained version of it. Virtually any evaluation model based on causal logic can be extended to embrace elements of the open-systems perspective at little cost and at an advantage to the original model.

The EvaluLEAD approach offers those developing evaluations the opportunity to venture into the systems realm to whatever extent feels right to them. That, in the final analysis, might be its greatest strength and contribution to the fields of leadership development and evaluation.

Resources

EvaluLEAD at www.evalulead.net provides access to the guide as well as contact information for the authors and other practitioners who can work with organizations to implement EvaluLEAD and related open-systems evaluation solutions.

Grove, J., Kibel, B., and Haas, T. *EvaluLEAD: A Guide for Shaping and Evaluating Leadership Development Programs.* W. K. Kellogg Foundation and Public Health Institute, 2005. This guide provides detailed information about and guidance for the EvaluLEAD process. The publication is available as a free PDF document at www.wkkf.org/Pubs/Tools/Evaluation/EvaluLEAD4_00447_03740.pdf.

Herda, E. *Research Conversations and Narrative: A Critical Hermeneutic Orientation in Participatory Inquiry.* Westport, Conn.: Praeger, 1999. In this book, Dr. Ellen Herda provides practical advice and examples on using research conversations as a technique for eliciting evocative information in applied research. The technique respects and engages the researcher as an active participant in creating meaning and interpreting for assessment.

Jacobs, J. *The Nature of Economies.* New York: Random House, 2000.

Senge, P., Jaworski, J., Scharmer C. O., and Flowers B. S. *Presence: Human Purpose and the Field of the Future.* Cambridge, Mass.: Society for Organizational Learning, 2004.

Wheatley, M. J., and Kellner-Rogers, M. *A Simpler Way.* San Francisco: Berrett-Koehler, 1996.

References

Grove, J., Kibel, B., and Haas, T. *EvaluLEAD: A Guide for Shaping and Evaluating Leadership Development Programs.* Chicago: W. K. Kellogg Foundation and Public Health Institute, 2005.

W. K. Kellogg Foundation and Development Guild/DDI. *Evaluating Outcomes and Impacts: A Scan of 55 Leadership Development Programs.* Battle Creek, Mich.: W. K. Kellogg Foundation, 2002.

CHAPTER FOUR

MAKING EVALUATION WORK FOR THE GREATER GOOD

Supporting Provocative Possibility and Responsive Praxis in Leadership Development

Hazel Symonette

An insistent chorus of hopeful voices from the future is vigorously calling our names! What is the leadership development world calling for from us, and in what ways can the tools of the evaluation profession rise up to the complex challenges of this rapidly emerging world of diverse leadership needs and interests? Authentically hearing the full spectrum of voices through their multifaceted channels of communication will help us more fully know and better understand the wide range of hopes, needs, and success vision expectations. They and we must *keep our eyes on the prize* in the midst of dynamic cross-cutting demands and often turbulent social relations.

What is the prize that various constituencies seek to keep their eyes on while vigorously exhorting us to do the same? It is the value reaped from engaging in responsive leadership development that facilitates each leader discovering and engaging his or her best self along with authentic ways to serve the greater good. More generally, it is embodied in the *success vision*—the envisioned changes in knowledge, skills, attitudes, orientations, relationships, and conditions of leaders, leadership, and other targets of a given intervention. Since evaluation is, at its core, about determining value, it is imperative that those involved in leadership development, and especially those involved in leadership development evaluation, understand the pivotal roles and implications of diverse lenses, filters, and frames for valid judgment making.

With an expansively refined set of polished lenses and filters, those involved in leadership development and its evaluation can cultivate others' capacities to do the same. Doing so increases the prospects of each of us empathically seeing, hearing, and feeling through multiple perspectives. This is especially crucial during times of fractured social contracts and eroded public trust. Leaders can help build capacities to craft authentic and productive border-crossing communications through which diverse stakeholders can hear and engage each other in full voice, increasing the prospects for speaking into their mutual listening. This is an especially critical role given increasingly diverse, globalized neighborhoods with many swiftly changing, cross-cutting needs and interests.

Mindfully exploring these considerations at the micro and macro levels spotlights evaluative thinking and being: what is deemed valuable, by whom, and via what sociocultural frameworks. Evaluation works best when it is directed toward the greater good of those whom our interventions exist to serve.

This chapter focuses on evaluation as a responsive development resource for excellence through processes that intentionally blur the lines among evaluator, program developer, and participant. By authentically including and engaging multiple voices and views in the evaluation process and by integrating evaluation into the natural rhythms of life and work, the evaluation itself becomes an ongoing and embedded component of effective program development, implementation, and improvement. The value of a participant's experience is enhanced while also being reflected more fully and accurately.

This form of evaluation serves as a self-diagnostic resource for critical and creative reflection on outcome promises, for empowered self-improvement, and for strategic image management. It offers program evaluators, designers, and facilitators strategies and tools to inform and improve as well as to prove. It is a resource for relevant knowledge creation, for continuous development toward excellence, and for accountability compliance verification.

Many program leaders, designers, champions, and others are facing strident accountability demands. Such pressures place many organizations on a course that is preoccupied with more and more precise measurements, often at the expense of meaningful understandings and thus viable pathways to excellence. Evaluation's intrinsic benefits, especially those of informing and improving, suffer under a myopic fixation on "prove it" demands.

Without diversity grounded vigilance, the process of specifying judgment criteria and determining value is often ethnocentric and one-sided. The resulting costs of embracing the potential gifts of evaluation are then too high. Those who are being evaluated often are on the receiving end of a barrage of disaffirming and disempowering evaluative messages—diagnostic pronouncements that magnify ways that they are judged as falling short and being "less than." Regardless of the evaluator's intent, which can range from seemingly benign, caring, and well intentioned to the opposite extreme, the sometimes unintended impact on participants is likely to be one of disengagement. As a result, the prospects for successful outcomes are suppressed.

The prospects for self-sustaining commitment and success are enhanced if evaluations work for and with, and not simply on, those who are closest to the intervention. More sustainable momentum toward excellence emerges when evaluation enters as a "sit down beside" critical friend rather than a "stand in judgment of" auditor.

Evaluative judgments are ubiquitous and often inescapably powerful. They are inextricably bound up with culture and context, so engaging diversity offers an essential resource. Excellence demands that leadership development programs and their evaluators "know the prize" from multiple vantage points: notably, the success vision, goals, outcomes, and desired benefits via a wide range of voices. (See Chapter Two for an approach for gathering and documenting from a variety of vantage points.) The ultimate prize resides in persons who receive an initiative's services or products vis-à-vis its intended outcomes: what the success vision pictures them experiencing, learning, being able to do, and so on. This is especially useful information when considering leadership development interventions or initiatives in which leadership development figures prominently.

In higher education, for example, in what ways and to what extent are curricular, cocurricular, pedagogical, and other intervention activities breathing life into the vision for all segments of the target population? How do we know what has been accomplished, and to what extent do evaluative judgments resonate with the realities of the persons evaluated?

Evaluators and their work often reflect non-neutral interventions, whether intended and desired or not. In such settings, people often tend to live up to or live down to expectations. Such self-fulfilling prophecies operate in many contexts. Given the frequency of such reactivity, why not intentionally make the evaluation process and the evaluator's presence work for and contribute to the greater good of those who are evaluated? To maximize excellence, then, leadership development programs and their evaluators need to proactively interrupt the operation of their own (and others') often ethnocentric default settings because they result in trust-eroding inaccuracies, truncated understandings, and twisted representations. Engaging the voices and views of anticipated participants during the design and the subsequent phases reduces the distance and potential distortions introduced by ethnocentric lenses, filters, and frames. Such collaborative approaches increase the prospects for sociocultural responsiveness and congruence, excellence, and ultimate success.

Evaluation may be further leveraged for the benefit of program developers and participants when they mindfully embrace evaluative thinking and being. By mainstreaming evaluation, assessment practices are embedded and integrated into the regular rhythms of work and life, rather than as episodic special events and products. By doing so, program developers and facilitators can more appropriately and effectively discern and respond to the full spectrum of voices and perspectives. By increasing evaluation practices at multiple levels, participants are encouraged to self-monitor with clarity and insight and to consciously align their values and goals with ordinary, ongoing work. Blending the program development and evaluator roles with multiple participant perspectives opens the door to provocative possibilities and responsive praxis.

Core Principles and Processes

In this chapter, I share some of my experiences and learnings with collaborative, integrated developmental evaluation as a resource for leader and leadership program development. Many of these insights are derived from and inspired by the Excellence Through Diversity Institute (EDI), a capacity-building leadership initiative at the University of Wisconsin-Madison (see Exhibit 4.1).

Harvesting Everyone's Wisdom: Participatory Approaches

Participatory, collaborative approaches are used to more fully engage participants in sustainable co-creation processes that model, seed, and support progressive change agendas. They provide a forum for enhancing insights into the particularity of one's own lenses, filters, and frames that can support fuller

EXHIBIT 4.1. THE EXCELLENCE THROUGH DIVERSITY INSTITUTE.

The University of Wisconsin-Madison Excellence Through Diversity Institute (EDI) is a nine-month campus workforce learning community for faculty, classified staff, academic staff, and administrators. It is one of five diversity-grounded professional development opportunities (the first initiated in 1998) designed to cultivate and support authentically inclusive and vibrantly responsive teaching, learning, and working environments that are conducive to success for all.

EDI operates as the campus capacity-building leadership development resource for facilitators with the other campus workforce learning communities as well as many other initiatives. It supports people who are committed to their own progressive leadership development journey, to supporting others in their journeys, and to organizational transformation. This intensive learning community cultivates leadership behavior across the campus community to help advance higher education's diversity and multicultural vision beyond a basic access agenda toward a much more challenging success-for-all and excellence agenda.

EDI helps each participant to discover and bring forward their best self by assisting them in making explicit their success visions and supporting them as they strive to embody and model the changes that we want to manifest in our students, in our colleagues, and in the world.

The EDI journey is ongoing, convoluted, and open ended. As EDI founder and director, program developer, fund-raiser, and developmental evaluator, I have challenged myself to stay responsive and adaptable—as have all others involved. We envision our efforts in terms of "making the path as it is walked" and "crafting the bridge as it is crossed." We have found collaborative, developmental evaluation approaches to be critical path-discovering, path-making, and path-navigating resources. Four core processes have informed and shaped the Excellence Through Diversity Institute experience: participatory approaches, multilateral self-awareness, appreciative inquiry, and the mainstreaming of evaluation.

---

and deeper understanding of the people and issues involved. Participatory approaches facilitate stakeholders' agency and commitment through opportunities to assert their voices and views while helping to build their capacity for genuine involvement in program development and evaluation processes. When such efforts are shared, they can more easily be owned and practiced by many. In this way, experience, knowledge, and wisdom can be passed on to others, creating the potential for multiplier effects beyond a small group.

Cultivating Multilateral Self-Awareness: Responsive Praxis

Listen as if you can't always tell

What the truth is.

Listen as if you might be wrong,

Especially when you know you're right.

Listen as if

You were willing to take the risk

of growing

Beyond your righteousness. (Williams, 1990)

Conscious self-calibration and mindful cultivation of self-awareness calls for a multilateral and responsive approach. This requires understanding of self in dynamically diverse contexts, including within power and privilege hierarchies. Unilateral self-awareness (one's view of self and what one believes one brings to a situation) is very important, yet insufficient. Even more important for building and sustaining viable, vital, productive transactions and relationships is multilateral self-awareness: who one is perceived to be by those with whom we seek to communicate and work.

Catalyzing Generative Momentum and Commitment: Appreciative Inquiry

Appreciative inquiry generates momentum by focusing program development and evaluation on the forces that connect with and fuel positive energy and action. Appreciative inquiry is a process by which individuals, groups, and organizations can explicitly identify the tensions of numerous competing forces, while spotlighting generative forces that drive movement in a positive direction. It involves discovering, tracking, and fanning the positive core of individuals, social relations, and social structures in order to fuel more of that which is desired and intended. Through appreciative inquiry, leaders can tap into and visualize the seeds, if not the full reality, of their success vision and build others' capacities to do the same.

Mainstreaming Evaluation: A Way of Thinking and Being

When evaluation operates primarily as a special event or simply provides a point-in-time assessment, its potential value is severely constrained. By internalizing and integrating evaluative thinking and doing into the natural rhythms of life and living, program lessons can be amplified. Mainstreaming evaluation helps refine and strengthens the program intervention itself and enhances its value and outcomes while engaging participants in their own tracking and measurement. This capacity-building process spotlights and clarifies the intimate interconnections among program visioning, development, implementation, and ongoing improvement. It creates a context through which these interconnected quality enhancement processes can be learned, applied, and moved out beyond the Excellence Institute.

Through mindful increases in these development practices, participants, evaluators, or both create more conscious and authentic alignment of their espoused values, beliefs, principles, and commitments. "Talking the talk" will more frequently and deliberately coexist with "walking the walk." As a result, participants, evaluators, or both can more dynamically self-monitor with clarity and insight and more consistently meet the demands of personal, professional, organizational, and institutional missions and visions. They walk their talk more frequently in alignment.

Creating Participatory Approaches

To better discern and take account of our own blind spots and biases, evaluators and program developers need to engage the many diverse voices of participants in their programs, projects, courses, or organizations. Through participatory approaches, we can harvest the wisdom of all and gain fuller and deeper understanding of the people and issues involved (see, for example, Exhibit 4.2). This richness of expression and understanding feeds into more meaningful evaluation while generating greater commitment to the work. Participatory approaches facilitate stakeholders' agency and commitment through opportunities to assert their voices and views while helping to build their capacity for genuine involvement in program development and evaluation processes. As John Shotter (n.d.) writes:

Far too often those we research into—who are outsiders to the disciplines within which our writing has currency—find what we have to say in our texts distant and inaccessible. This is because we do not often write from within any kind of involvement in their lives. Mostly, we write as external observers of their conduct. In so doing, we all too often claim that the analytic terms we use in attending to the features of their behavior we think important are the real influences shaping their lives. We feel able to ignore the actual influences which those others "over there" sense as important in their own shaping of their lives. But, in attempting to analyze and explain other people's lives rationally, in terms of *coherent and orderly systems of our devising, as academic professionals we have not only ignored their agency, but we have also ignored the fact that they live out almost every aspect of their lives dialogically.*

Jean King (2004) notes that all forms of participatory evaluation are characterized by "purposeful and explicit involvement of program participants in order to effect change" (p. 291). These approaches span the spectrum from narrowly soliciting input to full engagement in design, implementation, and interpretation; from the involvement of a small segment of stakeholders toward a comprehensively representative profile of stakeholders.

EXHIBIT 4.2. EDI AS A PARTICIPATORY INTERVENTION.

The Excellence Through Diversity Institute's (EDI) commitment to a participatory approach is explicitly reflected in its commitment to creating authentically inclusive environments—both within EDI itself and, most important, beyond EDI within the larger campus community.

Gaining full participation requires a commitment to embracing the many dimensions of diversity along with the associated turbulence and potential for conflict. EDI's work dwells in the unsettling tensions of the sometimes contentious convergence of diverse vantage points and views. Our work unavoidably occurs within contested terrain, so fully engaging the EDI journey summons all of us to lean into the inevitable turbulence when edges meet and sometimes collide. It requires a commitment to stay engaged even when one's impulse may be to run and disconnect. Doing so demands that we strive to know ourselves better while simultaneously decentering self in order to stay open and responsive to alternative views and pathways.

Key dimensions along which participatory evaluations may differ include

- The diversity of voices, views, and power positions represented
- The scope and depth of involvement across the evaluation design and implementation phases
- The extent to which various stakeholder groups control important decisions

The motivation for inclusion can range from symbolic desires to let stakeholders have their say (within a tightly proscribed format and structure) to an expansive frame that welcomes input and works to draw out the full array of stakeholder insights and contributions.

In complex work such as leadership development or learning, the evaluation process is compromised, is less rich, is incomplete, and is possibly inaccurate without full authentic involvement with key stakeholders. To work effectively, the experience should be perceived and received as open and inclusive, a space that welcomes multiple vantage points so that all voices can be fully heard. The focus ought to be centered on stakeholders, not evaluators. To the extent that evaluators intrinsically value stakeholders' voices and views, they are more likely to be closely attentive to the nature of the invitation to participate and, thus, tailor it for sociocultural congruency and relevance.

Basic democratic principles and methodological quality imperatives support the logic of participatory approaches. Jennifer Greene (2005) offers some very useful insights:

> The democratic approaches to evaluation are less about particular methods or strategies or tools—the usual technical aspects of evaluation—and more about the evaluator roles, stances, and value commitments. I've grouped these other aspects of evaluation into two clusters: one on the positioning of evaluation in society (for example, issues about whose interests are addressed, what's the purpose of the evaluation) and the other about the character of the evaluation practice—meaning the kinds of relationships that are established in the field between the evaluator and stakeholders and the kinds of interactions and communications the evaluator strives to have among stakeholders.

Actualizing a vision of full participation demands continuous learning and development of participants, facilitators, stakeholders, and evaluators. It requires the understanding that the program and the participants are all emergent projects in process. Underlying every interaction are several questions.

- When people come together, how do they engage in ways that allows each to bring forward their best selves to do their best learning, best engaging, and best work?
- How do we fairly navigate and negotiate where one person's needs and prerequisites for authentic inclusion end and another person's begin?
- What is the nature of the interface? Is it intersecting and interdependent with varied patterns of overlap or is it a mutually exclusive, non-overlapping pattern?

To work in the space of multiple voices, evaluators have a responsibility to specify parameters of involvement, build trust, engage all stakeholders, and work to minimize problematic sources of reactivity.

Specify Parameters of Involvement

Evaluators need to respectfully and proactively specify what aspects of the evaluation process are open to input and to what extent aspects are fixed and non-negotiable. Failing to proactively and explicitly articulate these boundaries implies that the terrain is wide open when in fact it may not be. Such assumptions can be a source of great anguish, angst, and anger. Being honest and straightforward about parameters reduces the risks of stakeholders feeling that their time and energy have been wasted or, worse, that they have been betrayed. Even though such parameters may be resisted or rejected, this approach is more likely to generate genuine and useful input.

To nourish participatory processes, evaluators and program developers need to provide feedback on the specific ways in which voices and views are used and ways they are not. Closing the loop with honesty speaks loudly in the voice of respect and appreciation, or signals otherwise. Furthermore, integrity in addressing participation paves the way—or sets up barriers—for the embrace of evaluation findings and future collaborations.

Build Trust. Evaluators need to build trust as a foundation for quality because their roles and responsibilities often engender fear and mistrust, especially when working across diversity divides. Lack of trust erodes access to data and undermines utility. Evaluators need to mindfully examine in what ways and the extent to which their communications and evaluation processes, practices, and products enhance versus erode trust. Triangulated, multiway dialogues with key stakeholders, especially with those who are being evaluated, are essential for addressing these concerns.

Dennis and Michelle Reina (1999) provide a comprehensive and highly nuanced framework for trust-building work. They detail three major types of trust: intrapersonal trust, interpersonal trust, and transformative trust. The components of interpersonal trust (also called *transactional trust*) are especially relevant:

- *Contractual trust:* Trust of character
- *Competency trust:* Trust of capability
- *Communication trust:* Trust of disclosure

Involve Stakeholders. Responsive evaluation summons all stakeholder groups to step forward in full voice to communicate their truths authentically. They should provide ongoing feedback and "feedforward" through periodic surveys and emergent oral check-ins to help modify intervention activities, increase alignment, and foster desired outcomes.

For example, the National Science Foundation-funded Howard University Evaluation Training Institute, with its focus on contextually and culturally responsive evaluation, spotlights "Engage Stakeholders" as a top priority. This task is repeated at five places in their conceptual model. More specifically, stakeholder engagement is the key connecting link within their five-step evaluation process (2005).

Minimize Reactivity. A significant aspect of generating participation and engaging the voices of many involves personal self-assessment and reflection on the part of leadership program developers and their evaluators.

Evaluations typically occur in social contexts, so reactivity abounds whether recognized, intended, or not. It abides and resides in the nature of the social relations constructed as well as emergent among the parties involved. Reactivity concerns typically focus on artificial effects related to research or evaluation instruments and strategies, but they also have direct relevance for the person who administers the instruments and designs the strategies. This multilateral process is shaped in varying degrees by all parties involved within and across diversity divides. That some voices and views are neither heard nor heeded does not mean they are not present and operative. (See, for example, Stern and Kalof, 1996.)

Even though reactivity is not solely controlled by the determinations of the evaluator or the researcher, one should actively work to minimize its problematic impacts. The following processes help in mindfully attending to such potential quality eroding impacts.

Map the Social Topography. Proactively survey the shifting sociopolitical and sociocultural terrain. This includes identifying and articulating (from multiple stakeholder perspectives) relevant and salient differences that make a difference in access, process, and success.

Use Multilevel Dynamic Scanning. Continuously assess and refine your sociocultural antennae for monitoring, reading, and engaging in social relations, which are embedded in the ever-present context of, for example, power and privilege hierarchies, while remaining aware of your own location in the social topography. Cultivate flexible micro and macro visioning—the ability to responsively zoom in for intrapersonal or interpersonal details and zoom out for the big-picture social structural context.

Cultivate Empathic Perspective-Taking. Acknowledge and regularly polish the lenses and filters that frame your perceptions, reflections, and interpretations. Discover what they illuminate and even more important what they ignore, obscure, or distort. Stay open and responsive to discovery of social processes and rhythms—those dissonant as well as those congruent with your own. Vigilantly monitor the culturally and contextually conditioned operational definitions regarding what is substance and worthy of engaging versus what is deemed noise and extraneous variation.

Responsive Praxis

Ultimately, the nature of social relations determines the quality and trustworthiness of the data collected, the soundness of the meaning making and possible interpretations, and the prospects for evaluation processes that facilitate excellence. Evaluation, like education and other social relations-rich professions, needs to mindfully attend not only to the disciplinary content of the field but also to modes of communication and relational processes. Such considerations are especially critical in seeking to appropriately engage key stakeholders.

Conscious self-calibration and mindful cultivation of self-awareness requires a multilateral and responsive approach. This requires understanding self in dynamically diverse contexts, including within power and privilege hierarchies. As mentioned earlier, unilateral self-awareness is very important yet insufficient. It involves exploration of, Who is the *I* that I know and believe myself to be? Knowing self is foundational to knowing one's own boundaries and, thus, the social borderlands vis-à-vis others. This provides the context for discovering and applying appropriate codes of engagement for respectful border crossings.

Even more important for building and sustaining viable, vital, productive transactions and relationships is *multilateral self-awareness*: Who is the *I* that others perceive and believe they know me to be? To what extent and in what ways do these images of *I* converge or diverge? What are some reasons for the likely disparities?

Relational processes are greatly influenced by our sociocultural lenses, filters, and frames. They configure and define our focus, inform our understanding of context, and selectively magnify some patterns vis-à-vis others. Consequently, they inform and shape the capacity-building processes that we design and implement as well as our assessment processes and evaluative judgment making.

We cannot grow ourselves beyond our default ethnocentric settings without mindful awareness and knowledge of what they are. Where one sits within a given social context influences where one stands on a variety of issues and how one shows up in ways of being, doing, thinking, engaging. We need to be fully conscious of the particularity of our lenses, filters, and frames—what they allow us to perceive clearly in a given context versus not. Furthermore, what we see and sense depends upon what we look at and look for. Failure to attend to these considerations often results in us doing violence to others' truths, whether intended or not.

We mindfully cultivate *multilateral self-awareness* through knowing and using self as responsive instrument. To do so requires knowledge and understanding of self from one's own vantage point as well as from the perceptual vantage points of others. This involves understanding self in dynamically diverse contexts within power and privilege hierarchies (specific point in time) and also understanding the contexts embodied in the self (across time—social identity and role socialization and status distribution and allocation processes).

Addressing the questions of identity as viewed by self and others requires empathic perspective taking and the ongoing development of the self as an expansively open and learning-grounded, responsive instrument.

Cultivating Empathy

Empathy is a foundational prerequisite for authentic communications and engagement. Empathic perspective taking involves one's capacity to stand in one's own perspective while consciously shifting and responsively standing in others' perspectives. Cultivating this competency lays the foundation for addressing some of the issues related to multilateral self-awareness.

Developing such competencies would place one at ethnorelative Stage 5 of Milton Bennett's (1986) Developmental Model of Intercultural Sensitivity: Adaptation to intercultural difference. In contrast, many well-intentioned evaluators and educators operate at ethnocentric Stage 3 (Minimization of intercultural difference). Unlike Stages 1 and 2 (Denial of intercultural difference and Defense against intercultural difference), this highest ethnocentric stage does recognize differences but judges them to be trivial and ephemeral vis-à-vis similarities and commonalities. Clearly, awareness of differences is necessary but woefully insufficient for excellence in communication and even much less so for assessment and evaluation excellence. These insights are especially critical in the leadership development arena.

Based upon extensive research that differentiates *sympathy* and *empathy*, Bennett (1998) outlines a comprehensive model and six-step process for developing empathy, "the imaginative intellectual and emotional participation in another person's experience," as compared to sympathy, "the imaginative placing of ourselves in another person's position" (p. 207). As a first step, contrasting to sympathy, empathy starts with the presumption of difference and multiple realities as opposed to presumed similarity and single reality. Step 2 involves a capacity-cultivating process that works from the inside out (Knowing oneself):

> The preparation that is called for is to know ourselves sufficiently well
> so that an easy reestablishment of individual identity is possible. If we
> are aware of our own cultural and individual values, assumptions, and

beliefs—that is, how we define our identities—then we need not fear losing those selves. We cannot lose something that can be re-created at will. The prerequisite of self-knowledge does not eliminate the possibility of change in ourselves as a result of empathizing. It merely makes such change a chosen option rather than an uncontrollable loss [p. 210].

Suspending self, Bennett's third step, calls for a temporary expansion of the boundary between self-identity and other people: "Suspension of the self-boundary is facilitated by knowing where the boundary is (self-knowledge), but only if one first has a self-reference assumption of multiple-reality which presumes difference" (1986, p. 210). Allowing guided imagination represents the fourth step:

In the extended state, we can move our attention *into* the experience of normally external events rather than turning our attention *onto* those events, as we usually do. This shifting of awareness into phenomena not normally associated with self can be called "imagination" [p. 211].

For accurate interpersonal empathy to occur, Bennett argues that in a fifth step (Allowing empathic experience), we must allow our imaginations to be guided into the experience of a specific other person: "If we are successful in allowing our imagination to be captured by the other person, we are in a position to imaginatively participate in that person's experience" (1986, p. 211). The last critical task and sixth step is Reestablishing self, reconstituting our boundaries by "remembering the way back to ourselves" (p. 212).

Developing Self as Responsive Instrument

Through mindfully attending to our ways of being and doing in the world, we discover that there are variations in the extent to which we are perceived as radiating and communicating respect, trustworthiness, caring, and soundness in our uses of self as knower, inquirer, and engager of others, notably, in "interpersonal validity" (Kirkhart, 1995).

In using the self as a pivotal instrument, we engage deliberately in *cognitive frame shifting* (border crossing in one's head) and in *affective frame shifting* (border crossing in one's feelings). Both actions require knowing and anchoring in one's own core values, beliefs, and expectations while knowingly extending one's borders, that is, the boundaries of the self. With expanded intercultural and other cross-boundary awareness and understandings, one can demonstrate appropriate and effective *behavioral code switching*: doing the right things right from multiple vantage points.

A critically reflective self-assessment inventory needs to be conducted in each context to ascertain the utility and value of the social identities, roles, and other attributes one brings to that context. What relevant attributes do you and others perceive that you bring into a given context? What attributes do you have to work with (assets and resources) and what attributes do you have to work on (blind spots, blank spots, triggers, issues)? What attributes can you (and are you perceived as being able to) call upon to facilitate and support the success vision? Most often, such self-assessments are automatic, swift, and informal, but the quality would be enhanced by a more mindfully conscious, contextually grounded, and responsive review process.

It is especially important to know the overall configuration of one's privileged identities and roles because they tend to automatically confer presumptions of competence, presumptions of worthiness, and presumptions of innocence (Cullinan, 1999). While such privileged identities often are a source of insensitivities, they also are a potential source of personal power that can be strategically exercised to support ethnorelative inclusion, equity, and more socially just evaluations.

We need to know our likely blind spots, deaf spots, numb spots: looking but not seeing, listening but not hearing, touching but not feeling. These represent places where our data-gathering and meaning-making capacities may be compromised. As evaluators and as responsive leaders, the following questions should always be highlighted on our radar screens:

- Given who I am—and am perceived as being—and, thus, where I stand and sit within a given context, what do my lenses, filters, and frames illuminate and allow me to accurately perceive versus what might they ignore, obscure, and distort?
- Which dimensions of diversity am I not discerning and attending to, whether by conscious choice or oversight?
- Who and what has been silenced, erased, distorted?
- How do I know what I think I know about this? To what extent does the full spectrum of stakeholders agree?

To maximize accuracy, validity, and excellence, evaluators must mindfully monitor and address the sources of reactivity in order to enhance illumination, insight, and understanding of the persons whom they seek to evaluate. We can address our limitations only with deep self-awareness, commitment, and initiative. Through ongoing efforts, we can cultivate our capacities to move from within our own sociocultural and sociopolitical boundaries into the shared space of social borderlands and perhaps even across the borders into others' spaces as an *inside-outsider.*

The dynamic insights and potential wisdom embodied in the Johari Window communications model provides an in-the-moment evaluative resource for pulling many disparate pieces together. This long-established communications model offers a useful developmental framework for cultivating multi-lateral self-awareness. It uses a four-paned window metaphor to facilitate processes for proactively giving and soliciting feedback to reduce the "hidden" and "blind" domains (Luft, 1982, p. 34). Disclosing personal intent and simultaneously seeking insights into the frequent blind spots of interpersonal impact helps interrupt nonproductive default responses. Left unchecked, defensive responses erode prospects for continuous learning, for personal responsibility, and for commitment to change. This model can be flexibly used to facilitate more authentic border-crossing communications that more effectively discern, navigate, and negotiate salient "diversity divides" (see, for example, Exhibit 4.3).

Appreciative Inquiry

Knowing what matters is a critical challenge for evaluators as well as for leadership program developers, facilitators, and participants. The many forces around us (people, issues, demands, and information) compete for our attention and energy. How do we judge each force as positive (energizing and enabling), negative (erosive and undermining), or neutral (irrelevant)? And which do we deem worthy of focus, exploration, and effort? Appreciative inquiry is one way to navigate and address such complex challenges and, in the process, mobilize momentum *for* positive action. It is a process by which individuals, groups, and organizations can explicitly spotlight positive generative forces and energize movement in a positive direction.

EXHIBIT 4.3. A CULTURAL COMPETENCE JOURNEY.

EDI cultivates participants' capacity to identify their lenses, filters, and frames through a Self-as-Instrument Portfolio that identifies the constellation of salient social roles, identities, and preferred ways of being, doing, knowing, and engaging. This portfolio is a resource for configuring and calibrating oneself as an instrument for appropriate and effective communications and actions in a given context.

Excellence in cultivating cultural competence demands that we embrace a twofold agenda.

1. *Inside/Out.* Understanding self in dynamically diverse contexts within power and privilege hierarchies (at a single point in time) and understanding the contexts embodied in the self across time through socialization and status allocation and distribution processes.

2. *Outside/In.* Expanding and enriching one's diversity-relevant knowledge and skills repertoire.

A critical segment of needed capacity-building work involves micro-focused assessment and evaluation processes that support the Inside/Out work. Such work calls for a mindfully conscious self that enables accurate discerning, navigating, negotiating, and understanding the shifting sociocultural terrain using appropriate codes of engagement. Over time, one develops a repertoire of cues and clues that signal when standing at or in the fault lines of diversity divides.

Appreciative inquiry is both a methodology and a mind-set. An appreciative mind-set, one that emphasizes positive possibilities, sets the stage for strategically organizing around assets and resources in ways that can neutralize or make irrelevant existing weaknesses, limitations, and barriers. Appreciative approaches help participants to tap into and visualize the seeds, if not the full reality, of their visions of success and to build others' capacities to do the same.

For evaluators, program developers, and participants, appreciative inquiry techniques involve strategic questioning and tracking practices. The more certain questions are asked, the more the organization, group, person is inclined to move in the direction of that inquiry. Grounded in and fueled by positive communications and relationships, it fosters the discovery and dissemination of best practices (Mohr, 2001).

Focusing on exceptional performance creates continuous opportunities to look back on those moments of excellence and use them to guide the organization toward a more positive future:

> The essence of appreciative inquiry in the context of evaluation is that it gives the organization as a whole a process by which the best practice of the organization can become embedded as the norm against which general practice is tested. . . . The embedded evaluation to which appreciative inquiry gives access is much less threatening and judgmental than many variants of traditional evaluation for it invites the staff—and indeed, in theory, all the stakeholders—to reflect on their best practice rather than to admit their failures and unsolved problems [Preskill and Coghlan, 2003, p. 18].

Appreciative inquiry declares that every voice matters, every voice deserves to be heard, and that every voice has something to lift up and contribute for the greater good (Royal, 2006). Thus, appreciative inquiry is foundationally participatory and grounded in embracing diversity, insistently inclusive, and expansively generative (see, for example, Exhibit 4.4).

Diligent application of conventional planning and evaluation strategies and instrumentation often squeeze the life out of innovation. Innovative and transformative interventions especially need expansively responsive evaluation strategies, processes, and instrumentation that fully engage and further fuel a stretch-inducing success vision. (See, for example, Kibel, 2003.)

EXHIBIT 4.4. ENACTING VIBRANTLY RESPONSIVE ENVIRONMENTS.

In all the University of Wisconsin-Madison campus workforce learning communities, appreciative inquiry approaches help us get in touch with the positive core and our personal power so that we more viscerally believe in progressive provocative possibilities. We strive to increase our capacities to discern, engage, and more effectively coalesce our collective power to actualize our campus success vision.

In EDI, we strive to mindfully anticipate, acknowledge, and move through the inevitable turbulence, uncertainties, anxieties, and conflict of border-crossing, bridge-building work. We cultivate an appreciative mind-set and skill set that help us acknowledge challenges, resistance, and structural constraints, yet we focus on generative visions of our best practices.

Mainstreaming Evaluation

Mainstreaming evaluation spotlights systematic inquiry and judgment in the service of an envisioned intervention—a deliberate resource for articulating and actualizing its success vision. Patton's (2004) concept of developmental evaluation most closely reflects this approach: "[It] helps make the program's development an R&D activity." This form of evaluation guides the design, implementation, and refinement of an intervention by "infusing evaluative questions, data, and logic" that supports empirical evidence-based decision making (p. 116).

Internalizing and integrating evaluation processes has the potential to continuously amplify program lessons. In contrast to evaluation as a special event or point-in-time assessment, mainstreaming evaluation regularly strengthens the quality of the intervention itself as well as its likely outcomes. It also engages participants in their own tracking and measurement and provides an engaging forum for learning about and applying those processes.

In a society, community, or organization that espouses and claims to be guided by democratic and humanistic values, diversity-grounded developmental evaluation is an essential leader and leadership competency. It is also an important resource for leader and leadership development. Developmental evaluation helps programs, processes, systems, groups, and individuals discover and declare their "best selves," to specify visions of provocative possibility for all that they can be and become. They can then envision and construct appropriate and effective scaffolding across the divide between the now and the yet to become.

A participant-centered, developmental evaluation model has been helpful in framing our efforts to mainstream evaluation and guide program development and refinements (see Figure 4.1). It is used as a resource for understanding and developing the EDI program and for driving its success vision. The model provides a framework through which EDI participants embody evaluative thinking and praxis in conceiving, developing, and refining their own projects and initiatives.

The center of this model and the focus of all efforts is the *who*. Who is being engaged and served by the program, course, initiative, organization, and so on? Who is engaging and providing the services? Who is judging the quality and efficacy of those efforts? It is important to consider *who* not simply as

FIGURE 4.1. A MODEL OF EVALUATIVE THINKING AND PRAXIS.

functional roles or personality characteristics but also in terms of salient dimensions of human difference that make a socially patterned difference for access, process, and success. Diversity groundedness helps one to understand and effectively work within a given context.

To maintain perspective, one needs to start with and stay grounded in the *who,* followed by the *what,* and then the remaining three W's and two H's: *why, where, when, how, how much?* The resulting understandings dictate the nature of the transformations, modifications, and adaptations that are summoned for whatever may have been initially perceived and received as appropriate and effective—notably, the default and often ethnocentric configurations. Such transformations need to simultaneously occur at multiple levels: self-to-self, self-to-others, and self-to-systems. Doing this work demands a conscious and conscientious array of knowledge, skills, attitudes, and orientations (habits of mind and practice) geared up for actualizing equity, excellence, and social justice.

Once one is grounded in the *who,* the *what* can be explored. This involves processes for getting clear on the current reality: What now? It also points to future states: What becoming? It includes assessing individual and personal assets and needs, as well as project strengths and limitations.

To get to the What now?, think about the ways in which you are now walking your path in the world, what is or appears to be the vision guiding and fueling your footsteps. How are you currently living the vision? The foundational groundwork begins with a baseline needs assessment, both at the individual and the project level. What do you know and understand about yourself within the context of sociocultural, power, privilege, and other social structures? What is the project calling for from you? Specifically, what are the requirements of the work compared with what you bring? Similarly, evaluate the project baseline needs. What is the current status of your project? What does it have to work with versus work on? Consider your answers from your vantage point and from various stakeholders' vantage points. Given multiple stakeholder perspectives, which of your attributes are perceived as relevant and can be engaged to catalyze and support the project's development?

To answer What becoming?, determine the success vision that you commit to for yourself by way of your project. Describe the transformation agenda that can become a bridge or scaffold between the current state and the future possibilities. Toward what ends are you aiming? What is the prize that you need to keep your eyes on? Consider the future state from three lenses: self-to-self, self-to-others, and self-to-systems.

- *Self-to-self vantage point.* What is your current self vis-à-vis your self-becoming? Assess and transform your own ways of being, doing, thinking, and knowing.
- *Self-to-others vantage point.* How are you working on relations with others? Seek ways to enhance patterns and levels of discernment, understanding, and engagement within and across salient diversity divides.
- *Self-to-systems vantage point.* In what ways do you address relations with systemic forces and factors (that is, social structures, norms, assumptions, expectations, philosophies, rules, roles, policies, protocols, procedures, and other regularized processes that specify, create, and sustain the terrain and the container within which you relate to and engage others)?

The By what? question is answered by the implementation strategies and means by which you breathe life into the vision of success and mobilize and manage your project development journey. This also involves the rollout of your vision of self as a responsive instrument for effective project implementation and success. Assess the ways in which and the extent to which envisioned processes and activities are actually implemented and experienced by whom, when, and where.

The answer to So what? can be found by determining the ways in which and the extent to which you are engaging and working in alignment with your project's success vision. In what ways and to what extent are your intervention activities yielding the results intended given your success vision? For whom is it making a difference, what changes are occurring for whom, when, where, and under what conditions? What else is emerging, whether intended or not? And, finally, who cares? For whom do these developments matter?

When you consider *Now what?*, monitor and review for excellence in order to maximize clarity, responsiveness, and alignment within the context of emerging needs, interests, and desires. In what ways can you use what you are learning to improve your practice, actualize the success vision, or make modifications as needed?

By using this developmental model to mainstream evaluative processes that are always focused on the *who,* I have seen a twofold benefit. First, the model has been a critical touchstone for ongoing development, monitoring, and improvement. In being responsive to internal as well as external evaluative feedback, EDI has been a substantially different intervention every year since its founding in 2002 (see, for example, Exhibit 4.5). Second, participants are using the model to develop and refine their EDI projects and campus work beyond the institute.

EXHIBIT 4.5. MAINSTREAMING EVALUATION AT EDI.

Mainstreaming evaluation is a conscious capacity-building component of EDI that works, first and foremost, for participants in the service of their work and purpose. EDI participants choose a project that they already have passion for and are committed to doing (and ideally may already be doing). This is either a self-to-others or a self-to-systems project because the self-to-self projects are automatically on the agenda for everyone.

We use assessment and evaluation as iterative program development resources through major midcourse changes in order to be responsive to changing internal cohort needs and interests as well as to shifting external context needs and expectations. Through this concrete project application focus, EDI more effectively serves as a collaborative, hands-on forum. The high personal intrinsic value of its projects also increases the attendance pull-power for some of the busiest and most in-demand members of our campus community.

Conclusion

Much of the EDI path has been uncharted, convoluted and frequently shifting through in-the-moment redesign and restructuring while participants have been engaged in it. As a crossroads intervention (notably, diversity and multicultural development and responsive assessment and evaluation), we have had a vision of provocative possibility but seldom a clear and definitive strategy. Developmental evaluation has been a core prospecting tool and trail-blazing resource: path-discovery, path-making, path-navigating, and path-negotiating. Such developmental resources help us constantly check the alignment of our aspirational rhetoric with our day-to-day footsteps on the ground, both from our own vantage points and the vantage points of others. Engaging in these iterative critically and creatively reflective processes is helping us breathe life into the EDI vision. It also models and cultivates a process that helps build participants' capacity to use developmental evaluation to breathe life into their own EDI projects.

Evaluation as a developmental resource is serving EDI, its participants, and others in the larger university community well. The four core processes (harvesting many voices, cultivating multilateral self-awareness, appreciative inquiry, and mainstreaming evaluation) are intrinsic elements of the initiative's success vision. Ongoing evaluation that informs and improves innovation has been the priority focus rather than the more conventional summative episodic approaches. This stance moves beyond the *do no harm* imperative toward honoring what I embrace as a core moral imperative: *leave better off!*

"People confronted with demands to cover [blend into the mainstream] should feel emboldened to seek a reason for that demand. Such [reason-forcing] conversations are the best—and perhaps the only—way to give both assimilation and authenticity their due. They will help us alleviate conservative alarmists' fears of a balkanized America and radical multiculturalists' fears of a monocultural America. The aspiration of civil rights has always been to permit people to pursue their human flourishing without limitations based on bias" (Yoshino, 2006, p. 37).

Resources

AI Practitioner, February 2005. For more information on applications of appreciative inquiry in evaluation, see this issue. Through five case studies, the editors demonstrate its value and compile a list of six synergistic benefits. These insights have great relevance for the configuration and operation of leader and leadership development initiatives as well as their evaluation.

Howard University Evaluation Training Institute. This program offers professional development to expand the number and capacity of mathematics and science project evaluators who can plan and implement evaluations that are technically sound, culturally and contextually relevant, and have increased utility. For more information, point your browser to www.howard.edu/school education/eti.

Johnson, A. *Privilege, Power, and Difference.* Mountain View, Calif.: Mayfield, 2001.

Reina, D., and Reina, M. *Building Trust in the Workplace.* Access at www.trustin workplace.com for information on the various forms of trust that can have major impacts on the accuracy, depth, and quality of data.

Style, E. "Curriculum as Window and Mirror." *Social Science Record,* Fall 1996, 35–42.

Thomas, V. "Building a Contextually Responsive Evaluation Framework." In V. G. Thomas and F. I. Stevens (eds.), *Co-constructing a Contextually Responsive Evaluation Framework: The Talent Development Model of School Reform.* New Directions in Evaluation, no. 101. San Francisco: Jossey-Bass, 2004.

References

Bennett, M. "Towards Ethnorelativism: A Developmental Model of Intercultural Sensitivity." In M. Paige (ed.), *Cross-Cultural Orientation.* Lanham, Md.: University Press of America, 1986.

Bennett, M. "Overcoming the Golden Rule: Sympathy and Empathy." In M. J. Bennett (ed.), *Basic Concepts of Intercultural Communication: Selected Readings.* Yarmouth, Maine: Intercultural Press, 1998.

Cullinan, C. C. "Vision, Privilege, and the Limits of Tolerance." *Electronic Magazine of Multicultural Education* 1:2, 1999. [www.eastern.edu/publications/emme].

Greene, J. "A Conversation with Jennifer Greene." *The Evaluation Exchange XI*(3). Published by Harvard Family Research Project, 2005. [www.gse.harvard.edu/hfrp/eval/issue31/index.html].

Howard University Evaluation Training Institute, 2005. [www.howard.edu/school education/eti].

Kibel, B. *Evaluating Activities That Ennoble*, 2003. [www.pire.org/resultsmapping/documents/EvalEnnobling.doc].

King, J. "Participatory Evaluation." In S. Mathison (ed.), *Encyclopedia of Evaluation*. Thousand Oaks, Calif.: Sage, 2004.

Kirkhart, K. "Seeking Multicultural Validity: A Postcard from the Road." *Evaluation Practice*, 1995, *16*(1), 1–12.

Luft, J. "The Johari Window: A Graphic Model of Awareness in Interpersonal Relations." In L. Porter and B. Mohr (eds.), *Reading Book for Human Relations Training* (7th ed.). Arlington, Va.: NTL Institute, 1982.

Mohr, B. "Appreciative Inquiry: Igniting Transformative Action." *The Systems Thinker*, 2001, *12*(1), 1–4.

Patton, M. "Developmental Evaluation." In S. Mathison (ed.), *Encyclopedia of Evaluation*. Thousand Oaks, Calif.: Sage, 2004.

Preskill, H., and Coghlan, A. T. (eds.). *Using Appreciative Inquiry in Evaluation*. New Directions in Evaluation, no. 100. San Francisco: Jossey-Bass, 2003.

Reina, D., and Reina, M. *Trust and Betrayal in the Workplace*. San Francisco: Berrett-Koehler, 1999.

Royal, C. "Organizational Development, Appreciative Inquiry and Diversity." In B. B. Jones and M. Brazzeal (eds.), *Organizational Development Handbook*. San Francisco: Pfeiffer, 2006.

Shotter, J. "Writing from Within 'Living Moments': 'Withness-Writing' Rather Than 'Aboutness Writing.'" Unpublished paper, n.d.

Stern, P., and Kalof, L. *Evaluating Social Science Evidence*. Oxford: Oxford University Press, 1996.

Williams, P. *A Nation of Lawyers*. Encinitas, Calif.: Entwhistle Books, 1990.

Yoshino, K. "The Pressure to Cover." *New York Times Magazine*, January 15, 2006, pp. 32–37.

CHAPTER FIVE

MEASURING RETURN ON INVESTMENT IN LEADERSHIP DEVELOPMENT

Jack J. Phillips and Patti Phillips

With increased expenditures in leadership development, many executives are questioning its value. Although leadership development endeavors are planned and executed with good intentions, not all engagements produce the value desired by either the individual being developed or the organizations paying for them. Measuring return on investment (ROI) for leadership development programs shows the value in terms that managers and executives desire and understand. This chapter describes how one process—the ROI methodology—collects six types of data (reaction, learning, application, business impact, ROI, and intangibles) and provides techniques to convert data to monetary value and to isolate the effects of the program from other influences.

Measuring ROI: Current Issues and Trends

Measuring ROI in leadership development has earned a place among the critical issues in the field of evaluation. For nearly a decade, ROI has been on conference agendas and at professional meetings. Journals and newsletters regularly embrace the concept. A 600-member professional organization has been developed to exchange information on ROI, and at least a dozen books provide significant coverage of the topic (a list of these can be found in the Resources section at the end of this chapter).

The Debate

Measuring ROI is a topic of much debate. Return on investment is characterized as flawed and inappropriate by some leadership development sponsors, while others describe it as the only answer to their accountability concerns. The same debate sometimes exists between providers and purchasers. For example, recently in Europe, a large respected organization initiated a multiyear, multimillion-dollar contract with a respected leadership development provider. Midway through the project, the organization requested an independent ROI study. The provider argued that ROI was not appropriate. The purchaser saw it differently, and the study was conducted. The truth in the debates probably lies somewhere between these extreme points. Understanding the drivers for the ROI methodology and the inherent weaknesses and advantages of ROI makes it possible to take a rational approach to the issue and implement an appropriate mix of evaluation strategies that includes ROI.

One thing is certain in the ROI debate: it is not a fad. As long as there is a need for accountability of leadership development expenditures and the concept of an investment payoff is desired, ROI will be utilized to evaluate major investments in leadership development and performance improvement. The concept of ROI has been used for centuries, with its beginnings in Europe. The seventy-fifth anniversary issue of *Harvard Business Review* (HBR) traced the tools used to measure results in organizations (Sibbet, 1997). In the early issues of HBR, during the 1920s, ROI was the emerging tool in the United States to place a value on the payoff of investments. ROI studies on leadership development were conducted as early as the 1980s. With increased adoption and use, it appears that ROI is here to stay.

The Challenge

Measuring the impact of leadership development using ROI techniques tests even the most sophisticated and progressive leadership development efforts.

While some leadership development professionals argue that it is not possible to calculate ROI, others deliberately embrace and develop measures and ROI calculations. Based on our experiences with hundreds of executives, the latter group is gaining tremendous support from senior management teams. Regardless of whether you think ROI is the best measure of development outcomes, the reasons and the need for measuring still exist. Almost all leadership development professionals share a concern that they must eventually show a return on major investments in leadership programs. Otherwise, funds may be reduced, or the leadership development function may not be able to maintain or enhance its present status and influence in the organization.

The dilemma surrounding the ROI process is a source of frustration among many senior executives and within the leadership development field itself. Most executives realize that leadership development is a necessity in an increasingly dynamic and competitive global environment. There are many situations in which leadership development could and would be helpful to an organization. Executives intuitively understand that there is value in providing leadership development opportunities, and they logically anticipate a payoff in important bottom-line measures such as productivity improvements, quality enhancements, cost reductions, and customer service. Yet the frustration comes from the lack of evidence to show that the process is adding economic value. While the payoffs are assumed to exist and leadership development programs appear to be necessary, more evidence is needed—or funding may be adjusted in the future. The ROI methodology represents a direct way to show this accountability using a logical, rational approach (Phillips, 2005).

Why ROI?

Several issues drive the use of ROI to measure the success of leadership development.

Visibility. Leadership development has taken on increased visibility in recent years. This visibility in corporate offices and attention in the press has brought new levels of scrutiny. A highly visible or perhaps even controversial project sometimes must be held to higher levels of accountability, including demonstrating the value with credible ROI data.

Accountability Trend. A consistent accountability trend is developing across all types of organizations, functions, programs, and projects. Many executives demand results from various processes and projects and ask for the actual ROI. It is a logical argument: money is invested, so there should be a monetary return on the investment.

Costs. Leadership development initiatives can be very expensive, and the costs of leadership development have continued to rise. Increased costs translate into the need for additional accountability, often at the ROI level. For example, one executive leadership development program at a large Canadian bank cost more than $100,000 per participant. Because of this, the board of directors requested an ROI impact study on the first rollout of the program (Phillips, Stone, and Phillips, 2001, p. 449). Executives asked the basic question, Do the monetary benefits of leadership development overcome the costs of leadership development? In this case the ROI study was able to demonstrate a positive ROI of 62 percent.

Soft Skills Concern. Because leadership development appears to be in the category of hard-to-measure or hard-to-value processes (typical of soft skill efforts), the results are not easy to link with hard measures such as productivity and quality. Because of this, executives are concerned about the return on investment. This investment is often considered a riskier investment since returns are not as clear.

A Familiar Term. The concept of ROI is a familiar term for executives who manage the business aspects of organizations. ROI is used for investments in plants, equipment, and other capital expenditures. The concept of ROI has been used for more than three hundred years as a business tool. So why shouldn't it be used for other major investments as well? Also, executives with MBAs and other management degrees have studied the concept of ROI, know how it is developed, and appreciate the usefulness of the concept.

These and other influences are prompting executives to raise the issue of ROI in leadership development. The good news is that it is being developed with limited resources, providing a credible value reflecting the payoff of leadership development. Exhibit 5.1 shows the leadership development programs for which ROI studies have been developed.

EXHIBIT 5.1. TYPES OF LEADERSHIP DEVELOPMENT
FOR WHICH ROI HAS BEEN DEVELOPED.

- Job rotation
- Management succession
- Front-line leadership
- University-sponsored leadership
- Executive leadership
- Middle management leadership
- Coaching and mentoring
- 360-degree feedback

ROI Methodology and Its Elements

The ROI process described in this chapter has been used by more than 2,000 organizations to show the success of a variety of human resource development programs, including leadership development, executive development, management development, and team building. It has been well documented in more than fifteen books that have been translated into twenty-five languages. More than 2,500 individuals have been certified to implement the ROI methodology internally in their organizations. Approximately 5,000 ROI studies are conducted each year, globally. The process has been formally implemented in more than forty countries. A global professional network, ROI Network, has been organized to share information.

Evaluating leadership development can be viewed as a puzzle that has been solved over time. The challenge is to develop a comprehensive measurement system with credibility and acceptance to a variety of groups. The methodology discussed here has five elements and collects six types of data, including the actual ROI. Figure 5.1 shows these various elements (Phillips, 2003).

An Evaluation Framework

The evaluation framework details the specific types of data arranged in a chain of impact that must occur if leadership development is to add business value

FIGURE 5.1. THE FIVE ELEMENTS OF ROI METHODOLOGY.

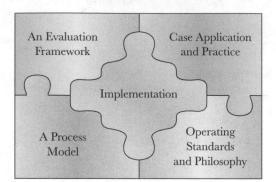

and ultimately ROI. These represent hard and soft data items collected at different times, often from different sources. Exhibit 5.2 shows the definitions of these types of data presented as levels that represent an update, modification, and addition to the four levels developed by Kirkpatrick (1959).

Reaction and Planned Action. At Level 1, the participant reacts to the leadership development program. A variety of data items are collected at this level, with particular focus on measures such as

- Relevance of the leadership development program to the current work assignment
- Importance of the leadership development program to job success
- Intent to use what is learned in the leadership development program
- Amount of new insights gained from the leadership development process
- Effectiveness of the facilitator

Although other measures can be developed, these are the critical ones that often correlate with the application of leadership development.

Learning. At Level 2, learning is measured usually on self-assessment scales. As new knowledge, skills, insights, and understandings are developed, it is important to measure the changes. Without learning, there will be no behavior

EXHIBIT 5.2. EVALUATION LEVELS AND MEASUREMENT FOCUS.

Evaluation Level	Measurement Focus
1. Reaction and planned action	Measures participant satisfaction with the leadership development and captures planned actions
2. Learning	Measures changes in knowledge, skills, and attitudes
3. Application and implementation	Measures changes in on-the-job behavior and progress with application
4. Business impact	Captures changes in business impact measures
5. Return on investment	Compares program monetary benefits to the program costs

change. Learning can be measured with skill practices, simulations, case studies, assessments, and traditional objective tests.

Application and Implementation. At Level 3, the application of leadership development is monitored. Here, the actions, steps, processes, and behaviors are captured during and following the leadership development program. The most common method is to use 360-degree feedback from other managers and direct reports. At this level, participants report on progress with action plans, individual projects, team projects, specific applications, and initiatives.

Business Impact. At Level 4, business impact measures are the consequences of the new behavior and program application. The leadership development program should influence one or more key measures, such as productivity, quality, costs, time, customer satisfaction, or job satisfaction. A key challenge at this step is to isolate the effects of leadership development from other influences.

Return on Investment. Finally, at Level 5, an ROI value is calculated. The cost of leadership development is compared to the monetary benefits of the business impact measures. This level requires the business impact measures to be converted to monetary values.

The levels of data are identified as they normally occur in a chain of impact. A process model is needed to provide consistency in options in collecting, processing, and reporting data.

A Process Model

Figure 5.2 shows the different steps in the ROI process model. For each step, options are available to address the variety of programs, participants, and settings. Because the situations can vary significantly, several options are needed to cover all the possible types of leadership development programs and scenarios. These are discussed later under key steps.

Operating Standards and Philosophy

Every process needs standards. In the ROI methodology, standards presented in Exhibit 5.3 provide the rules for collecting, processing, analyzing, and communicating data. These guiding principles represent a very conservative approach to ROI. Being conservative in approach—including only firm data on the benefits side and including all costs on the costs side—ensures the credibility of the process and of the data. One can be relatively sure the ROI value obtained is at the lower bound.

FIGURE 5.2. ROI PROCESS MODEL.

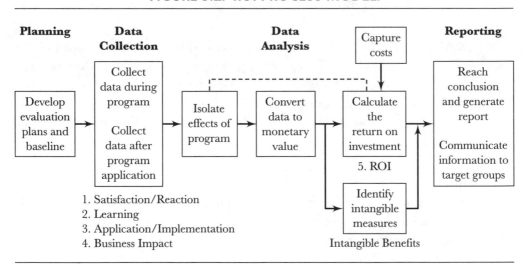

EXHIBIT 5.3. GUIDING PRINCIPLES (THE STANDARDS).

- When a higher-level evaluation is conducted, data must be collected at lower levels.

- When an evaluation is planned for a higher level, the previous level of evaluation is essential but does not have to be comprehensive.

- When collecting and analyzing data, use only the most credible sources, from the perspective of the project sponsor.

- When analyzing data, choose the most conservative alternative for calculations.

- At least one method and preferably more than one must be used to isolate the effects of the leadership development program.

- If no improvement data are available for a population or from a particular source, it is assumed that little or no improvement has occurred.

- Estimates of improvement should be adjusted for the potential error of the estimate.

- Extreme data items and unsupported claims should not be used in ROI calculations.

- Only the first year of benefits (annual) should be used in the ROI analysis of short-term solutions.

- Costs of the leadership development program should be fully loaded for ROI analysis.

- Intangible measures are defined as measures that are purposely not converted to monetary values.

- The results from the ROI methodology must be communicated to all key stakeholders.

In almost every case, the standards are aimed at being very conservative in the analysis, essentially understating the results of the leadership development program. This conservative approach translates into executive buy-in for the data and for the leadership development project. Without buy-in, the study would be virtually worthless. The standards represent the most important part of this overall comprehensive evaluation system.

Case Applications and Practice

Individuals who are involved in leadership development programs and who desire more accountability are encouraged to use this process to show the impact of leadership development. As with many new processes, a quick success story can be helpful in explaining how it might be applied. Published ROI case studies, tools, and templates are available, including software and many reference books (see the Resources list at the end of this chapter). In the most recent book of ROI case studies published by the American Society for Training and Development, five of the twelve cases are leadership development applications. Not knowing how to do it should not be a legitimate barrier today. Individuals who have a need to pursue ROI can achieve it, often with minimal resources (Phillips and Phillips, 2005).

It is important to obtain success with ROI within the organization and to document the results as impact studies. Consequently, the leadership development staff is encouraged to develop their own impact studies to compare with others. Impact studies within the organization provide the most convincing data to senior management teams that the leadership development is adding significant value and that the six types of data form the basis for actions for improvement. Case studies also provide information to improve leadership development efforts, as part of a continuous improvement process. The ROI methodology described in this chapter is rich in tradition, with application in a variety of settings and more than one hundred published case studies which can be used as examples in developing your own.

Implementation

Implementation addresses a variety of issues about the routine use of the ROI methodology in leadership development. This issue addresses how data will be communicated, how often studies are needed, who actually conducts the studies, and other issues that often hinder the routine use of the methodology.

A variety of environmental issues and events will influence the successful implementation of the ROI methodology. These issues must be addressed early to ensure that the use of ROI is successful. Specific topics or actions include

- A policy statement concerning results-based leadership development
- Procedures and guidelines for different elements and techniques of the evaluation process
- Meetings and formal sessions to develop and sustain staff capability with the ROI methodology
- Strategies to improve management commitment and support leadership development and the use of ROI

- Mechanisms to provide technical support for questionnaire design, data analysis, and evaluation strategy
- Specific techniques to place more attention on results
- Communication strategies for sharing information and results about ROI

The use of ROI can fail or succeed, based on these implementation issues; several books are devoted to this topic (Phillips, Phillips, and Hodges, 2004).

Key Steps

The following issues pertain directly to the use of the process model in leadership development and show the most likely scenarios to achieve success with ROI (Phillips and Schmidt, 2004; also, see Figure 5.2 for the process steps).

Objectives: Shifting the Alignment to the Right Level

The beginning point for ROI development is to establish objectives based on the commitment among the delivery organization, the client organization, and the individual participant. The outcomes for many programs are traditionally based on behavior needs, as individuals outline specific behaviors they are interested in changing through the leadership development process. However, for leadership development to add significant business value, it should be based on a business need. Thus, if the ROI in leadership development is desired, the initial alignment should be elevated to the business need level. Figure 5.3 shows the alignment of the upfront needs assessment with evaluation data (Phillips, Stone, and Phillips, 2001). The objectives provide the linkage between upfront assessment and evaluation.

In an ideal world, leadership development begins with a business opportunity, need, or challenge and migrates through different levels of analysis, which correspond with the levels of evaluation. Figure 5.3 shows the important linkage from the initial problem or opportunity that created the need for the leadership development program. Level 5 analysis defines the potential payoff and examines the possibility for a return on investment before the project is even pursued. Level 4 analysis focuses directly on the business needs that precipitated an intervention. Level 3 analyzes the specific issues in the

FIGURE 5.3. LINKING NEEDS, OBJECTIVES, AND EVALUATION.

workplace and focuses on job performance in detail. A Level 2 analysis uncovers the specific knowledge, skill, or attitude deficiencies as learning needs are identified. Finally, Level 1 analyzes the preferences for the structure of the solution. This connection is critical and important to understanding all the elements that must go into an effective leadership development solution.

If the need for the leadership development program is based on job performance needs (behavior), the most appropriate level of evaluation is application (Level 3). If the need is at the business needs level, it becomes easier (and sometimes even routine) to evaluate the program at the impact level. Subsequently, the ROI is developed from the impact data. It is not very difficult to elevate a job performance need (behavior) to a business need if there is a connection. The leadership development evaluator should guide stakeholders, especially the program sponsors, to the business need by asking So what? and What if? questions. Through this process the evaluator is attempting to pinpoint what will happen if a specific behavior changes. In some cases, it means that a specific business measure, such as productivity, cycle time, quality, project delivery, or retention will improve. When a business impact objective is established, the leadership development program has the best opportunity for developing the actual ROI.

In the Level 1 assessment, *preference needs* refer to the structure and process of the leadership development program (for example, timing, delivery, duration, location, format), taking into consideration the preferences of the leadership development staff, the participants, and the client. *Reaction* refers to the reaction of all parties on the structure and process of leadership development, as well as topics such as relevance, importance, usefulness, effectiveness, and perceived value of the content.

Achieving this alignment in practice is sometimes difficult. For example, in a first-level-manager leadership development program in a large car rental company, the leadership development team had to be creative. In an attempt to link the program to business needs and job performance needs, prior to attending the program, each manager was asked to identify at least two business measures in the work unit that represented an opportunity for improvement. The measure was to come from operating reports, cost statements, or scorecards. Further, the selected measures had to meet an additional two-part test:

1. Each measure had to be under the control of the team when improvements were to be considered.
2. Each measure had to have the potential to be influenced by team members with the manager using the competencies in the program. A description of the program was provided in advance, including a list of objectives and skill sets.

The initial needs assessment on competencies uncovered a variety of deficiencies across all the functional units and provided the information necessary for job descriptions, assignments, and key responsibility areas. Although very basic, the additional steps taken to connect the program to business impact were appropriate for a business needs analysis and a job performance needs analysis. Identifying two measures needing improvement is a simple business needs analysis for the work unit. Restricting the selected measures to only those that can be influenced by the team with the leader using the skills from the program essentially defines a job performance need. (In essence, the individual leader is identifying action that is not currently being pursued in the work unit that could be taken to enhance the business need.) Other factors that have significant impact on or influence over the areas selected will be sorted in the follow-up. Although more refinement and detail would be preferred, the results of the assessment process should suffice for this project (Phillips and Schmidt, 2004).

Planning

A leadership development evaluation begins with planning for data collection and analysis. We recommend two planning documents: a data collection plan and a data analysis plan (see Figures 5.4 and 5.5, respectively). In the data collection plan, specific types of data are identified corresponding to the levels of evaluation and objectives. For each objective, the data collection method, timing, and source are selected. The analysis plan focuses strictly on the business measures and addresses issues such as isolating the effects of the leadership development program on the business measures, converting the business measures to monetary value, identifying costs, and reporting data.

Data Collection

Both hard data (representing output, quality, cost, and time) and soft data (including job satisfaction and customer satisfaction) are collected as part of the ROI methodology. Data are collected using a variety of methods, including the following:

- *Surveys* are often administered to determine the degrees to which participants are satisfied with the program, have learned skills and knowledge, and have used various aspects of the program. Survey response options are often developed on a 1–5 Likert sliding scale and usually represent perception data. Surveys are useful for Levels 1, 2, and 3 data.
- *Questionnaires* are usually more detailed than surveys and can be used to uncover a wide variety of data. Participants provide responses to several types of open-ended and forced-response questions. Questionnaires can be used to capture Levels 1, 2, 3, and 4 data.
- *Tests* can be conducted to measure changes in knowledge and skills (Level 2). Tests come in a wide variety of formal (criterion-referenced tests, performance tests and simulations, and skill practices) and informal (facilitation assessment, self-assessment, and team assessment) methods.

FIGURE 5.4. PARTIALLY COMPLETED DATA COLLECTION PLAN.

Program: **The Leadership Challenge**   Responsibility: **Learning and Development Staff**   Date: **2003**

Level	Objective(s)	Measures/Data	Data Collection Method	Data Sources	Timing	Responsibilities
1	Reaction/Satisfaction • Participants rate the program as relevant to their jobs • Participants rate the program as important to their job success	• 4 out of 5 on a 5-point rating scale	• Questionnaire	• Participants	• End of program	• Facilitator
2	Learning • Participants demonstrate acceptable performance on each major competency	• 2 out of 3 on a 3-point scale	• Observation of skill practices • Self-assessment via questionnaire	• Facilitator • Participants	• End of program	• Facilitator
3	Application/Implementation • Participants utilize the competencies with team members on a routine basis					
4	Business Impact • Participants and team members drive improvements in at least two business measures					
5	ROI • Achieve a 20% ROI	Comments: _____ _____ _____ _____				

FIGURE 5.5. BLANK DATA ANALYSIS PLAN.

Program: _____

Responsibility: _____ Date: _____

Data Items (Usually Level 4)	Methods for Isolating the Effects of the Program/Process	Methods of Converting Data to Monetary Values	Cost Categories	Intangible Benefits	Communication Targets for Final Report	Other Influences/Issues During Application	Comments

- *On-the-job observation* captures actual skill application and use. Observations are particularly useful in leadership development. Using a 360-degree feed-back instrument is one way to collect observation data.
- *Interviews* can be conducted with participants to determine the extent to which learning has been used on the job. Interviews allow for probing to uncover specific applications and are usually appropriate with Level 3 data, but can be used to collect Level 1 and 2 data.
- *Focus groups* can be conducted to determine the degree to which a group of participants has applied learning to job situations. Focus groups are usually appropriate with Level 3 data.
- *Action plans* should be developed by participants during the program and are implemented on the job after the program is completed. Follow-ups provide evidence of program success. Level 3 and 4 data can be collected with action plans.
- *Performance contracts* should be developed by the participant, the participant's immediate manager, and the facilitator, who all agree on performance outcomes from the leadership development program. Performance contracts are appropriate for both Level 3 and 4 data.
- *Business performance monitoring* is useful where various performance records and operational data are examined for improvement. This method is particularly useful for Level 4 data.

The important challenge in data collection is to select the method or methods appropriate for the setting and the specific program, within the time and budget constraints of the organization.

The most efficient and cost-effective method, the questionnaire, captures data about the progress (or lack of progress) from the participant—and perhaps a coach or mentor. Specific changes in behavior are captured along with accomplishments. The most important part of the questionnaire—normally referred to as *chain of impact questions*—is where the individuals detail a specific impact chain to show the value of the leadership development contribution (see Exhibit 5.4).

The interview can be more flexible than the questionnaire, yet more time consuming and expensive. The same set of questions can be used in the interview, but with an opportunity to probe.

The action plan is appropriate and common for leadership development. With this approach, the participant develops action items that will be

EXHIBIT 5.4. CHAIN OF IMPACT QUESTIONS.

1. How have you and your job changed as a result of attending this program? (Skills and knowledge application)

2. What impact do these changes bring to your work or work unit?

3. How is this impact measured? (Specific measure)

4. How much did this measure change after you participated in the program? (Monthly, weekly, or daily amount)

5. What is the unit value of the measure?

6. What is the basis for this unit value? Please indicate the specific calculations you performed to arrive at the value.

7. What is the annual value of this change or improvement in the work unit (for the first year)?

8. We recognize that many other factors influence output results in addition to training. Please identify the other factors that could have contributed to this performance.

9. What percent of this improvement can be attributed directly to the application of skills and knowledge gained in the program? (0–100%)

10. What confidence do you have in the above estimate and data, expressed as a percentage? (0% = no confidence; 100% = certainty)

11. What other individuals or groups could estimate this percentage or determine the amount?

implemented during and, perhaps, after the leadership development session. The action plan not only indicates behavior changes (that is, particular steps in the action plan), but shows the business impact that will be driven with the behavior change. The business measures are defined and converted to monetary terms, possibly with assistance from a coach or member of the leadership development staff.

The performance contract is the action planning process with a pre-engagement commitment. The participant and his or her manager reach an agreement on the measures that need to change as a result of the leadership development program. In some cases, the immediate manager of the person being coached is in the loop. This technique is very powerful. In one leadership ROI study involving store managers in a restaurant chain, the performance contracting process produced impressive results, including a 298 percent ROI.

Data Analysis

Data analysis begins next. After the data are tabulated and summarized, five major processes are addressed: isolate the effects, convert data to money, capture costs, calculate ROI, and identify the intangibles.

Isolate the Effects of Leadership Development. An often-overlooked issue in most evaluations is the process of isolating the effects of the leadership development program. In this step of the process, specific strategies are explored that determine the amount of output performance directly related to the program. This step is essential because there are many factors that will influence performance data. The specific strategies of this step pinpoint the amount of improvement directly related to the leadership development program, resulting in increased accuracy and credibility of the ROI calculations. The following techniques have been used by organizations to tackle this important issue.

1. A control group arrangement, as described in Chapter One of this book, is used to isolate leadership development impact. With this strategy, one group participates in the program, while another, similar group does not. The difference in the performance of the two groups is attributed to the program. When properly set up and implemented, the control group arrangement is the most effective way to isolate the effects of leadership development.

2. Trend lines are used to project the values of specific output variables if the program had not been implemented. The projection is compared to the actual data after implementation, and the difference represents the estimate of the impact of the program. Under certain conditions, this strategy can accurately isolate the impact. In some cases, there can be a performance dip during the change process and then a climb to new heights. It is important to set the time for data collection to allow for this dip.

3. When mathematical relationships between input and output variables are known, a forecasting model is used to isolate the effects of the program. With this approach, the output variable is predicted using the forecasting

model with the assumption that no program is conducted. The actual performance of the variable after the program is then compared with the forecasted value, which results in an estimate of the leadership development impact.

4. Participants estimate the amount of improvement related to the program. With this approach, participants are provided with the total amount of improvement, on a preprogram and postprogram basis, and are asked to indicate the percentage of the improvement that is related to the leadership development program.

5. Supervisors of participants estimate the impact of the program on the output variables. With this approach, supervisors of participants are presented with the total amount of improvement and are asked to indicate the percentage related to the leadership development program. When estimates are used, the data are adjusted for the error of the estimate. While the process is perhaps inaccurate, there are some advantages of having senior management involved in this process.

6. Experts provide estimates of the impact of leadership development on the performance variable. Because the estimates are based on previous experience, the experts must be familiar with the type of leadership development program and the specific situation.

7. When feasible, other influencing factors are identified and the impact estimated or calculated, leaving the remaining, unexplained improvement attributed to leadership development. In this case, the influence of all of the other factors are attributed, and leadership development remains the one variable not accounted for in the analysis. The unexplained portion of the output is then attributed to leadership development.

8. In some situations, customers provide input on the extent to which the leadership development program has influenced their decisions to use a product or service. Although this strategy has limited applications, it can be quite useful in customer service and sales leadership efforts.

Collectively, these eight strategies provide a comprehensive set of tools to tackle the important and critical issue of isolating the effects of leadership development. The first three methods are more credible, but may not be feasible. The fourth method is always feasible and represents the fallback method. All methods should be explored.

Convert Data Collected into Monetary Value. Converting data to monetary value may appear to be a difficult issue, but it is actually one of the easiest. When a specific measure has been identified that is connected to the leadership development program, it is often a very simple and routine matter to convert it to monetary value. Ten approaches, described next, are available in leadership development situations.

Converting data to money requires a value to be placed on each unit of data connected with the program. The specific techniques selected usually depend on the type of data and the situation; many of the values indicated are already available in organizations.

1. Output data are converted to profit contribution or cost savings. In this strategy, output increases are converted to monetary value based on their unit contribution to profit or the unit of cost reduction.
2. The cost of quality is calculated and quality improvements are directly converted to cost savings.
3. For programs where employee time is saved, the participants' wages and employee benefits are used to develop the value for time. Because a variety of programs focus on improving the time required to complete projects, processes, or daily activities, the value of time becomes an important and necessary issue.
4. Historical costs, developed from cost statements, are used when they are available for a specific variable. In this case, organizational cost data establish the specific monetary cost savings of an improvement.
5. When available, internal and external experts may be used to estimate a value for an improvement. In this situation, the credibility of the estimate hinges on the expertise and reputation of the individual.
6. External databases are sometimes available to estimate the value or cost of data items. Research, government, and industry databases can provide important information for these values. The difficulty lies in finding a specific database related to the situation.
7. Participants estimate the value of the data item. For this approach to be effective, participants in leadership development programs must be capable of providing a credible value for the improvement.
8. Managers and executives provide estimates when they are both willing and capable of assigning values to the improvement. This approach is

especially useful when participants are not fully capable of providing this input or in situations where supervisors need to confirm or adjust the participant's estimate. If both inputs are equally credible, the lower value is used, following the conservative approach (Guiding Principle 4). This approach is particularly helpful to establish values for performance measures that are very important to senior management.

9. Soft measures are linked, mathematically, to other measures that are easier to measure and value. This approach is particularly helpful when establishing values for measures that are very difficult to convert to monetary values, such as data that are often considered intangible, like customer satisfaction, employee satisfaction, grievances, and employee complaints.

10. The leadership development staff estimates may be used to determine a value of an output data item. In these cases, it is essential for the estimates to be provided on an unbiased basis. This is often difficult, and thus this technique is the last resort.

Linking data to its monetary value is absolutely necessary for determining ROI from a leadership development program. The process is challenging, particularly with soft data, but can be methodically accomplished using one or more of these strategies.

Capture Costs. The costs of leadership development are needed for the ROI calculation. It is the number against which the value or monetary gain is compared. For example, it would be misleading to indicate a program led to $75,000 in gain per participant if the program itself cost $100,000 per participant. In this case, the program would actually be running at a loss. The cost of the leadership development program should be fully loaded—including both direct and indirect costs.

Among the cost components that should be included are

- The cost to design and develop the program, possibly prorated over the expected life of the program
- The cost of all program materials provided to each participant
- The cost for the facilitator, including preparation time as well as delivery time
- The cost of the facilities for the program

- Travel, lodging, and meal costs for the participants, if applicable
- Salaries, plus employee benefits of the participants who attend the program
- Administrative and overhead costs of the training function, allocated in some convenient way

In addition, specific costs related to the needs assessment and evaluation should be included, if appropriate. The conservative approach is to include all of these costs so that the total is fully loaded. Exhibit 5.5 shows the fully loaded costs for a leadership development program for senior managers at a hotel chain.

Calculate the Return on Investment. The return on investment is usually calculated in two ways. The benefits-to-cost ratio (BCR) is the monetary benefits of leadership development divided by leadership development cost. In formula form it is

$$BCR = \frac{Benefits}{Cost}$$

EXHIBIT 5.5. COST OF COACHING TWENTY-FIVE EXECUTIVES IN A LEADERSHIP DEVELOPMENT PROGRAM.

Item	Cost
Needs assessment/development	$ 10,000
Coaching fees	480,000
Travel costs	53,000
Executive time	9,200
Administrative support	14,000
Administrative overhead	2,000
Telecommunication expenses	1,500
Facilities (Conference room)	2,100
Evaluation	8,000
Total	$579,800

The return on investment uses net benefits divided by costs. The net benefits are the monetary benefits minus the costs. In formula form, the ROI becomes

$$\text{ROI (\%)} = \frac{\text{Net Benefits} - \text{Program Costs}}{\text{Program Costs}} \times 100$$

This is the same basic formula used in evaluating other investments where the ROI is traditionally reported as earnings (net benefits) divided by investment (leadership development costs).

Let's consider an example of the benefit-to-cost ratio and the ROI. The program, involving twenty-five executives participating in a leadership development coaching initiative at a hotel chain, generates monetary benefits of $1,861,158. As shown in Exhibit 5.5, the program cost $579,800, including the direct expenditures, the cost of the time involved, and other miscellaneous expenses. The benefit-to-cost ratio is 2.21. The ROI is the benefits minus the costs divided by the costs:

$$\frac{\$1,861,158 - \$579,800}{\$579,800} \times 100 = 221\%$$

Thus, the two values are directly related. For a shortcut method, it is possible to take the benefit-to-cost ratio, subtract one (1), and multiply that result by 100 to obtain the ROI as a percentage.

Identify the Intangibles. Intangible benefits associated with the leadership development program should be captured. *Intangibles* are those measures that are not converted to monetary values, and usually include other hard-to-value measures. If these measures cannot be converted to money credibly and with minimum resources, they are identified as intangibles. Intangibles are very important because they represent the human dynamics elements in the work environment, such as commitment to organizational goals, teamwork, and communication. That they cannot be feasibly or credibly converted to monetary values does not undermine their significance in the workplace. Exhibit 5.6 shows a list of typical intangibles. Intangibles are reported as the sixth type of data in the ROI methodology.

EXHIBIT 5.6. TYPICAL INTANGIBLES
LINKED WITH LEADERSHIP DEVELOPMENT.

• Job satisfaction	• Customer complaints
• Organizational commitment	• Customer retention
• Climate	• Customer response time
• Employee complaints	• Teamwork
• Engagement	• Cooperation
• Stress reduction	• Conflict
• Employee tardiness	• Decisiveness
• Employee transfers	• Communication
• Image	• Creativity
• Customer satisfaction	• Competencies

Report. The final step in the process is to report data to a variety of stakeholder groups. Each potential audience should be analyzed in terms of audience needs and the most effective method of communication for the audience. This should be determined prior to data collection so the data gathered are related to the type and level of communication needed. The communication must be timely; report as soon as the results are known and developed for presentation. Exhibit 5.7 shows the typical audiences and the rationale for communicating results to them.

In the very first impact study in an organization or for a certain client, a face-to-face meeting with key sponsors is desired and provides an opportunity not only to communicate the results of the study but also to gain support for the method used to conduct the study. If stakeholders were consulted prior to the study, this communication meeting would reinforce the support. A variety of options is available, ranging from a detailed impact study to an executive summary to a one-page description. The important point is to tailor the communication to the target audiences. Keep it as brief as possible. More communication time may be necessary early in the process to gain commitment to the methodology, assumptions, and standards as well as an understanding of the data.

EXHIBIT 5.7. TARGET AUDIENCES AND COMMUNICATION RATIONALE.

Reason for Communication	Primary Target Audiences
To secure approval for the project	Sponsor, top executives
To gain support for the project	Immediate managers, project team leaders
To secure agreement with the issues	Participants, project team leaders
To build credibility for HRD	Top executives
To enhance reinforcement of the processes	Immediate managers
To drive action for improvement	Sponsor, leadership development staff
To prepare participants for the project	Team project leaders
To enhance results and quality of future feedback	Participants
To show the complete results of the project	Sponsor
To underscore the importance of measuring results	Sponsor, leadership development staff
To explain techniques used to measure results	Sponsor, support staff
To create desire for a participant to be involved	Team project leaders
To build respect for the leadership development staff	Top executives
To demonstrate accountability for expenditures	All employees
To market future projects	Prospective sponsors

Conclusion

The use of ROI in leadership development evaluation is growing rapidly. ROI can be a very complex process, but doesn't have to be. Leadership development programs can and should be evaluated routinely. Only those programs that are high profile, especially expensive, and likely to draw scrutiny from top executives should be considered for evaluation to ROI. Figure 5.6 shows the approximate percentages of programs that should be evaluated at each of the five levels.

FIGURE 5.6. PERCENTAGE OF PROGRAMS
TO BE EVALUATED AT EACH LEVEL.

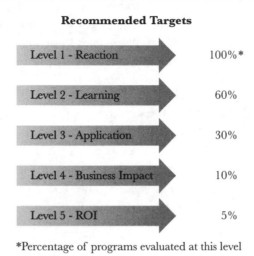

Recommended Targets

Level 1 - Reaction	100%*
Level 2 - Learning	60%
Level 3 - Application	30%
Level 4 - Business Impact	10%
Level 5 - ROI	5%

*Percentage of programs evaluated at this level

When using ROI methods to evaluate leadership development, it is important to keep several key principles in mind.

- Ensure that the leadership development program focuses on a business need. As discussed in this chapter, it is critical that the engagement expectations be pushed to the business level. Otherwise, the ROI may be negative.
- The participant (and manager or coach, if applicable) should be committed to providing data. This upfront, early commitment is critical to secure the quality and quantity of data needed. Although records can be checked, there is nothing more credible than information obtained directly from those whose performance has changed.
- Keep the process as simple as possible. The ROI methodology can morph into a complex process if not managed properly. Keep it simple and make it very conservative and credible.
- Follow the methodology. The process outlined here and contained in several of the books on ROI is a very disciplined process. It is a sequential, step-by-step methodology that must be strictly followed. Leaving out a part of the process compromises the integrity of the study and may lower the credibility of the outcome.

- Communicate results. The presentation of results is very critical. The appropriate target audiences should be selected and communication used to obtain buy-in for the methodology as well as buy-in for the data.
- Use the data. Evaluation data usually indicate changes are needed. Needed adjustments should be implemented. Improvements should be instituted to make the project more successful in the future.

Developing the ROI in leadership development can be very straightforward, if one follows the methodology defined in this chapter. A credible impact study can be developed using a systematic, step-by-step approach to define levels and types of data, collect and analyze data, and report the data to key audiences. The methodology uses very conservative standards (guiding principles) for analysis and has been utilized to develop thousands of studies, including hundreds in the leadership development environment.

Resources

The American Society for Training and Development (see www.astd.org), The ROI Institute (see www.roiinstitute.net), and the Society for Human Resource Managers (see www.shrm.org) all have members interested in ROI. The ROI Network at www.astd.org has been organized to share information. Case studies are available at www.roiinstitute.net. If you would like to receive a case study related to leadership development, please e-mail info@roiinstitute.net.

Phillips, J. *Investing in Your Company's Human Capital: Strategies to Avoid Spending Too Little or Too Much.* New York: AMACOM, 2005. This book presents five strategies for establishing appropriate levels of investment—monetary and otherwise—in workforce initiatives.

Phillips, J. *Proving the Value of HR: How and Why to Measure ROI.* Alexandria, Va.: SHRM, 2005. The human resources function must show its contribution and prove that HR policies, practices, and solutions add directly to the organization's bottom line. This book shows how to measure ROI and provides basic, step-by-step instructions to develop the ROI of HR. Includes a CD-ROM of tools, templates, charts, graphs, a case study, and more.

Phillips J. *Return on Investment in Training and Performance Improvement Programs* (2nd ed.). Woburn, Mass.: Butterworth-Heinemann, 2003. The second edition of this best-selling book guides you through a proven, results-based approach to calculating the return on investment in training and performance improvement programs.

Phillips, J., and Phillips, P. *ROI at Work: Best-Practice Case Studies from the Real World.* Alexandria, Va.: ASTD Press, 2005. This book presents best-practice case studies from the real world of measuring return on investment, including five case studies about leadership development programs. Case studies come from the government sector as well as a range of industries and provide valuable lessons for professionals working to contribute to the strategic goals of their organizations.

Phillips, J., Phillips, P., and Hodges, T. *Make Training Evaluation Work.* Alexandria, Va.: ASTD Press, 2004. This book provides the learning professional—newcomer or veteran—practical and specific ways to show value and communicate results, select the right model, find resources, get management buy-in, and overcome resistance.

Phillips, J., and Schmidt, L. *The Leadership Scorecard.* Woburn, Mass.: Butterworth-Heinemann, 2004. This book expands and discusses best-practice leadership development methods, incorporates ROI measurement and evaluation methodology, sets out a step-by-step process, presents case studies, and provides proven measurement and evaluation techniques. It is essential for CEOs, executives, managers, and professionals involved in leadership development, coaching and mentoring programs, action learning projects, and training and performance improvement programs.

Phillips, J., Stone, R., and Phillips, P. *The Human Resources Scorecard: Measuring the Return on Investment.* Woburn, Mass.: Butterworth-Heinemann, 2001. This book provides a comprehensive, step-by-step guide for measuring the impact of human resources programs and includes seven detailed case studies. This book is essential for human resource executives, professionals, CEOs, CFOs, consultants, professors, and other managers concerned with their business's bottom lines.

Phillips, P. *The Bottomline on ROI.* Atlanta, Ga.: Center for Effective Performance, 2002. This book offers the business case for ROI. It provides the basics, benefits, and barriers to measuring training and performance improvement programs.

Phillips, P. (ed.), and Phillips, J. (series ed.). *In Action: Measuring Return on Investment*, Vol. 3. Alexandria, Va.: ASTD Press, 2001. This book has eleven cases from a variety of industries including telecommunications, computer and technology, retail stores, automotive, and the government sector.

Phillips, P., and Phillips, J. *ROI Basics*. Alexandria, Va.: ASTD Press, 2005. This book provides the fundamental steps in developing a comprehensive evaluation, offering the reader basic skills in ROI, tools for selecting appropriate programs for ROI evaluation, and the ability to develop a strategy to integrate ROI as part of the ongoing learning process.

References

Kirkpatrick, D. L. "Techniques for Evaluating Training Programs—Part 2: Learning." *Journal of the American Society of Training Directors*, 1959, 21–26.

Phillips, J. *Investing in Your Company's Human Capital: Strategies to Avoid Spending Too Little or Too Much*. New York: AMACOM, 2005.

Phillips J. *Return on Investment in Training and Performance Improvement Programs* (2nd ed.). Woburn, Mass.: Butterworth-Heinemann, 2003.

Phillips, J., and Phillips, P. *ROI at Work: Best-Practice Case Studies from the Real World*. Alexandria, Va.: ASTD Press, 2005.

Phillips, J., Phillips, P., and Hodges, T. *Make Training Evaluation Work*. Alexandria, Va.: ASTD Press, 2004.

Phillips, J., and Schmidt, L. *The Leadership Scorecard*. Woburn, Mass.: Butterworth-Heinemann, 2004.

Phillips, J., Stone, R., and Phillips, P. *The Human Resources Scorecard: Measuring the Return on Investment*. Woburn, Mass.: Butterworth-Heinemann, 2001.

Sibbet, D., and the Staff of HBR. *75 Years of Management Ideas and Practice 1922–1997: A Supplement to the Harvard Business Review*. September–October 1997.

PART TWO

LEADERSHIP DEVELOPMENT EVALUATION IN CONTEXT

The nine chapters in Part Two are applications of leadership development evaluations in different contexts, across different sectors, and with different populations of people. Authors share the lessons they have learned from designing and implementing leadership development evaluations and discuss the issues and challenges that arose during the course of their evaluations. They provide advice about how to successfully undertake evaluations in similar contexts and how to be flexible in order to respond to new information and circumstances as they arise. Despite the diversity of contexts in which leadership development evaluations have been conducted, readers will notice many common themes emerging about how to successfully design and implement a leadership development evaluation.

The Importance of Context

Contextual factors influence leadership development evaluation design and implementation in ways that shape what is learned and how the evaluation is perceived and used. Some of the contextual factors that are most important to consider are the purpose and scope of the leadership development efforts, the history and circumstances of people and communities that are participating in the evaluation effort, the timing of evaluations, the availability of resources, the quality and availability of data, and the expectations of key stakeholders.

Purpose and Scope of Leadership Development Efforts

Leadership development efforts are designed and implemented for many different reasons. They are used to create opportunities for those who have historically been excluded or underserved to move into positions of leadership (Chapter Six); they are used to support people to become more authentic and to better align their values, beliefs, and actions (Chapter Seven); they are used to improve organizational performance (Chapters Eight and Nine); they are used to catalyze collaboration, community engagement, and improve neighborhoods and communities (Chapters Ten, Thirteen, and Fourteen); and they are used to seed systemic and social transformation by building a critical mass of leaders (Chapters Eleven and Twelve). The purpose of leadership development affects who will be recruited for participation, how they will be developed and supported, and what counts as success and how it will be measured.

History and Culture

Leadership development programs take place with people and communities that have vastly different histories and circumstances. A number of chapters in Part Two highlight how culture, past experience, and other factors influence the pathways of leadership for individuals, organizations, and communities. Paying attention to these factors throughout the evaluation process leads to a deeper understanding about what is occurring and why, and strengthens the validity of the evaluation findings.

People in communities and organizations have different experiences with leadership and evaluation, and those experiences need to be taken into account. The variation of leadership qualities, behaviors, and actions that are valued make it difficult for evaluators to define a single cultural standard that will apply to all individuals and communities. Likewise, the variation in past experiences with evaluation creates multiple expectations and concerns that become part of any evaluation process. In some communities, for instance, evaluation has been used in ways that undermine the community. Undertaking a successful evaluation in communities with this history and experience requires evaluators to engage in careful listening, processing of past experiences, and deeply engaging the community to own the evaluation process and its results.

History and circumstances are also important for defining what outcomes are desired and how success is measured. For instance, a significant outcome of leadership development programs in communities that have been divided by race or other issues may be to heal. Conducting evaluations in these communities would be incomplete without a focus on healing, but this outcome might not be central in another community. Individual leadership pathways are influenced by life history and circumstances as well. Some leaders may face tough circumstances that both motivate and disrupt their leadership. Their leadership pathways are not straight lines. Uneven pathways do not indicate that the leadership program was unsuccessful; rather, they point to the need to develop an evaluation design that accounts for personal circumstances.

It is important to identify key contextual variables early in the evaluation process because they can have dramatic effects on other program or initiative outcomes. For example, whether a program is implemented in a wealthy or a poor school district is an important contextual variable that may be useful in interpreting any other data that is collected.

Time

Time is an important contextual variable along several dimensions: the time period in which desired changes are believed to occur, the length of time the evaluation lasts, and when the evaluation takes place in relation to the program. Time affects how an evaluation is designed, implemented, and used (see the introduction to Part One for further discussion).

In leadership development evaluations, there are assumptions made about the time period in which outcomes and impacts can be observed. Frequently, there is an overestimation about the scope of change that will be observed in the time frame in which the evaluation takes place. Since most evaluations take place during the course of a program or shortly after, there is often not enough elapsed time to evaluate some of the desired outcomes, especially those at the community or systems level. Many chapters suggest that we need more longitudinal evaluation studies in order to assess the full impact of leadership development programs and initiatives.

Availability of Resources

One of the most significant contextual variables that influences the design and implementation of leadership development evaluations are the resources that are being invested. The knowledge, skills, and commitment of key stakeholders, money, and time all contribute to successful evaluations. While some of these resources are known in advance, others emerge during the evaluation. Having the flexibility to leverage existing and emerging resources strengthens evaluation outcomes.

There is a tendency to underinvest in leadership development evaluations. The questions that stakeholders want answered often require a greater investment of resources than organizations are willing to make. One of the important roles of the evaluator is to help stakeholders set realistic expectations given the available resources.

Quality and Availability of Data

In many complex evaluations, evaluators rely on others to collect information. Thus, the entire team of people engaged in evaluation activities needs to have the knowledge and capacity to collect quality data.

One of the challenges in measuring results is often the lack of available statistics that can be used to perform an analysis of the relationship between the program and the desired outcomes. Working with stakeholders to identify, track, and report on key performance indicators not only improves outcomes but also provides the data necessary to demonstrate impact.

Expectations of Key Stakeholders

In any leadership development process, there are multiple stakeholders involved who may have different expectations. One of the key challenges for evaluators is to manage these expectations throughout the design and implementation of the evaluation. Authors in these chapters describe how they have successfully managed expectations and what they would have done differently.

Chapter Summaries

Chapter Six. This chapter describes the evaluation of a pipeline program for evaluators of color that seeks to build their evaluation skills and develop their leadership capacity to use evaluation to advance social justice. Particular attention is paid to evaluating interns' leadership competencies.

Chapter Seven. This chapter's authors provide lessons learned from evaluating three personal transformation leadership efforts in three very different contexts. Based on extensive evaluation evidence and a review of relevant literature, a set of steps that occur along the path of personal transformation are presented.

Chapter Eight. This chapter describes a systematic evaluation approach that has been developed to assess the extent to which health sector teams in developing countries are transforming workgroup climate and achieving measurable change in organizational performance. The authors compare the challenges of evaluating outcomes in virtually delivered leadership programs and those delivered face to face.

Chapter Nine. This chapter demonstrates the return on investment for organizations when evaluation is intertwined with the leadership development process itself and when supervisors are accountable for the leadership development outcomes of their staff.

Chapter Ten. This chapter describes a multicommunity leadership initiative to develop more effective collective leadership. Special attention is given to using ethnographic approaches to evaluate the initiative. The challenges and opportunities for combining local and national evaluation strategies are highlighted.

Chapter Eleven. This chapter compares two leadership development strategies to transform educational leadership in urban K–12 school systems. New Leaders for New Schools is a well-defined intervention, and the Wallace Foundation's Leadership Development Initiative is a natural experiment with few prescriptive elements. Despite different intervention strategies, the authors have learned similar lessons about evaluating complex systems.

Chapter Twelve. This chapter addresses a complex multicountry evaluation to transform family planning and reproductive health leadership in developing countries. Considerable attention is paid to the challenges of evaluation design and implementation and how to address them when multiple programs, funders, and countries are involved.

Chapter Thirteen. This chapter describes how evaluating a leadership development initiative provided important evidence that led to some significant revisions in the initiative's theory of change and a definition of community-based youth leadership. The authors demonstrate how to use evaluation to clarify the initiative's theory of change and develop evaluation measures that are consistent with that theory.

Chapter Fourteen. This chapter describes a multilevel and multisite evaluation of resident leadership development efforts that are part of a multifaceted foundation initiative to transform tough neighborhoods. The chapter discusses how change is being documented at the individual, initiative, and community levels.

CHAPTER SIX

BUILDING LEADERSHIP DEVELOPMENT, SOCIAL JUSTICE, AND SOCIAL CHANGE IN EVALUATION THROUGH A PIPELINE PROGRAM

Prisca M. Collins and Rodney K. Hopson

Expanding representation of people of color and other underrepresented groups in various disciplines increases not only their numbers but also the diversity of ideas and thought and the potential for new intellectual discoveries. Various institutions and academic disciplines have adopted efforts to diversify with only limited success. Too often these efforts have not included integrating people of color (especially American-born) into positions of power and influence (Stanfield, 1999). A series of court challenges has diluted the institutional will and resources to diversify (The Woodrow Wilson National Fellowship Foundation, 2005).

Various professions such as teaching, nursing, dentistry, and medicine have developed and implemented pipeline efforts to recruit and train professionals of color. These professions have also made attempts to incorporate issues of multiculturalism into their curricula. In recent years the emphasis has been on increasing the number of minority students entering these fields (Griffin, 1990; JBHE, 1999; Olson, 1988; Post and Woessner, 1987). These pipeline efforts have focused on recruitment and to some extent on retention of students in training programs; however, very few professions have emphasized leadership development. Professions such as nursing have taken the next step of realizing that the demographics of the profession's leadership need to mirror that of the nation (Washington, Erickson, and Ditomassi, 2004). With the recent push to deliver health care and social services in a culturally responsive manner, it is critical to increase the racial and ethnic diversity of professional fields in order to improve access to services and the quality of services, as well as improve client satisfaction (Wallen, Rivera-Goba, Hastings, Peragallo, and De Leon Siantz, 2005; Washington and others, 2004). In order to increase diversity, a concerted effort needs to be made to create an environment of inclusion within various professions. Pipeline training programs are one way to do this; however, without a concerted focus on leadership development, social change, and social justice, these programs are unlikely to produce leaders who can effect change in these fields. For this to happen, pipeline efforts need to incorporate innovative ways to build a generation of ethnic and racial minority leaders who can be instrumental in developing new methods and frameworks of inclusion for communities of color and underrepresented groups that are rooted in a commitment to social change and social justice (Stanfield, 1999).

This chapter presents the evaluation of leadership development pipeline programs with a case presentation of the American Evaluation Association/Duquesne University (AEA/DU) Graduate Education Diversity Internship Program, a pipeline effort aimed at developing leaders of color within the evaluation profession. We begin by presenting examples of evaluations of various leadership development pipeline efforts found in the literature and then share our experiences evaluating the AEA/DU program. We present the rationale for developing the AEA/DU internship program as a leadership development pipeline effort; walk the reader through the design, planning, and implementation of the evaluation of this program; and share our findings through documentation of the journeys of the four members of the first-year cohort. We conclude by presenting the challenges, lessons learned through the evaluation process, and implications for the future evaluation of such efforts.

Type and Scope of Evaluations of Leadership Development Pipelines

Despite the abundance of pipeline efforts aimed at developing leaders in various professions, there seems to be a lack of well-designed in-depth evaluations demonstrating the effectiveness of these programs. Most of the evaluations we find in the literature are process evaluations providing descriptions of program components with special emphasis on success with recruitment and retention of participants. In this section of the chapter, we share a few examples of in-depth evaluations of leadership development pipeline efforts in teaching, library studies, and nursing.

Mason and Wetherbee (2004) conducted an analysis of trends in training programs for library leadership and evaluations of these programs. They lament the lack of in-depth impact evaluations of these programs. Most evaluations focused on descriptions of the training programs with very little emphasis on impacts or outcomes of the programs. The evaluations tend to be based on participant comments and personal recounting of their leadership experiences, rather than the results of pre- and posttests that assess what participants expect to learn and what they actually learn. The authors present a few in-depth evaluations that provide outcome measurement related to participant expectations and satisfaction; individual personal development; career advancement and mobility; development of desired leadership skills; formation of leadership cohorts; and organizational impact or performance. Based upon their literature review of leadership development evaluations in library studies, they conclude that few evaluation studies were designed in ways that produced legitimate results about the effectiveness of such efforts. Further, overreliance on self-report makes it difficult to validate program impact. Even when multi-methods, control groups, or longitudinal studies are used for data collection, there are still problems with data interpretation. The authors cite examples where some of the studies used control groups that were too similar to experimental groups, making it difficult to establish that two independent groups were used. They recommend that evaluations be conducted in a more systematic manner; include a clearer definition of what the profession of library studies really means by *leadership*; use trainee control groups to compare to the target group; and conduct longitudinal studies of two, five, or more years.

There are a few examples of evaluations of leadership development pipeline efforts specifically aimed at attracting people of color into positions of leadership in the nursing profession and in business. Wallen and others (2005) share the progression of one fellow through a pilot nursing research pipeline program aimed at increasing Hispanic nurse leaders. This case presentation focuses on individual short-term and long-term outcomes, including professional productivity. Roach (1999) reports on the PhD Project, a pipeline effort aimed at increasing minority faculty in business schools. Roach's work also relies heavily on self-reported data centered on recruitment and retention. More evaluation data is needed to determine if leadership development pipeline investments actively promote diversity, social change, and social justice.

The Need for Pipeline Leadership Development Efforts for Evaluators of Color

There is a need to build advanced training mechanisms in evaluation to expand the participation and leadership of diverse racial and ethnic groups in the profession. Despite the increased demands for accountability and evaluation in foundation and government sectors, during the past decade formal graduate programs have been decreasing and are not likely to expand (Fitzpatrick, Sanders, and Worthen, 2004). The low numbers of African Americans, American Indians, Mexican Americans, and Puerto Ricans who receive doctorates in research-based educational fields and in social sciences further limits the potential pool of evaluators of color (Frierson, 2003; Hood, 2000).

In recent years, there has been growing momentum to apply a cultural litmus test to evaluation processes, standards, use, and especially in situations where communities of color are participants and stakeholders in evaluations (Hood, 2001; Hopson, 2003; Thompson-Robinson, Hopson, and SenGupta, 2004). Without a significant increase in the number of evaluators of color, the ability of the field to respond to growing demands for cultural competence will be limited. Furthermore, without the presence of evaluators of color, the field of evaluation is unlikely to make speedy progress in becoming more conceptually and methodologically relevant to diverse communities. When evaluators are culturally responsive to a particular context they are able to derive deeper levels of meaning from the data they collect and analyze (Hood, 1998; Hood, 2001). The culturally responsive evaluator seeks and uses particular understandings, methodologies, and practices to ground her evaluation in a community context (LaFrance, 2004).

Inherent in the efforts to build innovative training mechanisms to increase diverse racial and ethnic evaluators is a desire to push the field to develop new ideas and paradigms to better understand diverse realities. A recent National Science Foundation workshop on the role of minority evaluator professionals finds a need to develop training programs for minority evaluators that expand potential strategies to a multiple agency/organizational approach. Models that involve colleges and universities, government agencies, and professional organizations, and use multiple strategies such as mentoring and job placement, increase the probability of fieldwide impact (Davila, 2000).

The AEA/DU Graduate Education Diversity Internship Program as a Leadership Development Pipeline Effort

The American Evaluation Association/Duquesne University Graduate Education Diversity Internship Program is a pipeline development program designed to increase the number of evaluators of color and train evaluators of color who have a potential to be future leaders in the profession. The design of the program and the types of participants who are recruited make it highly likely that this program will produce evaluators who will be leaders in the field. This evaluation training program has a significant leadership development aspect.

The AEA/DU internship program has several components: attendance and participation in evaluation seminars at Duquesne University, attendance at professional development workshops and sessions at the AEA annual conference, placement with a local sponsoring agency for providing practical, hands-on evaluation experience, matching of the interns with a facilitating mentor and an academic advisor, and an embedded communication and feedback system through a virtual classroom that includes a Web site blackboard and online reflective journaling. This type of classroom training, combined with developmental experiences and relationships and an embedded formal feedback system, has been described as one of the most commonly used strategies to develop effective leadership (Busch, 2003; Campbell, Dardis, and Campbell, 2003; Howe and Stubbs, 2001; Washington and others, 2004).

Even though the internship program is limited to nine months, the supportive mechanisms of mentorship and the communication and feedback system continue beyond the interns' graduation from the program. Short-term approaches to training leaders, such as two-hour or weeklong workshops, are not sufficient to develop leadership capabilities (Connaughton, Lawrence, and Ruben, 2003). They suggest that "leadership competencies are best developed over time through a program that fosters personalized integration of theory and practice and that conceives of leadership development as a recursive and reflective process" (p. 46). They suggest that to develop future leaders who are competent and ethical, colleges and universities must utilize highly focused multidisciplinary approaches.

The developmental relationship between the interns and their mentors and academic advisors are intended to last over a long term. Interns can call upon this resource even as they pursue their careers in evaluation. The interns are invited to continue their participation in an electronic communication system to share their evaluation experiences with the new cohorts of interns and seek feedback on projects from the internship staff and other members of the AEA leadership who work closely with the internship program. This type of long-term support is essential in leadership development for the creation of a community of practice among program participants that reinforces and stabilizes the new knowledge and skills the participants have developed (Howe and Stubbs, 2001).

The program recruits graduate students who are either in their second year of a master's program or are enrolled in a doctoral program. They have already been exposed to research methods and have substantive knowledge about their area of concentration, which better positions them for professional development in evaluation. The participants are admitted into the program based upon their academic qualifications and strong recommendations from professors that highlight the personal attributes, skills, and experiences that set the participants apart as potential leaders and that demonstrate their career interest in evaluation that promotes social justice and social change. The internship encourages and supports any personal interests the interns may already have in serving specific populations or pursuing certain social justice agendas. (See Exhibit 6.1 for an example of how the internship supports the personal interests of the intern.) The internship program, like other leadership development efforts, seeks to create context-specific learning opportunities that are compatible with the personality, skills, experiences, values, capabilities, and goals of the interns (Connaughton and others, 2003; Hernez-Broome and Hughes, 2004).

The program was conceived following the recommendation of the Building Diversity Initiative of the American Evaluation Association, a critical intervention funded by the W. K. Kellogg Foundation, to encourage the recruitment of diverse racial and ethnic persons to evaluation and to encourage the evaluation field to work in more diverse cultural contexts. Collabora-

EXHIBIT 6.1. AN APPLIED ANTHROPOLOGIST IN EAST AFRICA.

Based on her own personal background and experiences, Participant A joined the internship with the goal of gaining evaluation skills that would enable her to help needy populations. Of particular interest to her was to help Bantu-speaking people of Kenya and Somalia who have been displaced from their homelands. Her goals were to develop competencies in evaluation, especially related to integrating issues of culture into the evaluations, in order to facilitate service delivery for these marginalized populations. Through the internship program, she felt she had gained confidence in her skills as an evaluator. She reported having learned how to work well with organizations, how to engage them in the process, how to come across as an evaluator who is there to work with them as opposed to someone who is there to find fault. "I found ways to integrate things that interest me naturally, like some ways that organizations interact with their clients, or just the way organizational culture is versus that of clients."

From the experiences she was afforded at the American Evaluation Association annual conference, she felt like an "insider" in the profession, that she could think critically about some aspects of evaluation and make a contribution to the profession. At completion of the internship she acquired a position as an evaluation and monitoring specialist with an international organization that allowed her the opportunity to move to Kenya and work with the populations she always aspired to help. In preparation for her move she arranged to join the African Evaluation Association so as to be a part of the evaluation community there. She will present the evaluation work she did at the upcoming American Evaluation Association/Canadian Evaluation Society Joint Annual Conference. She was able to integrate her internship work with her academic work using the evaluation she conducted through the practical placement with a sponsoring agency as her final class practicum.

---

tion between AEA and the internship program staff is fostered during all phases of the internship through various joint committees that have been established to provide guidance, such as the curriculum planning committee and the evaluation design committee. The value of cross-program collaboration has been demonstrated by other leadership development program design and evaluation efforts (Busch, 2003; Connaughton and others, 2003; Packard Foundation Population Program and the Bill and Melinda Gates Foundation Global Health Program, 2003).

Evaluation of the AEA/DU Graduate Education Diversity Internship Program

The evaluation is planned through a collaborative effort between internship staff and a workgroup of the internship advisory committee. The purpose of the evaluation is to document the implementation process of the internship program and the impact of the program on the interns, the organizations involved (sponsoring agencies, universities attended by the interns, the AEA), and on the broader communities (local communities where the sponsoring agencies and interns are located, and the broader national and international evaluation community). Process and outcomes-oriented evaluations are essential for providing a comprehensive understanding of the program activities and their intended effects.

Process Evaluation

Process evaluation provides data on the implementation of the program, documenting the nature of people being served and the extent to which the program is operating as intended (Posavac and Carey, 1997). Program records are examined to determine whether the program is reaching its target population and implementing the appropriate intensity of program activities. A review of applications submitted to the internship provides information on the academic and personal backgrounds of all applicants. This helps us to examine whether there are any special attributes that set those who are admitted to the program apart from those not admitted to the program.

Furthermore, the process evaluation allows us to examine the extent to which program components were implemented, looking at whether the interns are successfully matched with mentors who are active senior AEA members with leadership roles in the organization and who have similar research and/or career interests with the interns. We also look at whether the interns select academic advisors from their local universities who have a concentration in their academic area. Also critical is whether the interns are matched with sponsoring agencies that work with populations that are of interest to them and address social issues in which the intern has a research interest. The evaluation seeks to determine what influence academic advisors, mentors, and networking activities with other key AEA leadership have on the leadership development of the intern. Because of the specific focus of the internship on social change and social justice, we review program documents related to the curriculum to ascertain if the topics covered reflect the program's focus.

Outcomes Evaluation

While the evaluation training approaches are aimed primarily at improving the individual interns' abilities to become culturally competent leaders in the evaluation field, change in organizations, communities, and society are key, desired long-term outcomes. The interns are the focus because they are the change agents (Grove, PLP Team, Leadership Evaluation Advisory Group, 2002). Like other evaluations of leadership development programs, the evaluation of the AEA/DU internship program seeks to identify changes at the personal, organizational, and at the community level. The evaluation framework incorporates both evidential and evocative approaches described by Grove and others (2002) in order to capture both the observable (evidential) and the not so observable but discernable changes (evocative) in participants, such as personal assumptions, attitudes, values, beliefs, and vision.

Developing a Theory of Change for the AEA/DU Internship Program

In designing, implementing, and interpreting the results of this evaluation, it is necessary to take into consideration the unique context of this internship program as described earlier. The collaborative nature of this internship program extends into the evaluation process. The theory of change maps out the activities of the program and how these activities contribute to the changes in the individual interns, the organizations involved, and the communities where the program and/or the participants are located. The theory of change model enables us to track the progression of impacts at the individual level, organizational level, and at the community level over the short and long term.

Individual-Level Impact

To assess impact at the individual level, we examine the immediate short-term gains in the interns' level of knowledge and skills in evaluation theory and practice. We assess the development of the leadership skills described by

Campbell and others (2003), which include intrapersonal qualities and interpersonal skills as well as cognitive, communication, and task-specific skills resulting from exposure to the activities of the internship program. This information is gathered through surveys, phone interviews, and postings on an electronic bulletin board.

Surveys are used to gather baseline information at the beginning of the internship program and after the fall, winter, and spring seminars. The surveys at the end of each seminar are critical in providing instant feedback on the interns' satisfaction with the training activities. This feedback is used continuously to improve the program.

A focus group is conducted in conjunction with the survey to gather baseline information at the beginning of the program. This is essential to complement the information provided by the interns in their application essays and to provide rich information on their background, goals, and career and topical interests. Sponsoring agency site visits are conducted halfway through the internship and at completion of the internship. The interns post weekly reflections on a Web site to facilitate discussions on their projects and get feedback from internship staff. The interns share the progress they are making on their evaluation projects, any challenges they encounter and their attempts to deal with them, post questions, and share with each other knowledge they gain from other sources. This helps foster a learning community for the interns and staff.

The internship coordinator conducts a site visit to each sponsoring agency and to the intern's academic institution to gather additional contextual information, such as organizational structure and relationship of agency with the local community; interview key sponsoring agency staff and academic faculty about their expectations of the intern and evaluation work she is doing, and whether these expectations are being met; and to foster a good working relationship between the program and the agency.

In examining the impact at the individual level, we reflect upon the activities of the program using the criteria of assessment, challenge, and support described by McCauley and Van Velsor (2004) to gauge the effectiveness of the leadership development strategies employed in this program. These criteria allow us to examine whether the activities provide the interns with adequate opportunities for gradual progression in evaluation-related knowledge gain and practice; whether the practical experiences provide them with learning opportunities that challenge their existing knowledge and skills, stretching them to learn and develop new capacities; and whether the supportive mechanisms are adequate to help the interns deal with the difficulties they encounter during their development. To minimize overreliance on intern self-reports, we use multiple data sources that include intern weekly postings on a Web site that highlight tasks achieved, challenges encountered, attempts to solve problems individually or through the intern groups; interviews with the interns' academic advisors, mentors, and supervisors at the sponsoring agencies; and sponsoring agency evaluation reports generated by interviews. (See Table 6.1 for a list of key questions and outcome indicators for measuring impact at the individual level.)

At the individual level, we also reflect upon the intermediate outcomes related to how the interns apply the knowledge they have gained in their projects with the sponsoring agencies and in their academic and professional work. This includes a look at how the interns incorporate the knowledge they have gained into the planning, design, and conduct of the evaluation project; how the interns negotiate their roles as evaluators in the field; how they define and solve the problems they encounter in the field; and the communication skills that they demonstrate in working with the various stakeholders. We also assess their ability to take the knowledge and skills they have gained and tailor it to a specific context in the field and whether the interns' work is beneficial to the sponsoring agencies. Of particular interest is how the interns apply the concepts of conducting culturally responsive evaluations; for example, evaluations that give voice to all the stakeholders, even the ones whose voices have traditionally been suppressed. (Refer to Exhibit 6.2 for a story of one intern's journey toward being a culturally responsive evaluator.) Information is gathered through interviews of interns, intern journaling, Web site postings, and evaluation project reports outlining the methods they used to engage all levels of stakeholders and documentation of findings in the intern evaluation report reflecting the multiple voices participating in the programs. Kirkhart's (1994) framework of multicultural validity is used to examine the extent to which the interns paid attention to threats to validity from a cultural perspective in their evaluation reports. Interviews with sponsoring agencies also provide data on the intern's interpersonal skills, such as how she engaged with the agency personnel, program participants, and other stakeholders.

Another measure at the individual level is the impact of the program on the interns' academic work and the evaluation profession, exploring how the

TABLE 6.1. INDIVIDUAL-LEVEL OUTCOMES.

Key Evaluation Question	Evaluation Subquestions	Outcome Indicators
1. How has the program impacted the interns? (Impact on a personal level)	What knowledge and skills have the interns gained?	• Scores of pretest (start of internship) and posttest (after every seminar and at end of internship)
	How have the interns applied the knowledge and skills they gained?	• Evaluation skills and knowledge demonstrated during the planning, design, and conducting of the evaluation project with sponsoring agency • Demonstration of problem-defining and problem-solving skills, communication skills during their field experiences • Quality of evaluation report examined using outline adopted from the Online Evaluation Resource Library (OERL) Web site • Integration of knowledge and skills gained into evaluation report, presentations, publications
	To what extent did the evaluation projects incorporate culturally responsive concepts that are reflected on the Culturally Responsive Evaluation Checklist?	• Review of evaluation reports using Karen Kirkhart's framework of multicultural validity
(Impact on intern at academic level)	How has the program enhanced or hindered the intern's academic work? (How has it contributed to the intern's dissertation or thesis?)	• Any incorporation of internship work into dissertation proposals or other class work

TABLE 6.1. INDIVIDUAL-LEVEL OUTCOMES, Cont'd.

Key Evaluation Question	Evaluation Subquestions	Outcome Indicators
	In what ways has the internship provided additional experiences that have enhanced the intern's academic work?	• Conference attendance • Presentation and publication opportunities • Networking opportunities with other evaluators
	How has the internship provided support mechanisms or resources (mentors, advisors, program staff, evaluation resources) and shared experiences that have facilitated the intern's ability to produce scholarly work?	• Publications or presentations generated from intern evaluation projects • Documentation of consultation with mentors, advisors, and internship staff on scholarly work
(Impact on a professional level)	What professional affiliations or networks has the intern developed as a result of the program?	• Intern's listing of professional affiliations or valuable networks developed during internship period and/or as a result of intern's affiliation with internship
	How has the internship contributed to the intern's decision on the career path or evaluation interest upon graduation?	• Intern's mention of specific events or experiences such as seminar topics, coaching experiences during workshops or with mentors, evaluation project experiences that steered intern to pursue further work in a particular area of evaluation
	What contributions has the intern made to the field of evaluation? What evaluation leadership roles has the intern assumed? How has the internship impacted the intern beyond evaluation experience?	• Evaluation-related publications or presentations • AEA Topical Interest Group (TIG) leadership roles • Evaluation-related volunteer work such as participation on student editorial board

TABLE 6.1. INDIVIDUAL-LEVEL OUTCOMES, Cont'd.

Key Evaluation Question	Evaluation Subquestions	Outcome Indicators
		• List of any leadership roles or participation in academic or professional activities that are not evaluation related where participation was somewhat influenced by the internship process (activities such as mentoring other students or community activism)
	What specific activities did the interns engage in academically and/or professionally that address issues of diversity/multiculturalism?	• AEA Multicultural TIG participation • Involvement in other professional, academic, or social activities that address issues of diversity and social justice • Publications or presentations addressing these issues by interns • Utilization of intern evaluation report findings

activities of the internship enhance the interns' schoolwork and their engagement in scholarly work. In addition to intern self-reports, the academic advisors provide information on how the interns are incorporating knowledge gained from the internship into their academic work and engaging in professional discussions and scholarly writing about multicultural issues in evaluation and beyond (see, for example, Exhibit 6.3). The mentors, who are senior members of the American Evaluation Association, provide information on intern participation in the association, networking with other evaluators, any leadership roles assumed by interns within the AEA and/or other professional associations, and any scholarly contributions to the field of evaluation.

EXHIBIT 6.2. BECOMING A CULTURALLY RESPONSIVE EVALUATOR.

Participant B was attracted to the field of evaluation and the internship program by the possibility that through evaluation he could provide a voice for people who have traditionally been marginalized in society. His research interest is in educational research, with a focus on the use of high-stakes test performance and how variables such as learning styles and socioeconomic status affect learning and standardized test scores of minority students. Upon entering the internship program, Participant B wanted to build a network with graduate students of color, work with a male role model of color, and gain a better understanding of what it means to be a culturally responsive evaluator. The program introduced him to readings and scholars who have done extensive work on cultural responsiveness in evaluation. It allowed him to begin to think more critically about these concepts and to begin to take progressive steps toward becoming a culturally responsive evaluator. Through the evaluation he conducted at the sponsoring agency, he was able to apply the concepts he learned and recognize some of his own shortcomings in conducting culturally responsive evaluations. He continues to work jointly with his mentor on a project developing a checklist for conducting culturally responsive evaluations. He feels that the networks he developed with the other interns and senior evaluation professionals during the internship are invaluable as he continues in his journey to be a culturally responsive evaluator. His doctoral dissertation will explore the theory of cultural responsiveness in evaluation. He believes that conducting evaluations that are culturally responsive can help provide a voice for many clients in human service programs who have been voiceless for too long.

Organizational-Level Impact

Outcomes at the organizational level address the impact of the internship program on the organizations that are affiliated with it. These organizations include but are not limited to the AEA, Duquesne University, the sponsoring agencies, and the academic institutions where the interns are enrolled. Considering the goal of the internship program to increase the number of evaluators of color and deepen the evaluation profession's capacity to work in racially, ethnically, and culturally diverse settings, particular attention is paid to the impact of the program on the diversity of the leadership of the AEA and scholarly contributions to the field of evaluation. Records of internship staff and intern publications and presentations around issues of diversity are

EXHIBIT 6.3. EXPANDING NOTIONS OF ENGAGEMENT, POWER, AND SOCIAL CHANGE THROUGH PSYCHOLOGY.

Participant C entered the internship program with an already established research interest in exploring power dynamics within social groups, agency, and civic efforts toward social change. However, she had absolutely no experience in evaluation. Her goals were to gain skills to better engage with the community, connecting the evaluation work she was learning to her field of study, and through that come out with a topic for her dissertation. She reported that by the end of the internship year she felt confident in her knowledge about not only what evaluation was, but about serious positions she could take in the field of evaluation and contributions she could make to her own field of study from what she had learned. The knowledge she gained and the work she did through the internship program helped highlight some holes or gaps and key issues in her own discipline of study. She commented that prior to the internship, "I was not really sure about where I was going and how research or an academic track including research would look for me, the areas I would like to focus, and through the course of the internship, social issues, cultural competence came up as an interesting intersection, and how I can tie evaluation into my discipline and everything, kind of interesting."

Through the process of interacting with other students of color in a classroom setting, she developed the confidence to speak publicly, something she had difficulty doing in the environment of her own discipline where she was always a minority. She was then able to present at three professional conferences nationally and internationally throughout the internship year. She also volunteered and was elected to a leadership position in the student topical interest group of the American Evaluation Association, and became a student member of an editorial board for an evaluation journal. Participant C is continuing with work at the sponsoring agency beyond her internship year for purposes of her dissertation.

---

maintained. Interns are interviewed about any leadership roles they assume in the AEA or other organizations. Interviews and surveys of the interns and key informants from the affiliate organizations are conducted to determine any activities related to issues of diversity (such as any volunteer activities, presentations, student leadership positions) that the interns have participated in and how the activities have impacted the organizations. For the sponsoring agencies, we seek to find out how they have benefited from hosting an intern, and how the evaluation conducted by the intern has impacted the agency. Table 6.2 shows a list of questions and indicators for measuring impact at the organizational level.

TABLE 6.2. ORGANIZATIONAL-LEVEL OUTCOMES.

Key Evaluation Question	Evaluation Subquestions	Outcome Indicators
1. How has the program impacted the field of evaluation?	What contributions has the internship program contributed to the literature in the field of evaluation?	• Evaluation-related publications or presentations by the interns or internship staff
	What contributions has the program made toward the racial/ethnic diversity of the American Evaluation Association (AEA) leadership?	• The number of interns in leadership roles within the AEA • Evaluation-related volunteer work such as participation on student editorial board
2. How has the program impacted the sponsoring agencies?	To what extent were the evaluation goals of the agency met?	• Agency goals as listed by agency
	What were the perceived benefits by the sponsoring agency of hosting an intern?	• Benefits listed by agency staff
	What did the interns perceive as their contribution to the sponsoring agency?	• Contributions listed by intern
3. How has the program impacted the academic institutions where the interns are enrolled?	What leadership roles have the interns assumed at their academic institutions?	• Any leadership roles listed by intern
	Has the internship or intern participation in the program stimulated any discussions or engagement in diversity-related issues at the institution?	• Speeches, publications in institutional newspapers, mention of any other diversity-related academic activity

Community-Level Impact

At the community level, long-term outcomes were established that are not likely to be evident until after the interns have completed the internship and academic training and are practicing evaluators. This could be years after graduation from the internship and after the interns had engaged in many other forms of training and/or professional development, which would also contribute to the long-term impact the individuals have at a community level. To begin measuring this impact, we examine the extent to which the implementation of the program may have stimulated discussions around issues of diversity/multiculturalism within the local community where the program is located and on the communities where the interns reside. This data is collected through interviews of the interns, mentors, and academic advisors, examination of publications in local newspapers about the internship, and documentation of participation of interns in various local community organizations that advocate for the betterment of communities of color. Table 6.3 shows the list of questions and indicators for measuring community impact.

Lessons Learned

During our evaluation work with the AEA/DU pipeline initiative, several lessons arose that may serve other evaluators working in similar contexts. These lessons fall into the areas of collaboration, stakeholder involvement, data collection strategies, understanding the importance of life experiences, paying attention to context, and the measuring of long-term outcomes.

The Importance of Collaboration During the Evaluation Process

The success of pipeline efforts such as the AEA/DU internship program depends heavily on effective collaboration and on engaging all stakeholders in dialogue during program planning, implementation, and evaluation. It is critical to engage the key stakeholders early in the evaluation design and throughout the evaluation planning process as outcome measures are selected and fine-tuned. The evaluation expertise of the AEA internship evaluation design subcommittee assisted with establishing realistic outcome measures and timelines. During the collaboration process, the internship staff also learned the importance of establishing reasonable time frames for engaging very busy stakeholders such as those who served on the evaluation subcommittee. Engaging experts from the field is essential when developing the program's theory of change because such experts have valuable information on best practices and expertise about how to maximize the impact of the program and the evaluation.

TABLE 6.3. COMMUNITY-LEVEL OUTCOMES.

Key Evaluation Question	Evaluation Subquestions	Outcome Indicators
1. What is the impact of the program on the broader community?	How has the implementation of the program stimulated any events/discussions related to issues of diversity/multiculturalism at the intern's institution or at any other organizations the interns are affiliated with such as the AEA local affiliates?	• Discussions on the Duquesne campus prompted by publications in the Duquesne and local newspapers • Discussions of issues of diversity at local AEA affiliates or intern academic institutions prompted by awareness of the AEA/DU program
	What activities have the interns or program staff engaged in to promote evaluation thinking/awareness about issues of diversity/multiculturalism at the interns' institutions or other organizations they are affiliated with?	• Presentations or newspaper articles highlighting the internship focus on promoting diversity in the evaluation profession • Presentation of intern evaluation findings highlighting these issues
	Do any of the interns engage in research work that addresses issues pertaining to communities or persons of color beyond the internship evaluation project?	• Intern mention of participation in research projects pertaining to persons of color in school or as professionals
	What is the perceived contribution of the internship program to the evaluation profession?	• Contributions mentioned during the interviews with key AEA board members, TIG leaders, and key evaluation professionals
(Evaluation capacity to work in culturally, racially, ethnically diverse settings)	How many interns pursue an evaluation career working in racially, ethnically, or culturally diverse settings?	• Numbers of interns working as evaluators in racially, ethnically, or culturally diverse settings
(Creation of a pipeline of evaluators of color)	How many trainees does the internship program enroll? How many of the interns pursue a career in evaluation?	• Number of interns enrolled in program • Number of interns who complete internship • Number of interns who pursue a career in evaluation

Engaging All Stakeholders

The AEA/DU internship program utilized mentors and academic advisors, and the interns worked under the supervision of program directors. All these individuals were in demanding leadership and/or managerial positions and had very busy schedules, which required flexible scheduling of interviews for data collection. Because most leadership development pipeline efforts, especially those specifically aimed at ethnic groups, tend to have a mentoring component and collect data from mentors, it is critical to establish reasonable timelines and interview schedules that will allow their participation in the evaluation process. Advance scheduling of a month or more ahead of the interview time, with multiple reminders, and scheduling of interviews at professional meetings can enhance data collection.

Using Multiple Data Collection Methods

Even though self-reporting seems to be the most common source of data for evaluating pipeline efforts, some evaluations of pipeline efforts have used nationally available databases for baseline data and for comparison groups. Use of multiple data collection methods such as validated questionnaires in conjunction with surveys to measure acquisition of leadership competencies can help enhance the quality of data collected and expand the ability to demonstrate the effectiveness of these efforts. Even though Mason and Wetherbee (2004) recommend use of carefully designed experimental designs using trainee groups that are truly different from the target in order to improve evaluation methodologies and better isolate the effects of programs, findings from a scan of fifty-five leadership development programs by the Kellogg Foundation (2002) alert us to the fact that such experimental studies tend not to be feasible learning approaches for many leadership development programs. The tendency of leadership programs to change and evolve over the course of their implementation and to respond to the learning needs of participants makes experimental controls unworkable.

According to Connaughton and others (2003), leaders learn to apply available theory and research findings in a way that is compatible with their own personalities, skills, experiences, values, capabilities, goals, and contextual assessments. This observation has significant implications for pipeline efforts for people of color that are aimed at promoting social justice and change. Evaluation of these efforts can not afford to ignore the role of lifetime experiences in shaping the leadership development of people of color (Davidson and Johnson, 2001; Washington and others, 2004). Exhibit 6.4 illustrates how lifetime experience shaped the development of an AEA/DU intern.

Paying Attention to Context

Grove and others (2002) remind us that context is critical in the design and implementation of a program and its evaluation and in the interpretation of results. This is especially important when evaluating leadership development pipelines because these efforts are designed to develop and support diverse leaders in professions or academic disciplines. In defining outcome measures, the specific purpose of the pipeline effort for the discipline or profession needs to be established so that outcomes can be selected that highlight those goals,

EXHIBIT 6.4. CROSSING BORDERS AND NEGOTIATING EDUCATIONAL POLICY, POSTSECONDARY EDUCATION, AND EVALUATION.

Based on her own struggles as a non-English-speaking immigrant student, Participant D developed a passion to help other students with similar backgrounds navigate the education system. Her goal when entering the internship program was to establish herself as an evaluator and gain credibility with program people and the students they serve. She wanted to learn how to effectively evaluate programs that serve Latino students and find ways to give them a voice. Her sponsoring agency placement, evaluating a transitional bilingual program for Latino students at a local college, afforded her the opportunity to design and conduct an evaluation in a very politically charged environment. She learned how to negotiate her role as an evaluator, deal with multiple stakeholders who held conflicting interests, and engage the commonly ignored voices of the student participants. The coaching from her mentors, internship academic advisor, internship staff, and exchanges with other interns via the virtual classroom helped her develop invaluable problem-solving and negotiation skills. Through her evaluation work at the college she had opportunity to use her personal experiences to help some of the students navigate through their struggles. She even received a request to be a mentor for one of the students and she felt that she had learned something that she could share with other people and that would be helpful.

avoiding an overemphasis on individual-level outcomes. Both organizational-level outcomes and field-specific outcomes can highlight how the profession may be transformed by these efforts. For the AEA/DU internship program, attention was paid to the overall goal of the effort to improve diversity in the field of evaluation by tracking how the participants contributed to discussions on issues of diversity and multiculturalism in the evaluation field and what changes in awareness and attentiveness to these issues are evident within the profession and academic institutions and ultimately within communities. Addressing contextual issues in evaluation allows an examination of how the program is impacting the institutions it is affiliated with and how those institutions may be impacting the implementation of the program.

Measuring Long-Term Outcomes

The leadership development process can span many years, and determining a realistic time frame for measuring long-term outcomes, especially community-level outcomes, is a challenge. This is also complicated by the fact that competencies needed for the practice of effective leadership vary within disciplines and/or communities. Furthermore, as time passes it becomes more and more difficult to isolate direct program impacts (Connaughton and others, 2003; Mason and Wetherbee, 2004).

Conclusion

Many pipeline programs tend to be established in a collaborative manner. Because these efforts tend to be discipline specific, evaluations should pay particular attention to the program's goals, target population, and context. Evaluations that are designed and implemented well can be very valuable in establishing best practices for effective leadership within the specific discipline the pipeline program targets (Connaughton and others, 2003; Grove and others, 2002; Hernez-Broome and Hughes, 2004).

Evaluations that are outcomes oriented and process oriented are able to highlight the critical components (the leadership development methods and experiences) that are essential in attaining specific outcomes. With the influx of pipeline efforts across many disciplines, evaluations of these programs will help provide valuable data that can be used to develop discipline-specific criteria for judging effective leadership development programs, establishing standards of leadership development practice and informing policies and/or decision-making processes relating to funding of these efforts.

Evaluating pipeline development efforts such as the AEA/DU Graduate Education Diversity Internship program that aim to address issues of social change and social justice provides an opportunity to explore outcomes beyond those at the individual level. Since the ultimate goal of such a program is to see change at the systems level, evaluation of this type of program needs to look beyond the short-term individual outcomes to document the changes in organizations and communities, thus providing information that is more likely to influence policy. In documenting outcomes at the systems level, it becomes increasingly difficult to attribute these outcomes solely to the program, hence the importance of the proliferation of evaluation information from multiple sources to validate individual program evaluation findings and the need to pay special attention to the context of the program and evaluation when interpreting the results.

Resources

The American Evaluation Association (www.eval.org) is an international professional association of evaluators devoted to the application and exploration of program evaluation, personnel evaluation, technology, and many other forms of evaluation. They serve as an important resource for tools, guides, and other materials related to evaluation.

The Association of American Colleges and Universities Web site (www.aacu.org/irvinediveval/index.cfm) provides an overview of the James Irvine Foundation Campus Diversity Initiative and an evaluation of its impact. The site also has a set of evaluation resources, such as an Evaluation Project Resource Kit, to help campuses create evaluation plans to measure outcomes related to their campus diversity initiatives.

The Diversity Web (www.diversityweb.org/research_and_trends/research_evaluation_impact/index.cfm) is a Web site created by professionals devoted to promoting diversity in higher education. It has descriptions and evaluations of various diversity efforts at multiple colleges and universities, including leadership development efforts.

The University Council for Educational Administration (www.ucea.org) is a consortium of major research universities with doctoral programs in leadership and policy. Their own consideration of leadership development and preparation and extant resources are a valuable reference for designing and implementing leadership development evaluations.

The W. K. Kellogg Foundation (www.wkkf.org) offers a variety of information sets, in particular toolkits and publications related to evaluation. It is a valuable resource for both the nascent and seasoned evaluator. You will find a document entitled "Evaluating Outcomes and Impacts: A Scan of 55 Leadership Development Programs" and another entitled "EvaluLEAD: A Guide for Shaping and Evaluating Leadership Development Programs."

The Wallace Foundation (www.wallacefoundation.org) has a document entitled "Beyond the Pipeline: Getting the Principals We Need, Where They Are Needed." This policy document addresses the need to design appropriate pipelines and policies to attract principals at school districts around the country.

References

Busch, J. R. *Leadership Formation: A Multimethod Evaluation Study of the Southern Tier Leadership Academy.* Published dissertation. State University of New York at Binghamton, 2003.

Campbell, D. J., Dardis, G., and Campbell, K. M. "Enhancing Incremental Influence: A Focused Approach to Leadership Development." *Journal of Leadership and Organizational Studies,* 2003, *10*(1), 29–44.

Connaughton, S. L., Lawrence, F. L., and Ruben, B. D. "Leadership Development as a Systematic and Multidisciplinary Enterprise." *Journal of Education for Business,* 2003, *79*(1), 46–51.

Davidson, M. N., and Johnson, L. F. "Mentoring in Preparation of Graduate Researchers of Color." *Review of Educational Research,* 2001, *71*, 549–574.

Davila, N. *The Cultural Context of Educational Evaluation: The Role of Minority Evaluation Professionals.* Arlington, Va.: National Science Foundation, 2000.

Fitzpatrick, J. L., Sanders, J. R., and Worthen, B. R. *Program Evaluation: Alternative Approaches and Practical Guidelines* (3rd ed.). Boston: Allyn and Bacon, 2004.

Frierson, H. T. "The Importance of Increasing the Numbers of Individuals of Color to Enhance Cultural Responsiveness in Program Evaluation." In C. C. Yeakey and R. Henderson (eds.), *Surmounting All Odds: Education, Opportunity, and Society in the New Millennium.* Greenwich, Conn.: Information Age, 2003.

Griffin, J. B. "Developing More Minority Mathematicians and Scientists: A New Approach." *Journal of Negro Education,* 1990, *59*(3), 424–438.

Grove, J., PLP Team, and Leadership Evaluation Advisory Group (LEAG) members. *The EvaluLEAD Framework: Examining Success and Meaning: A Framework for Evaluating Leadership Interventions in Global Health.* Oakland, Calif.: Public Health Institute, 2002.

Hernez-Broome, G., and Hughes, R. L. "Leadership Development: Past, Present, and Future." *Human Resource Planning,* March 2004, 24–32.

Hood, S. "Responsive Evaluation Amistad Style: Perspectives of One African-American Evaluator." In R. Sullivan (ed.), *Proceedings of the Stake Symposium on Educational Evaluation.* Urbana-Champaign: University of Illinois at Urbana-Champaign, 1998.

Hood, S. *New Look at an Old Question: The Cultural Context of Educational Evaluation: The Role of Minority Evaluation Professionals.* Arlington, Va.: National Science Foundation, 2000.

Hood, S. "Nobody Knows My Name: In Praise of African American Evaluators Who Were Responsive." *New Directions for Evaluation,* 2001, *92,* 31–43.

Hopson, R. K. *Overview of Multicultural and Culturally Competent Program Evaluation: Issues, Challenges, and Opportunities.* Woodland Hills, Calif.: The California Endowment, 2003.

Howe, A. C., and Stubbs, H. S. "From Science Teacher to Teacher Leader: Leadership Development as Meaning Making in a Community of Practice." *Science Teacher Education,* 2001, 281–297.

"JBHE's Survey of Colleges and Universities Taking Concrete Steps to Attract Black Students." *Journal of Blacks in Higher Education,* 1999, *24,* 28–31.

Kellogg Foundation. *Evaluating Outcomes and Impacts: A Scan of 55 Leadership Development Programs.* [www.wkkf.org]. August 2002.

Kirkhart, K. E. "Seeking Multicultural Validity: A Postcard for the Road." *Evaluation Practice,* 1994, *16*(1), 1–12.

LaFrance, J. "Cultural Competent Evaluation in Indian Country." In M. Thompson-Robinson, R. Hopson, and S. SenGupta (eds.), *In Search of Cultural Competence in Evaluation.* New Directions for Evaluation, no. 102. San Francisco: Jossey-Bass, 2004.

Mason, F. M., and Wetherbee, L. V. "Learning to Lead: An Analysis of Current Training Programs for Library Leadership." *Library Trends,* 2004, *53*(1), 187–217.

McCauley, C. D., and Van Velsor, E. (eds.). *The Center for Creative Leadership Handbook of Leadership Development* (2nd ed.). San Francisco: Jossey-Bass, 2004.

Olson C. "Recruiting and Retaining Minority Graduate Students: A Systems Perspective." *Journal of Negro Education,* 1988, *57*(1), 31–42.

Packard Foundation Population Program and the Bill and Melinda Gates Foundation Global Health Program. *Guide to Evaluating Leadership Development Programs.* Seattle: Evaluation Forum, 2003.

Posavac, E. J., and Carey, R. G. *Program Evaluation: Methods and Case Studies* (5th ed.). Upper Saddle River, N.J.: Prentice Hall, 1997.

Post, L. M., and Woessner, H. "Developing a Recruitment and Retention Support System for Minority Students in Teacher Education." *Journal of Negro Education,* 1987, *56*(2), 203–211.

Roach, R. "Groomimg the 21st Century Professoriate: Despite the Challenges Posed by Anti-Affirmative Action Initiatives, the Ph.D. Pipeline Continues to Deliver a Diverse and Much Needed Group of Professors." *Black Issues in Higher Education,* 1999, *16*(18), 20.

Stanfield, J. H. "Slipping through the Front Door: Relevant Social Scientific Evaluation in the People of Color Century." *American Journal of Evaluation,* 1999, *20*(3), 415–431.

Thompson-Robinson, M., Hopson, R., and SenGupta, S. *In Search of Cultural Competence in Evaluation.* New Directions for Evaluation, no. 102. San Francisco: Jossey-Bass, 2004.

Wallen, G. R., Rivera-Goba, M. V., Hastings, C., Peragallo, N. N., and De Leon Siantz, M. "Developing the Research Pipeline: Increasing Minority Research Opportunities." *Nursing Education Perspectives,* 2005, *26*(1), 29–33.

Washington, D., Erickson, J. I., and Ditomassi, M. "Mentoring the Minority Nurse Leader of Tomorrow." *Nursing Administration Quarterly,* 2004, *28*(3), 165–169.

The Woodrow Wilson National Fellowship Foundation. *Diversity and the Ph.D.: A Review of Efforts to Broaden Race and Ethnicity in U.S. Doctoral Education.* Princeton, N.J.: Author, 2005.

CHAPTER SEVEN

FROM THE INSIDE OUT

Evaluating Personal Transformation Leadership Efforts

Sally Leiderman

Personal transformation, as it plays out in leadership development efforts, is about supporting people to act in ways that are consistent with their deepest values. These efforts are distinguished from other kinds of leadership development by their focus on learning opportunities and development strategies that encourage change from "the inside out." Typically, this means they encourage individuals to become more fully conscious of their own values and personal and cultural identities, to see themselves as the locus for decision making, and to act in ways consistent with that internal sense of self and those personal values. The working assumption is that people who become fully aware of their values will find it difficult to continue working in ways that are not consistent with those values. Personal transformation is thus occurring when individuals continually act to align their behaviors with their values.

For many personal transformation leadership development efforts, a further assumption is that community, organizational, or institutional transformation occurs when a critical mass of transformed leaders acts individually and collectively to change norms and cultures of organizations and policies and practices of institutions and systems. Leadership tasks that are frequently valued include helping others to become more aware, freer, and more willing to act from their own values and supporting organizational, institutional, and community change in the direction of more decentralized power and autonomy.

Why do people choose to create personal transformation leadership efforts? Many designers of such efforts believe that these are among the most lasting ways to stimulate community change—particularly if a critical mass of leaders can be developed and if they can sustain their transformed behaviors over time. Others believe that leaders who continually align their values with their behaviors are necessary, though not sufficient, resources for community change. Why do the designers of these programs (and their participants) feel this is so important? From a deep belief that social and organizational problems are the result, at least in part, of the failure of all of us, including people in formal and informal leadership roles, to apply consistently our deepest moral, ethical, or spiritual beliefs. Personal transformation efforts use words like *selflessness, responsibility, reciprocity, love,* and *courage* to describe these values.

In addition, many supporters (funders, designers, and program alumni) believe that the skills needed to lead in the twenty-first century, such as the capacity to work effectively with people from many cultures and backgrounds, the ability to lead toward an uncertain future, and the ability to see patterns or find the big picture from many disparate parts (Heifetz, 1994; Senge, Jaworski, Scharmer, and Flowers, 2004; Wheatley, 1999), are best explored, understood, and internalized through a process of "inside out" leadership development.

Three Examples of Personal Transformation Leadership Programs

This chapter is based primarily on evaluations of three "inside out" leadership development programs that the Center for Assessment and Policy Development has evaluated. Designers, advisors, and participants from each of these programs have contributed greatly to the insights and learning that inform this chapter. A brief description of each program follows.

Healing the Heart of Diversity

This program was designed by Dr. Patricia Harbour. At the time of its evaluation, Healing the Heart of Diversity (HHD) was structured as a series of three-day retreats that cohorts of 20–25 people attended four times over the course of a year. Each cohort was diverse with respect to gender, race/ethnicity, sexual orientation, age, and other characteristics. Participants were selected who had been responsible for diversity or similar work in corporations, educational institutions, communities, and other settings. Two three-year program cycles were evaluated. One cohort was tracked during the year it participated in HHD and for two years following; another cohort was tracked for the year it participated and one year following.

An advanced leadership development program was available to participants who completed the initial four-retreat series. HHD considers itself a transformative learning process (rather than a program) that can be offered in a variety of delivery modes and applied in a variety of settings. Since its original evaluation, HHD has conducted implementation trials to refine the methodology and practice.

The Community Leadership Program

Designed by Dr. Susan Fowler and Dr. William Graustein, the Community Leadership Program (CLP) consists of a variety of reflective, experiential, and learning activities aimed at helping strengthen and transform nonprofit leadership in New Haven, Connecticut. Its mission is to "equip, support, and inspire" these leaders "in the practice of values-based collaborative leadership." Thus far, the program has served four cohorts, with 18–20 people in each. Participants are selected from New Haven's nonprofit sector organizations and include many executive directors, along with some board members, staff, funders, and volunteers. The group is diverse with respect to years in nonprofit leadership, age, and area of work (social services, arts, and faith communities, for example) and somewhat diverse with respect to gender and race/ethnicity. (There is a preponderance of white females, reflecting the composition of nonprofit leadership in New Haven.) The program's core offering (CLP 101) focuses on spirituality and leadership development. CLP is currently developing a series of more advanced program offerings that include CLP 201, advanced coaching, spiritually based retreats, and other alumni activities designed to deepen and sustain personal transformation of participants and move toward institutionalizing the program as a resource to social transformation in New Haven. CLP built evaluation into the work from its inception and is in its fourth year of evaluation.

Americans for Indian Opportunity (AIO) Ambassadors Program

This program, designed by LaDonna Harris, Laura Harris, and an advisory group of elders and other tribal leaders, supports leadership development of midcareer Native Americans. The program offers a structured set of learning and growth experiences, relationship-building and networking activities, and other strategies consistent with the values of reciprocity, relationship, responsibility, and redistribution (referred to as the four R's). These opportunities, lessons, and experiences are delivered to cohorts of selected leaders through four weeklong gatherings, held in different parts of the country and internationally, over one or two years. The Ambassadors Program is now in its eleventh year and has graduated more than 150 Native Americans in ten cohorts. The size of the cohorts has varied over the years. Participants are drawn from around the country. Each class is diverse with respect to tribal affiliation, home location, education, the sector in which leaders are currently employed (private, public, or tribal, for example), whether or not people are currently employed (there are workers, students, family caretakers, and volunteers), and the kind of work people do (corporate executives, writers and artists, entrepreneurs, information technology, advocates, and telecommunications, for example).

Exhibit 7.1 highlights the common goals, values, and approaches of HHD, CLP, and the Ambassadors Program, along with program-specific examples.

Theoretical Framework

The three programs draw on a number of theories to support their basic goals and approaches and to develop specific program components. These include adult learning theory, theories of liberation theology and pedagogy, and theories of the role of the individual in social change. As described by Susan Fowler (one of CLP's designers), liberation theology asserts that personal transformation happens in communities where one's identity is named and affirmed. In social learning theory, learning communities become communities of practice in which people also construct their identities (create personal histories of becoming) in relationship to the community. Thus, adult learning theory drives many of the decisions about how to help the participants master new ideas and materials; theories of liberation theology and pedagogy and

EXHIBIT 7.1. GOALS, VALUES, AND
APPROACHES OF THREE LEADERSHIP PROGRAMS.

| | Program-Specific Examples | | |
Common Features	Healing the Heart of Diversity (HHD)	Community Leadership Program (CLP)	Ambassadors Program
	Goals		
• Support personal growth along path of personal transformation, leading to organizational and community change, and improved well-being of individuals in communities	• Facilitates diversity leaders in a learning process, from the inside out, as a strategy to sustain change and reconnect with the inner values that brought them to their work • Expand their ability to live with differences, make conscious changes about how to behave, and apply transformative learning to their spheres of work and influence	• Help nonprofit leaders reconnect or strengthen connections with spiritual values that led them to this work • Encourage leadership consistent with these values • Support choice to apply these values in daily work and other spheres	• Help participants get in touch with their "medicine" and apply indigenous values to leadership activities • Increase their ability to "work in two worlds" simultaneously
	Values		
• Seeking and listening to one's inner voice • Making conscious choices about how to behave • Leadership that empowers others • Leadership for community well-being, collective well-being—not personal gain	• Valuing differences and diversity of all kinds • Servant leadership • Authentic listening, action	• Liberation and freedom • Equity • Servant leadership • Faithfulness • Authentic listening, action	Indigenous values of: • Relationship • Reciprocity • Responsibility • Redistribution

EXHIBIT 7.1. GOALS, VALUES, AND APPROACHES OF THREE LEADERSHIP PROGRAMS, Cont'd.

Common Features	Program-Specific Examples		
	Healing the Heart of Diversity (HHD)	Community Leadership Program (CLP)	Ambassadors Program
	Approach		
• Recruit and invite participants • Development of community (learning in relationship with others) • Periodic gatherings/retreats • Facilitated learning and self-directed learning • Storytelling • Reflection • Experiences • Network and relationship building • Sustained alumni networks • Assessment	(As originally designed): • Quarterly 2–4 day retreats over a year • Facilitation, ritual, exercises, reflection, journaling • "Train the trainers" model for alumni to replicate or adopt aspects for their work • African trip for alumni and trainers	• Monthly gatherings and two retreats over 10 months • Guest speakers and ongoing facilitation • Readings, reflection papers • Adult learning model • Consideration of multiyear design (in development) • Consideration of joint action (in development)	• Four-six gatherings over 12–14 months • Each session in a different location for a different purpose: reservation, Washington, D.C., New York, international with another indigenous leadership group (for example, Maori) • Alumni mentors • Community action project

theories of the role of the individual in social change help the programs develop materials, exercises, and experiences that help participants connect more deeply to their individual and group identities, surface their values, and align their behaviors with them.

An excerpt from a research brief written for HHD by Davido Dupree (see Exhibit 7.2) summarizes some of the key theoretical assumptions for that program that apply equally to other personal transformation leadership efforts.

The language of the people who design and participate in personal transformation efforts often reflects the focus on inner change leading to outer change. In particular, there is an openness to spiritual and values-based language. For example, in HHD, Patricia Harbour speaks of leading from

EXHIBIT 7.2. EXCERPT FROM HEALING
THE HEART OF DIVERSITY RESEARCH BRIEF.

Evaluation of HHD rests on a model or theory of transformation and change de-veloped from a set of assumptions. These assumptions address (1) consciousness (authentic change is a conscious choice that is a result of awareness and experi-ence); (2) consciousness and empowerment (when individuals make a conscious commitment to change inwardly, they take action outwardly); and (3) conscious-ness and healing (authentic interaction with others of different backgrounds may lead to inner awareness that contributes to individual and social change healing). In the context of the leadership development retreats, consciousness refers to *awareness.* Thus, changes in consciousness involve becoming more aware of that which one was previously unaware. A collection of readings on consciousness, *From Sentience to Symbols: Readings on Consciousness* (Pickering and Skinner, 1990) sug-gests that the ability to articulate what one is thinking or feeling is an aspect of emerging awareness. It is not that labeling experiences, feelings, and events with words brings them into existence, but rather that the meaning or significance of one's experiences, feelings, and events becomes much more evident as a result. Consciousness can represent a growing awareness of oneself, others, or the rela-tionships between oneself and others. Duval and Wicklund (1972) propose that a necessary condition for becoming conscious of oneself as a causal agent is to become aware that there are perceptions, thoughts, and behaviors that differ from one's own. That is, people are not necessarily aware of their own thoughts, per-ceptions, and behaviors until they are brought into conflict with the thoughts, perceptions, and behaviors of others. In HHD there is inquiry around diversity-related issues during the retreats. The retreats essentially serve as a laboratory in which participants develop an agreed-upon way of interacting with others of diverse backgrounds during the retreats. Further, there is the opportunity for par-ticipants to become aware of the meaning and significance of their words and actions for others of diverse backgrounds.

within, authentic communication, conscious awareness, healing, and "doing your own work" as ways to increase the skills needed to work effectively across similarities and differences (which include race, culture, gender, sexual ori-entation, physical and cognitive ability, and class). The CLP designers and many of its participants talk about love and courage as two of the essential ingredients of community change. The Ambassadors Program designers and many of its participants talk about understanding one's medicine and the four R's of indigenous values (reciprocity, relationship, responsibility, and redistribution).

Evaluation of Personal Transformation Leadership Development Efforts

As one might expect, there are a number of learning and methodological opportunities and challenges to evaluating these kinds of efforts. These are essentially of two kinds: (1) expanding what we know about the relationship, if any, between individual-level change and changes in organizations, institutions, systems, and communities; and (2) furthering the capacity to capture or measure changes that are often thought of as ineffable or intangible; for example, changes in consciousness or the role of spirit in transformation. This challenge is exacerbated by the need to consider different ways that people know things: intuitively, through experience, as expressions of cultural beliefs; in culturally or spiritually specific language, such as parables or stories; or through artistic expression. Many of these ways of knowing are not highly valued in traditional evaluations (that is, Western, white, counting-type evaluations). (See, for example, Potapchuk, Leiderman, Bivens, and Major, 2006.)

Evaluation Opportunities and Challenges

Evaluation provides an opportunity to examine whether or not, and under what circumstances, personal transformation does occur and to what end. Does inner change lead to outer change (sometimes called "ways of being in the world") and changes in leadership behaviors? (For two stories of how participants in personal transformation programs have aligned their values with their behaviors, see Exhibits 7.3 and 7.4.) What would a critical mass of leaders (or leadership) look like, and how would that contribute to a fundamental and sustained community change?

Evaluation can also shed light on the minimum bundle of opportunities, supports, incentives, and strategies it takes to promote and sustain individual-level transformation. Programs try many different components in different sequences to stimulate personal transformation. Evaluation could help programs be more efficient by identifying necessary elements and the intensity and duration of interventions that are sufficient to create the desired outcomes. Similarly, evaluation could help programs learn more about which strategies are

EXHIBIT 7.3. A STORY FROM A CLP PARTICIPANT.

In a nutshell, my agency had a contract to work with women receiving public assistance who were required to seek and retain employment in the face of significant obstacles. The contracting agent changed the scope of the contract and released a competitive request for proposal (RFP). In order to win the contract we would have had to submit a program design that would not have been in the best interest of the families to be served. We elected to submit what we believed to be a project design that would meet the outcome requirements of the contractor and serve the most vulnerable families in a fashion that afforded them some protection and support. We were not awarded the contract and we were told that it was because we did not integrate a key component of the system that we believed would harm families. Pre-CLP, I would have given the contractor what they wanted and then attempted to work within unreasonable constraints, taxing the organization and the staff. Articulating values and then operating from a values-driven place grounded decisions in the domain of human development rather than a marketplace perspective.

EXHIBIT 7.4. A STORY FROM AN AIO PARTICIPANT.

As an AIO alumnus, I have developed a deeper appreciation of my Native identity, a deeper sense of indigenous pride balanced with humility, and developed an outspoken voice for maintaining and building Native cultural identity and values as a stronghold for indigenous cultural perseverance. I instill this daily with my children, have instilled it in all my postsecondary papers and projects, and again daily with my colleagues and in my job. The AIO experience helped contribute to my knowledge and ability to do my professional work, which is working specifically with indigenous cultures and communities first, hemispherically at the National Museum of the American Indian, and now worldwide at National Geographic. I continue to keep abreast of the changing and current issues of indigenous people throughout the world due to my involvement in AIO, which first exposed me to the indigenous plight nationally and then internationally, both in tribal and urban settings.

necessary and sufficient to help create a critical mass of transformed leaders in a given place or directed at a given issue and the costs and benefits of doing so.

As people continue to offer personal transformation leadership development efforts and evaluate them, more opportunities exist to look across programs to build a base of knowledge about the common landscape or path of individual transformation. One way to do this is for programs to become involved in learning circles, such as the one described in Chapter Eighteen, devoted to this kind of information sharing and meaning making.

Multiple ways of knowing require diverse methods to capture the breadth and depth of changes that programs seek. For example, can storytelling more effectively and more systematically link individual change to community change? Can journaling, along with observation, measure inner change rigorously but efficiently? If people express much of their consciousness and values in art (as is true for some Native Americans), can that medium, along with more traditional methods, track personal transformation and leadership growth (or can we even use art alone for that purpose)?

Another methodological challenge is to develop generally accepted markers of individual and social transformation—in terms of leadership behaviors, actions, and their consequences—that are acceptable to funders and other stakeholders, and that are also consistent with the values and ways of knowing of the programs' designers and participants. That is, can questions be appropriately addressed, such as, What is success? Who says so? What evidence is acceptable to see whether or not it is occurring?

These opportunities and challenges are explored more fully in the remainder of this chapter, along with some tips for addressing them that have been garnered from experience.

Common Types of Evaluations

The most common evaluations of personal transformation leadership efforts are process or implementation evaluations, individual-level outcome evaluations, and organizational- or community-level outcome evaluations. Process or implementation evaluations are typically done to support program start-up, implementation, midcourse reflection, and replication. They often focus on the extent to which programs are able to enroll their intended participants; implement individual and collective processes that help individuals become more consciously aware of their assumptions, beliefs, and values; and take part in activities and experiences that encourage individuals to align their behaviors with those values. For a list of questions that are often asked in process or implementation evaluations, see Exhibit 7.5.

Outcome evaluations almost always focus on individual-level outcomes (the extent to which participants appear to be moving in a transformative di-

EXHIBIT 7.5. QUESTIONS FOR PROCESS OR IMPLEMENTATION EVALUATIONS.

Program Participation

- Is the program serving the people it wants to serve?

- Is their recruitment and selection process working as intended?

- Is their group diverse with respect to the characteristics, experiences, and perspectives they care about?

- Are they retaining certain types of participants but not others?

Program Implementation

- Are they implementing the program as designed?

- Are they putting in place each of the intended components?

- Do these program components meet research or best practice standards of quality?

- Are they of sufficient duration and intensity to meet what research suggests is required to stimulate consciousness awareness of values and efforts to align values with behaviors?

- Do they include individual and collective practices of reflection, dialogue, action?

Program Effects

- Are people taking up what we are offering?

- Are they learning what we are teaching?

- Are they engaging in the practices we believe lead to transformation (self-reflection, authentic engagement with others, questioning the alignment of one's values with one's behaviors, and so on?

- What lessons are they learning about how to improve the quality of implementation and their immediate results?

rection and/or are changing their behaviors to align with their values). The types of questions that are asked in individual-level outcome evaluations are featured in Exhibit 7.6.

Some evaluations also look at changes in the organizations, systems, or communities of which the leaders are a part or where they exert influence. Sample questions that focus on organizations, systems, and communities may be found in Exhibit 7.7.

EXHIBIT 7.6. QUESTIONS FOR OUTCOME EVALUATIONS THAT CAPTURE INDIVIDUAL CHANGE.

Inner Change

- What relevant inner changes are individuals experiencing in terms of conscious awareness of their values, identity, calling, and sense of service?

- What relevant inner changes are individuals experiencing in terms of attitudes, assumptions, beliefs, and knowledge relevant to the particular personal transformation leadership development program (for example, assumptions about people of different cultures than one's own (HHD); beliefs about how systems are transformed (CLP); knowledge of Indian history and sovereign rights (Ambassadors)?

Behavioral Change

- What relevant behaviors are individuals changing in terms of specific leadership skills? For example, is there evidence of authentic listening that creates opportunities for deep connection with others (HHD); of increased storytelling, of looking for the big picture while in the midst of organizational change (CLP); of organizing and carrying out an effective community change project (Ambassadors)?

- What actions are individuals taking in terms of increased or reduced leadership? For example, are they participating in a train-the-trainers facilitation program and taking HHD principles into new organizations (HHD); taking on new board positions or leaving jobs where they recognize that they are not effective (CLP); establishing projects where they are explicitly giving back to the Native American community, such as establishing a philanthropy that supports young Native American writers (Ambassadors)?

Aligning Values and Behavior

- In what ways are individuals aligning their values with their behaviors? For example, are they changing the board composition of an organization that does antiracism work so that people of color are leading the organization (HHD); working with staff of a nonprofit organization to articulate the organization's values and change its way of working with clients to reflect those values (CLP); exchanging a private sector health care position for a tribal health care leadership role (Ambassadors)?

- To what extent does it appear that the program is contributing to these changes in individuals? What proportions of participants experience these kinds of changes?

EXHIBIT 7.7. QUESTIONS FOR OUTCOME EVALUATIONS THAT CAPTURE ORGANIZATIONAL OR COMMUNITY CHANGE.

Leadership Contributions

- How and to what extent are transformed leaders directly contributing to change in the places where they have influence; for example, in the places where they have roles of positional leadership, or in their work, family, and community networks?

Critical Mass of Leaders

- How and to what extent does the existence of a critical mass of transformed leaders contribute to changes more broadly; for example, in organizations, institutions, systems, and communities?

Organizational, Institutional, and Systemic Changes

- Do we observe changes at the organizational, institutional, system, or community level consistent with the values of participants and the programs? Are organizational norms and cultures more empowering? Are there changes in the decision-making processes of public institutions and systems, or reduced privilege and oppression, for example?

Community Change

- What role do these personal transformation leadership efforts play in more comprehensive change strategies; that is, strategies that attempt to change an outcome at the community level (for example, the well-being of children; the redistribution of mineral rights) through attention to leadership as well as public engagement, system reform, policy work, and the like?

The most helpful outcome evaluations look at both individual- and community-, system-, or organizational-level outcomes, and they do so over a sufficient time period to determine whether or not individual changes are sustained after the initial flush of program effects and whether or not individual changes contribute to changes at broader levels. Typically this means examining change at least one to three years after the completion of the program. It can occur much longer afterward if community- and systems-level change is to be captured to allow change, if it is going to occur, to show up in systems- or community-level data (for example, improved rates of high school graduation, improved health outcomes for older citizens, or reallocation of funds that support housing).

It is useful to note that different personal transformation leadership development efforts place different weight on the importance (or even appropriateness) of holding themselves accountable (in an evaluative sense) for changes beyond those at the individual level. All of the personal transformation programs the Center for Assessment and Policy Development (CAPD) has evaluated have a desired outcome that participants move from changes in attitudes to changes in behaviors, and the staff of these programs is comfortable incorporating that expectation into the evaluation. Each program also hopes that participants will act in ways that promote social change (moving from personal transformation to social transformation). Further discussion about evaluating social change initiatives can be found in Chapter Thirteen. However, most consider this a long-term, not a short-term, goal, that is outside their immediate control. They also recognize that, by its nature, personal transformation that promotes freedom and autonomy encourages leaders to move in directions they set for themselves. Thus, while they are interested in tracking whether or not organizational, institutional, system, or community change occurs, they do not judge themselves as programmatic failures if these changes do not occur in a short time frame, and they are comfortable with outcomes not anticipated by evaluation.

Beyond these basic types of evaluation, there are some others that are rarely, if ever, undertaken. Doing them, however, would contribute substantially to our learning. For example, long-term and longitudinal evaluations could be implemented to track patterns of fading effects and the results of efforts to sustain or reinforce effects (for example, through alumni activities). Evaluations that incorporate social network analyses could review the extent to which individual connections forged or strengthened in personal transformation leadership development efforts contribute to organizational-, institutional-, system-, or community-level change.

Suggestions for the Field

Quasi-experimental evaluations of personal transformation leadership development efforts could systematically vary program components for randomly assigned cohorts and begin to tease out the value of particular program components. This information would be particularly useful for program designers, who are often asking what contribution a particular, and often expensive, component (international travel, four weeklong residential retreats a year) makes to the overall results of the program.

More cross-program evaluations and meta-analyses that look at individual and organizational, institutional, system and/or community changes across a number of personal transformation development efforts would also contribute greatly to our knowledge. These approaches can help separate findings and trends that are common across programs from those that are idiosyncratic to a particular program or approach. Even more important, these types of evaluation would help clarify

- A minimum bundle of personal transformation experiences, curricula, and programming necessary and sufficient to achieve individual outcomes
- A minimum bundle of change activities, including personal transformation leadership development efforts as one strategy, necessary and sufficient to achieve organizational-, institutional-, system-, or community-level change

Methodological Considerations

There are a number of special methodological considerations for evaluations of personal transformation efforts related to design, data collection and analysis, and to the use of the results of personal transformation leadership development evaluations. Some lessons about design from the evaluations of HHD, CLP, and the Ambassadors Program that might apply broadly are discussed next.

All of CAPD's evaluations of personal transformation leadership development efforts begin with support to program designers to articulate their theory of change (see Chapter Two); that is, to lay out in a formal manner the path by which they expect their strategies to produce their intended outcomes. Theories of change are useful in many evaluation contexts. Our experience suggests they are particularly helpful in designing evaluations of personal transformation programs. In our experience, designers of personal transformation efforts are often quite intuitive, with a strong understanding of the factors that support individual growth and change. They are able to trust that individuals with skills, values, and consciousness about their own identities, attitudes, and behavior will act in ways that can bring about positive change. The flip side is that often these same people tend not to think in linear terms and may not articulate (and may even resist articulating) short-, intermediate, and long-term outcomes for their work. This is often unsatisfactory to funders who sponsor people to attend personal transformation leadership efforts and others who demand "bottom-line"-type evaluations of programs. Theory of change pictures can be a bridge between these different ways of knowing. However, it is essential to do this in a way that fully respects the core values and assumptions of the program and accurately represents the designers' intents and understanding of how transformative learning is supported (for example, that people choose to change themselves, they are not changed by others [HHD]; that relationships are wealth [Ambassadors Program]; and that aligning one's values with one's behaviors may cause nonprofit leaders to reduce their formal leadership positions [CLP]). In addition, it means leaving room for the serendipitous, assuming that patterns will emerge from many different paths of individual transformation, and anticipating that change, resistance to change, backsliding, and forward progress mean that things may not happen in straightforward ways.

One effective way to help people do this kind of articulation is through the process of developing theory of change pictures and logic models. A *theory of change picture* typically lays out the strategies of an effort, the processes by which the program believes change will happen as a consequence of implementing these changes, and the expected results. It focuses on describing the program's assumptions and the relationships among them. A *logic model* lays out the ways in which change will be measured by specifying short-term, intermediate, and long-term outcomes. Figures 7.1, 7.2, and 7.3 illustrate three such representations. Figure 7.1 is a theory of change picture for CLP, Figure 7.2 is a logic model for CLP, and Figure 7.3 is a logic model for the Ambassadors Program. All of these are works in progress in constant revision, based in part on lessons from each evaluation.

The theory of change and logic model for CLP were developed over the course of several years, based on meetings with the program's designers and refined by discussions with a group of program advisors, many of whom are alumni of the program. They were also influenced by findings from the first year of evaluation. The program advisors and designers use these as touchstones for their planning work, and are considered works in progress. For example, the designers and advisors to CLP regularly revisit their theory of change and logic model to see if the strategies they are proposing are likely to be sufficient to produce the changes they intend. The flexibility to change the theory of change and logic model is one way to bridge between stakeholders who want to track change in a linear way and stakeholders who see change as an emergent, somewhat unpredictable process.

The Ambassadors Program has gathered stories around the outcomes in their logic model. They examine these stories to see if they are aligning their own programmatic behaviors with their values. The logic model was developed at a meeting of Ambassadors alumni, using an interactive discussion method developed by AIO. The method is built on indigenous decision-making processes that are intended to incorporate each voice in a gathering and establish a group consensus on priorities for action. The process begins with a question posed by the facilitator. Each person in the group gives one response. The group continues responding one at a time, going around the circle as many times as necessary to capture each person's full number of responses. To develop the Ambassadors' logic model, we asked people what questions we could ask of Ambassador participants (current and alumni) to capture the program's "medicine"—an indigenous term for the experiences, values, and forces that drive a person's life choices or a program's results. The results of the process became the frame for the outcomes noted in the logic model.

Another design task, particularly for individual-level outcome evaluations, is to develop a set of markers or outcome indicators that can help track movement along a path of individual transformation. A set of individual-level markers has been developed to guide all three evaluations (see Exhibit 7.8). These markers are based on an analysis of the common experiences of these three programs, a parent leadership development component of the Children's First Initiative, and the development of task force members in the Project Change antiracism initiative. In addition to program-level analysis, we also reflected on the theoretical assumptions that inform the program design in order to suggest a set of steps that occur along the path of personal transformation.

It should be noted that while these steps are presented as if they might occur in sequence, in fact, individuals experience them at their own pace. For example, some individuals immediately try out listening, storytelling, and other similar leadership skills well before they solidify their self-identification as a leader. However, across programs, in general, transformative Steps 1–3 can be observed for many participants while they are in the program, Steps 5–8 shortly thereafter (within a year), and Steps 9–12 within a year or two of

FIGURE 7.1. CLP EVOLVING THEORY OF CHANGE.

Process by Which Developed

Listened to NH nonprofit leaders; response to their felt need

Mission

CLP's mission is to equip, support, and inspire each other in the practice of values-based collaborative leadership

NH Context

Top down, business model, funder and numbers driven, competitive, more needs, fewer resources, burnout

(January 2005)

Create and convene Kitchen Cabinet

Create and implement engaging communication strategies

Identify and recruit participants via influentials, alumni, communication, word of mouth

Plan and implement program components (CLP 101, 201, and alumni activities)

Create and implement strategies for accountability, learning, and midcourse correction via evaluation, quarterly reports/conversations, and review of best practices

CLP 101

Creates space for change

Love fosters energy and courage that allows people to change themselves

Transformational leadership development

Internal spiritual transformation leads to social transformation

Community develops among participants that leads to peer support, opportunities for reinforcement of internal changes, allies and networks

Participants go deeper, acquire new skills, reinforce changes, strengthen ties

→ to A

Designers and the Kitchen Cabinet identify CLP core values, minimum bundle of program components to achieve intentions, criteria for new components

→ to B

The team has access to insights, stories, results, challenges, and lessons from regular reporting, meetings, informal communication, and evaluation, makes meaning from the results and acts on them

→ to C

Source: Community Leadership Program, New Haven, Conn.

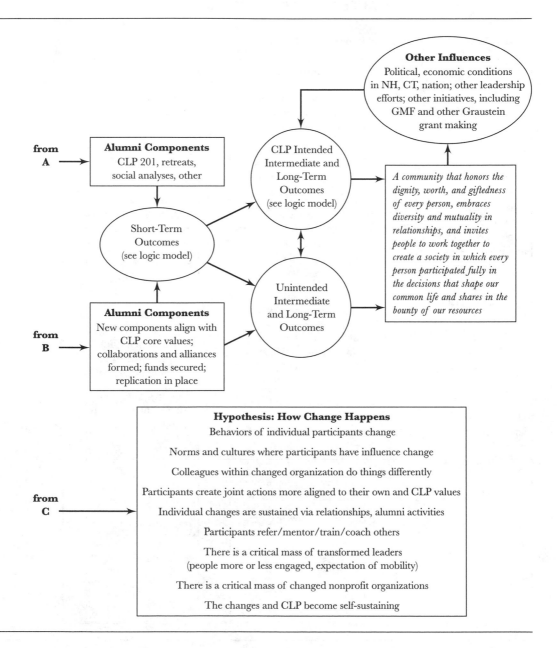

Other Influences
Political, economic conditions in NH, CT, nation; other leadership efforts; other initiatives, including GMF and other Graustein grant making

from
A

Alumni Components
CLP 201, retreats, social analyses, other

Short-Term Outcomes
(see logic model)

CLP Intended Intermediate and Long-Term Outcomes
(see logic model)

A community that honors the dignity, worth, and giftedness of every person, embraces diversity and mutuality in relationships, and invites people to work together to create a society in which every person participated fully in the decisions that shape our common life and shares in the bounty of our resources

from
B

Alumni Components
New components align with CLP core values; collaborations and alliances formed; funds secured; replication in place

Unintended Intermediate and Long-Term Outcomes

Hypothesis: How Change Happens

Behaviors of individual participants change

Norms and cultures where participants have influence change

Colleagues within changed organization do things differently

Participants create joint actions more aligned to their own and CLP values

from
C

Individual changes are sustained via relationships, alumni activities

Participants refer/mentor/train/coach others

There is a critical mass of transformed leaders
(people more or less engaged, expectation of mobility)

There is a critical mass of changed nonprofit organizations

The changes and CLP become self-sustaining

FIGURE 7.2. CLP LOGIC MODEL.

Mission: Equip, support, and inspire each other in the practice of values-based leadership

Inputs	Activities	Outputs
Ideas about how personal, organizational, and social change happen	Recruit and invite 20 leaders of nonprofit organizations to participate in CLP	Sessions implemented that are responsive and of high quality
Focused series of conversations with executives and observers of nonprofit organizations in New Haven about their opportunities, challenges, and needs as nonprofit leaders	Create syllabus, speakers, readings, reflection paper opportunities, exercises	Participants attend and engage in activities
	Implement monthly meetings and two retreats with intentional individual and group exercises, reflection, and discussion	Participants actively contribute to the content, inquiry, conversations, tone, inclusiveness of the sessions
Information (about leadership, personal transformation, spirituality in the workplace)	Facilitate sessions by responding to opportunities, guiding discussions, and being "in the moment" with the group	Participants form a community of shared inquiry and reflection
Experience, skills, intentions of the designers and facilitators	Refine syllabus as work proceeds, based on previous sessions, reflection, additional information, and inquiry	Alumni group forms and creates additional momentum for infusion of CLP learning into nonprofit organizations
Context: Existing leadership norms, values, reward structures, and behaviors; climate for nonprofit work in New Haven	Facilitate development of CLP alumni organization	Alumni organize and implement a collective action
	Create multiyear CLP program	
	Assess process and outcomes at baseline and follow-up	

 to A

Source: Community Leadership Program, New Haven, Conn.

Mission: Equip, support, and inspire each other in the practice of values-based leadership

Initial Outcomes	Intermediate Outcomes	Long-Term Outcomes
Participants are satisfied with what they have gained from the program	Individual organizations in which participating leaders and alumni work or in which they have influence as leaders change as a result of leadership actions and the manner in which participants do their work	Increased demand among leaders in New Haven for leadership development of this kind
Participants become resources to each other		CLP approach is shared and aspects are incorporated into leadership development ideas more generally
Participants are increasingly self-aware and more conscious and grounded in their choices with respect to leadership and nonprofit work	Participants are motivated to take new actions related to leadership and nonprofit work (or maintain current actions rather than "burning out")	Norms and cultures of nonprofit work (leadership) in New Haven are changed in ways consistent with this work
Participants challenge their current approaches to leadership and nonprofit work	Participants feel themselves to be more effective leaders	Changes in nonprofit leadership among CLP participants result in demonstrable benefits to people whom they serve
A Participants further consider the role of spirituality and their own sense of "calling" in their choices of action	Participants apply new leadership skills in their work	
Participants learn skills and different ways of thinking about how to be a leader	Participants apply new leadership skills in places where they have influence (boards, volunteer activities, networks)	
Participants become more aware of alignment among their values, roles, and actions in nonprofit leadership	Participants see themselves moving along a path toward greater alignment between how they want to lead and their activities	
Participants strengthen community within the group		

FIGURE 7.3. AMBASSADORS PROGRAM LOGIC MODEL.

Inputs	Activities	Short-Term Outcomes
Support from multiple funders	Community project experience	Participants have opportunities for leadership through relationships and networks linked in some way to their participation in the Ambassadors Program
Interest in developing leaders who could bring their Native values into their leadership activities	International experience	
	Washington, D.C./NYC experience	Communities begin to benefit in tangible ways from community projects
Recognition of a need to support the development of successive generations of Native American leaders	Mentoring	
	Tribal experience	Participants begin to recognize a change in their purpose in life
	Activities to develop leadership skills	Participants exercise leadership skills and values developed through the Ambassadors Program in other spheres of their lives (home, work, artistic, and cultural spheres)
Input from advisors and friends of the program	Activities to build community among each cohort	
The leadership traits that were instilled in the daughters of LaDonna Harris (the founders) as a consequence of their exposure to indigenous values, Native and other leaders, Indian advocacy and the spirit that flowed through the people, places, and other people to which they were exposed	Activities to understand your medicine	
	Selection of each cohort	Participants' relationships to their tribes are changed
	Curriculum design	Participants' relationships with their families, peers, coworkers, community are changed in ways that reflect indigenous values
	Overall program planning and planning for each cohort	
		Participants' actions embody indigenous values in ways that can be recognized by others
Individual medicine of the program's designers and advisors		Participants have increased confidence in their ability to lead and make a contribution through leadership that embodies indigenous values
Native American cultural values (the four R's): reciprocity, relationship, responsibility, and redistribution		Participants have increased awareness about global issues and global indigenous leadership and culture
		Reciprocal relationships are built among participants
		Individual participants reflect stronger knowledge of their own medicine

 to A

Source: Americans for Indian Opportunity, Albuquerque, New Mexico; www.aio.org.

Intermediate Outcomes

Ambassador alumni help others build different kinds of relationships and pass along skills and values developed within the program

Tribes and other organizations recognize the benefits of the training and seek out Ambassador alumni for tribal affairs and leadership

Ambassadors use their networks to take actions that are consistent with indigenous values and that benefit their communities

Ambassadors use their relationships to take actions on behalf of indigenous people domestically and internationally

A

Ambassadors choose to maintain formal ties to the program through alumni participation

Ambassadors give back to the Ambasssadors Program

Ambassadors maintain the relationships that were developed through the program

Ambassadors take steps that reflect movement toward their changed purpoзc in life

Ambassadors' nature, level, and quality of service to their tribe changes

Ambassadors maintain the leadership skills they developed

Community projects deepen and provide stronger benefits to their communities

Long-Term Outcomes

Communities benefit economically, culturally, or in other ways from activities led in part by Ambassadors

Ambassadors affect national policy

Ambassadors affect tribal policies

Communities in which Ambassador alumni live, work, and practice their culture and spirituality recognize benefits from the Ambassadors' participation in the program

EXHIBIT 7.8. INDIVIDUAL-LEVEL PERSONAL TRANSFORMATION OUTCOMES.

1. Deepened consciousness of one's values

2. Heightened awareness of the strengths of one's racial, ethnic, or cultural identity, heritage, or history

3. Ability to hold opposing points of view without having to reconcile them

4. Ability to put into words some aspects of leadership that one was vaguely aware of, but unable to articulate before

5. Increased sense of global consciousness, identification and solidarity with different others, and willingness and capacity to engage deeply with them

6. Increased sense of oneself as a leader

7. Increased awareness of leadership capacities in a wider variety of people

8. Compelling need to align one's values with one's daily behaviors

9. Greater use of deep listening, storytelling, and other skills offered by the programs as a way to forge more authentic connections or relationships with others

10. Feeling more connected to other individuals through relationships that are often less power-driven or hierarchical than previous relationships

11. Acting to change norms and cultures of organizations, systems, or communities or taking other public and political actions consistent with one's values

12. Taking steps to reinforce these behavioral changes (for example, finding peer supports, through introspection and spiritual practices, or by changing jobs or life situations)

13. Expressing and acting on a calling to give back to one's own group or community

14. Inviting others into the circumstances that promoted one's own transformative process (encouraging family members, work colleagues, other leaders to explore similar opportunities)

being in the program, particularly if they continue to be involved in reinforcing activities.

Another key issue in design is to establish the methods by which information will be obtained and analyzed. As is true for any evaluation, there are always technical, resource, and political issues to consider. The design task often becomes a process of trade-offs among these issues, a way to find the intersection that best meets the needs of key audiences, answers the research questions at an appropriate level of rigor and detail, and makes best use of available resources. The case example below illustrates how these dynamics can play out in an evaluation context.

Case Example: HHD Evaluation Design

Key audiences for the HHD evaluation include the board of the foundation that funded its original development. The program was originally developed to support professionals who were diversity consultants or trainers. Many of these potential participants expressed a need to push their own "edges" forward; for example, to address their own internalized superiority or racism or homophobia, to heal from deep feelings of anger, or to regain a sense of the efficacy of the work given constant resistance to it. While the designers and the original groups of participants reported very positive effects from their participation in the program, the board was skeptical about these reports because they were based solely on participant self-reporting. The board wanted an evaluation that had a strong theoretical framework and that could help it determine whether the results were attributable to the program or to the self-selection bias of the participants who chose to participate.

An important part of the design work was to illustrate to the board and the program designers what evaluation could and could not accomplish. For example, without random assignment, evaluation could not eliminate self-selection biases and isolate program impact. Both the program designers and the board recognized that random assignment was not a cost-effective or feasible evaluation strategy. Rather than randomly assign participants, stakeholders decided to use qualitative methods to explore with participants their reasons for applying to HHD, what they knew about the program in advance of participating, their expectations of benefits, what other options they explored, and other information that would help understand how self-selection might influence program effects. In addition, these data could be used to help create a profile of readiness for the program: What kind of participant is attracted to and benefits from this kind of program?

Another key challenge was trying to measure changes in consciousness, a critical part of HHD's theory of change (and that of most personal transformation efforts). To do that, one of the evaluation team members, Davido Dupree, a cognitive psychologist, reviewed literature on metacognition, behavior change, and transpersonal psychology. The results of that review, and some exploratory individual in-depth interviews, were used to create agree/disagree statements to help participants articulate changes in awareness, attitudes, and behaviors they might have experienced. Examples of these types of statements may be found in Exhibit 7.9.

EXHIBIT 7.9. AGREE/DISAGREE STATEMENTS
FOR EVALUATING THE IMPACT OF THE HHD PROGRAM.

- I became more aware of how my thoughts, attitudes, and beliefs influence my actions with respect to people of different racial and ethnic heritages, genders, religious beliefs, sexual orientation, and so on.

- I have a greater understanding of what personal action I can take to improve the quality of life for and among people of different racial and ethnic heritages, genders, religious beliefs, sexual orientation, and so on.

- I have forgiven a person or persons for any pain, confusion, or conflict they may have caused me with respect to my identity as a person of a particular racial and ethnic heritage, gender, religious belief, sexual orientation, and so on. (If not applicable, please indicate.)

- I have forgiven myself for any pain, confusion, conflict, and so on I may have caused others with respect to their identity as a person of a particular racial and ethnic heritage, gender, religious beliefs, sexual orientation, and so on. (If not applicable, please indicate.)

- I felt the freedom to speak and behave in ways that are indicative of the way I identify myself in terms of racial and ethnic heritage, gender, religious beliefs, sexual orientation, and so on.

- There was an experience that had such an emotional impact on me that it has influenced my thinking and actions with respect to people of different racial and ethnic heritages, genders, religious beliefs, sexual orientation, and so on.

Before finalizing the evaluation design, the program's designer invited the evaluation team to go through a full program sequence as a participant. The designer felt that this experience would give the evaluators a much deeper understanding of the nature of the work and its potential effects, thus broadening the evaluators' ability to design an evaluation that would know what to look for in terms of the full range of potential outcomes. This turned out to be a powerful strategy. It informed the areas of theory reviewed and the instruments that were developed to look at steps along a path of personal transformation. It suggested new data collection options; for example, conducting an in-depth follow-up interview at six months and a year after the program. Those interviews looked at the extent to which the immediate glow of program effects was sustained over time, steps participants took to reinforce changes, and whether or not individual-level outcomes translated to organizational- or community-level outcomes. Participation in the program thus enabled the evaluators to more effectively address the skepticism of the board.

Conclusion

The basics of good evaluation, particularly theory of change evaluations, apply to evaluation of personal transformation leadership efforts. However, there are some special considerations that also must be taken into account if evaluations of personal transformation efforts are to provide useful information at high levels of rigor. Key challenges include developing culturally competent measurements of individual-level change, especially of inner change or changes in consciousness, and of changes in awareness, consciousness, or attitudes that are linked with changes in individual behaviors. Other evaluation challenges include linking individual-level change to organizational-, system-, and community-level change, findings ways to incorporate and value multiple ways by which people know things, establishing reasonable expectations for what can and cannot be measured, and using creative and multiple methods to do so.

CAPD has learned something about how to do these things and something about approaches that are helpful. For example, CAPD has several articulated theories of change and logic models from personal transformation efforts on which to draw. These illustrate typical concepts, components, and outcomes. We are beginning to develop some useable markers along a path of transformation. These markers are consistent with personal transformation theory and with the theories that program designers are using in their personal transformation leadership efforts. They also seem to accurately reflect the kinds of individual changes that are being observed. In addition, we are beginning to take greater advantage of different kinds of data collection (storytelling; 360-degree observations of leaders; tracking social networks of program alumni and their links to changes in organizations, systems, and communities) that reflect a wider range of culturally valued evidence. Thus, there is a lot of evaluation experience on which to build.

At the same time, there are many opportunities to push the state of the art further. As evaluators, we support meta-analyses and synthesis of our learning across personal transformation programs. This might help us develop better ways of describing and measuring inner change, how inner change leads to changes in individual behaviors, and how changes in individual behaviors contribute to changes in systems, organizations, and communities.

In addition, we advocate for long-term evaluations that allow us to look at how and under what circumstances leaders are able to sustain their own transformation and support the transformation of others. We also advocate for the kinds of evaluations that will allow us to better describe the ratio of program costs to benefits, taking a very nuanced and broad look at the contribution of particular program components and the full range of benefits that accrue. All of this is within our current state of the art as evaluators.

Finally, we can challenge ourselves very particularly on some key questions. As evaluators, we can continually ask ourselves:

- What views of how the world works are incorporated into our evaluation? For example, what constitutes success, and who says so? What steps have we taken to make sure that multiple perspectives about leadership, transformation, inner change, and outer change inform every aspect of our work?
- In what ways, if any, does our evaluation reinforce privileged, racist, or ethnocentric worldviews? Is that intentional? Is it okay?
- To what extent does the evaluation create expectations about the timing, nature, breadth, and sustainability of personal change (and personal change that leads to organizational, system, and social change)? Are we explicit about the worldviews and assumptions on which those expectations are being created? Are we intentional about the expectations that the evaluation wants to set?
- To what extent are we, as evaluators, acting in the role of translator or bridge builder among different groups with different values and ways of seeing the world? Have we thought about the positive and the negative consequences of taking that role? Does that role protect people with more power from having to deal directly with groups whose approaches to the world are challenging to them? Does it make us the experts, rather than the program designers and participants? Is that okay?

As we continue to evaluate personal transformation leadership development efforts, we can use these questions to stimulate our own growth and, perhaps, even our own transformed leadership within evaluation circles.

Resources

Readers interested in learning more about the programs can access information at www.aio.org (Ambassadors) and www.leadingdiversity.org (HHD).

The full research brief for Healing the Heart of Diversity, as well as *Flipping the Script: White Privilege and Community Building,* may be found at the Center for Assessment and Policy Development's Web site at www.capd.org.

References

Duval, S., and Wicklund, R. A. *A Theory of Objective Self Awareness.* New York: Academic Press, 1972.

Heifetz, R. A. *Leadership without Easy Answers.* Cambridge, Mass.: The Belknap Press, 1994.

Pickering, J., and Skinner, M. *From Sentience to Symbols: Readings on Consciousness.* Toronto: University of Toronto Press, 1990.

Potapchuk, M., Leiderman, S., Bivens, D., and Major, B. *Flipping the Script: White Privilege in Community Building Work,* January 2006. [www.capd.org].

Senge, P., Jaworski, J., Scharmer, C. O., and Flowers, B. S. *Presence: Human Purpose and the Field of the Future.* Cambridge, Mass.: Society for Organizational Learning, 2004.

Wheatley, M. *Leadership and the New Science.* San Francisco: Berrett-Koehler, 1999.

CHAPTER EIGHT

EVALUATING LEADERSHIP DEVELOPMENT AND ORGANIZATIONAL PERFORMANCE

Nancy Vollmer LeMay and Alison Ellis

Through experimentation and the application of a variety of methods, the Management and Leadership (M&L) Program of Management Sciences for Health (MSH) has developed a practical yet thorough approach for evaluating the outcomes of its leadership development programs with health sector participants in developing countries. An overarching question is explored: How does leadership development contribute to measurable changes in organizational performance? Organizational performance is defined in terms of behavioral-level changes within participating teams and the results they produce that contribute to their organization's overall goals. Examples are provided from evaluations carried out by the M&L Program during 2003–2005 in order to illustrate the concepts presented in this chapter.

The M&L Program was a five-year cooperative agreement between the U.S. Agency for International Development (USAID) and MSH implemented from October 2000 to September 2005. The primary clients of M&L leadership programs are managers and their workgroups from ministries of health and nongovernmental organizations (NGOs), including private voluntary organizations (PVOs), faith-based organizations (FBOs), and community-based organizations (CBOs) working in the health sector of developing countries.

The purpose of M&L was to strengthen the leadership capacities of health managers and the management systems that are necessary to deliver high-quality health services. The M&L Program was charged with measuring and documenting the main outcomes of its leadership and management interventions according to the Leading and Managing for Results Model, as illustrated in Figure 8.1 (Galer, Vriesendorp, and Ellis, 2005).

While MSH continues to develop leadership capacity under a follow-on project called Leadership, Management, and Sustainability Program (August 2005–2010), all leadership development programs and evaluations described in this chapter were carried out under the M&L Program with funding from the USAID Office of Population and Reproductive Health, Bureau for Global Health, award number HRN-A-00-00-00014-00. The opinions expressed in these pages are those of the authors and do not necessarily reflect the views of USAID.

FIGURE 8.1. LEADING AND MANAGING FOR RESULTS MODEL.

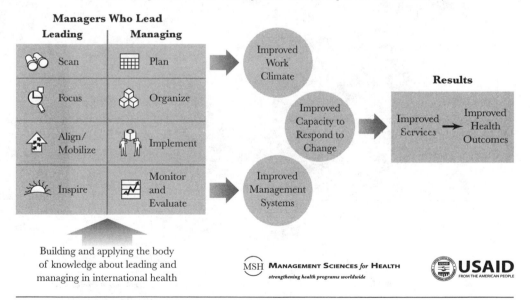

Source: Reprinted with permission from Management Sciences for Health. *Work Climate Assessment: Guide for Facilitators.* Cambridge, Mass.: 2005.

Design and Content of M&L Leadership Development Programs

Overview

M&L's approach to leadership development is to use a structured, participatory process in which health managers and their workgroups learn to apply a set of leading and managing practices to face an organizational challenge while receiving feedback and support from program facilitators. The Leading and Managing Process is visually represented in Figure 8.2 and summarizes the application of this set of practices.

The M&L Leadership Development Program, whether operating face to face or using distance learning, is intended for teams that already work together

FIGURE 8.2. LEADING AND MANAGING PROCESS.

Source: Reprinted with permission from Management Sciences for Health. *Work Climate Assessment: Guide for Facilitators.* Cambridge, Mass.: 2005.

on the job. The leadership program relies primarily on an action-learning approach to build capacity within teams at any level of an organization (Galer, Vriesendorp, and Ellis, 2005). The assumption of this approach is that capacity in leading and managing can be developed through an experiential learning process in which participants gain the skills to address real workplace challenges and produce desired results.

While specific program designs vary across countries and according to the type of organization that is targeted, all programs are founded on five guiding principles (Galer, Vriesendorp, and Ellis, 2005):

1. *Focus on health outcomes.* Good management and leadership result in measurable improvements in health services and outcomes. Only by focusing on real organizational challenges can managers develop their ability to lead.
2. *Practice leadership at all levels.* Good leadership and management can and must be practiced at every level of an organization. Working with their teams, managers at all levels—from health posts to national institutions—can confront challenges and achieve results.
3. *Leadership can be learned.* Leadership practices improve through a process of facing challenges and receiving feedback and support. By using this process, managers develop the leadership abilities of their staffs.
4. *Leadership is learned over time.* Becoming a manager who leads is a process that takes place over time. This process works best when it is owned by the organization and takes on critical organizational challenges.
5. *Sustain progress through management systems.* Gains made in health outcomes can be sustained only by integrating leadership and management practices into an organization's routine systems and processes.

Teams, Challenges, and Implications for Evaluation

The evaluation approach used by M&L is closely linked to the design of the leadership development program, in particular working with teams to implement the Challenge Model illustrated in Figure 8.3 (Galer, Vriesendorp, and Ellis, 2005). This model is a simple analysis tool derived from the Performance Improvement process (Luoma and Voltero, 2002).

The Challenge Model allows a team to analyze its local situation and select a specific organizational challenge around which the team members rally.

FIGURE 8.3. CHALLENGE MODEL.

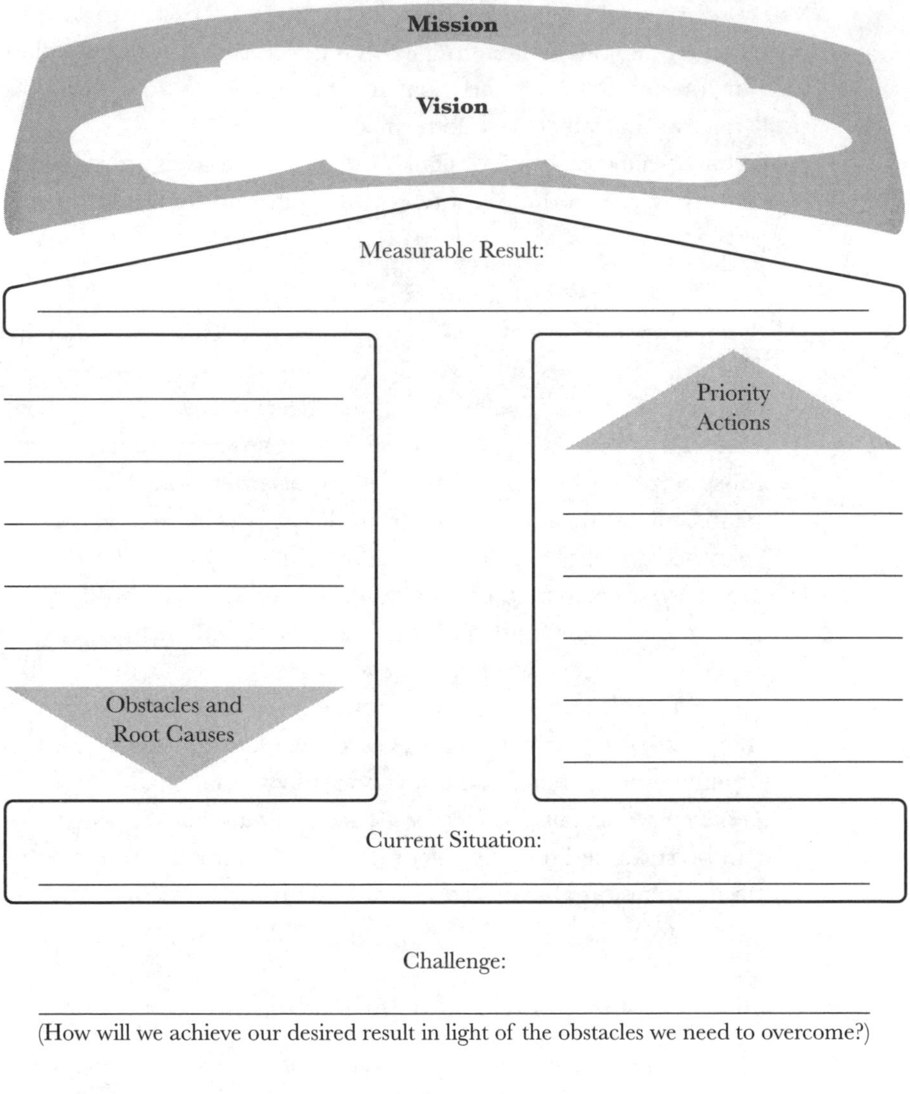
Mission
Vision
Measurable Result:
Priority Actions
Obstacles and Root Causes
Current Situation:
Challenge:
(How will we achieve our desired result in light of the obstacles we need to overcome?)
USAID
FROM THE AMERICAN PEOPLE
MSH MANAGEMENT SCIENCES for HEALTH
a nonprofit organization strengthening health programs worldwide

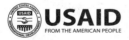

Source: Reprinted with permission from Management Sciences for Health. *Work Climate Assessment: Guide for Facilitators.* Cambridge, Mass.: 2005.

The team then measures their baseline (current situation) vis-à-vis the challenge, determines their expected or measurable result, identifies obstacles and their root causes that must be addressed to achieve their expected result and a series of priority actions or activities necessary to address the challenge, and defines indicators to measure whether it has reached the measurable result. This information is translated into an action plan that serves as a management tool for participating teams and forms one basis for the evaluation of outcomes.

Because the majority of M&L leadership development programs focus on working with teams rather than individuals, the team forms the unit of analysis for most evaluations. This program orientation is a departure from traditional leadership training, which tends to focus on top leaders and their individual development of leadership skills. These programs often reinforce the notion that some people are born with the natural ability to lead and others are not. In contrast, the M&L Program maintains that all members of a workgroup, regardless of their positions, are valuable contributors toward creating a positive work climate and achieving results. All have the ability to change the way they work with others when given the opportunity to reflect on their workplace interactions and to apply a set of leading and managing practices.

The Leadership Development Program invites managers and teams at all levels of an organization to participate. It demystifies leadership by encouraging participants to apply concrete leading and managing practices to the challenges they face in their unit or organization. The group decides how it wants to work together to create a more positive work climate. The role of the workgroup manager is to support the team in making a commitment to a new workgroup climate and to provide the direction to make needed changes.

Inherent to this design is the challenge of defining, recruiting, and evaluating teams. Our experience shows that intact teams who worked together before beginning the leadership development program and who continue to work together after the program ended are more successful in addressing their challenges. Teams that are formed artificially for the purpose of participating in the leadership development program have greater difficulty implementing their plans and measuring their progress after the program ends. These teams are often made up of individuals from geographically or administratively dispersed groups. They may work together well during the program, but after its completion, when they return to their normal routines, they may no longer be motivated to work together as a team. Teams that disintegrate after the program ends are usually lost to follow-up. Thus, not only for an effective program design, but also for evaluation purposes, it is preferable to recruit intact teams for leadership programs.

Delivery Mechanisms

MSH facilitates leadership development through face-to-face and virtual (distance learning) mechanisms. The face-to-face programs are delivered on-site to teams from a single organization, and the virtual programs are delivered to teams from one or more organizations in a single country or geographic region. The virtual programs extend our reach beyond those countries receiving on-site technical assistance. This section of the chapter defines the major content and design features of both delivery approaches.

Face-to-Face Leadership Development Programs. The face-to-face leadership development program lasts from four to nine months and is intended for members of intact teams from the public sector or NGOs, PVOs, CBOs, and FBOs. During the program, team members actively address their challenges through a series of workshops and follow-up assignments they complete together at their work site. Participants learn to adopt specific leading and managing practices to address their selected challenges and realize their desired outcomes. These outcomes are defined in the action plans the teams produce during the program. To help organize and support their work, five kinds of program activities are held.

1. *Senior alignment meeting:* An initial meeting that generates commitment and ownership of the program among key organizational stakeholders
2. *Workshops:* A series of workshops comprised of twelve half-day sessions during which participants learn core leading and managing practices and concepts
3. *Local team meetings:* On-the-job meetings between workshops in which participants transfer what they have learned to the rest of their work team, discuss strategies to address their challenges, and apply leading and managing practices
4. *Regular coaching:* Sessions in which local health managers support the teams in implementing the tools they have learned

5. *Stakeholder meetings:* Meetings in which stakeholders are periodically updated and enlisted as resources to support the teams

The Virtual Leadership Development Program. The Virtual Leadership Development Program (VLDP) is a twelve- to sixteen-week blended learning program that provides practical leadership training linked to organizational challenges selected by participants. The VLDP combines Internet-based facilitation, course material, and individual exercises with face-to-face (on-site) team meetings for reflection and shared learning. As additional support, all participants receive a printed workbook and CD-ROM containing the course content. Participants in the VLDP come from public sector and nongovernmental organizations, including PVOs, FBOs, and CBOs. They enroll in the program as teams that generally range in number from four to ten members.

The VLDP consists of seven learning modules on such topics as leadership in health institutions, facing leadership challenges, competencies in leadership, communication, and change management. During each module, participants carry out individual work on the VLDP Web site. They read the module content, case studies, and editorials; complete module exercises; and participate in electronic discussions. Following this, participants convene for face-to-face group meetings with other team members to discuss what they learned during the module and to complete group work assigned in the module. Two of the Web site features—the Café and the Forum—provide mechanisms for interaction between teams as they move through the modules. The Café is a location on the VLDP Web site where participants are encouraged to exchange ideas and questions on specific themes presented in a threaded discussion format. The Forum is another VLDP Web site element, where at the conclusion of each module a coordinator from each team describes how and what the team produced in response to the module exercise assigned to the group. Throughout the program, two facilitators provide virtual facilitation and coaching via e-mail and postings on the Web site.

Evaluating M&L Leadership Development Programs: Measures of Success

This section of the chapter presents the main outputs and outcomes of the M&L Leadership Development Program. *Outputs* are defined as the application of specific leading and managing practices by participating teams both during and after the program. *Outcomes* include both intermediate outcomes (work climate) and longer-term outcomes (expected changes in organizational results defined by participating teams). An overview of the methods used to measure each is discussed, including the challenges of measuring work climate as a robust outcome and the pros and cons of measuring health service delivery as a long-term outcome.

Leadership Practices and Competencies. M&L assumes there is a common set of leadership practices that can be developed and used by managers and workgroup members at any level of an organization to address their workplace challenges. These include four key leading practices (scan, focus, align and mobilize, and inspire) and the essential leadership competencies (communication, negotiation, change management) needed to achieve the given goal. The ability of the team to apply these practices in the workplace is the immediate result (output) of a leadership development process. Figure 8.4, the Leading and Managing Framework, defines the leading and managing practices and the expected organizational-level results (outcomes) of their application.

During its leadership development programs, M&L attempts to monitor the use of the four leading practices with a set of indicators described in the section following on evaluation instruments. Because the use of the indicators has been irregular across programs, information is also collected on the use of the practices and competencies through postprogram interviews and focus groups with participants and nonparticipants, including those who report directly to the workgroup manager and those who do not. This method has provided useful information on behavior change among program participants and the distinct processes the participating team used to achieve their results.

Workgroup Climate. M&L defines intermediate outcomes at the team level. The primary team-level outcome is workgroup climate, defined as the prevailing workplace atmosphere that is experienced by the members of a given workgroup. *Climate* is what it feels like to work together in a group (MSH, 2002). Every organization, office, and workgroup has a climate that affects how people behave at work and worker motivation. A positive work climate motivates staff because it provides conditions under which people can pursue their own goals while working toward organizational objectives (McGregor, 1966).

Workgroup climate is influenced by external and internal factors. Most external factors are beyond the control of the workgroup and include the

FIGURE 8.4. LEADING AND MANAGING FRAMEWORK.

Practices That Enable Work Groups and Organizations to face Challenges and Achieve Results

Leading

Scanning

- Identify client and stakeholder needs and priorities
- Recognize trends, opportunities, and risks that affect the organization
- Look for best practices
- Identify staff capacities and constraints
- Know yourself, your staff, and your organization —values, strengths, and weaknesses

Organizational Outcome: *Managers have up-to-date, valid knowledge of their clients, the organization, and its context; they know how their behavior affects others*

Focusing

- Articulate the organization's mission and strategy
- Identify critical challenges
- Link goals with the overall organizational strategy
- Determine key priorities for action
- Create a common picture of desired results

Organizational Outcome: *Organization's work is directed by well-defined mission, strategy, and priorities*

Aligning/Mobilizing

- Ensure congruence of values, mission, strategy, structure, systems, and daily actions
- Facilitate teamwork
- Unite key stakeholders around an inspiring vision
- Link goals with rewards and recognition
- Enlist stakeholders to commit resources

Organizational Outcome: *Internal and external stakeholders understand and support the organization's goals and have mobilized resources to reach these goals*

Inspiring

- Match deeds to words
- Demonstrate honesty in interactions
- Show trust and confidence in staff, acknowledge the contributions of others
- Provide staff with challenges, feedback, and support
- Be a model of creativity, innovation, and learning

Organizational Outcome: *Organization displays a climate of continuous learning and staff show commitment, even when setbacks occur*

Managing

Planning

- Set short-term organizational goals and performance objectives
- Develop multiyear and annual plans
- Allocate adequate resources (money, people, and materials)
- Anticipate and reduce risks

Organizational Outcome: *Organization has defined results, assigned resources, and an operational plan*

Organizing

- Ensure a structure that provides accountability and delineates authority
- Ensure that systems for human resource management, finance, logistics, quality assurance, operations, information, and marketing effectively support the plan
- Strengthen work processes to implement the plan
- Align staff capacities with planned activities

Organizational Outcome: *Organization has functional structures, systems, and processes for efficient operations; staff are organized and aware of job responsibilities and expectations*

Implementing

- Integrate systems and coordinate work flow
- Balance competing demands
- Routinely use data for decision making
- Coordinate activities with other programs and sectors
- Adjust plans and resources as circumstances change

Organizational Outcome: *Activities are carried out efficiently, effectively, and responsively*

Monitoring and Evaluating

- Monitor and reflect on progress against plans
- Provide feedback
- Identify needed changes
- Improve work processes, procedures, and tools

Organizational Outcome: *Organization continuously updates information about the status of achievements and results, and applies ongoing learning and knowledge*

MSH **MANAGEMENT SCIENCES for HEALTH**
strengthening health programs worldwide

Source: Reprinted with permission from Management Sciences for Health. *Work Climate Assessment: Guide for Facilitators.* Cambridge, Mass.: 2005.

organization's history and culture, organizational strategies and structures, and the external environment. What happens inside the workgroup, however, usually can be controlled. In fact, the practices and competencies of the manager and workgroup staff influence workgroup climate more than any other factor. Together, the manager and staff members can create a positive workgroup climate, even if the organization's overall climate is poor.

According to the M&L Results Model, workgroup climate is an outcome measure that is sensitive to change as a result of a leadership development process involving managers and their teams. There are two assumptions underlying the Results Model: (1) when team members work together on a shared challenge, a positive work climate is created; and (2) workgroup climate influences results (long-term outcomes). Research from the business and education sectors has shown that workgroups with a positive, supportive climate tend to perform well and to achieve their desired results (Goleman, 2000; Laschinger, Finegan, and Shamian, 2001). Positive workgroup climate motivates employees to improve their performance by going above and beyond job expectations. Better performing workgroups contribute to better organizational performance, which in our context translates into improved health service delivery.

Evidence was collected in several countries to show that as participants in the leadership development programs learn to adopt new practices and to address their challenges as a team, they create a positive climate that supports staff motivation. A brief assessment form (explained in depth in the section on evaluation instruments) was used to measure team members' perception of climate before the leadership program was implemented and at the conclusion of the program to demonstrate changes in workgroup climate. Without a comparison group, there are limits to showing change over time and attributing changes to the intervention.

Nevertheless, similar trends have been seen across participating teams that tend to corroborate the positive effect of the program on climate: teams in different environments have generally shown improved climate levels following participation in the leadership program (including teams from the central, provincial, and decentralized levels of a health system and among teams working in nongovernmental organizations). The operational settings and specific challenge of each team differ, yet most of the time internal climate levels improve as the teams go through the program and learn to adopt and apply leadership practices to solve their pressing management problems.

To help explain these climate data, evocative data (see Chapter Three for a discussion) and stories are collected through focus groups and individual interviews with the workgroup members, managers, and other key staff in the organization who might have been involved in the process. This provides insight into the processes that have taken place within the workgroup and throughout the organization during the implementation of the leadership program. It also allows the documentation of specific practices used by teams that are associated with improved climate. Over time a catalog of the commonly used approaches associated with improved climate has been developed and used to strengthen the content of the leadership programs.

Future evaluation plans include testing the relationships outlined in the Results Model (Figure 8.1), most likely using a quasi-experimental design. A control group may be used, but the random assignment of participants is not feasible in the context of these programs. Participation in the leadership program is not indiscriminate and teams are not uninformed; teams that participate are either self-selected or are recommended by an organizational executive or administrator. Nevertheless, the use of a nonrandom comparison group that has not received the leadership intervention would make the measurement of climate a stronger and more compelling program outcome.

Improvements in Health Service Delivery. M&L's approach to leadership development is guided by the belief that the proof of good leadership lies in the achievement of measurable improvements in health outcomes (for example, changes in the use of health services comparing one period to another; changes in the knowledge, attitudes, or practices of a target population or client group). The leadership program focuses on improving these health outcomes through the development of leadership capacity to improve the delivery of health services. Therefore, where possible, the results of the leadership programs are measured in terms of changes in health service delivery (for example, increase in the number of clients served or improved quality of services).

The expected outcomes of the leadership program are defined by the participants themselves and depend on the organizational challenge they choose to address during the program. In fact, a significant part of the program's design is the focus on challenges. The selected challenge connects leadership development content to the participants' work environment. The challenge involves overcoming obstacles to move from a state of actual performance to an improved state of desired performance, both of which should be measurable.

However, because of the donor's focus on reporting against its results framework, some M&L programs have felt the need to measure service results even when teams have not selected a service delivery challenge to address during the program. This has led to disappointing results in some programs, particularly when the scope or time frame of the program was too limited to accomplish outcomes at this level. In such cases, intermediate outcomes were also measured, such as changes in organizational management processes and systems and in workgroup climate—the necessary precursors to improving health services. The ability to measure change at the service delivery level is determined by a number of factors, including

- The length of time and comprehensive nature of our work with an organization
- The particular challenge selected by participants
- Whether interventions are focused on addressing organizational challenges at the central level or at the district or local level, closer to the point of service delivery
- The organizational functions, roles, and responsibilities assigned to the particular level involved in the leadership program (whether central, regional, or local)

Evaluation Instruments

This section describes three primary tools that M&L uses to monitor and evaluate the leadership programs: leadership indicators to measure outputs related to application of the leadership practices; the Work Climate Assessment, a simple and reliable tool designed to measure workgroup climate in teams; and action plans that form the basis for the evaluation of longer-term outcomes defined by each team. We discuss the advantages and disadvantages of each tool, including a detailed description of the validation of the climate tool and lessons learned associated with its use. Excerpts from the leadership indicators and climate tool are provided.

Assessment of Leadership Practices. In order to track the use of the four leadership practices (scanning, focusing, aligning and mobilizing, and inspiring), M&L developed a set of indicators (see Exhibit 8.1) to measure the practices

EXHIBIT 8.1. OUTPUT INDICATORS
FOR LEADERSHIP DEVELOPMENT.

Scanning. The workgroup can provide valid and relevant evidence about the nature of its internal and external environment, the quality and extent of its performance, and the resources available on best practices; and it can identify challenges within and facing the team.

Focusing. The workgroup has identified priority challenges to be addressed within a defined time period and selected measurable actions that address barriers to achieving results.

Aligning and mobilizing. Workgroup responsibilities and resources are internally aligned and workgroup goals are externally aligned in order to address selected challenges and meet stated objectives.

Inspiring. Workgroups are committed to the organization's mission and to continuous learning, improvement, and innovation.

and behaviors of managers and their teams. These indicators attempt to measure the extent to which workgroups engage in these practices as a matter of organizational routine, no matter what specific challenges they may face. The indicators are designed as a simple self-assessment tool that a team can apply periodically to monitor its use of the leadership practices.

Despite their simplicity, use of the leadership indicators in M&L programs to date has been limited for three reasons: (1) the leadership programs are relatively short (maximum nine months), leaving little time to monitor outputs along the way; (2) the programs have not adopted the indicators as a monitoring tool to use during program delivery; and (3) MSH and donor interest emphasizes final, often quantitative results, such as teams' achievements of objectives for improved health service delivery. The set of indicators were tested in Senegal by district-level teams participating in a leadership program, but have not yet been systematically used to measure progress and change during a program. The leadership indicators need to be further tested and refined by MSH so that leadership development programs will incorporate them as a program monitoring strategy. This way, participants may better understand and use the indicators to track their own progress during a leadership program and MSH will receive the necessary data to analyze the training processes linked to leadership outcomes. In the meantime, individual and group interviews are used once the program is complete to gain insights into the processes that took place.

Workgroup Climate Assessment. Workgroup climate is not directly observable, but is estimated through the use of a questionnaire measuring the perceptions of workgroup members. Because such an instrument did not exist for use in public health organizations in developing countries, M&L developed the Workgroup Climate Assessment (WCA) in 2002. The individual climate items in the survey are derived from the original work of George Litwin and Robert Stringer, who developed the first surveys to measure climate in corporate environments (Litwin and Stringer, 1968; Stringer, 2002).

The WCA is a self-scoring questionnaire with eight items, designed to measure climate among intact teams or workgroups in the health sector of developing countries (see Exhibit 8.2). Its secondary purpose is to engage workgroup members in a conversation about their particular climate so that together they can find ways to improve it. The WCA encourages a participatory process: team members individually respond to the survey and afterward they are encouraged to discuss and act upon the results together.

M&L validated the WCA in 2004 with forty-two workgroups from different administrative levels in Brazil, Mozambique, and Guinea (Perry and others, 2005). Respondents in the study represented a wide variety of settings, including central-level ministry staff, district-level managers, hospital admin-

EXHIBIT 8.2. WORKGROUP CLIMATE ASSESSMENT ITEMS.

1. We feel our work is important.

2. We strive to achieve successful outcomes.

3. We pay attention to how well we are working together.

4. We understand the relevance of the job of each member in our group.

5. We have a plan that guides our activities.

6. We understand each other's capabilities.

7. We seek to understand the needs of our clients.

8. We take pride in our work.

istrators, laboratory technicians, and clinic personnel. The WCA's validation items were tested against the Stringer Organizational Climate Survey, which served as the gold standard for measuring climate. The WCA was originally designed to measure three subdimensions of climate (clarity, support, and challenge), but the study did not confirm that these exist as separate subscales. Results of the validation showed that the eight items in the WCA survey do not discriminate between subdimensions of climate but rather capture a single perception of climate. Study results also indicated that the individual items cannot be analyzed or interpreted separately; they must be analyzed together as a composite score for climate. Finally, responses to the items were similar across gender, culture, language, and management level, thus confirming that the tool measures climate equally well in the different cultures and settings.

To date, the WCA has been used to provide pre- and postintervention measures of workgroup climate in the context of face-to-face leadership development in six countries (Brazil, Egypt, Guinea, Kenya, Mozambique, Senegal) and in nine VLDPs (three for Latin America, one for Brazil, one for the Caribbean region, one for Haiti, one for Iraq, and two for Africa). To apply the survey, all members of the workgroup (both managerial and staff) respond to the survey. Respondents rate how they feel about each item on a scale of 1 to 5. The scores are then tabulated across all items to produce individual-level composite scores and an overall workgroup climate score. An additional two items in the tool measure perceptions of the team's outcomes in terms of their quality and productivity, but these are not included in the climate measure.

Using the individual and workgroup composite scores, comparisons can be made between workgroups in an organization, between pre- and posttest assessments of the same workgroup, or between a single workgroup and a predetermined value of climate serving as a target goal.

Based on experience using the WCA, there are several lessons learned that affect the quality of the data produced by the tool. First, it is essential to apply the WCA with intact teams. Intact teams have a history of working together and as a result can respond to the survey items in a meaningful way. All members of the workgroup need to fill out the WCA in order to obtain a valid measure of workgroup climate. This is difficult to guarantee during the postintervention application of the tool when workgroup members may have already moved to positions outside their original workgroup. It is even more challenging with a nonintact team that does not continue to work together after the leadership program has ended.

Second, because the WCA is applied by program facilitators, the quality of the data depends on their ability to explain to participants the purpose of the tool and how it is used. It is especially important that participants understand the five-point scale used in the tool in order to correctly respond to the items. This scale has been a source of confusion in several cases. The facilitator must also be able to help participants interpret the results and determine ways to address the deficiencies in order to improve their climate. Finally, although the WCA is validated for use in different countries and languages, low literacy populations and those not accustomed to using a self-administered questionnaire tend to have trouble responding. As a result, difficulties in using the WCA are related more to respondents' education level than to their culture or language.

In addition, unless the WCA tool is properly introduced and explained by program facilitators, respondents may not understand the value in using the tool and the evaluation will suffer from incomplete data or poor response rates. For example, during the replication of the leadership development program in Egypt, the Egyptian facilitators did not include the use of the WCA in the program design. They perceived it as an external measure (used for M&L reporting purposes) that was not essential to the replication of the program. Hence they lacked postintervention climate data to use for comparison purposes.

Team Action Plans. During the leadership program, teams develop action plans and define indicators to measure their desired and actual performance levels. M&L has relied on the action plan as an evaluation instrument to measure organizational-level results achieved by participating teams. However, tying measurement to participant indicators has not worked well all of the time. The main difficulty is that the evaluation is dependent on the team's ability to use adequate methods to measure their progress and supply data. Except in the case of those programs that focus on using service statistics, teams often do not monitor their performance using the indicators in their plans; therefore, the data are not available for the evaluation. Reasons for this lack of data include the fact that some teams do not monitor their performance on a regular basis, so the data are not available; some do monitor performance but on a larger scale using organizational-level indicators; other teams do not fully implement their action plan and therefore have nothing to measure. New content has been added to the program design that will help teams to improve their selection and use of indicators to monitor progress. This should allow for better measurement of organizational results in the future.

Evaluation Methods and Key Questions Used

M&L evaluations use a mix of qualitative and quantitative methods, depending on the key questions to be examined, the specific content of the challenge being addressed by the teams, and the action plan under review. This mixed methods approach is in response to the absence of standardized metrics from the literature to measure organizational leadership outcomes. Quantitative methods include the use of specific questionnaires (such as the WCA) completed by program participants that measure changes at the team level and the use of indicators to measure organizational performance related to the expected results stated in the action plan. In cases where it is possible and logical to measure changes in services, service delivery data (usually service statistics) are analyzed.

The corresponding qualitative evaluation aims to understand and document behavioral and process-level changes that occurred in the workgroups as a result of the program. Methods used include document reviews as well as focus groups and semi-structured interviews with samples of program participants and nonparticipants. For virtual programs, e-mail questionnaires are sent to a point person from each team, followed by telephone interviews with carefully selected key informants from these teams.

For evaluating both face-to-face and virtual leadership programs, due to time and funding constraints, a purposive sample is most often used. *Purposive sampling* is a form of nonprobability sampling in which respondents are selected according to a specific plan or purpose. This sampling method differs from *probability sampling*, in which each member of the population has an equal chance of being selected for the sample and the results can be generalized to the sampled population. Purposive sampling is useful for reaching a targeted sample quickly and when sampling for proportionality is not the main concern. The disadvantage of a purposive sample is that it is hard to know how well the sample represents the population. As a result, it is important to qualify the findings from a purposive sample appropriately and note whether people left out of the sample might behave differently than those who were selected.

In the case of M&L evaluations, teams are selected for the purposive sample according to predefined criteria that are intended to ensure, as much as possible, maximum variability in terms of team performance. Teams are usually selected based on the quality of their action plan and their adherence to the criteria for SMART objectives (Specific: to avoid differing interpretations;

*M*easurable: to allow monitoring and evaluation; *A*ppropriate: to the problem, goals, and strategies of the organization; *R*ealistic: achievable, challenging, and meaningful; and *T*ime bound: with a specific time period for achieving them). Other criteria have been used, such as the quality of homework submissions and participation levels; however, these tend to lack context and must be interpreted with care as indicators of team performance.

Data Sources and Lessons Learned. As a result of using mixed methods to assess leadership outcomes, the evaluations are based on information from a variety of sources. The following is a review of the different information sources used by M&L, as well as a discussion of the challenges of implementing the evaluation and lessons learned.

- Evaluations start with a review of the project design and content of the learning modules. This is a necessary exercise in order to understand and make explicit the logic among inputs, outputs, and outcomes.
- Comparison of organizational results before and after the leadership program is usually based on indicators in the teams' actions plans and other quantitative and qualitative data supplied by participating teams. Along with climate data, these organizational data provide the evidential base for measuring outcomes. A prerequisite for using a participant action plan as the basis for an evaluation is ensuring that the plan meets the SMART criteria. To aid teams in improving their action plans during the program, M&L reviews them and provides guidance according to the following criteria or questions:

  - Are goals and objectives clear?
  - Are activities logically related to goals?
  - Are measurable indicators defined?
  - Is a timeline or time frame for implementation indicated?
  - Are resources indicated?

- Comparison of climate data before and after the leadership intervention is a measure of change within the team that tracks its growth and progress as a result of the program. An important challenge when using workgroup climate as a leadership outcome is helping participants understand how positive climate is created and that improved workgroup climate is an expected outcome linked to participation in the program. Some participants have tended to perceive climate as an external measure that serves the purposes of M&L reporting to its donor but that is not essential to action plan development or to improving team performance. As a result, some participants have not been motivated to complete the survey, and those evaluations have therefore suffered from poor response rates.

Part of the problem may be the role that workgroup climate plays in the program and how the WCA is introduced by the facilitators. The WCA should be presented as a way to measure workgroup climate and the results of its application by the teams must be tied to or used in the content of the program. When teams analyze their climate scores, the program should provide assistance with interpreting the data and guidance for strategizing ways to improve climate.

Finally, and especially in light of funding constraints, the program should ensure follow-up to systematically reapply the WCA with teams from face-to-face and virtual leadership development programs in the postcourse period to measure the maintenance of climate levels. Once the program ends, it is often difficult to gain access to the teams to request a reapplication of the tool. Therefore, follow-up should be incorporated into the initial project design.

- Semi-structured interviews and focus groups with participants can supply the necessary evocative data to explain outcomes achieved and to understand what changes have occurred within the team both during and after the program. Gathering quality evocative data depends on who is selected to provide the data and how they are selected. It is therefore important to select key informants carefully and ensure they represent the larger team. Likewise it is important that focus group participants are not selected by the program facilitators or the program team manager in order to help ensure more objectivity in the participants' views. Conducting focus groups with nonparticipants, as well as participants, is useful to gauge the degree of trickle over and trickle down that occurs between the two groups.
- For virtual evaluations, the use of e-mail questionnaires to gather process and outcome information from participants in the VLDP has had varied success. Due to frequent low response rates, different approaches have been tried. Sending the questionnaire to the team leader alone risks that this person either does not respond or does not have the detailed information required to report indicator data. Responses are usually richer when the

whole team is asked to fill out the questionnaire, and in this case, the e-mail questionnaire is sent to a representative of the team who will seek and compile responses from all team members. While this has improved the response rate, there is no guarantee that the questionnaire is actually completed by the team.

Interestingly, requesting teams to complete the questionnaire can serve as an intervention itself because it motivates team members to reunite with a shared purpose. What also works well is following e-mail questionnaires with semi-structured telephone interviews with selected course participants to verify and further probe questionnaire responses.

Review of Key Questions. M&L outcome evaluations are all based on a similar set of key questions in order to allow a synthesis of lessons learned across programs. The methods described provide the data sources for all of these key questions. It is useful to triangulate several data sources for the same key question in order to verify the information collected. Examples of the types of key questions addressed in the evaluations include

- What technical assistance approaches and tools were used in delivering the leadership development program?
- What are the organizational challenges that the teams have addressed through this program?
- What processes have participants established to address their challenges?
- Did teams develop action plans to address their challenges? If so, have all activities been implemented? Were other activities implemented that were not included in the action plan?
- What means do the teams and the overall organization use for monitoring their progress in addressing their challenges?
- To what extent have the individual teams and the overall organization achieved their expected results?
- What other results may have been achieved that are unrelated to addressing their challenges?
- What motivated participants to achieve their results? What prevented them from achieving their goals?
- Did the teams continue to work together to address another challenge after the formal leadership program ended? If so, what processes were used? Was this similar to or different from how they worked together during the for-

mal program? What motivated their participation and commitment after the formal program ended?

- To what extent was content from the formal program shared with other staff members who did not directly participate in the leadership program?
- In what ways has the formal leadership development program impacted staff as individuals, their teams, and the organization as a whole?

Lessons Learned from Field Applications

Choosing Where to Evaluate Workgroup Climate: Manager, Team, or Organization

Before designing an evaluation of leadership outcomes, it is necessary to determine the sample group that is most appropriate for measuring workgroup climate. Different options for the unit of measure include the manager; the manager's direct reports; all team members participating in the program; or staff from the whole unit, organization, or municipality, including those who did not directly participate in the program. Ideally, the decision about where to evaluate should be based on a working model that outlines the logical pathways among inputs, outputs, and outcomes for the particular program. According to the M&L approach to leadership development, the managers and members of a workgroup follow a participatory process to identify and address a workplace challenge. The act of going through this process together and adopting the leadership and management practices to address a given challenge tends to improve the climate in that particular workgroup.

For example, in Nicaragua, the municipal leadership program intervened in sixty-three municipalities over a period of three years. During the first two years, only the municipal management teams were directly involved in the program. The management team received the training, selected the challenge, designed the improvement plan, and deliberately worked on the challenge in the plan. The rest of the health workers in the municipality did not receive the training and were not involved in implementing the action plan. Many did not even know what purpose the plan served or what actions it contained. During the third year, however, the management team and all municipal health workers were trained, although the health workers still were not involved in implementing the action plans.

For the purposes of implementing the leadership programs, the intervention group was defined as the municipal management team. However, the unit of measure for assessing climate was defined as the management team plus all municipal health staff. According to the logic of the M&L approach, changes in climate likely would be seen at the level of the management team because only it was directly involved in the program. And yet results showed that climate generally improved among all municipal health staff, even in the absence of broad participation of all health staff in defining and addressing the challenge. It is possible that improvements in climate would have been even stronger had they been measured solely within the management team that had directly participated in the intervention. How can these documented results be explained? If a health worker does not go through the leadership process itself, can she still experience a change in climate? If the results in climate were not due to direct participation in the program, did the management team's improved practices have a trickle down or trickle over effect to the rest of the municipal staff? Were improvements in supervision and better working conditions brought about by the management team? Had a logic model been developed at the beginning of the program, it would have helped to explain the changes that were measured and their relationship to the program inputs. Because a logic model did not exist, there was no way to know for sure whether these outcomes were intended or unintended consequences of the program.

While much of MSH's leadership evaluation work, consistent with the literature, suggests that certain inputs will likely lead to certain outputs and outcomes (Goleman, 2000; Laschinger, Finegan, and Shamian, 2001; Litwin and Stringer, 1968; Stringer, 2002), further tests and models are needed to determine how strongly the inputs are linked to the actual outcomes.

Measuring Health Service Delivery Outcomes

If quantitative data are used to measure outcomes, it is important to select appropriate indicators that are correctly defined and calculated. In addition, the indicator definitions should be verified at the start of the program. For example, in Egypt the leadership program was delivered to teams of doctors and nurses at the district and health facility levels. Outcomes were defined as improved climate and improved family planning, antenatal, and postpartum care services. The action plans formed the link between program inputs and service outcomes because participants chose to improve service delivery as their challenge and they identified the necessary actions to achieve the service results.

The evaluation of the Egypt program relied almost entirely on service statistics to measure service outcomes. The program encouraged teams to select their own performance indicators from among the existing national indicators used by the Egyptian Ministry of Health and Population (MOHP). This was in line with MSH's philosophy to use data that teams are already collecting rather than creating additional requirements for data collection. The advantage of this approach was that it empowered the teams to own their challenge. The disadvantage was that it created a problem with measurement validity. Several teams chose to use couple years of protection (CYP) to measure family planning service performance. CYP is commonly used as an outcome indicator for family planning programs. Although participants followed the guidelines of the MOHP, the way in which the ministry instructed health facilities to compute CYPs was not conventional (did not follow international guidelines) and the unusual computation led to misleading results. By recalculating the CYP indicator and using additional data from the participating clinics' family planning service statistics, M&L was able to assess the teams' program outcomes vis-à-vis their expected targets for family planning services, and the teams themselves were able to accurately monitor their own progress.

In contrast, in Nicaragua it was not possible or appropriate to use service data to analyze potential relationships between climate and service outcomes, for two reasons. First, the Nicaragua program was designed to improve municipal climate as the outcome measure and did not intend to affect health services in any direct way. Each municipal team developed a plan to address the principal weaknesses in climate they had identified through the application of an organizational climate survey. Their plans did not address any deficiencies in services. In addition, the accompanying training units were directed at strengthening the leadership skills needed to overcome the identified limitations in climate. Therefore, in accordance with this program design, the evaluation framework of the Nicaragua program did not link changes in climate to service results.

Second, even if a logical link between program inputs and expected service results had been made, the available data (service statistics) on health services were insufficient to perform an analysis of these relationships. Data from service statistics should be defined ahead of time in order to ensure they are appropriate for the analysis. The service delivery indicators should be chosen and tracked from the beginning of the program in coordination with participating municipalities. This would serve two purposes: (1) to analyze the root causes of poor services and then design the program interventions to address these; and (2) to respond to municipal priorities for improving health services rather than measuring a standard set of indicators.

Using Mixed Methods to Evaluate Outcomes

Because leadership is as much about the process as it is about the results, evaluators should consider using a balanced mix of evocative (qualitative) and evidential (quantitative) data. Evaluations that rely solely on quantitative data such as service delivery results may conceal important changes in team practices and their interactions with the larger system around them. For example, in Egypt the monitoring and evaluation framework for the program relied exclusively on service statistics. During the evaluation, although significant improvements were measured in many of the outcome (services) indicators, the evaluator was not able to explain in any detail what had led to these changes.

A year after the conclusion of the program in Egypt, M&L evaluated the replication of the program carried out with another set of district teams. This time a mix of qualitative and quantitative methods were used to capture changes in outcomes. Quantitative methods were again based on an analysis of services statistics, using a control district for comparison to help rule out ecological effects of general improvements over time. Qualitative methods included postprogram interviews and focus groups with participants and facilitators. This second evaluation provided a much richer account of program results, with quantitative data on concrete changes in services coupled with evocative data to help explain how transformation in service delivery had occurred as a direct result of the leadership development program.

In Nicaragua, an evaluation of the leadership program was also conducted using both quantitative and qualitative methods. Data on pre- and postintervention climate levels were collected using an organizational climate tool developed by the Pan-American Health Organization (PAHO, 1989). This tool was chosen because the WCA was still under development by MSH and was not available when the Nicaragua program began. The PAHO tool contains eighty items that measure four broad areas of organizational climate: leadership, motivation, reciprocity, and participation. It was completed by all municipal health staff, both participants and nonparticipants (that is, managers and health workers). Analysis of the climate data included descriptive statistics and significance testing on the differences between pre- and postprogram climate levels.

Qualitative methods included focus groups with program participants (management teams) and nonparticipants (health workers supervised by the management teams) and in-depth interviews with municipal directors, selected participants, and program facilitators. In addition, action plans were reviewed with municipal directors and evidence of their implementation was solicited (for example, meeting agendas or other specific documents and observable modifications in health center organization or administration). These evocative data tended to substantiate the changes in climate captured with the PAHO tool and to strengthen the conclusions reached through evaluation.

Evaluating Results of Virtual Leadership Development Programs

M&L has conducted follow-up evaluations after six VLDP programs with the intention of documenting the outputs and outcomes produced by the participating teams. The intent of the evaluations is to capture medium-term outcomes of the program based on (1) results achieved through the implementation of the action plans developed during the course; and (2) changes in workgroup climate among participating teams. Without these data, it is difficult to document the concrete value of the program and relate the organizational outcomes to participation in the course.

Methods in these evaluations included review of action plans and WCA results, e-mail questionnaires sent to a representative of each team, and telephone interviews with a member of selected teams in order to document the progress they made in implementing their plans and to probe on specific actions they took as well as any behavioral outcomes produced. Selection of teams for the telephone interview has been based on stratifying teams into high- and low-performing categories based on such criteria as participation levels during the course and the quality of the action plan produced. Teams are then selected according to geographic representation within these strata. The goal is to acquire a sufficient spread of teams in terms of performance and geographic location to capture the variation in the cohort. In general about half of participating teams are selected.

The follow-up evaluations have on average taken place between six to eight months after program completion to allow sufficient time for teams to implement their plans. Nevertheless, only limited concrete data on outcomes have been documented. While teams have worked on some activities in their action plans, most have not measured their progress, despite the presence of indicators in their plans. Some teams do not implement their plan at all during or after the course. The ability to measure team results is dependent on their ability to supply the necessary data.

The lack of concrete performance data raises several questions: If a team does not fully implement its action plan, or does not measure its progress, does that mean the VLDP did not produce the desired outcome (increasing the ability of teams to address challenges and achieve results)? Or could it simply reflect the team's inability to implement their plan due to their level or role within the organization? Could it also mean that monitoring action plan progress is overlooked when teams are faced with other competing work priorities? Either way, if a team does not implement or monitor its plan, data for the evaluation are not available and alternative measures must be sought to document outcome-level results.

At the same time, basing the assessment of VLDP outcomes primarily on action plan implementation is a limiting and potentially misleading approach that may miss other important changes that occur as a result of the program. As a blended learning program, the VLDP engages participants in a unique way that builds effective teams that can affect the organization beyond the results of a single action plan. Accomplishments such as strengthened teams now serve as an intermediate outcome that can be produced during the life of the program and that is a necessary precursor to producing organizational results. Therefore the primary data source for assessing strengthened teams is the in-depth phone interview.

Assessing the structure and unity of a team complements the measure of the third outcome covered in M&L evaluations: positive work climate. The VLDP includes an online version of the WCA that teams complete during the first and last modules of the course. However, having tried repeatedly to gather climate data from VLDP teams, low response rates have prevented using climate as a robust outcome measure for the VLDP. More recently, the course diploma has been tied to completion of both pre- and postcourse WCA surveys, which has improved the response rates.

Experience in evaluating virtual leadership development programs shows that the most effective methods for soliciting information on intermediate outcomes from virtual teams are the following:

1. E-mail questionnaire sent to a point person identified prior to the close of the VLDP representing the team who will ensure that the team members

all contribute to responding to the questionnaire. Otherwise, if only the point person responds, he may have incomplete information on indicators and outcomes. Questions revolve around measurable progress on the action plan (including indicator data) and processes the team used to implement their plan.

2. The next step is to follow up with targeted, in-depth telephone interviews with a different team member to (1) verify information supplied in the questionnaire; and (2) probe key questions on results linked to the action plan as well as on progress in developing a cohesive team with a positive climate. A useful strategy for selecting teams for individual phone interviews is to first categorize them into high, medium, and low performers according to simple criteria such as the quality of their action plan and participation levels during the course (for example, posting to the Forum and Café, and completion of group exercises). Afterward, two to three teams are selected from each category for the phone interviews. This helps ensure an adequate spread of teams for interviews and enables a comparison of responses according to their performance levels. Participants complete a postcourse survey that provides their initial reactions to the course that are useful for developing the individual interview guide.

3. To round out the evaluation, participation data from the VLDP Web site is used to track participation during the course modules and on different site features such as the Café and Forum. However, these data have to be interpreted with care because they do not reflect participation that occurs offsite during team meetings.

4. The After Action Review (AAR) is an additional source of process data for the evaluation. The AAR is a very useful rapid assessment process for reflecting on and discussing what went well in implementing a project or set of activities and what did not go well. The exercise helps program designers and implementers think in a different way about mistakes, failures, and breakdowns without blaming. It also provides an opportunity to recognize successes. The lessons are then fed back into the group (or the larger organization) and combined with other lessons to create organizational knowledge and improved solutions. The AAR is a source of immediate feedback that can then be woven into an evaluation.

The use of the preceding methods to evaluate virtual leadership programs has yielded the following six lessons:

1. The timing of the follow-up evaluation is essential to capturing high-quality information from participants. The more time that passes after course completion, the lower the response rate to e-mail questionnaires and interview requests and the greater the risk of recall bias. Yet at the same time, delayed follow-up is necessary to allow teams enough time to practice new skills and implement their action plans. It is therefore necessary to strike a balance between recall and results: the evaluator must allow enough time to pass to be able to document organizational results and yet not too much time to compromise recall among respondents. Realistic and measurable outcomes should be identified at the outset of the program for the chosen time frame.

2. Without adequate preparation, e-mail questionnaires are a poor mechanism for gathering postcourse data from VLDP teams. Teams need to be informed ahead of time that e-mail questionnaires will be sent after the completion of the program. A point person should be selected to facilitate the dissemination and collection of questionnaires from all team members.

3. Similarly, participant interviews with respondents selected at random are an ineffective way to capture results on action plans or organizational results. Quality interviews depend on the knowledge of the interviewee who may or may not have accurate information regarding indicators from the VLDP action plan or data on organizational performance in general, depending on her role in the organization. Instead, each team should select a spokesperson or representative who will be prepared to respond to interviews or requests for information throughout the monitoring and follow-up period.

4. Strengthened teams, in addition to workgroup climate and action plan implementation, is a viable outcome measure for the VLDP. While quality action plans are needed to provide the basis for documented results, the richness of the process is in producing the plans. It is necessary to document the internal cohesion of the team that develops during the process of developing the plan.

5. WCA online response rates are generally poor. This may be because participants complete the survey on paper and do not upload their data to the Web site. Or it could be because the tool has not been presented as a useful way for teams to monitor their progress in working together. Linking the course diploma to WCA completion can improve response rates.

6. The AAR and tracking of back-end participation data are very useful for providing rapid process data on program implementation. Collecting this data provides a foundation for subsequent evaluations.

Challenges of Evaluating Leadership Development at the Team and Organizational Levels

Experience in numerous developing countries with managers and their teams from central and peripheral levels of the health sector has led M&L to identify key challenges and conclusions that may help to strengthen the evaluation of leadership outcomes.

- *The quality and availability of data is uneven.* Evaluations are highly dependent on the way in which the program facilitator introduces and uses measurement tools that supply data for the evaluation. Likewise, evaluations are dependent on the monitoring and evaluation systems and practices of the client organization. Evaluation data is only as good as the client organization's data. Participants from organizations with weak M&E systems are often unable to provide a suitable baseline measure, which only complicates the setting of appropriate targets to accomplish within the timeframe of a program. Often participants do not use the indicators in their action plans to monitor performance, and as a result postprogram data are unavailable to measure change in relation to a baseline. This is particularly the case when the team has identified an organizational process or system as its priority challenge; it is less often the case when the team has identified a service delivery-related challenge. The collection and analysis of qualitative data is usually carried out by the MSH evaluators. The value of this data is leading us to strengthen our qualitative approaches and consider offering M&E technical assistance to the client organization and participating teams to enhance their ability to collect qualitative data.
- *The design of the leadership development program affects the ability to measure outcomes.* Because of difficulties in attributing results to program inputs, evaluators and program designers need to define where and how they expect to see change as a result of the program. Logic models should be used to make explicit relationships between leadership inputs and expected outputs and outcomes and to define how the expected outputs and outcomes relate to the program content. Further, programs should develop performance benchmarks that can be used along the way during the program, especially if outcomes are likely to change slowly and if it will be difficult to gather process data from participants at a point after the program has ended. For example, programs can include and routinely use output indicators, such

as those presented in this chapter, that measure leadership competencies and practices and complement the measurement of outcomes such as climate. Finally, measuring change needs to become a program strategy so that participants learn to value the collection and use of data to measure their own progress. Programs should use simple measurement instruments that participants will also find useful in their own work. This is especially important if the program relies on participant data to measure its success or failure.

- *Ensuring adequate response rates to the WCA and the appropriate timing of data collection is essential.* Program facilitators that incorporate the WCA into the program in a way that is meaningful to participants increase their motivation to respond to the survey. Appropriate timing of follow-up data collection such as interviews and e-mail questionnaires maximizes the quality of the data collected (not too soon after the program to allow teams sufficient time to make progress and not too long after the program to affect participant recall). Also facilitators should enlist the key informants early in the program so they are aware of their responsibilities to represent the team in the interview.

- *Yearly funding pressures influence the scope, timing, and methods for collecting data.* Limited time frames for project implementation often inhibit the measurement of broad organizational change. Nevertheless, there is pressure from the donor to report results during these short time frames. Further, donors seek tangible, quantifiable evidence of outcomes in a largely qualitative environment in which qualitative methods are often more appropriate ways to capture change. Programs can respond to this pressure several ways. Participants should be oriented to select significant motivating targets that will contribute to organizational performance and at the same time can be measured at some point after the program ends. In addition, immediate program outputs can be defined and measured in order to satisfy the need to report results in the short term (immediately after program completion). Finally, more systematic reporting of results using mixed methods, such as climate outcomes combined with evocative data, may meet donors' need for hard data.

Resources

For a detailed explanation of climate, please see "Creating a Work Climate That Motivates Staff and Improves Performance" in *The Manager,* produced by Management Sciences for Health. This publication is available on the MSH Manager's Electronic Resource Center Web site (http://erc.msh.org/)

at http://erc.msh.org/newpages/english/leadership/workclimate.pdf. A hard copy can be ordered through MSH's e-bookstore located on the MSH Web site at www.msh.org.

We also recommend the seminal works by Litwin and Stringer, who pioneered the study of climate in corporate settings: *Motivation and Organizational Climate* (Litwin and Stringer, 1968), and *Leadership and Organizational Climate* (Stringer, 2002). The full references are available at the end of this chapter.

For information on the design and content of M&L leadership development programs, we recommend the publication by MSH, *Managers Who Lead: A Handbook for Improving Health Services*. The handbook is available for order through MSH's e-bookstore located on the MSH Web site at www.msh.org.

Another new manual recently developed by MSH provides guidance on applying the WCA as well as tabulating and interpreting the results: *Work Climate Assessment: Guide for Facilitators*. Copies are available for download from the MSH Manager's Electronic Resource Center Web site (http://erc.msh.org/).

For information on measuring leadership competencies, see the Leadership Assessment Instrument (LAI), a self-assessment tool developed by Linkages, Inc., with information at www.linkageinc.com/research_products/assessment_instruments.aspx. This tool is also available on the MSH Manager's Electronic Resource Center Web site (http://erc.msh.org).

For information on the performance improvement process that provides the foundation for our leadership programs, please see the International Society for Performance Improvement Web site, www.ispi.org.

Finally, the full evaluation reports for the leadership programs in Egypt, Nicaragua, and the VLDP are available from MSH on request. Brief evaluation notes summarizing the results of these evaluations are available at www.msh.org/projects/mandl/3.4.1.html.

References

Galer, J. B., Vriesendorp, S., and Ellis, A. *Managers Who Lead: A Handbook for Improving Health Services.* Boston: Management Sciences for Health, 2005.

Goleman, D. "Leadership That Gets Results." *Harvard Business Review,* March–April 2000, 78–90.

Laschinger, H., Finegan, J., and Shamian, J. "The Impact of Workplace Empowerment, Organizational Trust on Staff Nurses' Work Satisfaction and Organizational Commitment." *Health Care Management Review,* 2001, *26,* 7–23.

Litwin, G., and Stringer, R. *Motivation and Organizational Climate.* Boston: Harvard University Press, 1968.

Luoma, M., and Voltero, L. *Performance Improvement, Stages, Steps and Tools.* Chapel Hill, N.C.: Intrah, 2002.

Management Sciences for Health (MSH). "Creating a Work Climate That Motivates Staff and Improves Performance." *The Manager,* 2002, *11*(3), 1–22.

McGregor, D. *Leadership and Motivation: Essays of Douglas McGregor.* Cambridge, Mass.: MIT Press, 1966.

Guatamala GT: Organización Panamericana de la Salud (PAHO). "Organizational Development: Theories and Techniques." Sub-regional Project for the Development of Management Skills in the Health Services, Vol. 3, Module 2, 1989.

Perry, C., and others. "Validating a Workgroup Climate Assessment Tool for Improving the Performance of Public Health Organizations." *Human Resource for Health,* October 13, 2005, *3*(10), 1–8.

Stringer, R. *Leadership and Organizational Climate.* Upper Saddle River, N.J.: Prentice Hall, 2002.

CHAPTER NINE

THE IMPORTANCE OF LOCAL CONTEXT IN LEADERSHIP DEVELOPMENT AND EVALUATION

Larry Peters and John Baum

Effective leadership development should provide clear evidence of its added value in terms of changes in individual behavior, improvements in tangible results, and the production of desired business outcomes. The record to date shows that these outcomes are neither easy to come by nor often demonstrated. We argue that context (for example, reflected in opportunity, management systems, human resource (HR) systems, culture, and work constraints) is a big part of the reason why it is so hard to find evidence that investments in leadership development pay off. We believe that context does matter, and that it must be designed into leadership development efforts and the evaluation of these efforts. To achieve the outcomes important to business stakeholders, we suggest that a leader's immediate supervisor is one of the most important context factors in leadership development. We refer to this as *local context*, in large part because supervisors are the "face of the organization" to subordinates who are developing leadership skills. The positive roles that the leader's boss can play help to ensure that the investment has a chance to pay off. In short, we are arguing that leadership development needs to be conceived, designed, delivered, and evaluated with the role of the supervisor in mind and included! We provide two real-world examples of how creating supervisory involvement helped to produce meaningful evidence of the return on investment (ROI) in leadership development. We believe that the implications of this thinking are far reaching for leadership development efforts.

Introduction

Evaluating the effectiveness of investments in developing leaders has always been a difficult challenge. Partly this is because development programs are typically seen as events (for example, training programs) that are expected, in and of themselves, to have a measurable impact on individual performance, business outcomes, and financial results. And why not? The logic is clear. When leaders develop the skills and competencies needed to be successful, they should, logically, be expected to translate this learning into results that show and into outcomes that matter. And yet, evaluators of leadership programs have struggled to turn logic into results that clearly show a positive return on investment.

In this chapter, we offer a new argument and provide a new logic. We do not disagree with the logic of development described; we think it makes perfect sense in and of itself. It is just that this logic does not fit the realities of many organizations that are attempting to develop their leaders. The problem we see is that development does not occur in a vacuum; rather, it occurs in increasingly complex organizations.

Formal or intentional leadership development often occurs in organizations that resist change. It occurs in living systems in which people regard change as a virus that has to be expelled. It occurs in organizations that have come to expect that leadership development will have little or no meaningful impact on the outcomes that they really care about. When these limited expectations are then communicated to leaders and managers who are about to participate in formal development activities, it is not surprising that nothing much happens.

It is in these organizations that development is needed more than ever and where we, as evaluators, should expect to see the biggest impact on our investments in leaders. The new logic of development says that context matters; that the organizational conditions that receive the results of development activities may be just as important, or more important, than the quality of the development program itself.

Context Issues in Leadership Development

Context is an interesting issue in and of itself (see Johns, 2006, for a recent review). It refers to a variety of factors (for example, corporate culture, management systems) that make it more or less likely that a development effort will show a meaningful return. Figure 9.1 portrays several major context factors in leadership development. Consider, for example, the role that opportunity plays. Let's assume that a development activity is exceptional and helps participants to develop meaningful leadership skills. If participants then return to organizations where people are given limited opportunities to lead or where they are discouraged from or even punished for taking initiative, the investment in leadership development will not have an outlet and cannot produce any measurable return on investment. In this case, the real issue is not the quality of the development activity but is the opportunity to display the development and to demonstrate its value. It is the difference between *potential* and *performance:* developmental activities can create the potential for better leadership; the context, however, can act to reduce the display of that capability. Our experience suggests that, in most cases, the developmental activity itself will be blamed for the lack of results and not the context that the organization provides.

FIGURE 9.1. THE ROLE OF CONTEXT IN LEADERSHIP DEVELOPMENT.

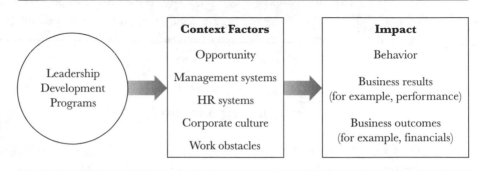

Other context factors include management systems (for example, appraisal, reward, and recognition systems), HR systems (for example, selection and promotion systems), and corporate culture (for example, where potential leaders are expected or encouraged and supported (or not) for taking actions to improve their organization's results). If new leaders see no near-term incentive to apply their newly developed skills (for example, a management systems issue), then they will leave what they have learned at the door of the training site. If they cannot see a long-term career advantage for leading (for example, an HR systems issue), especially if the social system (for example, a cultural issue) discourages such actions, they are likely to compartmentalize their leadership development from their daily work. To the extent that the work environment has factors beyond a person's control that impact results (see Peters and O'Connor, 1980), people may not have either the ability or the willingness to take on leadership opportunities.

The context issues that we speak of are not new. They have been stated for decades in terms of leadership development and evaluation (see, for example, Kotter, 1990) as well as in a variety of related arenas. One of the oldest truths about training and development is that it makes little sense to send newly trained people back into unchanged organizations (see Fleishman, Harris, and Burtt, 1955). The organization always wins. Conger and Benjamin (1999) make this exact point: organizational factors usually prevent people from stepping up to leadership challenges. Kotter (1990), on the other hand, notes that some organizational cultures support people who act as leaders, and therefore support leadership development.

We want to underscore the role that context plays and extend it. Not only does context affect the display of leadership resulting from development, but also, by extension, context has an impact on the evaluation of development efforts. Indeed, the new logic suggests that we must factor this contextual reality into our development planning and implementation if we are to expect to see new behavior, results, and outcomes on the job and in our evaluations.

Does Leadership Development Matter?

Does leadership development really make a significant difference in most organizations? We believe that it does, even though it has been hard to consistently demonstrate with empirical certainty. The natural state of life is for people to step up to their challenges and to connect with others who have the capabilities that are needed to meet these challenges. We see acts of incredible leadership in our daily, non-job lives, where people who are faced with major challenges take responsible actions to address them. Leadership is visibly seen in communities, where people have come together to handle crises and to support those in need of help (witness the events around Hurricanes Katrina and Rita in the United States, the 2005 tsunami in southern Asia, and the 2005 earthquake in Pakistan). We also see it in work settings, where people go beyond the call to meet the challenges that their organizations face. Indeed, McCall, Lombardo, and Morrison (1988) have documented how challenging work assignments (for example, turnarounds, changes in scope, moving to global work) have played important roles in developing leaders on the job. In these and other studies, it was the context that demanded growth by providing stretch opportunities that required people to grow in order to meet the challenges that were before them. It has also been argued that training is best received and best utilized when it is offered "just in time"—that is, when development efforts can be applied immediately. For these reasons, and others, the impact of development efforts is often taken on faith.

Let's look at a specific example. Some time ago, we interviewed the chief executive officer (CEO) of a successful high-tech business in the travel industry. This organization had become a major competitor in its niche and then started to grow through mergers with other high-tech travel businesses. Their growth strategy was to add breadth to their portfolio of technology solutions by expanding geographically into new markets in Europe. In the year prior to this interview, this strategy resulted in adding nearly 1,600 people to an organization comprised of only 400 people. The change in scope (from 400 to 2,000 employees) put new pressures on all of the executives, some of whom did not know how to lead in an organization that had grown fivefold almost overnight. The first executive to leave was the chief financial officer (CFO). He did not understand what it took to lead a large function that was spread halfway across the globe.

We asked the CEO if he planned to continue this growth strategy. He said that the organization would continue to grow through more acquisitions and mergers, at least in the foreseeable future. We then asked him if he had any formal plans to develop existing leaders to prepare them for the future that he envisioned for his company. He indicated that the only leadership development activity that they had engaged in was elementary succession planning, where each executive was asked to identify a replacement. This succession strategy was not backed by any formal, planned development and, when the CFO was released, they soon found what they should have expected. The named successor was no more prepared for the change in scope and geography than was his former boss. Succession is about identifying talent pools; development is about the depth of talent in that pool. In this case, the talent pool was very shallow.

We asked the CEO some very basic questions about leadership development:

- Have you identified critical competencies around which to build a leadership program?
- Have you identified any high-potential managers for development?
- Do you have a process in place to develop these high potentials?
- Have you thought about what jobs are critical for developing the new competencies that are needed to develop your next senior executives?
- How will you know that your leadership development efforts are leading to the outcomes that you desire?

He answered with a blank stare. Then, this CEO just leaned across the table and matter-of-factly asked, "I'm supposed to be able to answer these questions, aren't I?"

This CEO got the message loud and clear. He hired a director of leadership development who worked with us to develop and implement leadership programs for both the top succession pool and for a newly created pool of high-potential managers who would fill the pipeline with future leaders.

If you ask this CEO if leadership development matters, he will answer unconditionally "Yes." His experience in moving to an international business with a much larger scope demonstrated the need for new leadership (and management) talent. Did he see leadership development as the path to creating a deep talent pool? In his mind, it was the only solution. He told us that he watched his people grow as they transformed an entrepreneurial idea into a very successful 400-person company. He learned that people can develop new leadership skills to meet new business challenges. He is now convinced that he can accelerate the development of future leaders in planned ways to meet new growth challenges.

Is he interested in formal evidence of return on investment? Not really. His past experience has taught him that doing nothing (as he did in the past) has clear consequences that put the future of his business at risk. He is willing to take it on faith that leadership development adds real value in the near term and, more important, in the long run. He stated that he would not be caught with his "developmental pants at his knees again." In this instance, he equated the return on investment with the development activity itself.

Contrast this example with a CEO who did ask for evidence that the company's investment in leadership development had a positive payoff. The company is Bell Helicopter-Textron. The first author worked with training managers at Bell to jointly design a leadership program that was focused on leading change. At the time this program was developed, Bell was struggling with how to implement major changes that would directly affect their competitiveness and their future. This leadership program was aimed at leadership processes around change and the new skills needed to get these results. Our goal was to help these leaders develop the capacity to lead change in real time, by being willing and able to engage in tough conversations that had immediate impact. We helped them understand that these conversations were real opportunities to influence and to lead (see Peters and Grenny, 2003). The last two days of the program consisted of an interpersonal communications program (Patterson, Grenny, McMillan, and Switzler, 2002) aimed at helping the participants to develop the skills for addressing the crucial conversations that were identified during the first three days.

For each of the first six leadership programs, evaluation was based on participant feedback at the end of each day, and again at the end of the program. The feedback suggested that the program was well received by the participants and was on target to help them develop the needed skills. We urged participants to look for a practice field on the job to apply this learning. Two weeks after the training, the participants made an informal report on their training experience to senior leaders at Bell. At this time, they described the potential practice fields that they had selected to apply what they had learned in the program. Participants had no difficulty seeing where the material they had learned could be applied. The participants' general enthusiasm suggested that the program was effective and would produce the outcomes that senior management wanted to achieve. But no on-the-job evaluation was ever done.

Enter Mike "Red" Redenbaugh, Bell's newly appointed CEO. When Red came on board, he asked the question, What results have we seen from this development program and what difference does it make to the overall performance of the organization? In short, he wanted to be assured that Bell's investment in leadership development produced more than a promise. He wanted tangible results. It was no longer acceptable simply to speculate about how the development would help. Real results were needed.

Red's concern about demonstrating the impact of leadership development is becoming more common, especially in large companies that have invested large sums of money in development efforts that have produced no real evidence that these development dollars were well spent. Executives are now asking, Why will the next development program be any different than the last one? While some executives, as in the first example, will take it on faith that development is a solid and necessary investment that produces real returns, many CEOs are directly questioning the development proposals put before them: How will you show me that this investment in leadership development will produce a tangible payoff to the organization?

This perspective is important not only because it forces evaluation, but also because it clarifies that results do matter. Evaluation can no longer be an afterthought. Executive sponsors for training and development want to see something more tangible than a promise, more real than smile sheets, and with more impact than a subjective judgment that more talented people are in the succession pool.

Evidence of Impact Does Not Have to Be Financial

What evidence do executives want to see? This is an interesting question, and one that deserves considerable scrutiny. It is not uncommon to see people respond in financial terms. After all, that is the classic meaning of ROI. Stakeholders want hard evidence that the dollars returned make the dollars invested worthwhile. We have no problem with this perspective, except, of course, that it is an extremely difficult one to clearly and convincingly demonstrate in most organizational settings (see Chapter Five for a discussion and demonstration of using ROI to evaluate leadership development programs). The exception might be in those settings where leadership development is directly related to producing a financial outcome. For example, it is reasonable to see evidence of a financial return when the leadership development program is designed for the specific demands of, and conducted for, an intact team that has direct responsibility for specific project deliverables. If the participants attend a leadership development program that does not have such stated outcomes (for example, a public program where discussions of specific applications are more difficult to hold), is it reasonable to expect to see strong financial evidence of ROI? In this case, we would need to search for other criteria to evaluate the effectiveness of this kind of leadership development program.

This notion was captured years ago by Pat Smith (1976), who wrote that we need to choose criteria (outcomes) that are at the same level of abstraction as our independent (predictor) variables. She was concerned with the logic of hypothesizing and demonstrating relationships in applied research. While she was not considering leadership development specifically, her warning is highly relevant. She cautioned against measuring the independent variable (a leadership development program) at a micro (for example, individual) level and expecting it to relate statistically to criteria at a macro (or unit) level (financial outcomes at the business-unit level).

This is an important warning to heed regarding predictions of financial ROI. We all know that there are many factors beyond the control of a leader or leadership team that impact financial outcomes. They range from economic factors (for example, the rising price of oil), to market issues (for example, a new, strong competitor), to changes in laws and regulations (for example, the passage of the Sarbanes-Oxley Act in the United States), to internal issues (for example, contract problems with the union), to major external events (for example, the terrorist attacks of September 11, 2001), just to mention a few.

So, what can we conclude? First, financial ROI may not be the appropriate measure of success unless the leadership development effort is aimed specifically at more macro leadership issues. Second, ROI may be a complex issue to judge because context matters so much. We can seldom rule out the possibility that a failure to see a financial return on development dollars has more to do with external factors that are beyond the immediate control of leaders. Third, when we implement leadership programs at more micro levels, we need a way to assess ROI that is appropriate to those levels. Fourth, the most appropriate indicator of success may not be a financial measure at all.

It is unrealistic to expect that all leadership development activities will produce measurable financial results. Rather, we need to focus on the results that are possible relative to the development interventions that we select. To do this, we need to ask two fundamental questions:

1. What new results will the participants be able to produce (versus what they will be able to know or do) as a result of this development effort?
2. If they are able to produce these results, will the investment in development be worthwhile to the organization?

By asking the executive sponsors of leadership development to answer these questions, we move beyond faith and get down to what they really want to see in the way of results. If these executive sponsors really want hard evidence of ROI (quantitative financial results), then the leadership development effort has to be designed and evaluated in a way that makes it possible to measure effectiveness in this way. In the final analysis, we may need to engage executive sponsors of leadership development in a dialogue to identify the behaviors, results, and outcomes that can reasonably be expected as people develop leadership competencies, and then ask whether that would make the development effort worthwhile.

Context Revisited: The Notion of Local Context

It does not serve any purpose to bemoan the fact that context often conspires against realizing the effects of development efforts. Instead, evaluators need to identify how to use context to help ensure that investments in leadership development have a chance to pay off. This can lead to new ways of designing leadership development programs and to more meaningful ways of assessing results.

Since context refers to a wide variety of work and organizational factors (see Figure 9.1) that affect outcomes and that are beyond the control of leaders, it would be easy to conclude that it is impossible to control all of those factors simultaneously in ways that make the impact of leadership development observable. We would agree at this level. But context can also be viewed more narrowly, in the daily lives of people in their work settings. We call this *local context*.

We believe that one's direct supervisor is the key to creating local context. Supervisors are the face of the organization to those returning to work from a development program (see Exhibit 9.1). Supervisors provide focus by setting their direct reports' work agendas and goals. If they do not legitimize the development activity and allow the opportunity to apply what was learned (that is, to lead), not much evidence of ROI should be expected or measured. If the supervisors do not provide time and/or resources and support for leadership initiatives, not much can be expected. If they reward and punish in ways that reflect the status quo, again, the status quo is the most reasonable expectation and is what will be observed.

EXHIBIT 9.1. AN EXPANDED ROLE FOR SUPERVISORS' INFLUENCE.

Supervisors have always been regarded as an important part of their direct reports' context. This is not new. However, in recent years, more emphasis is placed on the impact that supervisors play on a day-to-day basis. Decisions to leave a job may have more to do with one's supervisor than with other context factors; people leave supervisors rather than jobs or organizations. Organizations have not done enough to reap the positive value of supervisors as stewards of precious human resources. We are not the first to underscore the critical role that supervisors play. But we want to extend that discussion by describing how direct supervisors might create context for leadership development, and thus for evaluating investments in leadership development.

Direct supervisors are the local context that matters most in evaluating leadership development precisely because they have the most impact on the factors that encourage or discourage direct reports to apply lessons from development activities on their jobs. We believe that supervisors, unlike ubiquitous HR practices, management systems, and corporate culture, can be aligned to support development efforts.

What would happen if supervisors' roles were defined as being accountable for the organization's investment in development? What could we expect if they took an active role in seeing that their direct reports applied their learning from development activities? We believe that if this were to occur, we would create a local context that would be a positive force toward application of learning, and that we would see the results from that learning in our evaluations.

How could this happen? At a minimum, supervisors would encourage and be supportive of participant-initiated leadership efforts. At the other extreme, supervisors would work with their direct reports to specifically identify how they will apply their lessons from a leadership development activity. This conversation should include an agreement about what application (that is, project or piece of the work) the participants will initiate, expected results and milestones, and what it will look like when they are successful. It should also include a clear understanding of what resources will be made available to better ensure success and how the supervisor will support this activity. In this way, the supervisor becomes an active participant in supporting the implementation of a leadership initiative.

How does this concept connect to evaluation? Quite simply, it is a model of evaluation that is intertwined with leadership development and application. Without the active participation of supervisors, there is less chance for real application, and evaluators are less able to measure whether leadership development efforts pay off. As a development model, it is based on the premise that real leadership development has to occur on the job. This premise is consistent with the research on the role that experience plays in leadership development (McCall, Lombardo, and Morrison, 1988), and that underlies action learning processes (see Conger and Benjamin, 1999). While people might learn about leadership in formal programs, people can really learn to lead only by leading. A leadership program that does not link lessons to leading misses the opportunity to create a practice field so necessary for leadership lessons to take root.

As a measurement model, when we involve supervisors in development processes, we end up with at least a demonstration project and, if formalized, an expected set of outcomes. This provides a much better opportunity for measurable results. Note that the results may or may not be financial in nature. In all cases, however, they should address the two key questions asked earlier: What should participants be able to produce (versus know or do) as a result of this development effort? If they are able to produce these results, will the investment in development be worthwhile? Thus, applications should be both meaningful, as judged by the supervisor, and matched to the level of intervention. As such, it provides an ROI opportunity that meets the expectations of the management audience that approved and supported it.

Case Studies of Leadership Development and Evaluation

To examine how context can be built into the design of leadership development programs and their evaluations, we report on the processes and outcomes in two organizations with which we have had direct experience.

Bell Helicopter

The Bell leadership development program (described earlier in the chapter) was a five-day program. Nine training sessions were conducted over a three-year period and at two different locations (Fort Worth, Texas, and Montreal, Quebec). For the first six sessions, participants were asked only to identify how they would apply their learning. After Mike Redenbaugh became CEO, however, the focus changed from potential to results. That only affected the two programs in Fort Worth and the one program in Montreal offered in 2004.

Prior to these programs, participants met for a kick-off meeting at which they were told that they would be expected to apply what they had learned to an on-the-job project. No attempt was made to focus them on any particular type of project. Rather, they were asked to identify a specific and important project in which they could apply what they learned from the development program. They were also asked to discuss this potential project with their immediate supervisors. Based on these discussions, the participants and their supervisors completed a written agreement indicating the nature of the issue, what specific problems they would tackle, what successful outcomes would look like, the timetable and milestones, and the support that the participant could expect from the supervisor.

We experimented with two methods of enrolling supervisors in the program. In Fort Worth, we simply informed supervisors of their responsibility for development, and we provided them with specially designed instructions to guide this discussion. In Montreal, we brought supervisors into a meeting to discuss their roles and responsibilities in this leadership development effort. This discussion ended with the company president asking them to work closely with their direct reports. He then provided them with forms to guide these discussions.

Forms were used to guide participants to identify a project that allowed them to apply learnings from the development activity. An example form is given in Exhibit 9.2.

Approximately four months after the training, we convened the participants and their supervisors to report out to the senior management team. Participants were asked to (1) summarize the types of projects and project results achieved; (2) review three to four "showcase projects" in greater detail; and (3) identify what they learned from the program that had positively impacted project outcomes and their ability to lead.

This report was facilitated by having participants complete a form summarizing results and learnings (see Exhibit 9.3) and having supervisors complete another form that summarized the results they observed and what their direct reports learned about leadership (see Exhibit 9.4).

Some projects were more focused on everyday leadership. They focused on changes in style (usually communications styles) or specific issues within the participants' level of authority. Some projects, however, were not as specific. They reflected leadership efforts that cut across functional and, in one case, national boundaries. These turned out to be the showcase reports. While all of the participants reported positive results (for example, better communication, better and more focused meetings, more effective performance feedback and coaching), some of the reports were especially noteworthy. Several projects were directed at developing a process for cross-functional or cross-national teams that united the team members in new ways. Others

EXHIBIT 9.2. APPLICATION PLAN.

Leadership development doesn't end with the end of the training program; it begins there! Application, on-the-job, is where you will learn how to put to use the concepts and skills that are learned. We want you to apply your learning to a project that both gives you a chance to practice what was learned on real challenges you face *and* that gives the company a return on its investment in your development. This does not need to be an additional, new project. It could be how you approach important, existing work to improve your results. In either case, you are to indicate what new and better result you will produce by applying what you have learned. Plan to report results at a meeting in approximately four months.

Pick a project that has some ambition to it, but that is doable within the next four months. That's a tight balance—we would rather you apply your learning to producing project results that matter, even if it means that you'll report on progress rather than results at our report out for this course.

Note: You can team up with other participants to work together on the same project.

Name _____   Dept. _____   Ext. _____

My Supervisor _____   Ext. _____

Other participants that will work with me:	
Project name and scope.	
Describe the project you will initiate.	
What results do you anticipate achieving? (improvements in quality, quantity, schedule, morale, safety, cost avoidance, cost savings, reduced cycle time, internal or external customer satisfaction, motivation, etc.)	
Describe what it would look like if you are successful (be specific here), and indicate any high-level steps and milestones that will guide your actions.	
What concepts and tools from the course will you use? Be specific here.	
What support (time, resources, unblocking obstacles, for example) was agreed upon in your discussion with your supervisor?	
Indicate the date you discussed this with your supervisor.	

EXHIBIT 9.3. FOLLOW-UP REPORT BY PARTICIPANT.

Name _____	Dept. _____
My Supervisor _____	
Other participants that worked with me:	
Answer the following questions. Project name, type(s) of changes or improvements I chose, and expected results.	
What are the tangible (for example, cost savings) and intangible (for example, improved morale) results of my leadership efforts?	
What learnings/skills did I attempt to apply in this project? What worked and didn't work, and what will I do differently next time?	
What did I learn about myself—how am I a better leader?	

EXHIBIT 9.4. FOLLOW-UP REPORT BY SUPERVISOR.

Name: _____	Dept._____
My employee: _____	
Please provide comments and feedback on:	
The name, scope, and importance of this project.	
The results achieved and why those results were important.	
What your direct report learned about leadership.	

focused more on tangible issues. At the Fort Worth site, senior leaders who had routinely provided positive evaluations for this leadership program were especially pleased to see real and tangible outcomes that justified their investment in their subordinates. Those outcomes can be seen in the following descriptions of the showcase projects.

One team took on a critical information technology issue that involved a process redesign that improved the availability of technical data across the corporation. Their challenge was to maximize time-to-market benefits of concurrent engineering, making data available to people who needed it, when they needed it, while maintaining control of the data. This project was critical because it impacted how the work of engineers could be used more effectively and the costs associated with using engineering work products.

This project had been stalled prior to the leadership program. In the four months following the program, this team tackled this issue and moved it forward through the third gate of Bell's gated decision process. They reported that concepts, processes, and skills taught during each day of the five-day program were used to get this project back on a successful track.

A second example involved a team working on a corporate project aimed at creating a center of excellence for communications services. If successful, this center would have a positive impact at not only Bell Helicopter, but also in all of the Textron family of companies. This team had been stuck. At the four-month mark, it was not only moving forward, but gaining momentum. The project leader reported that the team went back to basics, applying lessons from throughout the leadership program, to include creating a shared need, a common vision, a listing of obstacles to be overcome, and a plan for moving this project forward as middle managers across organizational boundaries.

A third showcase project was aimed at reducing materials costs in one of Bell's major test laboratories, where they were threatening to go well over budget. The leader of this team reported a savings of approximately $250,000 in the four-month period and also noted that the costs were now within budget. The leader of this team reported that their success reflected multiple aspects of the leadership program, especially the module on crucial conversations (Patterson, Grenny, McMillan, and Switzler, 2002). He also reported that a course in risk management contributed to the team's success.

A final example addressed delays in receiving component parts for helicopters being built for the Iraq war effort. The team leader reported that they resolved this issue within the four-month work period by applying their lessons about leading from the middle and the crucial conversations training they received. The result was an 83 percent (twelve days) reduction in cycle time. He not only spoke to this cycle time reduction, but also proudly spoke to more fully contributing to the war effort.

Similar results were reported at the Canadian facility. Jacques St-Laurent, president of Bell Helicopter-Canada, offered the following reaction: "[The follow-up process] was in my view a truly excellent tool to make sure participants had an opportunity to apply their learnings." He went on to say that the value was "in the fact that participants had to 'dig out' their course notes and try their best to apply them to a real situation, thereby truly leveraging the class training." Consistent with this reaction, Canadian participants reported that the leadership program made a big difference in their attempts to lead. Many could point to specific lessons, conceptual models, process tools, and other skills that they found helpful. A large percentage reported more confidence in applying the lessons from the leadership program.

These examples focused on enrolling supervisors in creating opportunity and support for a leadership development effort. We believe these ideas are scaleable, meaning that we can apply them anywhere we need to develop leaders to step up to leadership challenges. We turn now to an example of a leadership development effort that was more macro in its scope, since it impacted organization-wide outcomes.

Texas Instruments

Texas Instruments (TI) is a major player in the global semiconductor industry, specializing in the digital signal processing and analog segments of this market. Between 1983 and 1993, TI had positioned itself into a portfolio of businesses consisting of semiconductors, defense electronics, software, materials and controls, and personal productivity products. None were number one or two in their industry, and it showed. The market capitalization of the company stagnated and remained almost flat in the $3–$5 billion range during this period.

In 1994, CEO Jerry Junkins and his leadership team made the decision that it was time for major changes in the strategic direction of the company. Thinking back to other failed attempts to implement strategic change, Junkins adopted a different approach this time. Rather than huddling his senior executives to hammer out a new strategy and then asking the public relations department to announce it unilaterally to the TI workforce, he decided that the primary goal would be to create "strategic unity." Junkins knew from painful experience that leaders and key employees would not commit to executing any new strategy unless they had personal and active involvement in developing it. His goal, then, was to build a cadre of leaders who would work with their subordinate leaders to take the company to a more desirable future. Junkins's goal, just like in the Bell example, was to create leadership support for the leadership of others.

The Strategy Leadership Team (SLT), consisting of Junkins and his most senior executives, took personal ownership in developing the process for creating and implementing the new strategy. It was clear from the beginning that leadership development was a critical element in the planned strategic change. Junkins knew that strategy, no matter how compelling, would not implement itself. Leadership development was not considered an outside event (for example, attending a course). Rather, leadership development was conceived of as informing, engaging, and supporting the leaders who had to step up to the challenges of implementing the new strategy.

In 1995, the process of creating strategic unity was initiated. A series of weeklong meetings were held around the world to allow TI leaders to begin the work of crafting a new strategy. The first workshop was called "Creating Our Future" (COF), and it was designed to involve more than 200 leaders in the process of formulating the new strategy.

A key component of that strategy involved creating new revenue streams by creating new business lines. Junkins, again, moved to involve his cadre of leaders by holding another COF in 1996. At this workshop, attention turned to more than just improving the climate for innovation; it was the beginning of the process for identifying and bringing new businesses on line. Junkins realized that new business opportunities would depend on people stepping up to identify opportunities and then leading these efforts to create these new businesses. Importantly, many of these senior leaders knew that they would not be the ones to do this; their role would have to be one of supporting younger leaders who were closer to the emerging technology in the digital signal processing domain and who would be there long enough to develop, start, and stabilize those new businesses. Thus, the 1996 COF helped the top 200 leaders to (1) learn what it meant to create a climate for innovation; (2) develop capabilities for effectively identifying, encouraging, and sponsoring entrepreneurs within TI; and (3) understand how to identify and sort through potential innovation opportunities. The 1996 COF was based on the theme of "Achieving Our Vision through Innovation: The Leader's Role." Indeed, the agenda for the leader's role was clarified and the participants grew in their understanding of the company's direction and strategy. They were much clearer about their role of supporting innovators and entrepreneurs, and were much more confident in their own abilities to exhibit the leadership skills relating to this strategic focus. Since the hallmark COF workshops, additional yearly gatherings have taken place, each designed around a theme of continuing the strategic unity that was created and aimed at clarifying the support needed from the assembled leaders for the company's strategy implementation.

So what were the lessons learned from the TI strategic unity process? First, it became clear that the goal of creating strategic unity was attained by providing the opportunity for leaders to get personally involved in creating the new strategy. Second, the integration of leadership development into strategy formulation and execution was a powerful combination that gave leaders a business reason to improve their knowledge, skills, and abilities to align with the strategy. Leadership development was one of the stated goals of the strategic unity process and was embedded in all of the workshops and follow-up activities. Working on real business issues, as opposed to attending a training program dealing with hypothetical issues, became a very powerful motivator of individual development. Third, these leaders teamed with their subordinates to create a climate for innovation that spread throughout the organization. Fourth, this process was expensive, time consuming, and difficult to coordinate. Without the continuing ownership and involvement of the CEO and his senior team, it would not have been possible to sustain the effort for very long. That, as much as anything, legitimized and encouraged leaders to step forward.

Three metrics spoke to the outcomes of this development effort. They were shareholder value, customer value, and TI-people value. In the case of shareholder value, the market capitalization of the company had stagnated in the $5 billion range when the process began. TI's market capitalization is about $50 billion at the time this chapter was published. With its new business strategy, TI has positioned itself as the market leader in the digital signal processing and analog solutions segments of the semiconductor market. In terms of customers, TI has become a major player in wireless solutions (cell phones, PDAs), broadband, digital consumer products, and many others. TI's preferred position as the leader in these market segments put it in good position to expand its strong customer base in the growth segments of the market. In terms of employees, TI has been recognized by *Fortune* as one of the one hundred best places to work in America for the fifth consecutive year. While it is always hard to disentangle cause and effect in long-term, large-scale change efforts such as this, TI's leadership firmly acknowledges that these outcomes were made possible by the focused efforts to develop leaders who would create entrepreneurial results (indeed, create a whole new industry). These leaders, in turn, would not have emerged unless senior leaders created a supportive environment that allowed strategic unity to be linked with the development of a cadre of younger leaders who would enable the company to create a new future. George Consolver, director of the TI Strategy Process, summarized it this way: "We knew that we had to make huge changes in strategic direction to survive in the semiconductor marketplace. We put the company under a lot of stress by selling off profitable businesses and closing down others to make room for the new businesses that were created and acquired to give us a competitive advantage in the DSP and Analog segments. The strategic unity and leadership support that were generated by our leaders in COF helped us to get through this painful time and emerge as a much stronger company."

Role of the Direct Supervisor

In both of these case studies, supervisors are a major contextual factor in leadership development. They were intentionally designed into the development process. At Bell Helicopter, supervisors were asked to hold discussions with their direct reports aimed at identifying meaningful opportunities for leading. Those discussions included aspects of good performance management; for example, setting goals and milestones, discussing what success would look like, and deciding how these goals would be measured. The simple act of having supervisors help identify leadership applications acknowledged and reinforced the importance of applying new learnings on the job. This is an important local context feature. The supportive role of supervisors was intentionally designed into the process by including discussions of how supervisors would actively support their subordinates in performing the projects that they chose. This is a critical addition, since it acknowledges that the role of the supervisor includes direct support of the leadership initiative and the subordinate leaders who are on the firing line.

Patterson, Grenny, McMillan, and Switzler (1996) talk about this in their "six source" model of performance and argue, as do many others, that performance reflects both ability and motivation, and that ability and motivation have individual, social, and organizational determinants. They also argue that social determinants (for example, encouragement, social reinforcement, opportunity creation, coaching) are often overlooked as formal targets of influence when attempting to create change. They conclude that social roles may need to change in advance of individual-level changes in motivation and ability. Having supervisors create leadership opportunities and discuss their roles in supporting those opportunities can be a powerful social force. We think that this is what helps create the local context for applying leadership lessons and for realizing a return on those investments.

At TI, the importance of leadership development can be seen at a more macro level by the actions of the CEO and his team, who understood that strategic unity and leadership were needed for strategy implementation. Thus, they focused on the development of the next level of leaders, who in turn needed to assume a leadership support role for those who would actually be identifying and creating new business for the company. These managers were involved in strategy development and discussions about creating a climate for innovation. They learned about what it took to create a new, innovative business and how to identify ideas that would turn into prospects for new revenue streams. Their role was not so much to create these new businesses; rather, they were asked to provide critical support to subordinates who would actually do it. In effect, Junkins created the container for leadership development and encouraged the leaders that he produced to create the container for the leadership of others.

So what did these two organizations, Bell and TI, conclude about the return on their investments in leadership development? In both cases, the executive sponsors openly declared the organizational returns to be well in excess of the investment costs, even though no formal attempts were made to calculate financial ROI. The primary reason for this is that the sponsors did their homework in advance by addressing the two questions that were posed: What results will the participants be able to produce (versus know or do) as a result of this development effort, and if they are able to produce these results, will the investment in development be worthwhile to the organization? In both examples, the participants were able to deliver valuable results, and these results were deemed to be very worthwhile to both organizations. By designing the local context (supportive roles of supervisors) into the fabric of these development efforts, these leaders and their organizations were able to accomplish results that were obvious and powerful.

Conclusion

These findings have important implications for the design, development, and evaluation of leadership development efforts. First, this line of thinking acknowledges that leadership development, for the most part, occurs on the job. We can no longer be satisfied with leadership development efforts that wall off participants from on-the-job opportunities to lead, no matter how relevant the content or how good the delivery. This doesn't mean that formal leadership programs and workshops are irrelevant. It does mean that we need to intentionally link the lessons about leadership to the actual activity of leading (see Exhibit 9.5).

A second implication is that leadership development requires both opportunity and support in the work setting. Again, we learn to lead by leading, and in many organizations this requires creating real opportunities to lead along with active support for those leadership initiatives. Since many organizations conspire against making opportunity and support available, a third implication is that development opportunities need to be intentionally designed to promote both opportunity and support for applying leadership lessons on

EXHIBIT 9.5. CONNECTING LEADERSHIP DEVELOPMENT TO LEADERSHIP ACTIVITY WITH ACTION LEARNING.

Action learning is an increasingly more common way to link leadership development to leadership activity. Action learning has participants involved, individually or in teams, in a real issue of some significance to company leaders. It reflects a figure-ground reversal in that the leadership issue becomes the figure and the development is done in support of resolving that issue. There are a number of ways that program designers have attempted to approximate this within the context of a formal leadership program. Some programs, for example, have participants bring real issues to a leadership program to conceptually apply their learning. While not the same thing as leading, it provides a real-life application opportunity, even if only as a thought application. This is a more effective method if done as an in-company program where others in the room understand the issue and the company and, therefore, can contribute to the discussion by providing feedback, suggestions, encouragement, and support. Some companies send intact leadership teams to training with the goal of helping them address a specific leadership issue. Some companies organize training to be just in time and in support of individual or team leadership initiatives. Thus, individual leaders or leadership teams might have a coach assigned to serve them as needed and when needed.

the job. We think the best way to do this is to create local context by enlisting the active involvement of the supervisors of the individuals involved in leadership development activities. Thus, another implication is to leverage the involvement of the supervisor in leadership development efforts.

Yet another implication is that supervisors need to define their roles in ways that make them active participants in the development of their direct reports. They must see their role in providing the practice field, the resources, and the support needed for development to take root on the job. In this way, leadership development is not just about the development process or about the persons being developed: it is the marriage of both.

In this way, evaluation is designed into the leadership development efforts and, as a final implication, a hoped-for return is replaced by a design that better assures that one will be realized and measured. If organizations want to maximize the likelihood of a measurable return on their investment in leadership development, they must design their efforts in ways that create the local context that makes real development possible on the job and design evaluation to assess the relevant outcomes.

References

Conger, J., and Benjamin, B. *Building Leaders: How Successful Companies Develop the Next Generation.* San Francisco: Jossey-Bass, 1999.

Fleishman, E. A., Harris, E. F., and Burtt, H. E. *Leadership and Supervision in Industry.* Columbus: Ohio State University Bureau of Educational Research, 1955.

Johns, G. "The Essential Impact of Context on Organization Behavior." *Academy of Management Review,* 2006, *31,* 386–408.

Kotter, J. *A Force to Change: How Leadership Differs from Management.* New York: The Free Press, 1990.

McCall, M., Lombardo, M., and Morrison, A. *The Lessons of Experience: How Successful Executives Develop on the Job.* Lexington, Mass.: Lexington Books, 1988.

Patterson, K., Grenny, J., McMillan, R., and Switzler, A. *The Balancing Act: Mastering the Competing Demands of Leadership.* Cincinnati: Thomson Executive Press, 1996.

Patterson, K., Grenny, J., McMillan, R., and Switzler, A. *Crucial Conversations: Tools for Talking When the Stakes Are High.* New York: McGraw-Hill, 2002.

Peters, L., and Grenny, J. "Crucial Conversations and Transformational Moments." In L. Carter, D. Ulrich, J. Bolt, and M. Goldsmith (eds.), *Best Practice Leadership Champions: Leading, Learning, and Fostering Success in the 21st Century* (pp. 251–260). San Francisco: Pfeiffer, 2003.

Peters, L., and O'Connor, E. "Situational Constraints and Work Outcomes: The Influence of a Frequently Overlooked Construct." *Academy of Management Review,* 1980, *5,* 391–397.

Smith, P. "Behaviors, Results and Organizational Effectiveness: The Problem with Criteria." In M. Dunnette (ed.), *The Handbook of Industrial Psychology.* Chicago: Rand-McNally, 1976.

CHAPTER TEN

EVALUATING COMMUNITY LEADERSHIP PROGRAMS

Teresa R. Behrens and Maenette K. P. Benham

Beginning in the late 1990s, many philanthropic foundations that supported leadership development programs began to explore ways in which leadership development could be better incorporated into their broader missions and visions. Some drivers for this change included changing demographics across the United States that required leaders with abilities to lead across differences; a general shift in philanthropy toward more targeted, strategic grant making; and the increasing difficulty of justifying the high per-participant cost of individual leadership programs. Leadership for what? became a critical question that challenged philanthropic foundations to think about leadership development as a strategy that moves a larger, substantive social agenda.

For example, the Pew Charitable Trusts focused on strengthening cultural leadership to better support the operations of arts programs; the Northwest Areas Foundation sought to develop leadership to reduce poverty; the Annie E. Casey Foundation addressed leadership issues to enhance outcomes for children and families; the Ford Foundation's Leadership for a Changing World program identified emerging leaders committed to making a difference in their communities; and the W. K. Kellogg Foundation (WKKF) shifted its leadership strategy from individual leadership development toward collective leadership for community change. The emphasis across philanthropic foundations is increasingly on creating change that engenders civic engagement and social activism in the contexts where people live and work.

This chapter focuses on the evaluation of the first session of the Kellogg Leadership for Community Change (KLCC) series. KLCC was launched in 2002, signifying the W. K. Kellogg Foundation's continued commitment to leadership development in support of its overall programming objectives. The overall vision of KLCC is to develop diverse community leadership that can work across boundaries—including age, gender, geography, race, culture, class, and faith—and mobilize collective action to improve local conditions and the quality of life in communities. Additionally, KLCC works to create community environments where people, especially those who are not normally included in leadership roles, can participate in efforts to improve their communities. Those who see themselves as leaders for the first time and those who see themselves as established leaders learn to understand each other and fully use each other's knowledge, gifts, and wisdom in addressing community issues.

The Overall KLCC Program Design

KLCC is being implemented through several sessions, each one focused on a different, broadly defined content area. Session I (2002–2004) focused on building public will to improve teaching and learning. Session II (2005–2007) focuses on youth and adult partnerships for social justice. In each session, a grantee organization in each community (six communities in Session I, five in Session II) selects twenty-five community fellows. These fellows work with local leadership coaches and national intermediaries to learn and generate individual and collective leadership skills, to create a shared understanding of issues confronting their community, and to undertake a project or projects to collectively address the issues. While KLCC focuses primarily on developing and supporting leadership in the context of local communities, it also recognizes the value of enabling community leaders to learn from one another through national networking meetings and the importance of surfacing lessons learned across communities.

Community Leadership: Concepts and Implications

In the context of KLCC, *community leadership* means leadership that is firmly rooted in the traditions, culture, and experiences of a community. Community leaders are individuals who are committed to their community and to collectively working with others to create positive change. One of the values of WKKF is that all voices in a community must contribute to creating a shared vision. Communities are healthy and successful when they have a vision that is a vision for everyone. Community leaders are not necessarily or even usually those who hold traditional positions of authority, such as elected officials, business people, or leaders in the nonprofit or educational arenas. In many communities, these positions are still held by people from more privileged backgrounds, often representing the old interests and vested power. In the meantime, however, communities have changed, becoming much more diverse.

Collective leadership is seen as one of three elements that engage communities in activities that can effect sustained and systemic change. The other elements are partnerships (networks of individuals and organizations) and focal institutions (the community's schools or other learning institutions) to be affected. KLCC brings these elements together. Leadership is supported through the fellowship and the local host organization that implements the fellowship. Partnerships and alliances are generated through relationships of the individual fellows and staff from the host organization. From the national evaluator's perspective, community-based, collaborative leadership, therefore, can be defined as the result of a process that brings together a diverse community of people to influence the work and outcomes of community institutions. What remains to be further understood is how change happens or does not happen in light of (or not) the KLCC experience.

Theory of Community Change

WKKF echoes that evaluation of community leadership programs should address all three of the elements mentioned (leadership, partnerships, and institutions), since they are inextricably interconnected. (Throughout this chapter, viewpoints described as that of WKKF represent the views of Teresa Behrens, and do not necessarily reflect an official position of the W. K. Kellogg Foundation.) There is not necessarily, however, a universal theory about how community change occurs. For example, there are some who think of community leadership as synonymous with community organizing. Others see a "healing racism" approach to community change. The conceptual coherence for KLCC is provided by a fairly simple theory of change that involves the following dynamics:

- A diverse group of citizens are engaged around an issue of community concern.
- Through a variety of activities, the group exchanges and explores diverse points of view and arrives at a shared vision for the future.
- Commitment to the shared vision builds, and the group designs a plan of action.
- The sense of collective leadership continues to build, and the group, armed with a plan of action, mobilizes to implement the plan.
- In the process of mobilization and implementation, others are attracted to the collective energy and progress and are empowered.

The process is dynamic and cumulative, with the goal that as each community takes action to make community change, the imprint of collective thinking and shared leadership becomes more deeply embedded in the community's culture and institutions, and it becomes evident they are operating in new ways. The challenge for evaluation is to see if this self-reinforcing process actually begins in a community.

For KLCC, using a theory of change approach to evaluation seemed the only viable approach, yet it also had to include an empowerment evaluation approach (Fetterman, Kaftarian, and Wandersman, 1995). The theory had to be articulated at a level of detail that was sufficient to guide data collection but also broad enough to accommodate community variations. For example, in each community, what it takes to arrive at a shared vision is different. The experience in Session I was that each community had to address racism in some way in order to achieve a shared vision. For some, it was addressed early in the process. For others, the really explosive issue (for example, the school mascot) was put on hold while the community fellows learned to work together on other issues. The theory of change case studies, including site-specific details, helped to extract a general principle about racial issues being important to address.

From the national evaluator's point of view, before a community can tackle an historic and institutionally entrenched issue, such as racism, relationships have to be built. Thus, a key question was, What do community-based leaders and leadership teams need to know how to do? It was learned that the leadership team in each community had to have a set of skills and tools they could use to build trust and relationships. The precise tools and how they were used differed in each community.

The KLCC Evaluation Design

The KLCC evaluation design has both a local and national component. Each site engages a local evaluator to address the local outcomes based on a locally determined plan of action that includes the results each community site intends to achieve. The national-level evaluation addresses the broader learning about the content (in part a synthesis of the local evaluations) and what is being learned about how to motivate and sustain collective leadership. There are three features of the KLCC initiative that the national evaluators are focused on learning about:

1. How collective leadership is developed and how it enhances public will to build a foundation for sustainable improvements in teaching and learning
2. What a community needs to be ready for and have the capacity to move or create public will to create change
3. How organizational structures can enhance community building and leadership for change

The national evaluation includes two components: ethnographic studies and pre- and postsurveys of participants at each site. The ethnographic studies provide a detailed understanding of how the program works at the local site and across the sites. The surveys provide data on key aspects of community capacity, readiness to engage in change, and strength and nature of social networking patterns. The ethnographic approaches are used to further explore the changes that are noted on the pre- and postsurveys to determine if they are attributable to KLCC or some other factors. They are also used to help highlight processes and outcomes that are not captured in the survey. For a summary of the ethnographic design, see Exhibit 10.1.

EXHIBIT 10.1. OVERVIEW OF THE ETHNOGRAPHIC EVALUATION DESIGN.

Data Collection Strategies
- A short open-ended biographical questionnaire
- Pre- and postinterviews
- Document collection
- Electronic media (archived discussion)

Data Collection Matrix

Individual Leadership Story	Collective Leadership Story	Impact and Themes: Site-Based (Cases)	Impact and Themes: Cross-Site
Biographical Questionnaire			
Pre- and post-interviews of leadership fellows	Pre- and post-interviews of leadership fellows	Pre- and post-interviews of site coach	Post-interview with the leadership fellows
Post-interview with the site coach	Pre- and post-interviews of host agency and coor-dinating agency		
Documents: Critical life map	Documents: Critical leadership development map Organizational maps from leadership coaches, host agency, coordinating agency	Documents: Individual assessments	Collection of documents from host agency and coordinating agency Collection of documents from leadership fellows
Threaded discussions with leadership fellows with focus on leadership metaphors	Threaded discussions with leadership fellows, coaches, and invited guests with focus on organizational metaphors, context: community assets and needs, community processes and challenges	Threaded discussions with leadership fellows, coach, host agency, with focus on teaching and learning, building public will, and community capacity for change	

Specific tools employed by the national evaluator include Leadership Critical Life Maps, pre- and postproject interviews of KLCC participants (leadership fellows, coaches, host agencies, coordinating agencies), and an online threaded discussion midway through the project among participants across sites. In short, the critical life map process (see Figure 10.1) asks respondents to visually represent four to six critical events or defining moments in their lives (for example, major educational experiences and accomplishments, losses, phases of life and related issues, successful and unsuccessful leadership or learning experiences and/or initiatives, careers, and so on) that they believe

FIGURE 10.1. CRITICAL LIFE MAP.

Directions

Look back on your life and select at least four critical events or defining moments in your life that you believe define who you are as a youth/community leader and the work/advocacy that you currently do. Examples of these events may include major educational experiences and accomplishments, losses, phases of life and related issues, successful and unsuccessful leadership/learning experiences and/or initiatives, careers, and so on.

Next, write each critical event, in chronological order, by each of the stars below. You are not obligated to use this form; feel free to design a life map that illuminates who you are.

Finally, write a short statement or story that describes each of these events. We will share and talk about our individual journeys during our first visit.

define who they are as community leaders and the work that they currently do. At the end of the KLCC session, the fellows revisit this critical life map and add events that define their leadership. The story of each fellow's life illuminates who they are at the start of the session and how they have grown over the course of the KLCC journey.

The purpose of the leadership questionnaire, interviews, and electronic communications (threaded discussions) is to explore the professional and personal life and leadership experiences of the leadership fellows over time. That is, we are collecting rich text of the fellows' talk about their own leadership, the development of collective leadership in their cohort of leadership fellows, and how this collective leadership enhances public will to build a foundation for sustainable improvements in teaching and learning. Condensed versions of each of the instruments are provided in Exhibits 10.2, 10.3, and 10.4.

Data analysis of the ethnographic process is ongoing throughout KLCC, thereby providing opportunities for the evaluators to review each set of data as they are collected and to write memos that record impressions and potential synthesizing themes, and identify key ideas and questions for follow-up. Each process in this series of data collection over time informs the next process of

EXHIBIT 10.2. PREPROJECT INTERVIEW GUIDE.

Please share with me your Leadership Critical Life Map, talking about each one of the critical events or defining moments. Focus on (1) characteristics/qualities of leadership that are most commonly associated with successful community-based change initiatives; (2) the extent to which the agreement and/or tension among the economic, political, cultural, and social features of your community affects the educational/school environment; (3) what challenges you believe communities face today.

As you look ahead, what are your current expectations, hopes, and anxieties you might have regarding this initiative? And how might you advise the coach, the host agency, and the coordinating agency about their work with you and other leadership fellows?

Can you share your definition/perceptions of the following ideas/terms: leadership, educational leadership, community-based leadership, leadership for change, collaboration and/or networking, public will, community capacity building, social capital, cultural capital?

EXHIBIT 10.3. POSTPROJECT INTERVIEW GUIDE.

Note: Interviewer presents the respondents' initial Leadership Critical Life Map.

Look back over the last 18 months of the KLCC initiative and select four to six critical events or defining moments that you believe best define how your cohort of leadership fellows worked together to address teaching and learning in your community. Here's a piece of paper to add to your life map, and pencil and crayons. Please sketch these moments.

Please tell me about each of these moments.

What have you learned about yourself as a community leader?

What have you learned about your fellowship as leaders in the community?

In light of this experience, please define for me: *collective leadership* (provide me an example of this) and *theory of community change* (provide me an example of this).

In light of what you know, what do you still need to learn and/or what do you believe will be your next steps?

---

data collection as well as builds and deepens understanding of collective and community-based leadership for change.

KLCC Evaluation Challenges

The tricky part of the evaluation design, from WKKF's perspective, was to figure out how to look for common outcomes posited by the theory of change, understanding that it would be manifested in very different ways in each community. The in-depth, highly participative case studies served that purpose.

Another challenge in this evaluation is that the leadership development experience itself was highly customized for each community. There is a framework—a phased model of the steps that a group of community fellows go through together—but the way each community chooses to work through each stage varies. For example, one community tried to bring together five different ethnic groups in the city and began its work by having the five groups meet separately. In the other communities, the fellowship began with the whole group. In one community, the fellows had individual development accounts, while in others the grant funds were only used to support community projects.

EXHIBIT 10.4. THEMATIC PROBES FOR THREADED DISCUSSIONS.

Note: This is a midproject, online threaded discussion.

The following list of potential probes can be used during the course of the threaded discussion.

- What is the nature of individual leadership and group/collective leadership? How are they independent and interdependent?

- What defines the use (or not) of community assets that affect successful change initiatives? In particular, that affect successful teaching and learning initiatives in our schools?

- What community factors influence the level of public will to push for change? What is the level of contribution across different groups within a community?

- What are the unique factors (history, demographics, social economic status, and so on) that define/determine the perception and level of involvement in community initiatives and in particular school initiatives?

- Define the ideas/terms: *community capacity, social capital, cultural capital, community development, public will.*

- What are the perceived benefits of school-family-community networks/linkages to the governance of the schools? What perceived benefits of school-family-community networks/linkages are related to classroom teaching and learning practices?

- To what extent does community-based work impact policy and policy practice? What effect if any do these efforts have on the educational environment?

- How do race/ethnicity, gender, class, national heritage, languages (and other differences/uniqueness) impact community change? In particular, what effect do they have on school change related to teaching and learning?

- What is our perception/observation of the effect of collective leadership on change in the educational environment?

- How might community leaders and educational leaders utilize what they know and what they can know (through collaborative work such as KLCC, for example) in defining better educational policy and practices?

- What does the educational environment look like for students as a result of this initiative? What can it look like?

- In your observation, what changes have occurred as a result of KLCC? What changes still need to occur?

Ethnography seemed to be the only way to approach an evaluation with this level of complexity. Throughout the evaluation process it was important for the national evaluator to keep asking questions such as

- How has or has not the participation of fellows in their communities changed? Why and how?
- What are the attitudes and definitions of leadership to create and sustain change in teaching and learning arenas and how do they (or do they?) shift over the course of the KLCC timeline?
- To what extent have the fellows' levels of confidence and leadership skill changed (or not) in a way that constructively impacts and improves the lives of children, youth, and their families? What are the policy implications?
- So what do the fellows intend to do next? Why and how?

The national evaluator felt that by reflecting on these queries throughout the data collection and analysis process, she could stay true to both the rigor of the inquiry/evaluation discipline and also provide useful, practical information for the communities and for WKKF. She found that holding the tension between objective and participatory requires a bit of finesse. Evaluation of this sort is a holistic engagement process. *Engagement* means that the evaluator must be a part of many levels of participation (for example, participant-observer with leadership fellows, with the site management team, with the national evaluation team and other site evaluators, to name a few) and travel the pathway of this complex and messy journey. An external, objective reviewer is seldom accepted as part of the fellowship community and therefore does not have the respect of that community. Without those bonds of trust and respect, the usefulness of the evaluator's contribution to the ongoing development work of the fellowship is limited.

In addition to the challenges described, the nature of the KLCC intervention raised many interesting questions for the evaluation design. The remainder of this chapter is organized around these questions, providing insights and views from several vantage points, including WKKF, the national evaluator for Session I, and two KLCC site evaluators. The questions include

- How can evaluators address the "Leadership for what?" question in community leadership programs?

- How can evaluators address the role of organizations in community leadership development?
- How can the evaluation address the interests of the multiple stakeholders in assessing the intended outcomes of community leadership programs?
- How do concepts of culturally competent evaluation play out in community leadership development evaluations?
- What role does evaluation play in creating a reflexive, developmental, and useful leadership development tool?

Leadership for What?

The Leadership for what? question is more difficult to answer in community leadership programs than in traditional individual leadership programs. The tension between evaluating process and content outcomes is high. Although in an individual leadership program, the Kirkpatrick (1994) model (reaction-learning-transfer-results) is very useful, it fails in the context of community leadership. Learning, for example, has to be team learning and needs to encompass not only traditional leadership skills but also ways of finding common ground with people who may be very different. It may include being willing and able to surface mental models that are really stereotypes about other groups in the community. There is some element of individual transformation, to be sure, but there is a collective transformation component that is quite different.

While there is a value-based component to community leadership programs, the theory is that this more inclusive process will result in better content outcomes. In KLCC's Session I, with its focus on improving teaching and learning, the evaluation design had to address what the identifiable (measurable) changes were in building public will for teaching and learning; at the same time it had to assess if a sustainable process for developing and supporting collective leadership strategies was being put into place.

The in-depth case studies were tremendously valuable on the latter, but there was also an interest in quantifying process outcomes. In the context where the desired change is a change in processes (a systems change), quantifying the process outcome changes was a real challenge. Using an empowerment approach to the evaluation enabled the evaluation teams (national and site) to gain a deep understanding of the process changes that were occurring that might not be visible to an outsider, while allowing everyone to work together to clarify the content outcomes for both individual sites and the national network.

The KLCC longitudinal evaluation is another important component of how the community Leadership for what? question will be addressed. The KLCC Series provides an opportunity to assess how a group leadership development experience can contribute to improving conditions in communities. The evaluation of traditional leadership development programs typically focuses on the personal development and career paths of the individuals, the impact on their organizations, or both. The KLCC Series relies on collective leadership and the expected impact this will have on communities. Therefore, while the impacts of the experience on individual participants and organizations are important, the evaluation will also address the following questions:

- To what extent is the community and/or host agency able to sustain the capacity to develop collective community leadership?
- What was the relevance of context (that is, place, history, culture) in shaping and implementing effective practices?
- What mechanisms or programming elements were used by the communities to sustain changes? What was the role of impact services policy, evaluation, and communications?
- To what extent does the collective leadership approach create change related to community identified issues?
- How does the collective leadership model create change in communities?
- How is the collective leadership approach adapted to fit local contexts?
- To what extent is the Kellogg Leadership for Community Change approach propagated, both within the same communities and in others?

There will be a sample of the fellows, along with representatives of the host agency (grantee organization), and other community leaders from each site that will be followed over time in order to be able to answer these questions. The intent is to continue working with local evaluators to study the long-term impacts. This will be feasible in communities in which the evaluator maintains some relationship with the host organization.

The Evaluation and Grant-Making Models

From WKKF's perspective, it is important that the evaluation model fit the grant-making model. A collective leadership program requires an empowerment evaluation model, and thus an external expert wouldn't fit the spirit of the work. However, there is always a tension of wanting to document impact in an objective way that is credible to its board and other funders and a need to understand the bottom-line impact.

The national evaluator felt the need to push this evaluation toward a more communal process that included taking the pulse of the community, acknowledging that the evaluation would focus on both process and content outcomes and that reflective practice would be integral to the whole. There was careful consideration about evaluation of the sites, including whether there should be a focus only on collaborative leadership, only on the impact of the projects, or both. In the end, the qualitative team of evaluators, in varying partnerships with the site evaluators and host organizations, did a combination of the two.

This design tension was viewed as healthy by the national evaluator, as it encouraged thinking more deeply about how to evaluate site-based, collective leadership in a more collaborative and narrative fashion with site-based evaluators. More important, this presented multiple opportunities to learn more about the unique communities at each site and to build a common language and trusting working relationships with the site participants, thereby increasing the national evaluator's credibility and access at each of the sites, as well as ensuring the reliability of its evaluative conclusions.

However, leadership is not leadership if no one leads. In other words, once the fellows at each site develop their collective model of leadership, they need to do something. So, accounting for the work that engaged the fellowship and its impact on teaching and learning was an element that both the site-based evaluators and the national evaluators assessed. There are certainly limits to looking at impacts on teaching and learning in the short term because many indicators of impact take a longer time to be visible.

One example noted by WKKF of how it holds the process/content tension is in how it thinks about the role of the project or projects tackled by each community. For example, does the project result in pedagogical tools or is the project significant on its own? Are the sites accountable for the work done in the project or for gleaning learning and leadership insights from it? Interestingly, how the project is positioned within the leadership program differs across leadership programs funded by different foundations. In KLCC, the project has been viewed as emerging after some group development work that creates a shared vision; other programs have put the group of fellows together and had them begin with a project based on the theory that the project itself will lead to creating the group cohesiveness. Thus, there seems to be little consensus in the leadership development field as to whether projects are process or outcome focused.

One decision made by WKKF in the evaluation design was that evaluating the content outcomes of the work had to be the responsibility of the local evaluator and host agency. If it is going to help create local capacity to continue this work in the future, the mind-set of using evaluation as a local feedback mechanism had to be embedded from the beginning. This needed to be expressed even more explicitly and will be in future sessions. Using data to influence and inform decision making is a leadership skill. KLCC is casting a wide net with a hypothesis that different results endure in different communities. For some, the momentum will be on the issue; in others it will be the collective leadership approach. In some, it may be both.

This *Leadership for what?* tension has been important for the national evaluator, framed as the *So what?* as she worked to better understand how the KLCC Session I sites defined and enacted community-based, collaborative leadership. A cross-case comparative analysis of the *Leadership for what?* question must honor the disciplinary approaches to leadership and the local and cultural thought ways of leadership. Furthermore, conducting evaluation in a communal way that focuses on collective leadership requires that the evaluator and the process be inclusive of the place (ecological features and history of the community environment) and the social, cultural, political, and economic dimensions that influence the intent and the manner in which leadership functions. It was observed during the KLCC Session I that, for the most part, the fellows who came from ethnic minority communities were hesitant to participate in the evaluation process. Many ethnic minority communities have experienced evaluation processes that, while well intentioned, excluded local voices (at their worst twisted the meaning of respondents); conducted data collection and analysis processes that were not transparent, hence raising ethical concerns as well as concerns regarding the ownership of the knowledge generated by respondents; and disseminated assessments and recommendations that offered little to no usefulness to the site (due to the disengagement of the evaluator with the community).

Localizing the evaluation process was integral to the work of a communal evaluation process. According to the national evaluator, this was accomplished through the process of talking to, building relationships with, talking to again, collaborating on evaluative issues, and talking to again. Local evaluators had to meet the intent of WKKF's overall mission and KLCC Series vision, and Leadership for what? needed to be answered by and owned by the local site. The local or site evaluator, in partnership with the national evaluator and their local leadership fellows, needed to be engaged in this enriching process of definition. This called for some creativity on all parts as they worked to create a multilevel and multidimensional evaluation process (with appropriate tools) that had both an individual and collective focus, was local and national in scope, and provided opportunity to explore old organizational patterns in order to create new organizational patterns and bring to light traditional (culturally appropriate) leadership knowledge within a contemporary setting.

Social Network Analysis

To that end, one of the tools used was a social network analysis. WKKF notes that a big part of the reason it pursued collective leadership lay in changing which people relate to each other in the community. The individual fellows completed a network analysis instrument that asked about communications patterns with other fellows, a set of other key stakeholders in the community, and the local KLCC management team (the representatives of the host agency and the local coach).

The original thinking was that changes would be seen in these networks by doing this pre- and post-KLCC experience analysis. It was found that these instruments really were not that useful for a number of reasons, including that the list of stakeholders (generated by the host agency) was not necessarily a group that became involved with KLCC during this relatively short timeframe. In one community, the fellowship was so fluid that it wasn't really feasible to get the same individuals to complete the network analysis.

On the other hand, one of the communities used a different version of network analysis, the Spider Diagram (see Figure 10.2), that asked each fellow to identify who they knew and who they could talk to about an issue. This

FIGURE 10.2. MAKING A SPIDER DIAGRAM: MAPPING YOUR CONNECTIONS.

1. Think about all your roles—student, worker, neighbor, parent, church member. *Write each major aspect of your life in a circle as shown below.*

2. Think about all the individuals and organizations that you come in contact with in these roles. (For example, as a parent: your child's school, day care center, and parents of your child's friends. As a student: people in your classes, clubs, after-school activities, sports teams, teachers, and people on your school bus.) Begin to list those individuals and organizations *in surrounding circles.*

3. For every organization, think about specific subgroups of that institution. (For example, at a school there are the teachers, the administration, unions, parent groups, clubs, and after-school programs. In a worship community, there may be Bible or other religious study groups, the choir, deacons, and social action groups.) *Write these in circles.*

4. For every individual, think about other links they may have to other communities and groups. (For example, Jane, your friend from the Boys & Girls Club, might also be actively involved in her church.) Draw additional circles and write these names in them, connecting the circles with lines to show the relationships.

5. Surprise! Look how many connections you have after all!

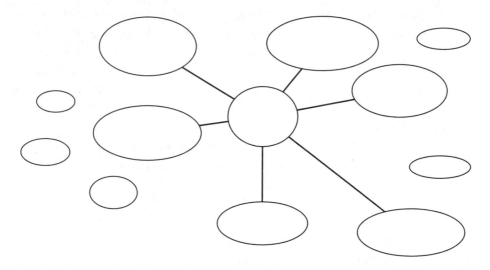

Adapted from D. Gehl, University Community Initiative, 2005.
Source: C. Ward, Northeast Action, 2004.

was very powerful for the fellows in terms of helping them visualize their own networks for change. WKKF is planning to use this approach in future KLCC sessions, beginning with asking the host agency representatives to map the other organizations with which they have working relationships. Changes will be tracked over time, repeating the mapping at midpoint and at the end of the initial (two-year) KLCC experience. It is hoped that this will provide a better picture of the real sustainable changes in relationships that may occur.

What Is the Role of Organizations in Community Leadership Development?

Organizations and institutions play a different role in community leadership programs than in traditional individual leadership programs. Traditionally, organizational impacts are assumed to follow from individual leaders behaving differently in the organization. In the KLCC community leadership model, the host organization is acting on behalf of the community; therefore, organizational leaders have to reach out to new constituencies that might not previously have been part of their network. The fellows, in most cases, are not employed by the host organization. The host organization is transformed by operating the program.

According to WKKF, when sites (communities) were first chosen to participate, one criterion was that a host agency could be identified—the grantee that would carry out the work locally—in whom there was confidence, based largely on having had prior experience working with them. In the original evaluation design, the impacts on the host organization were not incorporated very deeply into the evaluation. That is changing for future sessions. One lesson drawn from Session I is that the institutionalization of the work begun with KLCC is most likely going to occur through the efforts of the host agency. So, while individual fellows may have been drawn to KLCC because of their passion for the content (for example, improving teaching and learning), and they may continue working on the issue in meaningful ways, the host agency is likely to play a key role in developing new cadres of collective leaders, whether on the same issue or others. Further, the organization can have a broad reach in the community by changing how it interacts with other organizations by modeling collective behavior. For the next session, the host organization is completing a relationship map in which it identifies other organizations in the community with which it has relationships. This map will be repeated over time as one tool to assess how the host organization is impacted by their role in KLCC. (This is the Spider Diagram which was used at an individual level in Session I—see Figure 10.2—adapted for use at an organizational level.)

Individual fellows were not chosen as representatives of organizations, yet an unintended consequence of this process may be that they take a collective leadership model back with them to the organizations where they work. This may be another effective way to embed a new way of working in the community. As a sample of individual fellows are followed over time, this will be important to track via surveys in order to understand the real depth and breadth of the community change.

Opportunities of Diverse Cultural Situations

The national evaluator suggests that the diverse cultural situations of each KLCC Session I site present a powerful opportunity to understand more deeply the role of an organization in leadership development. Both organizational development theory and cultural and cross-cultural studies underscore the potential. (See, for example, Bolman and Deal, 2003; March and Simon, 1958; Ouchi, 1981; Peters and Waterman, 1982; Schein, 1992.) One way that a national evaluator can be helpful to local or site evaluators and the site's organizational team is to offer frameworks that might help them better understand the organizing power of culture. What is beginning to reveal itself is how local organizations learn to hold the internal dynamics of leadership development (for example, traditional cultural views of leadership and contemporary views of leadership) while interacting with external stakeholders and in some cases actively pursing external partnerships. For example, at several KLCC sites, evaluators observed empowered leadership fellows pushing and in some situations directing the work of the host organization toward practices that were more inclusive (less exploitive) and that further elevated the work of a collective community-based praxis.

Furthermore, the national evaluator indicates that a good deal was learned about how to do evaluation that promotes organizational learning while it supports collective leadership development. Involving the site-based evaluators and the fellows in the active process of accumulating knowledge (about place, context, culture, people, and so on) helps to inform their organizations' development, decision-making processes, and activities.

How Can the Interests of Multiple Stakeholders Be Addressed?

A community leadership program has a much larger and more complex group of stakeholders than does a traditional leadership program. In addition to the funder (which includes both a board of trustees and staff, who have different needs from the evaluation) and the fellows, there are representatives of the host agency, the broader community, and the organizations to which the fellows belong. Additionally, the organizations and institutions that might be impacted by the work of the fellows are other potential stakeholders. A multiple case study design that used multiple methods and enabled deep understanding of both the individual stories and the cross-cutting themes seemed most likely to satisfy the needs of a broad set of stakeholders.

The ethnographic approach has yielded insights into many facets of how KLCC has played out in each community. Another important way in which the evaluation can help address the needs of multiple stakeholders is by surfacing the fact that there are multiple outcomes, each with different timelines. Just making the complexity visible helps stakeholders. For stakeholders who are very results oriented, the longitudinal study will be important to addressing their interest in seeing content outcomes.

The national evaluator notes that by paying attention to the multiple audiences—what she terms the *social fabric* of each community—she came to believe that tacit knowledge about building strong communities of leadership lives within the individual, between people, and in community practices. The dynamic between people and community events and how this creates opportunities to become engaged in systematic, shared tasks was well understood among fellows. The ways in which this knowledge was encoded into practice (or not), within particular social justice actions, was less understood. The success of the fellowship's work depends to a large extent on their understanding of three factors: (1) the explicit and implicit dimensions of their community; (2) the explicit and implicit intention and rationale of their work (to what extent the project was embedded in relevant concerns); and (3) the nature of the fellowship.

In the end, according to the national evaluator, the nature of the fellowship became an integral influence that defined the outcome of KLCC programs—the extent to which a particular leadership team could affect the way in which a community thought about and approached teaching and learning. Knowledge about community-based, collaborative leadership emerges from the relationships people have with one another (see, for example, Exhibit 10.5). A community of leadership practice emerges from doing, which can be observed by viewing how this group shares, reframes, integrates, uses, and relearns information. This is a process that creates distributive awareness and ownership of particular problems, which can lead to powerful ways of crossing boundaries of difference, to inclusive engagement, to a definition of powerful programs, and to a fundamental change in the way a community thinks about the nature of learning, leadership, and to social advocacy. The KLCC theme emerges not as Descartes' famous dictum, "I think, therefore I am," but instead as "We think, therefore we create."

WKKF sees instances where the communities have built use of evaluative thinking into the leadership development experience itself, whereby the evaluation can meet the needs of local stakeholders. In one community, for example, there was a great emphasis on digitally documenting the work of the fellowship. The video content generated has been used very effectively in communicating to various stakeholder groups, locally and nationally, about the nature of the work of the fellowship and the results they have achieved.

EXHIBIT 10.5. A VIEW FROM THE SITES: A CONFLUENCE OF CONNECTIONS.

Incorporating the needs of multiple stakeholders proved to be a challenge. What eventually made sense to us was using a set of qualitative tools to view relationships. We were able to use the Spider Diagram, a community organizing tool, by looking at it through a different lens. Through our focus groups we saw the changes in the number and quality of connections not only between the fellows and the community, but also among the fellows. I remain struck by the importance of the host agency in facilitating these connections. At times it felt like making a crazy quilt. The evaluation helped people inside and outside the quilting circle to see the pattern that emerged from the individual pieces.

Danis Joyce Gehl, site evaluator

Building evaluative inquiry into the work of an inclusive community of leadership practice is integral to the KLCC initiative. The national evaluator identified a handful of principles of practice that emerged across all six sites.

- Members of the learning community must be able to honor, translate, and bridge traditional and local ways of knowing with contemporary worldviews of knowing.
- This learning community (fellowship) must work to establish and sustain a safe place for individuals and groups to learn. In particular, there needs to be local conversation and facilitated dialogue that helps community leaders debate difficult issues (for example, racial differences, views regarding learning priorities and approaches, territory, versions of history, and so on).
- To ensure lifelong learning and the sharing of lessons learned, fellows must engage frequently in a national conversation with other community leaders. This could entail visits to sister sites, a fellows exchange program, a resource and reading database, and cross-site focus group discussions on such topics as financing, efforts to sustain projects, communication, leadership development tools, evaluation tools, and youth involvement.

How Important Is Cultural Competence in Community Leadership Development Evaluations?

Given that the idea of respect for culture is embedded in the KLCC program, it was important to secure evaluators who brought cultural and intellectual diversity to the work. Each site chose an evaluator from their community. The ones who were most successful, in terms of having the evaluation add value, were the ones most in tune with the cultural issues. For the national evaluation, the evaluators have experience working across cultures in the United States and internationally. Bringing both qualitative and quantitative tools to bear was another way of being inclusive and respectful of different cultural ways of knowing.

To ensure culturally responsive evaluation processes, the site team and the national evaluation team were required to (1) have a clear and critical understanding of the cultures of the communities to ensure that all processes were culturally respectful; (2) recruit a diverse evaluation team (in some cases multiethnic, intergenerational, and so on) that included members of the community being evaluated; (3) know how to employ both spoken and written language to ensure a competent and sensitive understanding of cultural uniqueness and differences and an awareness of the political and social effects of words on communities; and (4) be open to evaluative review of the findings for the purpose of ensuring and correcting cultural nuance.

Overall, the national evaluator indicates that the qualitative team of evaluators worked diligently to learn more about each community through a variety of resources, including documents provided by the site, history texts, online information, films, and on-site fieldwork. In Texas, the site-based evaluation team was representative of its diverse fellowships. In New York, Wisconsin, Montana, and New Mexico, where there was a single evaluator, that individual was a member of the community and an integral participant in the development of the overall program. The Minneapolis-St. Paul site contracted a national evaluator.

Some key principles were applied by the national evaluator in the KLCC Session I evaluation process that are fundamental to the work of Session II. In particular, the national evaluator acknowledges the right of access that the local site evaluators have. It is understood that this right is also one of great responsibility, as the site evaluators must behave in a culturally respectful and ethical manner. In turn, national evaluators have a responsibility to respect the local people, to present themselves in a humble manner, to listen carefully before speaking, to be generous, to learn as much as they can about the people and the place, to not trample on the sovereignty and spirit of the community, and to work in partnership and reciprocity with the site participants.

Of particular concern in KLCC for WKKF was the notion that the very concept of leadership is culturally determined. The starkest example of this was that in one community, they referred to *the fellowship* rather than to *fellows*. The idea of having individuals selected for the honor of being a fellow was antithetical to the values of this community. They believe that individual engagement in community issues may ebb and flow depending on each individual's life circumstances at any given moment. Having evaluators who can see and interpret some of these nuances of language enriched understanding of how the concept of collective leadership was reinterpreted by each community.

Epistemology of Place

The cultural environment of a community is framed by multiple, oftentimes competing contexts. The national evaluator underscores that this can complicate the process of coming to common ground, identifying common goals, and defining a shared vision. From observations of the six KLCC sites, the national evaluator learned that it is important to understand the *epistemology of place*—the content of both the implicit and explicit knowledge of the community's history, geography, lineage, and the struggles that have defined how the community addresses issues of politics, economics, and demographics (to name a few). Furthermore, it is important to understand that this knowledge does not represent a singular view, but is instead defined by diverse cultural ways of knowing that are rooted in race, ethnicity, migration history, and socioeconomic status. In addition, this knowledge is dynamic because it has the capacity to evolve over time with the inclusion of new understandings.

In the case of the six KLCC sites, the epistemology of place became apparent as the evaluation sought to better understand how the fellows developed their group norms (for example, how they connected with one another and engaged with their broader community) and framed their initiative work (for example, the activities that were selected often reflected the attributes of the setting). A community's historical relationship with PreK–12 schools, for example, defined the work of the fellowship. In the urban settings, fellows realized that they needed to become better at understanding the history of their community schools and how demographics, economics, and social policy affected school policies and practices. In the rural settings, fellows worked to gain a deeper understanding of the families (new and old) that populate the region to better grasp the nature of their strongly held values and expectations of the schools. In both cases the complications of historical memory, demographics, power, and economics constitute key elements of the epistemology of place that define relationships and actions.

Indeed, according to the national evaluator, this deep understanding of place offers a diverse community an opportunity to define group norms that foster open communication, ongoing learning, and high expectations for performance and participation. It was found that when fellowships took the time to come to know their communities, adding place-based literacy to their learning leadership protocols, individual fellows moved outside an "I" perspective to a larger "we" community point of view (see, for example, Exhibit 10.6). Moving to this bigger picture generated new connections, stimulated critical questions and vital explorations, and ultimately guided the fellows to define, develop, and implement relevant projects. It was observed that the host organizations and fellowships that were respectful of historical, social, and cultural knowledge quickly engaged in empowering activities. In the end, if knowledge of place is not integrated into one's work, action has no meaning and no purpose.

EXHIBIT 10.6. A VIEW FROM THE SITES: THE COLLECTIVE "WE."

The collective "we" locally is a state of mind that is informed by context, culture, values, and actions. We have a collective responsibility to know and learn how to survive in the dominant world when we leave for college, employment, or to reside outside of our community. The beauty of this public action and will is that the fellows have learned to create this environment wherever they go. The ability to learn about individual and separated systems in our community and then act to weave them into a coherent social fabric is a skill that is transferable and very important to building responsive citizens, communities, and public systems. Certainly, the degree to which this is learned varies, but both youth and adults alike have learned from each other.

Miguel Guajardo, site evaluator

Relationships and Responsibilities

Practically speaking, what this meant from WKKF's perspective is that it had to be very clear as a foundation about what it expected the local site evaluators to do. There is a need to still improve on this. Early in the process of launching KLCC Session I, WKKF brought the local management teams together (the project director, the coach, and the evaluator) and described the overall evaluation process. A Venn diagram was presented that showed the evaluation questions that WKKF needed to have answered and how these overlapped in at least some way with the questions the sites would want to answer locally. Within the overlap, there needed to be a negotiation about what and how data would be collaboratively collected. For the questions that WKKF and the individual sites each owned, there was a need to be mindful of how to facilitate, rather than impede, each others' learning. Being transparent about this at the start and then living by that agreement was critical to welcoming the different cultural ways of thinking about evaluation—the different ways of knowing that each community brought to the work (see, for example, Exhibit 10.7).

In terms of cultural relevancy, the national evaluator underscores that it is tricky work. For example, several Native American communities participated in KLCC Session I, and it is important to acknowledge that there are features of evaluation that often oppose the *ethos* (lifeways) and *eidos* (thoughtways) of

EXHIBIT 10.7. A VIEW FROM THE SITES: EVALUATION AS SHARING, LEARNING, AND ACTING.

As local evaluators, it was important for us to be as organic as possible and from the beginning dismiss the prevailing understanding of research and evaluation. This was especially important because of the history our community has had with outside researchers and the present state of affairs in public education. The border area has traditionally been researched through the lens of the dominant academic culture, and the research questions have their origin in a deficit model of thinking. This type of research has perpetuated stereotypes about the region and the people and has done more harm than good. Additionally, since Session I focused on teaching and learning, we have had to frame this in a larger context than just what takes place in schools. Traditional pedagogy brings with it an accountability system that is high stakes and punitive. Evaluation and research within this political context is not constructive, it acts as a negative force that dulls teaching and learning. So for us as local evaluators, it was important to educate the fellowship on collecting data for the sake of sharing, learning, and acting. This reframing and use has proven to be very effective in the process and the impact.

Miguel Guajardo, site evaluator

an indigenous community. There are traditional cultural dimensions that can significantly constrain the work of the host organization and the leadership fellows. For example, because one site included the elders in partnership with the fellows in a more formal manner, the elders were held to agreed-upon participation norms. When an elder did not adhere to this group norm, and hence was not invited to participate in a group trip, the host organization found itself in a prickly political situation. Is the elder included or not? In the end, through discussion among the elders, the elder did not go on the trip, but the tension generated by this collision was one that all the fellows identified as a critical moment in their leadership learning journey. Holding the tension between what is traditional and contemporary and between internal and external objectives is complicated.

Regarding evaluation, one site evaluator had planned a fairly rigorous evaluation process with a survey and interviews; however, the fellowship (a mix of Native American and non Indian) refused to participate. In this case, the site evaluator came to understand that the Native people in his community no longer wanted to be passive respondents but instead wanted to be proactive partners in the process. Indeed, evaluation research is powerful because the findings shape a community's social, cultural, political, and economic landscape. It is prudent, if not obligatory, that evaluation conducted (and contracted) by WKKF construct culturally responsive methods and protocols.

How Can Evaluation Be Used as a Leadership Development Tool?

One important way that evaluation can be part of the leadership development process is to model the learning cycle of design, action, observation, and reflection. Funders and program implementers need to ask themselves, Is this an effective strategy to help these communities to help themselves? In KLCC Session I, the national leadership team (WKKF representatives, the national intermediaries, the national evaluators, and the national communications consultants) conducted a midpoint sense-making session, where the evaluation data was shared and interpreted. This process surfaced recommendations on both how to work with the Session I sites and what to do differently in future sessions. More frequent sessions of this type and a shared interpretation of data with the communities would have been beneficial.

The national evaluator indicates that more communication on a variety of levels and consistency throughout the process would indeed enrich the evaluation. The work of the qualitative team required planning and constant communication with the sites; therefore, the site-based evaluators became integral partners in this process. For the most part, site-based evaluators were excited by the new learning opportunity. Sustained conversation with other partners in the process, however, would have enhanced the analysis process. Other site evaluator characteristics that enhanced the evaluation process include

- The lead evaluator needs to have credibility with the fellows.
- The lead evaluator and site evaluation team must embrace the fundamental principles of a developmental approach to evaluation that is culturally relevant.
- The lead evaluator and site evaluation team must participate with the national evaluator and other site evaluators in an ongoing conversation that informs their practice and engages them in collaborative work within and across the sites.

- The lead evaluator and site evaluation team must be able to manage this important process (for example, data collection, data analysis, data reporting) in a timely manner.
- The lead evaluator and site evaluation team must have technological prowess or capable assistance in bringing their evaluative stories alive in a digital format.
- The lead evaluator and site evaluation team must learn to communicate (in written, digital, and oral texts) the successes of the fellowship.

WKKF echoes that more conversation would help it to develop a shared mental model of the role of evaluation. For WKKF, the mental model is that the role of evaluation is to help the foundation and its partners be successful in creating change, not to catch someone doing something wrong. Bringing a learning approach to the work of evaluation opens eyes to many opportunities to use data in support of the change process.

While the evaluation process is locally focused and participative in nature, it does not exist in a vacuum. That is, just as evaluation must be culturally appropriate (and linked to the needs of site and community participants), the work and the findings of evaluation should inform community aspirations. What was found in KLCC Session I was that when there was broad participation across the twenty-five fellows in the process of collecting and analyzing evaluative data, there was collective leadership. Evaluation at the community level functions as a valuable process that builds knowledge and capacity (see, for example, Exhibits 10.8 and 10.9). Lessons learned can then be shared with other leadership fellows in other communities nationally.

EXHIBIT 10.8. A VIEW FROM THE SITES: EVALUATION AS A REFLECTIVE TOOL.

In Buffalo, the evaluation team had to be aware of the inevitable conflicts and misunderstandings arising from an issue that is highly situated in race and class inequities. The evaluation helped everyone, including ourselves, to have the courage to face these conflicts. The evaluation data helped people recall their common interests and to put their work for improved education first. This happened because the project participants trusted the evaluation team. The evaluators were seen as respecting differences and accepting the integrity of people's expressed commitment to the work of the fellowship.

Danis Joyce Gehl, site evaluator

EXHIBIT 10.9. A VIEW FROM THE SITES: THE "I" TO THE PUBLIC "EYE."

Locally it was the willingness of the national evaluators to respond, adjust, and modify their evaluation process that made for a great collaboration. This willingness to negotiate with local stakeholders yields improved sharing and learning at both the micro and macro levels. This relational process and the willingness to share data collection strategies disrupted the traditional power dynamic that has typically prevailed among evaluators/researchers and local people. The ability to collect data and inform action created the on-time feedback loop necessary for the circular learning process of planning, action, and reflection employed by action research processes to be effective.

To me, the on-time, on-the-ground feedback provided by the local evaluators was part of the brilliance of the evaluation framework. This facilitated the data collection without overburdening the organization's staff. It also provided the opportunity for the local evaluators who are both community members and organizational participants to shift roles from the traditional public "I" to the necessary public "eye." As leadership and power goes, there is an instant redistribution and configuration of power when the observed becomes part of the observing process.

Miguel Guajardo, site evaluator

An important aspect of KLCC Session I was the networking meetings—"national gatherings" during which the focus was on the fellows and communities learning from each other, not on a lot of outside experts. There were two gatherings that included all of the fellows, and two that brought together the project directors, coaches, and evaluators. These gatherings were another way in which a learning environment was created for KLCC—living the example of shared leadership and learning. In the end, a primary goal of leadership is to be in tune with the pulse of the community. What we observed in KLCC Session I was that fellows who learned how to ask questions, collect and analyze data, and frame information in ways that could be easily managed by different audiences were more adept at generating new resources, partnerships, and sustaining efforts that made a difference in their communities.

Conclusion

In the end, this process taught everyone involved a great deal about how to work with diverse groups of people that bring to community work vast resources of knowledge and skills and deep passion for social justice. Framing an evaluation design that honors the history and current context of each of these diverse communities (their knowledge and ways of knowing and doing evaluation) and at the same time attends to the goals of the overarching project requires a good deal of flexibility and patience. The national evaluator went into the project with tentative data collection tools that were used as talking points with site-based evaluators. Over time, through conversation, an inductive and more robust evaluative process emerged that met both the site-level and the national-level goals. In retrospect, based on lessons learned, there are some things that would be done differently.

- Be more intentional about integrating the survey and ethnographic approaches. While it was found that both approaches were valuable, being able to write about them in a more integrated way would be helpful.
- Do more shared analysis; provide more frequent and more inclusive data interpretation, including with the sites, not just the national management team.
- Place more emphasis on understanding the effectiveness of different leadership development practices and strategies.
- Use network analysis at an organizational rather than individual level.
- Give more explicit guidance on the role and qualifications of the local evaluator.

In short, what should occur is that the evaluation should play a role in developing individual attitudes, beliefs, and skills, and in building community capacity. A key role of the evaluator is to shine a light on this process to make transparent a process that supports cultural identity, not to exploit it.

Resources

Atkinson, P. *Understanding Ethnographic Texts. Qualitative Research Methods Series 25.* Thousand Oaks, Calif.: Sage, 1992. This short, manageable monograph provides practitioners and evaluators with a set of thinking points to guide them in the complicated task of interpreting diverse contexts. Additionally, the author presents a more eclectic (cross-disciplinary) approach, what he calls *genres*, to ethnographic presentations.

Czarniawska, B. *A Narrative Approach to Organization Studies. Qualitative Research Methods Series 43*. Thousand Oaks, Calif.: Sage, 1998. This is a must-read monograph for anyone conducting an organizational ethnography. How one positions oneself in the field, defines a method (or as the author suggests, a *frame of mind*), and translates this to the storied text are key learning points offered by this resource.

Durland, M. M., and Fredericks, K. A. (eds.). Social Network Analysis in Program Evaluation. *Special Issue of New Directions for Program Evaluation*, no. 107. San Francisco: Jossey-Bass, 2005.

Simmons, A. *The Story Factor: Inspiration, Influence, and Persuasion through the Art of Storytelling*. New York: Basic Books, 2001. Storytelling is an ancient art that carries the soul and spirit of a community of people. For the practitioner or evaluator to employ this art to inform, to persuade, to entertain, and so on requires skill. The goal of this art is to be inspiring and illuminating; the book provides fundamental thoughts that all authors of organizational stories should know.

Stewart, A. *The Ethnographer's Method. Qualitative Research Methods Series 46*. Thousand Oaks, Calif.: Sage, 1998. A simply written monograph that provides the practitioner or evaluator with fundamental structures to understand and implement ethnographic studies.

References

Bolman, L. G., and Deal, T. E. *Reframing Organizations: Artistry, Choice, and Leadership* (3rd ed.). San Francisco: Jossey-Bass, 2003.

Fetterman, D., Kaftarian, S. J., and Wandersman, A. *Empowerment Evaluation*. Thousand Oaks, Calif.: Sage, 1995.

Kirkpatrick, D. L. *Evaluating Training Programs: The Four Levels*. San Francisco: Berrett-Koehler, 1994.

March, J. G., and Simon, H. *Organizations*. Hoboken, N.J.: Wiley, 1958.

Ouchi, W. *Theory Z*. Reading, Mass.: Addison-Wesley, 1981.

Peters, T. J., and Waterman, R. H., Jr. *In Search of Excellence*. New York: HarperCollins, 1982.

Schein, E. H. *Organizational Culture and Leadership* (2nd ed.). San Francisco: Jossey-Bass, 1992.

CHAPTER ELEVEN

EVALUATING LEADERSHIP AS A STRATEGY TO TRANSFORM COMPLEX SYSTEMS

Kimberly Jinnett and Todd Kern

This chapter describes the challenges of evaluating leadership development efforts within the broader context of complex systems. We use two separate but overlapping cases that focus on educational leadership within urban K–12 school systems to illustrate this dynamic. Each contains lessons that can be applied more broadly to other sectors and industries. The first case, New Leaders for New Schools (NLNS), is a well-defined intervention for preparing urban school principals with a clear theory of change that stretches from recruitment through training, placement into a principal position, and two full years of on-the-job support. The second case, the Wallace Foundation's Leadership Development Initiative, is a natural experiment of leadership development in various states and districts across the nation without common prescriptive elements. This chapter describes how a set of evaluation and research projects were designed around these complex leadership development initiatives. Though the focus of this chapter is on education leadership, we believe that the lessons apply to efforts to evaluate other types of leadership development in complex systems.

Evaluating Leadership Within Complex Systems

The New Leaders and Wallace initiatives have much in common. They identify leadership as key to transforming urban school systems. They are motivated by the same underlying premise: that effective leadership influences high-quality teaching and learning for all students, particularly for students of color and those from low-income families.

Yet, despite a commitment to similar objectives, the two initiatives take decidedly different approaches, and both face similar challenges associated with any effort to evaluate the impact of leadership development efforts in a systemic context. For instance, when trying to link leader effectiveness to positive student outcomes (for example, achievement), how can we be certain that gains derive from the actions of the leader and not, for example, from a student's home environment, school-level contextual factors, or the impact of recent local, state, or federal policy changes? In reality, each of these—along with leader effectiveness—likely contributes to the outcomes. Indeed, school conditions and state and district policy changes may affect leader effectiveness itself.

In the sections that follow, we share how New Leaders and Wallace developed evaluation approaches that are narrow enough to remain focused on their specific research concerns but broad enough to capture some if not all of the complexity inherent in the systems in which they operate. Indeed, deciding which elements of complexity to account for is a main challenge in designing evaluations of complex systems.

New Leaders for New Schools

To place the early lessons from New Leaders' evaluation work into context, it may be helpful to provide a quick description of the program and its history. Founded in 2000, New Leaders' mission is to "foster high academic achievement for every child by attracting, preparing, and supporting the next generation of outstanding school leaders for our nation's urban public schools" (New Leaders for New Schools, 2005). Within a decade, New Leaders aspires to build a national corps of 2,000 urban principals who impact the lives of a million students a day. Specifically, New Leaders expects to have two kinds of impact.

1. *Direct impact:* Dramatically increasing the academic achievement and success of individual students in schools led by New Leaders principals
2. *Catalytic impact:* Influencing how urban systems think about leader development and support as a systemic strategy to improve urban schools

Thus far, New Leaders has elected to devote the majority of its resources to implementing its direct model, for two reasons: (1) to ensure a focus on refining and perfecting the core model; and (2) because the ability to drive catalytic impact within systems rests, in many respects, upon having demonstrated the success and viability of the direct model. Figure 11.1 characterizes the components and immediate outcomes of the New Leaders' direct model.

The core New Leaders model consists of the following components:

- *Selection.* New Leaders has invested in a national infrastructure to recruit promising candidates from inside and outside of urban school systems. Applicants are admitted after a rigorous three-phase process that screens for qualities exhibited by highly effective school leaders. These qualities, called *New Leaders' Selection Criteria,* include a relentless drive to foster high levels of academic achievement for every child, integrity and inner strength, self-awareness and understanding of one's strengths and weaknesses, demonstrated leadership record with adults, demonstrated success with children, and excellent communication and problem-solving skills.
- *Residency training and support.* New Leaders residents participate in an intensive preparation phase that consists of two main elements: (1) Foundations, the yearlong, academic core of the New Leaders program, includes one five-week session in the summer and four five-day seminar sessions during the school year that are presented by leading national academics and practitioners and are aligned to the Principal Leadership Competencies (that is, proprietary standards for effective principal leadership); and (2) a yearlong residency in which residents work alongside a more experienced principal as a member of a school's leadership team.
- *Placement and job-seeking support.* New Leaders works with partner districts to help identify principalships (for all who are certified by New Leaders as ready to lead) that represent a good match with the skills of the New Leaders resident.

FIGURE 11.1. NLNS DIRECT IMPACT MODEL.

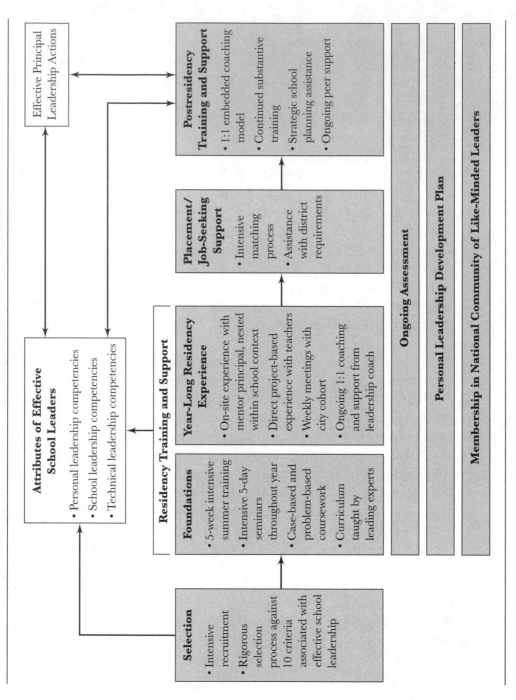

- *Postresidency training and support.* New Leaders provides two full years of direct support to principals in their first years on the job to help ensure their effectiveness as school leaders. This ongoing support focuses on the continued development of New Leaders on the skills and attributes of effective leadership. Leadership coaches visit schools regularly, providing feedback and coaching to each postresident, and lead weekly cohort meetings.

Additionally, three aspects of the model span the three years of training and support provided by New Leaders. New Leaders residents and postresidents receive ongoing assessment on their skill development, project-based learning and experiences, and direct work as school leaders. Based on these assessments, a personal leadership development plan is created and monitored to track residents' and postresidents' development and to identify specific areas of need and strategies to increase competency in these areas. New Leaders also provides membership in a national community of like-minded leaders, including residents and postresidents, coaches, mentor principals, staff, district partners, and other stakeholders.

New Leaders' direct model is nested within a broader conceptual framework, shown in Figure 11.2, which situates the specific intervention within school, district, and broader contexts and depicts the relationships through which New Leaders expects to influence schools and students.

The gray boxes in Figure 11.2 generally refer to the broad categories of model components in Figure 11.1 (also shown in gray). The link between the direct model and the conceptual framework is further anchored by the most immediate outcome of the model, *effective principal leadership actions,* shown in both diagrams. Taken together, these two figures capture New Leaders' theory of change—its expectations about how its model will bring about intended changes for schools and students situated within a broader context.

During its first five years, New Leaders received more than 3,800 applications for what has resulted in a total of 231 New Leaders currently serving in six cities (Baltimore, Chicago, Memphis, New York, Oakland-Bay Area, and Washington, D.C.). From inception, New Leaders collected and analyzed a range of internal data, with the goal of organizational learning that could lead to programmatic enhancements and refinements. In anticipation of increasing scale, and to begin to test the impact of the model, New Leaders launched a formal external evaluation during the 2004–2005 school year.

FIGURE 11.2. CONCEPTUAL FRAMEWORK FOR NLNS DIRECT IMPACT MODEL.

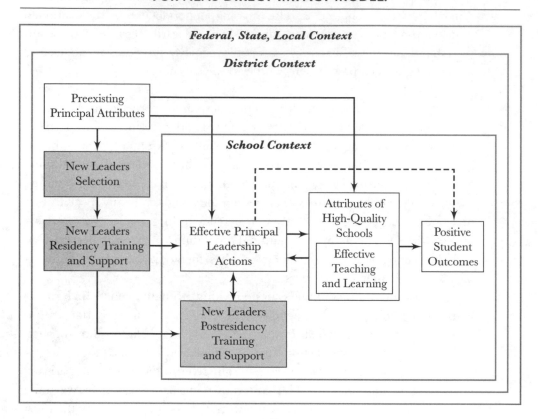

New Leaders Evaluation Design Considerations

Defining Outcomes and a Theory of Change

Effective principal leadership action, as described previously, is conceptualized both as the direct and immediate outcome of New Leaders training and support, as well as the driver of improvements in school quality and improved student outcomes. New Leaders posits that effective leadership actions lead to improvements in school quality and, in turn, also may be influenced by aspects of school quality. Based on existing research, as well as ideas that are core to the New Leaders approach but are not yet reflected in the research, New Leaders has identified six key attributes of high-quality schools that may be directly or indirectly influenced by principal action and will in turn lead to improved student outcomes. These attributes, which are mirrored in the New Leaders curriculum, are as follows:

1. Strong belief in all children, efficacy, and sense of personal responsibility
2. Effective leadership of the change process
3. Positive school culture, climate, and community
4. Effective management
5. Focus on data and outcomes
6. Effective teaching and learning

In particular, effective teaching and learning is central to New Leaders' theory and serves as a primary indicator of school quality. New Leaders' current conception does not yet offer hypotheses or speculation regarding the relationships between and among the individual attributes of high-quality schools. Indeed, shedding light on the interactions among these critical variables at the school level is among the top priorities of New Leaders' long-term research agenda.

Ultimately, New Leaders posits that the direct model will bring about positive student outcomes, defined as demonstrable, sustained gains in students' academic performance (for example, standardized test scores or promotion rates) and evidence of progress in nonacademic student outcomes (for example, motivation or sense of responsibility). It is anticipated that changes in school quality will likely precede and directly influence student outcomes, thereby providing an indirect link between principal leadership actions and student outcomes. While the conceptual framework also allows for the possibility of a direct line of influence between principal actions and student outcomes, this is seen as less likely, consistent with findings of current research that a direct impact of leadership on student outcomes is rarely found (Leithwood, Louis, Anderson, and Wahlstrom, 2004). Instead, principals are viewed as having an opportunity to directly influence many of the contextual factors that lead to school and student success.

These three key constructs (principal action, school quality, and student outcomes) and the relationships among them occur in and are influenced by specific school context. This includes a range of factors that may influence outcomes and help explain differences in how the model works in different settings. For example, school context includes aggregated student and teacher characteristics, such as the average years of experience among teachers. Principals working in schools with an abundance of new, inexperienced teachers may encounter additional challenges in ensuring that effective teaching practices are occurring. Generally, New Leaders believes that school context may play a strong role in influencing whether and how the competencies on which New Leaders trains its participants (that is, the attributes of effective school leaders) are translated into leadership actions.

More broadly, individual schools and the New Leaders' direct model as a whole are situated in a district context, which in turn is located in the local, state, and federal policy context. Contextual factors at these levels influence the enactment of the model and the outcomes that result. Different results between and within schools and between and within New Leaders' partner districts may be explained by these contextual factors. For example, district policies regarding level of principal autonomy over personnel, budget, and curricula will likely play a role in the degree to which principals trained by New Leaders can effectively enact changes in school quality and student outcomes.

Developing an Initial Evaluation Design

After a rigorous process to select a third-party external evaluation partner, New Leaders began work with the selected research team on the initial design of a multiyear (three- to five-year), multisite evaluation. (See Exhibit 11.1.)

From the outset, the New Leaders team knew the evaluation effort would need to meet both summative (program impact) and formative (program improvement) objectives. Given the complexity of the urban systems within which New Leaders operates, it also was determined early on that the evaluation would need to rely on mixed methods in its approach; for example, observation, interviews, surveys, review of materials, focus groups, and analysis of student achievement data.

In one sense, defining the formative aspects of the evaluation was more straightforward than defining the summative ones. Efforts to address the summative question regarding impact of the New Leaders model in driving gains in student achievement, however, were more nuanced.

The Design Challenges of Systemic Complexity

At its core, New Leaders is investing in principal leadership as a strategy to influence one of the most highly complex social organizations that exists: schools. As a result, while the model is quite simple, it is extremely difficult to

EXHIBIT 11.1. NLNS PROCESS FOR SELECTING A RESEARCH TEAM.

In contrast to the more traditional Request for Proposal (RFP), New Leaders relies on an iterative and somewhat less formal Request for Information (RFI) process. In repeating cycles over a few months, a draft RFI document—which seeks to define broad evaluation goals and objectives, core research questions, and the criteria used to identify an evaluation partner—is shared with experts across the field, inviting feedback on the document itself and recommendations for evaluation partner(s). Each new round of feedback sharpens the articulation of the desired objectives and broadens the list of potential partner candidates. With the help of a volunteer Evaluation Proposal Review Committee (EPRC), New Leaders uses the selection criteria to winnow the list from 12–14 down to 6–7 candidates. After a 90-minute phone conversation with each, a formal written proposal is requested from three evaluation firms. Again with help from the EPRC, proposals are rigorously assessed to select the best possible partner.

---

isolate the effects of a single intervention or strategy. The challenges can be reduced to a handful of core issues.

- *Small sample sizes.* Despite New Leaders' rapid growth, the still relatively small community—the number of New Leaders principals who have (or will have) served in the role for at least 2–3 years in the same school—could place additional constraints on the types of statistical analyses that are possible. This is especially true once the national community is further divided by program city (each of which relies on a different standardized assessment framework), school type, and grade level.
- *Comparison group.* As is true with any attempt to begin to determine program impact, it was critical that New Leaders identify an appropriate comparison group. This was challenging for a host of reasons, not the least of which was the fact that careful selection of candidates (which would not be true for a comparison group) is a core component of the New Leaders' model.
- *Causal attribution.* It is difficult to assign causal attribution in a model that lacks sufficient controls. As such, New Leaders would need to focus on first establishing a strong correlation while beginning to build a case for causation.

Together with the external evaluation team, New Leaders weighed the constraints mentioned in selecting an approach. Ultimately, New Leaders elected to move forward with a matched-pairs quasi-experimental design.

Through this approach, the external evaluator would attempt to match New Leaders and non–New Leaders principals on several key criteria (for example, tenure in the role, school- and student-level characteristics, historical student achievement patterns) and compare the performance of both schools over time. This design would satisfy a high standard for research-based methodology, while recognizing that it was neither possible nor desirable (given that it would limit New Leaders' impact) to conduct a true, randomized experiment. Figure 11.3 provides a diagram of the resulting Year 1 evaluation design.

As Figure 11.3 depicts, the two main components of the design are the Residency Study and the Principal Study, both of which are nested within a broader Global Descriptive Study. The Residency Study, formative in nature, focused on better understanding and illuminating the strengths and areas for continued improvement within the New Leaders' model during the residency training year. The Principal Study included both a formative focus (for example, What can be learned about the role of a Leadership Coach in providing effective ongoing support to first-year principals?) and a summative focus

FIGURE 11.3. NLNS'S YEAR 1 EVALUATION DESIGN.

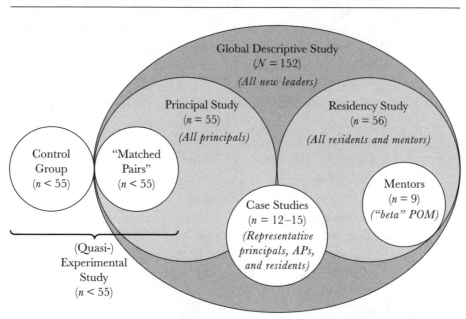

(a subset of principals was matched to similar non–New Leaders principals as part of the quasi-experimental design). The Global Descriptive Study was designed to capture as many relevant variables as possible for the full community of New Leaders, which could be used to further contextualize findings from the other studies. Finally, Case Studies were intended to follow a small number of individual New Leaders over time and provide a depth of analysis that, together with data and insights from the other aspects of the design, would further enable rich hypothesis development and testing. Taken together, these nested design elements were intended to strike the best balance of breadth, depth, and richness in evaluating the effectiveness of the New Leaders' model.

The Wallace Leadership Development Initiative

The Wallace Foundation education leadership initiative is based on the premise that effective leadership can lead to high-quality teaching and learning for all children, particularly for students of color and from low-income families. The particular focus of the initiative is on how district and school leaders generate learning gains for students, professionals, and the district as a whole. There is further emphasis on the role states play in supporting or impeding a district's ability to achieve learning gains. If the states play a supportive role, the initiative argues that district and school leaders can positively move learning throughout their systems by

- Having a strong, consistently engaged vision focused on teaching and learning
- Creating the conditions to continually improve the professional growth and development of adults in the system in order to promote learning gains for students
- Coordinating policies, practices, and incentives between states and districts and throughout district systems toward improvement in student learning
- Managing the change process and engaging key stakeholders around the learning agenda
- Using achievement data as a tool to identify strengths and weaknesses throughout the system and target specific efforts aimed at instructional improvement

The value of these leadership processes have been well documented (Elmore, 2000, 2002; Knapp, Copland, and Talbert, 2003; Snipes, Doolittle, and Herlihy, 2002).

Three complementary evaluation and research projects form the core of the evaluation strategy for this complex and ambitious initiative. With a combination of research efforts, the foundation set out to develop knowledge and tools around fundamental questions about education leadership and how it connects to improved learning and performance for adults and children in the K–12 public education system.

1. What empirical connections exist that link leadership actions to changes in classroom practice and student learning?
2. What is the effectiveness of various approaches to professional development for K–12 leaders and what options are there for improvement?
3. What are effective ways to assess leadership performance and what tools are needed to improve performance fieldwide?

It would be a mistake to see question number 2 as the only evaluation effort focused on leadership development. The development of leaders over time is not only a function of the targeted training they receive, but also the support they do or do not receive on the job, the conditions under which they work, the resources they can draw upon, and the incentives (monetary and otherwise) that do or do not exist for promoting effective performance. In the Resources section of this chapter we have provided links for each of the research projects attached to these three evaluation efforts.

Background Leading to Evaluation and Research Design

When the education leadership initiative was first launched in 2000, the Wallace Foundation commissioned several research efforts aimed at understanding the national and regional supply of principals. A widespread belief in the field was that there was a nationwide shortage of candidates for educational leadership. Rather than viewing the problem as a systemic one, the solution of increasing the supply (or stock) of principals was viewed by many in the field as a legitimate and sensible response to the perceived shortage. However, three independently commissioned investigations of this labor supply issue revealed remarkably similar conclusions: particular districts and schools experienced trouble attracting candidates mostly due to unattractive conditions. The Wallace Foundation (2003) summed up the findings across the studies, suggesting that strategies aimed solely at adding more candidates to the pipeline miss the critical challenges confronting states, districts, and schools if they are to be successful in attracting and keeping enough leaders needed to drive learning gains. It would be better to improve working conditions, to get the incentives right to attract job candidates, and to redefine jobs to focus on student learning. These are system changes that require more than the movement of dollars and people. They require that the rules (or policies) that govern the movement of dollars and people change. In this sense, the Wallace Foundation discovered early on that a system perspective was needed in order to fully understand the complexities of factors that contribute to improvements in leadership and learning. This perspective informed subsequent investments in research and evaluation.

At the same time, a parallel research investment aimed at synthesizing a set of insights about how leadership is linked to instructional improvement was close to completion. The action framework for education leaders, produced by the Center for the Study of Teaching and Policy at the University of Washington, identified a range of tools that leaders could draw upon to improve teaching and learning in their schools and districts (Knapp, Copland, and Talbert, 2003). The study synthesized the existing evidence on the linkage between leadership and learning and gathered additional insights from expert interviews and focus groups. Several other reports on district and school leadership practices were published around the same time and informed Wallace's commissioning of the three-part evaluation design presented in this chapter.

Knowledge about education leadership is richer today than it was even five years ago because of these and other studies. However, the field of education leadership requires a stronger empirical basis for understanding the relationship between leadership development efforts and changes in teaching, learning, and student achievement in large urban school systems.

Given this context, and the state of the field, the Wallace Foundation decided to invest in further knowledge development in the leadership development area with a specific focus on the empirical link between leadership and learning within a complex environment.

Designing an Evaluation Approach Around a Complex Initiative

In designing an evaluation strategy around a complex initiative, it is important to focus on a core question in order to anchor all research and evaluation studies to each other and to a whole. For the education leadership initiative, that core became the link between leadership and learning within a system

context. Wallace was interested in both intended and unintended consequences because professional development and other strategies can be used
effectively or ineffectively to bring about changes in classroom practice and
student learning via leader performance.

System Elements and Focus of Evaluation Efforts

A systems perspective focused attention around whether and how other
changes in the system, such as new incentives, restructuring of time, job re-
definition, grouping of students and teachers with relevant preparation in
classrooms, and other potential strategies, are utilized by leaders to affect adult
and student learning and the sorts of supports leaders need to enact effective
strategies. This shift in perspective required a corresponding shift in the evaluation strategy. Rather than soliciting a single evaluation aimed at a narrow
question, Wallace developed five broad system-related questions.

1. What evidence exists that shows how leaders improve teaching and learning?
2. Is there a way to connect leader performance to improved teaching and
   learning?
3. How do various conditions and incentives promote effective leadership?
4. What sorts of training and professional development best support effective leadership?
5. Are there useful ways to measure effective leadership and develop it over
   time?

A more detailed set of questions specific to each solicited research and
evaluation effort was included in the relevant request for proposals issued by
the Wallace Foundation. In addition, the RFPs requested information on proposed site selection, methodological issues, and expectations for public products. (The RFPs and detailed design features of each evaluation can be
obtained from the Wallace Foundation and the researchers involved. Relevant
contact Web sites are provided in the Resources section of this chapter.)

Choosing a Research Design

The Wallace initiative did not solicit an evaluation of a particular prescribed
intervention but funded a set of research and evaluation efforts aimed at understanding effective leadership in a systems context. Wallace remained flex-

ible about how the research would be designed in order to encourage creative approaches. Bidders were provided with a list of all districts and states that were part of the Wallace education leadership initiative. Bidders were further encouraged to select sites that would allow the greatest learning opportunities and whose findings would be widely applicable to large urban school districts. Therefore, bidders were not required to include all Wallace sites and were encouraged to consider studying sites outside of the Wallace-funded pool. The researchers were required to substantiate their site selection plan and use the same rigor of selection for both Wallace and non-Wallace sites.

The easiest and most straightforward approach to designing evaluations around leadership development efforts is to have a clearly articulated design for training and developing leaders that can be assessed and compared across sites using the same approach. This was not the case with the Wallace initiative. Though every site offered leadership training, the design of each program varied considerably and was completely under the control of the local site. In some sites the training was focused on principals, in others assistant principals. Sometimes attracting and training new leaders was the focus, other times providing ongoing training for sitting leaders was the focus. Whenever the design of programs is highly variable, it becomes infeasible to craft a meaningful comparative evaluation. Further, Wallace was interested in the performance of leaders, which required an evaluation design that included information about conditions and training, how these elements interacted with each other, and how they influenced leader performance—arguably, a much more complex evaluation than assessing different training programs.

Three Research Projects

Learning from Leadership, a study to link leadership actions to changes in classroom practice and student learning, was the first of the three research projects to be funded. Figure 11.4 outlines the framework for addressing this complex research project.

Variable 4 in Figure 11.4, school leadership, becomes in many ways the centerpiece and anchor for all the other research projects. Each of the three main research projects has school leadership as its central focus. The Learning from Leadership project puts school leadership at the center of its design, assessing how leaders are both influenced by people and conditions and how they in turn influence people and conditions. The School Leadership Study investigates principal training programs, exploring what works, what doesn't,

FIGURE 11.4. LINKING LEADERSHIP TO LEARNING.

1
State leadership,
policies, and practices
e.g., standards

testing

funding

2
District leadership,
policies, and practices
e.g., standards

curriculum alignment

use of data

9
Leaders' professional
learning experiences
e.g., socialization

mentoring

formal preparation

3
Student/family
background
e.g., family

educational

culture

4
School
leadership

5
Other stakeholder
e.g., unions

community groups

business

media

6
School conditions
e.g., culture/community

school improvement

planning

7
Teachers
e.g., individuals' capacity

professional community

8
Classroom conditions
e.g., content of instruction

nature of instruction

student assessment

10
Student
learning

Note: The research framework features ten interdependent variables. This figure cannot show the many complex relationships that actually exist among the ten variables. The relationships depicted in the figure are illustrative only.

Source: Kenneth Leithwood, Karen Seashore Louis, Stephen Anderson, and Kyla Wahlstrom. *Review of Research: How Leadership Influences Student Learning.* September 2004, p. 18.

and why in preparing school leaders. The Leadership Assessment System develops tools for assessing and improving the performance of school principals over time. We describe each of these projects in turn.

The researchers on the Learning from Leadership project proposed a multilevel approach to their evaluation. Their site selection involved random selection of states within geographic strata. In those states, schools and districts were selected based on variation in population size, skewed toward large urban centers. Schools and classrooms in these districts were further sampled. A set of surveys, administrative data collection, and observation at each level of the system were designed to allow the researchers to assess the effects of actions on outcomes at each level while controlling for contextual factors at each level.

Accordingly, for much of the proposed analyses, multilevel modeling or random coefficient modeling was used. We discuss these and other system-related methods in the next section and provide resources at the end of this chapter.

A companion research project, School Leadership Study: Developing Successful Principals, was funded at the same time. This project focused on how best to train and support school leaders through pre- and in-service professional development. This second study investigated eight exemplary programs, tracked performance on the job, and collected opinions from a set of graduates that were then compared to a nationally representative sample. A second component of this study seeks to understand the structure and financing of the eight exemplary programs as well as the structure and financing of the professional development landscape nationally. The tracking of on-the-job performance and linkage to financing mechanisms recognizes the systemic nature of leader development. System factors, such as working conditions and professional development funding, can influence whether training or ongoing professional development has an effect on leader performance.

The third study, Leadership Assessment System, develops a set of tools for assessing leadership performance and accompanying materials for improving leadership performance over time. This study recognizes the complexity of effective leadership performance and develops a distributed or team notion of effective performance. In this sense, the study recognizes leadership itself as a systemic concept; for example, leadership consists of people working together, not individuals working alone.

System Attributes and Methods to Handle Systems Analysis

Systems consist of many different types of components, and there are areas of agreement and disagreement about how to label such components depending on one's academic discipline, methodological preference, and life experience. Rather than attempt to propose the ultimate typology of system components, we offer a simple way of approaching systems analytically and provide references in the Resource section of this chapter.

With that caveat in mind, here's a simple three-part description of system attributes. *Systems* consist of people and things (also known as *stocks*), relationships between people and things (also known as *flows*), and structural levels in the system (also known as *rules*, which can enable or disable action). Understanding the nature and effect of these attributes requires different types of analytic methodologies.

Social Network Analysis. If the focus of the analysis is on the exchange of information, people, or money between two or more entities, then social network analysis (SNA) can be a powerful method for understanding structural features of networks and exchanges within the networks. As applied to leadership in particular, SNA can be used to understand how leaders both influence and are influenced by others. In the Resources section we provide a link to resources on SNA.

Multilevel Analysis. If the focus of the analysis is on the influence of policy and other organizational rules on leaders or others in the system, then having a way to account for the multilevel structure of the data is important. Students and teachers are nested in classrooms that are nested in schools that are nested in counties and states. Those in the same classroom are exposed to many of the same influences by virtue of being in the same classroom, and this clustering of like factors can be accounted for through the use of multilevel or random coefficients methods. In the Resources section we provide a link to sources on multilevel modeling.

System Dynamics Modeling. If the focus of the analysis is on the system overall, perhaps assessing leadership as a lever within that system, then system dynamics modeling may be the preferred method in order to assess both intended and unintended consequences. System dynamics is concerned with stocks, flows, and the rules that influence the level of stocks and nature of flows. In the Resources section we provide a link to sources on system dynamics modeling.

The messy and complex nature of systems is not a reason to shy away from quantitative methods. Methods like system dynamics modeling, social network analysis, or multilevel analysis are valuable tools, as are qualitative research efforts, for understanding the context of systems and how parts of the system relate to each other and to overall outcomes.

Key Lessons and Implications

There are a range of insights that can be gleaned from what is common (and uncommon) about the experiences of New Leaders and the Wallace Foundation.

Be Clear About the Needs Being Served

Multiple purposes are served by both the NLNS and the Wallace evaluations. Earlier, we described the three evaluation projects funded by Wallace. Each of these projects answers a slightly different question and serves a different purpose. All three projects, however, emphasize the need for practical and timely information over the course of the studies. For example, a project focused on developing performance assessment tools will produce useful information throughout the course of the project: a more coherent framework for understanding leadership performance at the piloting phase; comparative evidence from the field test phase; and a set of assessment products for widespread public use at the completion of the three-year project. The most complex study focusing on linkages between leadership and learning started with a literature review in the first year. In subsequent years, there are at least annual and sometimes more frequent reports on different aspects of the effects of leadership on teaching and learning. The professional development study has at least three major publications planned, starting with a literature review on what is known about exemplary training, followed by in-depth case studies and a final effectiveness report. A companion study will offer a tool for states and districts to better understand ways of structuring and financing programs and training activities for greatest effect.

Anticipate Reactions

As findings are disseminated, plan carefully for potential resistance. Wallace's (2003) position publication did go against conventional wisdom in the field. What initially started as three independent research studies on the supply of school leaders turned into a synthesis of findings on how the field needed to shift some attention away from a supply-side problem to more focus on the demand side or the conditions of schooling that were keeping talent away from those places most in need. Though on the face of it this is not a groundbreaking finding, the implications for the types of interventions needed to shift attention and intervention to the demand side were. The findings called into question vast amounts of activity being devoted to training and certification and encouraged more attention on why leaders would be attracted to and want to continue working in challenging schools and districts. In order to begin engaging with key decision makers who might use these findings, Wallace held a policy forum in Washington, D.C., with legislative staffers and other policy-making and membership organizations' representatives. At a grantee meeting, Wallace also devoted a panel discussion to the topic and sponsored a competition for the best ideas to tackle these conditions-oriented as opposed to training-oriented interventions.

Adopt a Dynamic Evaluation Model

There are many moving parts in a complex system. Key variables change during the evaluation. Adopt a dynamic, not static, evaluation model. The goal is to be as explicit up front (with both evaluators and stakeholders) about goals and activities, while acknowledging the need to be flexible and to modify along the way. As one example, NLNS is itself a young, dynamic, and rapidly growing organization. Further exacerbated by systemic complexity and an ambitious evaluation design, NLNS learned the value of limiting its scope to a smaller number of activities that can be well executed while maintaining flexibility regarding the broader elements of the design. Throughout the project there is the need to balance specificity with flexibility.

Recognize the Challenges of Collaboration

There is seldom time available to do a good job of inter- or intra-organization collaboration and knowledge sharing when designing and conducting evaluations and research. For the authors of this chapter, despite clear and common interests in the NLNS and Wallace initiatives (and our cowriting this chapter), there remained organizational barriers that limited the amount of joint learning or even swapping of notes. In a way, this mimics the dynamic in complex systems, where the incentive structure can often inhibit collaboration.

The Benefits and Challenges of a Systems Change Evaluation

The benefits of designing a multicomponent evaluation approach outweigh the challenges. Some benefits include obtaining better insights about complex problems, producing findings that are more reflective of real experience, and allowing multiple opportunities for the audience to engage in different ways with understanding leadership and leadership development.

The challenges are ever present and demand enormous patience, considerable resources, and the ability to juggle multiple evaluation approaches and research interests while producing timely products of relevance to the field. It is a challenge to communicate the findings from a complex research project, let alone a complex initiative, in a way that has practical relevance for those working day to day in the field to promote effective leadership and improved student learning.

If designs are too broad in the face of systemic complexity, they will fail to produce meaningful, interesting, or conclusive findings. This is a challenge for at least two reasons: (1) narrowly defined objectives may not be met; and (2) broadly defined objectives may undermine efforts to highlight the importance of complexity. Sometimes breaking the evaluation into separate, interrelated projects may allow a balance between these concerns about specificity and breadth.

Though this chapter is primarily focused on issues of evaluation and research design, there also needs to be considerable investment focused on communications activities for complex initiatives and initiatives whose findings might be counterintuitive or meet with resistance. Indeed, since improvement in a system's performance always requires change, we might expect there to be resistance present in the current system. Further drawbacks to receptivity of findings are that busy and overwhelmed people often want immediate results and simple answers. Leadership in complex systems is not simple. There needs to be considerable readiness preparation for findings, identification of leading voices to help carry the messages, and careful attention to making those messages as clear, coherent, and relevant to policymakers and practitioners as possible while staying true to the findings.

Recommendations

Before launching into a complex research design, some promising ways of getting started include concentrated work on framing the topics to be studied. Some approaches that we have found useful for launching a research effort (and also for beginning a stream of knowledge products) include starting with a summary of what is currently known through literature reviews and framing this knowledge for practical use in the field. An example of this from the Wallace initiative are the framing documents developed by the Center for the

Study of Teaching and Policy, which synthesized the existing evidence on the linkage between leadership and learning and gathered additional insights from expert interviews and focus groups. (For an example of these documents, see Knapp, Copland, and Talbert, 2003.)

In our experience, starting early in a complex initiative by synthesizing what is known through literature reviews and frameworks can also help sharpen the initiative's design and more targeted research and evaluation efforts. As more targeted research efforts are launched, interim publications can be topic specific, such as in-depth case studies on particular sites or programs, implementation studies, or journalistic accounts of particular strategies and activities. Finally, as targeted evidence begins to accumulate, the evaluation project can produce publications near the end stages of the study that address the effectiveness of leadership development policies and practices.

Know What You Are Trying to Accomplish

This is a principle that extends to any evaluation effort, but it is especially true in a complex, systemic context. If you do not clearly define your core evaluation or research question up front, the risk increases that you become lost in the complexity. For example, do you want to know whether a leadership development program is effective, whether your recruitment mechanisms are working, whether leaders have positive effects on teaching and learning, or some other point? The design required to answer each of these questions is considerably varied. The clearer you can be at the start, the better.

Choose the Right Evaluator

Clarity about what you are trying to accomplish will also help you select the right evaluator. For example, if your core objectives are primarily formative in nature, you may look for an evaluator with deep knowledge of schools and who specializes in ethnographic and/or qualitative research. On the other hand, you may likely seek out a different profile for your lead evaluator if your goal is a highly quantitative assessment of program impact. If you intend for the products to be highly valuable to policymakers and practitioners (as both Wallace and NLNS do), then you'll need to pay special attention to the past products and communications capacity of the selected researchers.

Select Appropriate Methods

Collecting data on various actors (students, teachers, principals, superintendents, and state chiefs, for example) who operate in a nested context (classrooms in schools in districts in states) demands methods that can handle both the interrelationships among the actors and the nested structure of the data. The sample selection must also match up with the multilevel analytic design. Being able to argue for the importance of such a design at the initial investment stages and to encourage development of useful products throughout the course of the project requires consistent and careful attention to the requirements of the research and the needs of the users of the knowledge being developed. As with any complex system, the main challenge becomes one of tackling the knowledge development in a way that embraces the complexity and yet develops clear and coherent evaluation and research products for widespread use.

Distinguish Carefully Between Causation and Correlation

It is critical that you determine up front the standard of evidence you need in order to answer various research questions in your evaluation because this will influence the design and the cost. Generally speaking, proving causation requires a more rigorous design and more resources than establishing correlation. Furthermore, if you need to distinguish the effects of training from the effects of context and conditions, you'll need to ensure your sampling frame and subsequent analytic methods allow that.

Establish Stakeholder Endorsement and Create Demand for Results

Just as it is helpful to be clear at the start what you're trying to accomplish and who your partners are, you should begin immediately to involve the primary consumers of the evaluation. Involving key players early can often yield better thinking to help shape the evaluation approach, but it also builds interest in and demand for the findings that the evaluation produces. For example, NLNS used an iterative process with a range of funders, board members, and other experts to select a lead evaluation partner, then transformed this group of informal advisors into a standing evaluation advisory board to provide input on the evaluation process and help interpret findings as they emerged. Within this forum, it is possible to test and develop policy arguments that may become relevant in the future. Similarly, Wallace used grantee and practitioner meetings to gather information for and report back on study plans. Wallace also has a communications unit that focuses on creating demand for results through policy forums, written briefs, marketing of knowledge products, online discussions, and various other media. Although the resources and capacity required to generate demand are often overlooked, without attention to demand-generating strategies the value of the knowledge products will never be realized.

Nurture Partnerships for Good Data

Every evaluation needs reliable access to quality data. We encourage you to develop a strategy to ensure access to data and to consider partnering directly with primary sources of data (for example, school districts). If research is sponsored by a funder, there is always the worry that sites may comply with the data request but not be forthright in their answers due to fears of confidentiality and potential loss of funding. This is not an issue that is unique to a complex design; however, for a complex design these issues become magnified as multiple sites and multiple levels are studied. Assuring respondents that their information will be kept confidential is essential.

Embrace the Complexity

Although a keep-it-simple approach can be helpful when operating in a systemic context, we encourage you to build in safeguards to ensure that you do not unintentionally miss the broader dynamics that often operate in complex systems. If complexity is core to your view of leader action, then you need to capture this complexity.

Explore the Use of Complex Methods

Because complex systems have multiple levels, nested activity, and lots of interrelationships, complex methods such as system dynamic modeling, random coefficients modeling, or multilevel modeling and social network analysis should be considered. Further complexity is added if you are trying to understand change in the system over time. For this reason, it is critical that systemic variables are captured even if you're not clear whether or how certain data will later be used. You may need them later as a deeper understanding of the dynamics at work in the system emerges, but you cannot go back in time to collect the data that may later prove most helpful. Having said this, however, whatever you capture ought to bear a plausible relationship to your outcomes of interest, otherwise you could be mired in irrelevant data and time-intensive data collection and cleaning activities that bear little fruit. Separating nonessential from essential system variables should be guided by your own core research concern.

Report Early and Often and Anticipate Reaction

Develop interim reporting timelines to lead to final products that have fewer surprises. Where possible, you can consider sharing interim reports and findings with key partners to reinforce their support and provide access to the data streams that will be needed. This early-and-often strategy should be married with the demand-generating strategies mentioned earlier to encourage stakeholders to pick up and use the resulting knowledge products throughout the projects. If you wait until all the evidence is in to produce a final capstone product, you run the risk of losing your audience. We have found this generally to be an unwise approach and certainly not a very useful one for policymakers and practitioners who do not have the luxury of waiting to act.

Maintain a Realistic Link Between Resources and Objectives

The efforts described in this chapter require considerable investment. For example, the Wallace research efforts amounted to roughly $6.5 million, representing 5–10 percent of the initiative's cost. Beyond dollars, research projects demand strong knowledge of research methods and adequate staff resources (internal and external) to assess, vet, and manage the process. It is important to recognize constraints when building your longitudinal research design and to be careful not to do too much. Although the complex context can lure you into ever greater nuance, it is much better to answer a few questions thoroughly than to address many questions superficially.

Expect Implementation Challenges

When working in a systemic context, everything takes longer, is more prone to political forces, and is less clear. A further complication is the tendency for initiatives to change considerably over time as on-the-ground lessons sharpen the focus and change the activities that are occurring in the sites under study. At the same time, what may appear to suggest bureaucratic dysfunction or inefficiency can open the door to creative problem solving.

Resources

For more information about the Wallace Foundation-funded research projects, you may contact the following researchers via their Web sites.

Learning from Leadership

Dr. Kyla Wahlstrom, Co-Principal Investigator,
　University of Minnesota
Dr. Kenneth Leithwood, Co-Principal Investigator,
　University of Toronto
http://education.umn.edu/CAREI/Leadership/default.html

School Leadership Study

Dr. Linda Darling-Hammond, Principal Investigator
Dr. Michelle LaPointe, Research Director, Stanford University
http://seli.stanford.edu/research/sls.htm

Leadership Assessment System

Dr. Andrew Porter, Principal Investigator
www.vanderbilt.edu/lsi/las/index.php

The Wallace Foundation

The Wallace Foundation's Knowledge Center on Education Leadership includes reports, stories, and other resources about strengthening the performance of education leaders to improve student achievement. Access at www.wallacefoundation.org/WF/KnowledgeCenter/KnowledgeTopics/EducationLeadership/.

New Leaders for New Schools

Preliminary results from the NLNS initiative may be found at www.nlns.org/NLWeb/Results.jsp.

Methods-Related Resources

System Dynamics Society. This group promotes the use of system dynamics by researchers and practitioners. They publish newsletters and the journal *System Dynamics Review* as well as hold annual conferences. More information is available at their Web site: www.systemdynamics.org.

Donella Meadows. A leader in the field of system dynamics, she wrote many accessible systems papers. Here is one of our favorites: Donella Meadows, "Places to Intervene in a System," available at www.rmi.org/sitepages/pid790.php.

Social Network Analysis. The International Network for Social Network Analysis is the main association for professionals (geared toward researchers) interested in social network analysis. The organization sponsors an annual conference and publishes *Connections,* a scholarly journal. More information can be found at their Web site, www.insna.org/. The group also maintains a useful listserv, *socnet,* for those interested in exchanging ideas about the use of social network analysis. Access at www.insna.org/INSNA/socnet.html.

Multilevel Modeling. There are a variety of resources on multilevel modeling. The organizations that have developed software packages tend to have useful links to other resources. One of the most useful links pages is maintained by MLWIN software developers: www.mlwin.com/links/index.html. A useful listserv for multilevel modeling is multilevel-mailbase@mailbase.ac.uk., which can be accessed at www.jiscmail.ac.uk/cgi-bin/webadmin?A0=multilevel.

References

Elmore, R. *Bridging the Gap between Standards and Achievement: The Imperative for Professional Development in Education.* Washington, D.C.: Albert Shanker Institute, 2002.

Elmore, R. *Building a New Structure for School Leadership.* Washington, D.C.: Albert Shanker Institute, 2000.

Knapp, M., Copland, M., and Talbert, J. *Leading for Learning: Reflective Tools for School and District Leaders, Leading for Learning Sourcebook: Concepts and Examples.* Seattle, Wash.: Center for the Study of Teaching and Policy, 2003.

Leithwood, K., Louis, K. S., Anderson, S., and Wahlstrom, K. *How Leadership Influences Student Learning.* Minneapolis: University of Minnesota, Center for Applied Research and Educational Improvement, 2004.

New Leaders for New Schools, 2005. [www.nlns.org/NLWeb/Index.jsp]. Accessed March 3, 2006.

Snipes, J. C., Doolittle, F. C., and Herlihy, C. *Foundations for Success: Case Studies of How Urban School Systems Improve Student Achievement.* MDRC, 2002. [www.mdrc.org].

Wallace Foundation. *Beyond the Pipeline: Getting the Principals We Need, Where They Are Needed Most,* 2003. [www.wallacefoundation.org].

CHAPTER TWELVE

EVALUATING LEADERSHIP DEVELOPMENT FOR SOCIAL CHANGE

Kim Ammann Howard and Claire Reinelt

Successful social change efforts typically depend upon mobilizing a critical mass of leaders around issues of common concern. Leadership development is a strategy for identifying, selecting, supporting, and connecting diverse leaders who together have a greater capacity to lead broadscale social change than they would have had individually.

The term *social change* refers to changes in how a broad group of people think and feel, how they act and relate to one another, how they organize themselves, and what kinds of structures and systems they create to identify and meet their needs. Leadership development for social change is an intentional effort to facilitate changes in people, organizations, communities, fields, and systems to produce specified outcomes. Other terms that have similarities to social change, and that you will see discussed throughout this book, are *systems change* and *community change*. Systems change focuses primarily on changes in policy, the allocation of resources, and the institutions that define and respond to the needs of people and communities. Social change has this focus as well, although it places more emphasis on values, beliefs, social norms, and relationships among people (how they interact and what they do together to lead change). Community change is similar to social change, although the location in which change is sought is usually a neighborhood, a rural area, a city or town. Community change is therefore typically smaller in scale than social change.

There are many approaches to developing leadership for social change. A program's design depends on the desired areas and direction of change and the assumptions about what will facilitate change. For instance, some program designers believe that what is needed is innovation, good ideas, and the ability to test and implement them. In this case, the preferred approach for developing leadership might be to identify and support social entrepreneurs. Other program designers believe that what is needed is to increase capacity for groups of individuals from diverse backgrounds to work collaboratively to address and solve shared problems. In this case, the preferred approach to developing leadership might be a shared leadership program in a community. Some programs use a combination of strategies.

This chapter discusses what we, the authors, are learning about how to assess the impact of leadership strategies that are designed to seed and/or catalyze social change around issues, practices, and attitudes regarding family planning and reproductive health (FP/RH) in developing countries. While the chapter draws on different evaluations, it focuses on one evaluation in particular: the evaluation of six population leadership programs funded by the David and Lucile Packard and the Bill and Melinda Gates Foundations. This evaluation serves as a case study. We walk the reader through the thinking and implementation of the different steps of the evaluation and share our reflections on the strengths and challenges of this experience and similar ones.

When to Conduct a Social Change Evaluation of Leadership Development Efforts

A social change evaluation approach is best suited for complex leadership development efforts in which comparisons across leadership programs are desired. While the leadership development efforts can vary in terms of specific goals, strategies, and activities as well as funding levels, length, and context, they should focus on the same types of ultimate social change outcomes (for example, reduction in teen pregnancy). Frequently, these leadership efforts take place as a broader initiative or funding strategy. For example, both the

Packard and Gates Foundations fund leadership development as one of their strategies to address FP/RH problems in more than ninety countries. The California Wellness Foundation supported leadership development as one part of a multifaceted initiative to reduce youth violence. Other components included policy, media advocacy, and community-based organizing and service provision.

For these types of evaluations, the Leadership development for what? question includes social change as the answer, or a significant part of the answer. That being said, we recognize that many times social change is a more distal outcome and one that typically is connected to other types of preliminary change, such as those at the individual and organizational levels. Sometimes funders desire assessments of social change when leadership development efforts are relatively new with not enough time passing or money invested to realistically expect this type of change. In these cases, evidence of progress toward social change may be seen, rather than social change itself. An advantage of conducting evaluations midway through such efforts is the opportunity to identify promising practices to date and make adjustments that enhance the likelihood that desired social changes will be achieved.

Due to the complex nature of social change, in regard to both the inputs and the processes that need to take place to achieve desired outcomes, these types of evaluations are typically more challenging than others. As a result, they require significant resources and benefit from a team of experienced evaluators who bring varied but complementary strengths to the work. In most cases, it makes sense to hire external evaluators who collaborate with program staff and internal evaluators. Ideally, this type of evaluation can build on and complement internal evaluations that usually focus more closely on short-term impacts of specific leadership development activities (for example, pre- and posttests of leadership development training sessions).

Leadership development evaluators have an important role in helping leadership programs and initiatives to focus on the social change outcomes they seek. Too often, programs do not focus on these outcomes because the outcomes are likely to occur too far in the future or lack attributable connections to the program; however, the failure to focus on desired social changes and consider pathways toward these changes may ultimately limit what can be learned and applied to accelerate social change efforts.

Overview of the Leadership Development Programs in This Evaluation

The Packard and Gates Foundations are jointly investing in six leadership development programs to create a critical mass of leaders to significantly improve access, coverage, and quality of FP/RH care services in developing countries. These programs are based on a theoretical assumption that individuals are critical catalysts in any social change process and that by working together more effectively these leaders can make a significant difference in the reproductive health of a country, a region, and the world.

Although they have a mutual interest in FP/RH, the Packard and Gates Foundations have taken somewhat different approaches to investing in FP/RH leadership development. The Packard Foundation concentrates its resources in selected focus countries where it believes it can develop and support a core of leaders; the Gates Foundation invests its resources in programs with a more global reach. Both foundations are interested in identifying and supporting national leaders who can influence policy. The Packard Foundation has an additional interest in reaching and developing leaders at the community level, particularly women, youth, and media representatives; the Gates Foundation targets leadership in research, academic institutions, and government. The Packard Foundation invests in building networks and collaborations to lead change; the Gates Foundation invests in building institutional capacity for research and training.

The six population leadership programs themselves vary in a number of ways. Grant allocations range from $3 million to $60 million. The number of participants for individual programs range from approximately 50 to more than 800 individuals and, depending on the particular program, represent from 4 to 35 developing countries.

Table 12.1 summarizes the formal activities of each leadership program; no one program includes all of the activities listed. All programs include some type of workshop or training that varies in focus, length, and location. Self-learning exercises and reflection or journaling take place in three of the programs. Three programs arrange site visits to leading FP/RH organizations when leadership program participants gather for trainings or alumni meetings. These visits provide opportunities to observe programs, learn about innovations, and ask questions. Three programs offer mini-grants for leadership

TABLE 12.1. FORMAL ACTIVITIES OF THE LEADERSHIP PROGRAMS.

	Workshops/ Trainings	Self-Learning	Mini-Grants	Formal Mentoring	Reflection/ Journaling	Site Visits	Formal Networking	Alumni Meetings
Population Leadership Program, University of Washington	X		X	X	X	X		X
Leadership Development Mechanism, Institute of International Education	X		X				X	
Visionary Leadership Program	X	X		X	X		X	
Gates Institute for Population and Reproductive Health, Johns Hopkins Bloomberg School of Public Health	X							
International Family Planning Leaders Program, Public Health Institute	X		X	X	X	X		X
Global Leadership Program, Partners in Population and Development	X					X		

participants to work individually or as a group on FP/RH related projects. While many leadership participants receive informal mentoring, three programs offer mentoring as a formal part of their program. Similarly, although informal networking was reported to be a frequent outcome of program participation, two programs offer regularly scheduled networking opportunities. While alumni attend program meetings occasionally, two programs hold regularly scheduled alumni meetings.

Evaluation Purposes and Questions

Similar to other foundations, the Packard and Gates Foundations have significantly increased their investments in leadership development because they believe that effective leadership is critical for catalyzing and sustaining positive change for people and communities around the world. However, few studies have systematically evaluated the intermediate and long-term impacts of these investments for social change. The Packard and Gates evaluation provided a unique opportunity to better understand and document these types of impacts across numerous programs and in a wide variety of contexts.

The Packard and Gates Foundations jointly funded this evaluation to assess the linkages among program design, implementation, and outcomes of the six population leadership programs. The eighteen-month evaluation took place when the leadership programs were from one to five years into their implementation. As a result, the funders viewed the evaluation as formative, with a primary focus on intermediate program outcomes. The foundations articulated a desire to better understand

- The outcomes that occurred as a result of participation in these leadership programs when program participants returned to their organizations and their countries
- The program strategies that best support participants to leverage their training experience
- The contributions of each program as well as their collective results
- The determination of which approaches and programs hold promise for producing long-term social change (for example, passage and implementation of progressive reproductive health policies)

The foundations also articulated their hope that evaluation findings and recommendations would inform their current and future investments in leadership development.

Based on our understanding of the evaluation purposes, we identified six questions to frame our inquiry for this evaluation. These questions were developed in an iterative process. First, the evaluation team reviewed relevant documents and spoke with foundation staff as well as representatives from all six leadership programs to obtain a better understanding of the goals, strategies, activities, and intended outcomes of the leadership investments as well as evaluation priorities. Next, we developed a proposed set of evaluation questions. We met with foundation staff to review the questions to ensure that they reflected their evaluation goals and information needs. The final set of evaluation questions included the following:

- To what extent are these six leadership programs identifying and supporting a critical mass of leaders who have the capacity to improve access, coverage, and quality of FP/RH services?
- What leadership development practices and approaches best support leaders to become effective FP/RH change agents?
- In what ways are leaders demonstrating more effective leadership as a result of their participation in these leadership programs?
- What improvements in family planning and reproductive health services; population policy, implementation, and allocation of resources; leadership training; research; and public attitudes are occurring within countries? In what ways are these changes linked to participation in these leadership programs?
- To what extent are the leadership programs and foundations effectively using their resources to deliver desired changes?
- What systems-level benchmarks may reliably indicate long-term impact of these leadership programs?

Evaluation Design and Implementation

In this section of the chapter we discuss critical steps in the evaluation design and implementation of leadership development efforts focused on social change. We begin by stating our approach to this type of evaluation followed by a description of our evaluation design team, theory of change model, and the evaluation measures, methods, and analyses.

Evaluation Approach

Our approach to the evaluation was rooted in the belief that learning is an ongoing and iterative process in which key stakeholders need to participate in order for learning outcomes to be meaningful and relevant to those involved. As a result, we regularly communicated with foundation staff through conference calls and in face-to-face meetings to provide feedback on what we were learning and to respond to questions that emerged during the course of the evaluation. We also engaged foundation and leadership program staff for input on many aspects of the evaluation, from selection criteria for evaluation participants to review of survey and interview protocols to interpretation and use of evaluation findings.

Evaluation Design Team

We put together a multidisciplinary evaluation design team comprised of individuals from three different organizations. This was critical, since no one organization comprised all of the needed skills—something that poses a common challenge for these types of large-scale evaluations. Members of the team came with different types of expertise in evaluation, leadership development, family planning, and reproductive health and a history of successful collaboration with each other and individuals from the countries in which the evaluation focused. Since the core team members resided in different locations, most of the work took place virtually, through e-mail and phone communication. In addition, three in-person meetings took place with the core team members during the course of the evaluation. These gatherings provided intensive periods of time to discuss the design of the evaluation, interim and final evaluation findings, and ways to make the evaluation most useful to the foundations, the six leadership programs, and the field in general.

Theory of Change Model

In preparation for this evaluation, staff from the six leadership programs and both foundations met with a consulting group, the Evaluation Forum, to develop a leadership development theory of change. (See Chapter Two for a more in-depth discussion about theories of change.) Each program staff worked on a theory of change for its program, and then came together to create a unified theory (see Figure 12.1). They also agreed on outcomes and priority indicators that they believed were most likely to occur for individuals, organizations, and systems and the collaborations within and between levels. This process of engagement, which took six months, deepened the knowledge that grantees and foundation staff had about what they were trying to achieve and how they would know whether they were successful. It allowed for an important time of reflection and discussion about leadership program assumptions and processes that may not have occurred otherwise (or at least to the same extent with such broad stakeholder representation). It also provided a shared starting point for continued learning during the evaluation. For example, over the course of the evaluation, we identified outcomes and contextual issues for possible inclusion into the theory of change model.

Based on this process, the Evaluation Forum produced a guide that describes the process of creating a leadership development theory of change (2003).

Evaluation Measures

The theory of change and associated indicators described previously provided an invaluable basis from which to identify evaluation measures. We used the documentation of this work, our experience measuring leadership for social change with other evaluations, and discussions with those involved with the leadership programs and the field more broadly to choose indicators that would assess program outcomes at multiple levels: individual, organizational, and systems. In addition to detecting changes that resulted from program participation at these different levels, we were interested in better understanding connections between and within them.

Since the internal evaluations of these programs focused most significantly on short-term individual outcomes and thus that work was already being done, we chose a minimal number of these types of measures. They were not excluded completely because it was hypothesized that these more immediate outcomes would in turn lead to other types of changes (for example, improved management skills and their application in participants' organizations). Examples of short-term individual outcomes include those on page 354.

FIGURE 12.1. LEADERSHIP DEVELOPMENT THEORY OF CHANGE MODEL.

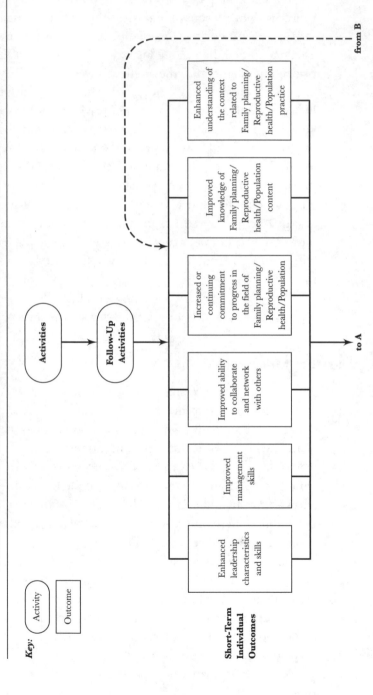

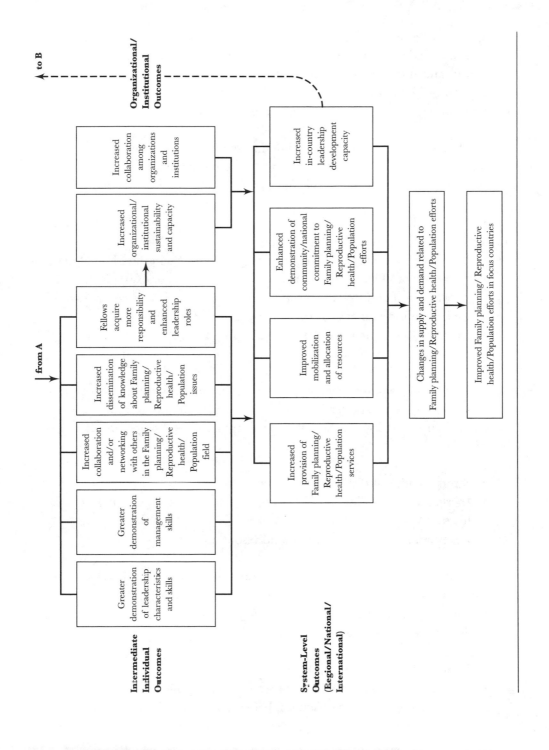

- Increased or continuing commitment to progress in the FP/RH field
- Enhanced understanding of the context related to FP/RH practice
- Enhanced leadership characteristics and skills
- Improved management skills
- Improved ability to collaborate and network with others

Second, we focused on choosing intermediate individual-level outcomes. These included measures that would capture more visible changes in participants once they returned home and to their work. Examples include

- Greater demonstration of leadership characteristics and skills (for example, participants were more able to promote controversial issues)
- Increased collaboration and networking with others in the FP/RH field
- More responsibility and enhanced leadership roles (for example, increased participation on FP/RH relevant boards, task forces, and commissions as well as honors and awards received for FP/RH work)
- Increased dissemination of knowledge about FP/RH issues (for example, participants served as mentors or were featured in the media)

Third, we looked at changes that took place in participants' organizations as a result of their experience in one of the leadership programs. These measures focused on organizational- and institutional-level outcomes. Examples include

- Strengthening and expansion of networks
- Increased collaboration on projects, meetings, or events with other organizations
- Leveraging of financial and in-kind resources

Next, we chose measures to assess system-level outcomes. These measures were used to capture more broadscale social changes that influenced systems across organizations as well as changes at community, regional, national, and international levels. Examples include

- Increased number and quality of FP/RH programs
- Increased in-country FP/RH leadership development capacity
- Changes in population policy, implementation, and allocation of resources

- Improvements in data collection and research capacity
- Changes in public attitudes toward FP/RH

Last, we asked questions to gain a better understanding of the organizational and country context in which program participants' FP/RH work took place. Examples include

- Recent significant changes in participants' organizations
- Current organizational practices (for example, strategic planning, use of data for planning, and collaboration with others)
- Reproductive health situations in countries (for example, significant FP/RH progress, most important FP/RH policies and initiatives, and cultural, historical, political, and religious supports and barriers)
- Cooperative action and collaboration across sectors

In addition to the outcomes identified at the outset of this evaluation, we continued to look for unanticipated outcomes and paid close attention to the role of contextual factors (for example, policy, technological, communication, and cultural) on the opportunities and challenges for individuals, organizations, and collaborative networks to achieve positive FP/RH changes.

Since the leadership programs were fairly early in their implementation (from one to five years), we thought about precursors of broadscale change that could be identified. For example, the introduction of a progressive national policy, even if it did not pass, could be seen as a positive step toward social change.

We constantly needed to weigh the time requested of those we surveyed and interviewed with our information needs. Closed-ended questions were used to measure clearly identified outcomes. Open-ended questions were used to gather more descriptive information to complement responses from closed-ended questions and to measure or capture less frequent or unanticipated outcomes. For example, in addition to asking a few batteries of survey questions about the impact of the leadership program on participants, we included an open-ended question: What is the most important thing you learned and/or experienced as a result of being involved in the leadership program?

Toward the end of the survey, another question we asked was, Is there anything that you have achieved in your FP/RH work that you think would not have been possible without your participation in the leadership program?

Open-ended questions also helped us better understand the process in which changes occurred. For example, Did the change in one program participant's ability to articulate FP/RH problems and potential solutions impact system-level practices directly or did the recognition of changes made at his organization contribute to the impact? Did the implementation of a national-level policy occur as a result of leadership participants' work, or was it a contributing or accelerating factor? During our in-person data collection, we also asked more questions about social change measures and the context in which program participants work (for example, interviews and focus groups that took place mostly in the evaluation focus countries). This focus was chosen due to limited resources and the desire to understand the impact of the program within a small number of countries in depth versus many countries incompletely.

Evaluation Methods

Since no one method provides a complete picture of a program's impact, we used a combination of quantitative and qualitative methods:

- Surveys
- Focus groups
- Interviews
- Participant-observation
- Review of secondary source data and program documents

To get a full and complete picture of program activities, their outcomes, and the context in which the leadership participants work, we collected information from a variety of sources:

- Foundation staff
- Leadership program staff
- Leadership program participants
- Colleagues and peers of program participants who worked close enough with program participants to observe changes that may have occurred as a result of their program participation
- Key informants, defined as individuals who can comment on the Packard and Gates leadership programs as well as the history and context in which FP/RH efforts take place

Next, we describe in more detail our processes and content of developing and implementing the different data collection tools. We start with a description of our sampling and then discuss each evaluation method individually.

Sampling. Since the leadership programs had already had more than 1,800 participants, decisions needed to be made about the breadth and depth of data collection. Taking into account available evaluation resources, we considered representation among the six different leadership programs and within each of these programs, the leadership program cohorts, and countries of participants. In other similar types of evaluations, sampling decisions may be based on other units such as communities, organizations, disciplines, or sites.

Because our primary interest was intermediate outcomes, we excluded those leadership participants who would not be completed with their initial leadership training prior to the start of our data collection phase. This resulted in a sample of 1,434 individuals. Second, we focused the more intensive in-person data collection efforts on four of the ninety countries represented by leadership program participants: Ethiopia, India, Mexico, and Nigeria. These countries were chosen in consultation with the Packard and Gates Foundations. Factors that led to their choice included the relatively large number of program participants located in each of these countries, representation of the six different leadership programs, geographic diversity of the four countries in comparison to each other, and the experience and availability of evaluation team members in these countries (for example, one evaluation team member's organization had current or former staff located in each of these countries). During the evaluation, each evaluation team member conducted two in-person site visits to one of the focus countries. Working closely with in-country evaluation consultants, the evaluation team members were afforded the opportunity to conduct in-person interviews, focus groups, and participant observations.

At the time of data collection, one of the leadership programs was relatively new, and the first cohort of participants had not completed its program. Since the evaluation focused on intermediate outcomes, we excluded these program participants from the survey and interview processes. We did, however, collect information from them through focus groups. This proved to be a relatively easy and informative process and provided information to inform the program and foundation staff about progress to date and our initial thinking about how this program compared to the other leadership programs in regard to inputs, strategies, and early indication of outcomes.

Surveys. We developed surveys for each leadership program to explore the priority outcomes and indicators that were identified in the theory of change work described previously. While each program survey was tailored with some specific questions related to that program, the vast majority of questions were the same. This allowed us to make comparisons across programs but also provided opportunities to query about a unique aspect of a specific program (for example, mini-grants offered by one of the programs).

The survey was pilot tested extensively among program staff and a select group of program participants in a variety of countries. Since program participants represented many countries, we made extra efforts to ensure that the survey was understandable and that participants felt comfortable answering survey questions. As a result of the pilot test, a number of changes were made to the survey instruments, such as shortening their length and changing some of the wording (for example, in one country, the word *leadership* could not be used due to government censorship).

Due to resource constraints, we chose to translate the surveys into Spanish only. After speaking with staff across the programs, we learned that this was the largest group of participants who attended trainings in another language besides English. With a few exceptions, all of the other program participants attended training programs in English.

Our survey collection strategy for each country and program was based on logistics (for example, the availability of Internet access), country visits, best-practice methods of survey dissemination, relationships, events in each country, and our face-to-face access to the alumni of the various programs. Based on these factors, along with our discussion with staff from each of the leadership programs, we decided to disseminate the survey to leadership participants using a two-pronged approach: e-mail and personal contact (as possible). Mail and phone did not prove to be the most effective options for disseminating the survey, with the exception of calls conducted in-country during site visits and those made by in-country evaluation consultants.

Leadership participants could respond online or by completing the survey, which was attached as a Word document. We used an online survey tool to help with e-mail and Web-based survey dissemination. In the e-mail, we asked leadership participants to tell us if they preferred to receive the survey by another method (for example, by mail or phone).

We obtained contact information for participants by using a database that one of the leadership programs kept on participants of all six leadership programs. This information was cross-referenced with information provided directly from the programs. If the contact information was incorrect, we made attempts to obtain information by contacting program directors and staff directly or others as relevant (for example, in-country contacts). The evaluation team made three attempts to contact all leadership participants to request their participation in the survey process. Prior to our request to complete the survey, program staff sent an e-mail to their leadership participants to announce our involvement in the evaluation and the coming survey.

For all program participants, we used our working relationships with in-country evaluation consultants to disseminate and collect surveys in person in the focus countries. This included using collaborative relationships established by the evaluation team during visits to focus countries and each evaluation team member's personal appeal to individuals they met to request their survey participation. When possible, we (or our collaborators) attended program sessions, alumni meetings, and conferences attended by program participants to collect and disseminate the surveys.

For the other countries, we made less intensive efforts to work with in-country staff from our evaluation team, in-country leadership program coordinators, and relationships established by the evaluation team with select program participants in those countries for survey dissemination and administration. The exception was the Philippines, Mexico, and Pakistan, in which we hired in-country consultants to help us with survey work. We chose these three countries because of their high number of leadership program participants.

Focus Groups. Focus groups were held with current program participants, alumni, and program staff in order to deepen our understanding of relevant issues and challenges in the field, to learn about experiences with the program, and to test some of our emerging findings. Focus groups were originally included as a minor element of the data collection strategy. However, over the course of the evaluation, they emerged as a more significant component. Focus groups (1) enabled us to gather more in-depth information about impact, and to benefit from interactive discussion among participants; (2) provided a targeted opportunity for disseminating and collecting surveys; (3) allowed us to engage program participants in the process of identifying and testing the validity of potential benchmarks for a summative evaluation; and (4) provided program participants with a networking and sharing opportunity.

Throughout the evaluation, we looked for relevant gatherings to conduct focus groups. In total, we conducted more than a dozen focus groups with program staff or leadership participants. Examples of focus groups include

- In-country staff from one of the leadership programs from five different countries at their annual staff meeting
- Leadership participants during their attendance at program-related gatherings, including alumni meetings as well as FP/RH meetings in which a significant number of leadership program participants attend (for example, Asian International Health Conference in Thailand)
- In-country selection committee members for one of the leadership programs

Interviews. We conducted interviews with more than 150 people. For each evaluation focus country, this included approximately ten program participants, two to three peers or colleagues of program participants, four key informants, and a few in-country program staff. In addition, we interviewed selected leadership program and foundation staff. A standard protocol was developed for each type of interview. These protocols guided the interviews and ensured the collection of comparable types of information. Interview questions were general enough in nature that they applied to different contexts; specific probes for each interview question helped evaluation team members guide interviews as appropriate. Interviews lasted on average one hour; however, they ranged from about thirty minutes to more than two hours.

Prior to focus country visits, each member of the evaluation team developed a sampling strategy based on an assessment of the program participants: which program they attended, their affiliation with different sectors (for example, government versus nongovernmental organization), the specific focus of their work (for example, program administration versus research), their longevity in the field, their geography (for example, urban versus rural), their gender and age. We also took into account a number of other considerations, such as opportunities to interview program participants face to face at meetings we attended, travel distance, and logistical challenges related to potential interviewees' locations.

In a few instances, there were multiple individuals in an organization who had participated in various leadership programs. This offered a unique opportunity to learn about the contributions and synergies that occurred by having multiple individuals within one agency attend leadership programs.

Where possible, for each program participant whom we interviewed, we chose one person from the participant's organization and one person external to the organization with whom the program participant had collaborated. The leadership participant, program staff, or foundation staff identified these individuals. We tried to select people who were knowledgeable about the participant's leadership from multiple perspectives (for example, supervisor or mentor). We asked these individuals about the leadership participant, how they knew them and in what context, and the ways in which they thought the leadership participant had been impacted by their program participation.

For in-country program staff and key informants, we asked questions about their perspective on the leadership programs and country context and the challenges and opportunities of building in-country leadership capacity. Key in-country informants were selected based on recommendations of foundation staff and in-country consultants who are deeply knowledgeable about the field. For interviews with key staff from each of the six leadership programs, we asked about recruitment and selection, program curriculum, follow-up activities, evaluation, and collaboration among programs.

Participant Observation. We sought, wherever possible and within the financial constraints of this project, to take advantage of gatherings of program participants to both observe program activities in action as well as to utilize the opportunity for survey and focus group administration. In our evaluation focus countries, participant observation included such activities as attending convenings of program participants and leadership trainings in the United States and abroad. The evaluation team used an observation protocol to guide their written documentation of these activities (for example, the who, what, where, why, and how) as well as their own reflections.

Review of Secondary Source Data and Program Materials. To learn more about each of the leadership programs, we asked for relevant program materials to review. These included program descriptions and plans, copies of training curriculum, and foundation and evaluation reports. Within focus countries, we also gathered materials that included documents that gave us a better idea of the context in which FP/RH work takes place. Types of program documents included copies of FP/RH policies and implementation plans and the results of national FP/RH surveys and descriptions of other FP/RH work taking place within country. We also used in-country consultants to research and assemble data from existing secondary sources and program participants to provide key organizational documents, including their dissemination pieces and relevant planning and evaluation documents.

Analyses

All survey data was entered into SPSS for data analysis. For quantitative data, the evaluation team ran frequencies and means for the aggregate data as well as for each program and focus country. We also conducted bivariate analyses to assess differences among programs and countries. In some cases, we looked at additional differences, such as reported success of leveraging funds as a result of program participation based on years of experience in the FP/RH field.

We analyzed qualitative data from the surveys, focus groups, and interviews in a number of ways. For each focus country, we identified key themes that emerged. We did the same for programs. This usually took place in an iterative process. For example, during our first site visits to focus countries we collected and analyzed an initial set of data that informed our data collection efforts during our second visit. We came together as an evaluation team a number of times during the evaluation to discuss our analyses to date and come to group consensus about findings within our focus countries as well as the other countries in which program participants reside and work. We shared these findings with individuals in the evaluation focus countries (for example, in-country program staff, technical support teams of the Packard Foundation, and in-country evaluation collaborators). Since a good portion of data relied on self-reporting from leadership participants, when assessing impact we looked for convergence from more than one source of information (for example, from the program participant as well as one or more of their colleagues).

Evaluation Reporting and Use of Findings

There were two primary audiences for this evaluation: the grantee organizations that implemented the leadership programs and the Packard and Gates Foundations' boards and staffs. A secondary but important audience for the evaluation was made up of other funders, leadership programs, and leadership development evaluators.

The overarching goal of our communication and dissemination plans for these audiences was to inform program decisions related to current and future leadership programs and to contribute to the knowledge of the field. Throughout the evaluation, a number of steps were taken toward this goal, including phone calls, e-mails, written communication, and in-person presentations and discussions with foundation staff and grantees. Planned sharing of evaluation findings included

- An external assessment of each leadership program that included reflections and recommendations on program strategies, initial findings about intermediate-term program impacts, reflections on learning strategies of the internal evaluation process, an analysis of the alignment of program activities and anticipated outcomes, suggestions for synergy across the leadership programs, and perspectives from the broader field of leadership development
- An interim and final report that addressed key findings from data collection and analyses and included reflections about the programs' selection processes, program interventions, and follow-up activities, as well as our recommendations to the foundations and to grantee organizations about how the programs' efficiency and effectiveness may be improved
- Individual reports that focused on each evaluation focus country that were included as part of the interim and final reports but also could be used as stand-alone products

A number of unplanned requests and opportunities surfaced during the evaluation. This facilitated our using evaluation findings in real time to inform discussion and decisions. Examples include

- Presentation and discussion about ways to leverage the leadership development efforts for broader support of FP/RH work at the annual Packard meeting of their technical support teams from their five focus countries
- Attendance at the annual International Family Planning Coalition meeting with staff from all six programs and both foundations to present findings to date, obtain input from attendees on the evaluation methods and processes, and discuss findings and their implication for program decisions
- Decision to write two executive summaries so the information needs for the board of each foundation could most effectively be addressed

- Foundation request for evaluation findings to review grant proposals and make suggestions about approaches to strengthen various program elements
- Providing input on leadership impacts for country-level strategy evaluations

For all evaluation products, we worked closely with foundation staff to ensure that the content and format of our reports and presentations met their needs. In addition to these formal reports and presentations, we conducted periodic phone conferences with foundation staff to address issues of timely concern. There were several venues where we shared what we were learning with the field more broadly. These included discussions at the annual gathering of the Leadership Learning Community and a presentation with foundation and program staff about the population leadership programs at the annual meeting of the International Leadership Association.

Evaluation Reflections and Lessons

In this section, we discuss our reflections on evaluating leadership development efforts that focus on social change. We include what we have learned about the key benefits and challenges of the design elements of evaluations, their implementation, and the usefulness and application of evaluation findings.

Key Design Elements

A multidisciplinary design team enriches the quality of the evaluation. Although collaboration across geographic boundaries sometimes poses logistical challenges (for example, vastly different time zones and support staff located in geographical distance offices), the evaluation process and products usually benefit from the greater breadth and depth of experience and expertise among these types of teams. For example, in addition to comparing these six leadership development programs with each other, team members could draw upon their knowledge about the strategies of more than one hundred other leadership development programs, including some that were part of social change initiatives. We also were able to leverage resources from the organizations of participating members. For example, the organizations with staff in the evaluation focus countries were critical to facilitate our access to leadership program participants and enhance the quality of data collected. This type of team seems especially important when working across different types of boundaries due to geography, sector, culture, class, and other factors.

Articulation of the theory of change among foundation staff and grantees is a critical step in the evaluation process. It is important for program and staff to articulate their goals, strategies, activities, and outcomes to make sure that there is alignment and agreement among key players. It also provides a strong foundation to build the evaluation on and enhances consensus among program and foundation staff. If such a process does not take place prior to the start of an evaluation, it should be one of the first steps. The amount of time devoted to this type of work can vary greatly; however, to do it well it is important to not underestimate the resources that are needed or the value of having a strong facilitator.

While the theory of change model provides a basis to build the evaluation, it is important to recognize the fluidity of such a model as programs evolve, contexts change, and unanticipated positive or negative outcomes take place. It was helpful to revisit the model periodically with the evaluation team as well as with grantees and foundation staff, both to test the theory of change and add to or modify it as needed. The limitations of these models also need to be recognized, as they appear to make the change process look more linear than takes place in reality. Open systems methods, discussed in Chapter Three, describe some newer methods that attempt to move understanding about change beyond a linear causal model.

Build flexibility into the evaluation for unexpected opportunities. At a number of points during the evaluation, we modified our plans due to a more realistic understanding of feasibility issues as well as unanticipated opportunities for data collection and/or sharing evaluation findings. Some examples include

- Taking advantage of leadership participant gatherings to distribute and collect surveys and increase the use of focus group discussions
- Responding to funder requests for the most up-to-date evaluation findings to inform decision making
- Attending program staff and funder meetings to obtain input on data collection, share evaluation findings, and discuss their potential application
- Developing a standard data collection protocol to gather information on clearly defined outcomes of interest and at the same time capture unanticipated outcomes
- Meeting with new foundation and program staff to inform and engage them in the evaluation (needed because of staff turnover)
- Identifying and hiring in-country consultants to increase survey response rates among leadership participants

Sometimes unexpected opportunities saved resources; however, more often than not, additional costs were incurred. Reserving a portion of evaluation budgets for these types of unanticipated but evaluation-enhancing activities seems ideal. However, many foundations seem uncomfortable with such a budget line item. As a result, in most cases it needs to be incorporated into all relevant evaluation tasks to the best extent possible. An alternative possibility would be foundation staff's access to a fund that could support emerging evaluation opportunities as needed. Regardless of the design, flexibility on the part of the foundation in terms of oversight of evaluation funds, and of evaluation teams in regard to their implementation plans, remains important.

Evaluation Processes

Ensure the alignment of evaluation values between evaluators and funders upfront. This helps to avoid conflicts between the grantor and grantee concerning the purpose of the evaluation, processes, and products. For example, on one end of the spectrum, a traditional stance on evaluation would have external evaluators collect data, synthesize it, and provide it to the client at the end of the intervention so the evaluation findings do not influence the intervention itself. On the other end of the spectrum, the intervention might be influenced by the evaluation findings in real time (for example, application of the interim evaluation report to make decisions that shift program goals and activities). Due diligence to ensure a proper match prior to entering into an evaluation relationship not only avoids conflicts but can increase the satisfaction and usefulness of the evaluation for all stakeholders. One caution is that even if the program officers who oversee the evaluation hold the same values as the evaluators, it does not necessarily mean that the senior foundation leadership does.

Identify funder and grantee expectations at the beginning of the evaluation and periodically reclarify. One of the most important and challenging aspects of these large-scale evaluations is facilitating discussions with key stakeholders to clarify the expectations for the evaluation and then to reclarify them periodically. This involves discussions and clarification about what the evaluation can and cannot answer, prioritization of key evaluation questions based on resources and feasibility issues, and the pros and cons of different evaluation designs and methods. This involves extra efforts when foundations experience change such as shifts in programmatic focus. For example, during the evaluation of the six population leadership programs, the Gates Foundation underwent a strategic planning process that resulted in shifts in its leadership investments. As a result, the evaluation team spent a day meeting with foundation staff to discuss evaluation findings and which ones to emphasize given these changes.

It typically is easier to maintain expectations with the program officers directly in charge of the evaluation than with their team members and/or the senior leadership of the foundation. For example, for the evaluation of the population leadership programs, we clearly defined goals for survey response rates that were approved by the program officers overseeing the evaluation. After exceeding those goals, we were unprepared for the central stage that generalizability took when we presented the evaluation findings to foundation staff, most of whom were not aware of the previous discussions and decisions regarding response rates.

Account for cultural differences throughout the evaluation process. Our evaluation team brought certain cultural competencies and sensitivities to the evaluation through previous travel and work experiences. Even though collectively we had a lot of experience working with diverse groups in a variety of cultural contexts, it was important that we continued to learn from each other and from others outside of our team, such as our in-country consultants. In-country consultants' understanding of cultural sensitivities helped with access to leadership participants as well as scheduling and organizing visits (for example, standard waiting periods, hospitality etiquette, and appropriate requests of leadership participants). They enhanced responses to our requests for input and the quality of data collected. For example, in some countries, in-country consultants helped explain the purpose of the survey and answer participants' questions in their primary languages.

In-country consultants' assistance with analyses and interpretation of evaluation findings were especially important. Many times we benefited from their observations and reflections during debriefs after interviews and meetings. For example, in one country an internal evaluator for one of the leadership programs criticized a participant as lacking leadership, citing her unwillingness to share her training materials with others. After interviewing this participant, it seemed as though her experience had greatly impacted her work and that she was sharing what she learned with others. After debriefing with the in-country consultant, it became clear that the disconnection resulted from local leaders having different expectations about what it meant to share.

We also asked evaluation questions about cultural sensitivity and competencies and reported on aspects of programs that seemed culturally inappropriate (for example, the use of 360-degree evaluations). Sometimes, leadership participants seemed visibly uncomfortable making criticisms of program leaders because it is viewed as disrespectful and improper in their cultures. An evaluation strategy that may be useful is to allow a group to work on their own with difficult questions and report results to the external evaluation team, without any clear attribution to any one individual.

Analyze and share evaluation findings in pieces over time to strengthen the evaluation and its usefulness for key stakeholders. In this evaluation and others, we utilized an iterative analysis process to cull and synthesize data at a number of points during the evaluation. This allowed each phase of data collection to inform the next phase. For example, in the evaluation of The California Wellness Foundation's Violence Prevention Initiative, the evaluation team met at three points in time to analyze findings: (1) after the completion of surveys of leadership participants; (2) after interviews of a smaller group of participants who completed the survey; and (3) after site visits with an even smaller group who completed an interview. Each stage of analysis informed our sampling and data collection for the subsequent phase. With the caveat that this type of analysis takes more time, it also provides an opportunity to share findings with foundation and program staff sooner to inform program implementation and funding decisions.

Evaluation Measurement

Clarify and define social change for each evaluation. The definition of social change can vary from initiative to initiative. It is important to make sure that the foundation and program staffs are clear as to what they mean by *social change* and their expectations for this type of change during the intervention period. The utilization of precursors and proxies for social change should be utilized as appropriate (for example, the passage of a policy through a government committee can be seen as progress toward positive social change regardless of its ultimate passage). Defining social change seems to be easier in retrospective evaluations when participants can reflect on the evolution and outcomes of their efforts rather than prospective evaluations in which the social change outcomes may lack clarity due to changing goals, strategies, and opportunities.

The maturity and scale of the leadership development efforts influence the breadth and depth of the evaluation. We utilize the evaluation of the population leadership programs and the violence prevention leadership programs to provide some examples. First, given the vast differences in resources of the population leadership programs ($3 million to $60 million), we had to make decisions about which program elements to include in the evaluation. For the largest investment, we chose to exclude some program components (for example, more traditional support for participation in U.S.-based master's and doctoral training) whose added value for learning seemed more minimal. Similarly, given the large number of countries from which program participants were drawn, we chose four countries in which we focused our most in-depth data collection efforts. This allowed us to better understand the impact of the leadership programs for participants in these countries and the context in which FP/RH efforts took place.

Second, we found that the type and content of questions needs to vary depending on the intervention period. For example, the length of time since program completion for participants in the population leadership programs varied from one to five years, while those in the violence prevention leadership programs ranged from one to nine years. Given this longer period of time, we tended to include more specific closed-ended questions about distal social change outcomes for those involved in the violence prevention programs as compared to those in the population programs.

Third, the intervention type influences the appropriate evaluation design. For most evaluations, retrospective cross-sectional designs involve one point of data collection. Ideally, longitudinal prospective designs would be used with multiple points of data collection over time. However, since the costs of longitudinal evaluations remain high (for example, an ongoing evaluation investment for such change would ideally last ten years), scaled-back retrospective evaluations that follow a portion of leadership participants when the intervention ends could be valuable.

Do not underestimate the resources and creativity needed to locate leadership program participants and garner their participation. In these types of evaluations, graduated times have elapsed between participants' completing the leadership program and a request to be involved in the evaluation. As a result, contact information frequently is outdated and enthusiasm to participate in an evaluation diminished. It is important to plan for more time than anticipated to update preexisting contact information, track down participants, and collect data. In our experience, in a number of evaluations this involves hiring additional consultants who live in the general area of participants, have flexible schedules to track participants down in a sensitive but effective manner, and who can be available to interview program alumni at their home or offices according to different schedules.

At times, changes needed to be made to evaluation protocols. For example, in the evaluation of the violence prevention leadership programs, we adjusted our protocol for the community leadership program to allow for in-person interviews rather than telephone interviews that were successfully completed by participants from the academic leadership program. We found that community leadership participants were much more willing to speak in person on their own turf than to talk with us by telephone. Another example is from one of the evaluation focus countries for the population leadership programs' evaluation in which high cost package carriers are the only reliable mail service and many leadership participants do not have phones, or at least reliable ones. As a result, for many leadership participants, we needed to distribute and collect surveys in person. For those leadership participants who did not attend relevant meetings, we delivered and collected surveys at their offices or homes. Due to the relatively low labor costs and the frequent travel of our in-country consultants and their staff, this became a surprisingly efficient and cost-effective way to obtain completed surveys.

The evaluation of large-scale leadership development efforts for social change demands data collection that utilizes multiple methods and perspectives. It is important to supplement self-reports about program impacts from leadership participants with data from other sources. Although leadership participants had the most intimate knowledge about what was changing for them personally, in their organizations, and in their collaborations with others, there could be an inherent bias in self-reporting. To address this bias, we also met with leadership participants' colleagues and with key informants to gather additional perspectives about program impact and the changes that were observed. However, a challenge exists with these interviews. Since these interviewees often have not participated in leadership programs, they do not necessarily recognize nor can they always articulate the changes in leadership that have occurred.

The issue of generalizability due to survey response rates also provides another reason to gather information from multiple sources. For example, many leadership participants who completed a survey also participated in a focus group and/or interview. This provided more in-depth information about their experiences, both in their leadership program cohort and their country. It also helped us to more fully understand the context in which changes occurred. Again, this was especially important due to the number of leadership participants, programs, and organizational and country contexts.

Establishing an attributable benefit for leadership development efforts focused on social change is inherently difficult. We asked leadership participants to tell us what changes occurred as a result of their participation in the leadership program. Proximal changes, such as changes in behavior and attitudes, as well as certain actions program participants took, were more likely attributable to program participation. Distal changes, such as changes in policy and quality of services, made it more difficult to establish attribution with certainty because it was difficult to isolate the impact of the leadership program. Many times, the best that can be achieved is establishing that the leadership program contributed to the outcome, something for which evidence can be collected from multiple sources. Case studies and more in-depth data collection in focus countries provided us with additional data and enhanced our understanding about these contributions and possible associations between program participation and social change outcomes.

Conduct cross-program comparisons with care and sensitivity. Few evaluations provide an opportunity to examine programs in relation to one another. The evaluations of the population leadership programs and the violence prevention programs were somewhat unique because they enabled the documentation of outcomes across programs. However, a number of cautions are warranted. First, grantees frequently become apprehensive that these comparisons involve a ranking or a grading of sorts. Second, funders many times desire an analysis and conclusion that involves a bottom line (for example, program A is a better investment than program B because of factor X). Typically, however, differences between program goals, strategies, intended outcomes, levels of resources, and contexts do not allow for such clear conclusions. For instance, with the population leadership evaluation, each program had particular strengths or weaknesses; however, the ideal program seemed to be a blend of the best elements across the programs. These types of results take extra efforts for evaluators to articulate and for funders to understand and apply.

To examine return on investments, program budgets need to account for and track costs in a similar manner. Leadership development investors frequently ask evaluators to assess the return on investment for different programs. For example, do programs that cost significantly more money deliver a value or achieve an impact that warrants the higher investment? In the population leadership evaluation, a comparison of the six leadership programs showed a cost per participant that ranged from $3,500 to $85,000. While we could make some comments based on these large cost differentials, we did not know their degree of accuracy because there was no uniform formula for reporting administrative costs per participant.

Typically we find a number of challenges to calculating return on investments that allow for these cross-program comparisons. These include

- Leadership development investments are often designed to address inequities in access and disparity in resources; thus the investment may be seen as a moral imperative, not a cost-driven decision.
- There is no standard in budget development that allows for an equitable comparison of actual cost per participant.
- Budget representation of training costs makes it difficult to cost out specific leadership program design components so that their costs can be understood relative to the value and impact.
- Cost may need to be tracked over time to capture the reduction of cost per participant as resources are shifted after program start-up phases.
- The costs of the same delivery strategy may vary across regions.
- There may be different costs associated with the training needs of different target populations.
- The impact of reflective time may be as significant, but more difficult to quantify and track, as a skills-based training such as strategic planning.

Foundations are in a position to request more standard and complete budgeting guidelines to increase learning about how programs invest their resources. Similarly, evaluators are in the position to bring attention to these issues. (See Chapter Five for a full discussion of return-on-investment methodology.)

Key Considerations

Based on the issues discussed, we provide some key questions to consider when deciding if, when, and how to evaluate leadership development efforts focused on social change. When we refer to stakeholders, we mean primarily funders and program staff.

Design Elements

- To what extent do leadership development program goals, strategies, and outcomes align?
- To what extent is the program evolving (that is, does the program's goals and/or strategies constantly change or does it have a high level of implementation fidelity)?
- Has enough time elapsed and/or resources been invested to expect changes in social outcomes or precursors of social change?
- What level of evidence of program effectiveness do stakeholders desire? Consider issues of generalizability and attribution.
- To what extent do stakeholders view the evaluation as formative versus summative?
- Are there enough resources and time to accomplish what is being asked of the evaluators?

Evaluation Processes

- How much interest do stakeholders have in the evaluation and how strongly do they endorse it (for example, what is their investment in evaluation findings, helping with data access issues, and other elements)?
- What types of cultural competencies are required for the evaluation? How will the evaluation design meet those needs?
- What type of information do stakeholders want and when do they need this information (for example, throughout the evaluation period or only at its end, for decision making to inform program implementation, or to be able to demonstrate effectiveness for the broader field)?

Evaluation Measurement

- How do stakeholders define social change?
- Do useful data exist? If so, what are the access issues? For data that needs to be collected, what are the feasibility issues?
- Does program monitoring or evaluation take place already? What value would an external evaluation add?
- What opportunities exist for gathering data from multiple methods and perspectives?

Conclusion

The support of leaders in efforts to improve the lives of individuals and communities through social change is terribly important. Given the lack of evidence of best practices regarding how this most effectively occurs, there is still a lot to learn and share among those who fund, implement, and evaluate leadership development programs. This is especially true given the complexity of the types of leadership initiatives that we focus on in this chapter. It remains important to support learning through evaluations that can inform program and funding decisions as well as the field. However, given the limited resources for both leadership development programs and evaluations, careful choices need to be made about where to focus evaluation efforts. The process of evaluating complex change processes requires foundations to balance cost, and the intrusion of the evaluation intervention, with the certainty of what can be learned.

As a field, improvements are needed in the reach and timing of how evaluation findings are disseminated and innovative evaluation approaches shared. Where it makes sense, the same measures could be used to make comparisons across different types of leadership programs and contexts. Since social change can have broad definitions and applications across disciplines, the audience with whom these conversations take place should be widened.

Resources

Leadership and Social Change

Here are some resources that we have found particularly useful in thinking about leadership and social change. These publications address how leaders and/or leadership development efforts catalyze change. Two that focus on leading innovative change are *The Tipping Point* (Gladwell, 2000) and *How to Change the World: Social Entrepreneurs and the Power of New Ideas* (Bornstein, 2004). Gladwell describes how ideas and innovations spread through the presence of certain types of people (connectors, mavens, and salesmen), the contagiousness of the message, and the context or environment that influences how quickly the innovations or ideas spread. Bornstein describes how Ashoka selects social entrepreneurs and supports them to scale up their ideas and achieve breakthrough results.

Other authors focus on how leadership emerges in communities. Margaret Wheatley (2002) discusses how to develop leadership through communities of practice. She believes that the community becomes an incubator where new knowledge, skills, and competencies develop. The diversity that exists within the community is a valuable resource for new ideas. Communities that value diversity and have developed processes of inclusion are much more likely to be successful at meeting their collective needs and solving problems that arise (Figueroa, Kincaid, Rani, and Lewis, 2002). They demonstrate collaborative or collective leadership (Chrislip, 2002; Morse, 2004).

Systems theories are also influential in helping us think about leadership and social change. Stephen Johnson (2001) argues that change does not require a champion or a pacemaker; rather, it requires the encouragement of clusters that generate the best ideas. It is through ever-shifting alliances of smaller groups that large-scale change occurs. A process of ongoing selection takes place that gives some ideas and solutions priority over others. These ideas and solutions attract energy and resources.

Evaluation, Leadership, and Social Change

As mentioned earlier, the Evaluation Forum's guide (2003) outlines the process and steps it used to assist programs to develop their theories of change and to construct a model of the underlying theory for the impact of the collective of leadership programs used to inform its evaluation design.

The evaluation model described by Figueroa, Kincaid, Rani, and Lewis (2002) is particularly useful for programs that emphasize community dialogue and collective action as catalysts for individual and social change. Outcome indicators are specified for measuring collective self-efficacy, sense of ownership, social cohesion, social norms, leadership, participation, and shared knowledge (what the authors call *information equity*). Questions and tools are provided for measuring each of these, including an easy approach to mapping network cohesion. There is also a very useful discussion of the social change process.

Last, the evaluation instruments and protocols used for the population leadership and the violence prevention leadership evaluations discussed in this chapter can be found on the Leadership Learning Community Web site at www.leadershiplearning.org.

References

Bornstein, D. *How to Change the World: Social Entrepreneurs and the Power of New Ideas.* Oxford: Oxford University Press, 2004.

Chrislip, D. *The Collaborative Leadership Fieldbook.* San Francisco: Jossey-Bass, 2002.

Evaluation Forum. *Guide to Evaluating Leadership Development Programs,* May 2003. [www.leadershiplearning.org/pools/evaluation/].

Figueroa, M. E., Kincaid, D. L., Rani, M., and Lewis, G. "Communications for Social Change: An Integrated Model for Measuring the Process and Its Outcomes." The Rockefeller Foundation and Johns Hopkins University Center for Communication Programs, 2002. [www.communicationforsocialchange.org/publications-resources.php?id=107].

Gladwell, M. *The Tipping Point: How Little Things Can Make a Big Difference.* Boston: Little Brown, 2000.

Johnson, S. E. *The Connected Lives of Ants, Brains, Cities, and Software.* New York: Scribner, 2001.

Morse, S. *Smart Communities: How Citizens and Local Leaders Can Use Strategic Thinking to Build a Brighter Future.* San Francisco: Jossey-Bass, 2004.

Wheatley, M. *Supporting Pioneering Leaders as Communities of Practice: How to Rapidly Develop New Leaders in Great Numbers.* Spokane, Wash.: Berkana Institute, 2002.

CHAPTER THIRTEEN

EVALUATING YOUTH LEADERSHIP DEVELOPMENT THROUGH CIVIC ACTIVISM

Hanh Cao Yu, Heather K. Lewis-Charp, and Michelle Alberti Gambone

Youth leadership development, as conceived by the majority of youth development practitioners, most commonly occurs within an organizational or programmatic context. The goal of this type of leadership development is to benefit individual youth by supporting them to lead others, set goals, and solve problems within youth-oriented programs. Accordingly, evaluations of these types of programs measure youth leadership in terms of opportunities for decision making and leadership skill building (Connell, Gambone, and Smith, 2000; Dormody, Seevers, and Clason, 1993).

As program practitioners gain an increased understanding of the necessary tasks of adolescent development, they recognize that youth need to understand that they are part of something larger, can contribute to their communities, and can develop a sense of mattering (Eccles and Gootman, 2002). Therefore, a number of youth programs have embraced a community focus, with the understanding that young people's involvement in their communities enables them to expand their knowledge of and access to resources within the community (Cahill, 1997; Hughes and Curnan, 2002; Irby, Ferber, and Pittman, 2001; Kahne, Honig, and McLaughlin, 2002). For some youth development programs, the emphasis on civic engagement continues to broaden the kinds of outcomes that young people need to achieve to become effective citizens. As educational and after-school programs strengthen civic participation among youth, for instance, they set higher performance outcome expectations related to increased political knowledge and community volunteerism (Kirshner, O'Donoghue, and McLaughlin, 2002).

The emergence of a civic activism focus in programming and evaluation of youth leadership raises interesting and underexplored elements of youth leadership that program leaders seldom promote or systematically evaluate (Ginwright and James, 2002). For instance, researchers and evaluators have most frequently studied the effects of youth leadership development at the individual level. Although youth leadership in civic activism has a strong element of individual benefit, a broader community and ideological focus alters thinking about traditional indicators of youth leadership development.

Zeldin and Camino's (1999) definition of youth leadership begins to acknowledge the areas of youth leadership development that civic activism programming promotes:

> Youth leadership, which is one type of youth development programming, is distinctive in three ways. First and foremost, it is grounded in a social cause. Second, it seeks to promote a relatively narrow set of youth outcomes, specifically those that allow young people to engage in collaborative action. And third, programming incorporates not only instruction and action, but equally important, membership and modeling. Indeed, we conclude that it is the experience of cause-based, collective, and visible action that transforms a youth group into a youth leadership team [p. 1].

This definition of youth leadership, derived from evaluations of five major youth leadership programs across the nation, helps to reframe youth leadership as something that occurs collaboratively across individuals.

In this chapter, traditional and popular conceptions of youth leadership are used as the foundation for evaluating youth leadership development. We examine how traditional concepts of youth leadership can be expanded to encompass youth leadership development within a community and civic context. We do this by presenting a case study of an evaluation of a national youth leadership initiative.

Youth Leadership Within a Civic Activism Context

In 1999, the Ford Foundation and the Innovation Center for Community and Youth Development launched the Youth Leadership for Development Initiative (YLDI) at a pivotal time in the research and funding of youth leadership development, civic engagement, and identity programs. The youth development field was embarking on a new direction: to explore how youth development programs could better address the community and family contexts where young people develop. Underlying the YLDI initiative were two basic assumptions about the value of civic activism as an approach to youth development: (1) civic activism, combined with leadership development, is a promising component of a comprehensive strategy for youth development; and (2) civic activism meets a number of young people's development needs and provides opportunities for youth to acquire a range of civic and leadership skills.

In 2000, Social Policy Research Associates (SPR) was selected as the initiative evaluator. Both the initiative and evaluation had many key stakeholders, including funders, program practitioners, youth, and researchers. From the outset of the evaluation, SPR sought to make the evaluation rigorous, participatory, and culturally proficient. We operated with the belief that the quality of the information we were gathering would be improved through the development of trusting and reciprocal relationships with participants in the YLDI advisory group of grantees. Toward this end, we created a diverse and culturally competent team of researchers to work with YLDI organizations. We engaged organizational leaders and youth in various aspects of tool development and data collection. Further, we gave both project leaders and young people opportunities to reflect and comment on our findings at the annual learning group meeting and during one-on-one meetings with YLDI leaders. (See Exhibit 13.1 for more details.)

The authors' experience evaluating youth activism organizations across the United States provided an opportunity to develop an evaluation framework that incorporated additional conceptions of leadership within a civic activism context. The goal of the YLDI evaluation study was to understand how civic activism differed from traditional youth development. The first step toward that goal was to develop an evaluation model for the project, drawing

EXHIBIT 13.1. PARTICIPATORY AND MULTICULTURAL EVALUATION APPROACHES.

Involvement of key stakeholders. The first opportunity in which learning group members could give input on the evaluation was when an evaluation workgroup of YLDI grantees reviewed and gave feedback on evaluation proposals and helped to select SPR as the initiative evaluator. The second wave of feedback occurred as site visitors worked with program directors to modify and add questions to the YLDI survey in order to capture information they needed for reporting to funders or for their own program improvement. Third, we worked with organizations in an ongoing way to improve their internal evaluation tools, methods, and procedures. Finally, we shared evaluation results in different formats with organizational leaders throughout the evaluation, soliciting feedback from them while also helping them to interpret the results for their own organizational improvement. For instance, we provided each organization with individualized survey results and guided them through a process of using the data to improve their program planning. We also presented cross-grantee results to grantees on several different occasions.

Involvement of youth in the evaluation. SPR also involved youth in different aspects of the evaluation. We hired a youth from one of the twelve organizations to help us with data collection and interpretation. A youth from one grantee organization worked at SPR as a youth evaluation intern for one year, and during that time she participated in site visits, reviewed and commented on our youth survey, and interviewed participants at the 2002 YLDI Youth Conference. Her perspective helped us assess the youth friendliness of our data collection tools and methods and provided a reality check for our early evaluation findings. In addition to hiring a youth intern, we involved youth from many of the sites as data collectors. We trained youth interviewers to videotape and conduct youth interviews at the YLDI youth conference. We also engaged young people at several sites as youth ethnographers, asking them to interview their peers.

Implementation of culturally appropriate evaluation strategies. We were intentional in using multicultural evaluation approaches to understanding diverse YLDI organizations' model of youth leadership. Internally, we involved eight highly diverse researchers in data collection and analysis, and to the extent possible we matched team members' expertise, background, and experience to the YLDI organizations, which worked with Asian, Native American, African American, Latino, and other youth. We also collaborated with a Blackfoot American Indian researcher to help us modify our evaluation design and to visit a Native American site. This researcher provided an external check on data collection and findings, as she reviewed and commented on our protocols, and reviewed and contributed to our site profile. Validity stemmed from the variety of cultural perspectives and interpretations that were solicited in project team meetings and review by YLDI organizational leaders.

on an established framework for evaluating youth development programs (Connell and others, 2000).

YLDI provided a unique opportunity to explore the relationship among identity, youth leadership, effective practices in civic activism and youth development, and positive youth outcomes. At the onset of the evaluation, a framework was developed for evaluating youth leadership development within civic activism (see Figure 13.1). This framework served as a starting place for understanding the relationships between core outcomes that cross-cut the various programs in the evaluation. The framework guided our evaluation by providing a conceptual lens through which to view program activities, strategies, and outcomes. As described later, we expanded this model considerably over time through the input of key initiative stakeholders as well as through the ongoing integration of evaluation findings.

The Initial Evaluation Framework

The evaluation framework reflected an understanding of the YLDI theory of change and articulated key organizational values, practices, and desired outcomes that would be tracked through the evaluation (Lewis-Charp, Yu, Soukamneuth, and Lacoe, 2003). This model identified high-level practices and outcomes that cut across the work of the twelve diverse grantee organizations, each of which had its own programming objectives and target population. At the beginning of the study, this framework was refined with input from the evaluation advisory board composed of prominent youth development researchers, evaluators, and YLDI leaders. Once it was finalized, the model guided the creation of quantitative and qualitative evaluation measures.

In this original framework, the core overarching principles of YLDI were represented as a continuum, moving from youth involvement to youth leadership to civic activism. The underlying assumption in this framework is that as an individual moves along the continuum, he or she moves from an inward focus on self-development to an outward focus on community change. Identity development, a core goal of YLDI groups, is presumed to occur as youth make connections between their own experience and social change issues.

This process can be visualized as an iterative cycle of reflection and action, occurring as youth move along the youth involvement-civic activism continuum. The cycle of reflection and action, what Paulo Freire (1992) calls

FIGURE 13.1. INITIAL FRAMEWORK FOR EVALUATING YOUTH LEADERSHIP DEVELOPMENT WITHIN CIVIC ACTIVISM.

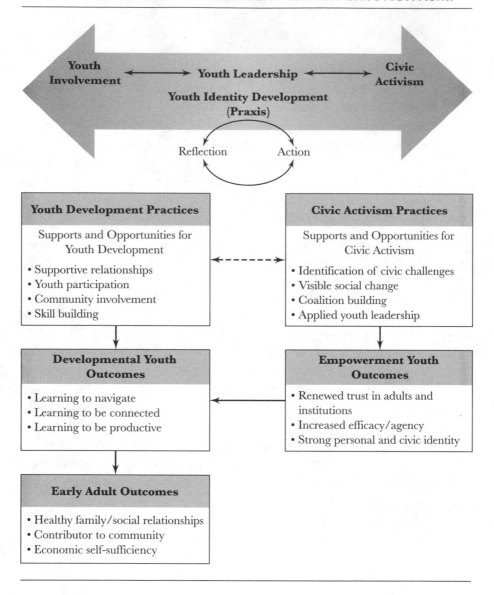

"praxis," is essential to the process of self-discovery. Freire contends that self-discovery "cannot be purely intellectual but must involve action; nor can it be limited to mere activism, but must also include serious reflection: only then will it be a praxis" (p. 52). The power of youth civic activism stems from a process of reflection and action that simultaneously engages the individual and the community.

Drawing on the change models of YLDI organizations, civic activist organizations seemed to actualize this ongoing cycle of reflection and action through their work with youth and communities, albeit using different starting points. For instance, some projects appeared to emphasize self-exploration as a precursor to leadership skill building, which they perceived as the basis for direct action. Conversely, other projects emphasized the need to first provide youth with an opportunity to take action, allowing them to channel their energy into social change efforts. Their change model suggested that skill building and work on self-improvement would naturally follow as youth learned to recognize gaps in their understanding that impeded their ability to be effective leaders and change agents.

In the original framework, some fundamental practices of youth development and civic activism that are instrumental to moving youth toward positive empowerment, developmental youth, and early adult outcomes were articulated. Following are definitions of core components of youth development and civic activism practices.

Youth Development Practices

The evaluation assessed YLDI grantees based on their ability to reach established benchmarks for each of the following core youth development practices, which remained consistent throughout the study.

- *Supportive relationships.* Youth need the opportunity to form caring, supportive, sustained, and equitable relationships with adults and youth across their multiple worlds (community, family, and peers).
- *Youth participation.* Youth need the opportunity to be in decision-making and/or leadership roles. They also need positive environments where they can experience a sense of belonging by joining others in developing and affirming shared goals and values.

- *Skill building.* Youth need increased opportunities to develop diverse academic, social, and creative skills. Such opportunities should provide a measurable sense of challenge, growth, and progress.
- *Community involvement.* Youth are integral to community health and benefit from the opportunity to engage actively and holistically in civic life.

Civic Activism Practices

The evaluation assessed the degree to which YLDI grantees implemented the following civic activism practices.

- *Identification of civic challenges.* Youth need the opportunity to engage in dialogue and action planning related to the critical issues facing the society they live in and their individual communities and neighborhoods and related to the unique contextual challenges they face as they grow and seek self-actualization.
- *Visible social change.* Youth need the opportunity to engage in work that will have lasting value in their communities. This work must be celebrated and acknowledged by adult and youth community members as a valuable contribution to community and institutional change.
- *Coalition building.* Youth need opportunities to build alliances with like-minded adults and youth. Through such activities, young people acquire the skills of teamwork, including accountability and negotiation. Furthermore, public relationships imbed youth in a broad network of services and institutional supports.
- *Applied youth leadership.* Youth need opportunities to apply their leadership skills in real-world settings around issues that they care about. Putting young people in positions of governance and decision making will contribute to the wellspring of ideas and creativity necessary to achieve social change.

Youth Outcomes

Factors outside of the organization (school, community, family, and peers) have such a profound influence on the development of these outcomes that it would be unfair to hold YLDI organizations accountable for their development. Instead, the evaluation sought to document developmental youth outcomes, linked to quality youth development supports and opportunities, as well as documenting empowerment youth outcomes arising directly from engagement in civic activism.

- *Developmental youth outcomes.* These outcomes include learning to navigate, learning to be connected, and learning to be productive.
- *Empowerment youth outcomes.* Empowerment youth outcomes include renewed trust in adults and institutions, increased efficacy and agency, and strong personal and civic identities.
- *Early adult outcomes.* The long-term goal of YLDI is to support the development of positive early adult outcomes and individual assets, such as healthy family and social relationships, contributor to community, and economic self-sufficiency.

Developing the Youth Leadership Measures

The process of developing the quantitative measures of youth leadership consisted of several steps and entailed replicating some standardized measures and creating new measures where none existed. This section of the chapter describes the process of administering, testing, validating, and refining these measures.

Quantitative Measures

Each of the components in the framework was operationalized according to the work and goals of the organizations in the YLDI project. The YLDI Youth Survey consisted of measures of youth development, civic activism, identity, and coping. The youth development measures were replicated from a standardized, national survey (Gambone, 2002). The survey was pilot-tested with one YLDI organization. The identity development and coping measures were adapted from the works of Phinney (1992) and Skinner (1996). The civic activism measures assessed the extent to which young people participate in identification of civic challenges, visible social change, coalition building, and applied youth leadership. They are of particular interest in this chapter because they underscore the types of leadership skills that youth learn within the course of performing civic acts. The civic activism measures and method of analysis paralleled the process of developing the youth development, youth participation/leadership measures developed by Youth Development Strategies. The indicators are based on extensive field testing with all of the YLDI organizations. The civic activism survey measures that we developed are identified in Exhibit 13.2.

Initially, two waves of the YLDI Survey were administered in 2001 and 2002 to all of the participating youth in nine of the YLDI organizations, including four identity-support and five youth-organizing groups. The original YLDI study was challenged by its lack of any comparison group against which youth developmental outcomes from YLDI organizations could be assessed. Additional funding was secured from the Center for Information and Research on Civic Learning and Engagement to conduct a follow-up study to administer a youth survey to a comparison group in 2003.

Eight predominantly urban organizations in five states for the traditional youth development programs were recruited and selected that met the fol-

EXHIBIT 13.2. QUANTITATIVE CIVIC ACTIVISM MEASURES.

(Answer scale: 4 = Strong Agree; 3 = Agree; 2 = Disagree; 1 = Strong Disagree)

Scales

Civic Action Measure

I have become an active participant in community events.
I have participated in a political event.
I have used the skills that I have learned at the organization.
I have expressed my opinions to people in positions of power.

Efficacy/Agency Measure

I am better prepared to take action against social injustice.
I am better equipped to make my community better.
I have figured out solutions to problems in my community.

Community Problem-Solving Measure

I have developed connections with people of different ethnic/racial groups.
I learn how to identify when something unfair is happening in my community.
I know more about problems that need to be fixed in my community.
I'm involved in activities that people in the community think are important.
I work on projects that make things better in my community.

lowing two criteria: (1) they targeted older, diverse youth; and (2) they had a programmatic focus that involved youth in their communities. The agencies included a boys-and-girls' club, conservation corps, a community garden project, arts organizations, and youth leadership organizations. These organizations were provided with a stipend for their participation in the study and given a thorough orientation to ensure their understanding and proper administration of the survey instrument.

We previously described our testing and analysis of the results of these survey measures relative to more traditional youth development organizations. For example, civic activism groups are significantly stronger than traditional youth development agencies at supporting youth leadership, decision making, and community involvement (Gambone, Yu, Lewis-Charp, Sipe, and Lacoe, 2006). Further, certain types of civic activism groups are significantly stronger than traditional youth development agencies at affirming youths' identities. This research underscores that civic activism organizations are similar to or more adept than traditional youth development agencies at providing developmental supports and opportunities to youth, such as quality relationships with adults, emotional safety, and skill building (Gambone and others, 2006).

Originally, each survey item (see Exhibit 13.2) was created with hypothesized outcome links back to the civic activism practices (for example, applied youth leadership, coalition building, identification of civic challenges, and visible social change). However, results of factorial analyses led to the development of three new scales of youth empowerment outcomes that result from youths' participation in civic activism: civic action, efficacy/agency, and community problem solving. Combined, these subscales are known as the *civic activism measures,* which measure the extent to which young people can participate in civic action with a sense of efficacy and the capacity for community problem solving.

Qualitative Measures

To augment and complement the quantitative measures, between 2001 and 2002 qualitative data was collected during two rounds of three-day site visits to the eleven identity support and youth organizing agencies. Each of these visits included observations and extensive individual and focus group interviews with program staff, youth participants, youth leaders, and community members. Youth participants were recruited for interviews based on their length of participation in the program and upon staff nomination.

The qualitative study had two primary goals: (1) to better understand each of the measures identified previously and how they played out within the YLDI organizations, and (2) to better understand how leaders and young people within the organization understood concepts such as youth leadership and civic activism. Our qualitative measures of youth leadership are mapped directly to the framework (Figure 13.1) and to the quantitative measures (Exhibit 13.2). Questions used to elicit how youth understood civic activism and their participatory and leadership roles are highlighted in Exhibit 13.3.

EXHIBIT 13.3. QUALITATIVE CIVIC ACTIVISM MEASURES.

Sample Interview Questions for Youth Participants

Youth Participation/Organizational Leadership

Describe what kinds of activities you've been involved in as part of this organization (for example, planning or organizing activities, participating in cultural events, discussing topics of interest).

How are decisions made in your organization? What role do you play in making decisions that affect you, the program, and/or your organization?

What additional roles or responsibilities would you like to have?

Identification of Civic Challenges

Do you talk about societal problems (for example, racism, class discrimination, homophobia) in your organization? Elaborate.

How do you talk about these issues? As a group? One on one?

Do you feel comfortable saying what you really think?

Do you get a chance to say how these problems affect you personally?

Do you talk about these issues outside of the context of this organization (for example, in your family, school, or among your peers)?

Do you think it is important to talk about societal issues and problems? Why or why not?

EXHIBIT 13.3. QUALITATIVE CIVIC ACTIVISM MEASURES, Cont'd.

Has your understanding of societal problems or challenges increased since becoming part of this organization? How?

How has this change affected you as a person?

Visible Social Change

Complete this sentence: The world would be a better place if . . .

Do you think you can make a difference (that is, make the world a better place)? Do you think your organization can make a difference? How?

Can you give an example of when you feel the work done by you has made a difference?

Can you give an example of when you feel the work done by your organization has made a difference in your school, neighborhood, or community?

Coalition Building/Sense of Connection to Community

Do others within your organization care about the same things that you care about? For instance?

Do you feel responsible to others within your organization (that is, do they rely on you to get things done)? How?

Do you know of other organizations that do similar work? Do you ever partner or share information with them?

Is the work that you do valued by your community? Is the work that your organization does valued by your community? By your family? By your neighbors? By your friends?

Applied Youth Leadership

What does it mean to be a leader?

Would you describe yourself as a leader? Why or why not?

Would you describe yourself as a leader in your family? In your friendship group? In your community? In this organization? Give examples.

Do you feel that people (in your community, school, organization) listen to what you have to say?

Moving Toward a Definition of Community-Based Youth Leadership

All YLDI organizations valued youth leadership, identifying themselves as youth leadership organizations, and yet they often promoted models of youth leadership that differed from popular or traditional notions of what youth leadership is (Lewis-Charp and others, 2003). The common thread among the civic activism groups in this study was that they did not exclusively promote leadership skills for individual advancement. Instead, they promoted community-based leadership for social change. Exhibit 13.4 summarizes some of the key distinctions that we will discuss in this section.

Looking across the sites, YLDI organizations often distinguished between being a leader and doing what it takes to be a leader. Van Linden and Fertman (1998) have described this distinction as the difference between transformational and transactional leadership. Transformational leadership focuses on

EXHIBIT 13.4. FROM TRADITIONAL/POPULAR CONCEPTION OF YOUTH LEADERSHIP TO COMMUNITY-BASED YOUTH LEADERSHIP.

Dimensions	Traditional/Popular Perspective	Expanded Perspective
Level	Individual level	Individual and collective levels
Type of Skills	• Decision making • Program design and implementation	• Problem identification • Coalition building • Working across difference • Problem solving in communities • Mobilization, advocacy
Context	Program and organizational context	Self, organizational, and community context
Purpose	Opportunity for individual development	Opportunity for social change
Timeline	Future leadership roles	Present and future leadership roles
Type of Leadership	Transactional forms of leadership	Transformational and transactional leadership

"the process of being a leader and how individuals use their abilities to influence people" (p. 9). Transactional leadership, on the other hand, focuses on doing tasks to achieve an end goal (for example, be in charge of meetings, make decisions, tell people what to do).

Rooted in a traditional youth development framework, the initial survey questions and interview protocols emphasized discrete transactional leadership tasks that provide evidence of individual growth and achievement. These modes of leadership were easier to observe and evaluate because they involved structural and organizational roles for young people. A qualitative typology of transactional decision-making models was developed based on the formal roles that existed for young people within YLDI organizations. This typology, highlighted in Exhibit 13.5, was useful for understanding various models of transactional youth leadership and differences between YLDI organizations.

Although many of the YLDI organizations—particularly those that were led by youth—were very effective at promoting transactional leadership, this was not their primary focus. The focus of YLDI groups remained squarely on transformational leadership, particularly on promoting the values and

EXHIBIT 13.5. TYPOLOGY: TRANSACTIONAL DECISION-MAKING MODELS.

	Youth-Led Organizations	Youth-Led Projects within Adult Organizations	Intergenerational Organizations	Adult-Led Organizations with Youth Input
Defining Feature	Youth make organizational and programming decisions. Adults advise, support, and guide.	Adults make organizational decisions. Youth provide input. Youth make designated programmatic decisions. Adults advise, support, and guide.	Youth and adults make organizational and programmatic decisions together. There is a goal of collaboration or consensus.	Adults make organizational and programming decisions. Youth provide input.

principles that characterize socially conscious leadership. YLDI organizations placed a high priority on the development of social justice values, universal human rights, critical thinking skills, and respect for and tolerance of diversity. They spent considerable time building political knowledge and skills, building a sense of group efficacy, and promoting personal and civic identity.

Finally, YLDI groups placed a high emphasis on group processes, consensus building, and collective action. In interviews, youth were reluctant to call themselves leaders and would repeatedly emphasize that leadership is a group rather than an individual construct. For instance, one young person said, "Activism is not about the individual. It's about the whole team. You can't make changes on your own; you need a group of people to work with you." A young person from another organization said, "A good leader is someone who speaks for the people and not just for themselves. For me that's what it means to be a good leader. You need to know that you are a part of something without taking it over." Similar quotes that echo this sentiment were gathered from all of the organizations. Youth and adult leaders emphasized leadership skills such as the ability to listen, empathize, cooperate, build consensus, and subsume personal interests and ideas to those of the collective.

This was a prominent finding emerging from the study in that civic activism puts emphasis on group leadership activities. YLDI sites that served Native American and African American youth were particularly focused on teaching young people that leadership is about being responsive to others, including looking to and relying on adults for guidance. Certainly, to the degree that almost all organizations stressed collective leadership and collective action, the data suggest that one of the defining features of civic activism may well be its focus on such group processes. This is not surprising, as community organizing and social change movements rely principally on critical mass and the power of groups to apply pressure on those in power.

Revisions to the Evaluation Framework

These findings, as well as engagement with key stakeholders, led to our substantially modifying the original evaluation framework. We have summarized our key changes below and highlighted changes in our understanding of civic activism practices, empowerment outcomes, and community outcomes.

Civic Activism Practices

Figure 13.2 summarizes how understandings of civic activism practices changed over the course of the study. Although identity was included as an area of interest in the original evaluation framework, it was not included as a civic activism practice. A hypothesis was made that positive identity development might occur organically as youth engaged in other civic activism practices, such as the identification of civic challenges. What emerged over the course of the study was that programs that were effective at supporting positive ethnic, racial, or gender-identity development used a very specific set of strategies. Thus, the final model included identity affirmation and exploration as a unique civic activism practice. As highlighted in Figure 13.2, evaluation findings were used to refine, narrow, or broaden concepts such as civic challenges, social change, and group processes.

Empowerment Youth Outcomes

As the evaluation unfolded, youth leaders articulated that youth empowerment is less about renewing trust in adults and institutions and more about building political knowledge and skills, personal and civic identity, democratic values, and sense of efficacy and agency. Figure 13.3 summarizes how understandings of empowerment youth outcomes evolved over the course of the study.

Community Outcomes

Originally, community outcomes were not included in the evaluation framework because it was not within the scope of the project to measure them systematically. Neither the resources nor the benchmarks to measure community impacts existed. The complexity of political and social factors that influence shifts in community attitudes or policy make it difficult to attribute community outcomes to any one factor or influence. For instance, community change, like that spurred by the Montgomery Bus Boycott, can be seemingly catalytic, arising from a single event. Yet in reality that single event was supported by years of ceaseless advocacy on the part of blacks and black churches throughout the South. Thus, community change is difficult to evaluate precisely because the effects of movement building are often invisible over a long period of time, with many battles seemingly lost before any are won. Despite the

FIGURE 13.2. REVISED CIVIC ACTIVISM PRACTICES TO PROMOTE YOUTH LEADERSHIP.

Original Concepts	Revised Concepts
None previously specified.	***Identity Affirmation and Exploration.*** Youth need to be affirmed in their identities so that they can develop a positive self-concept and positive relationships with peers who are both similar and different from themselves. They also need opportunities to explore different types and manifestations of identities so that they can develop a broad and integrated sense of self.
Identification of Civic Challenges. Youth need the opportunity to engage in dialogue and action planning around the critical issues facing us as a society, facing their individual communities and neighborhoods, as well as the unique contextual challenges they face as they grow and seek self-actualization.	***Identification of Community and Civic Challenges.*** Youth need the opportunity to engage in dialogue and action planning around the critical issues facing us as a society, facing their individual communities and neighborhoods, as well as the unique contextual challenges they face as they grow and seek self-actualization. This includes activities such as political education, popular education, historical analysis, community mapping, and power mapping.
Visible Social Change. Youth need the opportunity to engage in work that will have lasting value in their communities. This work must be celebrated and acknowledged by adult and youth community members as a valuable contribution to community and institutional change.	***Celebrating Incremental Social Change.*** Youth need ongoing opportunities to identify and celebrate incremental social change, so that they know that their work is making a difference. Indicators of incremental community change include press coverage of key issues, increased community participation in rallies or events, and the number of meetings they held with people in power.
Coalition Building. Youth need opportunities to build alliances with like-minded adults and youth. Through such partnership building young people acquire the skills of teamwork, including accountability and negotiation. Furthermore, public relationships imbed youth in a broad network of services and institutional supports.	***Engagement in Group Processes, Consensus Building, and Collective Action.*** Youth need opportunities to engage in group-level processes— including inclusion in consensus building (democratic group decision-making processes), identification with group norms of values, learning to sacrifice self-interest to the interest of the group, engagement in active listening and conflict mediation, and collaborative and collective action.
Applied Youth Leadership. Youth need opportunities to apply their leadership skills in real-world settings around issues that they care about. Putting young people in positions of governance and decision making will contribute to the wellspring of ideas and creativity necessary to achieve social change.	***Applied Youth Leadership.*** Youth need opportunities to apply their leadership skills in real-world settings around issues that they care about. This includes youth involvement in organizational decision making, outreach and education to community members, direct engagement with power brokers in the community, advocacy, and so on.

FIGURE 13.3. REVISED
YOUTH EMPOWERMENT OUTCOMES.

Original Concepts	Revised Concepts
Renewed trust in adults and institutions. We theorized that this would arise from youth-adult partnerships and the responsiveness of institutions to pressure for change.	Evaluation findings indicate that this was not a core outcome of YLDI civic activism groups.
None previouly specified.	***Political knowledge and skills.*** This included knowledge of democratic processes, including how institutions, systems, and ideology shape lives, as well as mechanisms for how citizens can transform social structures. Political skills include critical thinking skills and the ability to persuade others.
Strong sense of personal and civic identity. This included an understanding of how one's experience intersects with others, a sense of personal transformation and change, and a sense of membership in community, including connection and commitment to others.	***Stronger sense of personal and civic identity.*** This included an understanding of how one's experience intersects with others, a sense of personal transformation and change, and a sense of membership in community, including connection and commitment to others.
None previouly specified.	***Increased democratic values.*** This included empathy for others, appreciation for diversity, belief in universal human rights, and a sense of social responsibility to work toward improved social conditions.
Increased sense of efficacy and agency. We anticipated increases in young people's sense that they can make a difference.	***Increased sense of efficacy and agency.*** This included increased confidence and "voice," as well as a generalized belief that when people work together they can effect social change.

difficulty of measuring change within the hearts and minds of community members, awareness grew through interacting with the YLDI organizations throughout this evaluation that the impacts of civic activism and community-based youth leadership could not be fully assessed without proper attention to community change.

The evaluation field needs to develop indicators for measuring the types of incremental community change these groups worked toward on a day-to-day basis. Toward this end, we integrated into our evaluation model intermediate and long-term outcomes articulated by program leaders and youth during this evaluation (see Figure 13.4).

Intermediate Community Outcomes. The following are key intermediate community outcomes that were documented over the course of the YLDI evaluation.

- *Youth involvement in community decision making.* One of the primary goals of civic activism is to support grassroots involvement in decision making. Changed attitudes among adults in positions of authority about youth and their abilities is an important goal of civic activism work.
- *Youth issues on community agenda.* Community agenda is defined quite broadly and includes recognition by community representatives of the organization's work or issues, such as a place for youth to speak on the city council meeting agenda, coverage of a youth issue by a local TV station or newspaper, and meetings between youth and local businesses or school representatives.
- *Changes in policy, rules, and regulations.* During the course of the evaluation, YLDI groups achieved some relatively large-scale community wins involving the official reallocation of public resources and the changing of policy. Even such wins, however, are intermediate, since it takes ongoing pressure and oversight to ensure that institutions implement policies or allocate funds that improve youth outcomes.

Long-Term Community Outcomes. The desired long-term community outcomes of civic activism organizations include (1) reallocation of power and resources from those with the most to those with the least; (2) improved and more embracing attitudes of youth, marginalized social groups, and issues such as environmental preservation; (3) more widely practiced views of peace and social justice; and (4) healthier families and communities.

As a result of creating and refining the evaluation framework, developing the civic activism survey measures, and conducting the YLDI evaluation, we

FIGURE 13.4. REVISED EVALUATION FRAMEWORK LINKING YOUTH DEVELOPMENT TO CIVIC ACTIVISM.

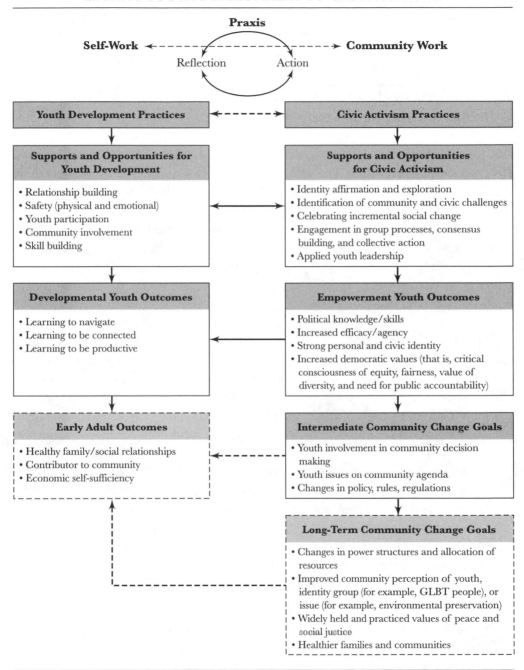

discovered a tremendous need for practical resources to help community-based organizations to evaluate youth leadership. Therefore, SPR, in partnership with the Innovation Center, developed a four-part train-the-trainer curriculum on evaluation for community-based youth development organizations (Soukamneuth, Lewis-Charp, Lacoe, Heiman, and Kebede, 2004).

Implications and Lessons Learned for Other Evaluations of Youth Leadership

In this chapter, we describe our experience evaluating YLDI. We discuss ways in which evaluators can expand the conceptualization and measurement of youth leadership to include youth leadership development within a community and civic activism context. While there are a few evaluations that have tried to capture similar measures of youth leadership, most current evaluations of youth leadership reflect practitioners' more narrow understanding of youth leadership (see, for example, Jakes and Shannon, 2002).

While current evaluations focus on individual outcomes such as mastering decision making and leading others within a program or organizational context, evaluations of youth leadership within civic activism aim to capture both the individual and collective changes around problem identification, coalition building, working across differences, mobilization, advocacy, and other key leadership aspects. Further, the context for change of youth civic activist leaders spans the domains of the individual, organization, and community. Interestingly, as discussed earlier, although the leader development activities of the majority of youth leadership programs are more observable and can be more readily captured (transactional forms of leadership, for example), youth are practicing for future leadership roles in adulthood. On the other hand, while civic activism forms of leadership have some easily measurable elements, the impact of transformational forms of leadership promoted by civic activism is more difficult to measure in the long run.

This study has provided lessons in two areas about how to study youth leadership: the research process and the measures.

The Research Process

As an emerging area in which the theory and research is still developing, there is much to be learned by departing from the traditional modes of study. For example, research methods need to include youth, organizational leaders, and researchers with expertise in particular communities to inform both the content and the process of the work. As described throughout this chapter, this clearly has significant benefits. Likewise, while it is necessary to start research with a theory, in this field it is also beneficial to maintain somewhat of an inductive approach to the work that allows for modifications to the theory based on emerging themes and lessons.

Traditional approaches to developing research methods and sharing data with stakeholders need to be expanded. There is great value to including stakeholders in the development of measures, engaging stakeholders in helping to interpret preliminary findings, and developing new strategies for sharing data with stakeholders. In traditional research, the research subjects are informed of the study process and methods but are kept separate from their development and implementation as a way of preserving objectivity. As research moves further into community settings and deeper into understanding the interaction between individual development and contextual influences, new approaches are called for. While objectivity must be preserved, the only way to ensure the validity or accuracy of the results is by shifting the role of the stakeholders. In this project the research process was made transparent to study participants through meetings before the onset of the study, by sharing data with groups of study participants through learning group meetings and a conference presentation during the course of the study, and by sharing information with individual sites, especially survey results and suggestions on how to use data to strengthen program activities.

The added benefit of this type of approach is that it creates a sense of participation and ownership of the information on the part of the study participants that creates the conditions for the use of the data as timely feedback on their work, thus allowing research results to serve both the purpose of understanding programs and interventions and the purpose of contributing to their improvement.

The Measures

Despite the promise and demonstrated effectiveness of the measures of youth leadership that were developed and presented here, there is clearly more work that needs to be done on measurement. More focus is needed to develop evaluation measures that extend youth leadership beyond a program or organizational context into the community context. In a pilot study that SPR co-conducted with the Funder Collaborative on Youth Organizing (FCYO) and Youth in Focus, we interviewed leaders of twelve youth organizing groups throughout the United States. Findings from this study suggest the importance of youth's leadership role in building solidarity with external allies. As part of a leadership group, youth learn to recognize the importance of alliance building and reciprocal support; in other words, they recognize that there is more power in numbers. Youth also learn the importance of developing ongoing relationships with other organizations. Further, youth learn to facilitate group consensus and decision making and to lend support to and participate in direct actions with other groups. While the process of providing leadership begins within their own organizations, the impact of their actions reaches well beyond their programs or organizations to create group solidarity with outside partner organizations. Better measures are needed to capture these kinds of transorganizational leadership outcomes.

There is also a need to reframe youth leadership outcomes as a collective or collaborative endeavor. SPR's findings and analysis from the FCYO study suggest that beyond impacting individuals, participation in youth organizing or civic activism impacts group-level dynamics. Group outcomes—such as increased power sharing between youth and adults, democratic group decision-making processes, group cohesion, group identification, and association with a larger social movement—are intentional goals of youth activism that are not typically emphasized by more traditional youth leadership programs. An important future direction for evaluation of youth leadership in civic activism is to invest in the development of collective youth leadership outcomes to accurately measure the multilevel impact of civic activism.

In conclusion, the YLDI evaluation represents lessons about evaluating youth leadership development and is among the first study of its kind. As more evaluations are conducted on youth organizing and other civic activism efforts, the ability to measure collective leadership and decision making, group synergy, group identity, and other leadership outcomes that extend beyond the normal purview of traditional youth leadership programs will undoubtedly increase.

Resources

Inouye, T. E., Yu, H., and Adefuin, J. *Commissioning Multicultural Evaluation: A Foundation Resource Guide,* 2005 [http://calendow.org/evaluation/reports.stm].

This guide was created for the California Endowment and provides guidelines for foundations and other organizations to effectively conduct a multicultural health evaluation. The publication also addresses the issues of monitoring and assessing the evaluation.

Soukamneuth, S., Lewis-Charp, H., Lacoe, J., Heiman, L., and Kebede, R. *Evaluating Civic Activism: A Curriculum for Community and Youth-Serving Organizations,* 2004 [www.evaluationtools.org/tools_main.asp]. This curriculum was created for the Innovation Center for Youth Development and is a comprehensive self-evaluation curriculum for youth and community serving agencies. The curriculum guides users through all the steps of self-evaluation, including building consensus for evaluation within the organization, creating a logic model, identifying evaluation questions, developing evaluation tools and measures, collecting data, as well as data analysis. Organizational and stakeholder empowerment through evaluation is emphasized.

References

Cahill, M. *Youth Development and Community Development: Promises and Challenges of Convergence.* Takoma Park, Md.: Forum for Youth Investment, 1997.

Connell, J. P., Gambone, M. A., and Smith, T. J. "Youth Development in Community Settings: Challenges to Our Field and Our Approach." In *Youth Development: Issues, Challenges and Directions* (pp. 281–300). Philadelphia: Public/Private Ventures, 2000. [www.ppv.org/content/youthdev.html].

Dormody, T., Seevers, B., and Clason, D. *The Youth Leadership Life Skills Development Scales: An Evaluation and Research Tool for Youth Organizations.* Research Report 672. Las Cruces: New Mexico State University, 1993.

Eccles, J., and Gootman, J. A. *Community Programs to Promote Youth Development.* Washington, D.C.: National Academy Press, 2002.

Freire, P. *Pedagogy of the Oppressed* (Myra Bergman Ramos, trans). New York: Continuum, 1992.

Gambone, M. A. *The YSDI Youth Survey.* Youth Development Strategies, 2002. [http://ydsi.com/ydsi/measuring/index.html]. Accessed March 2006.

Gambone, M., Yu, H., Lewis-Charp, H., Sipe, C., and Lacoe, J. "A Comparative Analysis of Community Youth Development Strategies." *Journal of Community Practice* Special Issue, 2006, *14*, 1–2.

Ginwright, S., and James, T. "From Assets to Agents of Change: Social Justice, Organizing, and Youth Development." In B. Kirshner, J. O'Donoghue, and M. McLaughlin (eds.), *Youth Participation: Improving Institutions and Communities.* New Directions for Youth Development Special Issue, no. 96. San Francisco: Jossey-Bass, 2002.

Hughes, D., and Curnan, S. "Towards Shared Prosperity: Change-making in the CYD Movement." *Community Youth Development Journal,* 2002, *3*(1), 2–8.

Irby, M., Ferber, T., and Pittman, K., with J. Tolman and N. Yohalem. *Youth Action: Youth Contributing to Communities, Communities Supporting Youth.* Community and Youth Development Series, vol. 6. Takoma Park, Md.: Forum for Youth Investment, International Youth Foundation, 2001.

Jakes, S., and Shannon, L. *Individual and Community Mobilization Survey,* 2002. [http://ag.arizona.edu/fcs/cyfernet/nowg/IndividualCommunityMobilizationSurvey-Packet].

Kahne, J., Honig, M. I., and McLaughlin, M. W. "The Civic Components of Community Youth Development." *CYD Journal,* Special Anthology Edition, Spring–Summer 2002, 85–88.

Kirshner, B., O'Donoghue, J., and McLaughlin, M. *Youth Participation: Improving Institutions and Communities.* New Directions for Youth Development Special Issue, no. 96. San Francisco: Jossey-Bass, 2002.

Lewis-Charp, H., Yu, H. C., Soukamneuth, S., and Lacoe, J. *Extending the Reach of Youth Development through Civic Activism: Outcomes of the Youth Leadership Development Initiative.* Oakland, Calif.: Social Policy Research Associates, 2003.

Phinney, J. "The Multigroup Ethnic Identity Measure: A New Scale for Use with Adolescents and Young Adults from Diverse Groups." *Journal of Adolescent Research,* 1992, *7,* 156–176.

Skinner, E. "A Guide to Constructs of Control." *Journal of Personality and Social Psychology,* 1996, *71,* 549–570.

Soukamneuth, S., Lewis-Charp, H., Lacoe, J., Heiman, L., and Kebede, R. *Evaluating Civic Activism: A Curriculum for Community and Youth-Serving Organizations.* Created for the Innovation Center for Youth Development, 2004. [www.evaluationtools.org/tools_main.asp].

Van Linden, J., and Fertman, C. *Youth Leadership: A Guide to Understanding Leadership Development in Adolescents.* San Francisco: Jossey-Bass, 1998.

Zeldin, S., and Camino, L. "Youth Leadership: Linking Research and Program Theory to Exemplary Practice." *New Designs for Youth Development,* Spring 1999, *15*(2). Accessed June 2006.

CHAPTER FOURTEEN

EVALUATING LEADERSHIP EFFORTS FOR NEIGHBORHOOD TRANSFORMATION

Nilofer Ahsan

Neighborhood transformation or comprehensive community change initiatives evolved in the 1980s to address the multiple challenges faced by children and families in tough neighborhoods: for example, high rates of school failure, abuse and neglect, poverty and financial instability, and poor health outcomes. These initiatives are based on the belief that many of these outcomes are linked and that it is impossible to address any one of them without addressing the entire constellation.

"Comprehensive community change initiatives aim to do more than remediate problems, such as teen pregnancy or insufficient income, or to develop assets, such as housing stock or social services. They aspire to foster a fundamental transformation of poor neighborhoods and the circumstances of individuals who live there. The change they seek is comprehensive, that is, inclusive of all sectors of the neighborhood—social, educational, economic, physical, and cultural—and focused on community building, that is, strengthening the capacity of neighborhood residents, associations, and institutions" (Kubisch, 1996).

In general, neighborhood transformation efforts share some key defining elements.

- They seek to address multiple issues and to recognize the interconnection between social issues.
- They involve multiple stakeholders. Thus, in contrast to community organizing initiatives that view residents of the community as their primary partners, comprehensive community change initiatives bring together residents, social service providers, political figures, community organizations, and others to solve problems.

Most comprehensive community change initiatives have a strong local planning component. This provides the infrastructure to develop a change model that is truly adaptive and responsive to community needs.

Background

Two pieces of work inform this chapter. The first is a multiyear documentation process of resident leadership development in one particular neighborhood transformation effort that is part of the Annie E. Casey Foundation's Making Connections initiative. The Making Connections initiative is a long-term effort to improve the lives of children and families in ten distressed neighborhoods across the country. The foundation is committed to the idea that change must be structured to meet local needs and build off local assets. Thus, there is not a single unified model within the initiative. Instead each site develops its own strategy guided by a set of common outcomes.

- Families have increased earnings and income.
- Families have increased levels of assets.
- Children are healthy and ready to succeed in school.
- Families, youth, and neighborhoods increase their civic participation.
- Families and neighborhoods have strong informal supports and networks.
- Families have access to quality services and supports that work for them.

Because of the complexity of the initiative, the foundation uses documentation as a key strategy in the learning process. Each site employs a diarist who is responsible for broader documentation of the work going on, and a variety of individuals help to document other aspects of the work from lessons learned within meetings to long-term documentation of particular areas of work. Resident leadership is one area where documentation work has been underway for the last four years. This work includes the following components:

- Interviews with resident leaders, Making Connections staff, and community partners working on resident leadership issues to identify and learn about the resident leadership strategies being used in sites (overall, nearly sixty individuals were interviewed)
- The review of materials and tools from the participating sites to enrich the understanding that was developed through interviews
- The development of a conceptual model that organizes strategies being used at the local level within sites into a logic model for framing and understanding the work
- Organization of material gathered from site interviews into written reports (site summaries) that are structured around the conceptual model described earlier
- Use of feedback and review by the original key informants to fine-tune and strengthen both the conceptual model and the site summaries

In addition to this documentation work, the other project that informs this chapter is a set of one-on-one interviews, also funded by the Annie E. Casey Foundation, with sixty resident leaders from around the country. This project, entitled "Leadership Journeys," seeks to learn more about how resident leaders become engaged in community change work, what keeps them involved, what discourages them, and how they want to grow and develop as leaders. The lessons learned from this project shed light on the role leadership plays in neighborhood transformation efforts.

Throughout the chapter, both pieces of work are used to

- Describe the documentation process and the ways it is both distinct from and contributes to the evaluation process
- Illustrate the complexities of evaluating resident leadership development within the context of a neighborhood transformation effort
- Delineate three separate levels of evaluation and specific focuses of evaluation and strategies for evaluation within each of these levels
- Describe how residents' own perceptions and experiences shape the evaluation process

- Provide practical guidance and thoughts on developing efforts to evaluate resident leadership development within neighborhood transformation efforts

The information in this chapter will be most helpful for those who are looking to evaluate resident leadership within the context of community change initiatives, especially those initiatives that seek to engage leaders who are directly impacted by the issues being addressed.

Understanding the Differences Between Documentation and Evaluation

Documentation is a different paradigm and framework for learning than is evaluation. The key difference between documentation and evaluation is how documentation is framed and understood by both the participants whose work is being documented and the researcher who is leading the documentation effort. Documentation is framed as a descriptive rather than an evaluative process, encouraging a rich dialogue between researcher and participant without fear that information will be used to make high-stakes decisions about funding or program structure. A documentation research design does not seek to prove or disprove hypotheses; rather, it seeks to learn what is available to be learned, to identify patterns, and to use these patterns to create broader conceptual frameworks for understanding the impact of what is occurring through the initiative.

Documentation avoids what is central to many, though not all, evaluation processes: the struggle to control interventions and variables in order to more rigorously understand causalities and impacts. Documentation sacrifices scientific rigor in favor of a commitment to learn by organically following the flow of events. Rigor is instead derived from looking across cases and seeing patterns and commonalities that make sense of an individual's or a single site's experience.

The narrative structure of the documentation process mirrors, in many ways, the process and structure for constructing case studies; however, the two processes are distinct. Case studies are generally illustrative examples that describe in detail a single case or experience in order to illuminate a broader phenomenon. While documentation may utilize case studies to illustrate points, it generally seeks to paint a more comprehensive picture of the activities and experiences that are taking place. Case studies use descriptive tools in an attempt to "go deep" to illustrate a phenomenon; documentation uses descriptive tools to "go wide" showing the full variety of experience and picking out themes and commonalities across this broad landscape. (For more information on case study and documentation methods, see the Resources section at the end of this chapter.)

Some key aspects of the documentation process include

- Being clear that the nature of the work is nonevaluative
- Beginning with no preconceptions about the activities or strategies one is looking for
- Interviewing multiple stakeholders and using other methods of data collection, such as observation and review of materials, to gain a rich understanding of the activities and strategies that one is noticing

Leadership Development Strategies in the Making Connections Initiative

Figure 14.1 shows the model for leadership development being used within the Making Connections initiative based on documentation of the strategies that sites are using. The figure reflects the complexity with which sites approach their leadership development work. Each of the communities involved in the Making Connections initiative is taking a unique approach to resident leadership development. Communities are also learning from each other and sharing the strategies they have found successful. The strategies represented in the figure are those that are being used by more than one site. If a strategy is being used by only one site, it does not appear in Figure 14.1.

These strategies group into five major categories:

1. *Opportunities for impact:* Helping resident leaders learn by doing in a supportive environment
2. *Owning information:* Equipping residents to be the experts on their own neighborhoods
3. *Network building:* Connecting resident leaders to each other and to other key decision makers

FIGURE 14.1. LEADERSHIP-BUILDING STRATEGIES IN MAKING CONNECTIONS SITES.

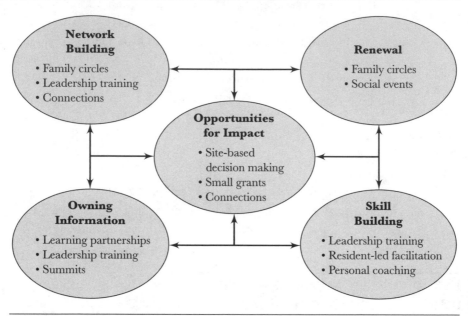

Source: Documentation of the Annie E. Casey Foundation's Making Connections initiative.

4. *Skill building:* Developing residents' leadership skills and capacity
5. *Renewal:* Preventing burnout and reenergizing resident leaders

No site uses the same combination of leadership development strategies as another site. Even within strategies there is broad variation. For example, nearly every site offers a leadership training program; however, each of these programs uses a different curriculum and has a slightly different structure.

Documenting Impacts of Resident Leadership

Impact of resident leadership development is documented at three separate levels: individual, initiative, and community. The evaluation strategies for each level are described next and suggested recommendations for how to conduct the evaluation at each level are provided.

Documenting Impacts at the Individual Level

Perhaps the easiest level of change to look at within the context of a neighborhood transformation effort such as Making Connections is what impact occurs for individuals who participate in leadership development activities. We pose several questions to help us better understand individual-level impacts.

- Have new skills and knowledge been developed?
- How are these skills and knowledge being used?
- Has the number of individuals that resident leaders can reach through their leadership been expanded or enhanced? Measures include how many individuals are in their networks, how many people they can get out to community change activities, and so on.
- Has the leader's ability to engage with those who have access to power and influence within the community been enhanced? This question looks at the extent to which a resident leader's network intersects with other types of leaders in the community.
- Has the resident leader's investment in the community change process been deepened? Measures include how energized or burned out they feel, how much time they are spending on community change activities, and so on.

Within a neighborhood transformation model, resident leadership development is a complex set of pathways that includes opportunities for resident leaders to develop skills, expand their networks, develop comfort with data and their own sense of expertise in their knowledge of the neighborhood, renew their energy, and most important, develop their sense of efficacy by engaging in concrete change activities.

The pathways of change are often not the focus of site-level evaluations. Often when sites are engaged in evaluation activities, they evaluate the impact of individual leadership development activities, such as a training program, but they do not examine how the combination of leadership development activities creates a leadership development pathway. For example, sites that have leadership training programs often use an evaluation tool to assess the skills and knowledge gained through participation in the program. Depending on the site, this could be an evaluation form filled out at the end of the training course, a pre- and posttest form, or some sort of postparticipation follow up. Sites tend to evaluate the structured parts of their leadership development activities, such as family circles or small grants programs, rather than informal activities such as network-building efforts, celebrations, and other efforts that renew energy. Our interviews suggest that these evaluations of resident leadership overlook the importance of informal activities for creating and maintaining active engagement in community change efforts.

Since we know that individual resident leaders participate in a unique basket of leadership development activities, or at the very least participate in leadership development activities within a unique ordering, it is important for us to understand how their leadership development was affected by the way they entered, the order in which they participated in leadership development activities, and the particular combinations of these activities. To fully understand this impact involves complex, sophisticated, flexible evaluation strategies.

Most resident leaders get connected with an initiative such as Making Connections because they have already been engaged with community change work before the initiative began, many for years if not decades. Parsing out the impact of the initiative-sponsored efforts to further develop their leadership versus the impact of their natural growth path is difficult, if not impossible, to determine.

Often resident leaders do not follow a linear progression in their leadership journeys. Because most neighborhood transformation efforts are focused on tough neighborhoods, the individuals they engage as resident leaders often face tough circumstances in their own lives. Many are motivated to engage with community change efforts because they themselves have gone through difficult circumstances in their lives. In the sample of sixty people we interviewed through Leadership Journeys, close to half (twenty-seven, or 48 percent) had some hardship or traumatic event that guided or motivated them to get engaged with community change efforts. We know from our interviews that those leaders who had experienced hardship did not have leadership pathways that were straight lines, but instead included dips, bumps, and breaks (see, for example, Exhibit 14.1). Sometimes this happens because some particular experience resurrects issues from the past, sometimes it is because someone in their extended network needed help or was in crisis.

Evaluating the Impact of Resident Leadership Development Efforts on Individuals

In order to more fully document the leadership experience, methods are needed that look at the ways in which multiple leadership development activities intersect to build a resident leader's skills, effectiveness, and commitment

EXHIBIT 14.1. THE COMPLEX PATHWAYS OF RESIDENT LEADERSHIP DEVELOPMENT.

T. has dealt with a lot of hardship in her life. Her father died when she was ten, leaving her mother with eight children. She and her siblings became the caretakers, paying the bills, taking care of the house, and generally keeping things going. Her childhood includes a history of sexual abuse. As a teenager she fell in love with one of her high school teachers and dropped out of school when she became pregnant. Her leadership pathway began more than nine years ago when she was approached to attend a leadership program by an organization that worked with women who had been on welfare. This organization has stood by her and kept her engaged despite the fact that at a number of points in her life depression, past trauma, involvement in an abusive relationship, or coping with problems with her children meant that she had to step away from her community change work.

"I lost three good jobs because I just couldn't keep it together. I'd end up being an emotional mess. There were some foundational issues from the abuse that I needed to deal with. Eventually I realized I needed to stop and work on me for a while, before I could move on and do other things. I decided to get back on the system (welfare). The folks from the leadership program kept on calling me to come and be part of things. After I lost the second job I remember they called me and I thought, 'Why do you want me? Can't you see that I'm just a mess—that I'm not worth it.' They kept on calling me, wanting me to come to things. Finally I agreed to go to a three-day leadership retreat. That was literally a turning point in my life. I was able to connect with other women and build supportive relationships. They helped connect me to what I needed."

T. now sits on the advisory board for the housing authority and is an active and effective advocate for community change. She couldn't have gotten to where she is today without an organization that believed in her—especially during the times that she didn't believe in herself.

---

to the work. Suggestions for documenting those experiences and activities include the following tactics:

- *Embed evaluation tools that look at the impact of a single strategy.* For example, build a posttest that looks at the knowledge and skills developed by a six-week leadership training course into a more comprehensive look at an individual's leadership pathway. This approach would look at the interplay between prior life experiences of resident leaders and the entire basket of leadership opportunities that are facilitated by the initiative. The Leadership Pathway

Case Study later in the chapter illustrates an example of this type of pathway analysis for a fictitious resident leader.

- *Use pathway mapping for both evaluative and leadership development purposes.* In interviews, most resident leaders had difficulty articulating how they wanted to grow and develop in their role as community leaders. Using an interview process to identify the different experiences that led them to their leadership role and how each one has contributed to their growth as a leader can help not only to identify critical aspects of a leadership pathway, but also help leaders to think strategically about future directions. For Leadership Journeys, we asked a series of simple questions.

  - How would you describe the community change work that you are involved in?
  - How did you get involved with community change work?
  - What keeps you motivated? What sometimes discourages you?
  - How would you get others involved?
  - How do you want to grow and develop as a leader?

- *Use social network mapping tools to help track changes in resident leaders' networks.* Leadership is in the end about interaction and the ability to leverage relationships. We need a better understanding of the relationships that resident leaders come in with and how interactions with leadership development opportunities impact those relationships. There are a number of software tools being developed to track network development in business and other sectors that could be used to aid evaluation efforts in this area. The Resources section of this chapter lists a few of these software models and provides a link where you can connect to social network mapping information.

- *Develop evaluation tools and strategies that have a long time horizon and take into account external factors.* For example, change or loss of a job, family illness, struggles with depression or other illness, and so on can affect a resident leader's ability to engage with community change work. Appropriate tools can allow the evaluator to factor in the impact of individual crisis and life circumstances that may affect a resident leader's growth in the short term. It also provides a better way to see how a given set of skills can impact later work. For example, a leadership training class may give someone a set of skills and tools that she will be able to fully utilize only after her network has expanded to give her more leadership opportunities. Following individual resident leaders over time gives us a better opportunity to understand how different leadership opportunities reinforce each other and how skills and commitment can be developed over time. An exploration of how different experiences allow individuals to develop their leadership skills over time can best be captured by using a pathways framework.

When reviewing the following case study, it is important to note that a number of activities or connections that might have appeared ineffective when doing a short-term evaluation contributed greatly to Lena's long-term impact. Figures 14.2 and 14.3 illustrate Lena's pathway.

Leadership Pathway Case Study

My name is Lena Perez. I grew up in East Rogers Park, Chicago. My mother was an activist and used to take me to community meetings in our Chicago neighborhood. At sixteen, I was selected to be a youth ambassador for human rights and civil liberties. The work involved traveling to other school districts to meet young people interested in social justice issues. This planted the seed for my present community work.

It wasn't until I was thirty-five that I started thinking about social justice issues again. By this time, I had a family of four and was working two jobs. I moved to the Pilsen neighborhood to be closer to my husband's family. In Pilsen, I had lots of family and friends to support me and my family when times got rough. It was also close to the church I attended regularly.

I had been living in Pilsen only three years when I noticed my third child, Olivia, began having major breathing troubles. Olivia at the time was a straight A student and a really good kid. More and more she was getting sick at school and falling behind. Doctor visits proved she had a rare form of bronchitis due to pollutants in the air. Our medical bills began to mount as her condition worsened.

By myself I didn't know quite what to do. I was frustrated and scared and felt powerless. One day I went and talked with my pastor about Olivia and what was going on. He was really sympathetic and listened to me and suggested I get in touch with a young woman who worked with a local organizing group that had been doing some work in the neighborhood. I called Rosa right away and she came to my house to meet with me and my family that week. She told us that Olivia wasn't the only one having this problem, but that many of the children in the neighborhood were getting sick from pollutants that were being dumped from one of the local factories. Talking with Rosa made me realize that I really needed to do something about this.

The next Sunday I talked with the pastor again and told him about what I had learned. I asked him if next week at the end of service I could have a little time to talk to the congregation about these issues. That week I worked with Rosa to put together my speech for the congregation. I had about fifteen minutes to speak and at the end of it I passed around a sheet of paper to see who would be interested and willing to come to a meeting to explore the issue more—I was thrilled when seventeen people signed up.

It took us awhile to get started and first I felt that we really weren't getting a lot done other than meeting and complaining. We came up with a strategy of trying to meet with our alderman to see if we could get him to take action against the companies that were the biggest polluters. I and a man from the group were picked to be the spokespeople. I was really nervous going into the meeting—but at first it seemed like it was going very well. The alderman was very courteous and polite toward us, but every time we asked him to take action he seemed to have some reason why it couldn't happen. We left the office with nothing more than an assurance that he'd "look into the issue."

I think we were all pretty frustrated around then; our meetings started becoming less regular. I was busy trying to support Olivia and working more hours to try to meet our medical bills. I frankly had pretty much given up. After about six months we basically stopped meeting. About that time Rosa called up to see if I was interested in being part of a leadership program that her community organizing group was putting on. I was flattered that she had asked but said No. Frankly I didn't feel like much of a leader at the time and making time with everything else going on. Rosa called back a couple of days later to follow up and try to convince me to participate. She told me that they could provide child care for my youngest and that another one of the participants lived down the street and could drive me. Eventually I told her that I would try to make it, but might have to drop out if things got too difficult.

I'm so glad I made the decision to join. Another woman in the program, Maria, also had a child suffering from asthma. We bonded immediately and it was great to have her to talk to. The program included both a research portion where they helped us to research an issue that we cared about and a small grants program to do a small project at the end. Well, of course, Maria and I decided to do our work on the pollution issue. With the information from the research portion we created these very powerful flyers on the impact of pollution on the kids in our community. I also contacted an old friend who had been a youth ambassador with me. Clive Johnson had gone on to become an environmental lobbyist in D.C. I felt awkward calling him after all these years, but I'm really glad that I did. He had a lot of ideas about next steps and agreed to come to Pilsen to meet with Maria and me when he was coming to Chicago three weeks later.

We decided that we wanted to use our time with Clive wisely—and maximize the impact of having a big D.C. lobbyist who worked on these issues. I went back to my

FIGURE 14.2. LEADERSHIP PATHWAY LEGEND.

	**Getting the Ball Rolling**
	**Family History**
	**Key Connections**
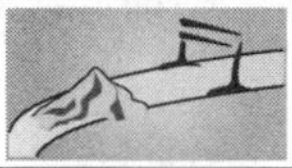	**Roadblocks and Barriers**
	**Crisis** Can serve as a lever for action
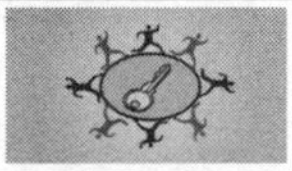	**Building Relationships**
	**Overcoming Obstacles**
	**Balancing Acts** Situation where the individual was forced to make difficult choices along the way due to many competing responsibilities
	**Skills Builder**
	**Breakthroughs**
	**Spiritual Insight**
	**Future Outlook**
	**Hitting the Wall**
	**Financial Concerns**

FIGURE 14.3. LENA'S LEADERSHIP PATHWAY.

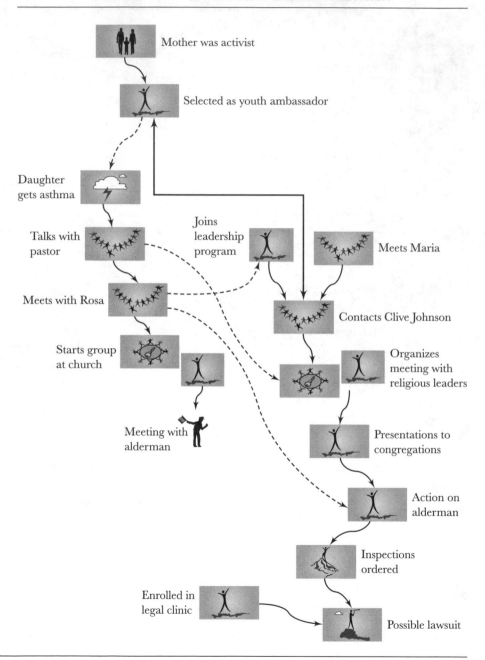

pastor to see if he would be willing to pull together a group of local religious leaders to meet with Clive while he was there. The meeting went great, and most of the leaders there agreed to let Maria and me come and talk with their congregations about the issues. The next few weeks were a whirl, but we went into them with a game plan. We worked with Rosa to plan an "action" on the alderman's office. Our goal was to get a group of 100 people together for a weekend picket of the office. The day of our action we had not 100 but over 250 outside of the alderman's office. A week later he had city inspectors out visiting the offending plants.

It's not over yet—there's still a lot left to do to make sure these plants clean up and keep things clean. Having that victory really helped to reinvigorate me though. Rosa has connected our group to a lawyer who is preparing a class action lawsuit on our behalf regarding the damage our children have faced. All the legalese was a little beyond me, so I enrolled myself in a community legal clinic that is helping me understand all this more.

Documenting Impacts at the Initiative level

Resident leadership is an important component of the theory of change within Making Connections. Part of the assumption is that for the initiative to be successful, residents must be involved as decision makers and implementers of strategies to transform their neighborhoods. Underlying this assumption are beliefs that

- Residents know the community better than outside experts, and thus can help guide the initiative to strategies that best meet the needs of the community.
- Visible resident leadership is necessary for full participation of community residents with the initiative.
- To create capacity for sustainable community change, leadership must be developed among those who live within a community.

Thus, at the initiative level there are several questions that need to be answered in order to assess whether or not there is meaningful resident participation.

- How many resident leaders are engaged in leadership roles in the initiative?
- How long do resident leaders remain engaged in the initiative?

- How fully do resident leaders participate in the various decision-making structures of the initiative?
- Are resident priorities reflected in the agenda of the initiative?
- Do those resident leaders who are engaged feel like their voices are heard?
- Is the support structure adequate? For example, are there resources available to compensate residents for costs such as transportation, child care, or the food they cook for meetings or events? Is staff available to support some of the planning and administration burden, mailing costs, or to arrange for space for meetings? Is there someplace for resident leaders to go to relieve stress or burnout?
- Are the resident leaders who are engaged with the initiative representative of key constituencies within the neighborhood? Are they trusted by community members?

One challenge in answering these questions is balancing insider and outsider information. Because these are internal process questions, it is easy to simply focus on the experience of those resident leaders who are connected to and participating in the initiative. If the initiative is structured so that a certain type of resident comes to the table (for example, only those with a high degree of education), then relying only on information from those residents who are part of the initiative will yield a false picture of how well the initiative is engaging the community. It is important to explore how unintentional messages and perceptions of the initiative get disseminated to the community and what impact these have on who participates. For example, when many neighborhood transformation efforts are initiated, the foundation forms a partnership with an institution that brings a particular set of resident leaders to the table. These partnerships and alliances often shape how the initiative is viewed in the community. If there are already fractures in the community, this may mean that some resident leaders are excluded.

This raises the issues of representation, accountability, and communication. In interviews with resident leaders, participants repeatedly described the problem of community leaders who were recognized by outside power brokers but in reality represented and were accountable to no one. It is tricky within the context of neighborhood transformation initiatives to be respectful and supportive of the resident leaders brought to the table by the partner institution and still raise questions about representation and accountability.

The evaluation needs to include the voices of those residents who are at the table and those who are not at the table.

A common evaluation challenge is the reliance on self-report. Often resident leaders feel pressure to please the foundation that is investing in their leadership development and giving them access to power, at the very least, within the structure of the initiative. In addition, resident leaders have an investment in giving meaning to the time they themselves have invested in leadership development activities, which may make them more likely to emphasize the transformative impact these activities have had on their lives.

Evaluating the Impacts of Resident Leadership Development Efforts on the Initiative

Paying attention to process measures ensures that the initiative is being responsive to and guided by those who live within the community. The following tactics and strategies can help foundations hold individual sites accountable to the larger vision of resident driven change that is central to so many comprehensive community change initiatives.

- *Evaluation strategies cannot just focus on the experience of those resident leaders who are active participants in the initiative.* Information should also be gathered from those who are not participating and those who came and left. This might involve following up with a subset of those who came to a single meeting and chose not to participate further. Another strategy is to conduct focus groups with other community groups not involved with the initiative to identify external perceptions about the initiative.
- *Initiative-level evaluation can provide valuable information to those planning the initiative.* Monitoring meeting attendance, the extent to which meeting objectives are reached, participation in activities, and meeting minutes can provide valuable data for the evaluation that can be used by the meeting planners to monitor and improve the meetings themselves. Combining evaluation and planning tools also helps to ground daily activities in both the larger goals and the principles of the initiative.
- *Conduct surveys and interviews with resident leaders that can be used to capture their experiences within the initiative.* For instance, consumer satisfaction surveys might be used to assess the extent to which the initiative is meeting the needs of resident leaders.

- *Gain a clear understanding of the representativeness and accountability of resident leaders.* This requires a clear map of who is in the community, what networks exist, how different groups interact, how information flows, and who the acknowledged leaders are. Collecting this information is both good practice and an important baseline for evaluation. Without this understanding it is hard to determine whether the resident leaders who are tied to the initiative are able to truly impact the broader community.
- *Create regular check-ins to identify whether the broader community is feeling that it is being heard and its voice and ideas are being integrated in the initiative.* Early in Making Connections, most sites did what were called "family summits," large town hall meetings of up to a couple of hundred individuals from the community who set the agenda for the initiative. It is in these types of settings that concerns about community voice often arise.

Documenting Impacts at the Neighborhood Level

Even though Making Connections is a ten-year effort, it has been from the beginning very intentional about framing itself as a point-in-time intervention that focuses on leaving long-term capacity for sustaining positive change in communities. In regard to resident leadership, there are a series of questions about the long-term community impact of neighborhood transformation efforts.

- Has the initiative contributed to the development of effective networks among resident leaders?
- Has the initiative contributed to the creation of an infrastructure for the identification and development of new leaders?
- Has the initiative supported the development of more opportunities for residents to exercise their leadership for change?
- Are the initiative's partner organizations creating resident leadership opportunities within their own structure?
- Have outcomes for children and families improved because of the enhanced leadership of residents within the community?

The value of an initiative like Making Connections is that it serves as a catalyst, bringing in outside experts, providing seed funds, connecting diverse community partners, and setting expectations for change in the way things are done. In the area of resident leadership, this is often especially explicit. Figure 14.4, for example, demonstrates a progression from the initial impetus for including resident leadership, which comes from the foundation, to its embrace by the individual site and community partners, and eventually coming to reside within networks of resident leaders.

One of the central measures of the initiative's success in this area is its ability to seed capacity in other organizations and institutions. This happens both explicitly and implicitly. The expectation that resident leaders will be active at all of the initiative's decision-making tables creates ties between resident leaders and community power brokers that might not otherwise have existed. For example, when Making Connections was asked to partner with the city of Indianapolis to fund Family Investment Centers, the initiative made the creation of a governance structure that includes resident leaders as one of the prerequisites for its participation.

One of the key evaluation questions within resident leadership development efforts relates to tracking impacts on partner organizations and demonstrating what the initiative has seeded that now has independent life. This involves a complex look at how ideas that began within the initiative have been implemented within other community institutions, how dollars that were invested by the initiative were matched, how the push by the initiative for greater resident participation changed how community partners get their work done, and how resident leaders work together, recruit others, and mobilize for change.

Often those parts of an initiative that have the highest sustainability are those parts that were developed most collaboratively with community partners and, in the case of resident leadership development, with resident leaders themselves. This can make evaluating the initiative's contribution very complicated to parse. It can also lead to a situation in which the very process of evaluation undermines community partnerships by creating a dynamic where one partner seems to be taking credit for work that was actually done collaboratively. Developing models of evaluation that specifically map the contributions of various players and show the intersections of efforts helps to address this problem.

The question of the impact of resident leadership development on outcomes for children and families is arguably the most important, yet difficult, to answer. In the end, neighborhood transformation efforts are about community-level outcomes, such as earnings, income, and assets of families, the level of youth participation, the quality and access that families have to services, the

FIGURE 14.4. CORE CAPACITIES IN RESIDENT LEADERSHIP.

Preparation	Ready for Action	Action	Sustainability
Foundation • Set expectation • Seed capacity-building programs • Influence strategic partners **Site** • Identify resident leaders • Engage community • Identify needs and perspectives • Influence strategic partners	**Foundation** • Engage resident leaders in cross-site learning opportunities • Provide some capacity-building support for resident leaders across site **Site** • Provide capacity-building opportunities • Create infrastructure to support resident leaders' participation in decision making and direction setting for the initiative • Engage individual resident leaders in leadership roles in the initiative	**Foundation** • Engage resident leaders in cross-site learning opportunities • Network resident leaders across sites **Site** • Continue capacity building • Expand resident leaders' decision-making authority in the initiative • Work with strategic partners to create decision-making roles for residents • Engage residents as experts—through paid consultation, staff roles, board members, and advisors **Resident Leaders Networks** • Provide support to resident leaders to prevent burnout • Identify and mentor new leaders	**Foundation** • Connect resident leaders from sites to national opportunities **Site** • Ongoing roles for resident leaders in community change efforts **Resident Leaders Networks** • Identify and mentor new leaders • Connect new leaders to opportunities for impact • Demand new opportunities for influence • Build new resident-led institutions

Source: Developed as part of a series of internal working papers for the Annie E. Casey Foundation.

strength of their networks of support, and the health and readiness of their children to succeed in school. As with most neighborhood transformation efforts, resident leadership is seen as a central component of the larger change effort. It is not, however, seen as a primary outcome or result of the initiative.

Because resident leadership is a precursor to rather than a central outcome of the initiative, the foundation's and sites' evaluation and tracking methods are not generally focused on evaluating the impact of resident leadership development efforts per se. The foundation's interest is in evaluating each site's ability to reach the core results. While it would be interesting to identify how resident leadership contributes to achieving the six results mentioned near the beginning of this chapter, the reality is that these results are not primarily achieved through resident leadership development. Even though Making Connections is a relatively well-funded initiative, the resources are still limited. The tension between investing time and resources in the change efforts themselves or in the evaluation of these efforts is particularly strong because determining what causes or contributes to long-term results requires considerable resources.

Evaluating the Impact of Resident Leadership Development Efforts on the Community

The complex challenge of determining cause and effect and tying those to results and impact at the community level can be met in some measure using the following strategies.

- *Clearly delineate how contributions in the form of dollars, ideas, connections, and impetus for change lead to an eventual outcome or impact within the community.* Just as a pathways model is useful for measuring the impact of resident leadership development efforts on individuals, it can be used to look at community-level impact. This might involve mapping how an idea or a pool of funding contributed by the initiative developed within the context of the broader community and with the support of key individuals and community institutions.
- *Track the development of infrastructure that supports the development of new resident leaders.* This might include

  - The development of new training programs, mentoring strategies, or leadership recognition programs

- Specific changes made by community partners in their decision-making structure to support the engagement of resident leaders; for example, additions of resident leaders to their boards, creation of new community planning processes, creation of new advisory committees, and so on
- The development of resident-led networks that are taking on community change issues (in this area new social network analysis tools can be used to track and monitor the growth of networks, their size and robustness, and the type of exchanges they facilitate)

While evaluation strategies that demonstrate the impact of resident leadership efforts on specific community outcomes would be ideal, striving for this goal may be counterproductive. There are many intervening variables between strong resident leadership and changes in outcomes for children and families. Tracking changes in child and family outcomes is difficult enough; attributing that change to resident leadership development programs is close to impossible. The danger is that this is where the resources get invested, and our failure to measure impact in this area will be seen as a failure in resident leadership development rather than a failure in evaluation.

Conclusion

Most evaluations of resident leadership efforts are focused on the specific impact within a single strategy and do not even begin to address larger questions such as, What is the impact on the individuals participating? Is the initiative effectively engaging residents in leadership and decision-making roles in ways that lead to broader community input? Are the resident leadership development efforts leading to broader changes that will support the ability of residents to play effective roles within community change efforts over the long term?

Addressing these larger issues requires that we focus more on mapping the pathways of impact for resident leadership development efforts. For an individual participant, this means understanding better his or her trajectory: How did he get involved in community change efforts? What is the entire basket of leadership development activities she has participated in and how have these opportunities interacted and intersected to amplify her community leadership? At the community level, we need to look at how the investments, ideas, and impetus for change that the foundation brings into the community blossoms into a new infrastructure to support leadership development, changes on the part of community institutions, and new resident-led networks.

It is easy to dismiss this type of analysis as storytelling, as it generally relies on more qualitative methods of information gathering: interviews, surveys, and mining of the existing data (such as meeting minutes, attendance records, strategic plans, and so on). Yet because the model of leadership development being used is so complex (and varies so much both across and within sites), this type of analysis is much more likely to give evaluators the information we need to make meaning of whether resident leadership development efforts have really made a difference.

Resources

More about the resident leadership documentation work can be found at the Annie E. Casey Foundation Web site at www.aecf.org/initiatives/ldu/.

The following resources on case study methodology can be helpful:

> Abramson, P. R. *A Case for Case Studies.* Thousand Oaks, Calif.: Sage, 1992.
>
> Gillham, B. *Case Study Research Methods (Real World Research).* London: Continuum, 2000.
>
> Hamel, J. *Case Study Methods. Qualitative Research Methods,* Vol. 32. Thousand Oaks, Calif.: Sage, 1993.

A brief chapter on the documentation process and some guidelines for documentation used within the Making Connections initiative can be found at the following Web address: www.aecf.org/initiatives/mc/llp/chapter8_1.htm. While some of this information is specific to the documentation work being conducted by local learning partnerships within sites, much of it is applicable to the projects described in this chapter.

There are several social network mapping tools that readers may find useful:

> InFlow 3.1-Social Network Mapping Software creates interactive visual models of social networks. You can access it at www.orgnet.com/inflow3.html.

UCINet is a general package for analysis of social network data. Access at www.analyitictech.com/ucinet.htm.

Pajek is a free Windows-based program for mapping social networks. Access at http://vlado.fmf.uni-lj.si/pub/networks/pajek/.

An overview of computer programs for social network analysis can be found at www.insna.org/INSNA/soft_inf.html.

Reference

Kubisch, A. C. "Comprehensive Community Initiatives: Lessons in Neighborhood Transformation." *Shelterforce Online,* 1996. [www.nhi.org/online/issues/85/compcominit.html].

PART THREE

INCREASING IMPACT THROUGH EVALUATION USE

Just as evaluation is mistakenly considered to be the activity that happens at the end of an intervention (such as a leadership development program), the use of evaluation is mistakenly considered to happen after an evaluation is over. In cases where this is true, an evaluation will be designed and implemented, a report and other documents will be created, and a presentation will perhaps be made, but no actions are planned as a result of the evaluation. As such, a significant outcome is that the evaluation, in fact, will not be used. The evaluation serves the purpose of reporting on the implementation and impact of a particular initiative, but does not lead to further development or learning. Is the evaluation in this case worth the time, effort, and funding that were required to make it happen? It is possible but not likely.

The American Evaluation Association feels so strongly about the importance of using evaluations and their results to create further action that several of the Program Evaluation Standards have been written to address proper use (other evaluation societies have their own versions of these standards).

- *Report timeliness and dissemination.* Significant interim findings and evaluation reports should be disseminated to intended users so that they can be used in a timely fashion.

- *Evaluation impact.* Evaluations should be planned, conducted, and reported in ways that encourage follow-through by stakeholders, so that the likelihood that the evaluation will be used is increased.
- *Political viability.* The evaluation should be planned and conducted with anticipation of the different positions of various interest groups so that their cooperation may be obtained and so that possible attempts by any of these groups to curtail evaluation operations or to bias or misapply the results can be averted or counteracted.

Although many evaluations are conducted to provide useful information for decision making, evaluations often fail because what organizations learn from the evaluation goes unused. Even more frequently, evaluations may be used, but only to a fraction of their potential.

It is important that evaluators, individual participants, organizations, and other entities understand that the evaluation process doesn't end when all of the data have been collected, analyzed, and interpreted. On the contrary, that is the time to revisit the reasons the evaluation was originally commissioned. The chapters in Part Three are targeted at different aspects of evaluation use: for strategic influence, program planning, communicating with stakeholders, building knowledge and capacity of the evaluation field as a whole, and for organizational learning purposes. Before we briefly introduce each of the chapters, we first address critical issues surrounding the use of evaluation.

Challenges to Effective Evaluation Use

Russ-Eft and Preskill (2001) discuss six challenges faced by evaluators that may prevent the findings from evaluation from being used.

1. *Changes in client membership or limited client involvement during evaluation.* An evaluation is strongest when the clients (or stakeholders) have been involved in creating the evaluation questions and in implementing the evaluation. When there is turnover of client membership during the evaluation, one of the outcomes can be that those who transition into responsibility for the evaluation do not hold the same value for it and do not make efforts to use its findings. A similar challenge occurs when the clients do not, in fact, become involved in the design and implementation of the evaluation. In both cases, the likelihood that the evaluation's findings will be implemented is diminished.

2. *Changes in the evaluand during the evaluation.* Especially in cases when a leadership development initiative is longitudinal, many factors can change over time that affect the results of the evaluation but that are not indicative of changes related to the initiative itself. For example, an organization's external environment may change in a way that necessitates changes in the organization's strategies. Or the primary set of instructors for a particular program are transitioned off of the program and replaced by a new set of instructors. Or the stakeholders for a particular program add a new component to it that inadvertently prevents participants from attending to one of the more critical components. In any of these types of situations, the evaluation should be reevaluated to be sure that it is targeting what are expected to be the new outcomes of the program. Failure to do so will result in the evaluation failing to represent all of the outcomes, limiting the usefulness of the results.

3. *Compromise of the evaluator's credibility.* Because the evaluator plays the lead role in data collection and interpretation, a great deal of weight is placed on the degree to which the evaluator can be trusted to do so responsibly and ethically. Reasons to question an evaluator's credibility can include the evaluator's perceived expertise, mistakes made in the conduct of the evaluation, or questions regarding potential conflict of interest presented by the relationship of the evaluator to the initiative being evaluated. If key stakeholders question the evaluator's ability to conduct a sound and ethical evaluation, their perceptions make it less likely that they will make use of the results of the evaluation.

4. *Changes in political winds.* There are inherent political effects for every evaluation. At some level, there are people who want the leadership development initiative to be proven effective, and potentially there are others who do not believe the initiative is the best way to address the challenges the organization faces. Were that a stable source of influence, the evaluation could be designed to account for the impact of these perceptions and motivations on the outcomes of the evaluation. However, the role of any leadership development initiative in key stakeholders' minds may shift over time. To the degree that their subsequent actions negatively affect the outcomes of the initiative, the results of the evaluation are less likely to be used because the stakeholders may no longer perceive the initiative and its results to be important.

5. *Insufficient communication channels.* Whether a leadership development initiative takes place in the context of an organization, a community, or a country,

appropriate communication channels must be established so that the results of the evaluation can be shared by all potential groups of key stakeholders. If the results are instead shared only with a small group of stakeholders, others do not have the opportunity to learn about the results and make use of them.

6. *Timeliness of the evaluation information.* Evaluation results must be shared in a timely manner to have maximum impact. Sometimes this means sharing results that are extracted during the course of the initiative, and sometimes it means sharing the results as soon as they are available following the end of the initiative. Whether the urgency is related to important timelines (such as budget cycles), attention span and interest of key stakeholders, or the needs of concurrently running initiatives, releasing evaluation results at a time that does not reflect the urgency of needs will result in decreased likelihood that the results will be useful and be used.

Finally, one additional challenge to evaluation use is the cultural context under which the leadership development initiative and the evaluation take place. The culture determines, in large part, whether and to what extent the results are used. For example, if an initiative takes place in an organization that values continuous learning, there are very good chances that the results of the evaluation will be used in an effort to improve the initiative and whatever aspects of the organization contribute to the success or failure of the initiative. Alternatively, if the culture of a given community demands that the most senior officials make the decision regarding the actions to be taken regarding evaluation results, and if those officials deem it inappropriate to implement the recommendations arising from the evaluation, the results will not be used. As these two examples show, evaluators need to understand the culture well and attend to it in the design of the initiative and the evaluation itself or the likelihood that the results of the evaluation will be used will diminish.

Misuses of Evaluation

There are also ways in which evaluation can be misused, posing an enormous risk to the credibility of evaluation. One example is when evaluation results are used to make judgments about the performance of individuals rather than about the effectiveness of the initiative itself. Evaluation of leadership development should never be used as performance appraisal or administrative decision making with regard to individuals. However, some stakeholders will ask evaluators to use the results this way or will request the evaluation data so that they can use the data this way themselves.

Another misuse of evaluation occurs when the results are used to draw conclusions that are not substantiated by the results themselves. For example, when evaluation results show that a leadership development initiative is effective for developing specific skills and abilities in individuals, but stakeholders ask that the results be reflected as representing the likely outcomes of a different initiative, the results are being misused.

These and other types of challenges are facing evaluators of leadership development in their efforts to ensure that the results of their evaluations are used. The chapters that follow in Part Three discuss different aspects of evaluation use. Together, they reflect the potential of evaluation to create impact beyond that of the leadership development itself.

Chapter Summaries

Chapter Fifteen. This chapter addresses the importance of using evaluation for strategic purposes. The authors argue that the design and use of an evaluation for strategic purposes will result in the initiative in question being more strongly linked to an organization's (or community's) vision and strategy. In doing so, the initiative is significantly more valuable to the organization or community than a program that is not strategically oriented. The authors provide guidance and case examples to support readers in designing and implementing evaluations that can be used to strengthen the linkage between leadership development and organizational strategic direction.

Chapter Sixteen. The premise of this chapter is that evaluation can be used to improve program quality and outcomes during the planning and implementation of leadership development programs. The author uses the Baldrige Education Criteria for Performance Excellence and case examples to demonstrate the use of evaluation for program planning.

Chapter Seventeen. This chapter focuses on a key component of evaluation use: communication. The author asserts that an evaluation's design and the resulting findings must be communicated to all key stakeholders in a way that makes sense to them and encourages them to use the processes or the findings. This chapter addresses issues such as identifying stakeholders and audiences, the ideal content and format of evaluation communication, and the timing of evaluation communication.

Chapter Eighteen. This chapter discusses the use of evaluation to create and strengthen communities of practice—in this case, the evaluation field. Through the use of learning circles designed to intentionally share the lessons of evaluations among evaluators working in the nonprofit sector, evaluation practices, designs, results, and implications have been shared as a way of strengthening individual and collective efforts to develop effective social change leadership. This has occurred by connecting the resources, learning, and practice of those committed to this work. The authors share collective learning strategies, tools, and tips to provide readers with support for using learning circles to affect change.

Chapter Nineteen. Finally, this chapter presents and discusses a continuous learning approach to the use of evaluation findings about leadership development programs. Its central argument is that evaluation designed and carried out in a way that supports ongoing use of findings within a particular organizational context will best support learning and change necessary to the development, delivery, and outcomes of leadership development programs. The author provides steps required in the process of engaging in continuous learning, the features of evaluation that facilitate continuous learning, and recommendations for a continuous learning approach to evaluating leadership development programs.

Reference

Russ-Eft, D., and Preskill, H. *Evaluation in Organizations: A Systematic Approach to Enhancing Learning, Performance, and Change.* Cambridge, Mass.: Perseus, 2001.

CHAPTER FIFTEEN

STRATEGIC USES OF EVALUATION

E. Jane Davidson and Jennifer W. Martineau

One of the catalysts for the development of strategic evaluation is that leadership development is being used to accomplish strategic objectives. As leadership development becomes focused on creating strategic-level outcomes and is highly dependent on organizations to support it for this purpose, evaluation must also be targeted toward the strategic purposes of the initiative. This not only ensures that the initiative remains focused on these outcomes; it is also a way of measuring the extent to which the outcomes are achieved. This chapter defines and discusses strategic evaluation, illustrates the value it provides, describes best practices and challenges, provides resources, and highlights future directions. As you read this chapter, assume that when we refer to an organization, the concepts we are describing and illustrating can apply to many different types of entities. Corporations, nonprofits, educational institutions, nongovernmental organizations, governments, communities, and other types of structures may all have strategies that guide the direction of their work. Thus, although we do not provide examples from all of these many different types of organizations, we believe that the content of the chapter applies to them.

Almost every major organizational intervention (leadership development or otherwise) has its origins in a strategic vision (a needed, or aspired-for, endpoint).

However, in some cases the strategic vision may not be well articulated or linked to specific actions (it may be more an inkling than a plan per se) and/or is not shared among stakeholders. In these cases, interventions become fractionalized and do not work in concert to support the strategic goals. Evaluative thinking can help to create a shared vision and strategy (for example, by identifying desired intermediate and long-term outcomes), and evaluation can then be used to measure the implementation of that strategy. From this strategic vision, strategic interventions such as leadership development initiatives are designed (see Figure 15.1). A common plea evaluators hear from clients is the need to link evaluation of these strategic interventions more effectively with the organizational strategy and vision from which they were derived. The purpose of this chapter is to explain why this is important and how it can be done.

All too often, strategies are operationalized very quickly, becoming a cluster of programs or interventions that rapidly become disconnected. Each program or intervention has a set of goals derived from (but smaller in scope than) the strategy. If the evaluations of those interventions amount to no more than program evaluations in the traditional sense (that is, evaluation against these lower-level goals, plus some investigation of unintended consequences), then the likelihood of achieving the original strategic intent is considerably diminished. Further, an evaluation that is conducted solely within the bounds of the program (that is, simply checking to see whether the program, in isolation from

FIGURE 15.1. RELATIONSHIPS AMONG ORGANIZATIONAL VISION, STRATEGY, AND INTERVENTIONS.

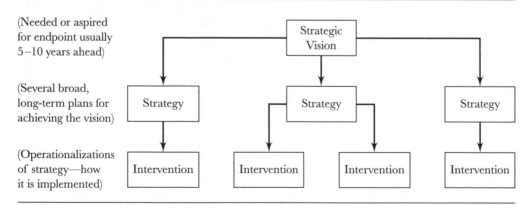

(Needed or aspired for endpoint usually 5–10 years ahead)

(Several broad, long-term plans for achieving the vision)

(Operationalizations of strategy—how it is implemented)

other events or initiatives, did what the implementers said it would do) cannot establish the overall value added by the program, let alone whether it is a good return on the strategic investment.

There is also the converse problem where some organizations evaluate large-scale strategic interventions simply by monitoring changes in long-term outcomes such as market share, financial performance, or whatever big-picture outcome the intervention is primarily designed to achieve. But as de Geus (1997) and Kaplan and Norton (1996) point out, outcomes such as financial data are measures of past organizational health; therefore, by the time bottom-line results turn up, it is usually too late to fine-tune the change effort. This type of approach therefore fails to measure the important markers and lever-age points along the way to the ultimate goal. Crucial early information about the likely effectiveness of a strategic initiative is missed, and the organization cannot take corrective action in a timely way. If the ultimate goal is not real-ized, stakeholders are not only left wondering what changes are needed in order to achieve success; it is likely too late to implement them anyway. And if the ultimate goal is realized, it is difficult to know which aspects of the ini-tiative (if any) contributed to it. Perhaps the long-term outcome was due to something else, or perhaps fewer resources might have been needed to achieve the success.

Strategic evaluations address this problem in two ways. First, they make sure that immediate and intermediate intervention outcomes are linked back to the overarching strategic goals. Second, they explicitly consider the other components of the strategy and how they work together to bring the organi-zation closer to its strategic vision. Because the focus of strategy (in contrast with programs and interventions) is broad and long term, strategic evaluations should also take a big-picture, long-term perspective.

Strategic evaluation, in its ideal form, is fully integrated into business processes. Thus, business decisions are data-driven, using information that has been collected specifically to determine the effectiveness of a particular busi-ness process or intervention in contributing to the organization's strategic per-formance. Further, this information is synthesized so that it is useful at a higher level, for example, to determine which business processes contribute the most to the strategy, which overlap and create redundancies, and whether the com-bined effects of the strategic interventions are greater or less than the sum of the effects of the strategy's components.

Strategic evaluation is relatively new and therefore its value is yet to be broadly accepted. At the same time, many organizations are hesitant to dedicate resources to evaluation because they assume the business process should be effective if they have designed it right. Some organizations enlist the help of an impact assessment specialist, who estimates the probable impact of a strategic intervention before it is implemented. But in many cases, this is not followed up with any serious attempt to see whether these predicted outcomes did in fact come about. Helping organizations understand the importance and power of incorporating strategic evaluation into business processes is the goal of this chapter. We hope to illustrate this point by demonstrating the outcomes of decisions made based on evaluation data in some particular organizations.

There are numerous forces in play that work against the evaluation of strategic interventions. Tichy (1993) identified several important technical, political, and cultural forces against evaluation. Tichy argued that the main technical difficulties are related to the measurement of attitudinal and cultural change, the development of internal staff to carry out monitoring and evaluation, and the availability of "conceptual frameworks for integrating measurement of change into management's thinking about organizational performance" (p. 364). We argue that most of these technical challenges have been more than adequately addressed by developments in the evaluation discipline since (and before) 1993. However, strategic evaluation does make an additional contribution to one of the technical difficulties Tichy raises, by providing a conceptual framework that meshes well with management thinking.

The other two forces that Tichy (1993) mentioned are still very much in play. Perhaps the most pervasive of these are the political forces, especially what Donald Campbell (1969) called the "over-advocacy trap." External consultants and internal advocates of change often need to sell a particular strategic change intervention to management as a solution that is virtually guaranteed to work. To suggest that evaluation might be useful is tantamount to saying that the solution is fallible or possibly flawed, an insinuation that clashes directly with advocates' views and reputations. Such an assumption is indicative of the fear that some people have about evaluation—that it will show that an intervention isn't doing what it is supposed to be doing. The truth is that strategic evaluation can be a provider's most useful tool, if the initiative and the evaluation are designed together, if the client for the initiative has had input to both (as well as to the outcomes intended), and if the evaluation provides the evidence that supports the role of the intervention in addressing the strategic goals. It can end debate of the value of an intervention because it provides the answers to questions about value.

A related issue is what Tichy (1993) calls the "career time bomb dilemma" (p. 365). Rapid career advancement, particularly in Western organizations, means that many managers move from position to position much faster than the timeframe for evaluating the effectiveness of their initiatives. Therefore, the focus is all too often on the short-term goals and immediate efficiencies implemented, rather than on the long-term strategic effectiveness of their work. This prevents managers from connecting their work and initiatives to the strategic goals of the organization, and results in numerous disconnected interventions.

The third set of Tichy's (1993) forces working against strategic evaluation are cultural. He describes how Western organizations have a "curious addiction to grand strategy" (p. 365) rather than incremental strategy. This leads to a monitoring approach that involves little more than watching the bottom line, or market share, or whatever major indicator was expected to be impacted by the large-scale change, as a gauge of whether the grand strategy was successful. While these are indeed important outcomes, much of the value of good strategic evaluation comes from the ongoing tracking of process (content and implementation) and intermediate outcomes that are logically linked to those long-term goals. Thus, a focus of this chapter is on how strategic evaluation is most effective when it is integrated into ongoing strategic management and business processes.

The strategic evaluation literature emanates from fields as diverse as radiology (Chan, 2002), community capacity building (Casswell, Ruenanga, and Paekaka, 2001), human resource development (Waight, 2004), and government (Silbert, Randolph, and Salmon, 2006). In the next section, we present our perspective on key definitions surrounding strategic evaluation for leadership development.

Key Definitions

Most organizations have what is referred to as a *strategic framework*. This consists of (1) an organizational vision, (2) a mission statement, (3) a set of overarching values, (4) a set of strategies, and (5) a set of specific strategic goals and actions.

An *organizational vision* is a desired end state of either what the organization hopes to become or what its target community will look like when its work is done. The organizational vision is often rather idealized and unachievable. Its purpose is to inspire organizational members by providing a clear view of the overarching goal the organization is striving toward. An *organizational mission* is a statement of what business the organization is in, that is, what part it plays in striving toward the vision. *Organizational values* are principles (statements about what is considered good, valuable, or important) that are used to guide decisions and actions. A *strategy* is one of the (usually four or five) key approaches an organization intends to use in order to achieve its mission and/or vision. *Strategic goals and actions* are the more specific operationalizations of strategy that guide the month-to-month running of the organization.

Strategic evaluation refers to the determination of the value of one or more business processes or interventions with particular attention to (1) its consistency with organizational values and (2) its contributions to organizational strategy and, ultimately, the achievement of the organization's mission or vision. Strategic evaluation differs from program or intervention evaluation primarily with respect to the type and scope of information provided and its intended users. Findings are designed and timed to be useful not only to those implementing the interventions that form part of a strategy, but to those reviewing and reformulating the overarching strategy itself.

Strategic evaluation is contrasted with *operational evaluation*. A typical operational approach to evaluation would have a primary focus on how an intervention could be improved through streamlining or changing existing processes. In other words, the greatest amount of attention is focused within the frame of the specific intervention itself, its inputs, processes, outputs, and the outcomes that relate quite directly to that intervention.

In contrast, a strategic evaluation is framed at a bigger picture and more long-term level. Even in an early formative evaluation, where long-term strategic outcomes could not possibly have been achieved, a strategic evaluation would explicitly consider the extent to which those long-term (that is, three to five years and beyond) outcomes are likely to be achieved. We do not suggest that strategic evaluation is somehow better than operational evaluation or that one should be chosen over the other. On the contrary, we believe that the optimal evaluation design is one that includes both operational and strategic evaluation.

A strategic evaluation asks (and answers) questions that go beyond program improvement or overall program quality, addressing the value of the program as a contributor to the broad strategic mix of initiatives and interventions. For example, to what extent does this particular initiative make a unique contribution to the strategic vision? How well does it fit with other initiatives in that respect? Are there any unnecessary overlaps? Is the initiative fundamentally consistent with the organization's overarching values? How much is it helping the organization make progress toward achieving its vision?

The Added Value of Strategic Evaluation

In this section of the chapter, we explore the ways in which strategic evaluation can add value to the key stakeholders of leadership development initiatives. Evaluation helps to keep the leadership development initiative connected to the organization's overarching purpose or strategy. In the evaluations we've been involved with, some of those long-term strategic outcomes include

- Making work more meaningful for employees
- Creating a better product for the customer
- Creating culture change
- Building stronger communities
- Building specific knowledge about where to invest in leadership development initiatives
- Building stronger schools and universities
- Improving the academic experience for all students, faculty, and staff
- Ensuring best use of resources
- Strengthening the leadership pool (related to succession planning)
- Strengthening organizational capability
- Creating shareholder wealth

Case Example: Government Agencies Initiative

Throughout this chapter, we use case study examples to illustrate our points. Our first case study is a recent evaluation of a senior leadership development strategy spanning thirty-five government agencies. Three main interventions (programs) fell under the umbrella of the strategy:

1. A multiyear, tailored executive development program aimed at very senior managers who would be ready to lead (or help lead) a government agency within three to five years

2. A three-week executive leadership course aimed at senior managers
3. A two-year Executive Master of Public Administration degree aimed at mid- to senior-level managers wishing to move into more senior positions

The primary strategic goal was to strengthen and diversify the pool of senior public service leaders so that there would always be talent available to fill senior roles. One of the great challenges with using strategic goals such as this in an evaluation is that they are usually long-term outcomes. This particular evaluation was conducted after the strategy had been implemented just eighteen months to two years, which is far too early to see any impact on the long-term strategic goals. A key requirement was to report back on a predetermined set of success criteria for Year 1. These indicators barely skimmed the surface of what the client really needed to know, and were primarily process and output focused. Thus, one challenge was how to make the evaluation strategic (in the sense of being long-term and related to high-level, big-picture outcomes) and not just a run-of-the-mill process evaluation with a few short-term outcomes tacked on.

In this particular case, the initiative being evaluated was itself a strategy. This made it doubly important to ensure that the evaluation was also strategic in its design and reporting. This was achieved in several ways. The first and most important step was to engage senior stakeholders, those who would be making strategic-level decisions based on the evaluation. They were interviewed to determine what it was that they needed to know about the strategy. As expected, most of the questions raised were high-level, big-picture issues, although important details were also sought. In addition, it was important to maintain a close working relationship with those overseeing the strategy to make sure that their questions were being answered along the way at a level that made the answers maximally useful for strategic decision making. This involved staying in frequent contact with the project manager and other key stakeholders in the client organization and sending through preliminary answers to important questions as the first data became available. This would often raise further questions, which could then be incorporated into the evaluation.

The second step was the development (by the evaluator, in consultation with the client) of a set of overarching evaluation questions, some of which were fundamentally strategic in nature. These questions guided the evaluation and helped ensure that all data gathered would somehow feed into answers to those high-level questions. In this case, the questions were

- What is the strength of the strategy's "brand" within the public service? What is its reputation or perceived strength in the eyes of those who might benefit from it?
- To what extent are the public service's best and brightest leaders attracted and encouraged into the strategy's various programs?

- What is the quality of the various strategy offerings (worthwhile content, effective delivery) and how effectively are participants and departments contributing to and taking advantage of these?
- What impact does the strategy have on participants' effectiveness as leaders within the public service and on their intent and success in pursuing careers as top-level leaders within the public service?
- What is the value of the strategy and its programs as an investment of time, money, and other resources?

What makes these overarching evaluation questions strategic are (1) some of the questions were derived directly from the stated intent of the strategy itself; (2) the use of concepts such as "brand," which are intrinsically high level and strategic in nature; (3) the inclusion of important macro-level contextual issues, such as the degree to which organizational cultures were enabling departments to get maximal benefit out of the strategy; and (4) this strategic evaluation included an overall value question to reflect the strategic decisions made about the allocation of scarce resources. It was not simply a question of whether the strategy achieved its objectives or even whether the benefits outweighed the costs. The question was, Was this the best possible use of the available resources to achieve needed and valuable outcomes?

One useful tool for helping make the evaluation strategic was to devise a logic model that showed how the main components of the strategy could be expected to achieve the long-term strategic goals (see Figure 15.2). This allowed us to identify the precursors of the truly strategic outcomes that might reasonably have been expected to have started emerging. (See Chapter Two for more on theory of change models, pathway mapping, and logic models.)

The second (and in hindsight, most important) part of the logic model was a set of "assumed inputs"—conditions that would have to be in place in order for the strategy to work. These included organizational cultures that supported leadership development, a diverse pool of talented recruits coming into entry-level positions, and untapped senior leadership potential (including women and minorities) within the current group of senior managers. By unearthing these assumptions about what was already in place, the evaluation was helpful in highlighting where the individual programs sat relative to related strategic initiatives (such as effective recruitment of a diverse group of high-potential employees to feed the talent pipeline). The logic model also helped to identify assumptions about cause and effect that were implicit in the strategy. (The long-term evaluation of this strategy includes more explicit testing of these assumptions than was possible at such an early stage.)

Another approach that helped make the evaluation strategic was the emphasis on going beyond the simple tangible data. Many of the evaluation questions probed what lay underneath. For example, if minority senior managers were being nominated for

FIGURE 15.2. SIMPLIFIED LOGIC MODEL SHOWING STRATEGY.

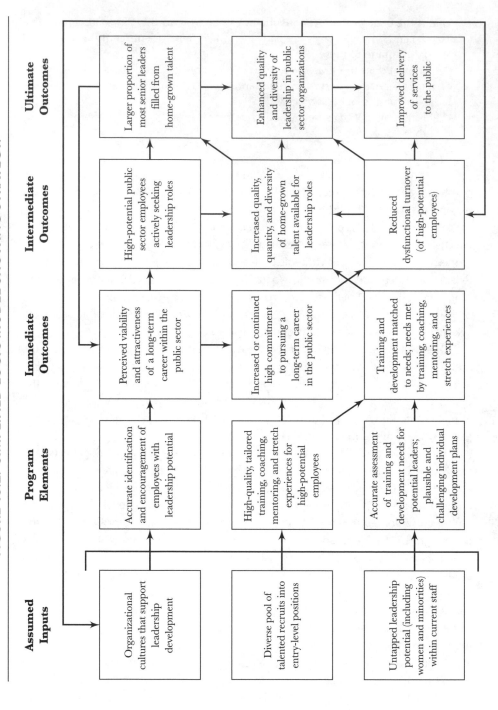

Note: The original version of this logic model was based on current theory and knowledge of organizational change and leadership development and on stakeholders' implicit theories. The model was revised in light of evaluation findings to more accurately reflect the cause-and-effect relationships in operation and relevant aspects of both context and initiative quality.

Source: State Services Commission, Wellington, New Zealand.

the executive development program at half the expected rate given their prevalence in senior positions, why was this? What aspects of the nomination process presented cultural barriers that made it less likely for a minority manager to be nominated? Was there anything about the program that made it somehow less attractive or relevant for minority managers?

For those in strategic roles, this probing of what lay underneath the data was extremely important for building an understanding of why and how things were happening. With information about the underlying causes of effectiveness and ineffectiveness, the client was better able to design solutions and enhancements that would address the true underlying causes. Strategic use was facilitated by conveying in-depth understanding, not just evaluative findings.

Case Example: Health Care System Initiative

Another example of strategic evaluation comes from an evaluation of a leadership development initiative conducted for a regional health care system. One of the largest not-for-profit hospital systems in the United States, leaders of this organization were acutely aware that strategic and successful succession planning was crucial to its future sustainability. Building a cadre of leaders capable of holding the reins was important, but ensuring those individuals imbued a strong sense of the organization's mission and values was imperative. Without holding the mission and values as a driving force, the organization risked becoming yet another health care system providing services to those in need in a cost-efficient way. Rather, the mission of this organization is foremost to serve the poor while running a cost-efficient operation. Therefore, decisions need to be made, and the hospitals and other types of health care facilities in this system need to operate daily, in a way that enables effective, appropriate service to the poor while allowing the organization's fiscal health to remain strong. To meet their development needs, the organization sought a state-of-the-art process that would align the organization's strategic priorities with five critical leadership factors.

1. Be passionate about the core values of the organization.
2. Exhibit servant leadership.
3. Utilize complex mental processes.
4. Exhibit bias for action.
5. Develop others.

The intervention designed and delivered to address these strategic goals was a fifteen-month development process that included the following components:

- A three-day, face-to-face orientation program
- Two five-day, feedback-rich, experiential leadership development programs
- Two phases of team-based action-learning leadership project and coaching work (action-learning leadership work is designed to build leadership capabilities while addressing real business needs; participants work in learning teams to explore, examine, and identify solutions to the organization's critical leadership challenges at the same time they are learning about leadership and development at the individual, team, and organizational levels)
- One-on-one coaching sessions

This intervention, named the Leadership Academy, was targeted at leaders who held hospital president, vice president, or similar positions. The roles they were being groomed to fill were at the regional chief executive officer (CEO) and executive team levels.

The needs assessment provided guidance for the design of the initiative as well as the design of the evaluation. Key stakeholders took part in a two-day, intensive, focus group session that provided a structure for first identifying the organization's overall challenges and needs (for example, to remain competitive, to develop a culture of ownership among employees) and linking leadership needs, leadership competencies, a conceptual design, and evaluation needs to them. Thus, stakeholders (the executive team in this case) identified the key organizational needs for which this leadership development initiative was required as (1) making the organization's mission a strategic advantage; (2) developing and retaining good people; and (3) remaining fiscally healthy. The strategic evaluation questions were

- How effective are the action learning projects? In this case, do they (1) provide an effective learning platform for participants and (2) lead to actionable recommendations that are adopted and put into action by the organization (and what are the outcomes of doing so?), and (3) lead to recommendations that are connected to the organizational challenges?
- How have participants enhanced the scope of their responsibilities (for example, promotions, roles on organization-wide task forces)?
- Are participants developing the critical competencies addressed in the initiative? How? What is the impact of developing these competencies for individual and organizational improvement?
- Are participants more committed to the organization as a result of the Leadership Academy (and therefore more likely to remain)?

Due to the issues addressed by the action-learning projects, the specific nature of the competencies being developed, and the relationship of the mission to questions about commitment, there is a strong link between these strategic evaluation questions and the overall intent of the initiative.

The strategic evaluation designed for this initiative was created alongside the design and development of the intervention itself. This enabled the collaborative design team (consisting of the two individuals most accountable for the initiative from the client organization, curriculum designers, and evaluators) to integrate evaluation tools into the initiative. Participants received feedback from the evaluation that enabled them to make changes in their own leadership practice, and the academy's stakeholders were able to make critical changes to the program and the support infrastructure while the academy was still underway. Evaluation tools were also used up to eighteen months after the program (at the time this book went to press; however, the evaluation of the initiative continues) to identify key outcomes.

The evaluation was designed for several purposes:

- To investigate the extent to which the intended outcomes were directly and indirectly met
- To provide evidence that the initiative contributed to desired changes such as

  Improvements in participants' leadership skills and behaviors

  A stronger corporate culture

  Improved retention of promising leaders capable of flexible movement

  Greater operational effectiveness through empowerment as leaders

- To demonstrate that the initiative contributed toward the mission of the organization, enhancing the vision of the organization
- To identify leverage points in the client organization infrastructure that either supported or got in the way of successful implementation of the initiative

Some parts of this evaluation are typically categorized as formative and some as summative. Formative evaluation describes evaluation designs that are meant to inform improvements in the effectiveness of an initiative, and summative evaluation describes those designs that are meant to draw overall conclusions about the value of a particular initiative. We do not address these aspects in this case example, but other chapters in this book do address them. We focus instead on the strategic components and use of the evaluation. We mention these operational components to illustrate that operational and strategic evaluation are not mutually exclusive. They are compatible and reinforcing of each other.

One of the ways this evaluation was strategic is that it enabled key stakeholders to support a culture of collaboration across upper levels of the organization. The action-learning projects provided a learning opportunity for participants to collaborate with each other and other nonparticipants across organizational boundaries. The evaluation enabled key stakeholders and participants to identify ways in which the initiative was successful and unsuccessful in doing so. For example, one of the projects focused on making a particular hospital more competitive in its market. This question had been addressed previously by employees of the hospital and surrounding area, with limited success. Project team members (none of whom were from that particular hospital) were not fully aware of these efforts initially, and therefore did not know to include the people who had worked on the project previously nor their learnings. By failing to do so, they alienated the very people who had information needed to address the problem. After stumbling and then reflecting (through the evaluation) on their mistakes, the team included some of the critical players and were able to get the information they needed to produce an actionable set of recommendations for the hospital and build a relationship with critical players rather than alienate them. By causing team members to reflect on the actions they had taken as a project team and the resulting outcomes, the evaluation supported them in approaching the task in a more strategic manner.

Another way that the evaluation was strategic was that it enabled key stakeholders to identify the role the organization itself facilitated in the success of the initiative. For example, one of the findings of the evaluation was that the Leadership Academy was not achieving its full potential because the participants' regional superiors were not closely involved with it. As a result, the strategy of the region was sometimes in conflict with the strategy of the organization as a whole. Regional strategies would typically be focused on local measures of success, such as the cost of providing services, yet a clear organizational strategy was to develop leaders who would be able to lead the organization overall to be more sustainable. It was possible, for example, for a participant to engage with a wide variety of colleagues across the system (that is, those outside of their own region or their own functional specialty) in learning about best practices for the work of the organization (for example, attracting and retaining specialty physicians in rural areas), at the same time that the leadership provided by that participant's CEO put his region in direct competition with the other regions by holding the participant accountable for attracting and retaining these physicians. Using the results of the evaluation, the organization has engaged a coaching process that is supporting regional CEOs to collaborate more as a team versus as competitors.

Learning from the Cases

These cases provide a powerful context from which to draw lessons. First, both cases illustrate that strategic evaluation adds value by questioning the assumptions behind the strategy that drove leadership development. In the second case, the assumptions made were that leadership development was the right tactic to addressing the organization's challenges and that relevant parts of the organization would support participants in collaborating across functions and regions. The evaluation enabled the organization to discover where leadership development was the right tactic and where the necessary support was not occurring. For the first case, the evaluation questioned the existence of the context and inputs that were implicitly assumed to be in place, and that were required in order to ensure success.

A second lesson is that, because strategic evaluation is focused on the strategy, attention is drawn away from the initiative as the object of interest. A focus on strategy translates to a focus on deep, systemwide, long-term outcomes. If, in the case of the health care organization, the Leadership Academy were created as a rite of passage for those entering a certain organizational level (rather than created to address a strategic need), the relevant evaluation question would be, Does the program have what it needs to be effective? By taking a strategic focus, the evaluation question is, Does the program have what it needs to be effective in supporting the organization in addressing its business needs? The answers to these two questions can be very different.

These cases also illustrate that strategic evaluation (and evaluative thinking) can be used on the front end to help the organization focus on what success looks like at the strategic outcome level. In other words, by encouraging stakeholders to think about what strategic outcomes will result from the leadership developing initiatives, strategic evaluation actually helps them to develop and implement precisely the intervention that will produce those outcomes. Hence, the stakeholders link the intervention to the strategy.

Strategic Evaluation's Best Practices

In order to enable strategic use of evaluation, there are five practices that are critical.

Integrate Evaluation at the Start

For best results, evaluation should be integrated into the design of a leadership development initiative. Ideally, the What outcomes do we need to achieve? question would be part of the first conversations about leadership development. Most important, these first conversations should occur not only with those at the operational level (who implement the program), but also those at the strategic level (who make high-level decisions about its future).

At the Center for Creative Leadership, clients routinely learn about its evaluation practice as they are learning about its other practices (needs assessment, design, and delivery). During the needs assessment process, clients focus on the questions their key stakeholders will ask once the initiative has been delivered. They identify the critical evaluation questions, the type of data most likely to answer the evaluation questions in a manner that satisfies the appropriate stakeholders, and the timing when the questions will be answered. For example, the critical evaluation question might be, How are the action-learning leadership projects contributing to the strategic goal of creating a more innovative culture in the organization? The type of data preferred might be evidence documenting the recommendations of the project, subsequent action by the organization on those recommendations, and outcomes of the action. The data may be collected one and two years after the intervention is completed in order to best capture changes in the organization's culture. The data gleaned from this needs assessment process are used to design the intervention itself in a way that will create the outcomes desired in addition to providing the information needed to design an appropriate evaluation.

We feel strongly about this practice because we have witnessed the outcome when evaluation is discussed after the initiative has been delivered. The worst case scenario occurs when, after an initiative is complete, its stakeholders request evidence of its impact and the impact discovered is not in the realm of what is expected, or different stakeholders discover that they had different expectations for the outcomes. Why does this happen? Precisely because the stakeholders' potential evaluative questions were not identified during the needs assessment phase and, therefore, the initiative was not designed in a way to lead to those outcomes. Even though the initiative was of high quality and deemed to be of value by the participants and the client organization's representatives, it was not designed to lead to the strategic outcomes expected by the stakeholders. If this happens, regardless of the quality of the initiative, it will be deemed a failure.

Develop and Use Strategic Evaluation Questions

The second important practice is to devise a set of overarching evaluation questions, based on conversations with stakeholders, that are fundamentally strategic in nature. They should address big-picture issues and should include strategic concepts, macro-level contextual issues, and a question about the overall value of the intervention.

Repeatedly, during the course of an evaluation, the evaluator is likely to be pulled in many different directions. There is a danger of getting lost in the details that are of interest to those on the operational side. Although it's important to provide such details if they are within the scope of the evaluation, it is also important to bear in mind the information needs of those who will make strategic (rather than operational) decisions about the program. Keep your eye on the big picture by frequently referring back to the overarching questions and asking yourself (and key stakeholders) what else you need to know in order to provide a robust answer.

We do not mean to imply that an evaluation cannot be both operational and strategic in nature. Rather, we are asserting that an appropriate amount of time and resources must be focused on the strategic aspects of an evaluation in addition to the operational components. It is easy to get caught up in the demands of day-to-day operational issues to the detriment of the strategic issues, yet the full power of an evaluation is not solely whether a particular intervention worked but also to what extent it worked and why. The answers to the latter questions provide direction for future development and organizational intervention.

Test Assumptions That Underlie the Strategy

All strategic interventions are infused with a number of inherent underlying assumptions, which must be tested if the evaluation is to be maximally useful to stakeholders (Rumelt, 1980). A logic model can be a useful tool for unearthing these underlying assumptions, and methodologies from theory-based evaluation can be useful for testing the theory of strategic change (see Chapter Two for more on theories of change). In particular, the most important cause-and-effect relationships should be critically evaluated and tested against reality to ensure that they are indeed operating in that way. In many cases, this testing illuminates alternate causal paths by which the strategy is achieving (or not achieving) both intended and unintended outcomes. (See Chapters One and Three, which offer two different approaches to thinking about causal paths.) It is also important in a strategic evaluation to check any assumed inputs that would be required for the strategy to be effective. In many cases there will be assumptions about resources, capabilities, aspects of organizational culture, and the nature of the organization's environment (or competitor capabilities). For example, in the case regarding the evaluation of the leadership development initiative in governmental agencies, the three assumed inputs identified were organizational cultures that were supportive of leadership development, a diverse pool of talent coming into entry-level positions, and the existence of untapped leadership potential within the current staff.

Employ Evaluation Expertise, Not Just Content Expertise

Strategic evaluations may be conducted by internal staff; an external contractor; or an evaluation facilitator or coach working with managers, internal staff, and community members, or any combination of these. (See Rose and Davidson, 2003, for a detailed discussion of the pros and cons regarding who designs and conducts the evaluation.) Regardless of who is doing the evaluation, it is critically important to ensure that the team has the right evaluation expertise to be able to design and conduct a good strategic evaluation.

Time and again we have heard regretful stories from clients who outsourced the evaluation task and hired absolutely the wrong person for the job. In 99 percent of such cases, the organization made the error of hiring a content expert with research skills rather than a trained evaluator. There was usually an assumption made that the individual clearly understood what was needed, and it was not until the final report was submitted that the client realized this was not the case.

Clearly, the situation described has as much to do with managing the evaluator-client relationship as it does with knowing the skills of the evaluator. But even in cases where the relationship has been managed carefully, clients we have spoken to still express disappointment with the evaluation they received. The fundamental problem (according to these clients) seems to be that content specialists without evaluation expertise tend to approach the work as research (testing hypotheses) rather than evaluation (finding out if the initiative is appropriately meeting the organization's needs). Situations like the one described highlight the very real benefits of involving organizational members in the evaluation process. They are in a unique position to ensure that the evaluation stays relevant to decision-making timelines and information needs. One challenge is that those who can be released from other work to be involved in the evaluation process are not necessarily those involved in strategic decision making. Therefore, it is important to create a mechanism that keeps the evaluation team in close contact with senior management as well as with operational staff.

In some cases, it may not be possible to involve organizational members in the evaluation process. For example, in the first leadership development evaluation case described, the government's cabinet had required that an independent evaluation of the strategy be carried out. This precluded any heavy involvement of internal people in the design of the evaluation. However, in this case, their input was sought and incorporated, particularly with respect to utilization issues (What were the main questions that needed answering for particular stakeholders? and, What kind of evidence would be particularly persuasive to those audiences?). Just because a particular evaluation is independent doesn't mean that it is somehow disconnected from the client. For strategic evaluation, it is essential that the evaluator gains a clear understanding of the information needs at the strategic level, and this can only be done effectively if there is good communication with key decision makers from the outset.

Whether a strategic evaluation is conducted by an internal, external, or a combined evaluation team, our experience highlights three essential capabilities: identifying the overarching evaluation questions, having a systematic evaluation framework for translating those questions into an evaluation plan, and being able to pull all the data together to speak to the original questions.

For this reason, we recommend that strategic evaluations be designed and led by a trained evaluator rather than a content expert with measurement or research expertise. Of course, it would be ideal to have an evaluator who also has content and research expertise, but in the real world it is often difficult to find such a person. In some cases, it is sufficient to have someone with relevant experience in this domain (or familiarity with it) rather than content expertise gained from formal education or training. The next best thing is to hire an evaluation team on which content experts are included. But if neither of these is available, the smart move is to hire a good evaluator and put them in touch with internal staff who have excellent content expertise.

Employ Methodological Rigor

Because there are often high stakes involved with projects being evaluated, it is dangerous to design the evaluation in a way that leads to fallible results. Four practices will help you maintain methodological rigor.

Gather Data from Different Perspectives. The strongest evaluations are those designed and implemented in such a way that their results cannot be called into question. Therefore, evaluations are strongest when they look not only at the outcomes of the initiative but also at the causal link between the intervention and those outcomes. With leadership development, the program itself is one of the independent factors that contributes to changes in the leader and her organization. But you cannot assume this to be the case. Participants and observers must be specifically asked about the relationship between the initiative (and its specific components) and the outcomes achieved. The evaluation must also examine other factors that may either lead to or provide a barrier to a particular outcome occurring. For example, in the second case described in the chapter, surveys, interviews, and workplace statistics (that is, examination of data collected by the client organization as part of their normal business practice) are designed in a way that short-term, midterm, and long-term outcomes are identified by both participants and others within the organization. In addition, these groups are asked to indicate the degree of support for development provided to participants by the organization. It is clear that the actions by organizational members and culture of the organization have an effect on the success of leadership development. Thus, it is important to examine the extent to which participants have had opportunities to receive feedback from their managers, peers, and direct reports after participating in leadership development in a way that makes them aware of whether the changes they are making are effective. Participants are also asked whether they have been given the time and space to try out new leadership practices, recognizing that trying anything new is often slower, less effective, less productive, and more likely to result in failure than is doing things the same way as in the past. An evaluation that points to the multiple factors that support or hinder the effectiveness of leadership development has a stronger methodological rigor than those that only point to the outcomes of the intervention.

Use Multi-Method and Triangulation Approaches. Related to the use of multiple strategies to infer causation is the practice of using multiple methods to evaluate a program. Rather than designing an evaluation that collects data via one approach only at one point from one perspective (a survey of participants two months after a program has been completed, for example), a multimethod approach results in data being collected through the use of multiple data collection strategies, from multiple audiences, at multiple points in time.

The evaluation for the Leadership Academy made use of surveys, observational techniques, interviews, focus groups, 360-degree assessment instruments, and document analysis. It gathered data from participants, the program's sponsors, the client organization's executive team, the coaches for the action-learning leadership projects, and participants' managers, peers, and direct reports. Data were collected before, during, and after the initiative. In fact, there are seven data collection points during the course of the fifteen-month initiative and at three additional points (three, six, and eighteen months after its completion).

The use of multi-method approaches for leadership development is critical because it is a complex form of development that often comprises many different elements, from training programs to assessment against competency profiles, individual development plans, manager support, and mentoring. Different stakeholder groups will see outcomes at different points in time, based on the character of the work relationship between participants and stakeholders. And they may place different levels of value or meaning on those outcomes. For example, if a leader is focusing her leadership development strategies on collaborating with peers in other units, groups, or departments, her peers will recognize changes in her collaborative efforts more quickly than may her manager and direct reports. Depending on the nature of the collaboration, some peers may evaluate it as more valuable than do others because the work in question may be of varying degrees of importance to the peers and their own organizational goals. Participants are able to identify changes they've made in their leadership practices more quickly than are their managers, peers, and direct reports. The specific types of outcomes are also then perceived differently by participants' workgroups.

Use Control or Comparison Groups Where Possible. Another form of methodological rigor is the use of control groups. Control groups are discussed in detail in Chapter One, so we provide only a brief highlight here as it relates to strategic evaluation. In our experience, control groups are difficult (although not impossible) to implement. Organizations make huge investments to provide leadership development to their employees. Effective leadership development takes the employee away from his or her work for days, if not weeks, over sometimes very long spans of time. (We do not assume that leadership development takes the form of face-to-face training programs only. Leadership development efforts may take other forms such as work-based projects and coaching. To be developmental, a nonprogrammatic effort must be different from normal work in some way. These efforts necessarily draw attention away from normal work.)

Due to the direct and indirect costs of taking employees out of their jobs for leadership development, it is the rare organization that sponsors a control group participating in some other form of activity that removed employees from their work for so many days without the intent of some form of improved outcome. It is often the case that the best design and selection methodologies for a leadership development initiative work in opposition to the appropriate use of control groups. The needs of the organization trump the need to create a powerful evaluation model, so control groups are often not a realistic methodology to use, however rigorous.

Additional Methods for Strategic Evaluation. There are many more methods apart from those suggested above that can be used to infer causation, even with qualitative or mixed method data. In fact, eight different strategies have been outlined that can be used for this purpose (Davidson, 2004).

1. Ask those who have directly observed or experienced the causal effect.
2. Check whether the content of the evaluand (that is, the program, strategy, or other object of evaluation) matches the content of the outcome.
3. Use the *modus operandi* method (Scriven, 1974) to check for telltale patterns that suggest one cause or another.
4. Check whether the timing of the outcome makes sense relative to the cause.
5. Check whether the "dose" is related logically to the "response" (that is, whether the magnitude of the outcome increases with the duration or intensity of the intervention received).
6. Make comparisons with a control or comparison group.
7. Control statistically for extraneous variables.
8. Identify and check the underlying causal mechanism(s).

The recommendation is to use at least two of these and preferably three, depending on the level of certainty required.

Challenges for Strategic Evaluation

As powerful as strategic evaluation is to an organization implementing leadership development, there are forces that act against its effective use. These include the traditional use of leadership development, the time that passes between strategic outcomes and development programs, a focus on financial results, costs, feasibility, and a lack of understanding about evaluation.

Traditional Use of Leadership Development

One of the most frequent nonstrategic uses of leadership development is as a perk or a reward for an individual who has entered a certain level of hierarchy in the organization. Some organizations provide a specific leadership development opportunity to all new managers, for example. In other organizations senior leaders use these programs and courses as a way to complete their leadership development responsibilities. However, participants attend the program without first discussing with their managers expectations for the application of newly developed skills or perspectives. Thus, the program simply becomes an isolated event for participants, however powerful it is to them as individuals. Such uses of leadership development make it impossible to utilize evaluation strategically since the initiative is not strategic in nature.

Time Delays Between Leadership Development and the Emergence of Strategic Outcomes

Another challenge to strategic evaluation occurs when leadership development occurs months or years before strategic outcomes are expected to appear (see also Chapter One). By its nature, leadership development's most direct beneficiaries are the individual leaders who participate in any given development opportunity. Often, however, the outcomes of greatest interest to the organization are those that address the organization's business and/or strategic needs. This makes it all the more important to use strategic intervention logic to identify the causal chain from intervention to strategic outcome. The extent to which any of its early outcomes can be considered strategic depends directly on the extent to which they can be shown to lead to long-term strategic outcomes. This, in turn, depends on the design of the opportunity and the soundness of the logic model or change theory that drives it (see also Chapter Two).

Focus on Financial Outcomes by Some Sectors

One of the questions often asked by stakeholders regarding the impact of leadership development is, What is the return on investment (ROI) of this initiative? Viewed as solely a financial indicator of impact, the answer is limiting (see Chapter Five for a full description of a methodology for evaluating development initiatives in this way, which includes but is not limited to financial indicators). When a leadership development initiative can be demonstrated to have a substantial positive financial impact on the organization, stakeholders are often assured that their investment has paid off. However, financial payback represents only one outcome of a leadership development initiative, and it is possible that this may not be a strategic outcome (in fact, it may actually act in opposition to a strategic outcome, as some outcomes may cost more in the short run but have payoff of different types later on). When all evaluative efforts are placed on financial outcomes rather than the achievement of strategic goals, such as increased diversity in senior levels, successful merger of two previously independent organizations, increased bench strength at specific levels of the organization, or decreased time to market for products launched, the question of Development for what? is not answered. Rarely can leadership development interventions be shown to be wise financial investments in purely dollar terms. It is not always possible, nor recommended, to seek financial outcomes from leadership development initiatives (see Kramer and Schein, 2005). Rather, financial outcomes should be evaluated only if they are the indicators that strategic outcomes have been met through the leadership development initiative. In which case, the ROI is part of a larger strategic evaluation.

Costs

Evaluation of any form requires an investment of time and other resources. Probably the largest single source of cost is in the time of the evaluator and the time required by participants, other observers, and key stakeholders to provide data of different forms to the evaluation. The rule of thumb in the field of evaluation is that an evaluation should be funded at approximately 10 percent of the other costs of the initiative. Thus, sponsors of a leadership development initiative with total direct costs of $250,000 should add an additional $25,000 to cover the direct costs of an evaluation. Of course, the actual range of costs for a strategic evaluation may be somewhat higher, based on the complexity and comprehensiveness of the evaluation design. Typical direct costs for an evaluation include the evaluator's fee, any survey or data collection instrument costs, travel, administrative costs related to the evaluation, supplies, and any overhead fees required. Even using an internal evaluator (which can help decrease the direct costs of any particular evaluation) requires the investment of resources to cover the evaluator's salary as well as the other activities listed.

These costs often cause program sponsors to exclude evaluation from the scope of an initiative (of course, in some cases, evaluation is required by government or foundation funders), but doing so prevents key stakeholders from systematically learning about the outcomes, their causes, and their value to the organization. The program may have been quite valuable in producing strategically relevant outcomes, but the sponsors do not know how to replicate the outcomes in future initiatives and do not have the data they need to illustrate the strategic value of the initiative to their own stakeholders. Conversely, funds could be being poured into a program that does not work. In such cases, by not investing in evaluation, the organization loses more significant resources. Using the previous example, the organization saves $25,000 by not including evaluation, but risks losing $250,000 by investing in a program that may not deliver the results it needs.

A related issue is that leadership development, like other organizational initiatives, can come under criticism from political opponents (within the organization, in government, or from shareholders or taxpayers). Without sound evaluative evidence in hand, leaders are unable to respond convincingly to such criticisms. This may put even the most effective leadership development initiative in jeopardy, risking a major loss to the organization when it is scaled down or discontinued.

Thus it is important that sponsors recognize the importance of strategic evaluation in leading to and illustrating the outcomes they need to produce in a way that enables them to learn and integrate those learnings into future initiatives.

Feasibility

Another challenge to strategic evaluation is feasibility. Rarely does the most valuable evaluation data magically make itself available to program stakeholders. Rather, it requires that the evaluator have access to the people, the documents, and databases where evaluative information resides. Furthermore, it requires that those who own the data have, and are willing to give, the time necessary to share and explain it.

Feasibility also relates to the question of whether the context is one that will produce accurate and actionable data. If, for example, the culture of the organization is such that participants and their observers are hesitant to be fully honest about their perspectives related to the outcomes of the program and the value of those outcomes, the evaluation will not produce valuable data if it relies solely on the views of those individuals. Thus, a valid evaluation in this situation would not be feasible unless there were other sources of data available that would allow independent verification of the initiative's effectiveness. Before initiating a strategic evaluation, evaluators and other sponsors for the leadership development initiative should determine the extent to which a strategic evaluation is feasible. It is better to not initiate such an evaluation than to waste time and money conducting an evaluation that is not capable of uncovering the necessary data.

Lack of Evaluation Understanding

Finally, another challenge for strategic evaluation is the failure to adequately understand evaluation and the role and skills of an evaluator. This most frequently results in program sponsors contracting the services of an available professional who is able to create, implement, and analyze surveys, interviews, and other forms of data collection using a semi-accurate set of evaluation questions. Too often, however, the work that is developed and carried out in this scenario is not evaluation but is a series of interesting (and yet not very valuable) questions asked about or with regard to the program. In the end, the program's sponsors will not have the data they need to make decisions about the program.

Future Directions for Strategic Evaluation

As the field of evaluation matures, so does strategic evaluation. The successes and failures of evaluators responsible for strategic evaluation are a rich source of ideas for new directions in which strategic evaluation specialists should focus in the future.

New Methodologies for Strategic Evaluation

As the strategic outcomes associated with leadership development become increasingly more complex, and the stakes associated with leadership development become greater, strategic evaluation practices need to advance similarly.

We believe there are a number of advances that can be made in developing methodologies for strategic evaluation.

One obvious area for methodology development is in making better causal links between strategic interventions and distal strategic outcomes. This is particularly important for some of the methodologies currently being used in business organizations that have been developed without reference to current knowledge in evaluation. For example, linkage research, which has its roots in marketing research and industrial-organizational psychology, uses a narrow form of intervention logic to track the supposed chain of impact from the intervention (if any) through employee satisfaction to customer satisfaction and the bottom line (Allen and Wilburn, 2002). The methods used to link the variables in the chain are often little more than correlational analyses. Clearly there is a need to make these links more robust by probing causal (not just correlational) links. Good strategic evaluation uses more sophisticated methods, but still has significant room for development. The eight causal inference strategies outlined earlier (Davidson, 2004) are useful in this regard. In addition, the fields of research methodology and philosophy have insights to offer in terms of the thinking behind establishing a logical argument for causation.

Evaluators need to have in their toolkits a variety of methods that enable the collection of data beyond the self-report and in addition to lagging indicators. For example, if two indicators of success in the health care case described earlier were a participant's report of increased collaboration across boundaries (self-report) and the subsequent decrease in costs associated with that collaboration (lagging indicator), what might strategic evaluation be able to contribute to the stakeholders' knowledge base if there were some way to objectively identify the collaboration taking place before a decision is made that results in reduced costs to the organization? For example, it would be possible to predict the direct organizational-level impact of the implementation of a new call center system on organizational revenues, based on an organization's current data and data provided by a vendor providing a call center system. However, for complex initiatives such as leadership development, it is not always possible to accurately predict (that is, create a leading indicator of) organizational-level outcomes due to the emergent nature of the outcomes of leadership development—the development that occurs in such an initiative forms each participant's action plans toward supporting the organization's strategic priorities. The results of an individual's actions may not be truly known for months (or longer). Strategic evaluation should be able to provide

predictive data to an organization regarding likely outcomes and their organizational value (financial or otherwise) as soon as possible so that the organization can take any necessary steps to support participants in creating their
anticipated outcomes.

Educating Clients About Strategic Evaluation

The difference between strategic and operational evaluation can confuse evaluators as well as clients. One of the key contributions that strategic evaluators
can make to the practice is in helping client organizations understand the difference and the relationship between strategic and operational evaluation.
That enables stakeholders to identify the key evaluation type required for each
situation, saving time, lowering costs, and decreasing the frustrations that may
arise when confusion exists.

One powerful step in clarifying the difference would be for evaluators who
practice strategic evaluation to come together (literally or figuratively) as a
community of practice to create common definitions, tools, and resources,
much as they have done in the past when creating other important evaluation-
related distinctions (for example, quantitative and qualitative evaluation, external and internal evaluation, objective and participative evaluation). There
is a wealth of knowledge that already exists and that remains to be discovered
that can help both evaluators and clients alike understand and manage the
differences (and similarities) in strategic and operational evaluation.

Building Better Theories of Change for Strategic Interventions

Good theories of change are powerful tools (as demonstrated in Chapter Two).
They can be used in the strategy development stage to identify underlying assumptions and check whether the strategy is both logical and consistent with
current knowledge and research. They can also be used to identify early outcomes that can be assessed to determine whether the strategy is on track for
success.

If strategic evaluations are conducted using intervention logic as a framework, this has the potential to not only add to our knowledge of what works
in strategic change, but also to help us learn how things work and why things
fail. The theory-based evaluation literature has much to contribute here.

A second source of potential synergy is between strategic evaluation and the application of systems approaches to evaluation (Williams and Imam, forthcoming). Because strategic interventions are by definition large scale and long term, it is extremely likely that their pattern of effects (and interactions with other influences and interventions) will exhibit some of the characteristics of systems (see Chapter Three). The very interesting work being done in this area has great potential to contribute not only to building better theories of change for strategic interventions but also for providing new perspectives on evaluating complex strategic interventions.

Conclusion

As we reflect on the themes and examples in this chapter, two key themes emerge. The first is the overwhelming importance of utilization as a central value in strategic evaluation. We have emphasized the importance of engaging senior stakeholders early in the process to gain a clear sense of their information needs: who needs to know, what they need to know, within what timeframe, to what level of certainty and detail, at what depth, and in what form. But even beyond this focus on the instrumental use of findings, strategic evaluation also brings with it an emphasis on conceptual use or enlightenment (Patton, 1997; Weiss, 1997). The intent is not simply to inform the improvement of an existing initiative or strategy but also to convey a deeper understanding of what lies beneath the findings. This is where we call for evaluators to question the assumptions inherent in the strategy (explicit or implicit) and to investigate the most important causal links between the initiative and long-term outcomes. This is the depth of understanding that truly allows clients to formulate better strategy and design more effective initiatives. These future-oriented needs are just as important as finding out how effective the current strategic initiative has been.

The second theme that strikes us is the reciprocal and synergistic nature of the relationship between strategy and strategic evaluation. It seems clear to us that strategy can be better formulated and operationalized if it is coupled with some high-quality evaluative thinking. Strategic evaluation will be able to add more value in situations where strategic outcome chains have been built into strategic initiatives right from the start. A valuable strategic evaluation is one that provides useful insights that inform both the streamlining of current strategy and the formulation of more enlightened strategy in the future.

Strategic evaluation, as it has been articulated here, may be a relatively new concept; however, it is one that we see as having great potential. The discipline of evaluation is continuously moving forward with the development of new and interesting approaches and methodologies, and strategic evaluation can both benefit from this and contribute to the mix.

Resources

Davidson, E. J. *Evaluation Methodology Basics: The Nuts and Bolts of Sound Evaluation.* Thousand Oaks, Calif.: Sage, 2004.

The Kellogg Report on Logic Models, 2004. [www.wkkf.org/Pubs/Tools/Evaluation/Pub3669.pdf].

Kramer, R. L., & Schein, L. *The Business Value of Leadership Development.* New York: The Conference Board, 2005.

Martineau, J. W. "Laying the Groundwork for the Evaluation of Leadership Development." *Leadership in Action,* 2003, *23*(6), 3–8.

Rose, D. S., Davidson, J., Carsten, J., and Martineau, J. "Strategic Evaluation: A New Perspective on the Value of I-O Programs." *Industrial-Organizational Psychologist,* 2001, *38*(4), 41–47.

References

Allen, D. R., and Wilburn, M. *Linking Customer and Employee Satisfaction to the Bottom Line.* Milwaukee, Wisc.: American Society for Quality Control, 2002.

Campbell, D. T. "Reforms as Experiments." *American Psychologist,* 1969, *24,* 409–429.

Casswell, S., Ruenanga, W., and Paekaka, H. "Community Capacity Building and Social Policy—What Can Be Achieved." *Social Policy Journal of New Zealand,* 2001, 22–35.

Chan, S. "The Importance of Strategy for the Evolving Field of Radiology." *Radiology,* 2002, (224), 639–648.

Davidson, E. J. *Evaluation Methodology Basics: The Nuts and Bolts of Sound Evaluation.* Thousand Oaks, Calif.: Sage, 2004.

de Geus, A. P. *The Living Company.* Boston: Harvard Business School Press, 1997.

Kaplan, R. S., and Norton, D. P. *Translating Strategy into Action: The Balanced Scorecard.* Boston: Harvard Business School Press, 1996.

Kramer, R. L., and Schein, L. *The Business Value of Leadership Development.* New York: The Conference Board, 2005.

Patton, M. Q. *Utilization-Focused Evaluation* (3rd ed.). Thousand Oaks, Calif.: Sage, 1997.

Rose, D. S., and Davidson, E. J. "Introduction to Program Evaluation." In J. E. Edwards, J. C. Scott, and N. S. Raju (eds.), *The Human Resources Program Evaluation Handbook.* Thousand Oaks, Calif.: Sage, 2003.

Rumelt, R. P. "Evaluating Business Strategy." In R. A. Burgelman, M. A. Maidique, and S. C. Wheelwright (eds.), *Strategic Management of Technology and Innovation* (3rd ed.). New York: McGraw-Hill, 1980.

Scriven, M. "Maximizing the Power of Causal Investigations: The Modus Operandi Method." In W. J. Popham (ed.), *Evaluation in Education: Current Applications* (pp. 68–84). Berkeley: McCutchan, 1974.

Silbert, J. H., Randolph, L., and Salmon, L. "Positive Transformation of Government." *AIPractitioner,* 2006. [www.aipractitioner.com/].

Tichy, N. M. *Managing Strategic Change: Technical, Political, and Cultural Dynamics.* Hoboken, N.J.: Wiley, 1993.

Waight, C. L. "HRD Involvement in the Investigative Phase of a Merger and Acquisition." *International Journal of Training and Development,* 2004, *8*(2), 157–169.

Weiss, C. H. *Evaluation* (2nd ed.). Upper Saddle River, N.J.: Prentice Hall, 1997.

Williams, B., and Imam, I. (eds.). *Using Systems Concepts in Evaluation.* American Evaluation Association monograph series, forthcoming.

CHAPTER SIXTEEN

EVALUATION FOR PLANNING AND IMPROVING LEADERSHIP DEVELOPMENT PROGRAMS

A Framework Based on the Baldrige Education Criteria for Performance Excellence

Karl E. Umble

This chapter discusses how evaluation during the planning and implementation phases of leadership development programs can improve program quality and outcomes.

First, it defines evaluation as the systematic collection and use of information to improve decisions. Second, it argues that such a mind-set should be promoted by a program's leadership. Third, it reinforces the idea expressed elsewhere in this book that evaluation activities should begin long before the program itself ever begins and can contribute valuable information to planning and goal setting.

Fourth, after a program starts, a disciplined process of continuous evaluation should help the staff make steady improvements and align the program with the goals of its key stakeholders. Fifth, evaluation should enable stakeholders to examine the program's results so that they can assess a program's merit and worth.

And finally, this chapter presents the Baldrige Education Criteria for Performance Excellence (Baldrige National Quality Program, 2006) as a framework based on these principles that can be very useful for evaluators. It briefly describes the Baldrige framework as a source of guidance for evaluation. Then it describes two programs organized by the North Carolina Institute for Public Health that have used some of the approaches to evaluation recommended by the Baldrige framework. Third, it briefly describes each category of the Baldrige framework, and shows how elements of the framework have been used to evaluate the example programs. Although the examples are from public health leadership development, the framework is applicable to any sector, organization, or program.

The Baldrige Education Criteria for Performance Excellence

The Baldrige framework (see Figure 16.1) emerges from organizational practices known as Total Quality Management (Evans and Dean, 2002) and performance improvement (Rummler and Brache, 1995; Swanson, 1999). Originally developed for business, the Baldrige framework has now been adapted for health care and education.

Baldrige recommends that organizations (or, for our purposes, leadership development programs) continuously evaluate and improve in several categories that contribute to overall program performance. The framework is focused on improving entire organizations, but nearly all aspects of the framework are also applicable to specific educational programs.

These categories include visionary and performance-oriented leadership; strategic planning; focus on students, stakeholders, and markets; focus on faculty and staff; and process management. The framework recommends that programs systematically measure and seek to improve specified requirements in each of these categories, such as the way the staff conducts market research or determines student and stakeholder expectations (under Student, Stakeholder, and Market Focus), or the way that they collect and use data about partners, competitors, and trends in the marketplace (under Strategic Planning).

The framework also recommends that programs specify their goals and objectives and systematically measure and improve their annual performance in reaching them. This approach is captured in the framework's reference to Measurement, Analysis, and Knowledge Management. A program's overall performance (Organizational Performance Results) includes its trends in improving its processes and outcomes.

The function of such evaluation models is to point out things that evaluators should pay attention to. The Baldrige framework is very useful because

FIGURE 16.1. BALDRIGE EDUCATION CRITERIA FOR PERFORMANCE EXCELLENCE FRAMEWORK.

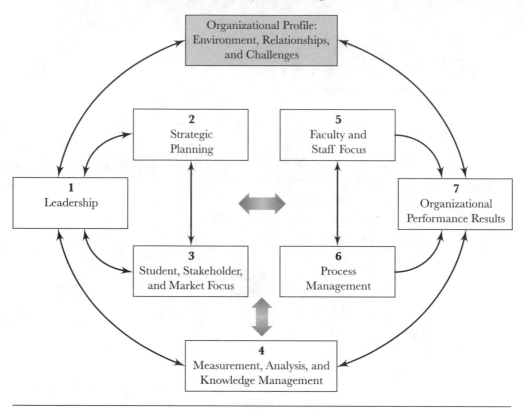

Baldrige Education Criteria for Performance Excellence Framework: A Systems Perspective

Source: U.S. Department of Commerce. National Institute of Standards and Technology, Baldrige National Quality Program.

it displays in one picture many factors that determine the results of educational programs, and because it offers guidance on how to measure and improve each factor over time. While many evaluators are familiar with the terms *needs assessment* and *process and outcome evaluation,* fewer evaluators think about (1) examining each of the Baldrige process areas, which are quite broad and linked to all stakeholders' interests and needs; and (2) measuring and tracking trends in a program's processes and results over time. The Baldrige framework is particularly useful because it is oriented toward progressively improving a program's performance in meeting stakeholder needs, and because it emphasizes achieving a program's intended results over time.

The framework is most useful for program managers and internal evaluators who are responsible for program improvement rather than for external evaluators who may be responsible only for measuring ultimate results.

To demonstrate how the Baldrige Criteria might help leadership development programs, this chapter describes how evaluators and staff at the North Carolina Institute for Public Health (NCIPH) have used elements of Baldrige to evaluate leadership development programs. While NCIPH has never used the entire Baldrige framework with a single program, as that would be very time consuming, it has used many aspects and parts of the framework.

The Two Programs Profiled

National Public Health Leadership Institute Program

The first example is the National Public Health Leadership Institute (PHLI), which is run by a partnership between the NCIPH, the University of North Carolina's (UNC) Kenan-Flagler Business School, and the Center for Creative Leadership (CCL). The program is sponsored by the Centers for Disease Control and Prevention (CDC). The one-year program (see Figure 16.2) enrolls teams of senior public health leaders and is focused on developing collaborative leadership skills through a major team action-learning project (Marquardt, 1999; Raelin, 2000; Umble and others, 2005). In 2003, PHLI began enrolling 5–10 individual scholars each year, due to market research suggesting that some senior leaders preferred to enroll as individuals rather than as team members.

PHLI's mission is to strengthen leaders' understanding and skills and to foster long-term collaboration and networks between the scholars and other public health leaders. Learning methods include assessments (multirater and leadership style profiles), feedback and coaching activities, readings, lecture-discussions, case studies, topical telephone conference calls with experts, and the action-learning project, which serves as a culminating and integrative activity. In Phase 1 (see Figure 16.2), the two-day program launch session, scholars learn to lead teams via a simulation, refine project ideas, and analyze their approach to change and interaction via leadership style assessment tools. Phase 2 involves

FIGURE 16.2. PHLI PROGRAM.

Phase 1: Lunch and Orientation (November)	*Phase 2: Scholar Retreat Preparation*	*Phase 3: Scholar Teams in Residency (May)*	*Phase 4: Retreat Learning*	*Phase 5: Learning Demonstration and Graduation (November)*
Envision the public health future	Distance learning telephone conference calls on significant leadership topics with national faculty	Transformational and adaptive leadership theory and application	Distance learning follow-up telephone conference calls on retreat topics with retreat faculty	Present final leadership project report before peers and faculty
Solve complex interorganizational and strategic problems via simulation	Complete 360-degree and personal assessment tools	Systems thinking to lead innovation and change	Individual leadership development planning	Team awards and diploma presentations
Develop and refine leadership projects	Leadership project work and postlaunch and midterm reports	Negotiation with partners and stakeholders	Leadership project work and postretreat report	Public Health Leadership Society (PHLI alumni association) educational session
Analyze one's approach to change and interaction via assessment tools		Effective communication in crisis situations	Personalized follow-up coaching (optional)	
Individual leadership development planning		Change management		
		Team building		
		Leadership project work		
		Personalized coaching and individual leadership development planning based on 360 assessments		

Source: North Carolina Institute for Public Health, Chapel Hill, N.C.

intensive project fieldwork plus conference calls, reading key texts, and completing individual and multirater assessments. Phase 3, a weeklong on-site program, includes team project work plus seminars and simulations in teamwork, systems thinking and change, negotiation, and communication. Leadership coaches trained by CCL provide in-depth, personalized coaching based on the feedback the scholars have received from the assessments, and scholars form a personal development plan. In Phase 4, scholars continue project work, attend conference calls, and may elect to receive additional coaching. In Phase 5, the final on-site program, scholars present their team's project results, share leadership lessons learned, and graduate. The action-learning project has regular written reporting requirements, and each scholar and team has a project coach who encourages reflection and provides resources.

PHLI accepts 50–56 leaders each year. Its primary audiences include state health officers and their deputies, health directors from populous counties and their direct reports, and leaders in key federal agencies. For example, one team from a large midwestern city included the health directors from the city and from an adjacent county, a senior leader of the city's medical school, and an epidemiology professor. Their project was intended to develop a public health institute to serve the city.

Management Academy for Public Health

The second program profiled in this chapter is the Management Academy for Public Health (MAPH), a national program for public health managers offered by the NCIPH in partnership with the Kenan-Flagler Business School (Orton, Umble, Davis, and Porter, 2002; Porter and others, 2002). This program is structured much like PHLI, but focuses on tactical management of people, finance, and data. In its capstone project, teams produce a business plan. This program is relevant because its curriculum and objectives include aspects of leadership and because it is similar in structure to programs that more exclusively focus on leadership (Baker, Johnson, and Sabol, 2006).

This chapter now describes in more detail how the Baldrige Educational Criteria for Performance Excellence can be used in leadership program evaluation. It presents one or two criterion areas at a time. Many of the Baldrige categories overlap in their concerns, such as Strategic Planning and Market Focus, which both recommend market research. Therefore, many of the examples given below could have been provided under several different categories of the framework.

Establishing an Overall Program Profile and Approach to Leadership: The Role of Evaluation

The Baldrige framework first recommends formulating an overall organizational profile. Leadership development programs should also develop a program profile (see Figure 16.1). A profile includes a specific target audience and a purpose, vision, and mission statement. It also means defining relationships and communication mechanisms with partners and stakeholder groups whose interests must be taken into account in planning and evaluation and defining an approach to using evaluation to improve performance over time.

Baldrige also advocates that program staff establish an approach to program leadership that enables them to communicate and negotiate effectively with partners and stakeholders during planning, evaluation, and implementation; that fosters individual and program learning; that defines and regularly reviews data on target audience coverage, processes, outcomes, and financial measures; and that supports continuous improvement and learning. With these leadership practices, it is much easier to conduct evaluations and to make sure that they are used by the program staff. In short, evaluation activities should be driven and shaped by these leadership practices (Stark, Briggs, and Rowland-Poplawski, 2002).

It is important to define the stakeholders (those influenced by a program, and those who influence it) (Mitroff, 1983) and to keep them involved. This helps staff tap stakeholders' concerns and interests as they manage the program. PHLI includes staff from its partners and sponsor in a monthly task force meeting to discuss and make decisions about curriculum and instruction, target audience selection, specific problems, and evaluation results.

PHLI also has a national advisory committee that includes senior staff from each of the partner organizations as well as from national stakeholder groups, such as the Association of State and Territorial Health Officers and the National Association of City and County Health Officials. This committee meets annually to review evaluation findings, target audience participation figures, the program's overall performance scorecard (described following), and to weigh in on other matters of concern.

Paying close attention to these groups is vital. By listening carefully to their concerns, interests, and ideas, PHLI has learned how to improve and stay in line with their interests and priorities. For example, at one national advisory committee meeting, some stakeholders explained that PHLI was not adequately enrolling enough of the most senior-level officials. In response, PHLI asked the sponsor to more carefully define that audience, which meant identifying target proportions of officials from certain leadership levels for each class. Then, the evaluator led market research that found that most senior officials thought the program should last one year rather than two, accept individuals rather than only teams, and use person-to-person promotions rather than relying on more passive strategies like brochures. PHLI implemented all of these strategies, and target audience enrollment significantly improved. Each year PHLI now examines its incoming class according to the defined targets and reports its progress to the sponsor and to the national advisory committee.

Of course, enrolling individuals has consequences for instructional strategies, which PHLI continues to adjust. For example, PHLI adapted its team-based action-learning strategy to accommodate individual learners. This example points out the systemic nature of change: changes in one program dimension (such as enrollment) have implications for others (such as instructional strategies). It also shows that the mission, vision, and target audience should be established early on, but that these aspects are subject to continuous renegotiation among the stakeholders during the lifespan of a program (Umble, Cervero, and Langone, 2001). By having representatives of important national groups on the national advisory committee, the program fosters a general give-and-take atmosphere among the stakeholders and yet seeks to meet the needs and interests of all.

Partly in response to the issues around target audience, PHLI developed an annual program scorecard that reports progress on enrolling target audiences, learner satisfaction, and learner completion of key portions of the program (see Table 16.1). This scorecard is reported annually to the national advisory committee, which appreciates it as a way to track program performance from year to year. The sponsor helped PHLI to develop the scorecard, which was based on the general concepts of the Balanced Scorecard (Kaplan and Norton, 1996) and performance management (McDavid and Hawthorn, 2006). Scorecards are like program report cards. Programs can use them to regularly keep track of and make public their results on several key aspects of the program over time (Karathanos and Karathanos, 2005). Program sponsors

TABLE 16.1. SCORECARD OF SUCCESS INDICATORS FOR PHLI.

	Goal	Year 10 Actual	Year 11 Actual	Year 12 Actual	Year 13 Actual
Category 1: Applications and Target Audience Enrollment					
1. Total number of applications	125	152	151	81	140
2. Percentage of enrolled units with State Health Officer or Direct Report	35%	23%	35%	31%	62%
3. Percentage of enrolled teams with health director from top 150 most populous metropolitan statistical areas or Direct Report	33%	62%	41%	38%	38%
4. Percentage of enrolled scholars who are members of ethnic minority groups	15%	13%	20%	31%	26%
Category 2: Participation and Completion of the Program					
1. On average, each learner in this class attended what percentage of the pretreat conference calls offered to this class?	75%	37%	42%	74%	73%
2. Percentage of scholars attending launch who are retained in the program (not counting people who withdraw for reasons unrelated to the program such as a work or family emergency)	100%	100%	100%	100%	100%
3. Percentage of teams that turn in a Final Leadership Project Report (that meets program requirements)	95%	80%	71%	100%	98%
4. Percentage of teams that give an oral report on the Leadership Project at conference or via conference call	95%	Not required until Year 12	Not required until Year 12	100%	100%

Category 3: Satisfaction with the Educational Process

1. Percentage of scholars who strongly agree or agree that participating in PHLI met their expectations for improving their leadership practice on the job (at 6-month follow-up)	95%	97%	85%	93%	
2. Percentage of scholars who strongly agree or agree that they would recommend PHLI to colleagues (at 6-month)	95%	100%	92%	100%	
3. Percentage of scholars who strongly agree or agree that PHLI improved their leadership competence (at 6-month)	95%	97%	96%	98%	
4. Percentage of scholars who strongly agree or agree that they intend to apply to their work what they learned in the distance learning conference calls for this year (mean of all calls each year)	95%	88%	88%	94%	

Category 4: Outcomes of the Program

1. From a list of leadership behaviors taught in the program and listed on the 6-month follow-up evaluation form, percentage of those leadership behaviors for which this year's scholars, on average, report statistically significant improvements in the extent to which they practice the behaviors ($p < .05$)	100%	100%	92%	100%	Data not yet collected
2. Percentage of scholars who strongly agree or agree that participating in PHLI improved their leadership practice on the job	95%	97%	100%	96%	Data not yet collected
3. Percentage of team projects in which activities have been implemented during the first year after the team graduated	60%	93%	73%	Data not yet collected	Data not yet collected

Category 5: Dissemination Activities

1. Total number of annual presentations at professional conferences or papers published in peer-reviewed journals and other practice-oriented publications pertaining to the *impact* of PHLI, by UNC staff or scholars (does not count promotional/marketing presentations)	2	0	0	2	2

Source: North Carolina Institute for Public Health, Chapel Hill, N.C.

and other stakeholders find them useful as a quick summary of how a program is performing in key areas like enrollment and graduation, learner satisfaction, and results. Program staff members find scorecards useful as ways to clarify what sponsors and stakeholders want the program to be accountable for. The NCIPH has found scorecards to be useful ways to track and report process variables like enrollment, satisfaction, and learner completion of assigned tasks, but it has been more difficult to develop measurable ways to count outcomes such as leadership learning and effects on organizations because these depend on the learners, teams, and communities' individual goals.

Program Planning: How Evaluation Can Help

The Baldrige framework recommends that organizations and programs regularly conduct strategic planning based on data on such factors as

- Student, stakeholder, and market needs, expectations, and opportunities, and student achievement
- Analysis of the competition
- Availability of technological innovations or other key environmental changes
- Strengths and weaknesses of the program and staff
- Budgetary, societal, and ethical risks
- Changes in the economic environment
- Partners' needs, strengths, and weaknesses

Baldrige also recommends that programs develop measurable action plans based on the strategic plans, and track their progress in implementing the plans.

The NCIPH has used evaluation methods during program planning in several important ways, including conducting needs assessments, using evaluation and needs assessments reported in the literature, benchmarking other quality programs and their evaluation activities, and using logic models and written program goals and objectives. Let's turn now to each of these activities.

Often, quality needs assessments may have already been conducted, and program planners are well served by studying these documents. For the Management Academy for Public Health, the sponsors had already conducted extensive needs assessments and determined that public health staff needed additional training in managing people, data, and money. The staff supplemented these data by conducting focus groups with managers to determine in more detail their typical skill needs. For PHLI, the staff based the curriculum on trends noted in the field of leadership development, such as the need for collaborative leadership, as well as on best practices in leadership development as defined by literature and by organizations recognized as leaders in the field, such as CCL. Program evaluators help conduct these kinds of assessments and determine their implications for program development.

Another important feature of program-planning activities includes preparing logic models and written statements of program goals and objectives (see Chapters Two and Three for methods addressing these needs). These activities can help a large and diverse group of sponsors, stakeholders, and staff members come to some degree of consensus, or at least accommodation, about a program's major goals, objectives, and theory of how it will improve learners' capabilities. The logic models also help program staff plan evaluation activities to perform at each step of the logic model.

Figure 16.3 displays the logic model for the Management Academy for Public Health. This logic model has proven useful in evaluation planning as well as in telling the story of the program. Starting from left to right, the logic model shows important inputs that shape the program and its results, such as participants, resources, faculty, and support for change in participants' organizations. Moving toward the right in the logic model, these inputs shape the initial classroom training methods and content, which in turn shape individuals' knowledge, confidence, skills, and perspectives. After receiving initial training, learners engage in two work-based or back-home learning experiences. The individual development plan is a personal, self-directed learning plan that learners write during the initial session. It includes key personal learning goals they have for the program and activities they will pursue to reach those goals. One learner, for example, decided to become a better financial manager and budget preparer by taking a class at a community college and by asking his supervisor to coach him through the process for budgets in their office.

The second work-based learning process requires each participant team to develop a business plan for a new public health program. The academy supplies learners with books, instructions, many examples, and coaches to help them with this very challenging assignment.

FIGURE 16.3. MAPH PROGRAM AND EVALUATION LOGIC MODEL.

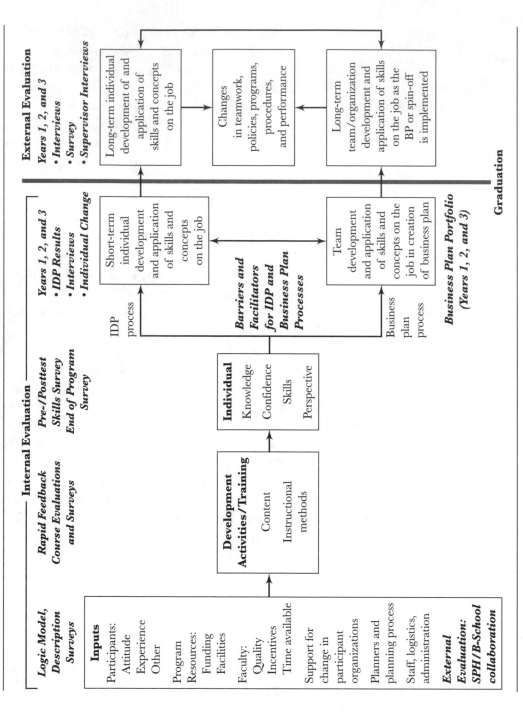

Source: North Carolina Institute for Public Health, Chapel Hill, N.C.

The logic model shows that completion of these learning processes is intended to lead to individual skill development, as well as team development and team application of skills on the job. The vertical arrow shows that the academy believes that individual and team-based learning activities will be synergistic, with the business plan process producing individual skill development and the individual development helping each learner become a more productive team member. After graduation, individuals and teams continue their development, leading, the program believes, to longer term improvements in teamwork, policies, programs, performance, and community impact.

This logic model spells out the academy staff's theory about how the program works, based on theories of training and training effectiveness, on several years of experience with the program, and on evaluation results. The logic model helps the program staff decide how to evaluate the program at each link (from left to right) and what to measure, as captured in the Internal Evaluation and External Evaluation methods shown in the model. The staff evaluates how each process is going and how to improve it. In addition, the staff evaluates dimensions such as learner motivation for enrolling, quality of faculty instruction, knowledge and confidence gains, individual development plan outcomes, application of skills on the job, and business plan quality. These evaluations lead to improvements in program activities, such as better courses and improved coaching for teams.

It is also important to use the logic model and written program objectives in developing the program. Too often, logic models and objectives are forgotten two or three years down the road. If the program's written objectives have been carefully thought through and negotiated with the program's staff and advisory groups, then they should be reflected in the teaching and learning activities. For example, if a program aims to develop collaboration skills and perspectives on shared leadership, learning activities of various kinds that develop them should be visible in curriculum diagrams.

In addition, as a program is modified over the years, the evaluator's job is to make sure that these changes are made in accord with the logic model and objectives, or conversely, that the logic model and objectives keep up with the changing philosophy of the program. If this does not occur, evaluators will not know what outcomes to measure or assess, and sponsors and partners are more likely to disagree on whether the resulting outcomes indicate success or failure or something in between (Wholey, 1994).

At a broader level, the Management Academy has conducted considerable strategic planning about how to sustain itself after its initial four years of demonstration project funding expired. This planning has included developing several models for funding and diffusing the program to other areas of the nation. This has included collecting data on potential partners and on how other executive education programs have organized themselves.

For its part, PHLI was a partnership between the UNC Kenan-Flagler Business School and CCL. The strategic decision to partner with these organizations was based largely on both partners' international reputations in creating customized executive education programs for leaders and managers and on a history of successful collaborations with the business school. Taking the time to carefully scan the environment for such opportunities helped UNC plan a leadership program that is much stronger than anything the School of Public Health could have offered alone.

Maintaining Student, Stakeholder, and Market Focus

The Baldrige framework recommends that educational organizations pay very close attention to meeting the needs of students and stakeholders, just as companies must pay close attention to customers (Cannon, Umble, Steckler, and Shay, 2001). Programs ignore such needs at their peril.

One way that PHLI stays in close contact with learners is by using evaluation forms to obtain student reactions to every major course offered and for each major face-to-face or on-site learning session. These forms ask questions about overall quality and instruction and ask for comments. Some of these forms also ask students to rate their levels of growth in skill or confidence. Evaluators immediately produce reports for the staff and faculty based on these forms and discuss the results in staff meetings within a few weeks after the event. An important evaluator role is to be present at such meetings to be sure that staff understand and use the data. If any major problems are evident, the staff consults with the faculty member to identify possible improvements. PHLI has also discovered that it is valuable for the evaluator, program director, and program assistants to mingle with students during the on-site sessions. Much can be gleaned about the attitudes of the group and their responses to the program and instruction through such informal discussions. The staff often decides that it wants to know more about a certain issue and fans out to ask informally of the learners questions, such as, How do you feel about the level of this course? How could it be made more relevant? These discussions always give staff new insights. Often, written evaluation reports merely amplify and confirm what staff already knows based on these conversations.

Of course, any single program cannot please all of the learners all of the time. When a program receives low evaluation scores from an individual or small group of individuals, the evaluator must help staff and faculty interpret these results in the context of the whole audience so that program alterations are not made inappropriately. Sometimes PHLI has overreacted to the vocal suggestions of a few participants and gotten poorer results the next year because it went too far in making changes or because most learners liked it the way it was.

The NCIPH has also learned that it is very important to gather and present data on what is working well and serving learners' needs, as well as what could be improved. It is tempting for evaluators with critical minds to focus on improvements needed and problems, and to give short attention in their conversations and reports to what is going well. This can irritate instructors and program staff and falsely create a negative impression of a program to stakeholders. It is crucial to be balanced and representative in one's interpretation of evaluation data so that a program can strengthen or keep what is going well and fix what is not. Maintaining an appreciative stance toward a program is the intent of a relatively new approach to evaluation called *appreciative inquiry* (see, for example, Chapter Four).

Measurement, Analysis, and Knowledge Management

This section of the chapter discusses how programs use data about processes and results to foster continuous improvement and innovation in processes and key results. It also refers to how the program or organization manages knowledge assets, such as successful practices, so that staff can learn from one another and rapidly deploy strategies that work well. Baldrige also recommends that programs gather data on best practices and results from similar organizations elsewhere, and compare their results to competitor or comparable organizations when possible.

As described previously, PHLI performs continuous assessment by using a scorecard to document annual results and student satisfaction indicators. The scorecard includes results from a six-month (postprogram) follow-up survey and allows PHLI to annually review student ratings of instructional methods and self-ratings of skill improvements. The Management Academy also uses a scorecard, tracking (among other results) student ratings of courses and coaches, applications and enrollment, learner and team retention, and intention to implement business plans (Orton, 2005).

Both PHLI and Management Academy have done significant benchmarking to identify and adopt successful practices. Two PHLI staffers spent a day at CCL to identify best practices that help PHLI improve its results. As a result, the staff has continued to hold discussions with CCL about how to improve its methods, and they have shared their lessons with other leadership development programs at the NCIPH. PHLI staff members also regularly consult books and journals and participate in leadership and human resource development organizations to gain new ideas.

Maintaining Faculty and Staff Focus

The faculty and staff focus of the Baldrige framework includes how faculty and staff assessments are conducted and how feedback is provided to faculty and staff to promote continuous improvements. It also includes how staff recommendations are collected and incorporated into program improvements.

In PHLI and Management Academy, course evaluation results are tabulated and given to each professor soon after each session. Staff work with faculty to solve any problems, as noted previously.

Immediately after each on-site program, the PHLI staff gathers and has an immediate postprogram debriefing about all aspects of the program. Staff assistants take notes, type them up, and the program director is responsible for implementing decisions taken. A few weeks later, the staff does a review based on the written evaluation reports. Sometimes the staff forms small study or action groups to undertake tasks such as revising a course, developing a case study, or revising an action-learning guide.

The leadership and planning role of the program leader is very important. The leader who supervises the PHLI program director is focused on continuous improvement and insists on having after-action reviews after every major session. In a very positive way, strong leadership keeps staff alert to the necessity of constant data-driven improvement. This is why a program's approach to leadership is so central in Baldrige.

It is also important that faculty and staff be satisfied with their roles in programs. In one distance learning leadership degree program at UNC, the evaluator interviewed each of the program's faculty members about the process. Many were teaching in a distance learning environment for the first time and needed more lead time to redesign their courses, better pay to cover the time needed to do that, and technical help for changing overheads into electronic formats. The evaluator presented these faculty needs to a group of program faculty and staff. Among other changes, the program later invested in a technical assistant to help faculty develop materials.

A faculty member in a different program recently came to the evaluator with a list of concerns about how the evaluation reports were inappropriately negative when in fact the data were much more positive. This faculty member was somewhat distressed because of unnecessarily negative portrayals of his teaching, but more concerned that the value of the program was being downplayed because of a vocal minority of disaffected learners. By carefully listening to this faculty member, the evaluator was able to revise the report to better portray the data to the stakeholders and sponsors and report problems that were pulling evaluation results down. This conversation would never have happened if the evaluator did not have an open and collegial relationship with the faculty and a habit of taking its concerns seriously.

Paying close attention to faculty concerns can directly improve instructional quality (Umble and Dooley, 2004). If the faculty are dissatisfied, they may teach poorly or quit. Learners readily pick up on negative attitudes and may lessen their commitment to learning. If distance education faculty lack technical help, instructional quality may plummet, because faculty hours are limited. In sum, programs should pay close attention to making sure that faculty and coaches are satisfied with their participation in the program, and make adjustments if they are not.

Process Management8

Process management is also a key area in the Baldrige framework. For example, how does the program design, evaluate, and continuously improve its key learning-centered processes, such as seminars, distance learning, action learning, and assessments? How are support processes, such as finance and budgeting, marketing, information and public relations, evaluated and improved over time? And how is knowledge about how key learning processes work best shared with similar programs in the organization?

All leadership development programs have key processes, such as recruitment of learners and marketing, faculty recruitment and development, curriculum and instructional development, distance learning design and delivery, communication, and evaluation. These key processes should run smoothly and effectively and be integrative. For example, marketing must accurately reflect the desired target audience and the nature of the curriculum, or learners may be disappointed. Action learning and coaching should work well and be integrated with the on-site curriculum and instruction and with evaluation methods. The left hand must know what the right hand is doing.

Previous examples have described how PHLI improved its marketing. In another case, PHLI asked its evaluator to determine why few learners were using the online discussion forums that the program offered, while many used the telephone conference calls. The evaluation found that the learners preferred the live human interaction of a call and could put a planned call on their calendars instead of having to remember to log on to a discussion forum. The program decided to use only conference calls for distance learning.

Both PHLI and Management Academy have used interviews, observations of retreats, seminar and program evaluation surveys to continuously evaluate and improve its processes.

Assessing Program Performance Results

The Baldrige framework also advises that it is important to use short-term and long-term program outcomes to continually improve programs. Sometimes evaluators and staff may focus on instructional suggestions from learners to guide improvements, but it is also crucial to examine the results programs are getting.

Having a clear logic model and written objectives is a big help. If a program is designed to improve certain areas of understanding, skill, perspective, confidence, or practice, the evaluation should of course try to measure those achievements over time. PHLI examines improvements in community health services, coalitions, or partnerships by carefully analyzing written action-learning project reports and through follow-up interviews with team leaders.

As previously noted, PHLI has used a six-month follow-up survey to measure students' self-reported learning outcomes and to compare these results from year to year. The evaluation also asks several open-ended questions to get more detail. By combining the qualitative and quantitative data, programs get a picture of highlights of learning and leadership changes for students. In this part of the Baldrige Criteria, it is critical that programs actually compare these results to objectives and ask, Is this what we are trying to achieve, and are we satisfied with this level of change?

In the program's first year, the quality of the Management Academy students' capstone business plan projects was not acceptable to the staff or to the sponsors. Since this assignment aimed to both develop and demonstrate the key skills taught, the staff immediately knew that they had to improve the instruction. The program hired coaches and developed a protocol for how the coaches would help the teams. The program also supplied examples of good projects and put together more detailed guidelines about what they expected learners to produce. Business plans dramatically improved. In Baldrige parlance, the program fixed a learning process to get better results.

As previously discussed, evaluation should be included from the start of program planning. If this occurs, the program knows what it wants to achieve and is designed specifically to achieve its objectives. Short-term and long-term outcome evaluations are then used to examine whether the program is reaching its key objectives, and if not, what might be done to improve the effort.

The program should consider spending considerable resources on measuring results that are most important to the program's sponsor. By being responsive to the sponsor's concerns, the program can help the sponsor assess the program's merit and worth. If a program does not discover early on that its results are below its hopes and expectations—or does not have clear hopes to compare those results to—the program may stagnate and get poor results for many years. This is why investment in performance-oriented evaluation is so important throughout a program's planning and implementation.

Conclusion

The Baldrige Education Criteria for Performance Excellence provides an integrated perspective on how evaluation can be used for program planning and for improving a program's quality over time. Using the framework can help staff define program goals and manage and evaluate the program in relation to them. The framework emphasizes the value of strong leadership, careful planning, student and stakeholder focus, faculty and staff focus, process improvement, and outcome measurement. Further, the framework suggests what is important in each category and indicates ways that staff can use measurement, analysis, and knowledge management to improve each domain and the overall program. Leadership development programs may benefit by using this framework to craft their evaluation strategies.

To be successful in the broad evaluation role described in this chapter, having a solid model like Baldrige is helpful but is not enough. Evaluators must be able to develop trusting relationships with staff, sponsors, and advisory committee members. They must also be able to take initiative to explain and negotiate for a strong role for evaluation in a project, especially if the program's leadership does not understand the need for comprehensive performance-oriented evaluation.

The evaluator also needs courage and mediation skills to fully represent points of view to a program's leadership. Faculty and staff may want more money to be spent on technical help with distance learning or wish that a principal investigator would give them more autonomy in operational decision making. Learners may be unhappy with some aspects of a program. Evaluators need to enter into uncomfortable situations, gain trust, listen carefully to all points of view, and represent them constructively and sometimes strongly and persistently. This can be difficult when the evaluator is part of the organization that offers the program, but to maintain integrity, the evaluator must find ways to faithfully represent the data to the stakeholders who need to hear it.

At the end of the day, evaluators can have a significant role in improving the results of leadership development programs with respect to the points of view of learners and all stakeholders. Doing so takes courage, initiative, persistence, mediation, and technical skills. A comprehensive model like the Baldrige Educational Criteria for Performance Excellence can be a useful guide.

Resources

Baldrige National Quality Program. *Are We Making Progress as Leaders?* Washington, D.C.: National Institute for Technology and Standards, 2005 [www.quality.nist.gov/PDF_files/ProgressAL.pdf]. This quick, handy checklist for leaders and managers can be used to assess their organization's adherence to key aspects of the Baldrige Criteria.

Baldrige National Quality Program. *Education Criteria for Performance Excellence.* Washington, D.C.: National Institute for Technology and Standards, 2006 [www.quality.nist.gov/Education_Criteria.htm]. The comprehensive Baldrige framework as applied to guidelines for evaluators, leaders, and managers who wish to improve the quality of their work.

Karathanos, D., and Karathanos, P. "Applying the Balanced Scorecard to Education." *Journal of Education for Business,* March/April 2005, 222–230. This resource provides concrete suggestions and examples about how to establish a useful set of indicators for an educational program; concepts are adaptable to leadership development institutes.

References

Baker, E. L., Johnson, J. H., and Sabol, B. J. (eds.). "Special Issue: The Management Academy for Public Health." *Journal of Public Health Management and Practice,* 2006, *12*(5).

Baldrige National Quality Program. *Education Criteria for Performance Excellence.* Washington, D.C.: National Institute for Technology and Standards, 2006. [www.quality.nist.gov/Education_Criteria.htm].

Cannon, M., Umble, K. E., Steckler, A., and Shay, S. "'We're Living What We're Learning': Student Perspectives in Distance Learning Degree and Certificate Programs in Public Health." *Journal of Public Health Management and Practice,* 2001, *7*(1), 49–59.

Evans, J., and Dean, J. W. *Total Quality: Management, Organization, and Strategy* (3rd ed.). Mason, Ohio: South-Western, 2002.

Kaplan, R. S., and Norton, D. P. *The Balanced Scorecard: Translating Strategy into Action.* Cambridge, Mass.: Harvard Business School Press, 1996.

Karathanos, D., and Karathanos, P. "Applying the Balanced Scorecard to Education." *Journal of Education for Business,* March/April 2005, pp. 222–230.

Marquardt, M. J. *Action Learning in Action: Transforming Problems and People for World-Class Organizational Learning.* Palo Alto, Calif.: Davies-Black, 1999.

McDavid, J. C., and Hawthorn, L.R.L. *Program Evaluation and Performance Measurement.* Thousand Oaks, Calif.: Sage, 2006.

Mitroff, I. *Stakeholders of the Organizational Mind.* San Francisco: Jossey-Bass, 1983.

Orton, S. "Scorecard: Management Academy for Public Health," 2005. [www.maph.unc.edu/reports/MAPH-Scorecard.pdf].

Orton, S., Umble, K., Davis, M., and Porter, J. "Disasters and Bioterrorism: Does Management Training Develop Readiness?" *Public Health Reports,* 2002, *117*(6), 596–598.

Porter, J., and others. "The Management Academy for Public Health: A New Paradigm for Public Health Management Development." *Journal of Public Health Management and Practice,* 2002, *8*(2), 66–78.

Raelin, J. A. *Work-Based Learning: The New Frontier of Management Development.* Upper Saddle River, N.J.: Prentice Hall, 2000.

Rummler, G. A., and Brache, A. P. *Improving Performance: How to Manage the White Space on the Organization Chart* (2nd ed.). San Francisco: Jossey-Bass, 1995.

Stark, J. S., Briggs, C. L., and Rowland-Poplawski, J. "Curriculum Leadership Roles of Chairpersons in Continuously Planning Departments." *Research in Higher Education,* 2002, *43*(3), 329–356.

Swanson, R. A. "Performance Improvement Theory and Practice." In R. J. Torraco (ed.), *Advances in Developing Human Resources,* Vol. 1. San Francisco: Berrett-Koehler, 1999, pp. 1–24.

Umble, K. E., Cervero, R. M., and Langone, C. "Negotiation about Power, Frames, and Continuing Education: A Case Study in Public Health." *Adult Education Quarterly,* 2001, *51*(2), 128–145.

Umble, K. E., and Dooley, L. "Planning Human Resource Development and Continuing Professional Education Programs That Use Educational Technologies: Voices That Must Be Heard." *Advances in Human Resource Development,* 2004, *6*(1), 86–100.

Umble, K., Steffen, D., Porter, J., Miller, D., Hummer-McLaughlin, K., Lowman, A., and Zelt, S. "The National Public Health Leadership Institute: Evaluation of a Team-Based Approach to Developing Collaborative Public Health Leaders." *American Journal of Public Health,* 2005, *95*(4), 641–644.

Wholey, J. S. "Assessing the Feasibility and Likely Usefulness of Evaluation." In J. S. Wholey and K. E. Newcomer (eds.), *Handbook of Practical Program Evaluation.* San Francisco: Jossey-Bass, 1994.

CHAPTER SEVENTEEN

COMMUNICATION IN EVALUATION

A Systems Approach

Darlene F. Russ-Eft

S everal years ago the vice president of human resources for a large pub-
lishing company asked for an evaluation of a leadership development program that the organization had implemented. The evaluation focused on the
extent to which first-line supervisors used the skills from the program and
what, if anything, might improve the program. In typical fashion, a final report was delivered to the client along with a briefing. As the evaluator, I kept in
touch with the client to aid in some of the implementation issues.

A few weeks after delivering the final report, the vice president suddenly
called me to ask for my advice. When I asked about the circumstances, he said
that a new president and chief executive officer (CEO) had been named and
the new president wanted him to meet him in an hour and describe the leadership development program. The vice president indicated that he thought
that the new president was considering canceling the program. I told him to
have the report available but to address the president's questions and to focus
on the major findings and recommendations from the evaluation.

The vice president called me a couple of hours later to tell me that the
meeting was a success. The president asked several questions and seemed gen-
uinely interested in what had been learned. Furthermore, based on the results,

the CEO had decided that the program needed to continue but with some possible enhancements.

This story reveals some of the critical aspects of effective communication of evaluation results. First, the initial report provided the client with details that addressed his key questions. Second, the evaluator recognized that, to encourage implementation of the recommendations, continued contact with the client was required. Third, because of that contact, rapport and trust had been established between the client and the evaluator. Fourth, because of that rapport, the client felt free to call the evaluator for some needed advice concerning an interpretation of the results to a new stakeholder. Finally, the evaluator and the vice president recognized the importance of addressing the new CEO's questions, rather than simply focusing on the details of the report. These issues of communicating evaluation results represent the focus of this chapter.

Evaluation is defined as the process of determining the merit, worth, or value of something, or the product of that process (Scriven, 1991). But an evaluation itself can only be considered worthwhile or valuable if it is used. To be used, its evaluation process and its findings must be communicated to all key stakeholders in a way that makes sense to them and encourages them to use the processes or the findings.

This chapter discusses the importance of communicating and reporting throughout the entire evaluation process. It begins by discussing the linkage between communication and reporting and evaluation use, as the previous vignette suggests. It then introduces a systems model for evaluation for considering the various factors affecting communication and reporting. It then discusses some communication steps and methods from the perspective of meeting stakeholder groups' unique needs. Finally, it includes the step of creating action plans from the communication of results.

Connecting Evaluation Communication and Evaluation Use

Communication and reporting of the evaluation process and the evaluation findings play a critical role in promoting evaluation use. Indeed, Patton (1997) introduced the notion of utilization-focused evaluation in order to emphasize the critical issue of evaluation use. Furthermore, he identified various types of evaluation use. Instrumental use focuses on judging the merit or worth of the program, improving the program, or generating some knowledge. Process use "enables the evaluators and the evaluation stakeholders and audiences to make use of the logic and process incorporated into the evaluation itself" (Russ-Eft, Atwood, and Egherman, 2002, p. 20).

Within the evaluation literature related to human resource development, some recent studies identify certain factors critical to evaluation use. Mattson (2003) suggests two factors related to the value of the evaluation information: the credibility of the information source and the organizational culture. Using an experimental design with a group of managers in a large financial services organization, he examined the effects of types of reports provided to decision makers on ratings of usefulness for decision-making purposes. Specifically, he compared an anecdotal approach, the critical outcome technique, and a utility analysis. The next paragraphs describe these various approaches as well as the results of the study.

Decision-making literature (for example, Brinkerhoff, 2003; Mintzberg, 1975) tends to support the use of an anecdotal approach. For example, Brinkerhoff introduces the success case method as one that "searches out and surfaces these successes, bringing them to light in persuasive and compelling stories" (p. 3). According to Mattson, such an approach may have "little or no basis in actual organizational data" (2003, p. 134). O'Reilly (1983) found that decision makers tended to use lower-quality information, such as an anecdote or an organizational story, because it was more accessible and easily understood. The anecdotal approach recognizes that managers and leaders use subjectivity in weighing various factors to make decisions.

The critical outcome technique (see, for example, Mattson, 2000; Mattson, Quartana, and Swanson, 1998; Swanson and Mattson, 1997) represents an approach to evaluate "intervention effectiveness in a systematic, post hoc manner" (Mattson, 2003, p. 133), meaning that the effectiveness measures can be determined after the implementation has taken place. Critical outcomes of a leadership development program, for example, are identified at the individual level (for example, improved budgeting skills), at the process level (for example, more efficient sales processes), and at the organizational level (for example, increased sales profitability). Each of these outcomes is then monetized to provide some form of financial results.

Utility analysis (for example, Cascio, 1989) transforms the outcomes of a program or intervention into expected monetary returns. Utility analysis determines "the cost of a . . . program, the incremental benefits derived . . ., the duration of those benefits, and the discount rate that represents the organization's minimum expected ROI (or return on investment)" (Mattson, 2003, p. 132). Thus, utility analysis first determines the effect size (or the true difference in job performance between the trained and untrained groups as expressed in standard deviation units). This is multiplied by the number of trainees, the length of time the improved job performance is expected to last, and the dollar value of the job performance of untrained employees (again, expressed in standard deviation units). The cost of the training is then subtracted to yield a change-in-utility value.

With business managers in this particular organization, Mattson found that the reports employing the utility analysis and the critical outcome technique were more likely than the anecdotal approach to receive high usefulness ratings for decision making and action. "The relative length and technical complexity of both the utility analysis and COT reports should have rendered them less easy to understand, and hence less useful for decision making" (2003, pp. 145–146). Mattson offered a possible explanation: the organization employed Six Sigma quality approach and required that managers use statistical reporting techniques. Thus, Mattson's results suggested that evaluation information needs to be tailored to the audience. The managers in this organization clearly preferred the more quantitative and more complicated methods. In other organizations, qualitative information would prove to be more persuasive.

More recently, Bober and Bartlett (2004) applied the Cousins and Leithwood (1986) framework to examine the factors influencing use of evaluation results in corporate university training programs, including leadership development programs. The twelve major factors were divided into categories representing evaluation implementation (including evaluation quality, credibility, relevance, communication quality, findings, and timeliness) and decision and policy setting (including information needs, decision characteristics, political climate, competing information, personal characteristics, and commitment or receptiveness to evaluation). The major users of the evaluation results included the evaluation staff, instructional design and development staff, deans or directors of the corporate university, upper-level and senior management, and student advisors and counselors. For these various users, seven of the twelve factors appeared consistently across the organization. These were ranked in order of importance: communication quality, timeliness, commitment or receptiveness to evaluation, evaluation quality, credibility, relevance, and findings. Most of these factors relate to the category of evaluation implementation.

Such results indicate the importance of considering communication and reporting within the context of the entire evaluation. The next section of the chapter introduces a systems model of evaluation that can help to identify the various factors influencing the evaluation, including those related to communication and reporting.

A Systems Model of Evaluation

Preskill and Russ-Eft (2001, 2003) introduced the systems model of evaluation, which is depicted in Figure 17.1.

The model recognizes that an evaluation takes place within a dynamic and changing environment. Any evaluation, and in particular an evaluation of leadership development, both affects and is affected by the system or organization in which it takes place. This model has been elaborated in subsequent work (Preskill and Russ-Eft, 2005; Russ-Eft and Preskill, 2001; Russ-Eft and Preskill, 2005).

The systems model begins with the evaluation processes themselves. These processes include focusing the evaluation, determining the design and data collection methods, collecting data, analyzing data, communicating and reporting, and managing the evaluation. Each of these evaluation processes is affected by and affects the other processes. Thus, communicating and reporting ultimately depends upon the other evaluation processes.

Consider, for example, an evaluation of a leadership development program within a large telecommunications company. The evaluation focuses primarily on the extent to which changes have occurred in the on-the-job behaviors of the participants. In addition, the executive team is concerned about travel expenses for the centralized training staff and is considering using some of the local managers to facilitate the sessions. As part of the evaluation, data were collected concerning the issue of centralized versus decentralized training. This additional information led to the need for revisions in the original dissemination plan. Rather than simply distributing the findings and recommendations to the vice president of human resources and the executive team only, the evaluator provided separate reports for the local management

FIGURE 17.1. A SYSTEMS MODEL OF EVALUATION.

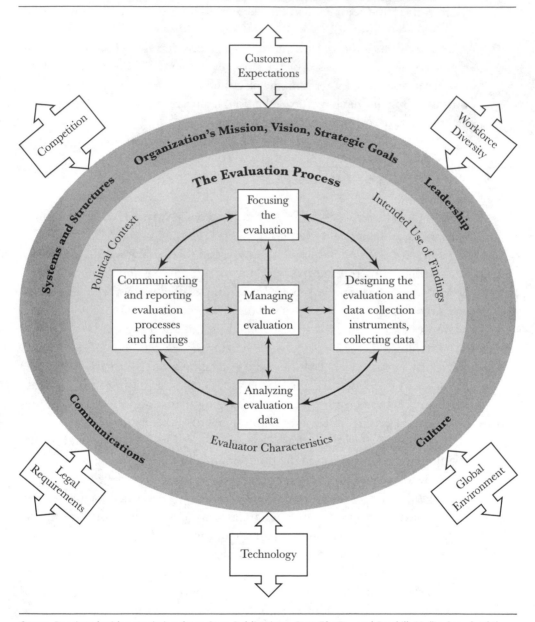

Source: Reprinted with permission from Sage Publications. Russ-Eft, D., and Preskill, H. "In Search of the Holy Grail: Return on Investment Evaluation in Human Resource Development." *Advances in Developing Human Resources,* 2005, *7*(1), 71–85.

teams who would be involved in any decisions regarding the use of local managers for such an initiative. These separate reports presented the results for each local area, along with specific recommendations for that local team. Such local reports provided the needed detail to ensure and encourage local implementation of the recommendations.

At the next level are factors separate from the evaluation process but directly tied to any evaluation. The political context in which the evaluation is being conducted is one such factor. In an evaluation of a leadership development program or initiative, for example, those in positions of power over the program will influence the evaluation and the needed communication and reporting, since such programs can impact the direction of the organization. Another factor of importance involves the stakeholders' reasons for conducting the evaluation and their intended use of the findings. Thus, stakeholders interested in formative types of information for improving the program will typically require different types of communication and reporting than those who are interested in summative information. A final critical factor concerns the evaluator's characteristics. This recognizes the effects of the evaluator's competence and expertise, the evaluator's relationship to the organization, and the evaluator's relationship to the program or process being evaluated.

As an example, the evaluator of a supervisory training program may be asked to examine the behavioral changes as well as the costs and benefits of the program. The primary stakeholder in this case may be the vice president of human resources. But, when the findings are presented to the executive council and show substantial benefits, including productivity gains, the chief financial officer may suggest that such gains would allow the organization to lay off some workers. The high power position of this person may lead to a potentially unexpected outcome from this evaluation.

Characteristics within the evaluation also influence the evaluation and are influenced by the evaluation. These include the organization's mission, vision, and strategic plan; the organization's infrastructure; the organizational culture and climate; and the leadership within the organization. The organization's mission, vision, and strategic plan should be examined and considered with any evaluation because they can determine the direction and extent of the evaluation and the likelihood that the evaluation can have some impact. The organization's infrastructure is also an important factor determining the ways in which the evaluation can be implemented and whether the findings are used (Preskill and Torres, 1999). The organizational culture can determine the level of participation, affecting the evaluation results and credibility. Indeed, this particular factor was emphasized in Mattson's (2003) research, discussed previously. In the case of Mattson's work, the managers within the organization, because of their exposure and use of the quality approach and statistical reporting techniques, appeared to favor more quantitative reports for decision-making purposes.

As with most organizational interventions and especially leadership development efforts and their evaluations, organizational leadership can provide needed support for the evaluation or can hinder or block the evaluation effort and possible use. The organization's systems and structures, in particular the communication systems, can facilitate data collection and help to ensure participation. As discussed in the following section, the communication systems can provide effective methods for disseminating the findings and for supporting future evaluation efforts (Torres, Preskill, and Piontek, 2005).

Finally, the model recognizes that the external environment influences organizations and any organizational evaluation. Such factors include competition, customer expectations, workforce diversity, legal requirements, technology, and the global context. For example, as part of an evaluation of a leadership development program within a manufacturing organization, the client and key stakeholders request that the evaluator survey customers to determine their expectations of the leadership and the organization. Thus, customer expectations became an integral part of the evaluation. In another example, a nongovernmental organization operates in multiple countries with both national staff and local staff. An evaluation for such an organization needs to take into account the global environment in which this organization operates as well as the various specific local contexts. Any of these external factors can influence the design, data collection, analysis, and reporting of the evaluation.

Given the various factors described, the next section of the chapter focuses on the specific factors that should be considered when developing a communication plan for the evaluation.

Developing an Evaluation Communication Plan

Recognizing the complexity of the organizational system within which an evaluation takes place, this section introduces the notion of building a communication plan for each evaluation. Creating such a plan helps to ensure that the communications are provided to the appropriate stakeholders, in the appropriate format, and within the expected time frame. Such a plan addresses such questions as

- What are the purpose and desired outcome of each communication?
- Who are the stakeholders and audiences for each communication?
- What are the resources available for each communication?
- What should be included in the content and what should be the format for each communication?
- What should be the timing of each communication?

What Are the Purpose and Desired Outcome?

According to Torres, Preskill, and Piontek (1996) and closely related to Patton's (1997) notion of instrumental use, there are three major purposes to communications in an evaluation: (1) to build awareness and support for the program, (2) to provide results and encourage accountability, and (3) to improve the program. A major outcome for any evaluation is to provide needed information to aid decision makers.

It is critical for the evaluation to undertake active communication efforts from the beginning. This means directing communication efforts to build awareness and support for the evaluation. To do so, key stakeholders need to be involved in decisions regarding whether and when to undertake an evaluation. They are the ones to help the evaluator identify factors both inside and outside the organization that can affect and be influenced by the evaluation. Furthermore, if key people are reluctant to proceed, it is likely that the evaluation will encounter difficulties throughout the process. Such reluctance toward the evaluation may be due to mistrust of the intentions of the evaluation or concerns about the costs and time commitments involved in the evaluation. Once stakeholders agree to the evaluation, the evaluator must ensure that these stakeholders are involved in the various key decisions regarding the evaluation. Such decisions include determining the overall purpose of the evaluation, recommending a design for the evaluation, developing data collection instruments, agreeing upon the logistics for the data collection, analyzing the evaluation data, and determining future communication activities.

Each of the proposed communication activities should involve some desired outcomes of these efforts, and it may be helpful to state these outcomes explicitly. Such outcomes include involvement in some decisions, information to stakeholders and audiences, and specific decisions, actions, and next steps. Exhibit 17.1 provides an example of such a statement from a proposal to undertake an evaluation of a leadership program designed for rural communities.

Who Are the Stakeholders and Audiences?

Presumably, early in the evaluation the stakeholders and audiences have been identified. If not, when planning for communications, some effort must be undertaken to identify all of the potential stakeholders and audiences. Examining the systems model described earlier may aid in determining important stakeholders and audiences. For example, for leadership programs within a corporate sector, the stakeholders will include upper management, middle management, human resource development, and the participants. Other possible stakeholders include the direct reports of the participants, customers, and competitors. In fact, the stakeholders will include all those who are affected by or who influence the program and the evaluation. Within nonprofit organizations, similar stakeholders would emerge, including upper management, middle management, human resource development, participants, employees, and those being served by the organization. Within a government agency, the stakeholders will include some of the same types of individuals, but would also include other government agency personnel, related nongovernmental organizations, and the general public.

EXHIBIT 17.1. A STATEMENT OF EXPLICIT OUTCOMES.

The purpose of this evaluation is to gain insight from program participants and related stakeholders to measure the effectiveness of the Community Trainer training program as measured against the Institute's goals and desired outcomes for rural communities. The insights gained from examination of the program will be used to inform curriculum revisions, delivery methods, and management of the Community Trainer program. The evaluation will also guide the Institute in the process for selection and training of new Community Trainer candidates.

Adapted from Stewart, G. (2006, April 13). Ford Institute Leadership Program: An Evaluation Model for Community Trainer Training Program, Oregon State University, Corvallis, OR. Used with permission.

It may be helpful to identify three levels of stakeholders. *Primary stakeholders* are those who will make decisions regarding the program using the evaluation results. Typically, these are the person or people providing the funding for the evaluation and/or the people supporting the program being evaluated. Such primary stakeholders can include organizational executives, the department or agency providing the funding, the program staff and developers, and the evaluation team. *Secondary stakeholders* are those who are not involved with the direct operation of the program but who have a stake in it. They include other managers and administrators, program participants, and customers and clients. *Tertiary stakeholders* are those who may be interested in the evaluation for making future decisions and planning, and can include potential users or adopters of the program, governing boards, professional colleagues, and other organizations.

Recognizing the importance of these various stakeholders, it is important in planning an evaluation to describe each one of them and to indicate the ways in which they can use the evaluation findings. Exhibit 17.2 provides an example of such an articulation taken from the plan for an evaluation of leadership development at a university.

When considering issues related to communicating and reporting the evaluation, the backgrounds and characteristics of each of the stakeholders and audiences must be examined. These can include such characteristics as accessibility, role in decision making, familiarity with the program, and familiarity with research and evaluation. As an example, a group that is highly educated in statistical presentations (as was the case in the Mattson work described earlier) may be interested in types of information different from those without much background in statistics.

In addition, there may be certain forms of communication and reporting that are considered more effective than others in a specific organization or setting. In one organization, the most effective communications might involve informal meetings with decision makers, followed by large-group formal presentations. In another organization, the most effective communications might involve large-group, formal presentations followed by small-group working sessions to formulate action plans to address the recommendations. In a third organization, the most effective communications might include a large-group formal presentation, followed by a formal written report from which several different working papers are developed to detail further actions.

EXHIBIT 17.2. SAMPLE DESCRIPTION OF STAKEHOLDERS.

Primary Stakeholders

Evaluator. The evaluator will use the evaluation results to determine in coordination with the training and development manager whether or not to move ahead with improvements to the Questioning Techniques Training Module within the Leadership Program. The evaluator will also help to gauge whether there is enough interest and reason to design further training as a supplement to other past and possible future communication skills training interventions.

University Training and Development Manager. The university training and development manager will use the evaluation's finding to ultimately make the final decision about whether or not improvements will be made and whether additional offerings will happen. The training manager will determine if there is sufficient need for this training based on coordination and consultation with the evaluator.

Secondary Stakeholders

Participants Old/New. The participants in the Leadership Program will be affected by the results of the evaluation because the outcome will determine whether or not they are offered any improvements or any additional training related to their previous instruction on leadership skills and communication.

Training and Development Assistant. This person is involved along with the training manager and the evaluator in assisting with any program improvements. In addition, this person would help with the development, set-up, and organization if an additional module or course is approved.

Tertiary Stakeholders

Other individuals affected by the evaluation's results include (1) participants' family members, coworkers, managers, administrators, and students, who may experience improved leadership and better communications with any improvements in the program; (2) university human resources, which may recognize the value in the training and provide additional funding for further program improvement; and (3) leadership development programs at other universities and nonprofit organizations that may be interested in the findings as support for their own initiatives.

Adapted from Boehme, L. (2003, June 10). Evaluation plan for development of Questioning Techniques Training Modules at Oregon State University, Corvallis, OR. Used with permission.

One stakeholder issue that must be considered involves the relationship between accessibility and decision-making authority. It is not uncommon to have executives and managers who are not very accessible but who will play an important role in decisions regarding the program. In such cases, the evaluator must identify the critical opportunities when input and involvement and communication with such high-level decision makers must be pursued. One example involves an evaluation of a leadership development program in a for-profit business services organization. In this case, the evaluator obtained advance information as to the scheduled meetings of the executive committee. Either a briefing was presented or a short memo was prepared presenting information as to the status of the evaluation effort.

What Are the Resources?

Before planning any evaluation communication (indeed before undertaking any evaluation effort), there needs to be some attention paid to the resources available. The level and type of resources will vary depending upon the type of communication. In-person meetings and presentations require available staff members and sufficient preparation time. Written communications require staff who can prepare those types of reports, as well as the time and materials to develop, edit, and produce them. Such activities must be considered part of the evaluation and the evaluation budget, and there may need to be decisions as to trade-offs between data collection and analysis and reporting.

What Should Be the Content and Format?

Based on an examination of the previous issues—purpose and desired outcome, stakeholder characteristics, and resources—the evaluator needs to consider the content and format of different types of communications. Content issues revolve around the amount and level of text, the level of description, discussion of quantitative and qualitative analyses, and the inclusion of graphs, tables, or pictures.

The formats available to an evaluator vary from those that require action and interaction from stakeholders to those that do not. Some examples of reporting formats include working sessions or meetings, oral presentations, memos, and formal written reports.

Working Sessions or Meetings. Working sessions or meetings are highly interactive sessions with stakeholders held primarily for the purpose of engaging stakeholders in the evaluation effort. Typically such sessions or meetings are facilitated by the evaluator and enable the various groups to express their own opinions and to listen and learn from the opinions of other stakeholders.

The desired outcomes of such sessions can include any or all of those previously mentioned. Such sessions or meetings should be designed to obtain stakeholders' active involvement and support in some decisions related to the evaluation. These decisions can involve issues related to the evaluation purpose, the key questions to be answered, the evaluation approach and design, the data collection instruments and tools, the analysis and interpretation of the findings, and the conclusions and recommendations. These sessions or meetings also provide excellent opportunities to inform stakeholders as to progress in the evaluation, to ask for suggestions as to solutions to impending problems, and to obtain continued support for the evaluation. Finally, such sessions or meetings enable the evaluator to engage stakeholders in specific decisions, actions, and next steps. Russ-Eft and Preskill (2005) provide some suggestions for holding such working sessions to aid in focusing an evaluation.

In some cases, informal meetings or gatherings may take place. These provide the evaluator with an excellent opportunity to update or brief individuals on the evaluation progress. Thus, the evaluator should be prepared for such encounters and should determine some desired outcomes from these communications. One typical question from high-level stakeholders is, What are the results? It is important to decide in advance on an appropriate response, perhaps indicating that all the data have not yet been analyzed but some information will be available by a specific date.

Another issue in today's workplace involves the widespread use of synchronous distance communications. These can include teleconferences, videoconferences, Web conferences, and chat rooms. Indeed, most global organizations make daily use of these types of communications to complete projects and tasks. The evaluator working with such organizations will need to know when and whether to use these options for working sessions or meetings. Torres, Preskill, and Piontek (2005) provide some guidelines for these synchronous distance meetings.

Oral Presentations. Oral presentations can take place during any phase of the evaluation and can be used to gain awareness and support as well as to provide details on the results of the evaluation.

One common type of oral presentation is that of the executive briefing. As stated previously, high-level decision makers typically have little time to devote to reading lengthy (or even shorter) reports. In these cases, the evaluator must simplify the complexity and reduce the details of the evaluation to a few salient points. It is appropriate to use tables, graphs, and anecdotes to aid understanding and decision making. In the author's experience, such executive briefings may be as short as ten to fifteen minutes and as long as a half hour.

With other stakeholder groups, particularly those heavily invested in the leadership program, longer oral presentations may be needed. As with the executive briefings, tables, graphs, and anecdotes can be very effective. With an increased amount of time available for the presentation, the evaluator can increase the level of participation and involvement of the stakeholders and audience. This can be done by simply including question-and-answer sessions at the end of the presentation. Alternatively, to encourage greater participation, the evaluator may request reactions or even action planning at various points throughout the presentation.

It should be noted that most oral presentations also involve the use of computer-generated and supported displays. These can include text notes and outlines, tabular and graphical displays, pictures and photographs, and video clips. A key value of such displays is to use them to enhance and clarify the oral presentation. Thus, textual, tabular, and graphical information should be brief and should use large characters. Pictures and videos should be directly related to specific points in the oral presentation.

Memos. Within organizational settings, brief memos provide a means for communicating with stakeholders and can be used to ensure awareness of the evaluation and to provide an overview of its findings and recommendations to wider audiences. Given their brevity, it is critical to craft such communications so that they capture audience attention and make one or two important points. Such memos can be delivered through a variety of communication methods, including internal newsletter, internal e-mail, faxes, and Web sites. Depending upon the organization's communication systems, the evaluator may want to use several or all of these methods in order to reach different audiences.

Comprehensive Written Reports. Comprehensive written reports represent the most commonly used formats for reporting on an evaluation and are usually a required part of any evaluation. Such a report presents a complete picture of the evaluation and typically includes the following components.

- Executive summary (providing a brief description of the program, process, or course; key evaluation questions; main findings; and recommendations)
- Background on the program, process, or course, and the reasons for the evaluation
- Purpose of the evaluation
- Key evaluation questions
- Key stakeholders and audiences for the evaluation
- Evaluation model or approach
- Evaluation design
- Data collection methods
- Sampling and sources of information
- Political or other constraints and limitations
- Results and findings
- Recommendations
- References and appendices

Such a report provides all the details needed by any of the stakeholder groups. Because of the report's length and complexity, however, some of the previously mentioned formats may prove more helpful and useful for certain stakeholder groups to augment the detail provided in the comprehensive written report.

It must be recognized that such comprehensive, written reports are static documents that tend not to promote interaction or even action among stakeholders. Thus, it is imperative that the evaluation attempt to engage stakeholders in the interactive and active communication methods of working sessions and oral presentations.

Alternative and Creative Formats. Evaluation findings can be reported in a variety of formats, including news releases, Web sites, Web conferences, blogging, Podcasting, photographs, cartoons, and drama. Torres and others (2005) detail these various formats and provide excellent examples.

What Should Be the Timing?

The timing of communications represents a critical factor affecting evaluation use. Findings that are communicated after decisions have been made can be useless. After all, any evaluation requires time, effort, and resources; if the major decisions have already been made, then the evaluation simply wastes precious resources. Therefore, determining the timing of each of the communication activities in advance can help both the conduct and use of the evaluation. (See Bell, 2004, for issues related to scheduling, and Torres and others, 2005, for the timing of communications.)

Evaluations take place within dynamic organizations. Thus, the timing of important organizational activities cannot always be anticipated in advance. A wise evaluator will remain in close contact with the various stakeholders in order to provide evaluation information when needed.

Managing the Communication Process and Risks

Even though an evaluator has undertaken thorough planning concerning the evaluation communications, events and circumstances inside and outside the evaluation can derail those plans. These risks can include a variety of anticipated situations, such as communication systems and organizational culture, as well as unforeseen events and circumstances, such as personnel changes among stakeholders, personnel changes among the evaluation staff, and the need to communicate negative findings.

One example of the impact of an unforeseen event on an evaluation appears in Russ-Eft, Atwood, and Egherman (2002). This involved an evaluation within an organizational setting undertaken for some key decision makers, including a CEO and a vice president. When the CEO left the organization and the vice president was replaced, the findings and recommendations from the evaluation were ignored by the incoming executive team. This did not, however, mean that no evaluation use occurred. In fact, later contact with the organization revealed extensive process use within certain segments of the organization. This process use happened because of the active involvement and communications with these stakeholder groups throughout the evaluation.

The following sections discuss some approaches to dealing with possible risks to the evaluation.

Undertaking Up-Front Assessment

In advance of any evaluation, the evaluator should undertake a thorough examination of the organizational context for the evaluation. The systems model
introduced earlier in this chapter can aid in identifying some of the supportive
elements as well as some of the possible barriers in the evaluation process.
Each element can be viewed from the perspective of these questions.

- To what extent and in what ways does a certain person or a group support
  the evaluation process and communication of the evaluation?
- How can these supportive elements be used and encouraged?
- To what extent and in what ways does a certain person or a group hinder
  the evaluation process and communication of the evaluation?
- How can these barriers be overcome?

Some other questions about the organizational context are outlined in Russ-
Eft and Preskill (2001). They include

- What is going on in the organization that makes this evaluation timely (or
  not)?
- How well prepared are the organization and its members to conduct an
  evaluation?
- What needs to happen to prepare organization members for the evaluation
  and the possibility of surprising results?

Another possible approach to examining the context for the evaluation
would be to use a diagnostic instrument such as the *Readiness for Organizational
Learning and Evaluation (ROLE)* developed by Preskill and Torres (1999) and
available in Russ-Eft and Preskill (2001). It helps to determine areas of strength
and weakness for supporting an evaluation that exist within an organization.

Using Risk Management Tools

One helpful approach to minimizing the effects of such risks involves the use
of some risk management tools. Specifically, the evaluator should consider
each of the above risks and determine their probability. Then, ideas should
be generated for overcoming or reducing these risks. Exhibit 17.3 presents a

EXHIBIT 17.3. A SAMPLE RISK MANAGEMENT TOOL.

Description of Risk. CEO may leave the organization and be replaced by another individual.

Possible Negative Consequences. New CEO may not be interested in the evaluation process or the findings.

Probability or Cost. 10 percent; but if CEO did leave, the costs would include (1) loss of support; (2) end of project; and (3) nonuse of findings.

Possible Strategies or Solutions. Involve not only CEO and vice president as clients requesting evaluation but also include regional managers and consultants.

risk management tool using the previous example in which the CEO of the organization was replaced.

This chapter now considers each of the risks described on page 503 and identifies some possible approaches to reducing the impacts.

Personnel Changes Among Stakeholders. The example given previously depicted a situation in which a key stakeholder was replaced. Although it may not appear very likely at the beginning of the evaluation, such changes can always take place, and clearly, removal and replacement of top leadership are typically not something that the evaluator can prevent. But, as part of the communication plan or as part of the management plan, the evaluator must consider actions that can ameliorate changes in key stakeholders.

One critical action that evaluators should consider for any evaluation consists of using a variety of methods for involving various stakeholders and audiences in the evaluation. When such involvement takes place throughout the evaluation (including meetings to focus the evaluation, sessions to develop a logic model of the program, interviews concerning the context, meetings to review data collection instruments, and so forth), these stakeholders become invested in the evaluation. Investment in the evaluation can mean that, even if one important stakeholder leaves or is replaced, other stakeholders can make use of the evaluation processes or the evaluation findings.

Personnel Changes Within the Evaluation Staff. Most evaluation projects involve a small number of staff, and typically each project member is responsible for certain aspects of the evaluation. It may be that one project member excels in data collection activities, specifically those involving building trust. Another project member may possess skills needed for specific analysis efforts or for presentation or writing tasks. As with key stakeholders, evaluation staff members may also decide to leave the project or the organization at any time. Thus, the person managing the evaluation needs to plan for such staff changes.

Keeping evaluation team members informed of progress not only helps the individual members, it can also allow for a smooth transition if one of those individuals leaves the team. Cross-training evaluation team members can be beneficial as well. Such training not only promotes the growth and development of team members, but it also enables a team member to substitute for another member who may leave or be unable to perform the needed responsibilities.

Communicating Negative Findings. Evaluations do not always reveal that programs and interventions are operating as expected, that is, with completely positive outcomes. The evaluator must be prepared to deal with negative findings. In many cases, the evaluation's purpose includes both formative and summative judgments. Therefore, the evaluator should consider ways to report negative findings in order to lead to program improvements.

Certain approaches to the reporting of negative findings need to be considered. It helps to identify the positive aspects of the program—all of the things that are working well. Such statements help stakeholders realize the value of the program or the intervention. In addition, careful wording of the findings is critical (Torres and others, 2005).

By involving stakeholders throughout the evaluation—in the design, data collection, and analysis—the results, whether positive or negative, will not be a surprise. Furthermore, holding working sessions to review the evaluation findings and to develop recommendations and action plans will aid stakeholders in identifying opportunities for improvement. If possible, the evaluator should try to work with stakeholders after the conclusion of the evaluation to implement the recommendations, particularly those leading to program improvements.

Conclusion

The chapter emphasizes the importance of communication, specifically in promoting use of the evaluation findings. The systems model introduced can be used to identify factors that may affect the program and the evaluation. Further, the chapter describes various communication and reporting methods as well as an approach to minimizing the risks that may accompany any evaluation effort. Recognizing the importance of good communication throughout the evaluation, tips and recommendations to promote evaluation include the following:

- Recognize and celebrate the connection between communicating evaluation findings and evaluation use.
- Recognize the variety of factors that affect the program, process, or product being evaluated and the evaluation. These include

  Factors and processes within the evaluation process
  Factors related to but outside the evaluation process
  Factors within the organization
  Factors outside the organization

- Create a communication plan for the evaluation that for each communication details the following:

  Purpose and desired outcome
  Stakeholders and audiences
  Resources available
  Content and format
  Timing

- Use a variety of reporting formats, such as

  Working sessions
  Oral presentations
  Memos
  Comprehensive written reports
  Alternative, creative formats

- Manage the communication process and risks by employing

  Up-front assessments
  Risk management tools

Resources

Bell, J. B. "Managing Evaluation Projects Step by Step." In J. S. Wholey, H. P. Hatry, and K. E. Newcomer (eds.), *Handbook of Practical Program Evaluation* (2nd ed.). San Francisco: Jossey-Bass, 2004. This chapter provides some basic approaches to managing evaluation projects, including issues regarding the scheduling of activities.

Figueroa, M. E., Kincaid, D. L., Rani, M., and Lewis, G. "Communication for Social Change: An Integrated Model for Measuring the Process and Its Outcomes." *Communication for Social Change Working Papers,* no. 1. New York: Rockefeller Foundation, 2002 [www.communicationforsocialchange.org/publications-resources.php?id=107]. This report provides a resource for community organizations, communication professionals, and social change agents. It clarifies some of the key components needed for an inclusive and participatory approach to social change.

Nadler, D. A. "Confessions of a Trusted Counselor." *Harvard Business Review,* 2005, *83*(9), 68–77. This article presents some practical suggestions about working with top executives. Many of these suggestions apply to working with stakeholders and communicating evaluation results.

Patton, M. Q. *Utilization-Focused Evaluation: The New Century Text.* Thousand Oaks, Calif.: Sage, 1997. This text represents a basic volume on evaluation and ways to enhance evaluation use. Many of the examples come from nonprofit and educational settings.

Preskill, H., and Russ-Eft, D. *Building Evaluation Capacity: 72 Activities for Teaching and Training.* Thousand Oaks, Calif.: Sage, 2005. This text includes various activities to introduce and enhance evaluations within organizations. These activities can be used with stakeholders in order to increase their understanding and use of evaluations.

Russ-Eft, D., and Preskill, H. *Evaluation in Organizations: A Systematic Approach to Enhancing Learning, Performance, and Change.* Cambridge, Mass.: Perseus, 2001. This text presents an overview to all phases of evaluation within organizations. It includes the *Readiness for Organizational Learning and Evaluation (ROLE)* instrument as an appendix.

Torres, R. T., Preskill, H., and Piontek, M. *Evaluation Strategies for Communicating and Reporting: Enhancing Learning in Organizations* (2nd ed.). Thousand Oaks, Calif.: Sage, 2005. This text provides an overview and details on communicating and reporting to support evaluation use. It includes suggestions and examples focused on a variety of reporting formats, including traditional formats as well as creative formats, such as photographs, cartoons, poetry, and drama.

References

Bell, J. B. "Managing Evaluation Projects Step by Step." In J. S. Wholey, H. P. Hatry, and K. E. Newcomer (eds.), *Handbook of Practical Program Evaluation* (2nd ed.). San Francisco: Jossey-Bass, 2004.

Bober, C. F., and Bartlett, K. R. "The Utilization of Training Program Evaluation in Corporate Universities." *Human Resource Development Quarterly*, 2004, *15*, 363–383.

Brinkerhoff, R. O. *The Success Case Method: Find Out Quickly What's Working and What's Not.* San Francisco: Berrett-Koehler, 2003.

Cascio, W. F. "Using Utility Analysis to Assess Training Outcomes." In I. L. Goldstein (ed.), *Training and Development in Organizations.* San Francisco: Jossey-Bass, 1989.

Cousins, J. B., and Leithwood, K. A. "Current Empirical Research on Evaluation Utilization." *Review of Educational Research*, 1986, *56*(3), 331–364.

Mattson, B. W. "Development and Validation of the Critical Outcome Technique." *Human Resource Development International*, 2000, *3*, 465–488.

Mattson, B. W. "The Effects of Alternative Reports of HRD Results on Managerial Support." *Human Resource Development Quarterly*, 2003, *14*, 127–151.

Mattson, B. W., Quartana, L. J., and Swanson, R. A. "Assessing the Business Results of Management Development Using the Critical Outcome Technique." In J. J. Phillips (ed.), *In Action: Measuring ROI.* Alexandria, Va.: ASTD, 1998.

Mintzberg, H. "The Manager's Job: Folklore and Fact." *Harvard Business Review*, 1975, *53*(4), 49–61.

O'Reilly, C. A. "The Use of Information in Organizational Decision-Making: A Model and Some Propositions." *Research in Organizational Behavior*, 1983, *5*, 103–139.

Patton, M. Q. *Utilization-Focused Evaluation: The New Century Text.* Thousand Oaks, Calif.: Sage, 1997.

Preskill, H., and Russ-Eft, D. *Building Evaluation Capacity: 72 Activities for Teaching and Training.* Thousand Oaks, Calif.: Sage, 2005.

Preskill, H., and Russ-Eft, D. "A Framework for Reframing HRD Evaluation Practice and Research." In A. M. Gilley, L. Bierema, and J. Callahan (eds.), *Critical Issues in HRD.* Cambridge, Mass.: Perseus, 2003.

Preskill, H., and Russ-Eft, D. "A Systems Model for Evaluating Learning Performance." In D. H. Redmann (ed.), *Academy of Human Resource Development: Defining the Cutting Edge.* Baton Rouge, La.: Academy of Human Resource Development, 2001.

Preskill, H., and Torres, R. T. *Evaluative Inquiry for Learning in Organizations.* Thousand Oaks, Calif.: Sage, 1999.

Russ-Eft, D., Atwood, R., and Egherman, T. "Use and Non-use of Evaluation Results: A Case Study of Environmental Influences in the Private Sector." *American Journal of Evaluation,* 2002, *23*, 19–31.

Russ-Eft, D., and Preskill, H. *Evaluation in Organizations: A Systematic Approach to Enhancing Learning, Performance, and Change.* Cambridge, Mass.: Perseus, 2001.

Russ-Eft, D., and Preskill, H. "In Search of the Holy Grail: Return on Investment Evaluation in Human Resource Development." *Advances in Developing Human Resources,* 2005, *7*(1), 71–85.

Scriven, M. *Evaluation Thesaurus* (4th ed.). Thousand Oaks, Calif.: Sage, 1991.

Swanson, R. A., and Mattson, B. "Development and Validation of the Critical Outcome Technique." In R. Torraco (ed.), *Academy of Human Resource Development 1997 Annual Proceedings.* Baton Rouge, La.: Academy of Human Resource Development, 1997, pp. 64–71.

Torres, R. T., Preskill, H., and Piontek, M. *Evaluation Strategies for Communicating and Reporting: Enhancing Learning in Organizations.* Thousand Oaks, Calif.: Sage, 1996.

Torres, R. T., Preskill, H., and Piontek, M. *Evaluation Strategies for Communicating and Reporting: Enhancing Learning in Organizations* (2nd ed.). Thousand Oaks, Calif.: Sage, 2005.

CHAPTER EIGHTEEN

ACCELERATING LEARNING ABOUT LEADERSHIP DEVELOPMENT

A Learning Community Approach

Deborah Meehan and Claire Reinelt

Imagine being asked as a leadership program evaluator, Is the investment we have made in this leadership program reducing poverty in rural areas, reducing violence statewide, reaching the critical mass of leaders it will take to have an impact on population growth in the developing world? Designing leadership development evaluations to explore and answer these questions is a complex process. It involves deepening an understanding of the questions being asked, identifying appropriate outcomes and indicators, developing robust methodologies for exploring what people want to learn, and preparing audiences to use findings effectively. No single leadership practitioner, evaluator, or funder can figure this out alone; it requires a broader community.

In this chapter we discuss our personal experiences with the creation of a leadership development evaluation learning community. We describe the use of collective learning methodologies and share stories about how our work individually and collectively has benefited. We hope you benefit from our insights and lessons about how to work collaboratively to accelerate learning and are inspired to try some of these techniques in your own work.

Understanding the Context of Nonprofit Leadership Development

Nonprofit leadership development initiatives and programs are supported primarily by public and private donors in an effort to accelerate change and solve social problems (such as health care access, student achievement, affordable housing, poverty reduction, racial equity), and to improve the quality of life in underserved and underresourced communities.

The long-term changes that nonprofit leadership approaches ultimately hope to achieve may not be realized for many, many years, if not lifetimes. As a result, success in the nonprofit sector has to be evaluated longitudinally and monitored with proxy measures of progress. This presents significant challenges because nonprofit organizations operate on very tight budgets that limit the resources available to invest in leadership development evaluation.

Most nonprofit sector leadership development evaluations are funded by foundations. As trustees of public resources, foundations bring a set of learning questions about the impact and cost of programs in which they invest. They want and need to know whether leadership investments are accelerating the desired results more effectively than other possible investments. These same questions are often ones that business leaders ask themselves about leadership development investments within the for-profit sector as they seek to determine the relative value of a program and its outcomes. Although this chapter is written about evaluation from the nonprofit perspective, our colleagues in the for-profit sector may find many similar opportunities and challenges.

A Brief History of Nonprofit and Philanthropic Investments in Leadership Development and Evaluation

One of the earliest nonprofit leadership development programs, Coro, was founded in 1942. An attorney and a business leader in San Francisco became concerned that there was no training available to prepare citizen leaders. Coro continues to offer leaders hands-on training designed to support them to make meaningful contributions to society. Other early nonprofit leadership development efforts include the founding of the Community Leadership Association (CLA) in 1979 and American Leadership Forum (ALF) in 1980. CLA is an umbrella organization that brings together hundreds of local programs that seek to create networks of informed, concerned citizens to guide the future growth of their communities. Working and learning together, participants enhance their leadership skills, capacities, and attitudes while they broaden their understanding of community issues. ALF was founded to address the need for more skillful, more ethical, more effective leadership on a local basis. Its founders were convinced that if a cross-section of a community's business, elected, academic, minority, and religious leadership could be brought together to work on public issues, no problem would be beyond solution. To our knowledge, these early leadership development efforts were not evaluated.

Philanthropic investments in leadership development span more than forty years. Some of the earliest efforts were supported by the W. K. Kellogg Foundation, such as the Kellogg Farmers Study Program, created in 1965 at Michigan State University, with the intent "to provide young agricultural and rural leaders with a broader view of society, as well as a greater sense of the world and how they fit into the bigger picture" (W. K. Kellogg Foundation, 2001).

In 1966, the Ford Foundation created a Leadership Development Program to identify and support grassroots leaders from around the country to improve rural life in America. The Smith Richardson Foundation supported the founding of the Center for Creative Leadership (CCL) in 1970 "to advance the understanding, practice and development of leadership for the benefit of society worldwide." CCL continues to be a recognized leader in the field of leadership development education.

From the earliest years there has been a strong philanthropic interest in documenting and assessing the impact of these programs. One of the earliest evaluations of the Ford Foundation's Leadership Development Program (1966–1977) led to the publication of *Left-Handed Fastballers: Scouting and Training America's Grass-Roots Leaders* (Nevin, 1981). Other early leadership development evaluation efforts include a study funded by the W. K. Kellogg Foundation to compare four leadership programs in Pennsylvania, Montana, Michigan, and California (Howell, Weir, and Cook, 1979).

During the past twenty years, philanthropic investments in leadership development have grown exponentially. This growth has been a response to the rapid expansion of nonprofit organizations and the recognition that the capacity of these organizations to lead change depends on strong leadership. Through foundation-funded programs and initiatives, leaders have been selected, nurtured, supported, and connected with one another in order to become more effective change agents.

With this expansion came an increasing interest in assessing the impact of leadership development programs. By the late 1990s, frustration was growing within the philanthropic community (and among programs themselves) about the capacity of evaluation to answer questions about impact. The Kellogg Foundation, one of the leading funders of leadership development and leadership development evaluation, commissioned a scan to find out which programs were evaluating outcomes and impact, how they were conducting these evaluations, and whether there were any promising evaluation models for the leadership development field. Its work surfaced a number of reasons why leadership development evaluations were not able to successfully answer questions about impact (W. K. Kellogg Foundation, 2002).

- Leadership development programs often lack a theory of change that surfaces the links between individual change and changes in organizations, communities, or fields.
- The most widely accepted methodologies for evaluating impact, such as randomized control experiments, are derived from the experimental sciences. In many cases, experimental methods are not appropriate for evaluating leadership development (see Chapter One for a further discussion of experimental and quasi-experimental methods for evaluating leadership development).
- Most evaluation learning occurs within the cycle of a program grant, limiting the breadth and depth of the knowledge that is generated.
- Few resources are invested in longitudinal evaluations that have greater potential for demonstrating leadership impact.

Because of findings like these, many funders, practitioners, and evaluators believe that learning can be accelerated if they develop stronger synergy among their evaluation questions, approaches, and methods.

The Value and Challenges of Learning in Community

Learning increases its breadth and depth by connecting diverse groups of leadership development stakeholders. Stakeholders can test their findings with each other, share resources and tools, and push each other to ask deeper questions.

One of the barriers to creating a learning community is that evaluators operate in a market economy, often bidding against one another for foundation contracts to conduct leadership development evaluations. As a result, evaluators have little incentive or opportunity to collaborate or share tools or knowledge with one another, often leading them to feel isolated in their work.

A competitive environment exists among leadership programs as well. Their dependence on foundation grants often makes program staff reluctant to share what works well for fear of losing a competitive advantage; they are equally concerned about sharing what has not worked for fear that perceived weakness or failure may be exploited by competitors. The guarded behaviors that emerge in a climate of fear and anxiety often occur without conscious thought or intention and are at odds with the values and mission-driven spirit of most organizations in the nonprofit sector.

Despite these challenges, many evaluators and leadership development practitioners believed that we could build a more compelling case for investing in leadership development strategies if we could aggregate findings about outcomes and impacts across our leadership development efforts. A cross-program examination of evaluation findings might also help us determine a cost-effective minimum bundle of program elements that could achieve a program's desired outcomes. Furthermore, we believed that by working together we could validate a diverse range of complementary qualitative and quantitative methods to create a fuller picture of leadership development program outcomes and impacts and effectively build support for the use of mixed methods among leadership development program staff, evaluators, and grant makers.

Our experiences suggest that when leadership program staff and evaluators are provided opportunities for collegial and collective learning, they are hungry for opportunities to both deepen their own learning and contribute to building the field's knowledge about the successful practice of leadership development and what it can accomplish and contribute to social change.

The Creation of the Leadership Learning Community

The Leadership Learning Community (LLC) was founded in 2000 by a diverse group of leadership development stakeholders: program staff, grant makers, researchers, evaluators, and service providers. One of LLC's core assumptions is that it is possible to strengthen individual and collective efforts to develop effective social change leadership by connecting the resources, learning, and practice of those committed to this work. Before forming LLC, we tested this assumption by working together as program staff and evaluators to develop a leadership development program and evaluation framework that we felt integrated our collective wisdom. The productivity of this process reaffirmed the value of and need for a sustainable community of learning and practice. We formed the LLC to support and structure continued opportunities for collective learning and knowledge development. Those who joined us in launching the LLC shared a commitment to building an open-source, publicly accessible knowledge base to strengthen the leadership development field.

Mission and Values

The mission and values of LLC encourage a culture of generosity. Within the LLC environment, leadership program staff, consultants, and businesses have responded to the call to contribute their knowledge about effective leadership development design and evaluation to elevate the practice of the entire field. Self-organizing groups, committed to a common issue or question, experiment with and develop the tools and methodologies that can support collective learning and knowledge generation.

Learning Circles

LLC primarily organizes learning through *circles*. Circles are "places where people . . . talk, celebrate, problem solve, sing and tell stories, and govern themselves" (Pond and Nielson, 2004). As the authors of a recent external evaluation of LLC reflected, "Ultimately the creation of these spaces [circles] is intended to help unfold creative social change agendas and strategies that are rooted in community and collective action" (Pond and Nielson, 2004).

LLC has found that learning is best supported in three types of learning circles, all of which are populated by those with an interest in learning more about how to evaluate leadership development: regional circles, affinity circles, and issue-focused circles.

Regional Circles. These circles bring together a diverse group of funders, service providers, and researchers who live in a particular geographic area. Proximity to one another makes it easier to gather more frequently, build relationships with one another across a variety of perspectives and work domains, and learn together around issues of shared concern.

Affinity Circles. These circles bring together people based on a shared role, such as being a funder of leadership development efforts or working in the field of health leadership development. The unique challenges of working within certain environments and the lack of opportunity to convene with colleagues who share those challenges make the opportunity to have a candid and open conversation about common concerns highly valued. While LLC encourages dialogue among diverse groups, some topics may be more fruitfully explored with those who have had similar experiences. For example, the meeting of the health affinity circle enables evaluators to look across the findings of multiple health-focused leadership efforts for synergy and leveraged impact in health outcomes.

Issue-Focused Circles. These circles convene around topics of interest to the community, such as evaluation and alumni network building. These circles have the advantage of consistent, deep focus that supports problem solving, tool generation, and direct application. The LLC evaluation learning circle has been critical to our ability to generate knowledge as a community of practitioners because we depend largely on the capacity of each participating program to successfully identify what is working and not working in their own leadership development practice. The ability of the evaluation learning circle to develop and disseminate tools that strengthen program learning lays the foundation for extracting important knowledge from front-line practitioners. We discuss the work of the evaluation learning circle in more depth later in this chapter.

In addition to circles, LLC has also developed a contract management model that generates learning and addresses financial obstacles to collaboration common among evaluators. For a description of the contract management model and an example of its use, see Exhibit 18.1.

An In-Depth Look at Learning Circles

A learning circle brings together a group of people in a process of mutual support and collective inquiry to explore issues, questions, and themes that are of

EXHIBIT 18.1. A COLLABORATIVE
CONTRACT MANAGEMENT MODEL.

Diverse teams of experts are recruited from the community to deepen collaborative learning through consulting opportunities that often focus on evaluation and scans of leadership development practices. This model builds evaluation capacity by supporting higher levels of collaboration and peer learning among field experts. Often these experts accept less compensation in order to participate in a collaborative learning experience. One such collaboration was pulled together to evaluate three leadership development programs that were part of a ten-year violence prevention initiative. The team included a biographer, a community leader committed to working with disenfranchised youth and adults to develop their leadership, a programmatic expert in the field of nonprofit leadership development, a public health program evaluator, a leadership development program evaluator, and a project manager. The diversity of this team improved the quality and relevance of the evaluation questions, ensured the use of appropriate data collection methods, and produced a report that was rich with stories and solidly grounded in leadership development program practice and theory.

Leadership development evaluators engaged in joint learning develop an appreciation for one another's particular areas of expertise and form stronger relationships. These experiences can seed collaborative projects that pool new combinations of expertise and perspectives to accelerate learning. For instance, a core group of team members from the violence prevention evaluation formed a collaborative team with another colleague who had international development evaluation experience in reproductive and maternal health to evaluate six family planning and reproductive health leadership programs.

mutual interest to the group and who are poised to advance the practice of participants and the field. Learning circles are based on several premises.

- Knowledge can be generated collectively that is not accessible to participants individually.
- Lessons extracted from one discreet experience may have transferable value beyond a specific context.
- Knowledge generated collectively has the potential to strengthen the leadership development work of participants individually while contributing more broadly to the effectiveness of the field.

Learning circles work best when people have burning questions they really want and need to find answers to, and when they feel isolated or frustrated about what they have been able to learn on their own. Learning circles are particularly useful for cross-program learning in fields of practice where there are not well-established venues for collecting, generating, and disseminating learning. Such is the case with leadership development evaluation. Often, knowledge exists in pockets, but there is no process for bringing that knowledge together and exploring what can be learned from this synergy.

In LLC, learning circles are used to generate and disseminate our collective knowledge about leadership development practices, outcomes, and impacts. Learning circles may be used to achieve other results as well, such as empowering communities to create changes that improve quality of life or facilitating learning across silos or teams within organizations to enhance services or products. For some tips on what to consider when initiating a learning circle, see Exhibit 18.2.

EXHIBIT 18.2. WHAT TO CONSIDER WHEN INITIATING A LEARNING CIRCLE.

- *Create a culture of sharing based on common mission and values.* It is important to balance concerns about competition with a higher commitment to strengthening all leadership development efforts. Allowing enough time to build relationships of trust and creating ground rules increases the comfort of participants.

- *Invite diverse stakeholders to participate.* Diversity is critical to the quality of the knowledge that is created. What constitutes diversity will vary by context, but every effort should be made to include people who do not normally have an opportunity to reflect and learn together.

- *Take time to deepen the questions that are being asked before exploring the answers.* The process of asking deeper questions often brings to the surface those questions that are most compelling and at the edge of current learning. Learning circles are more likely to hold the attention of participants when they are exploring the questions that matter most.

- *Engage people in a process of inquiry before meeting face to face.* Deeper learning occurs when people have engaged in their own learning process before coming together to share with others. This is particularly important when opportunities for meeting face to face are limited.

EXHIBIT 18.2. WHAT TO CONSIDER
WHEN INITIATING A LEARNING CIRCLE, Cont'd.

- *Good facilitation is a key to success.* Two elements of facilitation are particularly important: designing a variety of learning activities to tap different learning styles, and synthesizing the collective learning that has occurred so that people recognize what they learned together and can contribute to the field.

- *Document and disseminate the collective learning.* Learning is a cumulative process that builds on itself. Documenting the learning that occurs makes it accessible to people who may not have participated in the process but who can still benefit from what was learned. Documentation also provides participants with a synthesis that enables them to engage in further reflection and gain new insights beyond those they had when they first participated.

A Case Study of the Evaluation Learning Circle

Since the founding of LLC, there has been an interest among community members to

- Discuss evaluation with a diverse group of stakeholders, including those who fund, run, and evaluate leadership programs
- Share resources and tools to avoid reinventing the wheel
- Explore methodological, political, and longitudinal questions about leadership development evaluation that usually cannot be explored in the context of short-term program evaluation
- Create knowledge by mining data across multiple programs

A list of evaluation learning circle projects appears in Exhibit 18.3.

The first LLC gathering of leadership development evaluators occurred in March 2000, when about fifteen funders, evaluators, and practitioners developed a four-quadrant model that integrated leadership development evaluation and programming. The model encouraged learning and reflection about the individual and collective outcomes that occur for people as they engage in a leadership development process that supports changes and transformation over time. Using this model, we mapped outcomes that leadership programs frequently seek in each of the four quadrants (see Figure 18.1).

EXHIBIT 18.3. LLC EVALUATION
LEARNING CIRCLE PROJECTS (2000–2005).

Lessons from all of these listed projects, as well as evaluation reports, evaluation tools and guides, and cross-program evaluation learning materials, can be found in the LLC Evaluation Knowledge Pool. Readers can download those articles listed in parentheses.

- The development of a leadership evaluation and programming model ("LAMPS: A New Four Quadrant Tool" and "LAMPS: PowerPoint Presentation")

- The mapping and categorization of leadership development program outcomes across programs ("Outcomes Across Leadership Programs").

- A compilation of resources for evaluating leadership outcomes for individuals, organizations, and communities ("Guide to Leadership Evaluation Resources")

- A guide to participatory evaluation resources ("Participatory Evaluation Resource Guide")

- The exploration of personal transformation and its links to organizational and community transformation ("Exploring Personal Transformation and Its Links to Organizational and Community Transformation")

- The creation of a leadership development evaluation vision for ten years from now ("Illuminating the Interconnections between Personal and Community Transformation through Evaluation and Cross-Program Learning")

In November 2000, the evaluation learning circle engaged a broader group of stakeholders to identify challenges and questions we had about evaluating leadership development. It created a discussion guide about the politics of evaluation, program theory and evaluation, evaluation planning and design, measuring outcomes and impact, dissemination and communication, and utilization and application (see Exhibit 18.4).

By disseminating these questions to those with an interest in strengthening leadership development evaluation efforts, LLC began to build a shared framework of inquiry about evaluation in the context of leadership development.

In 2003, the evaluation learning circle convened thirty funders, practitioners, evaluators, scholars, researchers, and thought leaders to explore the benefits and drawbacks of creating a shared learning agenda. We invited participants from the Sustainable Leadership Initiative, a project funded by the W. K. Kellogg Foundation

FIGURE 18.1 FREQUENTLY DESIRED LEADERSHIP OUTCOMES.

Individual Outcomes

Improved skills, competencies, and abilities

Readiness for collaboration/cooperation

Improved self-reflection/self-awareness

Improved awareness of and value for diversity

Improved awareness of issues and opportunities for change

Leadership

Doing the work

Emergence of effective new leadership

Development of leadership networks and supports

Broadened perspectives

Sustained commitment and engagement

Support networks

Continuous learning

Youth development

Reflection and renewal

Leadership is shared and transferred

New and expanding leadership

Short Term ←——————————————————————————→ *Long Term*

Capacity of organizations is built

Enhanced effectiveness of organizations

Implementation of projects

Building of networks and relationships

Mobilized communities and movements for social change

Strong, responsive, and effective organizations

Responsive public policy

Responsive social services

Networks supporting social change

Expanding knowledge base informing practice

Available resources sustaining social change

Collective Outcomes

EXHIBIT 18.4. A DISCUSSION GUIDE
ABOUT LEADERSHIP DEVELOPMENT EVALUATION.

The Politics of Evaluation

- Why are we doing evaluations? What is the larger purpose?

- For whom are we doing evaluations and how does that affect what questions we ask and the methods we use?

- How do programs act as a catalyst within foundations? Are we "walking our talk"?

- Is a given program really necessary? Is it meeting a real need?

- What don't we ask that we should be asking?

- What are we afraid to ask because we don't know what to do with the answers?

- How do we manage the power relations that are inherent in evaluation?

- Who is going to evaluate our evaluations?

Program Theory and Evaluation

- What is the importance of having a coherent theory of social change for programming and evaluation?

- What do we know about leadership transformation?

- What will it look like if this program is effective? How will we know that?

- How do we know that what we are doing will get us to some result we want?

- How do we know that particular programs are making a difference for individuals, organizations, and communities?

- What works? What does not work?

- What are best practices in the field?

Evaluation Planning and Design

- What are models that address different evaluation needs and audiences?

- What are indicators for readiness for participation in programs?

- How do formative evaluations inform summative evaluations?

- How do you structure an evaluation?

- How can we use the evaluation to build the reflective capacity of participants?

EXHIBIT 18.4. A DISCUSSION GUIDE
ABOUT LEADERSHIP DEVELOPMENT EVALUATION, Cont'd.

Measuring Outcomes and Impact

- How can we evaluate the benefit of investing in an individual to their community?

- How do we measure leadership practice instead of position?

- What is the return on investment for individuals and in turn for the community?

- What are the prevailing outcomes from fellowship programs?

- How are outcomes measured?

- How do we evaluate the impact of leadership development programs?

- How can we develop indicators for social impact (transformational leadership) when most significant change takes place over decades?

Dissemination, Utilization, and Application

- How do we create short-term evaluations with a long-term message?

- How can the lessons from the evaluation of individual leadership programs be captured for broader dissemination and application?

- How can the lessons from leadership development programs be applied as a cross-cutting theme to other areas of foundation grant making?

and the U.S. Agency for International Development (USAID), to design and test a leadership development evaluation tool and to highlight their work and their use of an open-systems approach to evaluate leadership development. The Sustainable Leadership Initiative grew out of an effort by leadership development evaluators in the field of public health to strengthen their evaluation practice by developing and testing a tool that eventually became EvaluLEAD (see Chapter Three). While no shared learning agenda emerged from the meeting, the participants did express a commitment to continued collective learning (see Exhibit 18.5 for reflection on the process of creating a shared learning agenda).

To engage in meaningful collective learning requires consistency and duration. To deepen the quality of learning relationships, evaluation learning circle participants meet at least twice a year, for a daylong session and a half-day session at Creating Space, LLC's national gathering. Activities have included hands-on practice with evaluation tools, such as *A Guide to Evaluating Leadership Development Programs* (Evaluation Forum, 2003) and EvaluLEAD (Grove, Kibel, and Haas, 2005). These two approaches, while dif-

EXHIBIT 18.5. REFLECTIONS ON THE PROCESS OF CREATING A SHARED LEARNING AGENDA.

Creating a shared learning agenda is a complex process. It is not simple to figure out what questions we are asking in common and then set out to answer those questions. We bring vastly different learning needs to the discussion based on whether we are funders, practitioners, scholars, evaluators, or participants in leadership programs. Furthermore, we do not have well-developed approaches or methodologies for evaluating leadership development that are widely recognized as useful and valid. We have few ways to systematically capture and organize what we are learning. What we do have is a deep and abiding interest to continue working together to find a common language and to test and refine our approaches and methods so that we can all have more confidence in what we are learning. (LLC Evaluation Learning Circle, 2003)

ferent, support programs to be more intentional about what they are trying to achieve and how to evaluate their outcomes (Hsieh, 2003). Consistent with what we have learned about good leadership development, having the opportunity to apply concepts in practice deepens learning and makes it more likely that people will be able to use what they learn on their own. (Both the Evaluation Forum's *Guide to Leadership Development Programs* and the Sustainable Leadership Initiative's *EvaluLEAD Guide* are posted in the Evaluation Knowledge Pool on LLC's Web site. See this chapter's Resource section for more details.)

One of the challenges for any learning circle, whose members are scattered around the country, is how to effectively combine the use of virtual learning and face-to-face interaction, which is often very limited. The evaluation learning circle developed a "shared inquiry process" to support those with common interests to surface learning from their work and to share it virtually in advance of meeting face to face.

For example, there were a number of learning circle participants who were interested in exploring how to evaluate personal transformation and the connections, if any, between personal transformation and organizational and community transformation. For many evaluators, personal transformation is among the most profound yet illusive outcomes of leadership development programs that they seek to document and understand.

In order to use face-to-face time together effectively, participants were asked to commit to surfacing their own learning in advance using one of several methods: taking a retrospective look at data about personal transformation that they had already collected through their evaluations, gathering new data, or conducting a literature review. We provided participants with a list of questions to guide their inquiry, including the following:

- What do we mean by *personal transformation*?
- What are indicators of personal transformation?
- How do leadership development efforts support personal transformation?
- How do we evaluate personal transformation and its links to organizational and community transformation?

Participants were then asked to respond to these questions in writing and submit their responses via e-mail. We compiled the responses and shared them with the inquiry group before our daylong gathering. An analysis of the responses created a framework of understanding that was then tested when the group met. A series of facilitated exercises deepened our collective understanding about the questions that were posed (LLC Evaluation Learning Circle, 2004).

We emerged with a framework that reflected people's collective understanding about the types of changes that indicate personal transformation has occurred. They include changes in thoughts and feelings, changes in behavior, changes in interaction, and changes in collective action. Once we had this framework we recognized (or at least hypothesized) that it might be applicable to other domains of transformation (organizations, communities, fields, and systems). We also realized that change is not a linear process that begins with changes in thoughts and feelings progressing to collective action; rather, the process of change can begin in any of these dimensions. For example, someone might become involved in a community organizing campaign through which they clarify what they really care about and believe. Beliefs and values, in other words, do not need to precede collective action. The fullest potential of transformation requires change in every dimension, but there is no order in which this has to happen. We were excited about generating an approach to understanding transformation that was a product of evaluators surfacing individual lessons that were enhanced by learning in community.

During our face-to-face meeting, a group of participants with a shared interest in community leadership development became interested in sharing their theories of change. They wanted to deepen their collective understanding about how to support and evaluate community leadership development. This group organized a more focused follow-up meeting to explore how community leadership programs recruit and select participants, how they support connectivity among participants and in communities, what outcomes they seek in the short term, intermediate term, and long term, and how to align program outcomes with program activities. The meeting was attended by grant makers who each brought an evaluator who had worked with the community leadership programs they were funding. Participants at this meeting created a shared list of resources that have most influenced their thinking about communities, leadership and change, program design, and evaluation (LLC Evaluation Circle, 2005).

One of the group activities was identifying each program's short-term, intermediate, and long-term outcomes. After the meeting, we analyzed and categorized these collective outcomes using the categories of changes in thought and feeling, changes in behavior, changes in interaction, and changes in collective action that we had developed at our earlier gathering. We disseminated this analysis to those who participated in the community leadership development gathering and invited them to join us in a conference call to test the validity and relevance of the framework. While data has not been collected from participants about how they have applied what they learned, the systematic process of gathering data, creating a framework, and testing that framework against the experiences of diverse stakeholders appears to be a promising methodology for deepening knowledge about the leadership transformation process.

As you can see, our learning process is dynamic and emergent. Because initial efforts to create a learning agenda to guide collective work did not meet the needs of the learning community (see Exhibit 18.5), we moved toward exploring issues around which there was collective momentum and interest. We look for synergies in what we are learning along the way and seek opportunities to test and deepen our emergent knowledge. We have found that participants are willing to engage in virtual learning exercises designed to maximize the synergy and productivity of the learning that occurs in face-to-face time.

Becoming a Resource to the Leadership Development Evaluation Field

LLC has become a resource for the field of leadership development evaluation. For example, LLC was tapped for a research project on how fifty-five leadership programs evaluate their outcomes and impacts. Drawing on the resources of those leadership programs that participate in LLC, a list of the most frequent leadership outcomes for individuals, organizations, communities, fields, and systems was compiled (W. K. Kellogg Foundation, 2002). In addition, LLC worked with the Sustainable Leadership Initiative to recruit programs that could field-test the EvaluLEAD guide. The field-test process contributed to improving the usability and relevance of the EvaluLEAD guide.

Disseminating Evaluation Learning

One of our most deeply held commitments as a learning community is to share tools, resources, and knowledge with each other so that we can accelerate learning and increase the quality and use of evaluation findings to strengthen the practice of leadership development. On the LLC Web site we disseminate evaluation reports, guides, and tools that LLC community members have developed, and that may be valuable to those in the field of leadership development evaluation and to program staff who are trying to develop their internal capacity for continuous learning.

We always synthesize and share the learning process and outcomes from circle gatherings. We consider these circle syntheses as works in progress because they capture questions, visions, and lessons at one point in time. Waiting to share only polished products can stifle the exchange of valuable information and insights in favor of a more labor- and cost-intensive monograph that may not fully capture the learning that has evolved during the production process. It is our opinion that sharing work in progress accelerates the exchange of ideas and invites others to use and build upon this work more quickly.

We have begun to experiment with Web-based commentary vehicles that enable readers to respond to and comment on circle notes to expand and deepen learning. Reports are used to catalyze additional reflection and learning. In whatever ways we can, we seek processes that continually generate new knowledge.

We are still discovering ways to support dissemination face to face and through the Internet. One promising direction is modeling and documenting the learning circle process so that people can adapt it to their own settings to create new evaluation communities of learning and practice. By disseminating the process of learning (not just the results), capacity for generating knowledge grounded in experience, reflection, and mining of collective wisdom has a much greater opportunity to expand.

Assessing Circle Outcomes and Impacts

In a recent evaluation of the Leadership Learning Community, the evaluation learning circle was recognized for its conceptual and collaborative efforts as a knowledge developer in the area of evaluation.

This review of the evaluation learning circle was gathered from surveys and in-depth interviews, but there has been no systematic effort to capture how participation in circle projects and gatherings has influenced the evaluation of leadership development on a broader level.

We do have evidence that about one-fifth of all visitors to the LLC Web site visit the Evaluation Knowledge Pool. While this is encouraging, we do not know how visitors use the information they find. This would require more systematic tracking of those people who come to the site.

The strongest evidence of impact is in the relationships and bonds of trust that have been created and deepened through circle work, and some of the projects that have developed or been enhanced as a result. In fact, without the work of the circle, it is doubtful that many of the authors in this book would have been aware of each other, or for that matter that the editorial collaboration between CCL evaluation staff and the LLC's Evaluation Circle Convenor would have developed. Both the editors of this book and many of the authors met and/or deepened their relationships with each other through evaluation learning circle gatherings.

The collaboration on *The Handbook of Leadership Development Evaluation* was initiated after Creating Space in May 2003. At the evaluation learning circle gathering later that year, we began discussing the book project with several people who became contributors to the book. We generated excitement about the contribution this book could make to the field and affirmed the value of the work that people were doing. Because many of us knew each other through the LLC evaluation learning circle, the commitment we made to participate in this project was both personal and professional. In addition to the evaluation learning circle, there were other venues that contributed as well, including the leadership evaluation advisory group that was a learning community supporting the development of EvaluLEAD, and the American Evaluation Association topical interest groups, in which leadership development evaluators gathered with each other and strengthened their connections.

It is much more difficult to determine if participation in the learning circle has improved the quality of leadership development evaluation in the nonprofit sector. We have collected some individual stories. For instance, one circle participant, inspired by the process of cross-program learning that the LLC evaluation circle was using, sought funding to bring together three leadership development programs she was evaluating, each of which focused on personal transformation. Representatives from the three programs worked together to define what they each meant by personal transformation and to see where they had common and divergent understandings. They explored how to recognize when personal transformation was occurring and what they were learning about how best to support personal transformation. This process of cross-program learning deepened their collective understanding about what they were trying to achieve, and how best to achieve it (see Chapter Seven).

LLC may want to more systematically collect stories about the value that is created by participating in circles. Focusing on value creation will not only enable us to document outcomes, it will also accelerate our learning about how to create value through learning circles. For a description of what participants say they like about being part of the evaluation learning circle, see Exhibit 18.6.

EXHIBIT 18.6. BENEFITS OF PARTICIPATION IN THE EVALUATION LEARNING CIRCLE.

This list captures how participants describe what they like about being part of the evaluation learning circle.

- Being part of a community that values learning more than competition

- The acceleration of learning that occurs when diverse stakeholders participate

- The ability to make a more persuasive case for investing in leadership development and leadership development evaluation

- Reducing the sense of isolation by connecting with others and confirming that the challenges we face individually are the challenges we face collectively

- Having an opportunity to explore deeper questions that cannot usually be asked (such as, What do we mean by personal transformation and how is it linked to organizational and community transformation?)

- Being exposed to new methods, tools, approaches, and ideas

- Having time for reflection

- Imagining together how we want leadership development evaluation to evolve

- Contributing to building the knowledge of the field

Challenges of Generating and Disseminating Knowledge

There are challenges to generating and disseminating knowledge, beginning with how we think about and conceptualize knowledge itself. Knowledge is not static. It is accrued experience, the residual effect of actions, thinking, and dialogue that remain dynamic and contribute to an ongoing experience. Knowledge, in other words, lives in communities of practice in which people who share an issue, a problem, or an enthusiasm for a topic can increase their knowledge and expertise by interacting with one another (Wenger, McDermott, and Snyder, 2002).

Creating vibrant communities of practice is key to generating useful and meaningful knowledge. A vibrant community creates a shared vocabulary and core knowledge base that enables it to explore ever deeper and more complex questions. At the same time, a vibrant community is inclusive of multiple perspectives and experiences that enrich the body of knowledge and challenge truths that may be relevant to only one set of experiences. Stewarding a community of practice means holding these two needs in balance.

Perhaps one of the greatest challenges we face is how to disseminate knowledge beyond those who are active participants in its generation. There are both product and process challenges in this effort. We are learning, for instance, that tools that provide a step-based approach to evaluation embed knowledge that will emerge when people apply the tool. This seems to be an effective way to disseminate knowledge, because people want tools they can use to make their evaluations easier and better. While some people will pick up a tool and apply it, thus enhancing their learning and knowledge in the process, other people hesitate to use a tool unless they have a community or peer relationship to support them to try something new. These peer resources are more easily accessed through a learning community, as was clearly demonstrated with the EvaluLEAD field-test process.

The effective dissemination of knowledge requires a collective effort of all those who participate in generating knowledge to expand the people with whom they share knowledge. This is the "ripple effect" of knowledge generation, in which the spread of knowledge accumulates over time. Knowledge that is most valuable and useful will likely spread faster than knowledge that is not. After all, the validation of knowledge is ultimately in its ability to illuminate connections and provide insights that lead to improved practice.

Leadership Evaluation Ten Years from Now

So what is the collective vision of leadership development evaluation that is emerging from the evaluation learning circle? Where do we want our practice and learning to go? We asked evaluation learning circle participants to envision leadership development evaluation ten years from now, to explore the ways in which our roles and profession may need to change. Some of the insights that emerged from this exercise seem valuable for all of us to consider as we continue to engage in evaluating leadership development. Here is a summary of our vision.

- Evaluation is shifting from a process that is primarily external and conducted by consultants to a process that is integrated into the fabric of our work.
- Evaluation learning occurs in real time.
- Evaluation is more democratic; it is no longer done to us but is something that enables us.
- The validity of diverse ways of knowing is widely accepted.
- Technology creates access for many more people to document and interpret their experiences, resulting in a proliferation of knowledge.
- Integrating and synthesizing knowledge is a form of practice that accelerates change.
- Our frameworks of understanding are grounded in diverse cultural perspectives and experiences.

Areas for Further Learning and Exploration

The Leadership Learning Community and the evaluation learning circle continue to explore a number of questions.

- What is the minimum bundle of leadership development program elements that seed change in individuals, organizations, communities, fields, and systems?

- What are we learning about how to effectively use storytelling, case studies, and scenarios to place facts in context and give meaning to what we are seeing, hearing, and dreaming?
- How do we make evaluation more accessible and less costly? Can we use new technologies to democratize evaluation?
- What is the extent and strength of networks needed to foster individual, organizational, and community change? How can we better analyze social networks?
- How do we most effectively use evaluation as a tool for transformation and evolution?

In addition to these questions, we are challenging ourselves to integrate and synthesize what we are learning about effective leadership development practices that catalyze and seed positive change and to understand what the outcomes of these practices are. This effort will expand our shared knowledge base and make a stronger case for what we have learned. At the same time, we recognize the dangers of this quest. Knowledge may become detached from the source of its learning and lose its dynamic character. It may come to be seen as standing above practice, at which point it loses its usefulness. As a community we will continue to work with this tension, finding ways to establish a baseline of shared knowledge and honor context and complexity.

Conclusion

As we continue to learn more about how to evaluate leadership development, we need to pay attention not only to what we learn as individuals but what we are learning as a community and a field. We invite readers to join LLC to shape the field of the future and improve our collective capacity to develop and support leadership that can accelerate positive change in our world. While some of you may work in the for-profit rather than the nonprofit sector, LLC offers an opportunity for deeper connection and learning that is still valuable and useful. This book is a catalyst for a cross-sector conversation about leadership development. It is up to us to continue it. The synergy that might be created through this exchange could well enhance the usefulness of all our evaluation efforts, and accelerate changes that neither sector will realize alone.

Resources

The Evaluation Learning Circle's Knowledge Pool may be found at www.lead-ershiplearning.org. We invite and encourage you to read circle notes and become part of the learning process. Visitors to the site can join the evaluation learning circle by sending us an e-mail. You can upload your own resources in the community contributions section. Any visitor to the site can download anything freely. We believe learning will be accelerated through an open source environment.

Horton, M., and Freire, P. *We Make the Road by Walking: Conversations on Education and Social Change* (B. Bell, J. Gaventa, and J. Peters, eds.). Philadelphia: Temple University Press, 1990. This book offers an intriguing dialogue between Paolo Freire and Myles Horton that includes a chapter on educational practice that is instructive about how to create an effective learning environment among adult learners. Paolo Freire led a movement for democratic education in Brazil, and Myles Horton, a founder of the Highlander Center in the Appalachian region of Tennessee, developed "citizenship schools" in the early years of the civil rights movement.

Leadership Learning Community. The LLC Web site may be found at www.leadershiplearning.org. The site connects learning partners through an accessible leadership development program directory, shares resources through the knowledge pools, and has developed tools to support virtual learning activities.

Wheatley, M. "Supporting Pioneering Leaders as Communities of Practice: How to Rapidly Develop New Leaders in Great Numbers." Spokane, Wash.: The Berkana Institute, 2002 [www.berkana.org/resources/pioneering leader.html]. Accessed July 5, 2006. This article discusses how to use a "communities of practice" approach to develop leaders. Meg Wheatley is founder of the Berkana Institute. The institute initiated a global leadership initiative to organize ongoing circles of leaders in local communities across the world, and then connects these local circles into a global community of life-affirming leaders.

References

Evaluation Forum. *Guide to Evaluating Leadership Development Programs.* Seattle: May 2003.

Grove, J., Kibel, B., and Haas, T. *EvaluLEAD: A Guide for Shaping and Evaluating Leadership Development Programs.* Oakland, Calif.: Public Health Institute, January 2005.

Horton, M., and Freire, P. *We Make the Road by Walking: Conversations on Education and Social Change* (B. Bell, J. Gaventa, and J. Peters, eds.). Philadelphia: Temple University Press, 1990.

Howell, R. E., Weir, I. L., and Cook, A. K. *Public Affairs Leadership Development: An Impact Assessment of Programs Conducted in California, Michigan, Montana, and Pennsylvania.* Pullman: Washington State University, Department of Rural Sociology, 1979.

Hsieh, K. *Creating Space IV: How Do We Become More Reflective Leadership Development Practitioners, Individually and Collectively,* 2003. [www.leadershiplearning.org/creating_space/2003/].

LLC Evaluation Learning Circle. "Seeding a Leadership Development Evaluation Learning Agenda and Learning Process," 2003. [www.leadershiplearning.org/community/files/download?version_id=1753].

LLC Evaluation Learning Circle. "Exploring Personal Transformation and Its Links to Organizational and Community Transformation," 2004. [www.leadershiplearning.org/community/files/download?version_id=1750].

LLC Evaluation Learning Circle. "Theories of Change and Community Leadership Development," 2005. [www.leadershiplearning.org/community/files/download?version_id=1751].

Nevin, D. *Left-Handed Fastballers: Scouting and Training America's Grass-Roots Leaders 1966–1977.* New York: Ford Foundation, 1981.

Pond, A., and Nielson, S. *Leadership Learning Community: Program and Organizational Assessment,* unpublished evaluation report, Oakland, Calif., 2004.

W. K. Kellogg Foundation. *Evaluating Outcomes and Impacts: A Scan of 55 Leadership Development Programs.* Battle Creek, Mich.: August 2002.

W. K. Kellogg Foundation. *The Legacy of the Ag Leadership Development Program: Rich Heritage Cultivates Future Opportunities.* Battle Creek, Mich.: October 2001.

Wenger, E., McDermott, R., and Snyder, W. *Cultivating Communities of Practice.* Boston: Harvard Business School Press, 2002.

CHAPTER NINETEEN

CONTINUOUS LEARNING

Rosalie T. Torres

T his chapter presents and discusses a continuous learning approach to the use of evaluation findings about leadership development programs. Its central argument is that evaluation designed and carried out in a way that supports ongoing use of findings within a particular organizational context best supports learning and change necessary to the development, delivery, and outcomes of leadership development programs. The approach is very much embodied in the work of evaluators who have articulated the relationship between evaluation and organizational learning (Cousins, 1996; Cousins and Earl, 1995; Owen and Lambert, 1995; Preskill and Torres, 1999; Robinson and Cousins, 2004; Torres and Preskill, 2001; Torres, Preskill, and Piontek, 2005).

Here the approach is primarily presented in terms of, and in some ways most readily applies to, the use of evaluation findings within a single organization that is immediately responsible for decision making about the design and delivery of leadership development programs, and is highly interested in evaluation findings to inform program development and improvement. Audiences for evaluation findings about leadership development programs do, however, span a broader spectrum, including sponsors, funders, and clients external to the providing organization (see Chapter Seventeen). And, as evidenced throughout this volume, organizations that provide leadership development programs span a wide range from single-site nonprofits to multinational corporations to multisite collectives or collaboratives. These local, national, and international organizations serve the full gamut of leaders and prospective leaders from youth to very specialized sectors (for example, academic environmental scientists). These audiences and situations are addressed toward the end of the chapter after the case has been made for continuous learning based on significant engagement with evaluation findings within a single organizational context. Ultimately, this chapter argues that the organization (whether it is the funder, sponsor, corporation, governmental entity) within which evaluation use (formative or summative) occurs is the appropriate "unit of measure" for considering how learning can be maximized.

Continuous Learning Approach to Evaluation

The central tenet of a continuous learning approach to evaluation is that use of findings takes place on an ongoing basis stimulated by an abiding desire for data to inform growth and improvement. This notion stands in stark contrast to (and in some ways was promulgated by) evaluation use seen in the beginnings of the profession in the 1960s. At this time, evaluation primarily conducted by outside parties served an accountability function, and a sharp distinction between formative (for improvement/development) and summative (to determine effectiveness/worth) evaluation arose (see Scriven, 1967). Seeing little use of their primarily summative evaluation efforts drove evaluators to study factors influencing use. From those efforts a vast body of literature arose, much of which speaks to the virtues of participatory, collaborative evaluation for promoting ownership and use of evaluation findings (see, for example, Cousins, 2003; Cousins and Whitmore, 1998; Greene, 1988; Patton, 1978, 1986, 1997). Recent literature on use has focused on the relationship between evaluation and organizational learning.

"Organizational learning is a continuous process of growth and improvement that (1) uses information or feedback about both processes and outcomes (that is, evaluation findings) to make changes; (2) is integrated with work activities and with the organization's infrastructure (for example, its culture, systems and structures, leadership, and communication mechanisms); and

(3) invokes the alignment of values, attitudes, and perceptions among organizational members" (Torres and others, 2005, p. 6).

Thus, for continuing learning to occur, organizations must embrace evaluation "as a central tool for improvement rather than as mere paperwork required for funding" (Hernandez and Visher, 2001, p. 2). As much as possible, a spirit of inquiry pervades the organization, as opposed to the belief that the organization has all the information it needs for decision making until such time when a specific question or issue arises and there is engagement in some type of episodic learning to address it. This is not to say that there won't be times when a specific event or reporting requirement will be the impetus for a particular data collection endeavor. The intent, though, is that "each new learning both feeds back to inform . . . previous learning and feeds forward to set conditions for future learning" (Grove, Kibel, and Haas, 2005, p. 11). In this way the organization is in a continual process of making meaning from data about its functioning, but this meaning is never truly considered the last word.

This continuous learning approach to evaluation is particularly applicable to leadership development programs for at least two major reasons. First, the learning approach to evaluation and continuous learning as a major component of leadership has common roots in the organizational learning literature (see Senge, 1990a, 1990b, 1996; Watkins, 1996; Watkins and Marsick, 1993, 1996).

Second, the approach parallels the incremental growth and development processes that leadership development seeks to foster in individuals, organizations, and even at societal levels (see Grove and others, 2005, on episodic, developmental, transformative results from leadership development programs). The outcomes of leadership development programs are not necessarily realized or particularly visible in any one segment of time. So too, goes the use of evaluation findings, which does not alone necessarily result in immediate changes or decisions, but works in conjunction with any number of other sources of information and contextual circumstances and is as likely to manifest in changes in awareness and understanding as in direct action. Moreover, direct action partly attributable to evaluation findings is as likely (or more so) to take place at some later time as it is shortly after findings have been considered. Thus, from the standpoint of continuous learning, the use of evaluation findings is a process within a particular organizational context, not an end result.

Case Example for This Chapter

Throughout the remainder of this chapter a case example is used to provide nuance, meaning, and instances of practical application to the evaluation approach described here. This case describes the circumstances of a nonprofit organization that develops and markets leadership programs to K–12 school systems across the United States. The organization has a long-term relationship with an evaluation consulting group that provides both formative and summative evaluation findings for use by the nonprofit itself, the school systems that are clients of the nonprofit, and the foundations that fund the nonprofit. As described at the beginning of this chapter, there are many organization types through which leadership development programs are provided and means through which evaluation of these programs takes place. This case describes but one situation. It can be useful for learning and reflection about other situations because it describes the use of an approach to evaluation that has more to do with a way of thinking about evaluation (that is, in the context of continuous learning within virtually any type of organization) than it has to do with specific procedures that are applicable to one type of organization but not another. As with any learning materials, readers are invited to see how the tenets of this approach are applicable in the case described and also consider how the tenets relate to and can be useful in their own past, present, or anticipated experiences with evaluation of leadership development programs—which almost certainly are grounded in a variety of different circumstances. The basic elements of the case follow, and are elaborated upon throughout the chapter. Note that the elaborations of the case describe particular aspects of the evaluation work that illustrate the continuous learning approach to evaluation presented in the chapter. Due to constraints of space, the introduction to the case that follows and the elaborations as a whole do not describe every aspect of the evaluation work.

Center for Leadership Development in Education

The Center for Leadership Development in Education (CLDE) is an independent nonprofit organization that develops and markets a variety of leadership development programs to elementary and secondary school systems throughout the United States. The center was founded about twenty-five years ago with major foundation funding, and has continued to receive funding from multiple sources, including large and small foundations, and the state and federal governments. CLDE's flagship program is a leadership development academy for individuals who are currently serving as elementary school principals. The academy consists of a twelve-month program spanning two school years (January through December). Participants attend an initial weekend retreat, eight cohort group meetings, and six one-day seminars. They also receive sixty hours of individual coaching and support from an assigned mentor or coach.

Other smaller programs that the center offers provide institutes in educational administration for promising teachers, executive leadership development for superintendents, and leadership development for school boards. Over the history of the center, evaluation of its programs has occurred through a variety of arrangements, including both internal and external evaluators. Currently there is only a small-scale internal evaluation effort that compiles results from postprogram surveys completed by participants. CLDE has recently made a decision to expand its evaluation of the elementary principal leadership academy and has engaged the services of an evaluation consulting group that has conducted other evaluations for the center in the past. The major impetus for this evaluation effort is that the center's president feels that the academy could be more successful and marketable if revisions were made. He has some hypotheses about possible revisions, but wants a full-scale evaluation through which his ideas can be vetted, and in which the center's instructional designers can become involved as part of an organizational learning process. The president and lead evaluator began the evaluation effort by forming a team that would meet regularly to plan and guide the evaluation. In addition to the president, the lead evaluator and an associate evaluator from the evaluation consulting group, the team consisted of six representatives from each of the following CLDE departments: instructional design (two representatives), staff development (two), editorial (one), and marketing (one). Additionally, one past participant of the academy, who was also a consultant for CLDE, agreed to be a part of the evaluation team. The lead evaluator served as the facilitator for the team.

Processes of Engagement for Continuous Learning

Crucial to a continuous learning approach to evaluation is making meaning from evaluation processes and findings. Doing so requires significant engagement with the substance and circumstances of the evaluation and its findings. As detailed in Preskill and Torres (1999), this engagement can be realized through four interrelated learning processes: asking questions; dialogue; reflection; and examining underlying values, beliefs, and assumptions—applicable in all phases of an evaluation. In the following paragraphs, each is discussed as it applies to evaluation that supports continuous learning.

Asking Questions. Questions are part and parcel of any evaluation endeavor, from focusing the inquiry through interpreting and applying findings. In particular, a disposition of asking questions underlies the state of mind necessary for continuous learning from evaluation findings. Questions related to problems, issues, concerns, processes, and/or outcomes of leadership development programs are the impetus for many evaluation endeavors. Ongoing questioning stimulates continuous learning and a sense of connectedness, both of which are also enhanced when organization members begin with asking questions about existing levels of knowledge and understanding, and build data collection efforts from there.

In the case of CLDE, the lead evaluator invited the team to consider pertinent but sometimes overlooked questions related to various phases of the evaluation (see Preskill and Torres, 1999). These questions—intended to support continuous learning—and how they were used at different times during the evaluation are described following. (Note that what follows are snippets of the evaluation process; it is not meant to describe the evaluation processes and/or use of questioning in their entirety.)

Focusing the Evaluative Inquiry. During the first team meeting, the evaluator sought to establish a shared vision about the purpose of evaluating the academy. She posed the following questions for the team to consider.

- Why is it important that we collect additional data about the academy at this time?
- What are some of our hypotheses about how the academy is working now and why?
- What might we do if the evaluation findings do not support these hypotheses?

At this meeting the president was able to air his notions about how the academy might be revised, but others were able to do so as well. And, they were able to see that the president was open to learning from the evaluation and was not unduly tied to his current ideas.

Carrying Out the Inquiry. At another meeting, during which the team was invited to think about the use of data in the organization (so that existing data could be built upon in the evaluation of the academy), the evaluator posed these questions:

- What kinds of data does CLDE typically respond to? What does it ignore?
- What data already exist that might address the evaluation question we have developed?
- Where does this information reside?
- What new sources of data might we need to develop?

Here the team got to see that the existing sources of data were not adequate to inform the things they wanted the evaluation to address. This meeting helped develop shared buy-in for the work necessary to collect additional data.

Learning from the Inquiry. During a later stage of the evaluation, the evaluator and associate evaluator pondered the following questions themselves.

- What are some different analytic or reporting frameworks that might be appropriate for presenting findings about the academy (for example, the original evaluation questions, some organizational or programmatic framework, a new issues-oriented framework determined by the content of the findings)?
- How does each possible different framework meet the learning needs of the organization?

Once they had come up with some tentative answers, they included them in a presentation to the team and asked for feedback. They incorporated this feedback into an outline for organizing the evaluation findings, which they worked with once findings were available but refined again (based on "fit" with the findings) prior to the presentation of findings to the team.

As the evaluation work proceeded, the lead and associate evaluator periodically also discussed the following question between themselves.

- How can we best handle the communication of negative findings in a way that will support continuous learning?

Through their ongoing work with the team, the evaluators came to understand where certain team members' sensitivities were about the work on the academy for which they were responsible. In their initial draft of a presentation of the evaluation findings, some of the more negative findings about the academy curriculum were to be presented at the beginning. For their final version of the presentation, the evaluators decided to move this section to the middle of the presentation—after which they hoped that the team as a whole had become comfortable with receiving information about how well the academy had been working, and some desensitization had been taking place.

Dialogue. Throughout the evaluation, addressing questions such as these (in addition to the basic ones necessary for planning and conducting the evaluation) naturally leads to some form of discussion. Discussion involving the production of new knowledge and understanding (as opposed to telling, selling, or persuading) is dialogue. Discussion is often about preserving the status quo, whereas dialogue occurs when group members agree to suspend judgment in order to create new understandings. "Through dialog, individuals seek to inquire, share meanings, understand complex issues, and uncover assumptions" (Preskill and Torres, 1999, p. 52). A central feature of dialogue is bringing together multiple points of view that need to be addressed and negotiated, allowing group members to share meanings important for the continuous learning process.

For the CLDE evaluation team, dialogue conducted in a spirit of inquiry and learning resulted from many of the questions previously outlined. As described, the dialogue led to productive decision making for the academy evaluation.

Reflection. Reflection, a process through which individuals and groups review their ideas, understandings, and experiences, is almost always a result of asking questions and of the ensuing dialogue. Reflection enables group members to think more deeply and holistically about an issue, leading to greater insights and understanding; and it can help connect rational decision-making processes to affect and experience.

In the case of the CLDE academy evaluation, reflection was an important part of the evaluation team's action planning based on the evaluation findings. Through the evaluation, the team learned that one of the things most valued by the principals was the individual coaching and mentoring that they received. Although not addressed specifically, there were also hints in the evaluation data that principals wanted more opportunities for interacting with peers; for them this was another way of getting individual support around particular leadership issues they were facing. Because the team also saw ongoing peer support as a way of sustaining the program beyond the life of the formal academy experience, they were particularly interested in adding a peer support component. In the process of making this decision and specifying the details of a peer support component, they reflected on the following questions.

- What concerns do I have about adding a peer support component and why?
- How are participants likely to respond to the component, in particular as we have specified it?
- How will other stakeholders likely respond? District administrators? Our funders?

By systematically considering the addition of this component and its details from different perspectives, the team was able to better assure its ultimate success. As a result of the dialogue that resulted from these questions, they decided to make certain revisions to the peer support component as planned and to market the component in proposals they were currently developing to seek needed funding for redesigning the academy.

Reflection also takes place on an individual basis, and is often the basis for questions pertinent to inquiry activities that individuals may raise for consideration among colleagues and for input that individuals bring to any given dialogue.

Examining Underlying Values, Beliefs, and Assumptions. Another important outcome in the example of reflection just described is that it led to the uncovering of differing values, beliefs, and assumptions within the team; and it allowed the team to consider what values, beliefs, and perspectives might be invoked for others relative to a change in the design of the academy.

Another way to get at the perspectives individuals bring to an evaluation endeavor is to pose the following questions for individual reflection, followed by group discussion.

- What experiences have I had with respect to this issue or program? Were they positive, negative, or neutral?
- Have I had an experience where my expectations were not met? If so, why were they not met?
- How do I think this program/situation could be improved?
- Based on my answers to these questions, what underlying assumptions and values does my perspective on this program/situation/issue reflect?
- In what ways might my values influence my thinking about the evaluation endeavor?

Uncovering values, beliefs, and assumptions helps individuals understand that their perspective is one among many. Individually and collectively held beliefs and assumptions are significant mediators of action. Airing them supports mutual understanding. It can help individuals accept and modify their thinking and behavior, and can bring collective wisdom to decision making about evaluation activities and the use of findings. A climate of trust and safety is necessary for productive dialogue about individuals' values, beliefs, and assumptions. This topic is addressed in the following section on the characteristics of organizations in which continuous learning will be most successful.

Organizational Infrastructure to Support Continuous Learning

By now and probably more than once, readers may have thought, "This continuous learning approach is all fine and well, but it could never happen in my organization." It is most certainly true that continuous learning approaches thrive more readily in some organizations than in others. It is important to address this issue because the continuous learning approach described here recognizes that learning within any organization is significantly influenced by the organization's infrastructure: its culture, leadership, communication, and systems and structures (Preskill and Torres, 1999), all of which are interrelated.

Culture

In many ways, an organization's culture determines the extent to which learning takes place within it. Culture (the organization's traditions, customs, and philosophy) can be seen in "the patterns of interaction between individuals, the language that is used, themes explored in conversation, and the various rituals of daily routine" (Morgan, 1997, p. 130). "A learning culture requires that individuals be willing to take risks, that they view mistakes as opportunities for learning, and that a climate of trust and courage supports learning" (Preskill and Torres, 1999, p. 156).

In the case of CLDE, the team was able to approach the evaluation of the principal academy in the spirit of inquiry and discovery because the culture supported doing so. While CLDE staff sometimes acknowledged to themselves that their organization tended toward being overly academic, this characteristic served the evaluation effort well in that engaging in dialogue was viewed as a legitimate and necessary use of time; the dialogue was not unduly hampered by individuals feeling defensive about their areas of responsibility that the evaluation addressed; and members of the team felt safe in the presence of the executive director to air their views. As evidenced here, an organization's leadership plays an important role in its overall culture.

Leadership

Leadership in organizations that support continuous learning is operative at two levels: from the top of the organization, and also among lower levels of management as well as internal networkers or community builders (see Senge, 1996).

Organizations that design and deliver leadership development programs would reasonably be expected to practice what they preach. Thus, executive leadership would most likely have a vision for learning within the organization and actively promote it. For example, leaders would explicitly require that others within the organization devote time to the dialogue and reflection required for deep consideration and use of evaluation findings, and leaders themselves would actively participate in these endeavors. They would also make themselves readily accessible to those with evaluation responsibilities and see the value in tying evaluation to the organization's strategic objectives. Finally, they would provide resources for evaluation personnel to function in the networking capacity described following.

Those with evaluation responsibilities within an organization (and even in some cases external evaluators working with an organization over time) often function as networkers because they can bring together organization members from across various departments and functions, and they can also bring executive leadership together with other organizational members. Networkers exercise leadership supportive of continuous learning by (1) understanding contextual influences on the practice and use of evaluation within the organization, (2) working to maximize trust and credibility with all constituents, (3) aligning inquiry methods with the epistemological orientations of stakeholders, (4) raising and representing issues to those in authority, (5) educating senior management on the relationship between their perspectives and the perspectives of others, and (6) maintaining tolerance for ambiguity and incremental change (Torres, 1991).

Referring again to our case, it is obvious that CLDE's president exhibited many of the leadership qualities described here. He sought the evaluation to begin with, recognizing that his hypotheses about how and why the academy was working needed to be tested. He also realized that undertaking an evaluation inquiry without the involvement and support of those responsible for carrying out any resulting decisions to change the program would be destined to fail. Further, he was instrumental in seeking representation on the evaluation team by those individuals within the center's functional departments who were networkers. In particular, he advised the lead evaluator that certain individuals would be good team members because they had a broad view of how the academy operated, were trusted by their colleagues, and were not afraid to raise important issues—even those that the president himself might not want to hear.

Communication

It makes sense that communication systems and customs within an organization can either support or hinder continuous learning. Supportive organizational communication (1) uses information for learning, not personal power, (2) disseminates information that captures a diversity of voices, (3) uses information as a means to share learning among coworkers, (4) uses technology to manage, disseminate, and increase access to information, and (5) provides means for interpreting data (Preskill and Torres, 1999). Thus, communication systems cover everything from how and what information is shared and to whom, to how it is processed and used. As described earlier, continuous learning is an iterative process in which new learning informs and is informed by old learning. For this reason, information about what has gone before must be readily accessible.

In the CLDE case, the evaluators specifically addressed the organization's communication systems by determining what information already existed and/or was being collected that might inform the information needs of the evaluation. And earlier, in initial interviews with organization members (for more on the initial interviews, see following), they determined how information was typically used and shared within the center. This knowledge helped them support the evaluation team in devising plans for sharing results of the evaluation within the organization.

Generally, within leadership development organizations, communication systems that support continuous learning might include any or all of the following: the organization's strategic plan being available to all employees; a regular newsletter that describes evaluation findings from its programs; and an intranet or organizational database that captures basic, descriptive information about leadership development activities, routine evaluation findings, "lessons learned" and "best practices" entered by trainer-facilitators on a routine basis, and the results of periodic working sessions to review evaluation findings and refine practices.

Systems and Structures

The more integrated an organization's systems and structures are (that is, how it is organized to get work done), the more successful will be a continuous learning approach to evaluation. That is, functions and departments operating like silos within an organization are much less likely to learn effectively. Within any leadership development organization that is large enough to have an internal evaluation staff, it makes sense that working closely with and having ready access to others within the organization will facilitate learning. Though, regardless of the existence of an internal evaluation function or the number of persons with evaluation responsibilities, the more that the organization as a whole supports collaboration, communication, and cooperation among organization members within and across units and departments, the more learning can take place.

CLDE's external evaluators compensated for not having daily or routine access to organization members by working with a team that represented the major functional areas of the center. The work of the team built upon and helped to further existing collaborative efforts within the center.

Diagnosis of Organizational Infrastructure

Preskill, Torres, and Martinez-Papponi (1999) developed a diagnostic instrument, based on the organizational characteristics just described, to assess an organization's readiness for organizational learning and evaluation. The eighty-item instrument, *Readiness for Organizational Learning and Evaluation* (ROLE), available in Russ-Eft and Preskill (2001) and from this author, includes questions concerning the organization's culture, leadership, systems and structures, communication practices, use of teams, and evaluation. The results reflect the organization's (or department's) ability and commitment to sharing learning, asking questions, rewarding and recognizing individuals for learning, reflecting on practice, risk taking, working collaboratively, and engaging in evaluation studies. The results can be used to understand the organizational context as well as how an evaluation study may be perceived and supported. Additionally, by providing information about accessibility and information dissemination practices, the findings can inform evaluators about strategies to support continuous learning that might be especially beneficial and are most likely to be successful.

What is important to recognize is that continuous learning approaches can be promoted within any organization, regardless of its overall culture and leadership characteristics. The approach is multifaceted and permeates every part of any evaluation endeavor. A formal or informal diagnosis of the organization can take place, and the results can inform those promoting continuous learning of "teachable moments" along the way. Based on successes (small or large), the organization may become more and more open or able to embrace more of the approach, with the eventual result that aspects of the infrastructure begin to change.

For CLDE, the evaluator did not use a formal instrument to assess the organization's infrastructure, although it was considered. She discussed this possibility with the president, who was concerned that use of the instrument would raise too many issues that he was not prepared to address. Rather, the lead evaluator built her understanding of the infrastructure upon her prior knowledge of the organization as well as individual interviews that she and the associate evaluator conducted before the evaluation team was convened. This helped accelerate the evaluators' work with the team by allowing them to tailor questions for discussion to particular issues and circumstances that they would have only learned about, if at all, as the evaluation proceeded. Thus, the evaluators were able to make the evaluation more tailored and relevant to the center sooner than would have been possible otherwise.

Key Features of Evaluation Practice to Support Continuous Learning

This section describes various important features of evaluation practice to support continuous learning: evaluator role, the need for a programmatic frame of reference, the issue of boundaries between evaluation and program work, dealing with stakeholders external to the organization, and the time required for this approach. The following paragraphs address many of the issues and challenges of a continuous learning approach as well as its many promises.

Evaluator Role

A continuous learning approach can apply to evaluation regardless of the evaluator's role, whether the evaluator is internal to the leadership development organization (with dedicated or partially dedicated evaluation responsibilities) or is external to the organization. There are some particular advantages to functioning as an internal evaluator. These include having immediate knowledge of the organizational infrastructure, having daily access to others in the organization crucial to the success of the evaluation function, being in a position to advocate for the approach and build supportive communication and data collection systems over time, and being able to take an iterative and integrative approach to learning over time.

As was the circumstance in this chapter's case example, external evaluators can have many of these same advantages if they are engaged in a long-term evaluation rather than a single, short-term relationship with the organization. In any case, an external evaluator will initially need to spend more time articulating and advocating for the approach and understanding and learning about the organizational infrastructure, especially the organization's current communication systems. Where there is particular receptivity to the approach, the organization may be interested in an initial assessment of its infrastructure with an instrument like ROLE, described earlier. The evaluator would then spend time at the outset working with the organization to interpret its findings and build the evaluation activities in a way that takes advantage of positive aspects of the organization's infrastructure and helps to develop any less favorable aspects. Although in the CLDE case using a formal assessment instrument was not possible, the evaluators addressed infrastructure as described earlier with a set of initial interviews.

Programmatic Frame of Reference

Another strategy particularly supportive of a continuous learning approach to the evaluation of leadership development programs is to create and use a programmatic frame of reference. This is a written or graphic representation of the leadership development program, its activities, and intended and unintended results that can be referred to and revised on an ongoing basis. One such representation is a logic model (see Chapters Two, Ten, and Sixteen in this handbook; see also Preskill and Russ-Eft, 2005; Rossi, Lipsey, and Freeman, 2004; Torres and others, 2005; W. K. Kellogg Foundation, 2001); another is the results map of the EvaluLEAD approach (see Chapter Three; also Grove and others, 2005). The representation shows some sequencing of and/or cause-effect relationships between and among program activities and short- and long-term outcomes. Given the nature of outcomes for leadership development programs (that is, ranging from experiences in the program to changes in knowledge, skill, and attitudes; to on-the-job activities and changes; to intra- and extra-organizational networking; to organizational- and community-level changes), having a shared understanding about what is happening (or is intended to happen) over time across various levels and accounting for leadership development program activities and other influences is especially important.

The development and use of such a representation can serve a variety of uses throughout almost all phases of an evaluation: program description, articulation of underlying assumptions, shared understanding or consensus among stakeholders, prioritization of evaluation questions, instrument development, information sharing among stakeholders, and ultimately, evaluation use and program improvement. The representation is a shared and accessible reference point for continuous learning, and a place to capture shifts in programming or programmatic theory that may result from the learning. Specifically, a programmatic frame of reference can help organization members and other stakeholders develop a shared understanding around the multitude of activities and outcomes (short- and long-term) comprising each leadership development activity and/or program. Over time, the frame of reference can be revisited to reflect changes and improvements and support participants' shared understanding of them, which in turn supports more efficient and effective program operation. Finally, the frame of reference can show the relationship between and among the multilayered activities and outcomes of leadership development programs; point to nodes or program events or processes that suggest indicators and measures; and guide the organization of analyses and reporting activities.

For CLDE, the evaluators began their work with a logic model that they had helped the center build for a previous evaluation project. This evaluation project was not focused on the academy exclusively, but the academy's activities and outcomes had been included in a comprehensive logic model for all of CLDE's programs. Starting with this previously developed logic model was especially useful because some of the evaluation team members for the academy evaluation had been involved in developing it. The team worked through bringing it up to date, a process that helped both the CLDE staff and the evaluators see the relationship between the academy and both its other programs and CLDE's organizational mission and vision. They revisited the logic model once evaluation findings were becoming available (to establish a framework for presenting the findings) and again when decision making about revisions to the academy had been made. The team revised the logic model accordingly, and this helped sensitize them to the need for establishing progress-monitoring procedures for the new version of the academy.

Boundaries

It is important to recognize that taking a continuous learning approach to evaluation blurs the traditional boundaries between organizational development and evaluation, and between program development and evaluation. The first of these is inherent in the fact that the approach accounts for the role and influence of the organization in learning from evaluation. To maximize learning, the evaluator explicitly attempts to understand the organization's infrastructure, articulates its role in learning to organization members, and designs the evaluation activities to build on strengths and support weaknesses.

In some organizations there is a distinction between program development and delivery and evaluation largely mediated by differences in professional expertise. That is, program development personnel do not usually have training and experience in the systematic data collection and analysis required of evaluation; nor do evaluators necessarily have skill and experience in leadership development models and approaches (in some organizations an individual or group of individuals can have responsibilities for both). In the case of an external evaluator who is providing expertise to the leadership development organization, there could be a rather sharp boundary between program design or improvement work and evaluation work. Yet, a continuous learning approach works best when these two functions are integrated, such that use of and learning from evaluation findings is naturally seen as an extension of the evaluation activity. This means that whether internal or external, evaluators stay involved in helping program personnel use evaluation findings and even in planning and implementing indicated changes in program design and delivery.

In the CLDE case example, evaluation and program work was integrated through the work of the team, which comprised individuals with expertise in both areas. Additionally, because CLDE saw the benefit of doing so, the team did not disband once evaluation findings were available. They continued their work beyond consideration of the evaluation findings to action planning based on the findings and progress monitoring for the revised academy. (For a partial description of this, see the section of this chapter on Reflection.)

Stakeholders External to the Organization

Leadership development programs are likely to have one or more important external audiences for evaluation activities and findings. These audiences may be particularly concerned with the demonstration of outcomes, often in quantitative terms. At least two strategies are appropriate for external stakeholders. First, evaluators should explain and document the organization's continuous learning approach for these audiences. Increasingly, foundations in particular are recognizing the significance of ongoing use of evaluation findings to program quality (for example, The James Irvine Foundation, 2003; the W. K. Kellogg Foundation, 2006). In some cases, providing evidence of this can serve as important an accountability function as proving that a program has achieved its ultimate outcomes.

Second, you can pay particular attention to those aspects of the communicating and reporting processes that support continuous learning among external stakeholders. For example, you can specifically determine the stakeholders' needs and preferences with respect to evaluation findings and provide findings in easily understood and accessible formats. The latter can include well-formatted and appealing documents, video presentations, and even such creative formats as photography, cartoons, poetry, and drama (see Chapter Seventeen; also Torres and others, 2005).

Once the CLDE evaluation team had considered the evaluation findings and implications for future offerings of the academy, they turned their attention to reporting to both CLDE funders and clients. In addition to marketing the new peer component of the academy in proposals for future funding (as described in the section on Reflection earlier), the team also decided to devote considerable space in their reports to existing funders about the collaborative, learning-oriented process that had been undertaken for the evaluation of the principal leadership academy. This same information was shared with the CLDE board of directors. Feedback from both funders and board members indicated that they appreciated the value of this organizational learning effort. The board requested additional information about how the team had worked together. This request resulted in a presentation made by the evaluators to the board that more broadly described the elements of a continuous learning approach to evaluation. Ultimately, the board's support for this approach helped to institutionalize it within the center over time.

Evaluation findings were also shared with CLDE clients, namely those individuals who had participated in this expanded evaluation of the academy. A two-page executive summary was prepared and designed to read more like a newsletter or flyer than a dense report. The summary went to all participants and school district administrators; the document was also posted on the CLDE Web site.

Time

Whether thinking about, beginning to implement, or sustaining a continuous learning approach to evaluation, time is the "elephant in the room." As the CLDE case example attempts to show, the approach is both collaborative and participatory. This takes more time than in cases where the evaluator is making most of the decisions about evaluation design, data collection, analysis, and reporting. The approach requires abiding attention to the role and influence of the organization's infrastructure; this takes more time than ignoring it, and much more time if you design evaluation to work in conjunction with it. The approach requires continually integrating learning with what has gone before; this takes more time than exclusively looking ahead. The approach requires substantive and collective engagement with interpreting and using evaluation findings; this takes more time than one person writing and disseminating evaluation reports.

There will never be enough time. But there are opportunities to engage with any of the different yet interrelated aspects of a continuous learning approach. And out of these various engagements can come realization that the time is well spent and worth the effort. (CLDE's evaluation team concluded their work on evaluating the academy by deciding to make plans for more extensive and ongoing progress monitoring of the new version of the academy than was typically done.) Successes with the approach (again, both large and small) can make getting the time to further the approach easier. Both challenges and unique rewards await evaluators and stakeholders alike who are inclined toward continuous learning from evaluation.

Recommendations

The following list of recommendations summarizes many of the major requisites for successfully using a continuous learning approach to the evaluation of leadership development programs.

- Develop a deep understanding of how a continuous learning approach is invoked through all phases of evaluation activity—not just when findings are used.
- Advocate for a continuous learning approach, recognizing that it constitutes an ongoing process in which some state of static perfection is not the goal; but rather, adopting the approach parallels the developmental process that continuous learning itself is. Always, always seek and act upon "teachable moments."
- Assess and refine your skills for asking questions, facilitating dialogue, reflecting, and helping groups and individuals uncover and share their underlying values, beliefs, and assumptions.
- As do many models of leadership (see Meehan, 1999), recognize and embrace the role of relationships in facilitating this approach to evaluation.

- Conduct a formal or informal but systematic assessment of the organization's infrastructure. This can range from a single interview with a key informant to multiple interviews across the organization to the use of an instrument completed by all employees to assess infrastructure.
- Begin the work by establishing some programmatic frame of reference that is developed collaboratively, grounded in shared understanding, and used and refined throughout the evaluation activities and continuous learning that they are designed to support.
- Assess both internal and external stakeholders' learning needs and preferences. Design communicating and reporting processes to address them.
- Finally, recognize that this approach can be used regardless of the evaluation methods being used.

Resources

Preskill, H. S., and Torres, R. T. *Evaluative Inquiry for Learning in Organizations.* Thousand Oaks, Calif.: Sage, 1999. This book provides a comprehensive treatment of an approach integrating evaluation with organizational learning.

Schwandt, D., and Marquardt, M. J. *Organizational Learning from World Class Theories to Global Best Practices.* Boca Raton, Fla.: CRC Press, 2000. This book provides information on organizational learning.

Taylor-Powell, E., Jones, L., and Henert, E. *Enhancing Program Performance with Logic Models.* University of Wisconsin-Extension Web site, 2002. [http://www1. uwex.edu/ces/lmcourse/].

Torres, R. T., Preskill, H. S., and Piontek, M. E. *Evaluation Strategies for Com municating and Reporting: Enhancing Learning in Organizations* (2nd ed.). Thousand Oaks, Calif.: Sage, 2005. This book provides evaluation communicating and reporting strategies to enhance learning.

References

Cousins, J. B. "Understanding Organizational Learning for Educational Leadership and School Reform." In K. A. Leithwood, D. Tomlinson, and M. Genge (eds.), *International Handbook of Educational Leadership and Administration.* Boston: Kluwer Academic, 1996.

Cousins, J. B. "Utilization Effects of Participatory Evaluation." In T. Kellaghan and D. L. Stufflebeam (eds.), *International Handbook of Educational Evaluation*. Norwell, Mass.: Kluwer, 2003.

Cousins, J. B., and Earl, L. M. (eds.). *Participatory Evaluation in Education: Studies in Evaluation Use and Organizational Learning*. London: Falmer, 1995.

Cousins, J. B., and Whitmore, E. "Framing Participatory Evaluation." *New Directions for Evaluation*, 1998, *80*, 5–23.

Greene, J. C. "Stakeholder Participation and Utilization in Program Evaluation." *Evaluation Review*, 1988, *12*(3), 91–116.

Grove, J. T., Kibel, B. M., and Haas, T. *EvaluLEAD: A Guide for Shaping and Evaluating Leadership Development Programs*. Battle Creek, Mich.: W. K. Kellogg Foundation, 2005. [www.wkkf.org/Pubs/Tools/Evaluation/ EvaluLEAD4_00447_03740.pdf].

Hernandez, G., and Visher, M. G. *Creating a Culture of Inquiry*. San Francisco: James Irvine Foundation, 2001.

The James Irvine Foundation. *IQ: Irvine Quarterly, An Online Publication*. Winter 2003, *2*(3). [www.irvine.org/publications/iq/archive/vol2_issue3/iq.shtml].

Meehan, D. *Leadership Development Opportunities and Challenges: A Scan of the Leadership Development Literature and the Field of Leadership Development*. Technical report. Oakland, Calif.: Leadership Learning Community, 1999. [www.leadershiplearning.org/resources/].

Morgan, G. *Images of Organizations* (2nd ed.). Thousand Oaks, Calif.: Sage, 1997.

Owen, J. M., and Lambert, F. C. "Roles for Evaluation in Learning Organizations." *Evaluation*, 1995, *1*(2), 259–273.

Patton, M. Q. *Utilization-Focused Evaluation*. Beverly Hills, Calif.: Sage, 1978.

Patton, M. Q. *Utilization-Focused Evaluation* (2nd ed.). Thousand Oaks, Calif.: Sage, 1986.

Patton, M. Q. *Utilization-Focused Evaluation: The New Century Text* (3rd ed.). Thousand Oaks, Calif.: Sage, 1997.

Preskill, H. S., and Russ-Eft, D. *Building Evaluation Capacity: 72 Activities for Teaching and Training*. Thousand Oaks, Calif.: Sage, 2005.

Preskill, H. S., and Torres, R. T. *Evaluative Inquiry for Learning in Organizations*. Thousand Oaks, Calif.: Sage, 1999.

Preskill, H., Torres, R. T., and Martinez-Papponi, B. "Assessing an Organization's Readiness for Learning from Evaluative Inquiry." Paper presented at the annual meeting of the American Evaluation Association. Orlando, November 1999.

Robinson, T. T., and Cousins, J. B. "Internal Participatory Evaluation as an Organizational Learning System: A Longitudinal Case Study." *Studies in Educational Evaluation*, 2004, *30*, 1–22.

Rossi, P. H., Lipsey, M. W., and Freeman, H. E. *Evaluation: A Systematic Approach*. Thousand Oaks, Calif.: Sage, 2004.

Russ-Eft, D., and Preskill, H. *Evaluation in Organizations: A Systematic Approach to Enhancing Learning, Performance, and Change*. Boston: Perseus, 2001.

Scriven, M. "The Methodology of Evaluation." In R. Tyler, R. Gagne, and M. Scriven (eds.), *Perspectives of Curriculum Evaluation*. Chicago: Rand McNally, 1967.

Senge, P. M. *The Fifth Discipline.* New York: Doubleday, 1990a.

Senge, P. M. "The Leaders' New Work: Building Learning Organizations." *Sloan Management Review,* 1990b, *32*(1), 19–35.

Senge, P. M. "Leading Learning Organizations: The Bold, the Powerful, and the Invisible." In F. Hesselbein, M. Goldsmith, and R. Beckhard (eds.), *The Leader of the Future.* San Francisco: Jossey-Bass, 1996, pp. 41–57.

Torres, R. T. "Improving the Quality of Internal Evaluation: The Evaluator as Consultant-Mediator." *Evaluation and Program Planning,* 1991, *14*(3), 189–198.

Torres, R. T., and Preskill, H. "Evaluation and Organizational Learning: Past, Present, and Future." *American Journal of Evaluation,* 2001, *22*(3), 387–396.

Torres, R. T., Preskill, H. S., and Piontek, M. E. *Evaluation Strategies for Communicating and Reporting: Enhancing Learning in Organizations* (2nd ed.). Thousand Oaks, Calif.: Sage, 2005.

Watkins, K. E. "Of Course Organizations Learn!" *New Directions for Adult and Continuing Education,* 1996, *72*(Winter), 89–94.

Watkins, K. E., and Marsick, V. J. *Sculpting the Learning Organization.* San Francisco: Jossey-Bass, 1993.

Watkins, K. E., and Marsick, V. J. (eds.). *Creating the Learning Organization,* Vol. 1. Alexandria, Va.: American Society for Training and Development, 1996.

W. K. Kellogg Foundation. Home page, 2006. [www.wkkf.org/default.aspx?LanguageID=0].

W. K. Kellogg Foundation. *Using Logic Models to Bring Together Planning, Evaluation, and Action: Logic Model Development Guide.* Battle Creek, Mich.: Author, 2001. [www.wkkf.org/Pubs/Tools/Evaluation/Pub3669.pdf].

AFTERWORD

Future Directions for Leadership Development Evaluation

Kelly M. Hannum, Jennifer W. Martineau, and Claire Reinelt

Over the past two decades, the number of graduate programs offering degrees in leadership as well as those focused on evaluation has increased dramatically in order to meet the need for leadership development and evaluation services. As these two fields expand, the intersection between them, leadership development evaluation, is gaining ground as an area of growing sophistication and relevance. The complexity within and interplay between the fields of leadership development and evaluation, as well as other related fields, create the need for boundary-spanning learning and practice. In order to effectively and efficiently cross boundaries, we must engage in dialogue around common issues and do so with a shared vocabulary. In order to conduct leadership development evaluation appropriately—rigorously, ethically, and in a culturally responsive manner—we need to explore how and why evaluations of leadership development are conducted.

In this afterword we present and comment on a series of questions that we believe will help move the field of leadership development evaluation forward. We also synthesize the advice offered in the previous chapters and offer readers suggestions for where to find additional guidance.

By articulating what we know as well as our challenges and questions, we can better focus our resources and collaborate with other fields in order to increase our understanding and work together to find solutions to the growing challenges.

Questions from and for the Field

In conversations surrounding this book we, the editors, began to articulate questions that we felt were shared among many stakeholders and across contexts, and that were important to address. We share these questions here and offer our perspective on them as a means of encouraging further discussions and work in these areas. We have separated the questions into discrete units, but recognize that these questions are somewhat interrelated.

What is the best way to identify and match the "right" individuals, teams, and communities with the "right" leadership development?

Identifying the right individuals, teams, and communities for leadership development is a task that every leadership program or initiative must address. In some cases, individuals or their bosses decide whether they should participate in a leadership program. In other cases, participants are selected for their potential to advance within an organization, lead policy change in a field, or become a boundary-crossing leader of community change. Teams and communities are often selected when leadership initiatives seek systems and social change, or when organizations seek better strategic alignment. More sophisticated programs are beginning to look at readiness factors in order to determine who will benefit most from leadership development. Further inquiry in this area is needed.

There are also issues of fairness and power that can be raised about the selection process. Who gets to decide which individuals, teams, or communities will have access to leadership development? What individuals, teams, or communities are being excluded from the development opportunities, and what consequences might that have for the strategic direction of a company, or for perpetuating injustice?

Another aspect of this question is determining the right leadership development. In some cases, individuals have been identified for leadership development based on a needs assessment or a learning plan review process; in other cases they may choose to go themselves. There is little guidance about how to choose a program that will meet the individual's learning needs. For teams and communities, engaging in collective learning experiences is even more complex, and many organizations and initiatives are seeking better guidance about what kinds of teams or networks best support organizational and social change. We need more evaluations that examine readiness, and the appropriateness of programs or initiatives to respond to the learning needs that exist.

How are leadership development outcomes affected when leadership is developed "at home" or "in place"?

It's no secret that participants in off-site leadership development programs sometimes return to their work environment or community only to realize that they no longer want to be there. On the less extreme end, leadership development participants may return home knowing what changes they want to make but feeling trapped in a system that resists making those changes. On the bright side, participants can return home and get the support they need, flourish, and provide positive role models for others. What's thought provoking is that the same leadership development program can have a very different impact on individuals or teams depending on the context in which they are embedded. This raises issues about organizational and community readiness for leadership development and how that can be effectively assessed.

Increasingly, teams within organizations or networks of leaders within communities are recruited and selected. Often, it is most feasible and valuable to develop teams and networks at home or in place.

The process of leadership development is increasingly collective and democratic, even when the focus of leadership development is personal. Developing leadership at home or in place makes it much more likely that systemic, cultural, and historical issues will be addressed. It is these issues that often influence interpersonal dynamics, power differences, and historical injustices, and make it difficult for change to occur and be sustained. Similarly, participants who attend leadership development (even when it takes place away from the home setting) with a group of participants from the same organization or community are also able to address critical issues and create higher-level impact because they are developing within the context of their organization or community.

What program components are most strongly related to which program outcomes?

Leadership development program designers make decisions about what components to include based on little firm empirical evidence that links desired outcomes to particular program components. We also know little about the effects of combining program components. What synergies, for instance, are created by combining training and mentoring? Is investing in programs with multiple components necessary for achieving the desired outcomes, or can the same outcomes be achieved with less investment?

Determining links between program components and program outcomes is complicated further by context. It may be that one combination of components works well in one context but has disappointing results in another. Still others question whether outcomes can ever be directly linked to program inputs. They look instead to positive outcomes that are occurring and consider in what ways the leadership development efforts may have contributed to what they have documented.

Understanding what components tend to be associated with what outcomes can help different stakeholders with a wide variety of tasks, such as designing programs for specific outcomes, setting appropriate expectations, and better managing resources by focusing on or including program components that are more likely to result in desirable outcomes. Most participants in leadership development programs are very busy. If a program can be designed in a way that utilizes only the most effective components, a three-day program can achieve roughly the same outcomes as a five-day program. Thus, resources, including the participants' time, can be saved and perhaps reallocated to areas of greater need.

What are the stages or pathways for individual and collective leadership development?

Developing a framework that captures the interplay among individual, contextual, and programmatic factors and mapping when and how different changes or shifts take place would help stakeholders better design, implement, and evaluate leadership development.

Logic models and theories of change are described as helpful tools in many of the chapters in this handbook. A future direction for the field of leadership development evaluation might be to scan the existing logic models and theories of change and the evidence gathered in support of (or in contrast to) them to begin to develop a more generalized framework of leadership development.

Another promising approach is finding common themes and threads in leadership stories. Over time, these stories yield evidence and in-depth descriptions about the change process in particular contexts. Sharing and analyzing these stories may provide a rich and nuanced understanding about pathways and stages of change that will enable us to more effectively design, implement, and evaluate leadership development.

What are promising methods for evaluating collective leadership development?

Most of our current evaluation approaches have been developed and tested to assess individual leadership development (360-degree assessments, for example). There are fewer evaluation approaches that have been designed to assess collective leadership (although some have been described in this handbook). One promising technique that several authors mention is social network analysis, which maps and measures relationships and flows among individuals, teams, organizations, and communities. In addition to resources that are mentioned throughout the book, a special issue of *New Directions for Evaluation* on "Social Network Analysis in Program Evaluation" (Durland and Fredericks, 2006) discusses the potential of social network analysis as an evaluation tool.

Ethnography is another method that is being used to evaluate collective leadership. Evaluators participate in events, converse with people formally and informally, observe, and talk to key informants in order to develop nuanced understandings of how collective leadership is being developed. A recent GrantCraft (2006) guide, *Getting Inside the Story: Ethnographic Approaches to Evaluation,* provides some good resources on this approach.

Finally, many organizations are looking for a relatively straightforward measure to illustrate the organizational impact of leadership development. The ROI method creates a single score and is the right measure in specific situations. However, it requires significant resources to adequately collect the data needed to calculate ROI, and many types of leadership development initiatives do not have financial outcomes as the ultimate goal. Nevertheless, other than ROI, there is no readily accepted score that both appropriately indicates the organizational impact of leadership development and satisfies the needs of many users of leadership development. This is an area on which evaluators of leadership development should focus attention.

How does culture influence leadership development initiatives and evaluations?

Cultural assumptions are deeply embedded in our concepts of leadership development and evaluation. As our communities, workplaces, and nations become more multicultural, it is critical that our approaches to developing and evaluating leadership become more culturally inclusive and transparent. Cultural competency has become an important component of leadership programs in some fields, such as health. As a result, resources are being developed to help grant makers and evaluators assess cultural competency. A good resource to consult is *Commissioning Multicultural Evaluation: A Foundation Resource Guide* (www.calendow.org/reference/publications/pdf/evaluations/TCE0510-2004_Commissioning_.pdf).

Culture has an impact on whether leadership development content and format is relevant and appropriate, what kind of evaluation approaches are appropriate, and how information should be interpreted.

Joining the Dialogue

If you are interested in engaging with others around issues related to leadership development evaluation, the Leadership Learning Community's Evaluation Learning Circle explores questions similar to those we've introduced. Chapter Eighteen provides more information about this community. Another option is to contact one of the evaluation organizations to see if they have a group focused on leadership development. Another organization that may be of interest to you is the International Leadership Association, a global network of people who practice, study, and teach leadership. More information about this organization can be found at www.academy.umd.edu/ila/.

Guidance for Leadership Development Evaluations

Leadership development evaluation is undoubtedly a complex, culturally sensitive, and often politically charged endeavor. In order to maintain the relevance and credibility of this work, those involved in it must periodically address and communicate how this work is best conducted. In general, the following advice is offered to those responsible for designing, implementing, and using leadership development evaluations:

- Involve stakeholders at all stages of the process in order to appropriately consider multiple needs and perspectives. (Note that different stakeholder groups may need to be involved at different stages.)
- Design the evaluation before the initiative is implemented. Ideally, the initiative and evaluation design processes would be conducted in conjunction with one another.
- Clarify outcomes to the extent possible with stakeholders, recognizing that there may be different kinds and levels of outcomes.
- Discuss the purpose of the evaluation and how information will be used before beginning the evaluation.
- Use multiple measures to gather information about complex or vague outcomes from multiple perspectives.

Two additional sources of guidance are the evaluation standards and the guiding principles set forth by various professional evaluation groups. Exhibit A.1 provides the guiding principles of the American Evaluation Association (AEA). These principles are not necessarily prescriptive, but offer a framework for exploring evaluation practice. While the AEA is a large organization, with approximately 4,000 members including evaluators from more than sixty countries, it is by no means the only evaluation association, nor are these the only guidelines. Exhibit A.2 provides a list of evaluation associations focused in various regions. There are also evaluation associations that focus on specific sectors, such as the International Development Evaluation Association. As has been described in this book, different contexts can present different challenges; accessing a network of evaluators familiar with the culture in which evaluation work is being designed, conducted, and/or used can provide useful, and sometimes necessary, information. A special issue of *New Directions for Evaluation* (Russon and Russon, 2005) is devoted to "International Perspectives on Evaluation Standards." This issue provides an overview of the challenges faced by those formalizing standards for program evaluation in cross-cultural contexts as well as insight into differing perspectives on standards. Another special issue of *New Directions for Evaluation* (Thompson-Robinson, Hopson, and SenGupta, 2004), titled "In Search of Cultural Competence in Evaluation Toward Principles and Practices," shares perspectives on what it means to be culturally competent.

As the editors of this handbook, we hope the information we've assembled is helpful to you in your current role and propels you to engage with leadership development evaluation colleagues in order to learn from each other and to drive the profession forward.

EXHIBIT A.1. AMERICAN EVALUATION ASSOCIATION GUIDING PRINCIPLES FOR EVALUATORS.

Revisions reflected herein ratified by the AEA membership, July 2004.

Preface: Assumptions Concerning Development of Principles

A. Evaluation is a profession composed of persons with varying interests, potentially encompassing but not limited to the evaluation of programs, products, personnel, policy, performance, proposals, technology, research, theory, and even of evaluation itself. These principles are broadly intended to cover all kinds of evaluation. For external evaluations of public programs, they nearly always apply. However, it is impossible to write guiding principles that neatly fit every context in which evaluators work, and some evaluators will work in contexts in which following a guideline cannot be done for good reason. The Guiding Principles are not intended to constrain such evaluators when this is the case. However, such exceptions should be made for good reason (e.g., legal prohibitions against releasing information to stakeholders), and evaluators who find themselves in such contexts should consult colleagues about how to proceed.

B. Based on differences in training, experience, and work settings, the profession of evaluation encompasses diverse perceptions about the primary purpose of evaluation. These include but are not limited to the following: bettering products, personnel, programs, organizations, governments, consumers, and the public interest; contributing to informed decision making and more enlightened change; precipitating needed change; empowering all stakeholders by collecting data from them and engaging them in the evaluation process; and experiencing the excitement of new insights. Despite that diversity, the common ground is that evaluators aspire to construct and provide the best possible information that might bear on the value of whatever is being evaluated. The principles are intended to foster that primary aim.

C. The principles are intended to guide the professional practice of evaluators, and to inform evaluation clients and the general public about the principles they can expect to be upheld by professional evaluators. Of course, no statement of principles can anticipate all situations that arise in the practice of evaluation. However, principles are not just guidelines for reaction when something goes wrong or when a dilemma is found. Rather, principles should proactively guide the behaviors of professionals in everyday practice.

D. The purpose of documenting guiding principles is to foster continuing development of the profession of evaluation, and the socialization of its members. The principles are meant to stimulate discussion about the proper practice and use of evaluation among members of the profession, sponsors of evaluation, and others interested in evaluation.

EXHIBIT A.1. AMERICAN EVALUATION ASSOCIATION GUIDING PRINCIPLES FOR EVALUATORS, Cont'd.

E. The five principles proposed in this document are not independent, but overlap in many ways. Conversely, sometimes these principles will conflict, so that evaluators will have to choose among them. At such times evaluators must use their own values and knowledge of the setting to determine the appropriate response. Whenever a course of action is unclear, evaluators should solicit the advice of fellow evaluators about how to resolve the problem before deciding how to proceed.

F. These principles are intended to supercede any previous work on standards, principles, or ethics adopted by AEA or its two predecessor organizations, the Evaluation Research Society and the Evaluation Network. These principles are the official position of AEA on these matters.

G. These principles are not intended to replace standards supported by evaluators or by the other disciplines in which evaluators participate.

H. Each principle is illustrated by a number of statements to amplify the meaning of the overarching principle, and to provide guidance for its application. These illustrations are not meant to include all possible applications of that principle, nor to be viewed as rules that provide the basis for sanctioning violators.

I. These principles were developed in the context of Western cultures, particularly the United States, and so may reflect the experiences of that context. The relevance of these principles may vary across other cultures, and across subcultures within the United States.

J. These principles are part of an evolving process of self-examination by the profession, and should be revisited on a regular basis. Mechanisms might include officially sponsored reviews of principles at annual meetings, and other forums for harvesting experience with the principles and their application. On a regular basis, but at least every five years, these principles ought to be examined for possible review and revision. In order to maintain association-wide awareness and relevance, all AEA members are encouraged to participate in this process.

The Principles

A. Systematic Inquiry: Evaluators conduct systematic, data-based inquiries.
   1. To ensure the accuracy and credibility of the evaluative information they produce, evaluators should adhere to the highest technical standards appropriate to the methods they use.
   2. Evaluators should explore with the client the shortcomings and strengths both of the various evaluation questions and the various approaches that might be used for answering those questions.

EXHIBIT A.1. AMERICAN EVALUATION ASSOCIATION GUIDING PRINCIPLES FOR EVALUATORS, Cont'd.

3. Evaluators should communicate their methods and approaches accurately and in sufficient detail to allow others to understand, interpret, and critique their work. They should make clear the limitations of an evaluation and its results. Evaluators should discuss in a contextually appropriate way those values, assumptions, theories, methods, results, and analyses significantly affecting the interpretation of the evaluative findings. These statements apply to all aspects of the evaluation, from its initial conceptualization to the eventual use of findings.

B. Competence: Evaluators provide competent performance to stakeholders.

1. Evaluators should possess (or ensure that the evaluation team possesses) the education, abilities, skills, and experience appropriate to undertake the tasks proposed in the evaluation.

2. To ensure recognition, accurate interpretation, and respect for diversity, evaluators should ensure that the members of the evaluation team collectively demonstrate cultural competence. Cultural competence would be reflected in evaluators seeking awareness of their own culturally based assumptions, their understanding of the worldviews of culturally different participants and stakeholders in the evaluation, and the use of appropriate evaluation strategies and skills in working with culturally different groups. Diversity may be in terms of race, ethnicity, gender, religion, socio-economics, or other factors pertinent to the evaluation context.

3. Evaluators should practice within the limits of their professional training and competence, and should decline to conduct evaluations that fall substantially outside those limits. When declining the commission or request is not feasible or appropriate, evaluators should make clear any significant limitations on the evaluation that might result. Evaluators should make every effort to gain the competence directly or through the assistance of others who possess the required expertise.

4. Evaluators should continually seek to maintain and improve their competencies, in order to provide the highest level of performance in their evaluations. This continuing professional development might include formal coursework and workshops, self-study, evaluations of one's own practice, and working with other evaluators to learn from their skills and expertise.

C. Integrity/Honesty: Evaluators display honesty and integrity in their own behavior, and attempt to ensure the honesty and integrity of the entire evaluation process.

1. Evaluators should negotiate honestly with clients and relevant stakeholders concerning the costs, tasks to be undertaken, limitations of methodology,

EXHIBIT A.1. AMERICAN EVALUATION ASSOCIATION GUIDING PRINCIPLES FOR EVALUATORS, Cont'd.

scope of results likely to be obtained, and uses of data resulting from a specific evaluation. It is primarily the evaluator's responsibility to initiate discussion and clarification of these matters, not the client's.

2. Before accepting an evaluation assignment, evaluators should disclose any roles or relationships they have that might pose a conflict of interest (or appearance of a conflict) with their role as an evaluator. If they proceed with the evaluation, the conflict(s) should be clearly articulated in reports of the evaluation results.

3. Evaluators should record all changes made in the originally negotiated project plans, and the reasons why the changes were made. If those changes would significantly affect the scope and likely results of the evaluation, the evaluator should inform the client and other important stakeholders in a timely fashion (barring good reason to the contrary, before proceeding with further work) of the changes and their likely impact.

4. Evaluators should be explicit about their own, their clients', and other stakeholders' interests and values concerning the conduct and outcomes of an evaluation.

5. Evaluators should not misrepresent their procedures, data or findings. Within reasonable limits, they should attempt to prevent or correct misuse of their work by others.

6. If evaluators determine that certain procedures or activities are likely to produce misleading evaluative information or conclusions, they have the responsibility to communicate their concerns and the reasons for them. If discussions with the client do not resolve these concerns, the evaluator should decline to conduct the evaluation. If declining the assignment is unfeasible or inappropriate, the evaluator should consult colleagues or relevant stakeholders about other proper ways to proceed. (Options might include discussions at a higher level, a dissenting cover letter or appendix, or refusal to sign the final document.)

7. Evaluators should disclose all sources of financial support for an evaluation, and the source of the request for the evaluation.

D. Respect for People: Evaluators respect the security, dignity, and self-worth of respondents, program participants, clients, and other evaluation stakeholders.

1. Evaluators should seek a comprehensive understanding of the important contextual elements of the evaluation. Contextual factors that may influence the results of a study include geographic location, timing, political and social climate, economic conditions, and other relevant activities in progress at the same time.

EXHIBIT A.1. AMERICAN EVALUATION ASSOCIATION GUIDING PRINCIPLES FOR EVALUATORS, Cont'd.

2. Evaluators should abide by current professional ethics, standards, and regulations regarding risks, harms, and burdens that might befall those participating in the evaluation; regarding informed consent for participation in evaluation; and regarding informing participants and clients about the scope and limits of confidentiality.

3. Because justified negative or critical conclusions from an evaluation must be explicitly stated, evaluations sometimes produce results that harm client or stakeholder interests. Under this circumstance, evaluators should seek to maximize the benefits and reduce any unnecessary harms that might occur, provided this will not compromise the integrity of the evaluation findings. Evaluators should carefully judge when the benefits from doing the evaluation or in performing certain evaluation procedures should be foregone because of the risks or harms. To the extent possible, these issues should be anticipated during the negotiation of the evaluation.

4. Knowing that evaluations may negatively affect the interests of some stakeholders, evaluators should conduct the evaluation and communicate its results in a way that clearly respects the stakeholders' dignity and self-worth.

5. Where feasible, evaluators should attempt to foster social equity in evaluation, so that those who give to the evaluation may benefit in return. For example, evaluators should seek to ensure that those who bear the burdens of contributing data and incurring any risks do so willingly, and that they have full knowledge of and opportunity to obtain any benefits of the evaluation. Program participants should be informed that their eligibility to receive services does not hinge on their participation in the evaluation.

6. Evaluators have the responsibility to understand and respect differences among participants, such as differences in their culture, religion, gender, disability, age, sexual orientation, and ethnicity, and to account for potential implications of these differences when planning, conducting, analyzing, and reporting evaluations.

E. Responsibilities for General and Public Welfare: Evaluators articulate and take into account the diversity of general and public interests and values that may be related to the evaluation.

1. When planning and reporting evaluations, evaluators should include relevant perspectives and interests of the full range of stakeholders.

2. Evaluators should consider not only the immediate operations and outcomes of whatever is being evaluated, but also its broad assumptions, implications, and potential side effects.

EXHIBIT A.1. AMERICAN EVALUATION ASSOCIATION GUIDING PRINCIPLES FOR EVALUATORS, Cont'd.

3. Freedom of information is essential in a democracy. Evaluators should allow all relevant stakeholders access to evaluative information in forms that respect people and honor promises of confidentiality. Evaluators should actively disseminate information to stakeholders as resources allow. Communications that are tailored to a given stakeholder should include all results that may bear on interests of that stakeholder and refer to any other tailored communications to other stakeholders. In all cases, evaluators should strive to present results clearly and simply so that clients and other stakeholders can easily understand the evaluation process and results.

4. Evaluators should maintain a balance between client needs and other needs. Evaluators necessarily have a special relationship with the client who funds or requests the evaluation. By virtue of that relationship, evaluators must strive to meet legitimate client needs whenever it is feasible and appropriate to do so. However, that relationship can also place evaluators in difficult dilemmas when client interests conflict with other interests, or when client interests conflict with the obligation of evaluators for systematic inquiry, competence, integrity, and respect for people. In these cases, evaluators should explicitly identify and discuss the conflicts with the client and relevant stakeholders, resolve them when possible, determine whether continued work on the evaluation is advisable if the conflicts cannot be resolved, and make clear any significant limitations on the evaluation that might result if the conflict is not resolved.

5. Evaluators have obligations that encompass the public interest and good. These obligations are especially important when evaluators are supported by publicly generated funds; but clear threats to the public good should never be ignored in any evaluation. Because the public interest and good are rarely the same as the interests of any particular group (including those of the client or funder), evaluators will usually have to go beyond analysis of particular stakeholder interests and consider the welfare of society as a whole.

Source: American Evaluation Association. Retrieved from http://www.eval.org/Publications/ Guiding_Principles.asp.

EXHIBIT A.2. EVALUATION ASSOCIATIONS.

African Evaluation Association
www.afrea.org/

American Evaluation Association
www.eval.org/

Australasian Evaluation Society
www.aes.asn.au/

Canadian Evaluation Society
www.evaluationcanada.ca/

Danish Evaluation Society
www.danskevalueringsselskab.dk/ (with limited information in English)

European Evaluation Society
www.europeanevaluation.org/index.html

French Evaluation Society
www.sfe.asso.fr/ (in French)

German Evaluation Society
www.degeval.de/ (in German)

Ghana Evaluators Association
www.isodec.org.gh/

International Organization for Cooperation in Evaluation (IOCE)
internationalevaluation.com/

Israeli Association for Program Evaluation (IAPE)
www.iape.org.il/

Italian Evaluation Society
www.valutazione.it/ (in Italian)

Japan Evaluation Society
www.idcj.or.jp/jes/index_english.htm (in Japanese)

Malaysian Evaluation Society
www.mes.org.my/

Nigerian Monitoring and Evaluation Network
www.pnud.ne/rense/index.html

EXHIBIT A.2. EVALUATION ASSOCIATIONS, Cont'd.

PREVAL for Latin America & the Caribbean (in Spanish)
www.ird.ne/rense/

Russia International Project Evaluation Network (IPEN)
www.eval-net.org/

Spanish Public Policy Evaluation Society (SEE)
www.sociedadevaluacion.org/

Sri Lanka Evaluation Association
www.nsf.ac.lk/sleva/semina.htm

Swedish Evaluation Society
www.svuf.nu/ (with limited information in English)

Swiss Evaluation Society
www.seval.ch/en/index.cfm

United Kingdom Evaluation Society
www.seval.ch/en/index.cfm

Utvärderarna
www.statskontoret.se/utvarderarna/english.html (in Swedish with English link)

Walloon Evaluation Society
www.prospeval.org/ (in French)

Conclusion

While this book represents a variety of current perspectives, there is a great deal more to be learned and shared. We hope this book has provided you with useful information that you can apply immediately as well as engaged you in thinking about the more enduring and emerging issues related to leadership development evaluation.

References

Durland, M. M., and Fredericks, K. A. (eds.). "Social Network Analysis in Program Evaluation." *New Directions for Evaluation*, Special issue, 2006, *107*,

GrantCraft. *Getting Inside the Story: Ethnographic Approaches to Evaluation,* 2006. [www.grantcraft.org/index.cfm?fuseaction=Page.viewPage&pageID=618].

Russon, C., and Russon, G. (eds.). "International Perspectives on Evaluation Standards." *New Directions for Evaluation,* Special issue, 2005, *104.*

Thompson-Robinson, M., Hopson, R., and SenGupta, S. (eds.). "In Search of Cultural Competence in Evaluation Toward Principles and Practices." *New Directions for Evaluation,* Special issue, 2004, *102.*

NAME INDEX

A

Abramson, P. R., 425
Adefuin, J., 7, 11, 400–401
Ahsan, N., 403
Allen, D. R., 459, 462
Ammann Howard, K., 343
Anderson, A., 51, 69
Anderson, S., 321, 342
Atkinson, P., 313–314
Atwood, R., 489, 503, 510

B

Baker, E., 469, 485
Bartlett, K. R., 490–491, 508
Baum, J., 261
Behrens, T. R., 284, 286–287
Bell, J. B., 503, 508, 509
Benham, M.K.P., 284
Benjamin, B., 264, 272, 283
Bennett, M., 124–125, 135
Bergson-Shilcock, A., 55, 69
Bickman, L., 51, 69
Bivens, D., 206, 227
Bober, C. F., 490–491, 508
Bolman, L. G., 302, 314

Bornstein, D., 374, 376
Brache, A. P., 465, 486
Briggs, C. L., 470, 486
Brinkerhoff, R. O., 489, 508
Burns, J. M., 5, 11
Burtt, H. E., 264, 283
Busch, J. R., 177, 179, 196

C

Cahill, M., 377, 401
Camino, L., 378, 402
Campbell, D. J., 177, 182, 196, 436, 462
Campbell, D. T., 46, 47
Campbell, K. M., 177, 196
Cannon, M., 478, 485
Cao Yu, H., 7, 11
Carey, R. G., 180, 197
Carsten, J., 462
Cascio, W. F., 489, 508
Casswell, S., 437, 462
Cervero, R. M., 471, 486
Chan, S., 437, 462
Chrislip, D., 375, 376
Clark, H., 51, 69
Clason, D., 377, 401

Coghlan, A. T., 7, 11, 129, 136
Collins, L. M., 28, 46
Collins, P. M., 173
Conger, J., 264, 272, 283
Connaughton, S. L., 177–178, 179, 192, 194, 196
Connell, J. P., 49, 69, 377, 381, 401
Consolver, G., 279
Cook, A. K., 513, 535
Cook, T. D., 46, 47
Copland, M., 325, 327, 336, 342
Cousins, J. B., 490–491, 508, 536, 537, 555, 556
Craig, S. B., 19, 36, 47
Cronbach, L. J., 36, 47
Cullinan, C. C., 126, 135
Curnan, S., 377, 402
Czarniawska, B., 314

D

Dailey, P. R., 36, 47
Dardis, G., 177, 196
Darling-Hammond, L., 340
Davidson, E. J., 3, 11, 433, 454, 459, 462, 463
Davidson, J., 450, 462

575

SUBJECT INDEX

A

Academic achievement outcomes, 316, 317, 327

Accountability: of neighborhood resident leaders, 418–419, 420; for social change, 212; of supervisors, 271, 272–283, 282

Accountability requirements and concerns. *See also* Foundations; Funder reporting; Stakeholder expectations: of business executives, 265–270; continuous learning approach and, 552–553; multiple viewpoints and, 112; neighborhood resident leadership development and, 418–419; open-systems approach and, 108; pathway mapping and, 65–66; ROI measurement and, 138, 139, 140, 145–146

Action, cycle of reflection and, 381, 383

Action learning: connecting leadership development and, 282; on-the-job development and, 272, 282; in public health leadership program, 467, 469, 471, 482; strategic evaluation of, 444–445; in team leadership development programs, 231, 467, 469, 471

Action plans: in Baldrige framework evaluation, 474; in health management team evaluation, 240, 244, 245, 246, 250–251, 253–254, 257; in ROI measurement, 153

Activities approach models, 51–52. *See also* Logic models

Adaptability, measurement of, 25

Administrative decision making, 431

Adult learning theory, 202

Advocacy. *See also* Civic activism; Social change: for continuous learning approach, 554; evaluators' role in, 9

Affective frame shifting, 125–126

Affinity circles, 517. *See also* Learning circles

African Americans, in youth leadership evaluation, 392. *See also* People of color

African Evaluation Association, 572

After Action Review (AAR), 255, 256

Agency, sense of, 395

AI Practitioner, 134–135

Alignment: of behavior and values, 199, 206, 207, 210; of evaluation model to grant-making model, 297–299; of evaluator and funder values, 366; as leadership competency, 236, 237, 240–242; mainstreaming evaluation for, 117, 130–133; for ROI measurement, 147–150; of stakeholders, 234

Alliances. *See* Coalition building; Partnerships and alliances

Alumni meetings, 346, 347, 360

Ambassadors Program. *See* Americans for Indian Opportunity (AIO) Ambassadors Program

Ambition, as preexisting difference, 21–22

American Evaluation Association (AEA): annual conference, 179; Building Diversity Initiative, 178; Guiding Principles, 565, 566–571; mentors from, 186; Program Evaluation Standards, 427–428; Topical Interest

ABOUT THE CENTER FOR CREATIVE LEADERSHIP

The Center for Creative Leadership (CCL) is a nonprofit, educational institution with international reach. Since the Center's founding in 1970, its mission has been to advance the understanding, practice, and development of leadership for the benefit of society worldwide.

Devoted to leadership education and research, CCL works annually with more than two thousand organizations and twenty thousand individuals from the private, public, education, and nonprofit sectors. The Center's five campuses span three continents: Greensboro, North Carolina; Colorado Springs, Colorado; and San Diego, California, in North America; Brussels, Belgium, in Europe; and Singapore in Asia. In addition, sixteen Network Associates around the world offer selected CCL programs and assessments.

CCL draws strength from its nonprofit status and educational mission, which provide unusual flexibility in a world where quarterly profits often drive thinking and direction. It has the freedom to be objective, wary of short-term trends, and motivated foremost by its mission—hence our substantial and sustained investment in leadership research. Although CCL's work is always grounded in a strong foundation of research, it focuses on achieving a beneficial impact in the real world. Its efforts are geared to be practical and action oriented, helping leaders and their organizations more effectively achieve their goals and vision. The desire to transform learning and ideas into action provides the impetus for CCL's programs, assessments, publications, and services.

Capabilities

CCL's activities encompass leadership education, knowledge generation and dissemination, and building a community centered on leadership. CCL is broadly recognized for excellence in executive education, leadership development, and innovation by sources such as *Business Week,* the *Financial Times,* the *New York Times,* and the *Wall Street Journal.*

Open-Enrollment Programs

Fourteen open-enrollment courses are designed for leaders at all levels, as well as people responsible for leadership development and training at their organizations. This portfolio offers distinct choices for participants seeking a particular learning environment or type of experience. Some programs are structured specifically around small group activities, discussion, and personal reflection, while others offer hands-on opportunities through business simulations, artistic exploration, team-building exercises, and new-skills practice. Many of these programs offer private one-on-one sessions with a feedback coach.

For a complete listing of programs, visit http://www.ccl.org/programs.

Customized Programs

CCL develops tailored educational solutions for more than one hundred client organizations around the world each year. Through this applied practice, CCL structures and delivers programs focused on specific leadership development needs within the context of defined organizational challenges, including innovation, the merging of cultures, and the development of a broader pool of leaders. The objective is to help organizations develop, within their own cultures, the leadership capacity they need to address challenges as they emerge.

Program details are available online at http://www.ccl.org/custom.

Coaching

CCL's suite of coaching services is designed to help leaders maintain a sustained focus and generate increased momentum toward achieving their goals. These coaching alternatives vary in depth and duration and serve a variety of needs, from helping an executive sort through career and life issues to working with an organization to integrate coaching into its internal development process. Our coaching offerings, which can supplement program attendance or be customized for specific individual or team needs, are based on our ACS model of assessment, challenge, and support.

Learn more about CCL's coaching services at http://www.ccl.org/coaching.

Assessment and Development Resources

CCL pioneered 360-degree feedback and believes that assessment provides a solid foundation for learning, growth, and transformation and that development truly happens when an individual recognizes the need to change. CCL offers a broad selection of assessment tools, online resources, and simulations that can help individuals, teams, and organizations increase their self-awareness, facilitate their own learning, enable their development, and enhance their effectiveness.

CCL's assessments are profiled at http://www.ccl.org/assessments.

Publications

The theoretical foundation for many of our programs, as well as the results of CCL's extensive and often groundbreaking research, can be found in the scores of publications issued by CCL Press and through the Center's alliance with Jossey-Bass, a Wiley imprint. Among these are landmark works, such as *Breaking the Glass Ceiling, The Lessons of Experience,* and *The Center for Creative Leadership Handbook of Leadership Development,* as well as quick-read guidebooks focused on core aspects of leadership. CCL publications provide insights and practical advice to help individuals become more effective leaders, develop leadership training within organizations, address issues of change and diversity, and build the systems and strategies that advance leadership collectively at the institutional level.

A complete listing of CCL publications is available at http://www.ccl.org/publications.

Leadership Community

To ensure that the Center's work remains focused, relevant, and important to the individuals and organizations it serves, CCL maintains a host of networks, councils, and learning and virtual communities that bring together alumni, donors, faculty, practicing leaders, and thought leaders from around the globe. CCL also forges relationships and alliances with individuals, organizations, and associations that share its values and mission. The energy, insights, and support from these relationships help shape and sustain CCL's educational and research practices and provide its clients with an added measure of motivation and inspiration as they continue their lifelong commitment to leadership and learning.

To learn more, visit http://www.ccl.org/connected.

Research

CCL's portfolio of programs, products, and services is built on a solid foundation of behavioral science research. The role of research at CCL is to advance the understanding of leadership and to transform learning into practical tools for participants and clients. CCL's research is the hub of a cycle that transforms knowledge into applications and applications into knowledge, thereby illuminating the way organizations think about and enact leadership and leader development.

Find out more about current research initiatives at http://www.ccl.org/research.

For additional information about CCL, please visit http://www.ccl.org or call Client Services at 336-545-2810.